THE BACK TO BASICS HANDBOOK

A GUIDE TO BUYING AND WORKING LAND, RAISING LIVESTOCK, ENJOYING YOUR HARVEST, HOUSEHOLD SKILLS AND CRAFTS, AND MORE

T0072063

ABIGAIL R. GEHRING

Skyhorse Publishing

Skyhorse Publishing books may be purchased in bulk at special discounts for sales promotion, corporate gifts, fund-raising, or educational purposes. Special editions can also be created to specifications. For details, contact the Special Sales Department, Skyhorse Publishing, 307 West 36th Street, 11th Floor, New York, NY 10018 or info@skyhorsepublishing.com.

Skyhorse® and Skyhorse Publishing® are registered trademarks of Skyhorse Publishing, Inc.®, a Delaware corporation.

www.skyhorsepublishing.com

10 9 8

Library of Congress Cataloging-in-Publication Data

Gehring, Abigail R.
  The back to basics handbook : a guide to buying and working land, raising livestock, enjoying your harvest, household skills and crafts, and more / Abigail R. Gehring.
      p. cm.
  Includes bibliographical references.
  ISBN 978-1-61608-261-1 (alk. paper)
  1. Sustainable living. 2. Country life. 3. Home economics. I. Title.
  GF78.G439 2011
  640--dc22

                                                    2011017179

Printed in China

Contents

Part One

Land: Buying It—Building on It

The homes of the settlers conformed naturally to the great architect's precepts. People built slowly in those days, over generations, and they understood their land as only those who spend their lives on it can. Their building materials were the very stuff of the earth around them—trees from their woods, rocks from their fields, adobe mud beneath their feet—so it was small wonder that their homes blended well with the surrounding countryside. Above all, they built their homes themselves, and so each mitered beam, each length of floorboard, each hand-riven shingle took on a special meaning of its own. In "Land: Buying It—Building on It" the process of creating a home the traditional way is described, from the acquisition of a site to the construction of the house to the installation of walls and outbuildings. Some of these jobs are difficult; others are within the capabilities of the average person. All help impart a personal touch to a house. In the final analysis that is the ingredient that makes a house a home.

Buying Country Property

Realizing the Dream Of Owning a Place In the Country

With careful planning and a modest investment almost anyone can turn the dream of owning a small farm or a few acres of country land into a reality. And with some effort this land may provide a significant portion of life's amenities: wood for the fireplace, fresh produce for the table, a pond for fishing or swimming—even waterpower to generate electricity. But as with any other major purchase, care and caution are required.

The first step is to have, in general terms, a strong notion of what it is you want. Those desiring year-round warmth will obviously have different priorities than those who wish to see the seasons change. Prospective part-time farmers will look for one kind of land, whereas weekend sojourners will look for another. Whether you enjoy isolation or prefer neighbors nearby is another consideration to ponder. And, of course, there is the matter of money: how much you can afford to put down, how much you can pay each month for a mortgage and taxes. Once you have made these decisions, pick an area or two to investigate. Get the catalogs of the Strout and United Farm real estate agencies, and look for ads in the Sunday paper real estate section. Also subscribe to local papers from the regions of your interest; these may provide lower priced listings plus information on land auctions.

When a property appeals to you, investigate—first by phone and then in person. When looking, do not neglect small matters, such as television reception, the contours of the land, and the style of the farmhouse; but never lose sight of your ultimate goals or basic priorities, and gauge the property in that light.

To Buy or Not to Buy: Resist That Impulse

Once you have found a piece of property that appears to meet your needs, resist the temptation to come to terms. This is the time for an in-depth investigation rather than a purchase. After leaving the parcel, think about it, talk about it, try to remember its contours, and list all the things you do not like as well as the things you do. If after a week or so the land still is appealing, arrange to spend an entire day tramping about it.

Walk slowly about the property in the company of your family. Among the subjects of discussion should be these: Is the ratio of meadow to wood-lot about what you have in mind? Does the woodlot consist of hard or soft woods? (The former are generally more valuable as timber and fuel.) Is the meadow overlain with ground cover, indicating some fertility? Is it swampy? Is there a usable residence on the property? If not, can you afford to build? Is there a road that cuts across the property into a neighbor's driveway? If so, there is likely to be an easement on the parcel, conferring on the neighbor the right to cross at will. If there is no electricity, gas, or telephone service, ask yourself honestly how well you can get along without these conveniences. And if your goal is to be a part-time farmer and full-time resident, check into employment possibilities in the area.

If the answers to most of these questions are satisfactory, then begin a more formal survey of the property. For those who plan to grow vegetables, grains, or fruits, the question of soil fertility becomes a major factor in any ultimate decision. Take a spade and dig down—way down—in several widely scattered places. Ground that is adequate for good crops will have a layer of topsoil at least 10 inches deep; 12 or 15 inches deep is better. The topsoil should be dark, and when handled it should feel soft, loose, and crumbly to the touch. If the topsoil seems rich enough and deep enough, make doubly certain by taking several samples to the nearest county agent; he can analyze it for acidity (pH) and mineral content and tell you what crops are best to grow on it. Another way of discovering what crops the soil will support is to find out what the neighbors are growing. If the farm over the fence has a healthy stand of corn, and a thriving vegetable garden, the chances are good that the land you are looking at will also accommodate those crops.

When walking the land, look for evidence of soil erosion. Gullies are a sign of erosion, as are bared roots of trees and bushes. Parched, stony, light-colored soils indicate that erosion has carried off the rich topsoil. If you are only planning a small kitchen garden, erosion and lack of topsoil can be repaired. But if extensive cropping is your goal, the cost of restoring scores of acres to fertility may be beyond your reach.

Check the drainage capacity of the land. If the subsoil is so compacted or rocky that it cannot quickly absorb water, then the plants you sow are likely to drown. Also bear in mind that poor drainage can make it difficult to install a septic system, since sewage will tend to back up or rise to the surface. Inspect the property in the wake of a heavy rainstorm. If the surface is muddy or even very spongy, it is a sign that the drainage is poor. Dig several widely spaced holes in the ground, each one about 8 inches around and 3 to 4 feet deep. Check the soil near the bottoms. If it is hard-packed and unyielding to the touch, chances are it is relatively impermeable to water. Or pour a bucket of water on the ground, wait 10 minutes, and dig to see how far the water has penetrated. For the most accurate information, a percolation test by a soil engineer is necessary.

If you are planning on building a house, carefully inspect possible construction sites. The land for the house should be reasonably flat, with easy access to a public road. Do not overlook the site's relationship to the winter sun. A house with a northern exposure, particularly if it is on a slope, is likely to cost considerably more to heat than one with a southern exposure that can take advantage of the warming rays of the low-lying winter sun.

Finally, there is the all-important matter of water— the lack of a reliable source of water for drinking and irrigation can make an otherwise desirable site worthless. The subject is discussed in detail below.

In all events, try to delay a commitment until you see the land in all seasons; both the blooms of spring and the snows of winter can hide a multitude of evils.

Buildings Are Important But Water Is Vital

In assessing country property the most important single consideration is the availability of an adequate supply of fresh, potable water. With water virtually anything is possible; without it virtually nothing. Consider, for example, that a single human being uses between 30 and 70 gallons per day; a horse between 6 and 12; a milk cow about 35; and a 500-square-foot kitchen garden, if it is to thrive, must have an average of 35 gallons of water per day. Even if the property is to be used only as a country retreat, a family of four will require a bare minimum of 100 gallons every day for such basic needs as drinking, washing, cooking, and sanitation. In short, complete information about water availability is an imperative when assessing country property. This is not to say, however, that a piece of land should, in all cases, be rejected if the existing water supply is inadequate, since in most instances a water system can be developed (see pp.42–46). Nevertheless, this can be an expensive,

Plants that provide clues to water in dry country

Rushes and cattails are a sign of marshland or of water very near the surface.

Pickleweed indicates the presence of salty water at or just below the surface.

Saltbush indicates water near the surface, but the quality may be poor.

Mesquite indicates that water is to be found from 10 to 50 ft. beneath the ground.

Reeds signify the existence of good quality water very close to the surface.

Black greasewood generally means that mineralized water exists 10 to 40 ft. down.

Rabbit brush will grow only where there is water no more than 15 ft. below the ground.

Elderberry shrubs are a fairly good sign that there is water about 10 ft. down.

laborious, and time-consuming effort, and it is far more satisfactory if a water system is already in place.

Existing systems. If there is a well or other water source, along with plumbing in the house, in the out buildings, and at the fields, test the system out as completely as possible. Try all of the taps: one at a time, several at once, all at once. Is the flow sufficient for your purposes? Does the water pressure drop significantly when several taps are on at once? Has the water been tested for potability and for minerals, particularly salt? Water with even a relatively low salt content may be useless for drinking or irrigation. Remember that a fast flow in spring may become but a trickle in the dog days of summer. This is another reason to visit a property in different seasons before purchase.

Aboveground water. A river, stream, brook, or pond on the property may provide adequate water, particularly for irrigation. A freshwater spring bubbling up from the earth can usually provide drinking water, but again, such sources may dry up during the summer. If you plan to use a river or pond for recreational purposes, such as swimming or fishing, make certain that pollutants from logging operations, sewage treatment plants, and factories are not being dumped upstream. Pollutants, of course, can make the water unusable for irrigation as well. Check with local and state authorities on the amount of water you may take from a watercourse. Also make sure that the source is properly positioned to allow you to get the water from where it is to where it will be needed. A stream below a building site and garden plot will be useful only with the installation of pumps. Even one above these areas may require siphons and considerable piping if it is to be useful.

Marshlands. Though marshes and swamps indicate a high water table and, under the proper conditions, a possible pond site, they are considered negative factors by most builders, since they provide breeding grounds for mosquitoes and other insect pests and the land is useless for construction unless drained and filled.

Public water supplies. In a number of rural areas water is supplied by an outside utility company. Some utilities are owned by the government, others are owned privately with rates established by law, and still others are associations of landowners who have pooled their resources to bring water in from distant sources so that they can irrigate their lands and provide for themselves and their livestock. Hookups to any of these water utilities can be expensive and, in the case of the landowners' associations, impossible to obtain. It may be, however, that the owner from whom you are obtaining the land already has shares in the local cooperative water association. If so, make sure that the transfer of these shares is included as part of the purchase price and that you know in advance the amount of water to which your shares will entitle you.

Water rights. The fact that a parcel has water either aboveground or underground is not necessarily a guarantee that the owner has the right to exploit the resource. In some states even underground water must be shared. Before purchasing any property, have your lawyer check on your water rights.

Sizing Up the House and Barns

The extent and condition of improvements play a large role in determining the worth of any piece of property.

Clues to a building's age

Irregular lath marks on beams indicate building dates from 18th or early 19th century.

Accordion lath marks (rarely seen) were produced by a technique not used after 1830.

Straight lath marks, regularly spaced, indicate post-1850 construction.

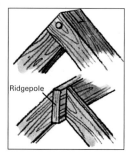

Ridgepole

No ridgepole on roof (top) usually means pre-1800; presence of ridgepole indicates later date.

Hand-sawed beams, with irregular, slanted saw marks, date from before the 1750s.

Vertical cuts in regular patterns usually indicate lumber was sawed before 1860.

Curving saw marks point to post-1860s construction–the more even, the later.

Blunt wood screws with no taper were not made after 1840. Hand-cut notches in heads can give clues to age of screws.

Tapered screws with pointed ends were made after 1840. Notches in heads were cut by machine rather than by hand.

Wrought nails, with square, tapered shanks and hand-forged heads bearing hammer marks, were made before 1800.

Cut nails, sliced from a sheet of iron, were not made before 1800. They are still manufactured for use in flooring.

Benchmarks for the buyer

Major points to consider when contemplating the purchase of a piece of country property are listed below. Use them as a checklist to avoid costly mistakes.

Contract of sale. The contract describes the terms under which the property is being sold. It should include a description of all encumbrances on the property and should be made contingent upon a successful title search and the ability of the buyer to secure adequate financing. Have your lawyer draw up the contract of sale rather than accept a real estate agent's standard form.

Easements. If land has no direct access to a highway, make sure you have an easement (legally binding right-of-way) across intervening properties. Know also if neighbors have an easement on the property you plan to buy.

Eminent domain. Many public and quasi-public agencies have the right to condemn land (with compensation to owners) for roads, drainage canals, dams, airports, school construction, power lines, rights-of-way into bordering state-owned property, and the like. Check with the local planning board to ascertain if any condemnation proceedings are contemplated.

Land contracts and mortgages. Land contracts are the least advantageous means of buying land because the seller or financing agency holds title until the purchase is fully paid off. The title holder may, during this interval, encumber the property by using it as collateral; the purchaser can lose the land if the title holder fails to make payments. Mortgages in which the buyer has title to the property and uses it as collateral offer greater protection against foreclosure.

Mineral and other encumbrances. The seller or an earlier owner may have sold or reserved the right to exploit minerals, timber, or even the water on the land. These encumbrances, if properly recorded, are legally binding.

Survey. Check with county recorder to determine if a legally binding map of the property has been made. If not, insist that a licensed surveyor draw such a map, preferably at the seller's expense.

Taxes. Check with local authorities to find out the amount of taxes (property, school, water, sewer) on the property you contemplate buying. Also try to determine if these taxes have been rising rapidly in recent years. Some states tax standing timber, mineral deposits, and water rights. Make sure there are no liens for unpaid taxes on the property.

Title search and insurance. Have your lawyer or a title insurance company check records to make sure you are buying land free of liens and encumbrances. Purchase title insurance—a one-time expense—that will guarantee the accuracy of the title search.

Water rights. Contract of sale should include clause in which seller guarantees a minimum water supply. Make sure the clause is in accordance with state laws on water rights.

Zoning laws. Check with the local zoning board to be certain you may use your land in the manner you intend. Also check building and health codes for the same purpose.

Direct access to a county highway via well-maintained internal roads is a major factor when considering a piece of land. A house, barn, and other outbuildings in good condition, the presence of primary utilities, and a central heating system all add to the market value of any parcel. When assessing improvements, look beyond the appearances and into such matters as structural soundness, electrical service capacity, the age of the heating system, and the relationship of the house to the winter sun.

First examine the house as a whole. Is it big enough for your needs? Does it afford sufficient privacy? Does it appear to be well maintained? Very important is the placement of the house. To take full advantage of the low-lying winter sun, it should present a broad front to the south and have a large proportion of its window openings facing south. Look at the windows themselves. Are storm windows and tight-fitting screens installed? Make notes as you move along the outside of the house and as you inspect the inside. Check for wood rot both inside and out, using an ice pick to jab at the beams and supports. If the pick goes in easily, there is probably wood rot, an expensive condition to repair. Look for signs of termites and carpenter ants, particularly along the baseboards of the ground floor and in the exposed joists in the basement. Also check the main fuse box to see if the electrical service is sufficient for your needs (modern service is at least 100 amps at 240 volts), then inspect the water heater as to age and capacity. A four-person family requires a 30-gallon gas water heater or a 50-gallon electric model. As you move from room to room, look up and down as well as around. Stains on the ceilings or evidence of recent plastering may mean roof leaks; horizontal stains on the lower part of basement or ground floor walls indicate flooding. Finally, hire a building engineer for an in-depth analysis. The deficiencies he finds may not necessarily be overwhelming, but they could provide you with a strong bargaining position for lowering the price by thousands of dollars.

Many people considering a move to the country seek out the charm of 18th- or 19th-century structures. Real estate agents recognize this and often emphasize that a house is one or two centuries old. Generally, it is best to verify such claims. Some tips on what to look for in dating a house are given on opposite page.

Sources and resources

Books

Nash, George. *Old Houses: A Rebuilder's Manual.* Needham Heights, Mass.: Prentice Hall, 1979.

Orme, Alan D. *Reviving Old Houses: Over Five Hundred Low-Cost Tips and Techniques.* Avenal, N.J.: Random House Value, 1994.

Poore, Patricia, ed. The *Old House Journal Guide* to *Restoration.* New York: NAL-Dutton, 1992.

Sherwood, Gerald E. *How to Select and Renovate an Older House.* New York: Dover, 1976.

Planning Your Home

The Key Ingredient In Home Design Is You

A well-designed home, like a well-tailored garment, should fit your taste, needs, and pocketbook. In years gone by, homesteaders achieved this goal by designing and building their own houses. One reason they were successful was that they were guided by traditions handed down over the centuries. Another was that their homesteads evolved over many years, each generation altering and enlarging the original to suit its particular needs so that the house slowly became better and better.

Nowadays, the best way to ensure that the home you build will have the right feel for you and your family is to take an active part in the design process. This is true whether you intend to put up a vacation cabin, a family residence, a retirement home, or a full-fledged homestead. Learn about design, look at as many homes as you can, and if you plan to hire an architect, shop carefully before you choose one.

Choosing a Building Site

The main house—even if it is just a cabin or cottage—is almost always the focal point of any site development plan, and the first step in designing it is to decide where it will be located. To choose a site intelligently, you should have a good idea of how you want to live. Do you favor a secluded home far from the road? Are you interested in a sweeping vista? Do you plan to put up a sprawling one-story structure or a more compact two-story house? (The former is useful if stair climbing presents a problem for anyone in the family; the latter is generally more energy efficient.) Do you foresee the need for future additions and, therefore, a larger site? Do you require a full basement? (If you do, avoid a site that will require expensive blasting of bedrock.)

Frame dwelling in the Northeast has sloping roof to allow snow to slide off easily in the winter. Having the barn attached to the main house makes it easier to care for the animals in poor weather.

Log home is well protected by trees against fall or winter winds. If built in a hot climate, log homes can be built on piers to allow air to circulate beneath.

Stone cottage has an eyebrow dormer to allow extra light into the second floor. Like brick, stone is fireproof and maintenance free. Attic helps retain heat, partially compensating for poor insulating ability of stone.

Next, examine what your property has to offer. Consider the general lay of the land, the bearing strength of the ground (see *Preparing the Site,* p.21), the soil's ability to absorb rainwater and sewage, the frost depth, the availability of drinking water, the height of the water table, the amount of annual sunlight, and the direction of prevailing winds. Pay particular attention to accessibility. How far is a proposed site from existing electric and telephone service lines? How many feet of driveway will have to be installed to provide access to the nearest public road? Of all development costs, road building is often the most extreme. In general, a well-chosen building site should suit the terrain and provide adequate drainage away from the foundation. For this reason, gently sloping ground is usually best but not always necessary, since pole or pier foundations that compensate for uneven ground can often be constructed.

Energy efficiency is becoming a basic element in site selection just as it was in the past. Significant savings in heating can be realized by building on the lee side of a rise or by locating the building site downwind from a stand of trees. A site that takes advantage of the low winter sun—even if the home is not designed for solar heating—can reap major long-term energy savings.

Most sites require some shifting of earth. Because of the labor and expense involved, thorough planning is a must. The goal is to move as little earth as possible. Of the three methods of leveling—cut, fill, and a combination of the two—the last is easiest and most economical.

Using the Lay of the Land to Your Advantage

A detailed map can be an invaluable planning aid. To make your own map, you will need a plane table (a board mounted on a tripod is best, but a card table will do), straight pins, a ruler, a spirit level, and a 10-foot pole marked in feet and inches. Start by drawing the

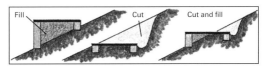

Cut-and-fill leveling technique requires least movement of soil.

outline of your property on a large sheet of paper; if you do not have a boundary map, you can get one at the town assessor's office. The remainder of the job consists of plotting as many distinct features as possible. If your property is relatively open, you can also find the height of each point and sketch in equal-altitude contour lines. When mapping, concentrate on features that will tie the map together, such as a road, a stream, a hedgerow, or an old stone wall. Either pace off the distance to each feature or else take sightings on it from two different locations: the intersection of the two lines of sight will pinpoint the feature.

Getting Your Ideas Down On a Sheet of Paper

Settling on a design for a home reflects a series of compromises between the ideal and the possible. The most fundamental compromise involves size: the expense of building a home is directly proportional to the number of cubic feet of interior space it contains. In addition, a larger home requires more energy to heat and cool and is more expensive to maintain.

One way to cut down on cubic feet without sacrificing comfort or floor area is to keep the ceilings low. Typically, a traditional two-story farmhouse will have 8-foot ceilings on the ground floor and 7-foot ceilings upstairs where the bedrooms are located. Another energy saver is an attic. The heat that rises to the peak of a cathedral ceiling is almost totally wasted. An attic not only eliminates this waste but also functions as a jumbo-sized insulating space, moderating the temperature both summer and winter.

Space in houses divides three ways: communal (living room, dining room, recreation room), private (bedroom, studio, study), and service (kitchen, bathroom, garage, laundry, closets). The allocation of these spaces into rooms depends on the needs and tastes of the family. When sketching your designs, pay particular attention to the way the different spaces interact. Traffic flow between areas should be smooth, and a private space should never lie in the flow between two communal areas. Service areas generally function as appendages to communal or private areas. The kitchen, for example, must be adjacent to the dining room, and the bathrooms should be convenient to the sleeping quarters. Separation can be important; a noisy family room should be far away from an area used for studying.

Home design should take into account future needs. A growing family will either have to build extra space into the original house or plan on future additions. The escalating cost of building materials argues for the first alternative, but any excess space will mean unnecessary heating bills, property taxes, and mortgage payments until the day that it is put to use. Plan your addition so that it meets the following criteria: it should not interfere with natural lighting or spoil the view; it should not conflict with local zoning requirements; and, in the case of a second floor addition, the original structure should be strong enough to support it.

Drawing Accurate Floor Plans

After a basic layout has been developed, the next step is to draw carefully scaled floor plans. Try to base room dimensions, ceiling heights, and the widths and lengths of floors on increments of 4 feet insofar as possible. This is because standard sheets of plywood and other building materials are sold in 4- by 8-foot sheets. In addition, keep in mind the following design criteria:

Closets. Minimum depth for a closet is 2 feet.

Counter space. Allow 2 feet from the wall for kitchen counters, since most kitchen equipment protrudes about that amount.

Doors. Interior doors are generally 2 1/2 feet wide; the front door should be 3 feet wide.

Hallways. Widths run from 2 feet up to 4 feet and more. The longer the hallway, the wider it should be.

Kitchen aisles. Small is not necessarily convenient. A minimum aisle width of 4 feet is recommended when equipment is laid out along parallel walls; increase this dimension to 5 feet if the kitchen is U-shaped.

Room dimensions. The ratio of room length to width should be no more than two to one. Overall size varies from 5 feet by 5 feet for a small foyer to 20 feet by 30 feet or larger for a living room. In general, the bigger the room, the higher the ceiling should be.

Walls. Allow a thickness of 1/2 foot for both interior and exterior walls. If the walls are masonry, allow 1 foot.

When drawing plans for a two-story house, trace the structural elements of the ground floor, then use the outline to draw the rooms on the second floor.

Architects and Other Outside Aids

A home is the most expensive possession that a family is ever likely to own. With so much time, labor, and money invested, it is vital that the house plans be accurate and sound. In most cases this means that outside design aid will have to be enlisted.

The most straightforward way to get help is to hire an architect. A good architect does not come cheaply—a fee of 10 percent of the cost of a home is not unusual. One

Idealized 15-acre parcel illustrates how natural features of land can be put to best use. Land use principles apply to small parcels as well.

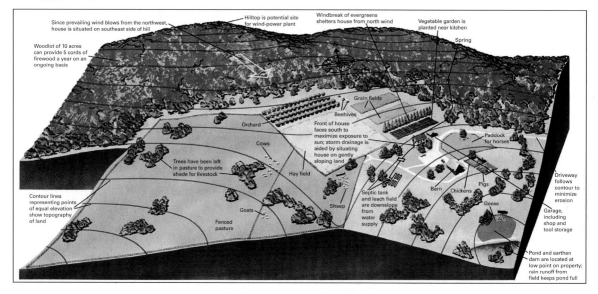

Since prevailing wind blows from the northwest, house is situated on southeast side of hill

Hilltop is potential site for wind-power plant

Windbreak of evergreens shelters house from north wind

Vegetable garden is planted near kitchen

Spring

Woodlot of 10 acres can provide 5 cords of firewood a year on an ongoing basis

Grain fields

Beehives

Orchard

Front of house faces south to maximize exposure to sun; storm drainage is aided by situating house on gently sloping land

Paddock for horses

Cows

Trees have been left in pasture to provide shade for livestock

Hay field

Barn

Chickens

Pigs

Driveway follows contour to minimize erosion

Contour lines representing points of equal elevation show topography of land

Goats

Sheep

Septic tank and leach field are downslope from water supply

Geese

Garage, including shop and tool storage

Fenced pasture

Pond and earthen dam are located at low point on property; rain runoff from field keeps pond full

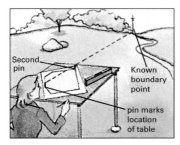

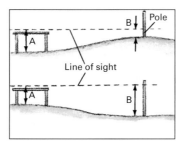

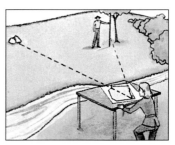

1. Set up table at a corner of your property line, insert pin at corresponding point in map outline, and adjust table so it is horizontal. Then sight from pin to another known boundary point, align map along line of sight, and insert second pin.

2. Sight from first pin to other distinct features. Have assistant pace off distance to each point. Then have him hold measuring pole while you sight to it. Height of table (A) minus height from base of pole to line of sight (B) equals height of point.

3. Move table to one of the points you have already mapped, reorient map as in Step 1, and map more points as in Step 2. By setting up table at a number of locations, you can map enough points to sketch in the topography of your land.

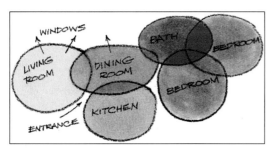

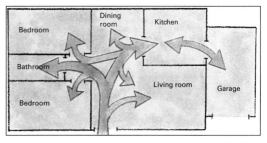

Layout of space can begin with a series of informal "bubble" sketches. Each bubble represents a particular use of space. The more of these diagrams you draw, the nearer you are likely to come to sensing the best floor plan. You should also make a point of visiting and examining as many homes as possible.

Sketch of floor plans, with rooms in approximately correct proportion, follows space layout. With such sketches, defects in the location of doorways and patterns of personal movement can be discerned. Bathroom in sketch shown, for example, might be considered too long a walk from kitchen.

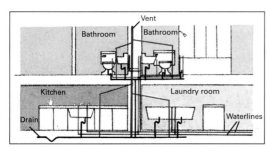

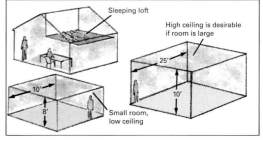

Clustering of utilities, such as waterlines and drainpipes, in one area of the house is advisable from point of view of economy, ease of installation, and ease of maintenance. In a typical layout the kitchen sink and laundry room are placed back to back with a bathroom located above.

Room size should be suited to function—large and spacious for a main communal area, small and cozy for a den or child's bedroom. Cathedral ceilings are attractive, but they waste heat. A sleeping loft can reduce heat loss in a room with a cathedral ceiling without destroying the ceiling's dramatic impact.

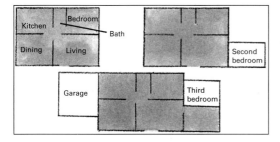

Build small and add on later is often preferable to building everything at once, particularly for a growing family. As the years pass, you will know more accurately whether you need that extra bedroom or studio. However, the initial design should take possible additions into account.

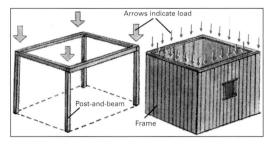

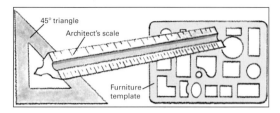

Frame construction and post-and-beam construction are the two principal building methods. In the former, house weight is borne by all segments of each wall; in the latter, by separate posts. Frame construction costs less and is more widely used; post-and-beam permits larger spaces, bigger windows.

Inexpensive tools can aid in drawing floor plans and vertical views. A triangle makes it easy to draw lines at right angles; an architect's scale lets you choose from 12 different scales that automatically convert feet to inches; and a furniture template helps you indicate such items as chairs, sofas, and shelves.

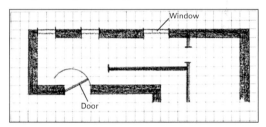

Quadrille paper with four or five squares to the inch is handy for sketching floor plans. If the side of each square in sketch is set to 1 ft., the area of each room can be quickly determined by counting the number of squares it encloses.

Model of house can be constructed out of foam core board or corrugated cardboard. Carefully draw the outlines of floor plans, house sides, interior walls, and roof on the cardboard, then cut out pieces along outlines, including doorways and windows, and put the model together with rubber cement or transparent tape. With a little imagination you can place yourself in each room, sense how it feels, and make design adjustments. By setting the model outdoors on a sunny day (or simulating the sun with a high intensity lamp) you can tell how much natural lighting can be expected.

way to save money is to have the architect make only a basic sketch, then let a contractor work out the practical details. This procedure still gives you the benefit of the architect's ability to establish lighting, space relationships, flow patterns, and environmental harmony.

When choosing an architect or contractor—or for that matter when doing your own designing—there is no substitute for examining actual houses: no floor plan or rendition can replace the real thing. Visit all the homes you can (most homeowners will be happy to show you around if you explain your purpose), and note which homes give you a good feeling and which leave you with a negative impression. Try to spot the features you like or dislike; sometimes the difference between a desirable and undesirable home comes down to nothing more than carpeting, wallpaper, or furniture. Before you pick an architect or contractor, quiz him closely; especially if you are interested in energy efficiency, solar heating, or other special technology. Do not rely on verbal assurances alone. Rather, ask the architect or contractor to show you examples of his work.

An alternative to hiring an architect is to purchase standard plans. Magazines containing floor layouts and artist's renderings are available at building supply dealers and magazine stores. After choosing a plan, you can order complete blueprints for a few hundred dollars.

Sources and resources

Books and pamphlets
Ching, Francis D.K. *Building Construction Illustrated.* New York: Van Nostrand Reinhold, 1991.
DeCristoforo, R.J. *Housebuilding: A Do-It-Yourself Guide.* New York: Sterling Publishing, 1987.
DiDonno, Lupe, and Phyllis Sperling. *How to Design & Build Your Own House.* New York: Knopf, 1987.
Kern, Barbara, and Ken Kern. *The Owner-Built Homestead.* New York: Scribner's, 1977.
Ramsey, Charles G., and Harold R. Sleeper. *Architectural Graphic Standards,* 7th ed. New York: John Wiley, 1993.
Shemie, Bonnie. *Houses of Wood: Northwest Coast.* Plattsburgh, N.Y.: Tundra Books, 1994.
Sherwood, Gerald H. and Stroh, Robert C., eds. *Wood Frame House Construction: A Do-It-Yourself Guide.* New York: Sterling Publishing, 1992.
Uniform Building Code. Whittier, Calif.: International Conference of Building Officials, 1994.
Wagner, Willis H. *Modern Carpentry.* South Holland, Ill.: Goodheart-Willcox, 1992.
Walker, Les, and Jeff Milstein. *Designing Houses: An Illustrated Guide.* Woodstock, N.Y.: Overlook Press, 1979.
Wood Frame House Building. Blue Ridge Summit, Pa.: TAB Books, 1991.

Preparing the Site

Carving Your Homestead From the Wilderness

A small cabin on a minimal foundation normally needs little site preparation. For a larger home, however, the work of clearing the land, leveling a building site, developing an access road, excavating, and laying a foundation sometimes requires as much labor, time, and expense as erecting the house itself. Pioneer settlers, lacking power machinery, searched for building sites that required a minimum of preparation. Though such sites are scarce today, the loss is more than offset by modern techniques and equipment that permit the development of lands that the pioneers would have been forced to pass up.

Planning and Preparation

The job of site development starts in the winter, when trees are bare and the features of the terrain are clearly visible. This is the time of year to lay out your plans in detail. It is also the time to cut and haul away any trees that have value as lumber or firewood.

Start actual clearing as soon as possible after the spring thaw, when the ground is firm and dry: land cleared later in the year seldom develops enough ground cover to prevent erosion. The initial stages require only hand tools—a chain saw, an ax, and a brush hook. Later, heavy equipment must be brought in for grading and excavation. A rented gasoline-powered chipper is useful for shredding brush; the chips make excellent mulch for gardening, landscaping, and erosion control. If you have the time and energy, hand clearing has advantages over machinery: far greater numbers of trees and shrubs can be left undisturbed, and there will be less damage to the natural features of the surrounding area. Hand clearing also saves money and gives you additional time to plan the final construction.

It takes two to survey. The assistant (right) will point to a spot. When that spot is in line with the surveyor's scope, the assistant will measure its height above ground. That height, minus the height of the scope, will give the ground elevation where the pole stands.

The Four Stages of Site Development

1. Start clearing in winter by cutting down trees that are on the building site. Winter is the best season for logging, since wood is driest and snow on the ground eases the job of hauling. Leave 3-ft. stumps to ease the job of removing them later.

2. Wait until spring, when the ground is fully thawed, to pull stumps. Use animals or a mechanical aid, such as a winch, unless they are to be removed by bulldozer. Ordinary cars and trucks do not have enough traction for the job.

Batter board

3. Erect batter boards to mark building lines and excavation boundaries. Simple foundation trenches can be dug by hand, but a powered backhoe with an experienced operator is usually more economical in the long run.

4. Pouring a foundation is the last step before construction begins. You will need plenty of assistance, since the job is long and difficult even if you hire a cement mixer. For maximum strength the entire footing should be poured at one time.

Surveying the site, grading the land, and excavating the foundation and drainage field are jobs for professionals unless you happen to have experience in this type of work. A home is too important to risk the consequences of trial-and-error learning, so assess your abilities fairly before you begin.

Clearing the Land and Building an Access Road

The job of site development starts with clearing the land and constructing an access road. There was a time when this work was accomplished with the sweat and muscle of animals and men, but today the fastest and cheapest method is to hire a bulldozer run by an experienced operator. Prepare in advance for the job of clearing by marking features that might affect the grading of the site and access road on your development map. Also rent a builder's level and measuring rod; you will need them to make sure that the building site and access road are graded to the proper angles.

Tree removal should be thought out carefully. Generally speaking, stands of native hardwoods are more valuable than evergreens and should receive priority if a choice has to be made to cut one type or the other. An exception would be a case where dense evergreens can serve as a windbreak or where diseased hardwoods may eventually fall and damage the house. Trees less than 4 inches in diameter, along with brush and undergrowth, usually can be cleared away with little worry. Consult a forester, however, before removing large numbers of bigger trees; he can help you work out a plan for gradual removal that will allow the remaining growth to adjust to altered water-table characteristics. Use paint or plastic ribbon to distinguish trees that are to be removed; mark trees that are to be saved with paint or ribbon of another color. Trees that are cut should be carried away as lumber or sawed into firewood and left to season. Stack firewood nearby, between standing trees; it will be easier to haul after it is seasoned.

Access roads should be 10 feet wide or more—a wide road will last longer than a narrow one because

Homemade tools for grading

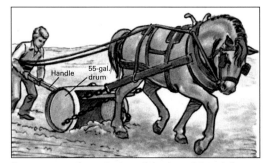

Fresno scraper, for moving loose dirt and gravel, is made from 55-gal. drum cut in half with ends left intact. Bolt or weld a blade of 1/2-in.-thick steel along bottom edge, and add braced handle made of 2 × 4 s or thick poles.

Buck scraper smooths high spots left by fresno. Use sturdy 2 × 12 s for buckboard, 1/4-in.-thick steel for blade, strap iron for bracing. Handle is bent iron pipe. Operator stands on trailer board, applies pressure to handle to regulate blade.

Taking elevations with a builder's level

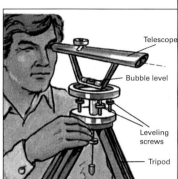

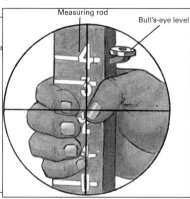

1. Mount builder's level on tripod and adjust until bubble is stable throughout 360° rotation of telescope. Measure height of scope above the ground.

2. Have assistant hold measuring rod at point where elevation reading is desired, then sight rod through scope. Rod marking, minus scope height, is elevation.

3. Take elevations of surrounding points by rotating telescope; tripod must remain fixed. In each case, subtract scope height from rod reading to obtain result.

wear and tear is spread over a larger surface. Grade all curves to an inside radius of 30 feet for a car, 45 feet if large vehicles, such as oil trucks, will use the road. A turnaround at a garage or dead end should be a minimum of 30 feet by 40 feet. Drivers must have at least one car length of unobstructed vision at all points along the road, so foliage should be kept low along curves. Similarly, trim trees and shrubs far enough back from the shoulders to prevent them from interfering with traffic. Try, however, to leave a screen of foliage for soil control, privacy, and encouragement of wildlife.

If a road is being put in on a steep slope, do not cut it directly uphill. Instead, traverse the slope by following the contour lines. Slope gradients should be no more than 10 percent (a 1-foot rise for every 10 feet in length) to minimize vehicle strain and road damage from braking and wheel spinning. In order to prevent landslides, embankments should be smoothed back to their angles of repose–the point at which a given material ceases to slide downhill of its own accord. Incorporate gutters, ditches, and culverts into the roadway to minimize erosion, mud formation, and frost heaving.

Road surfaces of dirt, gravel, or crushed rock are adequate in most parts of the country although occasional routine maintenance will be necessary. Regrading and smoothing require little more than hard work and often can be accomplished with the simple homemade equipment shown below.

Laying the Groundwork Gets You Started

After the building site has been cleared and leveled, actual construction can begin. The first step is to set up accurate building lines to mark the structure's perimeter. Once that is accomplished, the area can be excavated for the foundation. Start by setting the corner stakes, which identify the exact locations of each corner of the proposed building. Make these stakes of 2 × 2 lumber, 2 to 3 feet in length, and sharpen their ends symmetrically to keep them from twisting when driven into the ground. Drive the first stake so that it is centered over the spot selected for the first corner of the building. Locate the second corner by measuring from the first, then drive another stake into the ground at that spot. The two stakes define the corners, length, and position of one side of the building. The other corners and sides can now be found by measuring out from the established corners according to the ground plan of the building. Each time a new corner is established, drive a stake into the ground to mark it. Square or rectangular structures require only four corner stakes. If the building is L-shaped or has additional projections, stake out a central rectangle, then lay out the extensions.

Precise right angles are essential throughout. One method of achieving them, explained in Step 1 on following page, is to use the Pythagorean theorem. Another way is to build an oversize try square in the shape of a right triangle; construct it from a metal angle iron or from lumber carefully selected for straightness. Place the square at a known corner of the site so that one arm lies along the established straight line and the other arm extends at right angles to it in the direction of the corner location you wish to find. Measure along this arm to establish the new corner.

The corner stakes are usually removed during excavation, since their locations normally place them in the path of any foundation trenches that must be dug. In order to keep a permanent record of their location, horizontal boards known as batter boards are set up on stakes several feet outside the site at each corner. The boards are then notched with saw cuts so that strings stretched between them will intersect directly over the corner stakes. Batter boards are used to record other information as well, such as excavation boundaries and footing widths, and are generally left in place throughout most of the building process.

Setting Corner Stakes and Batter Boards

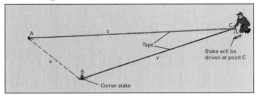

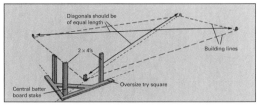

1. Locate corner stakes at right angles to known building lines with help of Pythagorean formula. Stakes A and B mark corners of known line x. Length of side y is specified in plans. Compute length of z by adding together square of side x and square of side y; z equals the square root of sum ($z = \sqrt{x^2 + y^2}$). Now attach tape equal in length to z to stake A and another tape equal in length to to y to stake B. The point on the ground where both tapes are stretched tight when held together is correct spot for C.

2. Complete corner stake layout by using methods described in Step 1 to locate remaining stake. Check final rectangle by stretching tape between diagonally opposite stakes: both diagonals should be equal. Next step is to erect batter boards. Set central batter board stakes 6 ft. behind corner stakes along extended diagonals. Use homemade oversize try square built of metal or lumber to locate the remaining batter board stakes, and drive them about 6 ft. from each central stake, making sure they are parallel to the building lines.

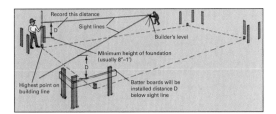

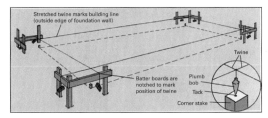

3. Horizontal 1 × 6s complete the batter board assemblies. Set up a builder's level, and have an assistant hold a measuring rod at the highest corner stake. Sight to the rod, and record the difference (D) between the rod reading and the minimum height of the foundation above grade. Next, have the assistant hold the rod alongside each batter board stake in turn. In each case sight to the rod, subtract the distance D, and mark the stake at that point. Nail on the 1 × 6s with their top edges touching the marks.

4. Record location of building corners by stretching twine between batter boards so that their intersections fall directly over the centers of the corner stakes. Achieve precise alignment by hanging plumb bob from intersections as shown. (Use thumbtacks to mark centers of stakes.) Make saw cuts in batter boards to establish twine locations permanently, and note on boards which corner each cut represents. Stretch twine and make cuts to record other information, such as excavation boundaries.

Excavating for a Firm Foundation

Excavation for the foundation can begin as soon as the building lines are established. Be sure to dig deep enough so that the base, called the footing, will be safely below the level of frost penetration. Freezing ground expands and can crack an improperly laid foundation. Local building authorities can provide you with precise specifications for building safe foundations in your area. You should also consult a government soil engineer who will analyze the type of ground upon which your site is located and determine its weight-bearing ability, drainage characteristics, and other factors that influence the kind of foundation best suited to that spot.

Power shovels and backhoes are the most efficient and economical tools, for excavation unless the amount of digging is very small. Try to hire equipment and operators by the job rather than by the day or hour so that you do not have to pay for wasted time due to problems and delays that are not your fault. Be sure that the plans for digging are fully understood by the excavator beforehand, and be there yourself when the work is performed. To lessen the chance of cave-ins, which are not only potentially dangerous but also time-consuming to repair, have the scooped-out earth placed at least 2 feet from the rim of the excavation. Topsoil should be stripped from the site and piled in a separate area to prevent it from becoming mixed with the subsoil. (Mixing would change the vitally important drainage and weight-bearing characteristics of the subsoil. The topsoil can be used later for landscaping.) The excavation itself should extend at least 3 feet beyond the building lines to give space for such work as manipulating building forms and laying concrete block. Do not backfill the excavation until the entire foundation is laid and the floor of the building has been attached; only then will the foundation walls be well enough braced to eliminate any danger of collapse. It is also important that the excavation be no deeper than called for in the plans, since refilling to the correct level does not restore the weight-bearing capacity of the original undisturbed soil upon which the foundation rests.

There is always plenty of trimming to be done with hand shovels, so be safety conscious. Do not let debris collect in and around excavations. Use a ladder to avoid jumping in and out of trenches, and do not work so near a partner that you risk injuring each other with your tools. Brace all trenches more than 4 feet deep with boards placed vertically along the banks. For added strength, especially if heavy equipment is used nearby, install crosspieces that span the width of the trench between the vertical boards. If possible, slope the sides of the excavations back to their angles of repose. Watch for cave-in signals: cracks developing nearby or earth trickling down the sides. And check the site carefully after heavy rains or a weekend break.

Bracing for trenches

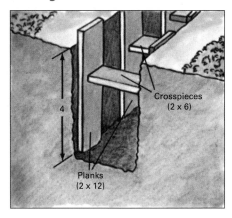

Light bracing (above) consists of vertical planks placed at 3- to 5-ft. intervals, held apart by cross-pieces. For heavy bracing (right) set planks almost side by side. Horizontal walers tie planks together and distribute pressure. Nailing is not necessary; wedging holds boards tight.

Common types of foundations

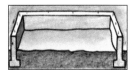

Perimeter foundation made of poured reinforced concrete, masonry block, or stone is strong, provides basement or crawl space, and conforms to most codes. Excavation and formwork are often necessary, usually requiring heavy equipment.

Wooden pole foundation made of logs, ties, or telephone poles leaves underside of building exposed but requires little excavation and is good for steep sites and remote areas. Pole foundations are not suitable on soft ground.

Concrete slab foundation of reinforced concrete also serves as basement or ground floor and is especially suited to passive heat storage in solar designed buildings. Steep site or high water table may preclude use.

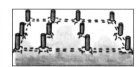

Concrete pier foundation is inexpensive and needs little excavation. Piers are suitable on steep sites but do not provide the anchoring strength of perimeter or slab foundations. Piers can be either precast or poured.

Suitability of various soils for building

Soil description	Value as foundation material	Frost action	Drainage	Angle of repose
Gravel	Excellent	None	Excellent	
Gravel-sand-silt mix	Good	Slight	Poor	40°–55°
Gravel-sand-clay mix	Good	Slight	Poor	
Sand	Good	None	Excellent	
Sand-silt mix	Fair	Slight	Fair	50°–60°
Sand-clay mix	Fair	Medium	Poor	
Inorganic silt	Fair	Very high	Poor	
Organic silt	Poor	High	Impervious	55°–70°
Clay	Very poor	Medium	Impervious	
Peat or organic soil	Not suitable	Slight	Poor	40°–45°

Foundation is only as strong as the earth beneath it; chart gives key characteristics of common soils. Frost action refers to amount of frost heaving that can be expected.

Sources and resources

Books
Bureau of Naval Personnel. *Basic Construction Techniques for Houses and Small Buildings Simply Explained.* New York: Dover, 1972.
Church, Horace K. *Excavation Handbook.* New York: McGraw-Hill, 1980.
DiDonno, Lupe, and Phyllis Sperling. *How to Design and Build Your Own House.* New York: Knopf, 1987.
Nichols, Herbert L. *Moving the Earth: The Workbook of Excavation.* New York: McGraw-Hill, 1988.

Converting Trees Into Lumber

Processing Your Timber Into Hand-Hewn Beams and Top-Grade Lumber

Making your own lumber is practical and economical. You not only save the cost of buying wood but of having it delivered. You can cut your lumber to the sizes you need rather than shaping your projects to the sizes available. And you can use your timber resources to the fullest, harvesting trees when they are mature, converting the best stock into valuable building or woodworking material, and burning imperfect or low-quality wood in your fireplace.

Most important of all is the quality of the wood you get. Air-dried lumber of the type demanded over the years by furnituremakers, boatbuilders, and other craftsmen is rare and expensive—lumbermills today dry their wood in kilns rather than wait for years while it seasons in the open. The lumber you cut and stack yourself can match the finest available and in some cases may be your only means of obtaining superior wood or specially cut stock at a reasonable cost. You may even be able to market surplus homemade lumber to local craftsmen.

Logs and Logging Techniques

Once a tree has been felled and trimmed of limbs, it is generally hauled elsewhere for conversion into boards. Trunks that are too long or heavy to move must be bucked into sections. Make your cuts near crooks or defects to preserve good board wood. Log lengths may range from 2 to 16 feet, depending on intended use and your ability to haul them.

Horsepower is often the best way to log rugged timberland.

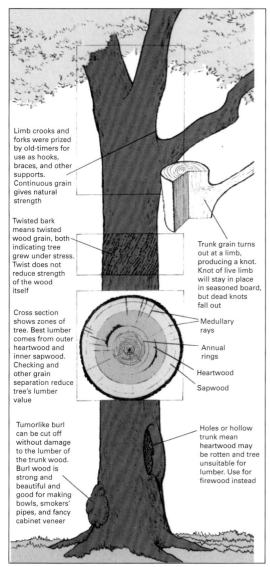

Limb crooks and forks were prized by old-timers for use as hooks, braces, and other supports. Continuous grain gives natural strength

Twisted bark means twisted wood grain, both indicating tree grew under stress. Twist does not reduce strength of the wood itself

Cross section shows zones of tree. Best lumber comes from outer heartwood and inner sapwood. Checking and other grain separation reduce tree's lumber value

Tumorlike burl can be cut off without damage to the lumber of the trunk wood. Burl wood is strong and beautiful and good for making bowls, smokers' pipes, and fancy cabinet veneer

Trunk grain turns out at a limb, producing a knot. Knot of live limb will stay in place in seasoned board, but dead knots fall out

Medullary rays

Annual rings

Heartwood

Sapwood

Holes or hollow trunk mean heartwood may be rotten and tree unsuitable for lumber. Use for firewood instead

For best lumber and greatest yield per log, select trees with smooth, straight trunks at least 1 ft. in diameter. Trees that have branches at the top only are best, since limbs cause knots in finished boards. Avoid hollow trees or trunks with splits; both probably signal extensive interior decay.

A good deal of lumbering is still done with horses, especially in hilly areas inaccessible to motor vehicles or where there is a risk of environmental damage. Horses are ideal when only a few trees are being culled or where forest growth is dense. In flat country a four-wheel-drive vehicle with tire chains can be more efficient. Buy a good tree identification handbook (see *Sources and resources,* page 21), and use it to identify your trees so that you will know what you are cutting. Pay particular attention to bark characteristics, since logging is often done in winter, when there are no leaves. (Logs can be moved more easily on snow, and winter-cut logs season better.)

The Lumbermen's Tools

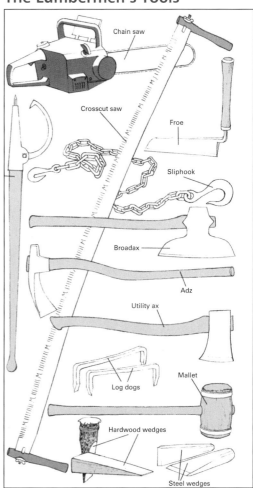

Chain saw

Crosscut saw

Froe

Sliphook

Broadax

Adz

Utility ax

Mallet

Log dogs

Hardwood wedges

Steel wedges

Many home-lumbering tools are available from hardware stores. Some, however, such as froes, broadaxes, and adzes, are manufactured by only a few firms and are difficult to find. Wooden mallets can be homemade; log dogs can be fashioned from steel reinforcing rod (rebar) sharpened at both ends.

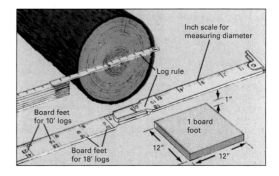

Inch scale for measuring diameter

Log rule

Board feet for 10' logs

1 board foot

Board feet for 18' logs

12"

12"

1"

Use a log rule to estimate board feet. Varying scales exist, each yielding slightly different results; the Doyle rule shown above is typical. To use a log rule, determine length of log, measure diameter at small end, then read board feet directly from tables on rule corresponding to those measurements.

Use straight grain, 2- to 4-ft. sections for splitting shingles and shakes

Two men, one to guide, one to pull operate crosscut bucking saw, one man can operate chain saw

Keep areas with deep defects at one end of section

Sections with surface defects can still yield usable lumber

Buck at or near crook unless naturally curved lumber is wanted

Tips on bucking

Plan bucking cuts to avoid wasting wood. Group defects together to minimize scrap; allow only enough extra length for trimming logs to final board dimensions.

Hauling logs

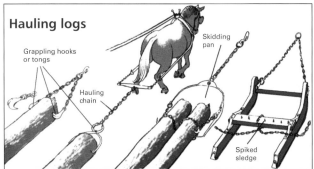

Grappling hooks or tongs

Skidding pan

Hauling chain

Spiked sledge

Horses and oxen are versatile haulers, good in deep woods or over rough terrain. Shovellike skidding pan or heavy sledge with spikes holds log end and eases the job. Tongs or hooks on hauling chain grip the log. Keep the animal moving forward slowly and steadily, and avoid following routes that take you along the side slopes of hills. Never haul logs down an icy or steep grade; instead, unhook the log at the top of the slope and let it roll or slide down.

All About Boards, Beams, Shingles, and Shakes

Making lumber is simpler than most people realize. A chain saw and lumbermaking adapter are almost indispensable accessories if you plan to make boards. The chain saw can also be used to make beams and heavy building timbers, but you may wish to hew these by hand instead. The broadax is the traditional tool for hand-hewing; however, an ordinary utility ax costs less, is more widely available, and will perform almost as well. Of course, axes and chain saws are potentially dangerous tools and should be used with extreme caution. To split shakes and shingles, a special tool called a froe is needed. Froes are available from a few specialty hardware suppliers or they can be made by a blacksmith from a discarded automobile leaf spring. The key to making shingles is not your tools but the wood you use. Choose only straight-grained wood

of a kind noted for its ability to split cleanly, such as cedar, oak, and cypress.

Seasoning is probably the most important step in making your own lumber. During this stage the wood is slowly air dried until ready for use. Freshly cut lumber must be stacked carefully to permit plenty of air circulation between boards; at the same time it must be protected from moisture, strong sunlight, and physical stresses that can cause warping. Done properly, drying by air produces boards that are superior in many ways to the kiln-dried stock sold at most lumberyards. Air drying is a gradual process that does not involve the high temperatures used in kiln drying, and the wood cells are able to adjust to the slow loss of moisture without damage, toughening as they dry and shrink and actually becoming stronger than when fresh. Moreover, sap and natural oils, which do not evaporate as quickly as water, remain in the wood for long periods of time, further assisting curing. Air-dried lumber is not only strong but also durable, attractive, highly resistant to moisture damage, and well conditioned against seasonal shrinkage and swelling caused by changes in humidity.

Using a vehicle

Four-wheel-drive vehicle that has tire chains and power winch is efficient but less maneuverable than a draft animal. Keep the vehicle away from deep mud, heavy snow, and thick woods. Use a pulley chained to a tree to maneuver logs around sharp turns. Pad the chain to prevent damage to tree trunk.

Pulley

Keep vehicle wheels straight when pulling

Pad

Pitsawing was once the standard method for making boards, and it can still be used. Place the log on trestles or over a pit. The upper man stands on the log, starts the saw cut with short strokes, then continues cutting by pushing the saw blade down from shoulder height (a heavy saw works best). Lower man guides saw and returns blade but does no actual cutting.

Hat with protective netting

Trestle

Common woods for lumber

Beech is hard, strong, heavy, and shock resistant. It is good for furniture, floors, and woodenware and can be steam bent. Beeches grow in all states east of the Mississippi River.

Shagbark hickory is strong, tough, and resilient, making it ideal for tool handles and sports equipment. It can be steam bent. Hickory grows in most of the eastern and central United States.

Black cherry, or wild cherry, is medium weight, strong, stiff, and hard. Straight-grained cherry is excellent for making furniture or cabinets. It grows in the eastern United States.

Shortleaf or yellow pine is a tough softwood with good grain. Formerly used for sailing ship masts and planking, it makes good clapboards. It grows in the southeastern United States.

Black walnut is medium weight, has beautiful grain, is easy to work, and is strong and stable. Reserve this wood for special paneling and furniture. It grows throughout the United States.

Sugar maple, excellent for furniture, floors, and woodenware, is hard, strong, easy to work, and extremely shock resistant. It grows in New England and the north-central United States.

Douglas fir is light, easy to work, and very strong. A leading structural wood (building timber, plywood), it is also used for Christmas trees. It grows on the Pacific Coast and in the Rockies.

Western white pine, similar to Eastern, resists harsh weather and is a good board wood for house frames and panels. It grows best in the mountains of the northwestern United States.

Eastern red cedar is light, brittle, easy to work, and decay resistant. It grows in the eastern two-thirds of the country and is used for fence posts and as mothproof closet or chest lining.

White oak is similar to red but stronger and more resistant to moisture. It can be steam bent and is often used in boats. It grows in the eastern United States from Canada to the Gulf.

Eastern white pine is light, semisoft, easy to work but strong, and has been used for everything from clapboards to furniture since colonial days. It grows mostly in the northeastern United States.

White spruce is light, strong, and easy to work. It can be used for house framing and paneling but is not decay resistant. It grows in the northern United States from Maine to Wisconsin.

Northern red oak is tough and strong but heavy and hard to work. It is excellent for use in timber framing and as flooring. It grows in the northeastern third of the United States.

Yellow birch is heavy, hard, and strong, with a close, even grain. It is excellent for furniture, interior work, and doors. It is easy to work. It grows in the Northeast and the north-central states.

How to Slice a Log

Quality of lumber varies depending upon what part of the tree it comes from. Innermost heartwood is relatively weak; use it only for heavy timbers and thick planks. Best boards come from surrounding area. Avoid using extreme outer sapwood next to the bark. Lumber cut so that rings are perpendicular to the sawn sides of the board when viewed from the end is less likely to warp. Boards whose ends show curving lines tend to cup as they dry. Two basic ways to cut boards are plainsawing (slicing through the full diameter of the log) and quartersawing (cutting the log into quarter sections before ripping it into boards). Plainsawing yields the widest boards and the most lumber per log; quartersawing yields less lumber, but boards are of higher quality.

Uneven shrinking

Cupping

Best lumber

Plainsawn

Quartersawn

Lumbermaking With a Chain Saw

Chain saw can be used without guide to rip logs into boards, but skill and practice are needed to cut long lengths. Raise log off ground to avoid blade damage and kickback; wedges in cut prevent blade from being pinched.

Saw

Insert wedge

Support log off ground

Simple adapter attaches to chain bar; 2 × 4 nailed along length of log acts as guide for making straight cuts. Support log off ground; attach and test entire assembly before starting saw. Reposition board after each cut.

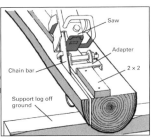

Saw

Adapter

Chain bar

2 × 2

Support log off ground

Portable chain-saw mill, best manned by two men, cuts horizontally, permitting operation with log on ground. Rollers keep saw blade level and adjust vertically to make boards of different thicknesses. Mill fits any chain saw.

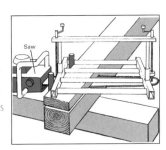

Saw

Hand-Hewing a Beam

Squaring a log into a beam is easier if you use green freshly cut timber. You can also save a lot of extra labor by hewing the logs where they have fallen instead of hauling them to a separate site. Before you begin, be sure to clear the area of all brush and low-hanging branches that might interfere with your ax work.

Choose logs that are only slightly thicker than the beams you wish to hew. Judge this dimension by measuring the small end of the log. Place the log on wooden supports (notched half-sections of firewood logs will do) with any crown, or lengthwise curve, facing up. The two straightest edges of the log should face the sides. Do not remove the bark; its rough surface helps hold the ax to the mark and also diminishes your chances of striking a glancing blow with possibly dangerous results. It is not always necessary to square off all four sides of a log. Old-time carpenters often hewed only two sides, and sometimes, as in the case

of floor joists found in many old houses, they smoothed off only one. Rafters, in fact, were often left completely round.

Seasoning and Stacking Lumber

Commercial lumber mills season new wood in ovens, called kilns, to dry it quickly. Seasoning wood by exposing it to the open air will do the job as well or better, but the process takes much longer—at least six months for building lumber and a year or more for cabinetmaking stock. A traditional rule of thumb is to let wood air dry one year for every inch of board thickness.

The best time of year to begin seasoning new lumber is in the early spring, when the dryness of the cool air coupled with the windiness of the season combine to produce optimal drying conditions. A spring start also permits the curing process to continue uninterrupted for as long as possible before freezing winter tempera-

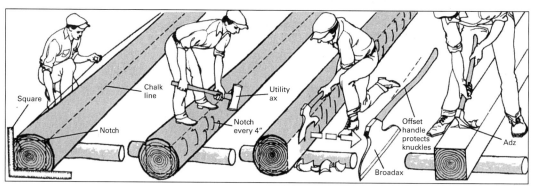

1. Scribe timber dimensions on log ends. Cut notches for chalk line; attach line and snap it to mark sides.

2. Notch logs with utility ax. Make vertical cuts at 4-in. intervals to depth of chalk line marks.

3. Hew sides with broadax. Keep ax parallel to log, and slice off waste by chopping along chalk marks.

4. Smooth hewn surface with adz if desired. Straddle beam and chop with careful blows of even depth.

Splitting shingles and shakes

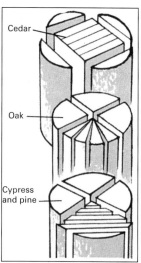

Billets are log sections from which shakes and shingles are split. Use straight-grained logs, 2 ft. or more in diameter, with no knots. Cut logs into 11/2-to 2-ft. lengths for shingles; for shakes use 2 1/2- to 4-ft. lengths. (Longer clapboards can also be split but only from exceptionally well-grained timber.) To make cedar billets, split off outside edges of log section to form squared block. Split block in half, then halve each piece again. Continue until all pieces are of desired thickness. With oak, split the log first into quarters, then radially. Discard heart and outermost sapwood. Cypress and pine are quartered, like oak, then split along the grain at a tangent to the growth rings.

To make shingles with a froe, rest billet on a stump. Drive froe blade into top of log using a heavy wooden mallet or homemade maul. Twist blade to split wood by pulling handle toward you.
To make wood shakes (oversize shingles), brace billet in fork of tree or other improvised holder. Stand behind upper limb of fork, drive froe into wood, and twist blade to start split. Then slide the froe farther down into the crack while holding the split wood apart with your free hand. If the split starts to shift off-center, turn wood around so that opposite side of billet rests against upper limb of fork, and continue twisting with froe.

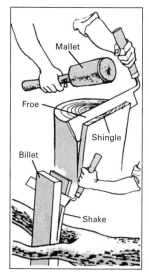

tures temporarily halt evaporation. Set aside or build a sheltered area such as a shed (it may be no more than a roof set on poles) to protect the wood from harsh weather and direct sunlight. Seal the ends of each newly cut board with paint or paraffin to prevent checking, and stack the lumber in one of the ways shown at right so that it receives adequate ventilation and support. Place the poorest quality pieces on the top and bottom of the pile, where weather damage and warping is greatest. Date and label each stack for future reference.

Sources and resources

Books

Collingwood, G.H., and Warren D. Brush. *Knowing Your Trees.* Washington, D.C.: The American Forestry Association, 1984.

Constantine, Albert, Jr. *Know Your Woods.* New York: Scribner's, 1975.

Hoadley, R. Bruce. *Understanding Wood.* Newtown, Conn.: Taunton Press, 1987.

Schiffer, Herbert, and Schiffer, Nancy. *Woods We Live With.* Atglen, Pa.: Schiffer Publishing, 1977.

Seymour, John. *The Forgotten Crafts.* New York: Knopf, 1984.

Sloane, Eric. *An Age of Barns.* New York: Henry Holt & Co., 1990.

Sloane, Eric. *A Museum of Early American Tools.* New York: Ballantine Books, 1985.

Soderstrom, Neil. *Chainsaw Savvy.* Dobbs Ferry, N.Y.: Morgan & Morgan, 1984.

Underhill, Roy. *The Woodwright's Shop.* Chapel Hill, N.C.: University of North Carolina Press, 1981.

Wittlinger, Ellen. *Noticing Paradise.* Boston: Houghton-Mifflin, 1995.

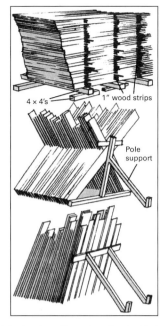

Flat stack lumber that will remain undisturbed for long periods. Place 4 × 4 s on floor or on ground treated with pesticide. Lay boards side by side, 1 to 2 in. apart, then stack in layers separated by 1-in.-thick wood strips.

Pole stack saves labor and space, requires less foundation, and allows lumber to shed rainwater. Lean boards against pole support so they are nearly vertical, crisscross pieces for maximum exposure of surfaces.

End stack is used only for nearly seasoned wood because it provides limited air circulation. Lean boards against wall or frame with spaces between boards at bottom. Boards can be removed without disturbing pile.

Building a Log Cabin

An American Symbol of the Pioneering Spirit

Log cabins have long symbolized the American pioneering spirit and love of independence—and with good reason. Made from inexpensive, locally available materials, they are well suited to homesteaders of any era. For the early settlers, most of whom were neither woodsmen nor carpenters, they provided sturdy, economical housing that did not demand expert skills or require scarce materials and tools. In colonial days trees were plentiful and free. A rough cabin of logs and split lumber shakes or shingles could be put up quickly by one or two people using little more than an ax. Such a structure would last a lifetime; some survive after more than two centuries. Nowadays, cabins are still comparatively economical to build, and with the help of modern techniques and materials they can be made to last even longer. When putting up a log cabin from scratch, the greatest investment remains time and labor rather than trees and tools. But another option also exists: instead of cutting and peeling your own logs, you can buy an entire log cabin kit complete with precut logs.

Traditional log-building methods were brought here from Scandinavia. The first American log cabins were probably built by Finnish colonists at New Sweden, near the mouth of the Delaware River, in 1638. By the 1800s log cabins were common from the Atlantic to California and from Alaska to the Southwest. Only a few decades

Most early log cabins consisted of only one room. Ease of construction plus availability of timber contributed to the enormous popularity of log cabins in colonial America. In turn, log cabins helped make possible the settlement of lands from New England west to the Great Plains.

Logs with the bark removed dry faster and are less susceptible to insect damage. Peeling logs with a drawknife or spud is easiest when logs are freshly cut. Stack logs off the ground to prevent warpage and decay. Let them season three to six months.

ago cabins were still being built by traditional methods in backwoods areas of the United States and Canada. The chain saw, however, has ended the need for many centuries-old skills, and few men exist today who can notch logs with an ax as skillfully as their grandfathers once did.

Choosing Trees and Preparing Logs

Evergreens—pine, fir, cedar, spruce, and larch—make the best cabin logs. You will need about 80 logs for an average one-room cabin. Should you decide to cut your own, be sure of your logging skills and your ability to transport the logs out of the forest. Select trees that are about equal in age, thickness, and height. Look for stands that are dense but not crowded and are located on level land. Avoid trees with low limbs. Good building logs should be between 8 and 14 inches in diameter. Once you select a size, all should be approximately the same. Logs should be straight and free of structural or insect damage. Allow at least 4 feet extra per log so that the ends can project beyond the corner notches.

Cutting is best done in winter when the sap is out of the wood: the logs weigh less, season faster, and resist decay better. In addition, hauling is easier and less damage will be done to the environment, since the ground will be frozen and foliage will be at a minimum.

The Tools You Will Need

Proper tools make the job of building a log cabin much easier and help achieve a high level of craftsmanship. Shown at right are some of the tools needed. In addition, you should have an assortment of basic carpenter's tools, including a handsaw, chisels, measuring tools, and sharpening equipment. A small winch can save a good deal of sweat and strain, and you will also need a chain or a stout rope. Traditional log-building tools are usually hard to find and expensive if bought new or from antique dealers. Begin collecting the ones you will need well in advance. Farm auctions, flea markets, and tag sales are possible sources. If you are buying a chain saw, get one with an instant chain brake and a 16- to 20-inch bar. Learn how to use it safely, keep it sharp at all times, and always wear protection for your ears and eyes.

Foundation and Siting

Although the pioneers often built their cabins directly on the ground, it is better to build on a raised foundation for protection against both termites and damp rot. The crawl space beneath the floor can be used for storage, wiring, plumbing, and under-the-floor insulation. One type of foundation, shown at right, consists of reinforced concrete piers strategically placed around the perimeter of the building and beneath important floor girders. Other possibilities are concrete slab foundation or stone masonry block foundations. Stone is the traditional foundation material. Piers can be of wood rather then concrete. Use log posts of black locust or treated cedar set into the ground on stone or concrete pads.

Locate your cabin in a sheltered, well-drained area, and design it to take advantage of the sun's changing angle throughout the seasons. Make batter boards to mark the corners of the site and stretch string between them to form the exact outline of the foundation. Consult standard building texts for complete advice.

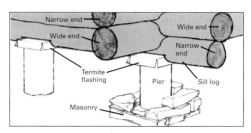

Sill logs are notched flat and drilled so tops of piers will seat firmly and take rebar anchors. Compensate for log taper by alternating wide and narrow ends when building walls. Termite flashing should also be inserted in any area where this insect poses a problem. Concrete piers can be faced with stone to make them attractive; leave wooden piers exposed.

Ordinary garden hose with 6 in. of clear tubing in each end can be used to find equal heights above grade level at widely separated points. Attach one end of hose to reference point, the other to new location. Fill end near reference point with water until water reaches mark. Water level at the other end will then be at same height.

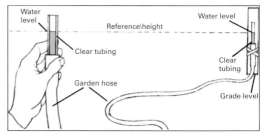

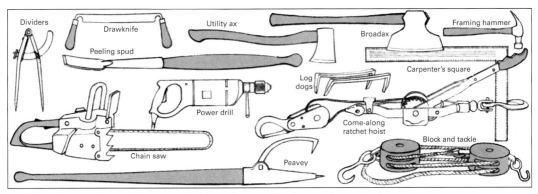

Log builders' tools: a basic kit includes such old-fashioned tools as a broadax as well as modern implements.

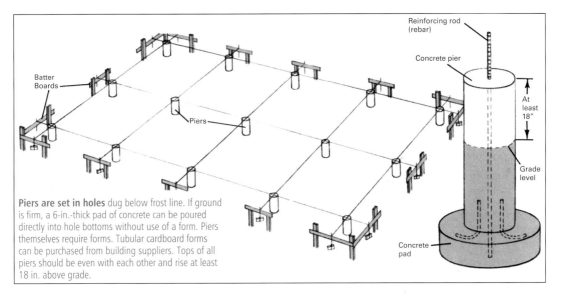

Piers are set in holes dug below frost line. If ground is firm, a 6-in.-thick pad of concrete can be poured directly into hole bottoms without use of a form. Piers themselves require forms. Tubular cardboard forms can be purchased from building suppliers. Tops of all piers should be even with each other and rise at least 18 in. above grade.

Tight-Fitting Notches Mean Sturdy Walls

Well-made notches lock wall logs in place and prevent water from collecting inside the joints. They involve as little cutting away of wood as possible to avoid weakening the logs. Many builders spike the logs together at the joints, but spiking is not necessary for the types of joints shown here. Except in chinkless construction, shown on page 29, notches are generally cut so that a 1- to 2-inch gap remains between parallel logs. This makes chinking easier and more durable.

Round notch is easy to make and very effective, especially when combined with the chinkless construction method. It is a Scandinavian technique and represents one of the earliest notching styles. A sturdy pair of wing dividers with a pencil attached to one leg is essential for scribing a perfect joint. To make the notch, follow the step-by-step procedure shown at right.

V-notch is one of the favorite styles in the Appalachian Mountains. It can be cut with only an ax—the fit is accomplished by trial and error. By adding a carpenter's square to your tools, perfect first-try joints can be made.

Chamfer and notch, probably of German origin, is a more complex notching style but has the advantage of holding the logs in two directions. It is often found on hewn-beam cabins. Since there is no projection beyond the notches, the logs form a flush corner that can be easily covered with clapboard siding. In many parts of the country this notch is called the half-dovetail.

Cutting a chamfer and notch

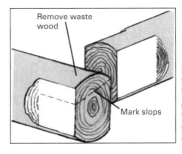

1. Hew sides of log parallel. Then mark slope to angle from top of one side, about one-third of way down other side. Remove wood with ax.

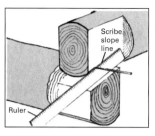
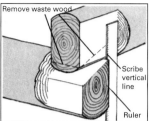
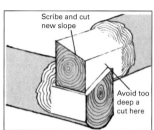

2. Place second log on top of first as shown, its end flush with side. Hold ruler along bottom log and scribe slope line on both sides of top log.

3. Hold ruler against vertical face of lower log and scribe line on upper log so that it intersects slope line. Scribe both sides and end of log.

4. Hew or saw wood from scribed area. Avoid too deep a cut. Carefully trim for a snug fit, then scribe and cut new slope in top log as before.

5. Chamfer-and-notch style is intricate—careful measuring and skillful cutting are required. Results, however, are attractive and durable.

Scribing and cutting a round notch

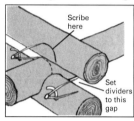
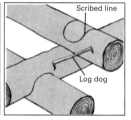
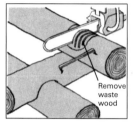

1. Place log at corner. Set dividers to space between logs. Scribe top log on both sides by drawing dividers over surface of lower log.

2. Roll log over and pin in place with log dogs. If you are unable to buy log dogs, you can fashion your own from rebar (reinforcing bar).

3. Rough out notch with chain saw or ax. Deepen center and trim edges to scribed line with chisel. Roll log back into place.

4. Finished notches shed water, since they are cut only in underside of logs. Ends of logs should project about 1 1/2 ft. beyond corners.

Hewing a V-notch with ax and square

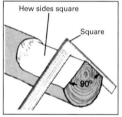
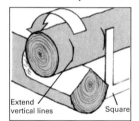
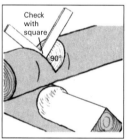

1. Mark 90° angle on butt of log, then hew peak with ax or chain saw by removing wood outside of lines. Keep sides straight. Check accuracy of cut with carpenter's square.

2. Place next log on peak and mark notch width by extending vertical lines upward. Then roll log 180° toward center of wall and pin in place with log dogs.

3. Cut V-notch by hewing wood from between side marks. Maintain 90° cut, and roll log into proper position occasionally to check notch for solid fit.

4. V-notch on underside of one log fits over peak of log below. Experienced woodsmen can cut the joint by eye, but using a square improves accuracy.

Windows and Doors, Then Roof and Floors

The initial step in building a cabin is to prepare the site. Construction of the foundation, walls, and roof comes next. One of the final jobs is to install the windows and doors. Although windows and doors are among the last items completed, they must be planned from the first to ensure that the rules of sound building design are followed. One rule is that wall openings for doors and windows should be located away from corners. Another is that the openings must not penetrate either the sill log or the top plate. Normally at least two logs should span the space above a doorway or window, although in a small cabin with no upper loft the log below the plate can be partially cut away.

Cut out door and window openings after the walls are completed or prepare them for cutting during the building process. Kit homes save on lumber by using logs that have been precut to conform to the precise window and door openings specified in the plans. Once the wall is up and the openings are made, use rough-cut commercial lumber to build the frames. Since the bottom of a door frame serves as a threshold, it should be made of a hardwood, such as oak. Notch and flatten the top and bottom logs, and then fit in the frame by one of the methods shown below. Be sure to slope the flattened surface of the bottom log toward the outside so that water can drain away. Allow several inches for settling between the frame and the top log, and chink the gap with fiberglass insulation protected by metal flashing as shown below. It is best to have the doors and windows on hand when the wall openings are cut.

Installing a splined frame

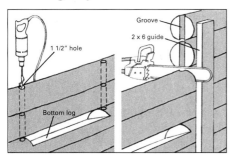

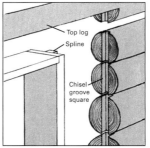

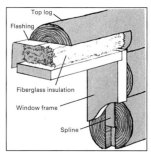

Flatten log that will be at bottom of window, and mark width of frame on it. As each log is laid in place, bore 1 1/2-in. holes through it (left). Bore outside of the mark on both sides of the opening. When top of frame is reached, attach 2 × 6 guides and saw down through each log (right), cutting through the edge of the holes nearest the opening to form vertical grooves.

Splined frame fits in grooved opening. Chisel groove square or trim with tip of chain saw. Assemble frames and nail 1 1/2-in.-sq. strips along outside edges. Work frame into place before attaching top log. Caulk gaps with sealer.

Log walls may settle up to 4 in., so provide an extra space allowance above openings. Fill the gap with fiberglass insulation that compresses as logs descend. Install protective copper flashing on the top log above the insulation for weather seal.

Fitting a nailed frame

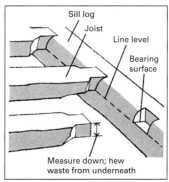

Nailed frame can be fitted after wall is completed. Saw out opening to match frame dimensions. Allow extra room at top. Assemble frame and nail it onto log ends through slotted frame sides to allow settling. Caulk with sealer.

Notch joists carefully into sill logs for a level floor. Use string and a line level to ensure that bearing surfaces of all sill notches are at the same height. When cutting the ends of joists, hew top surfaces flat, then measure down from the top and trim excess from beneath. Commercial 2 × 10's can also be used as joists.

Putting a Floor in Your Cabin

Unless your cabin is set directly on the ground, the floor must be supported by joists. These are beams spanning the distance between sill logs or between sills and a center floor girder if the distance between sills is more than 10 feet. The girder, like the sills, must be supported by the foundation. Notch the sills (and girder) to take the joist ends after the second round of logs is in place. All notches must be carefully cut to the same depth.

Logs for joists should be 6 to 8 inches in diameter and be hewn flat on top. Joists of 2 × 10 commercial lumber can also be used. They generally produce a more level floor and are just as strong as logs. Space joists at even intervals, between 16 inches and 2 feet apart center to center. The flooring itself consists of two layers: a subfloor and a finish floor. The subfloor can be made of 1 × 8 tongue-and-groove lumber, 3/4-inch plywood, or particle board. Traditionally, the finish floor is made of wide pine planks; hardwood, such as oak or maple, will wear better, however. Fasten the finish floor with cut nails for an authentic appearance. Or simulate a pegged floor by countersinking screws and concealing them beneath dowel plugs. Tar paper is often placed on the subfloor to prevent dampness. Insulation beneath the subfloor will cut down on heat loss.

Raising the Roof Beams

Two traditional roof styles—rafter and purlin—are illustrated on following page. Rafter-style roofs require ceiling joists or tie beams to prevent the walls from spreading outward, since the vertical load of the roof exerts downward pressure at an angle on the cabin sides. Purlin roofs produce no spreading even under tremendous snow loads because vertical pressure is not transferred at an angle but instead is supported directly beneath by long horizontal logs resting on the end walls of the cabin. Although tie beams are not required for the walls when a purlin roof is used, they are generally installed anyway as parts of the trusses that support the purlins themselves. Without trusses the purlins of any but small cabins may sag under their own weight.

The first step in making either style of roof is to install plates—large logs similar to sills that are notched to take the ceiling joists, tie beams, or truss supports. The plates should also be notched to take the rafter ends unless extra, courses of wall logs are to be added to form a second-story loft.

Gable ends rise to a peak at each end of the cabin. In a rafter-style roof they can be built after the rest of the roof is completed. One type of gable consists of horizontal or vertical log sections spiked together and trimmed to the angle of the roof pitch. Another kind, shown at right, is built like an ordinary exterior frame wall. Panel the exterior of the gables with lumber siding or log slabs. Gables for a purlin roof (also illustrated at right) are made of horizontal log sections spiked one on top of another and notched to take each purlin as it is set in place during the building sequence. Afterward, the angle of the roof pitch is marked and the log ends are trimmed off with a saw.

Details of rafter installation

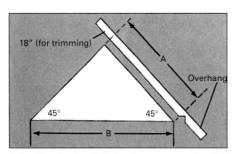

Traditional angle of roof pitch is 45°, steep enough to shed snow from roofing. To determine rafter length (A), divide length of end wall (B) by 1.4, then add additional 18 in. for trimming (more if an eave overhang is desired).

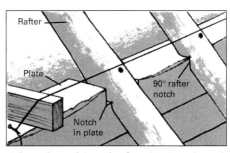

Cut right-angle notch in each rafter where it attaches to the plate. Vary the depth of the notches to compensate for variations in rafter thicknesses. If the plate is uneven, notch it to equalize depths, using level line as guide.

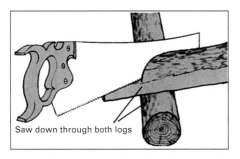

To match rafter ends at peak when ridgepole is not used, overlap each pair and saw both at once. Before cutting, make sure plate-notched ends are set correct distance apart. Nail 1x 6 collar tie across joint for extra strength.

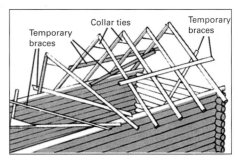

Raise preassembled rafter pairs by resting ends on plate logs, then pushing peak upright with pole. Spike rafters to plate at notches; brace until decking is installed. Permanent braces are required in windy or heavy snow areas.

Rafter-style roof with framed gable ends

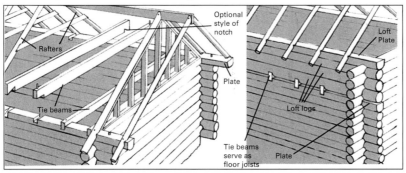

In rafter-style roofs, plates are spiked or pegged in place (far left). Install tie beams in plate notches cut on 2-ft. centers. For rafters use logs or 2 x 8 lumber spaced 2 ft. apart. Notch rafters and spike to plate. Nail tops to ridgepole, or assemble rafter pairs on ground and erect as units. Logs can be added above plates (near left) to increase attic space.

Purlin roof with log gable ends

Roof pitch determines purlin location. Cut vertical posts to height of roof peak and set them against center of end walls (far left). Stretch wire from posts to wall sides as a guide when installing purlins and trimming final angle of gable ends. Allow for the fact that purlins will be set in notches that are half their diameters. Support purlins with trusses every 12 ft. (far right).

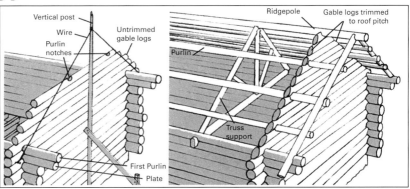

Raising the Walls

After the foundation has been laid and the sill logs and end logs that form the base of the cabin have been set in place, the next step is to raise the walls. Decide before starting how the floor will be built (see p.26), whether or not to use the chinkless method of stacking the logs described on page 29, and also whether you will use short precut logs to frame the window and door openings as the walls go up, or saw out these openings later from the solid walls as builders of traditional cabins usually do.

The basic steps in constructing the walls are hoisting the logs into position, aligning them so that they are vertical and at right angles to each other at the corners, and notching them so that they lock permanently in place. Since logs weigh several hundred pounds each, lifting is best done with mechanical assistance. Two traditional methods are shown below. Plenty of manpower helps too—not just to make the job easier but to make it safer as well. Once a log is up it should be carefully positioned for notching with the help of carefully aligned sighting poles driven into the ground a short distance from each corner. Sight along the log's length to make sure its center is lined up with the poles.

After a log is in place for notching, scribe it at both ends, roll it over, and use log dogs to fasten it to neighboring logs while you cut the notch. For safety, always roll logs toward the center of the wall. Most logs have a crown, or slight bow along their length. This should face upward on the finished log so that as the cabin settles the logs will flatten and their fit will improve. To keep walls level, alternate the wide and narrow ends of the logs as shown. Use a plumb bob to check verticals and an oversized square made from 2 × 4 lumber to make sure corners form right angles.

Hoisting logs into place

Hauling logs to the top of the wall is a major undertaking. One common system uses a block and tackle hung from the top of a gin-pole tripod. Another combines a block and tackle for mechanical advantage with poles for leverage. Instead of a block and tackle, a so-called come-along ratchet hoist can also be used. It is slow but can be operated safely by one person. A come-along can also be used to draw wall logs tightly together.

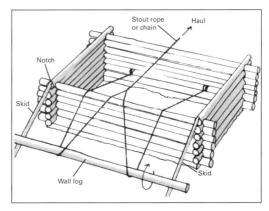

Inclined skids, a pioneer device, can be used to roll logs upward. Skids should form a 30° angle and be notched at ends to hold them in place on the wall. Tie ends of rope to a wall log already in place; pass center of rope under the log being raised. Tie another rope to center of first rope, and haul on free end to roll log up ramp. Have two persons guide the log, and never stand between the skids when hauling the log upward.

Alternate courses to keep the walls level

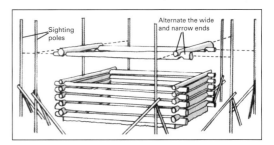

Precise leveling of log walls is not necessary. Compensate for the natural taper of logs and prevent the accumulation of large errors by laying each course of logs so that the thick ends join the thin ends. Alternate the thick and thin ends vertically as well to avoid high corners when the walls are completed.

Working with short logs

Short logs can be lapped and spiked together end to end provided the joint does not occur over a wall opening or beneath a joist or beam requiring support. Many kit homes make use of this joint. The French-Canadian pioneers introduced the piéce-en-piéce construction method. Slotted vertical posts are used to anchor short horizontal logs notched to fit the grooves. Piéce-en-piéce construction is excellent for building long walls, even with small diameter logs. Be sure to provide a firm foundation. Horizontals may be pegged after settling is completed.

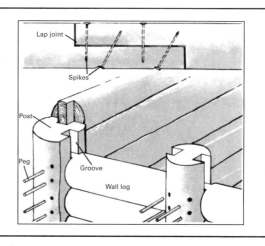

The Finishing Touches: Shakes and Chinking

Rafters stand a few inches above the sills they rest upon, with the result that there are narrow spaces between the top of the wall and the underside of the roof. These spaces are generally filled with short segments of lumber known as snowblocks, or birdstops. Fit them as shown in the illustration at upper right, either between rafters or on each side of the plates. In warm areas the gaps are often screened without being plugged in order to provide increased ventilation.

Most cabin roofs are surfaced with wooden shakes or shingles, materials that can either be purchased in a lumberyard or made by hand (see *Converting Trees Into Lumber,* p.16). Standing-seam sheet-metal roofing or asphalt shingles may also be used; both are long-lasting, durable, and attractive. Shakes are slabs of wood split from straight-grained, knot-free sections of logs. They should be about 1/2 inch thick and 18 to 30 inches long. Shingles are thinner and less rough-hewn

than shakes. Both are traditionally made from cedar, oak, or cypress and must be completely seasoned before use; otherwise splitting will occur at the nailing points as the wood shrinks. Shakes and shingles are sold in lots called squares. Each lot contains four bundles, and each bundle will cover 25 square feet of roof. Nail shakes and shingles along the roof in overlapping rows.

Old-fashioned roofs were not insulated. The shakes or shingles were nailed directly to the purlins running the length of the roof or fastened to rows of furring strips nailed horizontally across the rafters. Skins or rugs were sometimes placed on the floor of a full loft to retain heat in the lower room; the upper story remained cold. Modern roofs are decked over, sealed with a moisture barrier to prevent condensation, and completely insulated with urethane, styrofoam, rock wool, or fiberglass. Openings for the chimney, stovepipe, and vent stack should be flashed with aluminum or copper to prevent leaks. There are several methods of constructing insulated roofs; two of the most common are shown below. Insulation requirements vary according to climate zones (see *Making Your House Energy Efficient,* pp.58–64).

Two Ways to Insulate

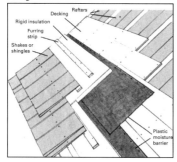

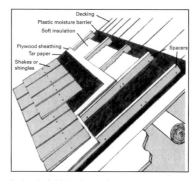

Rigid insulation is more expensive than the soft type but requires less lumber when it is being installed. Nail pine decking boards across rafters. Cover with plastic moisture barrier. Lay insulation board over plastic. Nail 1 x 3 furring strips through insulation to rafters. Cover with shakes, shingles, or metal.

Soft insulation is laid in channels between spacers and is protected by plywood sheathing. Allow airspace as shown. Lay plastic moisture barrier atop decking and toenail 2-in.-thick spacers through decking to beams. Install insulation and sheathing, and cover with shakes, shingles, or other roofing.

Covering the Roof

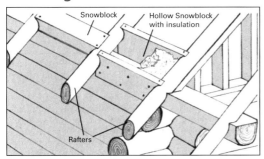

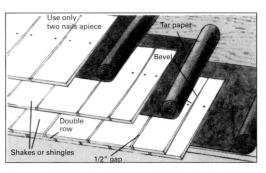

Snowblocks, also called birdstops, seal gaps between rafters along the wall tops. Trim log sections or lumber to size; bevel to match roof pitch. Insulation can be placed as shown. In warm climates screening is often installed instead of snowblocks.

Start roof with double row of shakes (or shingles) at bottom. Overlap each row, leaving exposed only a third of length of shakes beneath. Space shakes 1/2 in. apart and use only two nails per shake. Tar paper between rows reduces leakage.

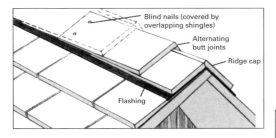

Use galvanized nails to fasten shingles at ridge cap. Alternate the butt joints of top course shingles and blind-nail them as shown. For added moisture protection install metal flashing over roof peak beneath final row of shingles.

Chinking the Gaps

Unless you have used the chinkless construction technique shown at right, your most important finishing-up job will be to chink the gaps between logs. Traditionally, chinking was done with clay and had to be repeated frequently until the logs were completely settled. Fiberglass insulation, temporarily covered with strips of plastic and later chinked permanently with mortar, saves labor and requires little additional maintenance.

Once the cabin is weathertight, other finishing projects may be completed at leisure. These include wiring, plumbing, any interior partitions, wood stoves, fireplaces, and chimneys. Interior log walls can be covered with two coats of clear urethane varnish for a durable, washable finish. Spray the exterior of the cabin with preservative every two to three years.

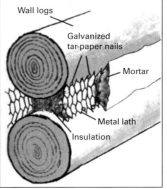

First step in chinking is to pack insulation between logs, cover it with metal lath, and seal it temporarily with strips of clear plastic sheeting. After logs have seasoned (up to one year) apply mortar over lath. Use one part sand, three parts Portland cement, plus a handful of clay or lime for a stickier mix. Repair chinking periodically as logs settle.

Chinkless construction

Chinkless notching eliminates gaps between logs, making periodic chinking with clay or mortar unnecessary. Extra building time is needed, however, since each log must be grooved and filled as it is laid in place. First, cut round notches in ends of top log to approximate fit, allowing a gap of about 2 in. between it and lower log. Then, with dividers or log scribing tool, scribe both sides of log, transferring contours of bottom log to underside of top log. Finish cutting the round notches to the newly scribed lines, then make V-notch and channel along the length of the log, using the scribed lines as a guide. Pack channel with fiberglass insulation, and roll log into place on wall.

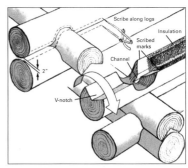

Tips on wiring

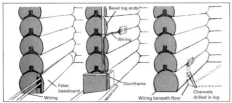

Plan ahead for wiring. Chinkless construction and wiring that runs beneath floors or drops from above may require boring holes through logs during assembly. Wiring can also run behind baseboards and between logs. Bevel log ends to run wires vertically behind a doorframe molding. Check local codes and have an electrician supervise.

Building a Stone House

A Home Made of Rock: Beauty Plus Strength

People have a natural love for stones. Children climb on them, collect them, and skim them over ponds. Our most magnificent structures are made of rock, as well as some of our most ancient. To this day, a house made of stone provides a special feeling of security, comfort, and coziness.

For years stone houses were made by expert masons using the time-tested technique of laying each rock individually in place. More recently, however, the slipform method has become popular, especially among do-it-yourselfers. A slipformed house can be built for less than two-thirds the cost of a similar home made of wood and will compare favorably with mason-built stone houses in terms of durability and attractiveness.

Choosing Your Stone

There are many variables to keep in mind when selecting building stones. Perhaps the most important consideration is availability: stone is heavy and if good stone cannot be found locally, shipping costs can be prohibitive. Stone for building should be durable and waterproof, qualities that depend not only on the type of rock but also on climate. Limestone, for example, is among the most durable of construction materials in arid areas but will weather rapidly in a wet climate. Attractiveness is also important. Ideally, stone buildings should fit in with the prevailing architecture and blend with the local topographical features as well.

The chart at right gives some of the common rock types and their suitability as building stone. However, you can tell a lot about a stone without knowing what type it is. Start by examining it carefully to determine its features. Compare its weight, texture, and appearance with other stones. Good building stone is heavy and therefore less likely to absorb moisture. Break open a sample with a sledgehammer. The rock should be difficult to fracture and should break into rough-textured, irregular chunks. Stone that crumbles or splits easily along flat planes is probably weak and porous. Though the stone may still be suitable for building under many conditions, water may seep in, hastening erosion and causing cracking in freezing weather.

Streambeds, mines and quarries, rocky pasturelands, lakeshores, and abandoned stonework are all likely sources for building stone. Maps published by the U.S. Geological Service show locations of abandoned mines and quarries. In suburban areas talk to contractors who may be involved in demolition work. In the country ask local farmers; you may find all the rock you need free for the hauling. If the stone is not on your property, be sure to talk to the owner before you take any, and always put the emphasis on working safely.

Fieldstone is loose surface rock. It is rough textured and worn from exposure to nature and the passage of time.

Creek stone is polished smooth by running water. Its unusual character lends it to decorative uses, such as fireplace facings.

Quarried stone is cut from massive outcrops. Its surfaces are freshly exposed, sharp, clean, and regular.

Suitability of rock types for building

Rock type	Durability	Water resistance	Workability
Basalt	Excellent	Excellent	Difficult
Gneiss	Good	Good	Moderate
Granite	Excellent	Good	Moderate
Limestone	Fair	Poor	Easy
Marble	Good	Excellent	Moderate
Sandstone	Fair	Fair	Easy
Schist	Good	Good	Moderate
Slate	Good	Excellent	Easy

Principles of Traditional Stonemasonry

For centuries the only way to erect a stone house was to lay the stones individually like bricks. The skill of the stonemason involved selecting the proper stone to lay in place and then adjusting the stone to fit securely, either by shaping it to fit or by filling in around the stone with specially chosen smaller rock fragments called shims.

The first stone structures were dry, that is, built without mortar. Later, clay, lime, or cement was used to set the rocks in place. In either type of masonry, structural integrity depends on the same two forces—gravity and friction—and the key to building enduring stonework has always been to make full use of both forces. For gravity to do its job, keep the stones' bedding surfaces horizontal or canted slightly inward toward the center of the wall. Maximize friction by creating as much contact between stones as possible. Follow the old rule "one over two and two over one" so that each stone rests across at least two stones beneath; gravity then locks the stones together and unifies the structure. Maintain solid bedding surfaces by shaping or shimming any stones that fit poorly. Shaping is done with a hammer and chisel. Shimming is done by inserting small pieces of filler rock in spaces between stones, thereby providing support and increasing surface contact. However, do not use shims as wedges to hold stones in place. If you do, the wedged stones may eventually work free. The best use of shims is for leveling and stabilizing the bedding surfaces, always with the goal of keeping them as horizontal as possible in order to make the fullest possible use of the force of gravity, which pulls straight down.

Mortar eliminates much of the shaping and shimming needed in dry-wall construction. It does not, however, glue the stones together. Portland cement, the active ingredient in mortar, cures as hard as stone and automatically provides a perfect seat for the rocks as they are laid, filling the smallest gaps.

For maximum structural integrity each stone should weigh straight down on the ones beneath it (left). Stones in a mislaid wall (right) tend to slide out; the higher the stones are stacked, the greater the tendency to crumble. Shape the stones with hammer and chisel or use small fragments as shims to keep bedding planes horizontal or tilted slightly inward.

Shaping the stones to fit

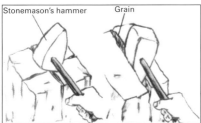

Large rocks should be broken into random chunks with a sledge or stonemason's hammer. Use the wedge-shaped end of the mason's hammer to split the stone along the grain.

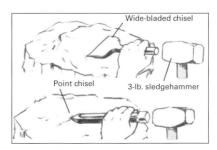

Wide-bladed chisels are used when scoring, smoothing, and splitting soft stone. A point chisel is employed when working with hard stones where impact must be concentrated.

When hewing stone, chip rock away gradually to avoid breaking entire block. Place stone on bed of sand and score with chisel. Chip off small pieces using flat face of hammer. Work from edge toward line with steady blows. On hard rock you may have to hammer quite a while before cracking begins. Wear safety goggles to prevent injury from rock chips.

Mortaring the stones in place

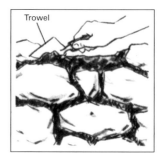

1. Mortar proportions are one part portland cement to three parts sand. Add only enough water for a firm mix.

2. Stones should be clean and surfaces wet. Shape stone and test for fit before laying down bed of mortar.

3. Lay mortar on bedding face with a trowel. Do not smooth. Use only enough to provide firm support.

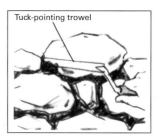

4. For effective seating drop stone in place from a few inches above. Once stone is set, do not move it farther.

5. Scrape off excess mortar and pack it into vertical joints. Use a trowel; mortar will irritate skin.

6. Use tuck-pointing trowel to trim mortar. Clean stones with cleaning compound from building supply dealer.

The Slipform Method Of Casting Walls

Slipforming is a method of building with stone that does not require advanced masonry skills. Rather than shaping, shimming, and mortaring each stone into place individually, loose stones are simply packed into removable forms and cemented together by filling in around them with concrete. In a slipformed wall an entire layer, or course, is built as a unit. A number of forms are connected end-to-end and filled. While the mix hardens, a second chain of forms is placed on top of the first and also filled. When the bottom layer has set, those forms are removed and reattached above the second to form a third layer. In this way wall building proceeds vertically like a game of leapfrog. Properly done, the results are excellent. A slipformed wall is sturdy, weatherproof, and almost indistinguishable from old-style mortared masonry—and can be put up in half the time it would take to lay it stone by stone.

For ease of handling, forms are usually 18 inches deep and about 8 feet long. Stones to fill them should also be of manageable size—no more than 50 pounds each—and have at least one fairly flat face. Stockpile a wide variety so that you will have plenty to choose from. Cast the walls at least 14 inches thick. Place stones in the form with their flat faces against the side that will become the exterior wall. Try to follow the "one over two, two over one" rule that holds for mortared masonry so that gravity will help bind the stones together.

Stone is a poor insulator and, in addition, joints between stones tend to develop small leaks. As a result, most slipformed walls are built so that the stones extend no more than two-thirds of the way through the wall from the exterior to the interior. The inside face is smooth concrete. Furring strips are usually embedded in the concrete, and the wall is finished with insulation and paneling. If you want your interior wall to be of stone, place a 2-inch layer of solid insulation in the middle of the form and fill in on either side with stones and concrete. This type of wall will be thermally sound as well as leakproof.

Apply a coat of oil to the slipforms before using them so they can be removed more easily later on. As you pour the concrete, tamp it down, striking the forms occasionally with a hammer to dispel air bubbles. Your aim should be to surround each stone with 1 to 2 inches of concrete. It is vital that the bonding between successive layers be strong and weathertight. Try to complete an entire course on a single pour to avoid vertical through-seams, which will weaken the walls. Horizontal seams tend to form on the top of a course. To keep them from allowing moisture into the house, slope the top of each pour downward to the outside. Do not cap the courses with concrete; instead, finish each course with stones that protrude vertically, so they will mesh with those in the next layer. Surfaces that have cured for more than 48 hours may require application of a commercial bonding agent or a paste of portland cement and water before the next layer is poured on top.

Good Concrete Is the Secret of Slipforming

When building slipformed stonework, the quality of the concrete is most important. Concrete is made up of portland cement, sand, and gravel. For slipforming, 1/2-inch-diameter gravel is best. Recommended proportions are one part cement, three parts sand, and four parts gravel. Proper water content is the secret of strong concrete. There must be enough water so that the mixture can be worked and the chemical reaction that hardens the cement can go to completion. Too much water results in weak concrete. Generally, for a batch of concrete mixed from one sack of cement (94 pounds), 5 gallons of water are needed. Adjust this figure to accommodate the moisture content of the sand and gravel. To obtain good results when you are mixing by hand,

use the method shown below. With a power mixer, blend the dry ingredients first, then add water gradually until a workable mix is obtained. It helps to have an experienced person on hand when you make your first batch.

Concrete must not dry too fast. Water evaporating from the mix while it cures has the same effect as adding too little water at the start. Nor must ordinary concrete be exposed to freezing temperatures for at least a week after it has been poured. The chart describes different types of portland cement, each suited to a particular building condition. Type I is suitable for all but severe conditions. Type III is excellent for slipforming because its rapid setting time allows forms to be removed sooner. So-called air-entrained cement will trap microscopic air bubbles as it hardens, causing it to resist frost damage. Use Type III A in all areas where heavy freezing occurs.

The measuring box

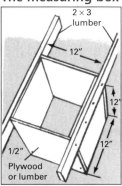

Measuring box for dry ingredients has a 1-cu.-ft. capacity. Box has no bottom. Sides are 1/2-in. plywood or 3/4-in. lumber with 2 × 3 boards for handles. Join parts with screws, not nails, for extra strength. When mixing concrete, place box in mixing trough, fill, and lift up. Each filling equals one unit of a particular ingredient.

Mixing the components

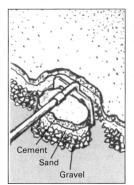

To mix concrete by hand, first wet the mixing trough. Spread correct proportions of ingredients in layers over three-quarters of the bottom; then pour water into remaining area. To mix, pull sections of dry material forward into water with mason's hoe and blend until proper consistency is reached.

Assembling the Forms

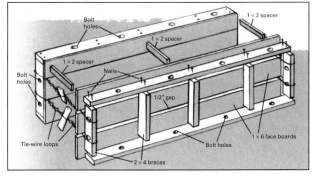

Build your own slipforms using 1 × 6 boards or sheets of 1/2-in. plywood for the faces. Nail them to 2 × 4 braces as shown. Leave 1/2-in. gaps between face boards or drill holes in plywood so that tie-wire loops can be threaded through to hold the sides together. Bore holes in end, top, and bottom braces to bolt forms together end-to-end and in vertical layers. You will need enough forms to assemble two end-to-end chains the length of the wall section being poured. The forms will be stacked one on top of the other leapfrog fashion as the wall is raised. For efficiency and economy use standard commercial lumber sizes for forms, and make them interchangeable by planning walls to be even multiples of form dimensions.

Getting Ready to Build

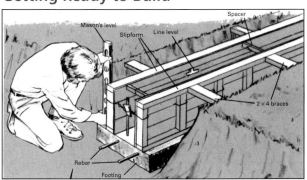

Reinforced concrete footing poured below frost line ensures firm base for heavy masonry walls. Footing should be 4 in. wider on each side than width of wall and at least 10 in. thick. Set forms in place along footing marked with a chalk line. Make tie-wire loops by inserting light wire through holes or between boards and tying around vertical braces. Twist loops tight with nails while inserting 1 × 2 wood spacers cut to width of wall to maintain correct dimensions. Use mason's level, and line level to make sure forms are plumb. Adjust by tapping forms with hammer. If additional support is needed, nail extra braces across the tops of the forms or prop the sides with 2 × 4 s set in the ground as shown in the illustration.

Filling the Forms

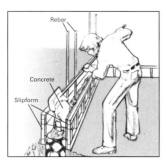

Place stones 2 in. apart with flat faces against form. If rebar (steel reinforcing bar) and furring strips are being used, install them now. Pack remaining area with concrete and tamp well, allowing the concrete to flow beneath stones.

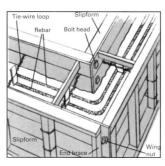

Corners are built as a unit with special forms that can be bolted together at right angles. Lay a 6-ft. length of 3/8-in. rebar, bent at a right angle, into corners every 10 in. vertically. Use cornerstones that have two faces at right angles.

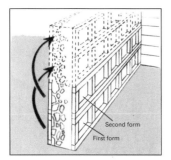

While masonry cures in first form, second form is placed on top and filled. After 48 hours first form is removed and placed atop second form as its contents continue to cure. Clip tie-wires flush; they will remain embedded in the wall.

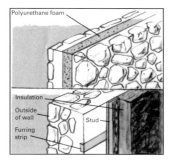

Stone is cold unless insulated. Sandwich-type wall (top) with core of 2-in. polyurethane foam provides exposed stone inside house. Or embed treated furring in wall as it is built, then attach studs, insulation, and paneling.

Movable Slipforms: an Old-fashioned Home Using Modern Methods

Stone houses have the quality of blending into the landscape, especially if they make use of stone gathered from the building site itself. Plan a house that will harmonize with the environment. Choose an area of well-drained solid ground upon which to build, since masonry will crack if settling occurs. Stone walls are not easily modified, so plan your house large enough to accommodate any anticipated needs for more space in the future, and take into account plumbing, heating, and electrical arrangements. Wall openings for these systems are far easier to incorporate during the construction process than to drill afterward.

Stretch string between batter boards to guide excavation and wall building. A perimeter footing of poured concrete with horizontal rebar (steel reinforcing bar) ensures rigid foundation. Below-grade walls can be poured, slipformed, or made of laid stone and mortar. Vertical rebar is optional if the base of the foundation wall is keyed into footing notch. Drainpipe next to footing carries water away from foundation, preventing water damage and settling. Use sealant to weatherproof joint between foundation and stonework.

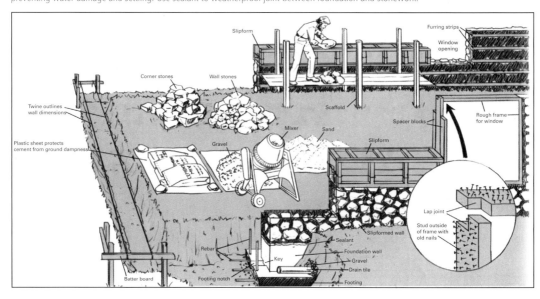

Sandwich-type wall, with stone face inside, stores heat from fireplace or sunlit windows. Paneled stud walls permit easy installation of shelves, plumbing, and wiring. Flagstone or slate floors are laid at ground level. Wood floor is raised, since crawl space is needed to prevent rot. Gable ends are wood. Roof may be simple truss type. Since slipformed walls can withstand the outward thrust of the rafters, few tie beams are needed. This allows architectural freedom to include such features as the skylight and cathedral ceiling.

Types of cement and where to use them

Type I	General purpose: Moderate-weather building conditions in areas where light to moderate freezing will occur
Type IA	General purpose, air-entrained: Moderate-weather building conditions in areas where heavy freezing occurs
Type III	High strength, early set: Early or late season building conditions in light to moderate freeze areas where conditions require rapid concrete setting and early form removal
Type IIIA	High-early, air-entrained: Early or late season building conditions in heavy freeze areas where conditions require rapid concrete setting and early form removal

Begin by collecting stone. The more you have on hand the better. Unless you plan to pour a concrete floor along with the foundation, it is a good idea to stack the piles of rock in the center of the site. That way you will have less distance to carry the stone and will be able to keep all possible choices in view. Store bags of cement where they will stay absolutely dry, stacked on wooden platforms with an airspace beneath and covered with plastic. Cover sand also if rain is frequent.

Build enough forms to be able to "slip" them properly. This means having on hand as many forms as are needed to construct a wall section two courses high. Ideally, you should build enough forms to reach between natural openings in the wall plus special forms for corners or odd shapes. Remember to make forms from standard lumber and to plan wall dimensions in multiples of form sizes. That way you will not have to construct a number of different forms and can use them interchangeably.

You might design your house with low walls for greater ease in handling stone. Extend windows and doors all the way to the top plate to eliminate the need for lintels. Frames are studded with nails on the outside and laid up directly in the forms, with spacer blocks on each side to prevent concrete from being pushed behind them if they are not as thick as the wall itself. Use heavy timber joined with pegged lap joints. Soak the frames and any of the wood that will make permanent contact with masonry in preservative to prevent dry rot.

Sources and resources

Books
Basic Masonry. Menlo Park, Calif.: Sunset Books, 1995.
Burch, Monte. *Brick, Concrete, Stonework*. Saddle River, N.J.: Creative Homeowner, 1980.
McClintock, Mike. *Alternative Housebuilding*. New York: Sterling Publishing, 1989.

Raising a Barn

Timber-Frame Method, Now Centuries Old, Still Means Quality

Farm families have long valued a sturdy barn as much as a comfortable home. Barns are a symbol of the farmer's relationship with the land and of his personal goals and values. Eric Sloane, the noted historian and artist of Americana, describes the sturdy old barns of New England as the "shrines of a good life." Their simple, honest lines and lasting strength seem to reflect the farmer's steadfast love of the soil and enduring belief in a secure and bountiful future.

Care, pride, and dedication go into the construction of a good barn. Very often details of craftsmanship hidden high in the hayloft are likely to be of finer quality than those displayed in the parlor of the family house. Old-fashioned barns had massive, carefully fitted frameworks of hand-hewn timbers, joined together with stout wooden pegs instead of nails. This construction method, called timber frame, or post and beam, had its roots in medieval European architecture. In spite of the time, labor, and skill necessary, the great-grandfathers of today's farmers built in this style because of its proven ability to last, even though the faster, cheaper, and easier method called stud framing—building as we do today with 2 × 4 s and nails—was available to them as early as the 1830's.

Stud framing requires the additional strength provided by wall sheathing and siding. A timber frame, however, is self-supporting. The heavy posts and beams—the principal frame members—are joined together at right angles, then braced with additional diagonal timbers notched into them. The result is a strong and stable triangular support. Barn siding, necessary only to enclose the structure, is usually made of low-cost lumber, such as rough-cut 1-inch pine boards, nailed vertically to the frame.

Sections of a barn frame are generally built on the ground in units called bents. When all the bents are completed, they are raised upright and joined

This sturdy old barn is a testament to old-time craftsmanship. Gambriel roof was a favorite style among thrifty farmers because of the increased interior space it provided. The original shingles have been replaced with more modern roofing, but the frame remains sturdy, largely due to the amazing durability of post-and-beam construction.

A minimum kit

Barn-framing tools shown here can be obtained at most quality hardware stores. In addition, you will need several standard carpentry tools, including a claw hammer, pry bar, and jack plane.

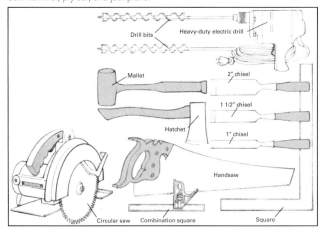

Old-fashioned specialties

Old-timers had a tool for every job. Mortising was done with a special ax or with a combination of boring machine, corner chisel, and slick (for smoothing). Frames were pounded together with a 40-lb. beetle. Pegs were shaped by driving them through a steel sizer. Pikes helped in raising the barn sides upright.

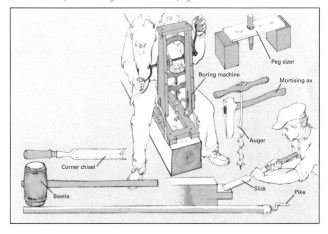

together to form the completed frame. Because the bents are so massive, community effort is usually required when the barn is ready to be erected. In fact, part of the beauty of an old-fashioned barn lies in the spirit of community friendship it reflects. A hundred years ago an entire town might turn out on the "raisin' day" of a barn like the one shown on previous page; to raise a small barn, such as the one described on page 41, a dozen or so friends should suffice.

Tools Should Be Big and Sturdy

Timber-frame construction requires heavy-duty tools. Chisels should be the strongest type available, with socket ends to prevent the handles from splitting under repeated malleting. Three blade widths are helpful: 1 inch, 1 1/2 inch, and 2 inch; the overall length of the chisels should be at least 15 inches. You will also need a six- or eight-point crosscut saw, a 1 1/2 to 2-inch auger (or brace and bit), a mallet, a sledgehammer, a hatchet, measuring tools, and a level. A chain saw is valuable, and if electricity is available, a great deal of sweat can be saved with a sturdy power saw and a rugged electric drill. Keep edged tools sharp for safety, accuracy, and ease of use.

In the 19th century, carpenters had special tools designed expressly for timber framing. As a result, framing a barn back then was easier in many ways than it is now. You may be fortunate enough to locate some of these valuable old tools at specialty tool stores, farm auctions, or through advertisements in collectors' magazines.

Some Tips on Timber

Seasoned hardwoods-usually oak or chestnut-are the traditional timbers for frames. Pine, hemlock, fir, or spruce can also be used, provided that all vertical posts made of

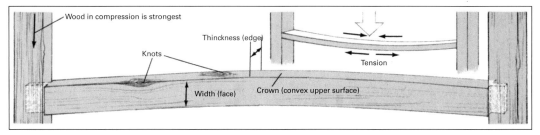

Wooden members can support the greatest loads when stress is along the direction of the grain, as in the vertical post at far left. Horizontal beams sag because stress crosses grain. Compression, which forces wood together along beam's top surface, creates tension along the bottom, stretching wood apart. For maximum horizontal strength, place beam on edge with its natural arc, or crown, facing upward, like an arch. However, if large knots are present on the concave edge rather than the crowned edge, place that edge up instead so that the knots will be pressed into the wood, not loosened and forced out by tension.

these weaker woods are at least 6 inches square and that horizontal beams measure at least 6 inches by 8 inches. Seasoned wood is best, but framing timbers can be green if allowances are made for later shrinkage. Try to obtain the timber from trees felled during the winter months. Winter-cut wood contains less sap, so seasoning is faster, shrinkage is less, and the wood is more resistant to decay. You may choose to hew your own beams (see *Converting Trees Into Lumber,* pp.16–21), or you can order them from a sawmill. Stack lumber off the ground and protect it from wet weather. Insert 1 × 2 boards between layers to allow air circulation.

Timber-Frame Joinery: Like Giant Furniture

Timber framing is cabinetmaking on a grand scale. Except for size, the frame of an old-fashioned barn hardly differs from that of a traditional blanket chest, cabinet, or bureau of drawers; each is basically the framework of a box. Even the individual elements of construction are the same.

The principal joint used in both barn framing and furniture framing is the mortise and tenon. This joint has been used by carpenters and cabinetmakers since ancient times because of its great strength and simple construction. When accurately cut, fitted, and pegged together, a mortise-and-tenon joint will be virtually as strong as the wood from which it is made. The technique of making mortise-and-tenon joints for timber-frame structures differs from that used when working on a piece of furniture. The tools are larger, the timbers

Wooden pegs and well-made joints hold frame of barn together.

are harder to maneuver, and the entire process must take into account the greater physical forces at work as well as the sheer weight of the materials involved.

Old-timers recognized that a tight fit was the key to a sound, long-lasting joint and summed it up in the motto "Measure twice, cut once." They made and fitted each joint individually, paring the sizes to the last sliver of wood, then took the joint apart until the

Making a Mortise-and-Tenon Joint

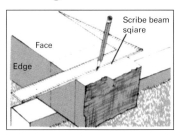

1. Make tenon first. Scribe rough end of beam square on all sides, then measure off tenon length and scribe it on all sides. Tenon length should be half thickness of receiving timber.

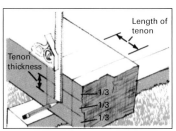

2. Place beam on its side. Use combination square as gauge to mark tenon thickness on both edges of the beam. Tenon thickness should be one-third the width of the receiving timber.

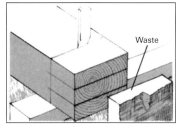

3. Saw off the rough end of the beam, being careful to cut along all four squaring-off lines. Then connect the ends of the tenon-thickness lines with a combination square.

4. Saw the tenon shoulders next. Cut must be square. For accuracy, score line with chisel, and begin cutting with saw tilted back. Rock saw forward as rear thickness line is reached.

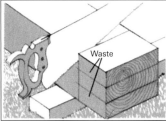

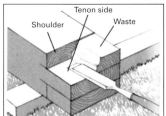

5. Remove waste from tenon sides. Use either ripsaw, chisel and mallet, or a sharp hatchet. To use hatchet, begin chopping at end of beam near surface; work along grain.

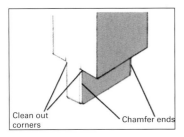

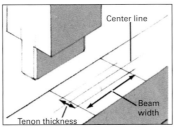

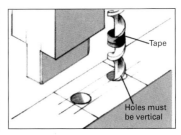

6. Smooth tenon and shoulder with an extra-sharp wide-bladed chisel or a block plane. Take special care to clean out corners. Chamfer (bevel) ends to ease final assembly.

7. To lay out mortise, place tenoned piece across timber and scribe width of beam. Remove, then scribe center line, adding tenon-thickness dimensions on either side as shown.

8. Bore out waste with bit slightly smaller than mortise width. Use tape on bit for depth gauge, and hold drill at precise 90° angle to work. Bore the two end holes first.

9. Smooth mortise sides with wide-bladed chisel and mallet, and carefully square corners. Use exact-sized chisel to trim mortise ends. Be sure walls remain square and vertical.

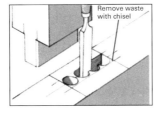

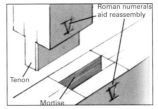

10. Check final fit by measuring both mortise and tenon; some trimming is usually necessary. Mark each piece to aid later assembly (chiseled Roman numerals are traditional).

barn was ready for assembly. Since no two joints were quite alike, the pieces were marked to avoid mistakes on raising day. Roman numerals were used as labels because they were easy to cut with a chisel; they can often be seen inscribed in the sturdy timbers of 19th-century barns.

From Beams to Bents

Before a barn raising can begin, mortised posts and tenoned beams must be fastened together and then braced with diagonal timbers to form bents, the basic units of barn construction. Styles of bents vary; in all cases, however, they consist of combinations of posts, beams, and braces—nothing else.

Each joint should be pegged, not nailed. Wooden pegs are stronger and longer lasting than nails, screws, or bolts, and, unlike metal fasteners, they will never rust. In addition, the pegs shrink and swell in harmony with the surrounding timbers, producing very tight joints with little or no splitting during moisture changes. Pegs should always be made of harder wood than the timbers that they join; oak and black locust are best. They must be made of completely seasoned wood; otherwise they can shrink and loosen in their holes. Ideally, a peg will tighten with age as the wood around it shrinks.

Braces, which make the framing rigid, must be installed carefully so that the structure remains square. The best way to ensure precision is to fit the braces after the main timbers have been joined and pegged.

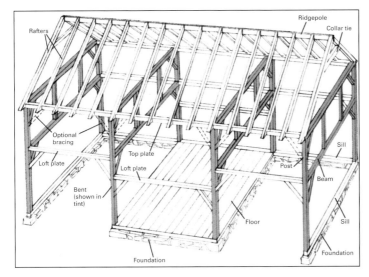

Timber-frame barn is less complicated than it appears. It is basically a series of bents joined together.

Making pegs

Stock can be driven through steel peg sizer instead. Notches in sides of finished pegs give tighter fit.

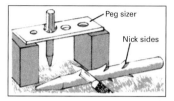

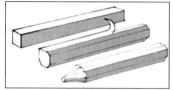

Whittle hardwood pegs by shaving corners to form rough octagon. Diameter is one-third tenon length.

Fitting braces

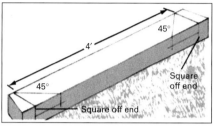

1. Mark 45° angle at one end of timber and scribe across ends. Mark length of brace, then scribe second 45° angle.

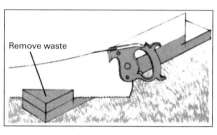

2. Measure, then saw halfway through brace by cutting along angle lines. Remove triangular waste sections with chisel.

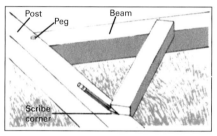

3. With post and beam pegged at 90° angle, hold brace in place and scribe outline of corner on each timber.

4. Scribe depth of notch on inside edge of timbers, then remove waste with chisel. Fit the brace; drill and peg securely.

Drawboring

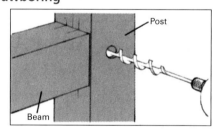

1. Driving pegs through offset holes draws joints tight. Begin with joint assembled; bore through one side of mortise only.

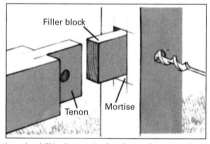

3. Replace the drill in the mortised timber and continue boring through the other side. Use filler block to steady bit.

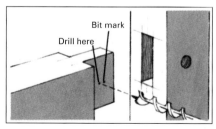

2. Remove tenon and locate bit mark. Drill hole through tenon, centered a fraction of an inch closer to its shoulder.

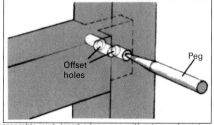

4. Reassemble joint. Insert a long peg with a tapered point, and drive it in until full thickness of peg travels through both timbers.

Construction Plans for a Small Barn

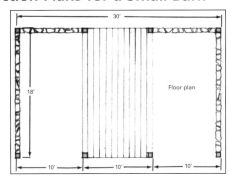

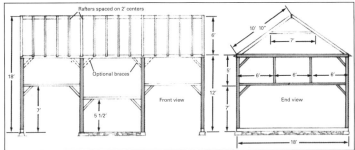

Sources and resources

Books

Benson, Tedd. *Timber-Frame Home*. Newtown, Conn.: Taunton Press, 1996.

Fitchen, John. *The New World Dutch Barn*. Syracuse, N.Y.: Syracuse University Press, 1968.

Halsted, Byron D., ed. *Barns, Sheds and Outbuildings*. Battleboro, Vt.: Alan C. Hood, 1977.

Kelley, J. Frederick. *Early Domestic Architecture of Connecticut*. New York: Dover, 1963.

Sloane, Eric. *An Age of Barns*. New York: Henry Holt & Co., 1990.

Wallas, Elliott. *The Timber Framing Book*. Kittery Point, Maine: Housesmith's Press, 1977.

Specifications can be adjusted to suit individual needs, especially if you hew the timbers yourself, as the builder of the barn pictured here did. Before building this or any barn, seek professional advice to be sure that timber sizes and span lengths are correct for the conditions and type of wood being used. Braces are especially important. For extra strength include as many as possible.

Developing a Water Supply

Reaching Downward To Tap the Reservoirs Beneath Our Feet

Water is one of the elementary staples of life, and the existence of a dependable supply of drinking water is probably the single most important factor in determining whether a homesite will be livable or not. Virtually all the water we use arrives as rain and collects either on the surface of the ground or beneath it. Most of the privately owned residential water supply in the United States comes from wells. Aboveground sources, such as ponds, lakes, reservoirs, and rivers, supply the remainder, almost always for large-scale users, such as heavy industry and population concentrations in urban and suburban areas.

Digging for water is a centuries-old practice with significant sanitary benefits. Due to natural filtration, well water is relatively pure, whereas water in ponds and streams is highly susceptible to bacterial pollution from human and animal waste. But digging wells manually is hard, sweaty work and at depths greater than 10 to 20 feet can be extremely dangerous as well.

Modern methods of well construction, which rely on boring and driving equipment, water pumps, and drilling machinery, avoid most of the danger but still take time, work, and money. In addition, they remain almost as chancy as ever when it comes to striking water. Old-time dowsers and water witches—people who seem to have a special knack for locating subsurface water—are still consulted, but recourse to common sense, a knowledge of local geology, and a professional well digger's experience are likely to prove better guides. Assistance in finding and developing a well on your property can also be obtained from your state's water resources agency.

Where to Find Water

Of the rain that falls on the land areas of the world, the major part collects in lakes and rivers, some evaporates, and the rest, called groundwater, filters slowly into the earth. In many areas groundwater is the most dependable water—often the only water—available.

Old wells were dug with a pick and shovel. When the water table was near the surface and the well shallow, a long counterweighted pole with a bucket at one end sufficed to lift the water up. For deeper wells (they were sometimes dug down 100 ft.), a windlass was used to crank up each bucketful of water. When not in use, such wells should be covered as a safety measure and to keep out dirt and debris.

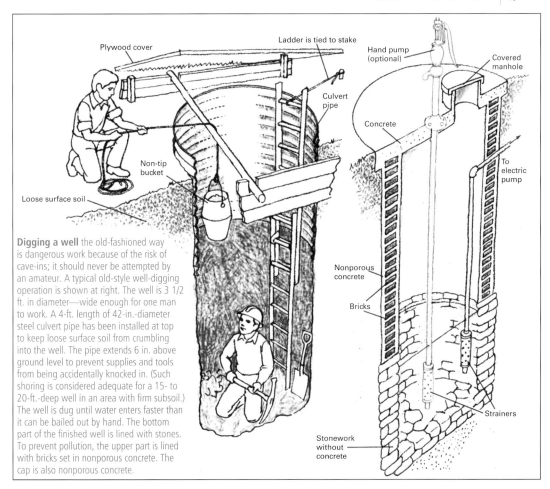

Plywood cover

Ladder is tied to stake

Hand pump (optional)

Covered manhole

Culvert pipe

Concrete

Non-tip bucket

To electric pump

Loose surface soil

Nonporous concrete

Bricks

Digging a well the old-fashioned way is dangerous work because of the risk of cave-ins; it should never be attempted by an amateur. A typical old-style well-digging operation is shown at right. The well is 3 1/2 ft. in diameter—wide enough for one man to work. A 4-ft. length of 42-in.-diameter steel culvert pipe has been installed at top to keep loose surface soil from crumbling into the well. The pipe extends 6 in. above ground level to prevent supplies and tools from being accidentally knocked in. (Such shoring is considered adequate for a 15- to 20-ft.-deep well in an area with firm subsoil.) The well is dug until water enters faster than it can be bailed out by hand. The bottom part of the finished well is lined with stones. To prevent pollution, the upper part is lined with bricks set in nonporous concrete. The cap is also nonporous concrete.

Strainers

Stonework without concrete

The top of a groundwater reservoir is known as the water table, a level that moves up and down according to the rate at which water is being taken out and replenished. In some locales the water table is a few feet from the surface—a relief to well drillers; elsewhere, the table is so far down even drilling becomes impractical.

Groundwater is frequently confined within rock formations, where it forms an aquifer, or underground stream. If the aquifer originates from a high elevation, the water may be under enough pressure to bubble up spontaneously to the surface when a drill bit reaches it. This type of natural flow is called an artesian well and does not require a pump. Water tables also break the surface, creating seeps, springs, swamps, and ponds.

Spring (where water table touches surface)

Pond

Narrow-diameter well

Dog well

Artesian well

Horizontal well

Water table

Water-bearing formation

Impervious formation

Confined water-bearing formation

Variety of water sources (above) is equaled by the variety of ways water can be tapped. Because of the complex structure of aquifers, wells quite close to each other can nevertheless differ markedly in output.

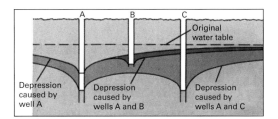

Original water table

Depression caused by well A

Depression caused by wells A and B

Depression caused by wells A and C

Wells draw the water table down in their vicinity, sometimes causing neighboring wells to dry up. In the example shown above, well A was dug first, creating a dry cone-shaped volume around it. Next came well B, which produced water until well C was put in.

Small-Diameter Well Construction

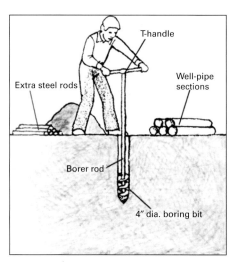

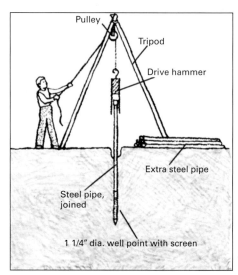

Bored well can be put in with inexpensive hand tools. First a 1-ft.-deep hole is driven with a pick or crowbar, then the borer introduced. As the borer penetrates, segments are added to its rod to accommodate increased depth. Periodically, the borer must be lifted to empty the hole of loosened cuttings. Boring is impractical for wells deeper than 50 ft. Moreover, if a large stone or a rock formation is met, the operator has to abandon the hole and start again elsewhere. After water is encountered, the well pipe and water intake are installed.

Driven well is put in by hammering a pipe directly into the earth. The point of the pipe is screened to keep dirt out, since it will serve later as a water intake. The pipe is hammered in by repeatedly dropping a heavy weight on it. Well depths of up to 150 ft. can be achieved with equipment like that illustrated. To check for the presence of water, lower a weighted string down the pipe, then raise the string and examine the end to see if it is wet. Once water is detected, drive the pipe down another 20 to 30 ft. to guarantee water supply.

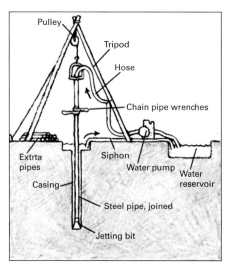

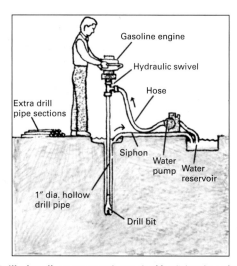

Water-jetted well can be put in fairly rapidly with a pump that forces water down a pipe. The water pressure jars the soil loose and forces it up the well hole to the surface. As the well deepens, the pipe should be rotated periodically to help keep it vertical. The mud in the upward flowing water helps to line the well wall and prevent crumbling. A casing, installed as the well is being jetted, will further reinforce the wall. If no rock formation is encountered along the way, a strong pump can jet a 1-ft.-diameter well to a depth of 300 ft.

Drilled well can penetrate thousands of feet below the surface; the depth is limited only by the power of the drilling engine and the quality of drill bit used. For very hard rock, diamond-tipped bits are required. A hand-held, 3-horse-power drilling unit like the one shown can reach a depth of about 200 ft. A water pump is used to wash soil and rock cuttings to the surface and to cool and lubricate the bit. After the hole is drilled, the hole is reamed to a diameter of 3 in., and the well pipe and screen (or submersible pump) are installed.

Aboveground Storage In Pond or Cistern

Of the various types of surface water the most valuable for a home water supply is a spring. Springs can be thought of as naturally occurring artesian wells, the water being pushed to the surface by gravity. A mere trickle can support the water needs of a home if it is collected in a cistern or holding tank. A spring's flow can be measured by timing how long the spring takes to fill a 5-gallon container. For example, if the container takes 30 minutes to fill, the spring will provide 10 gallons an hour, or 240 gallons of water a day—enough to support a small homestead. Remember, however, that springs can run dry at certain times of the year.

In some areas the most practical way to obtain drinking water is to channel rain falling on a roof into gutters that lead into a cistern. In a region of moderate rainfall (30 inches per year), a roof with a surface area of 1,000 square feet will collect an average of 50 gallons of water per day, enough for a two-person household with modest water needs. Since rainfall varies over the year, the cistern must hold enough water to cover expected dry periods. For example, a 50-gallon-per-day requirement could be supported for 30 days by a cistern that is about 6 feet on each side and 5 1/2 feet deep. Cisterns up to five times this size are practicable.

For large-scale water storage a pond is usually the best alternative. Ponds are excellent for such major uses as irrigation, livestock maintenance, and fish farming. In addition, they attract and support wildlife and provide water for fire protection if located within 100 yards or so of the structure to be protected. A pond can be a simple excavated hole if the water table at the site is close to the surface, or an earth embankment can be built to collect runoff. Unless the pond is also intended for power generation (see *Waterpower,* p.69), you should not attempt to impound a running brook. (There are legal restrictions that govern the development and use of waterways, and, in addition, a large and expensive spillway may have to be constructed.)

The probability is high that water from ponds, brooks, and similar aboveground sources will not be healthy enough to drink, particularly if livestock have direct access to the water source or if the source is located in areas suffering from pollution, such as mining regions. If necessary, water can be purified with ceramic filters or by chlorination. In emergencies the water can be boiled.

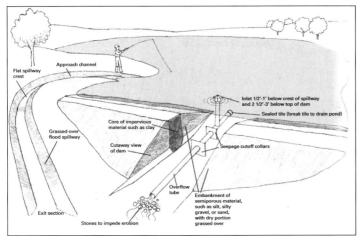

Pond formed by an earth embankment must have an adequate spillway, preferably excavated from undisturbed soil. The spillway is only for emergencies. Overflow is generally handled by an overflow tube built into the dam. To prevent undermining by water seepage, a core of impervious material should be included in the structure.

Use map to estimate acreage you will need to maintain a pond of a chosen size in your part of the country. The map is derived from annual rainfall data and specifies how many acres of rain-runoff area are required for each acre-foot of pond water. For example, to create a 1/4-acre, 4-ft.-deep pond (1 acre-ft.) in eastern Nebraska will require 12 to 35 acres of runoff area.

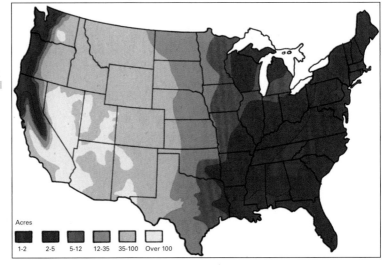

Acres

| 1-2 | 2-5 | 5-12 | 12-35 | 35-100 | Over 100 |

Ways to Collect and Store Rainwater and Spring Water

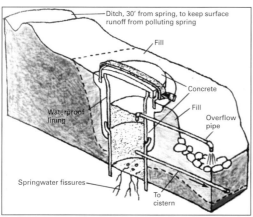

Spring water collection structure, formed primarily of concrete, helps stabilize water flow and protects water from surface contamination. Take care when excavating to avoid disturbing the fissures; otherwise the flow can be deflected.

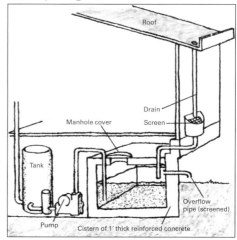

Typical cistern can hold 180 cu. ft. of water. Since water weighs 62.4 lb. per cubic foot, the cistern and its foundation must be massive enough to hold 5 to 6 tons of water. The entire system should be screened and sealed against insects.

An old-style springhouse

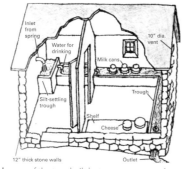

Springhouse of the type built last century put a spring to work to keep food cool. Such perishables as milk and butter were placed in containers, and the containers were set in a trough through which cool spring water flowed, keeping the food at refrigeratorlike levels even in summertime.

For pure water

Drinking water should not be considered safe until tested by your county health or sanitation department. These agencies will send an inspector to your property to collect a water sample, then mail you a report on its purity. In particular, be suspicious of water taken from a surface source, even if it comes from a sparkling brook and is clear and odor free.

Sources and resources

Books and pamphlets

Campbell, Stu. *Home Water Supply: How to Find, Filter, Store, and Conserve It.* Charlotte, Vt.: Garden Way Publishing, 1983.

Manual of Individual Water Supply Systems. Washington, D.C.: Environmental Protection Agency, 1987.

Matson, Tim. *Earth Ponds: The Country Pond Maker's Guide.* Woodstock, Vt.: Countryman Press, 1991.

Wagner, Edmund G., and J.N. Lanoix. *Water Supply for Rural Areas and Small Communities.* Geneva, Switzerland: World Health Organization, 1959.

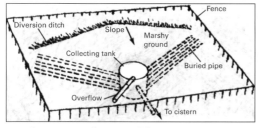

Marshy area can be tapped for water with a system of perforated or open-joint pipes draining into a tank. Pipes are buried in packed gravel faced by a plastic barrier on the downslope side to help concentrate water near them.

Springhouse is made of stone and built into the hillside to keep the interior cool in all seasons.

Sanitation

Disposing of Waste Without Wasting Water

Modern sanitation methods, such as flush toilets, septic tanks, leach fields, and sewerage treatment plants, have come to be taken for granted. Not only is their vital role in preventing the proliferation of contagious bacteria all but forgotten, but their imperfections are often ignored, particularly the enormous amount of water they consume. In addition, the sheer volume of waste that now pours into our lakes and rivers is beginning to overtax the ecosystem, destroying wildlife and polluting the waters.

In recent years attention has begun to focus on new kinds of waste disposal devices that greatly reduce water consumption and at the same time convert the waste into nonpolluting material. Some new types of toilets have cut water usage to 2 quarts per flush, others go further, doing away with the flush method entirely. Among the latter are toilets that incinerate the refuse, toilets that partly decompose the refuse through anaerobic (oxygenless) digestion—outhouses are a somewhat primitive example—and toilets that turn the refuse into high-quality compost via aerobic decomposition. Some of the newest approaches are finicky to operate, and others are costly to install; but most hold promise for saving water and energy while reducing pollution.

Primitive but functional outhouse is still standing from the early 1900s. Familiar crescent moon ventilating hole once meant "For ladies only."

Pit Privies

Pit privy, or outhouse, must be located where it will not pollute the water supply. Place it downhill from any spring or well and be sure that the water table, even at its highest level, is several feet below the bottom of the privy's pit. A pit with the dimensions shown will last about five years if used continuously by a family of five. Once the pit fills up, it must be covered and the privy moved to a new site. Though safe and sanitary if properly constructed, pit privies tend to be smelly. They are also uncomfortable to use, especially in winter.

Incinerating Toilets

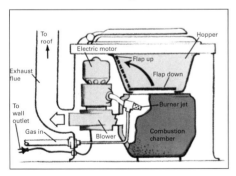

Refuse is converted to sterile, odorless ash in incinerating toilet. When top lid of seat is lifted, flap beneath the seat opens and a cycle timer is set. When lid is closed again, the flap drops down and refuse burns for about 15 min., after which unit is cooled by blower. Burner is fueled by natural or LP (liquid propane) gas. Hopper should be washed once a week and ash removed from combustion chamber with a shovel or vacuum cleaner. Toilet is effective but relatively costly to run and cannot take overloading—as might happen if the owner were to host a large party.

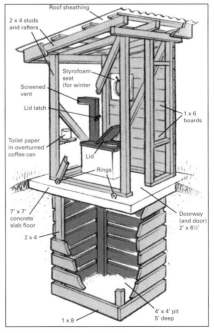

Privy is built on precast concrete slab to stop rodents and divert rain from pit. Rings cast in slab permit entire structure to be hauled by tractor to a new site when pit becomes full.

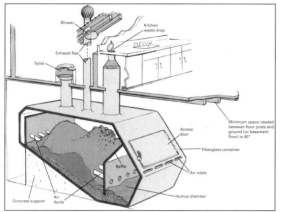

Large size of container in this composting toilet means that system likely requires almost no attention in normal operation. Mass of waste matter slides slowly down incline, decomposing as it moves. By the time it reaches lower end of container, it will have turned into high-grade fertilizer. System of perforated pipes and baffles helps supply oxygen to aerobic bacteria that digest the refuse. To keep bacteria at peak efficiency, the wastes should include such vegetable refuse as kitchen scraps and lawn clippings. The chimney exhausts occasional odors and supports air flow through the container.

Freezer toilets are odor free but require an energy-consuming compressor to freeze the waste; like chemical toilets, they must be emptied at intervals.

Vacuum toilets are fairly expensive. They work like waterless flush toilets, using special plumbing and a pump that sucks the waste into a collecting chamber.

Nonaqueous flushing systems imitate conventional toilets, but instead of water they recycle treated oil. Like vacuum toilets, these systems are expensive.

Composting Toilets

Unlike outhouses, composting toilets are just about odorless. Their chief requirement is a steady supply of air to maintain the aerobic (oxygen-loving) bacteria that feed on the refuse inside the fiberglass composting container. These bacteria function best between 90°F and 140°F—temperatures considerably higher than normal room temperature. A properly designed container can lock in the warmth generated by the bacteria themselves, helping to maintain the ideal temperatures.

In principle, a composting toilet does not require energy to operate. In practice, however, this is likely to hold true only in warm climates. In colder areas, during the winter, the composter will generally draw warm air from the house interior, venting it to the outdoors. In extremely cold regions, such as Maine, northern Minnesota, and Alaska, the composter may even require an auxiliary heater to maintain the proper composting temperature. Occasionally, a blower must be added to the exhaust flue to prevent odors from seeping into the house via the toilet seat or kitchen waste access port.

A composting toilet must usually be supplemented with a small standard septic tank and leach field to handle greywater (water from the bathtub, washer, or sink). Generally, a composting system is most economical where water is in short supply or where soil and topography combine to limit the effectiveness of more conventional waste disposal systems.

To offset the rather high cost of commercial models, some homeowners have tried building their own composting containers out of concrete block or other material. The job is difficult and can lead to problems, such as compost that does not slide properly and solidifies in the tank. Should that happen, the container must be broken open and the compost chipped out.

Other Toilets

A number of new waste-disposal devices have recently appeared on the market. Most are for special needs, such as a vacation home or in arid climates.

Chemical toilets employ a lye solution to destroy bacteria; the waste must be emptied and disposed of periodically. They are safe but have a tendency to give off an offensive odor.

Greywater disposal

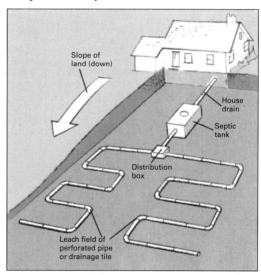

Typical septic system has a 200-cu.-ft. holding tank and a 120-ft. leach field. The field consists of pipe made of clay tile or perforated fiber buried 1 1/2 to 3 ft. deep. The tank can be concrete, fiberglass, or asphalt-lined steel, with an access port to pump out accumulated sludge. Dimensions of system can be reduced one-third if waterless toilets are used. Excavation for system can be by hand, but the job is more easily handled with mechanized equipment, such as a backhoe.

Sources and resources

Books and pamphlets
Hartigan, Gerry. *Country Plumbing: Living With a Septic System.* Putney, Vt.: Alan C. Hood Publishing, 1986.
Kruger, Anna. *H Is for EcoHome: An A to Z Guide to a Safer, Toxin-Free Household.* New York: Avon, 1992.
Wagner, E.G., and J.N. Lanoix. *Excreta Disposal for Rural Areas and Small Communities.* Geneva: World Health Organization, 1958.
Whitehead, Bert. *Don't Waste Your Wastes—Compost 'Em: The Homeowner's Guide to Recycling Yard Wastes.* Sunnyvale, Tex.: Sunnyvale Press, 1991.
Wise, A.F., and Swaffield, J.A. *Water, Sanitary and Waste Services for Buildings.* New York: Halsted Press, 1995.

Stone Walls

Mortarless Masonry: The Natural Alternative To Concrete and Tar

Stone is one of nature's finest building materials. It is plentiful, free, attractive, and enduring. Long before mortar was developed, stone was used to build walls, walks, roads, towers, and monuments. Some of these structures, like Stonehenge in England or the great monolithic statues of Easter Island, have withstood the ravages of time for millennia. In America mortarless stone construction is chiefly associated with New England. There, colonial farmers made a virtue of necessity by using stones from their rocky fields for everything from walls to root cellars.

The principles of mortarless, or dry wall, construction have remained unchanged over the centuries: walls must be perfectly vertical, their individual stones should overlap each other, and the base of the wall should be as wide or wider than the top. Materials have remained largely unchanged, too, although brick has been added to the dry mason's repertoire and is especially useful for walkways, driveways, and patios.

Almost any size, shape, or variety of rock can be used for dry wall construction. Old foundations, loose rubble from an abandoned quarry, a rock-strewn field, or the bed of a stream are likely sources of building stones. If it is not your property, be sure to get the owner's permission before removing any rock. And never attempt to quarry rock without professional help; rock is massive (170 pounds per cubic foot for granite) and can break unexpectedly.

Tools and Supplies

The tools and equipment needed for dry wall stonemasonry tend to be simple and rugged. Most, if not all of them, will already be part of your home stock of tools; others can be purchased as the need arises: there is little point in investing in special chisels and a set of steel wedges, for example, if you are not going to split stone.

Whatever tools you buy, be certain their quality is high. Rocks can be enormously heavy, and sudden, unexpected failure of a piece of equipment can cause serious injury. You should also be sure to purchase and use the three items most connected with safety: heavy-duty steel-toed work shoes, a pair of sturdy leather work gloves, and safety goggles with plastic lenses to wear whenever you chip, shape, or otherwise dress stone.

Old stone wall is constructed from fieldstone. The turnstile allows ramblers to explore the moors more easily.

Stone masonry is an art when practiced by a dedicated craftsman. In the richly variegated wall shown above, stones have been carefully placed for strength as well as beauty: the largest rocks are at the base with stone decreasing in size as the wall gets higher. Like all dry walls, it has a certain amount of flexibility, or "give," making it relatively immune to frost heaving.

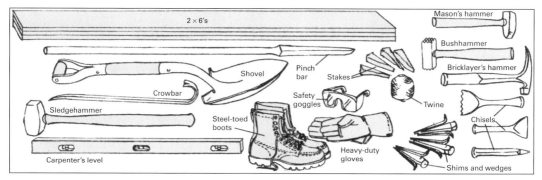

Most stonemason's tools are available in any good hardware store. Sturdiness is vital, but avoid tools that are too heavy for you.

Moving and Lifting Large Stones

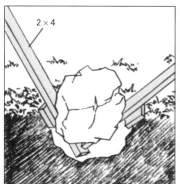

Pair of 2 × 4 s, worked in opposition, are employed as levers to raise large stones. Pry first with one, then the other, until one can be used as a ramp. Do not stand in hole with rock when raising it.

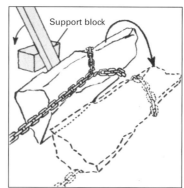

Large rocks can be dragged short distances with a chain hooked up to a winch, vehicle, or draft animal. After attaching chain, flip rock over; tension of chain will keep rock from digging into earth.

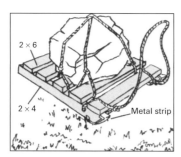

Stone boat is good for moving large rocks. Make the boat's bed of 2 × 6 s, the runners of 2 × 4 s. Line the front of each runner with a metal strip. Tie boulders to the bed to prevent them from rolling off.

Boards and rollers serve as a temporary roadway over limited distances. Pick rollers up from rear, lay them down in front of advancing rock. Effort can be saved by levering the rock forward from behind with a 2 × 4.

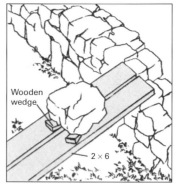

Stones can be rolled up ramp to wall top. Wooden wedges keep stones from slipping back. Make ramp out of long boards so that the slope will be gradual. Before moving a stone, measure it to be sure it will fit wall.

Shaping Stone

Shaping, or dressing, stone can be tough, exhausting work and should be avoided if possible. Moreover, the rough, natural surface of a rock will add much to a wall's character and beauty. Occasionally, however, a bit of dressing is essential. Use a chisel to chip off an unwanted protuberance on a flat side, a mason's hammer to dull a jagged edge, or a bushhammer to powder a point. Brute force blows with a sledgehammer can pulverize a lump or even an edge, but they may also split the rock. If a rock is too large to handle, it can be split. Whenever you split or shape rock, be sure to wear your goggles—a flying stone chip can blind you.

To split a rock that has a stratified (layered) structure, mark a line along the grain, then chip on the line with the sharp end of a mason's hammer until a crack starts to form. Widen the crack gradually by driving wedges into it at several points. When the crack is wide enough, pry it apart with a crowbar.

Shim and wedge

Granite and other rocks with uniform textures are difficult to split. Start by drilling holes about 6 in. apart along the split line with a narrow-bladed chisel that is rotated after each blow. Next, hammer thin wedges into the holes. Follow these with progressively larger wedges until the rock cracks in two.

Attention to the Basics Gives Lasting Results

There are three types of dry walls: freestanding, breast, and retaining. Breast walls are simply rock pavements laid into sloping ground to prevent soil erosion. Retaining walls are similar to freestanding walls except that they require dug-in foundations and are open on only one side—the other side butts against an earth terrace. Both retaining walls and dry walls are held together by friction and gravity. Friction is maximized by laying each stone so that it makes the greatest possible surface contact with the greatest number of stones around it. Since gravity works in only one direction—straight down—the wall must be perfectly vertical. If it is, the overlapping weights of the individual stones will effectively knit the structure together along its base line. If the wall is out of plumb and leans, it eventually will be reduced to a pile of rubble. When constructing either a freestanding or retaining wall, set up stakes and stretch a line between them at the planned wall height. Along with a carpenter's level, the string and stakes will act as guides to keep the wall even and vertical.

Principles of a Freestanding Dry Wall

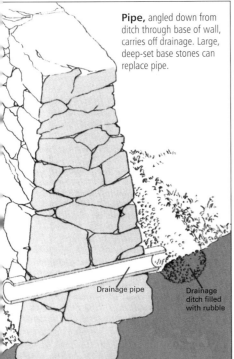

Pipe, angled down from ditch through base of wall, carries off drainage. Large, deep-set base stones can replace pipe.

Cap the wall with heavier stones set aside during the building. Slablike stones provide a level top.

Long stones should be set into wall; they help tie the wall together.

Drainage ditch must be dug on uphill side of a wall built on a slope. Fill ditch with stone rubble.

Drainage pipe

Drainage ditch filled with rubble

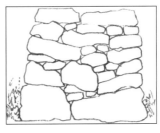

Cross section shows rocks placed so that each major stone bears on at least two others beneath it. Note chunky rocks wedged inward by small slivers driven beneath them. Use small stones in interior only; set largest stones at base.

7 1/2'
5'
3'
0'   2'   3 1/3'   5'

Proper wall width depends on height. Minimum width of base is 2 ft. For walls higher than 3 ft., width of base should be two-thirds of height, and wall should be tapered upward symmetrically so that center line is plumb. For attractive appearance top the wall with flat slabs.

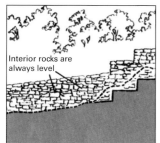

Keep wall level across uneven ground. Cut trenches through small rises or build up base to fill small depressions. Wall running up a gentle slope can have a sloped top, but interior rocks must be laid level. When slope is steep, wall should be built in stepped sections, each with a horizontal top.

Interior rocks are always level

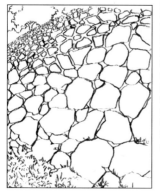

Breast walls help stabilize soil on slopes. Build wall from bottom up. If the wall is so high that the entire slope cannot be paved from ground level, pave as much as you can, then allow several weeks for bottom section to set before doing higher portions. Use chunk-type rocks set level with each other in holes spaced as close to each other as possible. Fill gaps with soil topped with pebbles. Grass seed can be added.

Retaining and Breast Walls

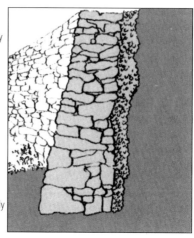

Retaining walls buttress earth terraces. They are wider than other dry walls with bases that are set well into the ground (2 to 3 ft.). Occasionally they are designed to lean slightly into the terrace. If a retaining wall is more than 2 ft. high, its base should be wider than its top but only on the open side. Pebbles between soil and wall help water drain through openings. Pipes or drainage holes in the wall should angle down toward the open face and be designed to prevent undermining of the wall by runoff. The ground in front of the wall should slope down to help carry off water.

Fences

Building Fences for Beauty as Well as Practicality

The poet Robert Frost took exception to the old country notion that "Good fences make good neighbors." But there is no disputing the fact that good fences can be useful and attractive. Fences keep livestock in and pests out; they prevent small children from wandering off; they serve as boundary markers, windbreaks, sunshades, and privacy screens. And while some fences are merely utilitarian, others are true adornments: a rambling split-rail fence or an old-fashioned zigzag can be every bit as pretty as the countryside in which it is set.

Choosing a Fence to Fit Your Needs

Choosing a fence is an exercise in common sense. First, you should decide exactly what functions the fence is to serve, then you should consider such factors as cost, appearance, and durability. If the main purpose of the fence is privacy, it should be tall and free of gaps. So-called stockade fences made of upright poles fulfill this

requirement as do tightly spaced picket fences and fences of woven redwood slats. If you want to enclose a play area, the fence should be strong enough to resist the wear and tear of children and tall enough and tightly woven enough to prevent their squeezing out or climbing over. It should also be free of dangerous projections and open enough to let you keep an eye on the kids. A welded wire fence would meet these requirements.

In rural sections barbed wire is an economical way to fence in livestock. The barbs are dangerous, however, and their use is forbidden in most residential areas. A better choice, especially for smaller lots in built-up locales, would be a split-rail fence. Not only will it do the job, but it is safe and attractive as well. In addition, split-rail fences are easy to erect, require little lumber,

Fence styles have evolved throughout the centuries into a panorama of varieties designed to suit specific needs.

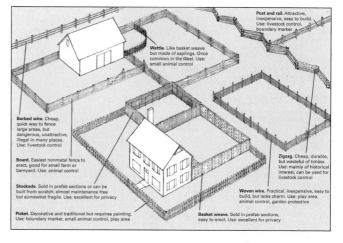

Post and rail. Attractive, inexpensive, easy to build. Use: livestock control, boundary marker

Wattle. Like basket weave but made of saplings. Once common in the West. Use: small animal control

Barbed wire. Cheap, quick way to fence large areas, but dangerous, unattractive, illegal in many places. Use: livestock control

Board. Easiest nonmetal fence to erect, good for small farm or barnyard. Use: animal control

Stockade. Sold in prefab sections or can be built from scratch; almost maintenance free but somewhat fragile. Use: excellent for privacy

Picket. Decorative and traditional but requires painting. Use: boundary marker, small animal control, play area

Zigzag. Cheap, durable, but wasteful of timber. Use: mainly of historical interest, can be used for livestock control

Woven wire. Practical, inexpensive, easy to build, but lacks charm. Use: play area, animal control, garden protection

Basket weave. Sold in prefab sections, easy to erect. Use: excellent for privacy

and are longer lasting and more maintenance free than most fences. (A picket fence, for example, requires periodic painting and is relatively fragile.)

Fences require planning. To calculate the amount of wire or boards you will need and the number of fence posts that you will have to set, mark off the corners of the fence line with stakes and measure the distances between; the sum of these measurements is the amount of fencing you must obtain. In order to figure the correct number of posts, allow one for each corner and a pair for each gate. Along a straight fence line posts are usually spaced at 16-foot intervals for woven wire, at 12- to 14-foot intervals for barbed wire, and at 5- to 8-foot intervals for board or rail fences, depending on the lengths of lumber available. When laying out a wire fence around a curve, space the posts more closely.

Take special care when building a fence along a property line. Unless you and your neighbors agree on legal provisions, you will have to make certain that the fence is on your own land. Zoning laws often stipulate that a professional boundary survey be made.

Making Post-and-Rail Fences

The familiar split-rail fence is an updated version of the rustic post-and-rail fences built by homesteaders out of timber cleared from their lands. Like the picturesque zigzag fence, a split-rail fence can be built by anyone who has timber and some simple tools.

Split-rail fences are economical to construct: they require relatively little lumber, they can be built from wood you harvest yourself, they require no hardware to hold them together, and they can be left unpainted—weathering will eventually turn the wood a soft silver-gray that blends unobtrusively with the landscape. Any of the woods shown in the chart above can be used, although the difficulty of splitting certain woods, particularly elm, can add considerably to the work.

When splitting rails, you will find it easier to work with green freshly cut logs rather than seasoned timber. Also, since wood tends to split more readily in cold weather, try to do your rail-splitting in the winter and early spring. You will need an 8-pound splitting maul or sledgehammer and three or four sturdy wedges. Old-fashioned wooden wedges as well as wedges made from steel can be used, but you will need at least one steel wedge in order to make the initial opening. Poles can be employed rather than split rails if plenty of 3- to 4-inch-diameter timber is available; the fence will still be attractive, and a good deal of labor can be saved. Milled 2 × 4 s also can be used as rails, but the fence will cost more and lose much of its rustic charm. When working with either split rails or poles, use a saw to taper the ends of the rails so they will fit side by side in the slotted posts. It is not necessary to taper the 2 × 4 s; simply place the rail ends one on top of the other in the slots.

For posts try to select a longer-lasting variety of wood, and be sure to treat the belowground portions by soaking them in creosote or other commercial preservative, such as pentachlorophenol. Digging post holes is usually done by hand with a clamshell-type post-hole digger, but gasoline-powered augers are also available on a rental basis. In soft

Life expectancy of fence posts

Wood type	Untreated	Treated
Birch	2-4 yr.	10-20 yr.
Black locust	20-30 yr.	Not needed
Cedar	15-20 yr.	20-30 yr.
Douglas fir	3-7 yr.	15-18 yr.
Elm	4 yr.	15 yr.
Hickory	5-7 yr.	15-20 yr.
Maple	2-4 yr.	15-20 yr.
Oak	5-10 yr.	15-20 yr.
Osage orange	20-25 yr.	Not needed
Pine	3-7 yr.	20-30 yr.
Redwood	10-15 yr.	20-30 yr.
Sassafras	10-15 yr.	20-25 yr.
Spruce	3-7 yr.	10-20 yr.

ground, fence posts can be sharpened with a chain saw and simply hammered directly into the earth with the aid of a post maul or sledge.

The number of tiers of rails that you should install depends on the use to which the fence will be put. For a boundary fence or for penning such small animals as sheep, a two-tiered fence is sufficient. Larger livestock require three to four tiers. The vertical distance between rails, and between the bottom rail and the ground, should be about 15 inches. Some livestock owners staple a strand of barbed wire across the top of the posts, inside the fence, to keep heavy animals from rubbing against rails and dislodging them or loosening the posts.

Fences for Farm, Home, Pastures, and Stockpen

Many traditional fence styles evolved as by-products of the land-clearing process, which produced enormous amounts of timber suitable for fencing. In heavily wooded sections of the country, such as Tennessee, Virginia, and Kentucky, the zigzag rail fence was the most popular type, especially for enclosing pastureland. Beautiful examples of the zigzag still stand in Cades Cove in the Great Smoky Mountains National Park. For small stockpens designed to contain sheep or pigs, portable wattle fences were common. Built of saplings, shoots, or branches, the wattle fence was a holdover from the settlers' European heritage, since fence timber had long been scarce in the Old World. The stockade fence was originally a protective structure around forts and settlements; the relatively flimsy modern version serves mostly as a fence for privacy.

Barbed wire and, later, woven wire replaced wood for use by settlers who reached the treeless prairie states. Not only was barbed wire less expensive than scarce lumber, it was far easier to install. It came into such widespread use among cattlemen and sheepmen that

Splitting the rails

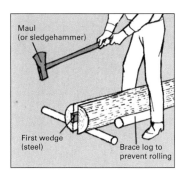

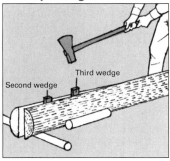

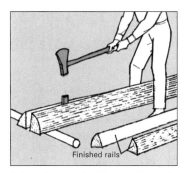

1. Use straight-grained logs with 9- to 12-in. diameters. Drive wedge into butt end to open a 2-ft.-long crack.

2. Lengthen crack by driving additional wedges until log splits along entire length. Work to keep crack centered.

3. Lay split trunks flat side down. Then split each half into quarters (finished rails) by repeating Steps 1 and 2.

Setting the posts and assembling the fence

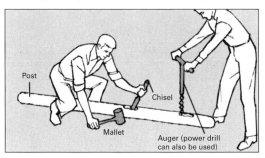

1. Use 5- to 6-in.-diameter logs for posts. To make slots for rails, bore groups of 2-in.-diameter holes in upper parts of logs, and trim away waste with a heavy chisel and mallet.

2. Post holes should be 2 1/2 ft. deep or one-third length of post, whichever is greater. Set post in hole on gravel base. Fill with layers of earth and gravel; concrete capping is optional.

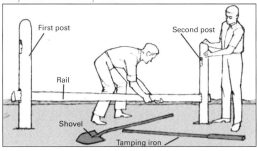

3. Set the first post, and tamp soil firmly around it using an iron bar or tamping iron. Place second post in its hole; fill but do not tamp. Install rails between posts.

4. Tamp firmly around the second post. Continue assembling the fence by setting the next post loosely in place, installing the rails, then tamping the soil around the post, and so on.

A variety of wooden fences

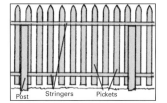

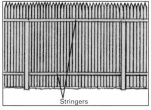

Wattle fence is constructed of woven saplings. Uprights are set in base of flattened logs. Fence can be permanent or built in portable 8-ft. panels. Pile stones on base logs for added stability.

Picket fence is made with 2 × 4 stringers nailed to 4 × 4 posts. Pickets are 1 × 3 slats nailed to stringers at the top and the bottom. The tops of pickets are generally pointed for style as well as to shed water.

Stockade fence is built like picket fence, but stakes are longer and more closely spaced. Stakes can be round or half-round. Stakes can be nailed to stringers or woven together with wire.

historians claim its invention in 1870 deserves more credit than the six-gun for the taming of the West.

Gates and Stiles for Getting Through

Fences, whose primary job is to bar passage, must still be designed to permit legitimate movement. Gates of one sort or another are the most common solution to the problem, but for livestock fences around large pastures, an old-fashioned stile—a device that bars animals but lets people through—can suit the purpose admirably.

Decorative gates for yard and garden fences may need to be only wide enough for a person to pass through, but a minimum width of 4 feet is required for gates that must accommodate such devices as lawnmowers, wheelbarrows, and garden machinery. Gates in farm and pasture fences should be 12 to 16 feet wide in order to admit livestock and large machinery. Regardless of size, the gate and its support must be strongly built, since it will receive more wear and tear than any other part of the fence. To prevent sagging and lessen stress on the far end of a gate, a diagonal brace of wood, wire, or steel cable is usually installed between the gate's low corner at the hinge side and its high corner at the far end. Gateposts must be sturdy, firmly set, and absolutely vertical. To keep them from loosening, shore them with lumber, strategically placed boulders, or poured concrete slabs.

Post and rail wood fencing systems use the least amount of wood, making them well suited for larger, more open areas of land. Zigzag fencing is made of overlapping tiers of split rails with a 1-ft. overhang. The rails zigzag, creating a 120° angle at each bend. No hardware is needed for zigzag fences, but they use much more lumber than post and rail fencing.

The art of stringing barbed wire

Barbed wire is used for fencing in horses and cattle. Popular types of wire are 12-gauge (heavyweight), with 4-point barbs, and 14-gauge (lightweight), with 2-point barbs. Use heavyweight wire for small areas, since small fences receive more pressure from animals; use lightweight wire for open pastures.

Barbed wire is stretched between posts, then stapled in place. A reel is needed for safety and to keep the wire from tangling; a stretching device makes the wire taut. Installers should wear thick gloves and should stand with a fence post between themselves and the wire during the stretching operation.

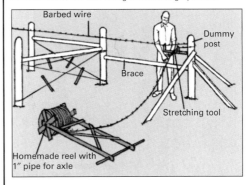

1. Corners are braced by fitting poles and wires between corner posts and neighbors on either side. Wires should be twisted tight. Corner posts are set deeper than others—about 3 1/2 ft.

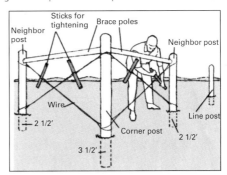

2. Fencing is stretched between corners, using stretcher tool or block and tackle, then stapled to line posts. Temporary brace and dummy post (set 18 in. deep) support corner post during stretching.

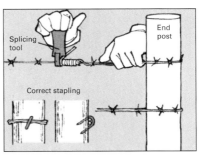

3. Final step is to splice each wire around last post. Each strand is drawn tight against post, stapled in place, then wrapped back on itself and twisted several times, using pliers or splicing tool.

Planting sturdy gateposts

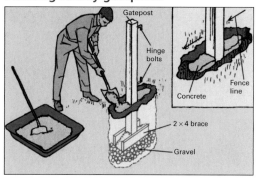

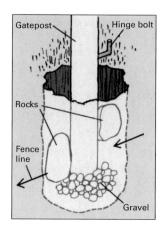

Gatepost above is braced by 2 × 4's at base and cap of concrete at top. Nail 2 × 4 braces to bottom of post, set in hole with braces parallel to fence line, and fill with earth to within 1 ft. of surface. Then pour slab, using about 1 cu. ft. of concrete.

Boulder-braced gatepost (above) is kept in place with rocks—the bigger the better. Place them firmly against the post parallel to the fence line.

A strong and simple gate

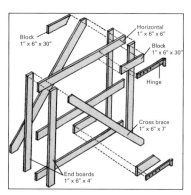

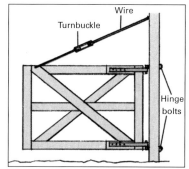

Heavy-duty gate, 6 ft. wide, is made of 1 × 6's fastened together with 3/8-in.-diameter carriage bolts. Sandwich three horizontal members between cross braces and vertical end boards. Use heavy steel strap hinges to attach the gate to the post, and string wire diagonally from the top of the gatepost to the end of the gate. Install a turnbuckle in the wire to adjust tension. Gate can be doubled in size by increasing the length of each horizontal board and adding a second pair of cross braces and end boards.

Stiles: an old idea that still works

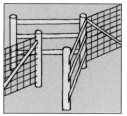

Zigzag stile is built into fence. Openings in stile should allow a man through but bar livestock.

Ground rods safeguard people and animals against lightning.

Lightning protection

Wire fences with nonmetal posts are a lightning hazard unless metal ground rods are installed. Make ground rods from 8- to 10-foot lengths of 1-inch-diameter pipe. Attach them within 150 feet of each end of the fence and at 300-foot intervals in between. The rods should extend 6 inches above the fence posts and be sunk into the ground far enough to be in constant contact with moist soil. Attach the ground rods to the wire side of the posts.

Sources and resources

Books and pamphlets
Barnett, Jim. *Walks, Walls and Fences.* Saddle River, N.J.: Creative Homeowner, 1996.
Fences and Gates. Menlo Park, Calif.: Sunset-Lane, 1996.
Martin, George A. *Fences, Gates and Bridges: A Practice Manual.* Brattle-boro, Vt.: Alan C. Hood, 1992.
Snow, Diane. *How to Design and Build Fences and Gates.* San Francisco: Ortho Books, 1985.

Part Two

Energy From Wood, Water, Wind, and Sun

The energy joyride—that brief delusion of 20th-century man that the supply of cheap fuel was limitless—came to a sudden stop in 1973 with the Arab oil embargo and subsequent price rises. But long before then, farsighted individuals had been advocating a change to what have come to be called alternate energy sources: waterpower, wind power, solar energy, wood, and other nonfossil fuels. Conservation was one reason, saving money was another, but equally important were ecological considerations, for the growing use of oil and coal was polluting the earth, the air, and the oceans. *Energy From Wood, Water, Wind, and Sun* is both an overview and a detailed look at small-scale applications of these "new" sources of energy. The techniques needed to use them in the home are described as well as the methods for determining if a particular system—be it wood stove, waterwheel, windmill, or solar heater—makes good economic sense for the individual homeowner.

Making Your House Energy Efficient

Energy-Saving Measures That Cost Least

The most effective way to save money on fuel bills is to use less fuel. At one time this philosophy was taken as a matter of course in America. Heavy shutters helped homeowners keep their houses warm in winter, cool in summer. Shrubbery was planted with an eye to protecting the home from weather and not used merely for decoration. Chimneys ran through the center of the house rather than along the exterior. Homes were compact, not sprawling, and designed to draw family members together not only for conversation but also to share body heat. In many farm homes even animal heat was used occasionally by sharing living quarters with a goat or cow, or by housing large animals in a space alongside or beneath the family's living quarters. The need to save fuel influenced customs and manners too. Bundling, the practice of permitting unmarried couples to occupy the same bed without undressing, allowed courtships to proceed with a minimal cost in firewood.

With the advent of the energy crisis, many old practices are being revived. These techniques, when combined with modern insulation and weather stripping, allow us to immunize our homes against the vagaries of the weather to a degree unimagined by our ancestors.

Where heat leaks out and cold leaks in

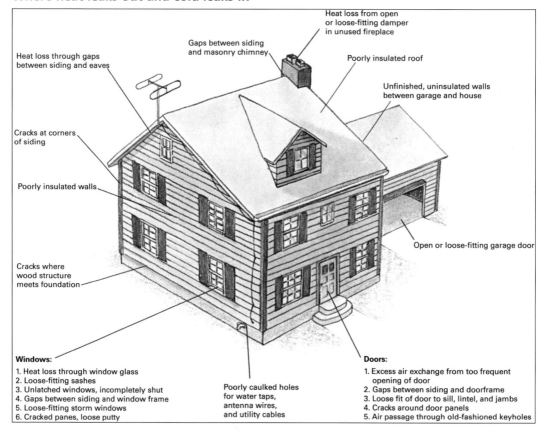

Heat loss from open or loose-fitting damper in unused fireplace

Gaps between siding and masonry chimney

Poorly insulated roof

Heat loss through gaps between siding and eaves

Unfinished, uninsulated walls between garage and house

Cracks at corners of siding

Poorly insulated walls

Cracks where wood structure meets foundation

Open or loose-fitting garage door

Poorly caulked holes for water taps, antenna wires, and utility cables

Windows:
1. Heat loss through window glass
2. Loose-fitting sashes
3. Unlatched windows, incompletely shut
4. Gaps between siding and window frame
5. Loose-fitting storm windows
6. Cracked panes, loose putty

Doors:
1. Excess air exchange from too frequent opening of door
2. Gaps between siding and doorframe
3. Loose fit of door to sill, lintel, and jambs
4. Cracks around door panels
5. Air passage through old-fashioned keyholes

Reducing Air Infiltration

Every house has gaps and cracks through which outdoor air can enter and indoor air escape. In most houses air exchange takes place at a rate of one to two changes in an hour. Inevitably, this turnover of air causes a substantial loss of heated air in wintertime.

Caulking and weather stripping are the basic means for reducing this loss. Properly applied, they can lessen the air exchange rate by 50 percent and cut fuel bills by 5 to 20 percent, depending on how leaky your house is.

Caulking is used to seal construction cracks in the body of the house, such as those between window frame and siding. The usual way to apply caulking is with a caulking gun loaded with a cartridge of caulking compound. When the trigger is pressed, a continuous bead of compound is squeezed out, like toothpaste from a tube. The compound is also sold in a ropelike strip that can be pressed into place. Caulking is not a modern development. In pioneer days homesteaders would plug leaky cabins with such materials as moss, mud, clay, and pitch-impregnated rope. Today's caulking compounds are superior. They are easier to apply, last longer, and insulate better. Oil-based compounds are still very common. Others include acrylic latex types that permit cleanup with water before they set. Butyl compounds are more flexible and stick to more materials.

Weather stripping is used to seal gaps between moving parts, such as those between a window sash and frame, and at door closures. To minimize wear, match the weather stripping to the motion of the parts. For compressive contact, as in a door closing, use felt or foam. For a sliding motion select a tough plastic or metal strip. Whatever type you buy, be sure it is thick enough to fill the gap. Foam stripping is available with a wood backing or with a self-stick adhesive backing. Where considerable compression is likely, as in a front door closure gap, use an open-cell foam, such as urethane. For light compression use a closed-cell type, such as vinyl. Adhesive-backed weather stripping bonds best when the temperature is above 50°F. During cold weather warm the surface to which the stripping is to be applied with a heat lamp or hair dryer. In some cases inexpensive felt stripping can be used for sliding as well as compressive contact. Where sliding motion is involved, the felt must be mounted carefully so that contact pressure is adequate but not excessive, since friction shortens the felt's useful working life. Felt stripping is usually held in place by tacks or staples. Wherever possible, with any type of stripping, make a trial fit with a short length before doing the complete job. Check that the seal is snug enough to block drafts but not so tight that the window cannot open or the door catch fail to hold.

Caulking

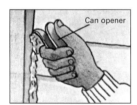

Before caulking, clean away any crumbling old caulking, flaking paint, and dirt with either a putty knife or the point of a can opener.

Apply caulking in continuous bead, working it into cracks. To flow freely, caulking must be warm. In winter keep it indoors until you use it.

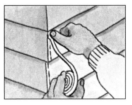

Rope-type caulking is less messy than cartridge caulking and does not require a gun to apply. Press caulking firmly into cracks.

Stuff large gaps more than 1/2 in. wide with oakum, fiberglass insulation, or other insect-proof material before sealing with caulking.

Weather stripping

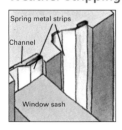

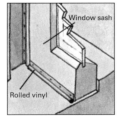

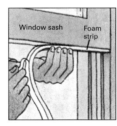

Windows can be sealed against the weather in a number of ways. The most effective method is to tack specially designed strips of spring metal in the channel between sash and jamb. You can also nail rolled vinyl along sash border. Adhesive-foam strip can also be attached along border; it is simple to install but should not be used where window sash rubs against window frame.

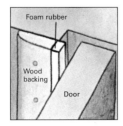

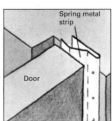

Doors as well as windows can be weatherproofed by various methods. Adhesive-backed foam along the jamb is easy to install but wears out quickly. Longer lasting is a strip of foam rubber with wood backing nailed to fit snugly against the door when closed. More durable yet is a strip of spring metal.

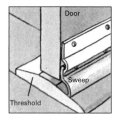
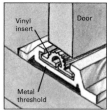
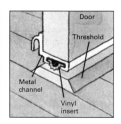

Maximum toughness is a requirement for weather stripping put in between door and threshold. A sweep nailed to the door bottom works well if there is no carpet or rug to interfere with it. More troublesome to attach are channels of metal with vinyl inserts that you can screw either to the threshold or to the door bottom to seal space between door and threshold. Unless the threshold is worn out or absent entirely, it is preferable to attach a channel to the door bottom.

Keeping Heat In (and Cold Out)

One of the most effective ways to save energy in the home is by adding insulation. The concept is simple: keep the flow of heat through walls, ceilings, floors, and roofs to a minimum. As the chart shows, different materials have a wide range of insulating abilities. Among traditional building materials, only wood—and that in thicknesses found in log cabins—is an effective insulator. The chart also indicates that stone masonry is a particularly poor insulator; a castle may be magnificent to look at, but it is a chilly place in which to live.

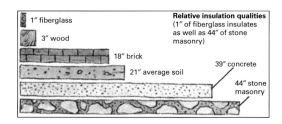

Relative insulation qualities (1″ of fiberglass insulates as well as 44″ of stone masonry)

1″ fiberglass
3″ wood
18″ brick
21″ average soil
39″ concrete
44″ stone masonry

Because heat rises, the attic and roof are the first targets for insulation. Next in importance are walls and windows, then crawl spaces and basements. Insulating materials are rated in terms of their R value: the higher the R value, the more insulation they give. Typically,

Floors and walls

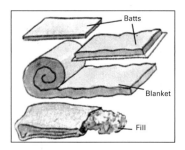

Insulation comes in different forms for different purposes. Batts and blankets fit well between joists and studs; loose fill and pumped-in foam are used for areas more difficult to reach.

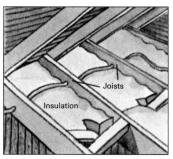

To insulate attic floor, select batts or blankets so that they fit snugly between attic joists. Place batts with vapor barrier face down. Be sure not to cover any attic vents or light fixtures.

Loose fill works well on attic floors. Use a board or garden rake to spread it evenly. If joists are boarded over, hire a contractor to drill holes into boards and blow fill into spaces between joists.

Finished homes with wood-frame walls can be insulated with loose fill or foam that is blown or pumped in through holes drilled into outside walls. This job is best handled by professionals.

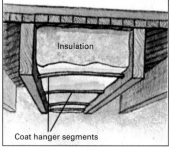

Floors over cold cellars are worth insulating. Press batts or blankets between joists, vapor barrier facing up, and secure with wire mesh or pieces of coat hanger cut to fit between joists.

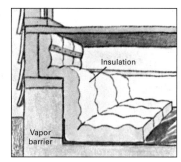

Crawl spaces can be insulated with batts or blankets. Note: Because of possible frost heaving, always provide proper perimeter drainage.

R-30 insulation might be used for an attic and R-20 insulation for the outside walls. However, the optimum values for your house can depart significantly from these. When selecting insulation, a key point to be aware of is that doubling the amount of insulation (using R-60, for example, instead of R-30) will not double fuel savings. More likely you will achieve barely enough savings to compensate for the cost of the added insulation.

When putting in insulation, it is important to install a vapor barrier to prevent moisture from condensing in the insulation. Blankets (rolls of insulation) and batts (precut lengths of blanket) often come with a vapor barrier already attached in the form of a waterproof layer of plastic or aluminum foil. Always install the barrier so that it faces toward the interior of the house. In older homes a vapor barrier can be created by applying two coats of paint to the inside of walls to be insulated, and sealing penetrations. If there is wallpaper, remove it before painting.

Windows

Shutters are a traditional means for containing house heat. Leave them open during daylight hours so that sunlight can get in; close them at night to keep heat from radiating out through windows. Slatted shutters are used in summer for shade.

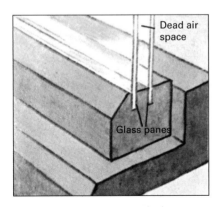

Double-pane windows (and storm windows fitted over existing windows) reduce heat loss by creating a layer of dead air between the panes that acts like insulation. For maximum benefit, windows should fit tightly and joints should be fully weatherproofed.

Heat-Saving Vestibules

For years vestibules have been looked on solely as repositories for umbrellas, galoshes, dirty boots, old toys, and snow-covered children's togs. Lately, they have been rediscovered as the heat-conserving structural devices they were originally meant to be, and many owners of homes that lack vestibules are having them installed or building them onto their houses themselves.

Pipes, ducts, and heaters

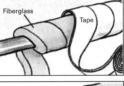

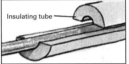

Hot-water pipes to distant faucets often waste heat. Wrap pipes with 1/2-in.-thick fiberglass and seal with plastic tape or else install ready-to-use foam-type insulating tubes with self-sealing aluminum backing. Insulation also protects pipes from freezing. If used on cold-water pipes, it will keep water cool in summer and stop pipes from sweating.

Exposed heating and air-conditioning ducts in unused cellars or attic spaces raise fuel bills unnecessarily. To cut down on the waste, first seal joints and other leaky spots with aluminum-foil tape or silicone caulk. Then cover ducts with 2 in. of blanket-type fiberglass or similar insulation.

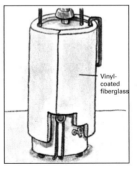

Hot-water heaters can waste fuel the year round. Special insulating material of 2-in.-thick fiberglass with a vinyl outer coating should be used. Wrap entire heater in material except for bottom and controls. Complete water-heater insulation kits are available that can be slipped on, then trimmed to size.

A vestibule saves heat and increases the comfort of your house in two ways. First, it acts like an oversize storm door to provide a barrier between the front door and the outside. Second, it serves as an air lock, cutting to a minimum the transfer of cold air indoors as you enter or leave the house. And the same qualities that make a vestibule an efficient heat saver in winter also conserve energy in the summer, when the air conditioner is on. As an added bonus, a well-designed vestibule is an attractive addition to any home.

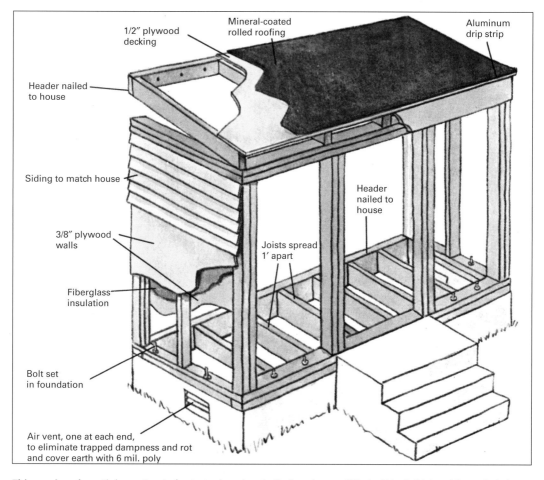

1/2″ plywood decking

Mineral-coated rolled roofing

Aluminum drip strip

Header nailed to house

Siding to match house

Header nailed to house

3/8″ plywood walls

Joists spread 1′ apart

Fiberglass insulation

Bolt set in foundation

Air vent, one at each end, to eliminate trapped dampness and rot and cover earth with 6 mil. poly

This version of a vestibule uses 2 × 4 s for structural members. Inside dimensions are 40 in. by 84 in. Prefabricated door and window units will save time and work. You can use a conventional storm door with a small window on each side or a fenestrated door with matching stationary windows, as in the picture. Door is hung on studs made of doubled 2 × 4 s. A solid masonry foundation extending below the frost line is essential. The depth of the frost line for your area can be obtained from a local weather bureau. In many localities you can simply dig a trench the width of the vestibule wall and fill it with concrete. The foundation should protrude at least 8 in. above the ground. Install wiring before putting in inside wall.

If you are thinking of adding on a vestibule, design it to blend in with the overall look of the house. The vestibule should have room for a bench and enough space for coats, overshoes, and other such items. Otherwise it need not be large—in fact, the smaller it is, the more efficiently it functions as an air lock.

Protecting Your Home With Trees and Earth

Winter winds, like a forced-air cooling system, can cause substantial heat loss from a house. The loss is due to various effects: lowered air pressure, conduction, and evaporative cooling. These combine to produce a temperature drop called the windchill factor. The chart at right shows how large the factor can be. For example, if during January the average outdoor temperature in your area is 10°F, an average wind speed during the same period of 10 miles per hour will make it seem like –9°F—a net difference of 19 degrees. If your house stands fully unprotected from the wind, the drop of 19 degrees that it is therefore subjected to might be virtually eliminated if you can find a way to block the wind. As an estimate of how much fuel such a step might save, check your fuel bills for January and for a month in which the average

1. Winter

2. Summer

3. Autumn and winter

4. Summer

Trees shade house from summer sun

S

Trees and shrubs can be planted in a variety of ways to redirect the wind. If the cold winds of winter arrive mostly from one direction, a single line of evergreen trees will do a good job of blocking them (Fig. 1); more rows at other angles to the house may be needed if the wind is variable. In the summer, however, these same trees may interfere with cooling breezes. One solution (Fig. 2) would be to plant a row of deciduous trees (trees that shed their leaves in autumn) to deflect summer winds onto the house. Once autumn arrives and the leaves have fallen (Fig. 3), the evergreens will function as before to protect the house. Deciduous trees are also valuable as shade trees (Fig. 4) to keep the rays of the hot summer sun off the house. Their advantage over evergreens is that sunlight will be able to get through during the winter to warm the house.

A thoughtful, step-by-step approach to planting windbreaks is advisable. Wind patterns can vary considerably during the year. In many cases, not until the windbreak is in place can you be sure what its net effect will be. Phone or write your state energy office or local utility company for further information. Local agricultural extension offices can help and may provide you with lists of additional resources.

outdoor temperature was 19 degrees above January's temperature. The difference between these costs would be the saving for January. Such savings can range up to 30 percent in a year.

Various methods exist for keeping wind away from a house. One of the most esthetically pleasing is a strategic placement of trees and shrubbery to block the wind. Planted near the house, trees can also shade it in summer and save on air-conditioning costs. Walls, trellises, and parapets can also be built onto or near the house to deflect air currents. When planning a new structure, consider the shape of the land—slopes and hills strongly affect the way the wind blows.

Underground Houses

Houses that are built into the earth or beneath it are virtually immune to fuel shortages. This is because very little fuel is necessary to keep them heated comfortably

above the surrounding temperature of the earth in which they are buried, a temperature that stays remarkably close to 55°F the year round.

This impressive fuel-saving advantage is offset, however, by the desire of most people for open space and

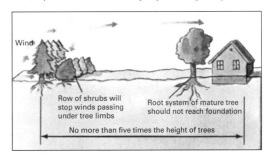

Wind

Row of shrubs will stop winds passing under tree limbs

Root system of mature tree should not reach foundation

No more than five times the height of trees

Shrubbery windbreaks are most effective when planted no farther from the house than five times the height of the windbreak (150 ft., for example, for a windbreak with 30-ft.-high trees). The trees should be far enough away from foundations and sewer pipes to prevent root damage. The distance can be inferred from tree size; root systems of mature trees usually extend about as far as the trees' branches.

Windchill

Wind speed	Temperature when there is no wind				
	50°F	30°F	10°F	–10°F	–30°F
5 mph	48	27	7	–15	–35
10	40	16	–9	–31	–58
15	36	11	–18	–45	–70
20	32	3	–24	–52	–81
25	30	0	–29	–58	–89
30	28	–2	–33	–63	–94
35	27	–4	–35	–67	–98
40	26	–6	–36	–69	–101

When the wind blows at speeds listed in left-hand column, your body—and outside walls of your house—will react as if the temperature were as given in the remaining columns.

Structures that impede air flow past the house, such as fences, walls, and parapets, can also serve as windbreaks. Even a trellis—which is normally used to support vines—or a similar wind-spoiling attachment serves this purpose.

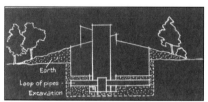

This New England structure is essentially a two-story house buried halfway in the earth. A sunken courtyard-greenhouse, like a solar collector, supplements the fossil-fuel heating system. In winter, heat is extracted by a heat pump from a deeply buried air pipe; in summer, cool air is pumped inside the same way.

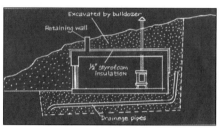

Built into the side of a hill, this Midwest home is nearly impervious to the effects of wind, storms, and tornadoes. An asphalt coating waterproofs the concrete roof and walls, which support more than 1 million lb. of earth. Drainage tiles below footings channel away water that collects there as a result of soil seepage.

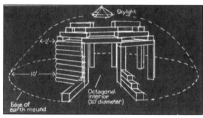

Traditional Navaho hogan is the basis for the design of this octagonal log-supported home in the Southwest. The logs rest on footings of stone and form the roof as well. The structure is covered by a mixture of earth and pumice. A vapor barrier of asphalt paint and stucco protects the logs from moisture.

sunlight rather than the cavelike atmosphere of an underground dwelling. Moreover, since subsurface structures are surrounded by tons of earth, some individuals worry that the walls may collapse or that escape may be difficult in case of fire or other emergency.

Many underground houses have been built in this country. Those that have been are often only partly buried. This type of design can still achieve major fuel

savings if the layout of the house permits the residents to live aboveground during the warm months of the year and belowground during the cold months. Even if a house is embedded more deeply in the earth, its design can still achieve a degree of airiness by incorporating skylights, sunken courtyards, and aboveground panels that deflect the sun's rays down light shafts. Another variant is to build the house into the side of a hill. That way one or more walls can be left exposed to let in sunlight and provide views of the countryside.

There are a number of special problems associated with underground structures. Erosion of the earth that covers the house must be kept in check. Usually this can be done by planting grass or shrubs that stabilize the soil. The shrubs should have short roots so they will not penetrate the walls or ceiling. An underground building must have enough strength to sustain the heavy load of earth pressing down on the dwelling. To achieve extra strength, underground houses are often built in the shape of a circle or octagon, designs that achieve a relatively even distribution of load. Roofs reinforced with steel beams and heavy concrete walls are also used.

Extra effort has to be made to keep belowground homes dry. Even with a waterproof vapor barrier around the structure that blocks moisture from the earth, the house must cope with condensation that accumulates inside. Surface houses have enough openings to let interior dampness quickly evaporate. Underground houses, however, need special ducts and blowers to keep them dehumidified. The problem is similar to the one many homeowners experience with their basements; but while a small portable dehumidifier will handle the moisture problem in the average basement, a much larger system is needed to control the humidity in an underground home.

Wood as a Fuel

A Reliable, Renewable Home-Heating Fuel

Wood, as the old saying goes, warms two times: when you cut it and when you burn it. The saying sums up the chief virtues of heating by wood—healthy exercise, comforting warmth, and the homey pleasure of a wood fire. In addition, wood is widely available and economically competitive with fossil fuels. And if you gather your own firewood, the savings can be tremendous, cutting your yearly fuel bill from hundreds of dollars to practically nothing.

Managing a Woodlot

A woodlot can supply wood indefinitely if the quantity you take out of it each year is no more than the amount replaced by natural growth over the same period. As a rule of thumb, 1 acre of woodland can produce 2/3 cord of hardwood each year. (A cord is a stack measuring 4 feet by 4 feet by 8 feet; it is illustrated in the picture above.) If you own or have access to 10 acres of woodland, you should be able to harvest 6 to 7 cords a year—enough to heat an average three-bedroom house.

The better you manage your land, the less acreage you will need. Woodlot management is like tending a garden, except it takes longer to see the results—years instead of months. In execution, it is a program of selective cutting based on the age and condition of each tree and how closely one tree grows to the next. As in gardening, experience is the greatest asset.

The first trees to cut down are those in an advanced state of decay and those damaged by disease or insects. These conditions are usually obvious, even to the inexperienced eye. As an exception, a tree with damage only to its leaves might be left for another season to see whether or not it is able to recover. Also, an occasional dead tree should be left standing as a home for wildlife. After damaged trees have been removed, harvest trees that have no potential value as lumber or trees that crowd others and inhibit their growth. Your county agent and state forester can both provide additional information on tree harvesting. The state forester may also be willing to go over your woodlot, marking the trees that should be culled.

Obtaining Wood

The cost of fuel wood depends very much on where you live and on the type of wood you are buying. In cities and treeless parts of the country you will probably have to pay much more for wood than in forested regions; and in either locale a cord of hardwood (generally more desirable for burning) is likely to be priced considerably higher than the same amount of softwood.

Wood is usually sold either by the cord or by the face cord. A cord is a stack of split or unsplit logs that measures 4 feet by 4 feet by 8 feet, but the amount you actually get in a cord will depend on how the wood is piled—in the old days some woodcutters developed an uncanny ability to stack cordwood with a maximum of airspace and a minimum of wood, and the practice, regrettably, has not entirely died out. The so-called face cord is not a cord at all but rather any pile that measures 4 feet high by 8 feet long. The width of the pile can be almost anything; sometimes it is no more than 12 inches and it is rarely more than 2 feet.

Wood is sometimes sold by the truckload. A 1/2-ton pickup will hold roughly 1/3 cord of wood. When buying by volume, keep in mind that the heat value of wood is directly indicated by its dry weight. Unfortunately, when wood is still wet, it is not always easy to estimate the amount of water in it. Try to avoid woods with a high resin content; resin adds to creosote buildup in a chimney.

On many occasions you can obtain fuel wood at nominal cost or for free. Public parklands and forests, town dumps, and lumber mills are sources for such wood. Even private owners may let you on their land to clear dead or unusable timber.

Tools and Techniques for Harvesting Wood

The best way to get fuel wood is to cut it yourself. Every step in the process—from felling the tree to bucking it into usable lengths to splitting and stacking it—provides vigorous outdoor exercise that is healthful and satisfying. With proper equipment and convenient access to the forest area in which you are working, you can harvest a cord of wood a day. A week or two of heavy work and you should have enough wood split and stacked to heat a reasonably well insulated house for one year (more wood will be needed, of course, in the colder parts of the nation, less in warmer climates).

Felling and bucking with a two-man saw can be quiet and sociable, but the efficient chain saw is the best choice for heavy work—it can cut through wood 10 to 30 times faster. Some chain saws run on gasoline, others on electricity. Gasoline models, although more expensive, are better for most purposes, since the electric versions require an extension cord (impractical in the deep woods) and are not as powerful. Chain saws can be dangerous. Make sure the model you get has all the

Chain-saw operator is in process of making a 45° angle face cut, the second of three cuts made when felling a tree.

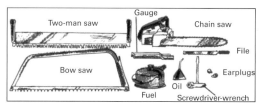

The blade of a bow saw is cheap. Replace blade when it gets dull. You can sharpen cutters on a chain saw, but be sure to use proper file and file guide and to follow instructions in your owner's manual. If in doubt, take chain saw to your dealer.

available safety features, and read the instruction book carefully before using it. Chain saws are also noisy; operate them with consideration for your neighbors.

All your woodcutting tools, including the chain saw, should be kept sharp. Dull edges require much more labor and create hazards. Your chain saw will stay sharp longer if you avoid cutting through dirt-encrusted logs or allowing your saw to dig into the earth beneath a log. There are several signs of a dull chain saw: the chips become smaller, more force is required to make the saw bite into the wood, the wood smokes due to increased friction, and the saw does not cut straight.

Felling a Tree

To get a tree to fall where you want, first make a notch on the side facing the desired direction of fall. This is done with two cuts: first the undercut, then the face cut. A third cut, the backcut, is then made at a slight angle downward, approaching the undercut about 1 inch above it. Leave an inch or two of uncut wood to act as a hinge to encourage the tree to tilt in the direction you want. If the tree does not fall of its own accord, push it with a long pole or peavey. Do not cut through the hinge.

Felling a tree can be dangerous. A side may be rotten, the tree may twist or bounce off another tree, or the trunk may rip loose and kick back in the direction opposite to its fall. Dead branches may also fall on you. For these reasons it is vital to have at least one, preferably two, clear escape routes and to get out of the way as soon as the tree begins to fall.

From Tree to Firewood

Winter is the best time for felling and bucking. The underbrush is thin, you sweat less, and there are no biting insects. Also, it is easier to spot dead trees and to choose safe paths of fall and good escape routes. Should there be snow on the ground, you will be able to slide logs about with less effort. On the average, a tree with a diameter of 12 to 14 inches will yield about 1/4 cord of wood. One to two dozen such trees will probably satisfy the heating requirements of your house for one season.

When you cut a tree down, make sure the area is clear of people, particularly children. If the tree is near a house, attach a strong rope high up on the trunk and apply tension so that the tree will fall in a safe direction. You can get the rope up by weighting one end with a rock and throwing it over a limb. To apply tension, you can either have a helper pull on the rope from a safe distance or else attach the rope to another tree.

Once cut, a tree may hang up on another tree instead of falling all the way to the ground. If you cannot pry it loose with a peavey, tie a rope to its trunk and use a block and tackle attached to another tree to pull it loose.

Diseases and other undesirable characteristics found in trees

Fruiting body or a canker (an open wound caused by rot) on the trunk of a hardwood tree indicates serious disease. Damage by insects is typified by holes left by oak borers and a sawdustlike residue at the base of trunk that results from infestation by certain types of bark beetles.

Disease that often afflicts evergreen trees is blister rust. Wilting branches may indicate an attack by weevils, while extrusions of pitch from the trunk of the tree are signs that pine beetles are present. Even slight symptoms may mean extensive internal damage.

Wolf trees are trees that take up large amounts of space and are too twisted and gnarled to have value as lumber. Due to advanced age they grow very slowly, robbing smaller trees of sunlight and nutrients and underutilizing the sunlight that they do absorb.

Cull trees from groups that grow too closely together. Saplings, for example, should be about 6 ft. apart, trees with trunk diameters of 12 in. should be 18 ft. from each other. Sell straight, tall, unblemished trees to a mill, since they are worth more as lumber than as fuel.

Characteristics of different kinds of firewood

Wood species	Approx. weight of 1 cord (in pounds)	Value of air drying	Resistance to rot	Ease of splitting
Shagbark hickory	4,200	Little	Low	Intermediate
Black locust	4,000	Little	High	Intermediate
White oak	3,900	Some	High	Intermediate
American beech	3,900	Some	Low	Difficult
Red oak	3,600	Some	Medium	Intermediate
Sugar maple	3,600	Some	Low	Intermediate
Yellow birch	3,600	Some	Low	Intermediate
White ash	3,500	Little	Low	Intermediate
Cherry	2,900	Little	High	Easy
American elm	2,900	High	Low	Difficult
Sycamore	2,800	High	Low	Difficult
Douglas fir	2,800	Variable	Medium	Easy
Eastern red cedar	2,700	Variable	High	Easy
Tulip (yellow poplar)	2,400	High	Medium	Easy
Hemlock	2,300	High	Low	Easy
White pine	2,100	Variable	Medium	Easy
Basswood	2,100	High	Low	Easy
Cottonwood	1,900	High	Low	Intermediate

Use the table at left when choosing firewood and making cost comparisons. When you buy by the cord, heavier wood gives more value per dollar, since weight is equivalent to heat. To find out how many pounds of wood of a particular species you get in a cord, look down the weight column. The figures assume that the wood has been air dried (20 percent of its weight remains water).

Before drying wood, check the column on value of air drying. Some woods have too little water in them to benefit much from drying; others should be dried six months or longer. Dealers often describe the wood they are selling as hardwood. In general, hardwood is heavy and softwood is light. The division is only approximate, however. Some hardwoods are light, some softwoods heavy.

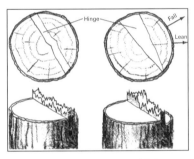

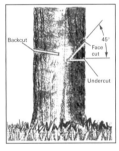

Pivoting technique lets you coax a tree to fall the way you want, even if it leans another way, provided the difference is not too great. Make backcut so that hinge is thicker at one end than the other. As tree falls, trunk will cling to wider end of hinge, causing it to pivot in that direction. Practice this technique in open woods before you try it in a tight spot.

A notch cut about one-third of way into trunk guides tree to fall in direction of notch. Set backcut higher than point of notch to prevent tree from falling backward. Tree will fall as planned unless it is leaning in some other direction. You can follow a similar cutting procedure with an ax, though control of fall will not be as precise.

Keeping your ax sharp

Chain saw may bind when making backcut into a large tree. You should have a wood, plastic, or aluminum wedge with you to free the saw. Knock wedge into backcut until pressure is eased, then resume sawing. (By using more than one wedge you can also encourage the tree to fall in the direction you want.)

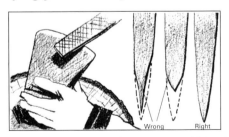

Sharpen ax with carborundum file or use ax stone lubricated with light oil (avoid motor-driven grinders). Maintain original blunt taper. Do not try to take out every nick; you will only remove more metal than is necessary, shortening life of ax.

When you remove a limb from a felled tree, make it a practice to stand on the side of the trunk *opposite* to the limb; that way you will minimize the risk of cutting your foot with the saw or ax. During

the bucking operation (sawing the tree into logs), the weight of the tree as it sags can pinch your saw blade and bind it. The pinching is caused by compression, either along the top side of the fallen tree trunk or the bottom side. With practice, you will learn into which side to cut to avoid binding. When binding does occur, hammer a wedge into the cut to free the saw. The wedge should be made of wood, plastic, or other soft material to avoid damage to the saw.

Sawbucks, cutting cribs, and woodsheds

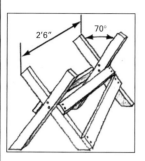

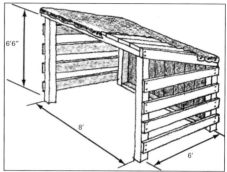

Sawbuck holds log so that it will not shake or shift as you cut. Make sawbuck taller than necessary; use it, then trim it to most comfortable height.

Cutting crib lets you cut many logs at once. An easy way to make one is to drive four posts into ground, then rope tops together so posts do not spread.

Woodshed can be made from scrap lumber. Protect stored wood from rain and snow, but allow enough air circulation inside to dry the wood. Store wood off the ground.

Limbing and bucking

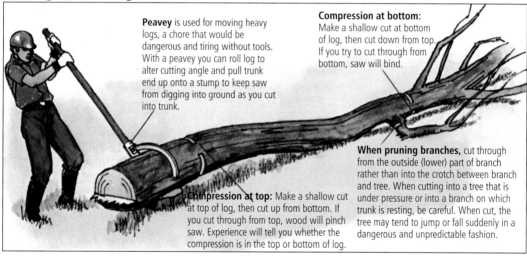

Peavey is used for moving heavy logs, a chore that would be dangerous and tiring without tools. With a peavey you can roll log to alter cutting angle and pull trunk end up onto a stump to keep saw from digging into ground as you cut into trunk.

Compression at bottom: Make a shallow cut at bottom of log, then cut down from top. If you try to cut through from bottom, saw will bind.

Compression at top: Make a shallow cut at top of log, then cut up from bottom. If you cut through from top, wood will pinch saw. Experience will tell you whether the compression is in the top or bottom of log.

When pruning branches, cut through from the outside (lower) part of branch rather than into the crotch between branch and tree. When cutting into a tree that is under pressure or into a branch on which trunk is resting, be careful. When cut, the tree may tend to jump or fall suddenly in a dangerous and unpredictable fashion.

Splitting and stacking

When splitting logs with an ax or splitting maul, proceed as if cutting a pie (left). However, if wood is twisted and fibrous (like elm), split it into tangential segments.

Heavy logs are better split with a sledgehammer and steel wedge. Never use the ax as a wedge or its poll (blunt end) as a hammer. You will ruin the ax.

Splitting screw, which attaches to the rear axle of a car, is one of several splitting devices on the market. Be sure to follow the manufacturer's instructions when using it.

One way to stack wood so that pile does not topple is to build up the ends log cabin style, as shown here. To protect from rain, place cordwood with bark up.

Sources and resources

Books and pamphlets
Drying Wood With the Sun. Washington, D.C.: U.S. Department of Energy, 1983.
Harris, Michael. *Heating With Wood.* New York: Carol Publishing, 1980.
Hogencamp, Robert. *Heating With Wood.* Washington, D.C.: U.S. Department of Energy, 1980.
Sharpe, Grant W., et al. *Introduction to Forestry and Renewable Resources.* New York: McGraw-Hill, 1995.
Smith, Robert A. *The Backyard Woodcutter: A Guide to Preparing Your Own Firewood.* Bristol, Wis.: Huron Group, 1994.
Thomas, Dirk. *The Harrowsmith Country Life Guide to Wood Heat.* Buffalo, N.Y.: Firefly Books, 1992.

Waterpower

Streams and Rivers Provide Energy Free for the Taking

The use of waterwheels to free human beings from heavy labor is almost as ancient as the use of draft animals. The earliest applications of such wheels were

Making your own stove

Small wood stove can be made from a 15-gal. closed-head heavy gauge grease drum after cleaning drum of any residue of grease. Tolerances need not be precise. One weld and some furnace cement to hold stovepipe flange to stove top are needed. All other parts bolt on. Cut rectangular openings for fuel loading and ash removal; then cut doors from sheet metal to overlap the openings 1/2 in. all around.

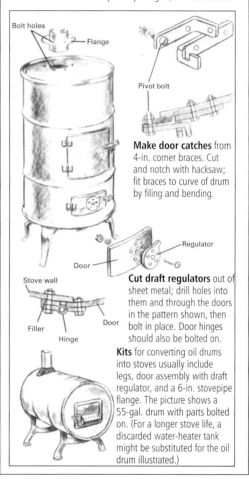

Make door catches from 4-in. corner braces. Cut and notch with hacksaw; fit braces to curve of drum by filing and bending.

Cut draft regulators out of sheet metal; drill holes into them and through the doors in the pattern shown, then bolt in place. Door hinges should also be bolted on.

Kits for converting oil drums into stoves usually include legs, door assembly with draft regulator, and a 6-in. stovepipe flange. The picture shows a 55-gal. drum with parts bolted on. (For a longer stove life, a discarded water-heater tank might be substituted for the oil drum illustrated.)

to raise water from wells and to turn millstones to grind grain. Later, waterwheels were adapted to provide power for other processes to which a slow, ponderous, unceasing rotary motion was suited. In early America, textile factories and sawmills were generally built on riverbanks to take advantage of waterpower.

With the advent of steam power in the 19th century, the massive, wooden waterwheel became obsolete, and water did not again compete as a power source until the invention of the high-speed turbine for generating electricity. This development not only led to huge hydroelectric installations but also made small, private hydropower installations possible.

A personal hydroelectric power source has the potential to sustain every household energy need and provide an unexcelled level of independence. Having enough water flow is less a problem than one might imagine, particularly in hilly areas where hundreds of thousands of potential hydroelectric sites remain untapped. With a drop of 50 feet from water source to turbine, for example, a brook small enough for a child to jump across can provide enough power for a single-family dwelling. However, bear in mind that the smaller the installation, the higher will be the construction cost for each kilowatt generated. Scaled against the cost of power from a public utility, it may be 10 to 20 years before a small installation pays back its initial expense, though rising fuel costs may substantially shorten the payback period.

Traditional Waterwheels

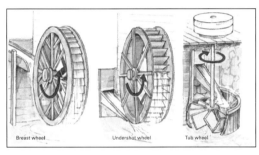

Breast wheel   Undershot wheel   Tub wheel

Individuality and variety marked the waterwheels of the past. Their diameters ranged from 3 ft. to 20 ft., and they incorporated every conceivable water-flow scheme. The most efficient type was the overshot wheel shown above, but if the water source was not high enough, a breast wheel or undershot wheel was employed. Of low efficiency, but simplest to build because it used no gears, was the tub wheel. A typical large wheel made 10 to 20 revolutions per minute; with wooden gearing this could be stepped up to 10 times the rate. A number of traditional waterwheels are still in operation in America, turning out the stone-ground meal so highly prized by home bakers.

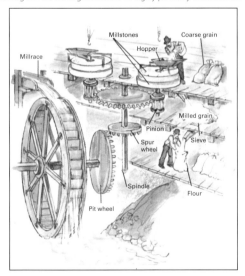

Old-fashioned gristmills could grind 5 to 10 bushels of grain an hour. The miller poured the grain into a hopper from which it trickled down through the eye of the upper millstone onto a bed stone. As the 1/2-ton upper stone rumbled over the bed stone, it scraped off husks and pulverized the grain. The husks were then separated with a sieve, leaving flour.

Modern Waterpower Systems

Waterpower achieves its greatest usefulness when it is converted into electricity. Lighting fixtures, heating systems, small appliances, cooking ranges, and machinery of all sorts are some of the common applications. The conversion is made possible by electrical generators that transform rotary motion into electric current.

Though not originally designed for the purpose, old-fashioned waterwheels can actually be used to run generators, but not without overcoming a major obstacle: electrical generators do not operate efficiently except at high speeds, on the order of 1,500 revolutions per minute. To reach these speeds, a large step-up in the waterwheel's rate of rotation is required, somewhere in the vicinity of 100 to 1. Wooden gears simply will not work—friction alone would destroy them. Instead, rugged, well-made gears or pulleys are required that are not only highly efficient but also capable of handling the huge forces present in the shaft of a waterwheel. Heavy-duty tractor transmissions have been adapted for the purpose and can provide several years of service. The design and construction of a system that will last 20 years or more calls for a high level of mechanical ingenuity plus persistence and luck in finding the appropriate used or abandoned equipment.

Gearing problems can be circumvented by using a turbine instead of a waterwheel. Turbines are devices that convert water flow directly into high-speed turning motion. Little in the way of supplementary gearing is needed to achieve generator speeds. In addition, turbines

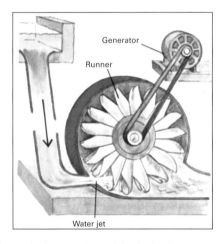

Generator

Runner

Water jet

Pelton turbines operate best with heads of 50 ft. or more. The high-velocity jet of water that results from such heads spins the bladed runner up to generator speed without the need of additional gearing. Pelton runners can be any size from 12-ft. diameters for megawatt installations down to 4- to 18-in. diameters for home installations. Very little flow is required to run a small Pelton turbine, in some cases no more than the water issuing from a modest spring. The need for a high head, however, restricts installations to hilly or mountainous locations. Also, springs tend to dry up during some parts of the year and freeze up during other parts, so care must be taken to select a water source that will provide year-round power. A recent improvement in impulse turbines is to orient the jet at an angle to the blades, as in Turgo turbines. These units are smaller and faster than Peltons.

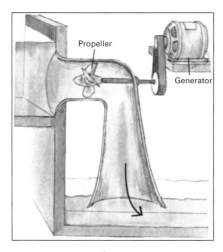

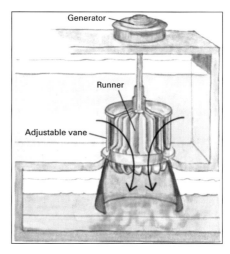

Propeller turbines are most effective at relatively low heads of from 3 ft. to 30 ft. The propeller is completely submerged and is impelled more by the dead weight of the water than by the water's velocity. In high-head installations, propeller turbines suffer wear from cavitation. In addition, they work well only over a narrow range of speeds, so care is required to match the size of the turbine to the available stream flow. For example, when flow drops to 50 percent of a propeller turbine's optimum, the power output will drop by about 75 percent, and when the flow drops to 30 percent, the output becomes nil. To overcome this limitation, some large hydroelectric installations use several turbines in tandem, shutting down one or more whenever the flow lessens. Others employ Kaplan turbines, which have automatically adjustable blades that compensate for flow changes.

Francis turbines can be used over a wide range of heads 4 ft. and more. As with a propeller turbine, the runner is immersed in the head water, which is guided onto the blades of the runner by a ring of adjustable vanes. The Francis turbine is highly efficient at its optimum flow but easily damaged by grit and cavitation. It is frequently used in large hydroelectric stations and is relatively expensive. As with propeller turbines and other interior-flooded turbines, a draft tube beneath the unit with its bottom rim immersed at all times in the tail water (the water flowing out of the power station) is a valuable adjunct: as water drops from the turbine runner down the draft tube, it sucks more water down with it, adding to the effective head of the system. This added head can be of substantial importance whenever the overall head of the remainder of the installation is small.

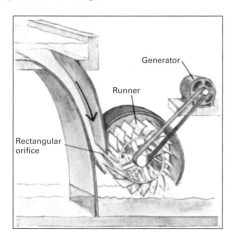

Cross-flow turbines work well when the head is greater than 3 ft. Water from a rectangular orifice passes through a barrel-shaped runner in such a way that the water strikes the ring of blades on the runner two times. This turbine is a relative newcomer; it has not yet been built in megawatt sizes but shows a great deal of promise for use in small installations. Moreover, it is simple enough for a person with a home machine shop to make; yet it can match the performance of the other turbines shown, whose fabrication requires a high level of technology. It works well over a wide range of water flow, is relatively free from problems caused by silt and trash, and is not affected by cavitation. To improve efficiency, the rectangular orifice can be partitioned and parts of it closed off during periods of low flow. Some step-up gearing may be needed for optimum generator speed.

are much smaller than waterwheels of the same power output, hardly larger than the generators with which they are coupled. Turbines run with a high-pitched whine—not as soothing as the rumble and splash of the old mill wheel—and some are subject to cavitation (wear caused by air bubbles).

Before you buy a turbine, you should measure the characteristics of your stream, particularly its head, so you can match the turbine to them. ("Head" is the vertical drop the water makes from the point where it is diverted from the stream to the point at which it reaches the power–generating equipment.) Pelton wheels, for example, perform best under high head conditions; propeller turbines, the reverse. "Flow"—the volume of water carried by the stream past a stationary point each second—is also a factor in turbine design.

Finding Out How Much Your Stream Can Do

To determine the amount of power available in a stream, it is necessary to measure the water flow and make calculations from these measurements. This is not a hard job, since a rough estimate is usually all that you will require. Generally, wide seasonal variations in flow put a limit on the degree of precision that makes sense when measuring a stream.

Changes on the order of 100 to 1 in the volume of water carried by a stream are not uncommon from one part of the year to another. In the Southwest, large rivers as well as smaller streams often dry up completely for long periods of time.

The key information that your measurements should provide is whether or not a stream will yield enough kilowatts of electricity to make its development worthwhile.You will also want to get an idea of how large the equipment has to be to generate these kilowatts and what type of installation should be used.

A rough estimate, however, may fail to provide sufficient precise data to determine how the installation should be constructed or what specifications the turbine and generator should have. For greater precision professional surveying instruments may be needed; but before involving yourself at this level of complexity, consult the turbine supplier with whom you expect to do business. He should know the degree of accuracy required.

A stream should be measured several times during the year so that its overall potential can be estimated and the power-generating equipment tailored to the variations in flow. The measurements will have value even when the flow is so large that only a small fraction will satisfy your power needs. It is particularly important to measure a stream near its low point during the year. Also, potential flood level should be ascertained if equipment is to be installed near enough to the stream so that it could be destroyed by a flood. When a dam is to be constructed, knowledge of flood potential is crucial.

If you are not familiar with your stream's annual ups and downs just by living near it, contact the nearest U.S. Geological Survey Water Resources Office (a branch of the Interior Department) for information on water runoff in your area. The information is free and likely to include rainfall and river flow data going back many years. If a stream is too small to have been directly measured by the office, a knowledge of local water runoff will help you form a profile of its behavior.

What You Must Measure

To find out how much power a stream can deliver, you must know three key measurements: the stream's head, its velocity, and its cross-sectional area.

When the stream is tiny

Flow from a spring can be measured by funneling it into a 5-gal. container and timing how long the container takes to fill. For example, if it takes 20 seconds, the flow is 5/20 gal. per second, or 0.035 cu. ft. per second (multiply by 0.14 to convert gallons to cubic feet). Flow, measured by a container, is the equivalent of the velocity times area, factors that are separately measured in larger streams. Water behind the embankment should not change elevation during the period of measurement.

Head refers to the vertical fall between the water source and turbine. In other words, it is the difference in elevation between the point where the water will be diverted from its natural streambed to the point where the water will be piped into the turbine.

Velocity refers to how fast the stream flows.

Cross-sectional area is a product of the width and depth of the stream.

To make the measurements, follow the procedures outlined on this page and the next. Once the three quantities are determined, multiply them together to obtain a power product. The greater the product, the greater the power available.

Measuring head

Head is measured in step-by-step fashion proceeding downstream from the water source to the planned hydropower location. You will need an assistant to help you make the measurement plus the following equipment: a carpenter's level, a camera tripod or similar support, an 8-foot-long pole, and a tape measure.

Set up the tripod near the water source and place the carpenter's level on the tripod's table. Adjust the table to the horizontal, then vary the tripod's height until the sight line along the level's upper surface is lined up with the water source. Next, have your helper hold the pole vertically at a location downhill from the tripod so that you can sight from the other end of the level to the pole. Call out instructions as you sight toward the pole, and have your assistant make a chalk mark on the pole at the point where the sight line intersects it.

Now set up the tripod and level downhill from the pole at the location where the sight line, looking back uphill toward the pole, will intersect the pole at a point near its base. The assistant should now mark the new point of intersection, measure the distance between marks, and jot the measurement down. Once this is done, both chalk marks can be erased and the pole set up at a new location downhill, where the entire procedure is repeated. Once the power site is reached, add up the figures you have jotted down and you have the head.

What the Power Can Do

After measuring the head, velocity, and area, multiply together the numbers you have obtained and divide the result by 23. You will then have the usable stream power in kilowatts. Expressed as a formula, the calculation is:

$$\text{Power in kilowatts} = \frac{\underset{\text{in feet}}{\text{Head}} \times \underset{\text{in ft./sec.}}{\text{Velocity}} \times \underset{\text{in sq. ft.}}{\text{Area}}}{23}$$

The divisor, 23, is in the formula to make the answer come out in kilowatts and to reflect an overall system efficiency of 50 percent.

For example, for a head of 10 feet, a stream velocity of 1.4 feet per second, and a cross-sectional area of 4.8 square feet, the usable power output is:

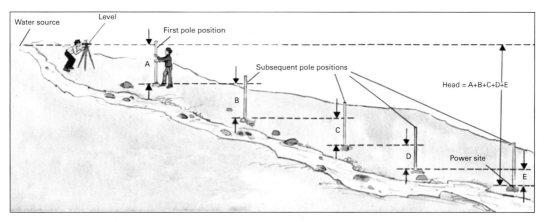

Measuring velocity

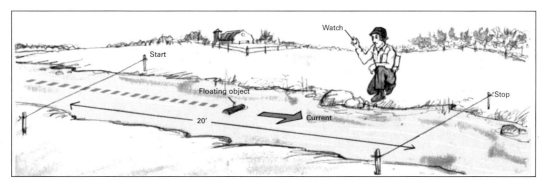

Estimate of velocity can be obtained clocking how rapidly floating objects move down the center of the strem. Select a portion of the stream that is reasonably straight and without obstructions, turbulence, or eddies. Tie strings across the stream at two locations spaced 20 ft. apart, with each at right angles to the direction of flow. Toss a cork, or other object that floats, into the center of the water upstream of the first string and time how many seconds it takes for the stream to carry the cork from one string to the other. Divide this amount into 20 ft., multiply the result by 0.7, and you will have the stream velocity in feet per second. (The factor of 0.7 is necessary to reflect the fact that portions of the stream flowing along the banks and near the bottom move more slowly than the surface of the stream where the measurement is made.) As an example, suppose the cork took 10 seconds to traverse the 20-ft. distance from string to string. Dividing 20 by 10 and multiplying by 0.7 gives a velocity of 1.4 ft. per second. For greater accuracy, repeat the measurement several times, then average the results.

Measuring area

$$\text{Power} = \frac{10 \times 1.4 \times 4.8}{23} = 2.92 \text{ kilowatts}$$

To find out how much electricity is available to you over a period of a month, multiply the figure you have obtained for power by 720—the number of hours in an average month. In the example above the 2.92 kilowatts (if this output is constant) would provide 2.92 × 720 = 2,104 kilowatt-hours per month.

Cross-sectional area of a stream must be measured at the same location at which you measured the stream velocity. Mark off one of the strings in equal intervals. Six to 12 intervals should be enough, depending on the size of the stream. Measure the depth of the stream at each of the marked points on the string, record each measurement, and calculate their average after all the measurements have been made by adding the figures together and dividing by the number of measurements. Multiply this result by the width of the stream, measured from bank to bank, and you will have the area.

As an example, suppose your stream measures 6 ft. across and you have marked your string at five points, each 1 ft. apart with depth measurements at each marker 1/2, 1, 11/4, 3/4, and 1/2 ft. respectively. The measurements add up to 4 ft.; 4 ft. divided by five gives an average of 4/5 ft.; and 4/5 ft. multiplied by six results in an area of 4.8 sq. ft.

The computation is similar if a container is used to measure flow. Just take out velocity and area from the formula and substitute the flow measurement in their place.

Making the Calculations

Once you determine a stream's power, you can estimate its usefulness. One way to do this is to compare the kilowatt-hours stated on your electric bill with the stream power you have calculated; you will then have a quick estimate of the proportion of your needs the stream will be able to satisfy. For the comparison use a bill with a monthly charge that is high for the year.

Another way to estimate what the stream can do is to use a capability chart like the one above. In an approximate way the chart indicates the number and type of appliances various power outputs can handle. It assumes that the use of these appliances will be fairly evenly distributed over each month and also assumes that a storage system, such as a bank of batteries, is used in the power system to take care of peak power demands (see *A Power System for Hilly Areas,* p.75).

One measurement of the stream is not likely to be enough to make a reliable estimate. Because stream flow varies, measure the stream's velocity and area at several times during the year (over the course of a number of years if possible) and use the lowest measured power to estimate usefulness.

Leading the Water To the Powerhouse

A small dam—one up to 4 feet high and 12 feet across—can often be built of locally available materials such as earth, stones, or logs. Such a dam can provide a dependable supply of water at an intake to a race (a canal for diverting water from a stream to a power station) or at a penstock (a pipe that serves as a race).

To moderate the effects of monthly and seasonal variations in stream flow, larger dams can be built. These will store excess water and release it during periods of low flow, providing more dependable power year round. Also, larger dams offer additional head (vertical drop from pond surface to turbine), a factor that can be critical in locations where the terrain is flat.

As the dam is made larger, however, its design becomes more and more complex and the number of potential problems increases. Particularly serious are cracks that may develop because of the varying stress and strain characteristics of the materials used in constructing the dam. In addition, rock formations under the dam may permit unexpectedly large amounts of groundwater seepage that threaten the dam's stability. As a result, dam builders must proceed with extreme caution. A failed dam can be awesomely destructive.

The best way to design against flooding is to obtain rain runoff data for the stream's watershed going back a substantial number of years. If such data are not available, the dam's construction must incorporate a large safety factor. Extra safety precautions must also be taken in earthquake-prone areas. If you are considering building a dam and have any doubts about the design of either the dam or its race, consult a professional engineer. In addition, you should check local regulations governing structures that affect stream flow. For dams above a certain size, a permit must be filed and limitations on construction observed. For further information, write to your state's water resources agency.

When building a dam and race, the area to be flooded, plus a marginal strip around the area, must first be cleared of trees and bushes. This is to prevent any undesirable tastes and odors that may later result from the decay of the plants. The foundation site of a dam itself should, at the very minimum, be cleared of all soil (earth containing organic matter). If a rock fill or concrete dam is to be built, the site should be dug down to bedrock, hard clay, or other stable formation.

While construction is in progress, it will be necessary to divert the course of the stream. One way to do this is to dig a temporary channel around the construction site. Another method, useful for small streams, is to build a wooden flume that straddles the dam, carrying the water overhead while construction proceeds beneath. A third solution is a drainpipe installed under the dam works. By fitting the pipe with a valve, it can be made a permanent part of the structure for use in emergencies. However, such pipes may crack and silt up with the passage of years, so they should not be relied on as the only flood control device.

Types of Dams

A dam impounds many tons of water. If its mass and strength are not sufficient, the weight of the water may be enough to topple the dam or slide it downstream. Also, water seepage under the dam can cause it to settle, crack, and eventually rupture. To protect against this, a variety of cores, barriers, and asphalt blankets are usually incorporated into the dam structure. Another hazard is the possibility of flood waters that may overflow a dam, eroding and disintegrating it as they pour downstream. To meet the danger, an

Power capability

The amount of kilowatt-hours per month that can run the appliances listed:
300 kilowatt-hours will run all those in **A**
700 kilowatt-hours will run all those in **A** and **B**
1,500 kilowatt-hours will run all those in **A**, **B**, and **C**
8,000 kilowatt-hours will run all those in **A**, **B**, **C**, and **D**

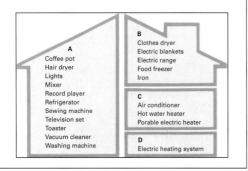

A Low-Head, High-Flow Power Site

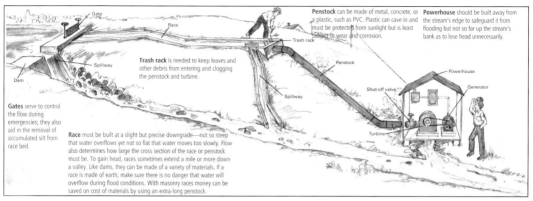

Penstock can be made of metal, concrete, or a plastic, such as PVC. Plastic can cave in and must be protected from sunlight but is least subject to wear and corrosion.

Powerhouse should be built away from the stream's edge to safeguard it from flooding but not so far up the stream's bank as to lose head unnecessarily.

Trash rack is needed to keep leaves and other debris from entering and clogging the penstock and turbine.

Gates serve to control the flow during emergencies; they also aid in the removal of accumulated silt from race bed.

Race must be built at a slight but precise downgrade—not so steep that water overflows yet not so flat that water moves too slowly. Flow also determines how large the cross section of the race or penstock must be. To gain head, races sometimes extend a mile or more down a valley. Like dams, they can be made of a variety of materials. If a race is made of earth, make sure there is no danger that water will overflow during flood conditions. With masonry races money can be saved on cost of materials by using an extra-long penstock.

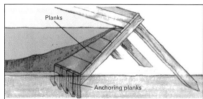

Frame dam is fabricated from planks that have been coated with such preservatives as creosote or pentachlorophenol to prevent rotting. To forestall seepage, face upstream side of dam with asphalt or a layer of fine silt or clay.

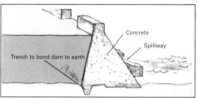

Concrete dam is preferred whenever overflowing is possible, since a spillway can easily be incorporated. To prevent erosion under the spillway, pile rocks at the base or shape the base to deflect the downward rush of water.

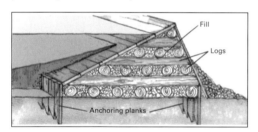

Log dam can be built of treated 6-in. logs, such as oak, with stone or gravel used as fill. Face the upstream side with seepage-proof planks. Wood dams do not last nearly as long as stone or earth dams and should not be more than 4 ft. high.

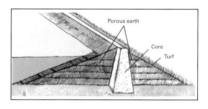

Earth dam is the oldest and most common type. For stability its slopes must be very gradual. To inhibit seepage, a core of impervious clay or concrete may be used. (See *Developing a Water Supply*, page 42, for more information.)

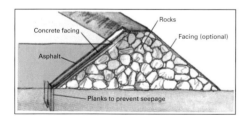

Rock-fill dam (and concrete dam as well) requires solid foundation of bedrock, compact sand, or gravel to prevent settling and rupture of watertight facing. When constructing on bedrock, anchor dam with bolts and seal joint with concrete.

overflow spillway should be built, either in the dam itself or as a separate pond-exit channel cut into the hillside to one side of the dam. On a site where the flood potential is great a spillway may be the dam's dominant feature.

A Power System For Hilly Areas

A high head system relies on a long vertical drop rather than a large volume of water in order to generate power. The minimum head needed is 50 feet, but even at that minimum surprisingly little flow is required to develop usable wattages. For example, with a 50-foot head a flow of only 1 gallon of water (1/8 cubic foot) per second will yield an average power output of 300 watts.

Energy storage is a key factor in many hydroelectric systems. In some, a pond or lake serves as the main storage element. In other systems, especially small ones like the one shown, a bank of rechargeable batteries plays a similar role, helping the system to adapt to daily and seasonal variations in stream flow and power demand. Perhaps the most important function of the batteries is to store power during periods when little current is being drawn so that it can be tapped at times of peak usage.

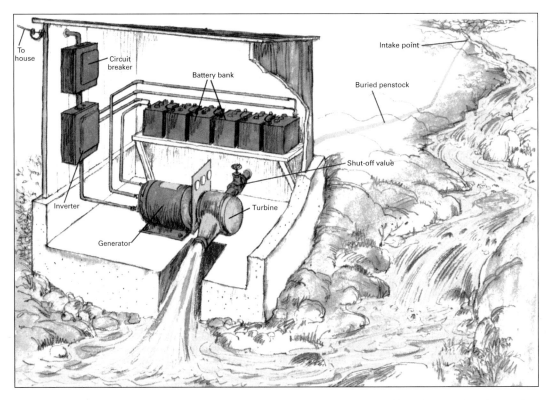

To house

Circuit breaker

Battery bank

Intake point

Buried penstock

Shut-off value

Inverter

Turbine

Generator

Powerhouse is built on concrete foundation to minimize vibration. Batteries are a special type that can withstand repeated charging and discharging; they are not conventional auto batteries. An inverter converts the 32 volts DC (direct current) delivered by the generator and batteries to the 60-cycle 115 volts AC (alternating current) on which most appliances operate.

Demand is generally lightest after 10:00 P.M. and heaviest in the morning and between 6:00 and 8:00 P.M. in the evening.

The batteries in the system shown here will tolerate a power draw of up to 3 kilowatts. If peak demand exceeds this, or if the batteries become completely discharged, a circuit breaker discontinues service in order to protect them. A power outage will also occur if the waterline (penstock) becomes clogged. The inconvenience of an outage can be eased if there is an emergency backup system to switch on: either a small gasoline-powered generator or power from the local utility.

Clogging in the penstock is most likely to occur inside the turbine (the narrowest point along the line). To reach the nozzle and clean it, first close the shutoff valve and open up the turbine. Unclogging a plugged line is particularly important in winter, since the stopped-up water may freeze in the penstock and burst it. In cold areas of the country the safest procedure is to bury the penstock below the frost line.

Storage batteries currently on the market can last as long as 15 years if a somewhat reduced charging capacity toward the end of the period is not critical for the homeowner. Eventually, however, they must be replaced. The cost will not be out of line for a small system, but for a large system the number of batteries required would make replacement too expensive. For such a system a storage pond becomes the preferred alternative.

Power Storage, Regulators, and Inverters

All but the simplest waterpower systems have some means of storing power to compensate for irregular stream flow and to hold power for periods of high user demand. It is also important to have some means of regulating the power output so that it matches the demand placed on the system. Power when it is generated has to be sent somewhere, whether to appliances, batteries, or the power company. If no loads of this type are present, or if most or all of them happen to be switched off, the generating equipment may freewheel up to a point where it eventually burns out its bearings and self-destructs. The diagrams below show several methods to store and regulate power.

Where it is necessary to convert from DC to AC, an inverter is used. Inverters come in two forms. One is the rotary type, which consists of a combined motor and generator plus built-in controls for maintaining a constant 60-cycle 115-volt AC output. The inverter motor is run electrically by the 32-volt turbine generator. The other type of inverter is electronic. It is less bulky than the rotary type and roughly 30 percent more efficient (the rotary type is only 60 percent

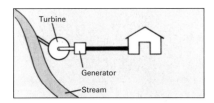

System without storage is the least costly to install but very limited in application. The output from the generator has a voltage that varies widely according to how much water is flowing in the stream and how many appliances happen to be switched on. Usually the only appliances that work well with such a system are ones with simple resistance elements for heating, such as hot water heaters and hot plates. The temperature of the heater's water may not be constant, but the arrangement is satisfactory if sudden demands on hot water are avoided.

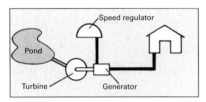

Pond formed by damming a stream is the traditional means for storing energy and smoothing the effects of erratic stream flow. A speed regulator, such as the hydraulic model in the installation shown below, is needed to take care of varying electrical demands as appliances are switched on and off. Hydraulic regulators are expensive, however, sometimes costing more than everything else in the powerhouse. Regulators currently being developed to accomplish the same task electronically may become a cheaper alternative.

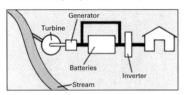

Battery storage works well for small systems such as the one shown on the facing page. Since batteries store and deliver DC electricity, an inverter is required to convert to AC. An attractive feature of battery storage is that it acts in part like a regulator, automatically diverting power into the batteries when house power demand is low and releasing it when demand is high. But to accommodate periods when the batteries have become fully charged, the turbine must be sufficiently rugged to withstand the resulting no-load condition.

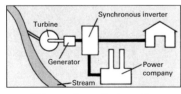

Local power utilities usually permit private citizens to sell their excess power to them. In this way the power company becomes a substitute for batteries or a storage pond. A device called a synchronous inverter automatically sends out the excess when the home system overproduces and draws power from the company when the home system underproduces. Power companies tend to pay less for your power than what they charge for their power. Even if they pay nothing, the arrangement still saves the cost of a regulator or batteries.

efficient). In addition, electronic inverters consume much less power than rotary inverters when all the appliances are turned off.

Something for Nothing: Water Pumping Itself

Hydraulic Rams

Although a stream or other water source may be considerably below the level of your house, it can be tapped for fresh water without relying on electrical motors, windmills, hand pumps, or buckets. The trick is to use the water to pump itself. The Amish system described below is one method. A more common approach is to use a hydraulic ram, a century-old invention that at first glance seems to give something for nothing.

The heart of a hydraulic ram is a special pump, or ram, that uses the energy of a large mass of water dropping a short distance to raise a small amount of water far above its source level. A typical installation is illustrated on the next page. Ideally, for a fall of 10 feet and an elevation of 50 feet, 50 gallons per minute of water flowing down the drivepipe would be able to pump 10 gallons per minute into the storage tank, with the remaining 40 gallons being returned to the stream. In actual practice, however, rams operate at about 50 percent efficiency so that the water delivered would be half the ideal figure—5 gallons per minute in the example.

Rams pump at a cyclic rate of 20 to 150 times per minute. The ram shown at right has two built-in rate adjustments: a sliding weight that regulates spring tension and a bolt that limits valve movement. Increasing tension and restricting valve motion speeds the rate and decreases the amount of water pumped. Such a control is useful when waterflow in the stream drops off. If a ram's pumping capacity exceeds the stream's flow rate, intermittent and inefficient operation results.

Waterwheels to Pump Water

The Amish people of Pennsylvania have for many years been applying stream power to pump water from their wells. Their method is to use small waterwheels that turn at 10 to 20 revolutions per minute located on streams as much as 1/2 mile away from the well. Power is transmitted between waterwheel and well by a wire, attached at one end to a crank on the wheel and at the other end to the pump handle. As the waterwheel turns, the crank translates its circular motion into reciprocating motion. The wire carries the movement to the pump.

Both undershot and breast wheels are used. The wheels are from 1 to 3 feet in diameter and are fabricated from steel sheet, with curved cups for blades. The length of the crank arm is critical; it must be just long

Hydroelectric Power Output (in watts) Flow Rate (in GPM)									
5	**15**	**20**	**30**	**40**	**50**	**75**	**100**	**150**	**200**
Head (Vertical distance, in feet)									
5		5	8	10	15	20	30	40	
10	7	12	18	23	30	45	60	80	100
15	5	15	20	30	40	50	75	100	125	150
20	8	25	32	50	65	85	125	170	210	275
30	12	35	45	70	90	120	180	240	300	400
40	16	48	60	95	125	160	240	320	450	600
50	20	60	80	120	160	200	300	400	600	
75	30	90	120	180	240	300	450	600		
100	40	120	160	240	320	400	600			

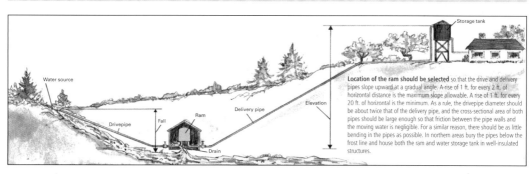

Location of the ram should be selected so that the drive and delivery pipes slope upward at a gradual angle. A rise of 1 ft. for every 2 ft. of horizontal distance is the maximum slope allowable. A rise of 1 ft. for every 20 ft. of horizontal is the minimum. As a rule, the drivepipe diameter should be about twice that of the delivery pipe, and the cross-sectional area of both pipes should be large enough so that friction between the pipe walls and the moving water is negligible. For a similar reason, there should be as little bending in the pipes as possible. In northern areas bury the pipes below the frost line and house both the ram and water storage tank in well-insulated structures.

The ram pumping cycle

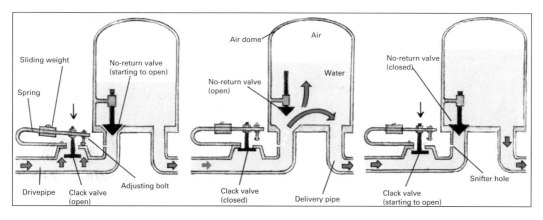

1. The cycle begins with the no-return valve closed and the clack valve open. Water starts to flow down the drivepipe, out of the clack valve, and onto the floor of the ram enclosure from which it is drained off and returned to the stream. As the flow builds up momentum, pressure against the clack valve increases. Within a second or so the pressure rises to a point where it overcomes the force of the clack valve's weighted spring. The valve closes and the water stops pouring out of it.

2. With the clack valve closed the water in the drivepipe begins to push against the no-return valve, opening it. Water now flows into the air dome, compressing the air trapped inside while at the same time forcing water into and up the delivery pipe. After about a second, the air pressure inside the dome becomes great enough to exert a counterpressure that closes the no-return valve again. With both valves closed waterflow down the drivepipe momentarily stops.

3. With the no-return valve closed, pressure in the dome continues to drive the water in the delivery pipe upward toward the storage tank. At the same time the clack valve's spring opens the valve again because the pressure of the now stationary water in the drivepipe has fallen off. At this point, the conditions are the same as in Step 1 and the cycle repeats. Note that the flow of water up the delivery pipe is continuous, largely because of the cushioning action of the air in the dome.

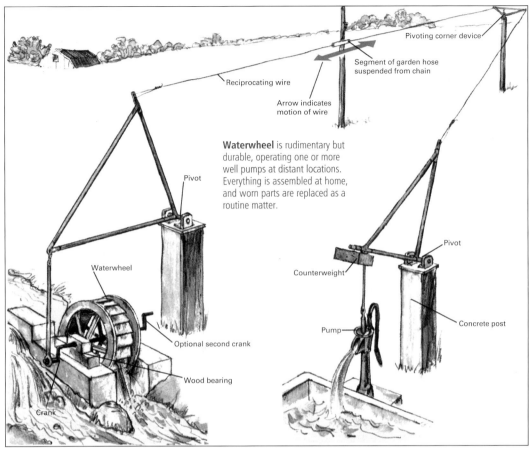

Pivoting corner device

Segment of garden hose suspended from chain

Reciprocating wire

Arrow indicates motion of wire

Waterwheel is rudimentary but durable, operating one or more well pumps at distant locations. Everything is assembled at home, and worn parts are replaced as a routine matter.

Pivot

Pivot

Counterweight

Waterwheel

Concrete post

Pump

Optional second crank

Wood bearing

Crank

enough to produce the back-and-forth motion needed by the pump, usually 4 to 6 inches. The crank is connected by a rod to a triangular frame that pivots at the top of a post. The frame is made of 3/4-inch-diameter galvanized pipe welded or bolted together. A similar frame is used at the pump end of the system. A counterweight weighing about 100 pounds is attached to a corner of this frame.

Commercially made rams can be purchased in a variety of sizes with drivepipes ranging from 1 1/4 in. to 8 in. in diameter. Or a person who has plumbing experience can actually build a ram at home. For plans write VITA Publications, 1600 Wilson Blvd., Suite 1030, Arlington, Va. 22209, info@vita.org.

The wire that connects the frames so that they move in tandem is smooth, galvanized 12-gauge fence wire. If the wire is very long, poles spaced 75 feet apart are used to support it. If the wire is to traverse a zigzag course around obstacles, a device for negotiating the corners, such as the one illustrated, can be constructed.

The system can also be rigged to operate an additional water pump by attaching a second crank to the opposite end of the waterwheel shaft.

Sources and resources

Books and pamphlets
Allen, Inversin. *Hydraulic Ram*. Mt. Rainier, Md.: Volunteers in Technical Assistance, 1979.
Design of Small Dams. Washington, D.C.: U.S. Department of the Interior, 1984.
Eshenaur, Walter C. *Understanding Hydropower*. Arlington, Va.: Volunteers in Technical Assistance, 1988.
Holland, Peter R. *Amazing Models: Water Power*. Blue Ridge Summit, Pa.: TAB Books, 1990.
Marier, Donald, and Stoiaken, Larry, eds. *Alternative Sources of Energy: Hydropower*. Melaca, Minn.: ASEI, 1988.
Naudascher, Eduard. *Hydrodynamic Forces*. Brookfield, Vt.: Ashgate Publishing, 1990.
Ovens, W.G. *A Design Manual for Water Wheels*. Mt. Rainier, Md.: Volunteers in Technical Assistance, 1988.
Rickard, Graham. *Water Energy*. Milwaukee, Wis.: Gareth Stevens, 1991.

Wind Power

Clean, Cheap Power From an Old Idea and a New Technology

Wind power has been used for hundreds of years to pump water and grind grain. Its use in milling grain was once so common, in fact, that all machines with blades turned by the wind became known as windmills, even though they were and are used for other purposes than milling. Traditional windmills of the type associated with Holland were ponderous and inefficient. As a result, wind power did not become popular in this country until mills with multiple metal blades were developed. Such mills performed admirably at pumping water from wells and proliferated rapidly after 1850, particularly across the Plains States. Millions of them were erected on farms and placed along railroad rights-of-way to supply water for the boilers of steam locomotives.

In the 1930s it became possible to buy a windmill that could generate electricity. This was a new development based on a mill using two or three propellerlike blades turning at high speed. The best of these wind-electric systems were made by Marcellus Jacobs, whose product is still admired today. Many of these depression era wind-powered generators, along with their water-pumping brethren, have fallen into disuse or been sold for scrap. But with the steady rise in the cost of electricity, wind generators may yet become a competitive alternative in areas of the country where the average yearly wind speed is high. However, it takes a very large wind plant to supply the entire power needs of a typical modern home, so unless the family is willing to budget its household electricity usage stringently, a wind plant can only act as a supplement or serve as an emergency backup during utility blackouts.

Traditional windmills with four arms in the Dutch style are rare in America. Such mills used cloth sails that were reefed when stormy weather threatened. The top of the mill was swiveled by hand to keep the arms facing into the wind.

Modern Windmills

Turning speeds of greater than 1,500 revolutions per minute are necessary to generate electricity. To attain these speeds, propellers with only two or three blades must be used. Traditional multibladed windmills do not work because they operate well only at relatively low speeds. At higher rates of rotation the blades spin so fast that the air cannot pass between them, and as a result the whirling blades act like a solid disc.

High-speed wind generators are subject to stresses that can quickly destroy them if they are not carefully designed and built. Exhaustive testing of a variety of prototypes has led to several key discoveries. The most important was that the propeller blades should have an aerodynamic design similar (although not identical) to that of airplane propellers. In addition, it was found that the blades should be constructed from a durable lightweight material such as Sitka spruce or carbon fiber. Finally, engineers determined that either two or three blades will work well. Wind generators in both styles are being produced in sizes over 1000 kilowatts—electricity for more than 400 U.S. homes.

High-speed windmills behave like gyroscopes. When the wind changes its direction and pushes at the tail vane to swing the mill around, the windmill balks and exerts a gyroscopic counterforce that can either break the blades or tear the entire propeller-generator unit off its base unless it is sturdily moored to the tower and cushioned at critical points by shock absorbers.

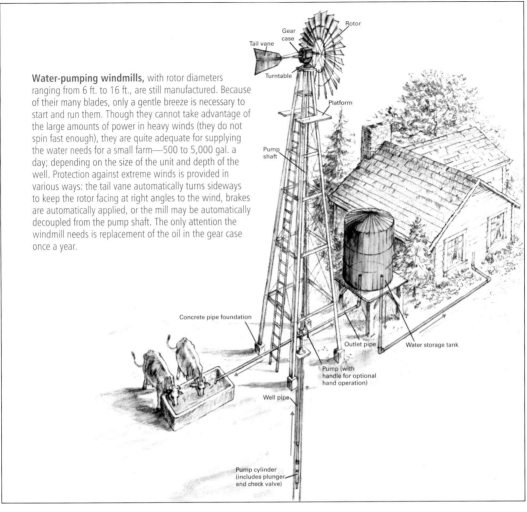

Water-pumping windmills, with rotor diameters ranging from 6 ft. to 16 ft., are still manufactured. Because of their many blades, only a gentle breeze is necessary to start and run them. Though they cannot take advantage of the large amounts of power in heavy winds (they do not spin fast enough), they are quite adequate for supplying the water needs for a small farm—500 to 5,000 gal. a day; depending on the size of the unit and depth of the well. Protection against extreme winds is provided in various ways: the tail vane automatically turns sideways to keep the rotor facing at right angles to the wind, brakes are automatically applied, or the mill may be automatically decoupled from the pump shaft. The only attention the windmill needs is replacement of the oil in the gear case once a year.

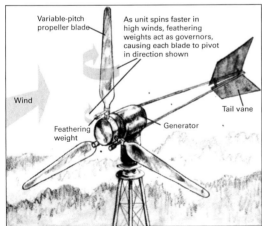

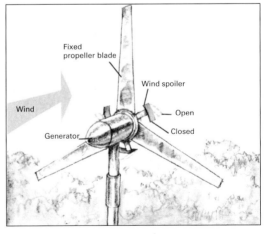

Wind-powered generators are manufactured in two configurations: with a tail vane and without one. Generators without a vane pivot on an off-center support point so that the force of the wind keeps them oriented toward the wind on the downwind side of the pivot. In heavy winds the generator shown with a vane has weights on each propeller shaft that turn outward like governor weights and "feather" the blades. (Feathered blades are edged into the wind; in this way they lose their propulsive power and keep the unit from overspeeding.) The wind spoilers shown on the downwind generator serve the same purpose, but instead of feathering the blades, the spoilers spread centrifugally outward in rising winds to act as a brake.

Windmills for residential installations that meet these requirements can be obtained from manufacturers in the United States, Europe, and Australia. The propeller diameters of the units (diameters of circles swept by the blade tips) range in size from 3 feet up to 30 feet, corresponding roughly to power outputs of 25 watts to 6,000 watts at a 25-mile-per-hour wind speed. Most of the plants are designed to run for 20 or more years with little or no attention. Lubrication is relatively permanent, parts are moisture-proof and noncorrosive, and some means is built into each unit to keep the windmill from running wild and destroying itself in extreme winds. Two such safety devices are illustrated below.

Wind-electric technology is no longer in its infancy, yet a variety of ways to tap the wind continue to be investigated. The Darrieus rotor shown at the right solves the problem of twisting stresses since it does not have to swivel its axis with each change in wind direction. A virtue of sailwing plants is that extreme winds are likely to do no more damage than rip the sails—a considerably safer consequence than a broken propeller blade flying downwind. They are also easier to repair.

Experimental designs

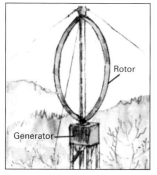

Darrieus rotor resembles a two- or three-bladed eggbeater. Because it spins on a vertical axis, it does not have to swivel into the wind to catch it every time the wind shifts direction. It does not start by itself, however, so a small motor is usually built on to get the unit going after each spell of no wind.

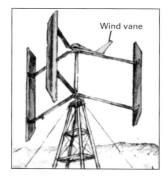

Variable-pitch blades on this type of Darrieus rotor give the unit a means to start by itself. A small wind vane on top of the rotor shaft makes starting possible by sensing any new direction from which the wind may be rising and altering the angle that the blades make with respect to the new direction.

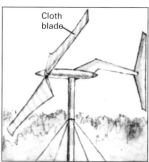

Sailwing windmills use blades made of nylon. The cloth is kept taut by a framework of aluminum poles and takes on the airfoil profile of a sail on a sailboat whenever the wind blows. Since the cloth is flexible, the blades bend with the wind and so are less likely than solid blades to break.

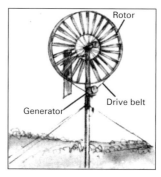

Bicycle-wheel rotor is a modern cousin to the old multibladed windmills. The rotors weigh very little. To operate a generator, the rotor perimeter is employed as a drive wheel in a pulley system with a large step-up ratio. Fair amounts of power can be produced in this way in the low wind-speed range within which these mills are most effective.

Measuring the Wind In Order to Reap It

Although the most accurate way to calculate the power potential of the wind in your area is to measure it yourself, a fair estimate can be obtained by using wind data accumulated by the government at over 270 locations around the country. It can be obtained by writing the National Climatic Data Center, Federal Building, Asheville, North Carolina 28801; ask for data collected by the station nearest you. Also check with your local newspaper and television and radio stations—they frequently maintain files on wind and weather dating back many years. The most useful information you can get is the average wind speed for each month of the year as well as for the year as a whole. For most parts of the United States the average falls between 8 and 12 miles per hour. Localities that

have an average wind speed of more than 12 miles per hour are definitely worth considering for a wind power installation; areas with an average below 8 miles per hour are marginal at best.

What the Wind's Power Can Do

After an optimum location has been selected, use the wind speed measured at that location and the monthly power output chart (far right) to determine the number of kilowatt-hours available if a wind-powered generator is installed. The output will depend, of course, on the wind-plant model planned for the site. The manufacturer will probably specify a power rating that is the maximum power the wind plant will deliver—usually it will be the power generated when the wind speed is 25 miles per hour. Use this rating in the chart.

Having determined the expected monthly output in kilowatt-hours, you can estimate what value it can have for you. One way to do this is to compare the kilowatt-hours on your electric bill with the expected output of the wind generator. This will tell you how much of your electric power needs the wind plant will satisfy. For the comparison, use a bill that is typical of the year.

Alternatively, use a power capability chart like the one below for the estimate. The chart indicates in an approximate way the number and type of appliances that various monthly power outputs can handle. It is expected that the use of these appliances will be fairly evenly distributed over each month and that batteries are used to store power and absorb peak power demands.

If you make your own wind speed measurements, you should obtain periodic readings at a number of locations around your property, particularly at higher elevations, to find the optimum site. One shortcut is to measure for a week or two only; if the ups and downs of the data over this period are similar to those reported by the nearest weather station, you can assume that the station's readings for the remaining 11 months will also be similar. For example, if your measurements consistently turn out to be 10 percent higher than the station's reported wind speeds, augment the remaining reported figures by 10 percent to achieve a year-round estimate.

A variety of instruments are available for measuring wind speed. Some, costing only a few dollars, simply measure the speed at a given moment. To obtain a reliable average over a period of time with these devices requires that you make many observations, a chore that can quickly become tedious. At the other end of the spectrum are sophisticated instruments costing hundreds of dollars that automatically provide a complete printout of wind data over an extended period. The best choice for the individual homeowner may be a compromise, such as the semiautomatic anemometer-odometer arrangement shown at the right.

Power capability

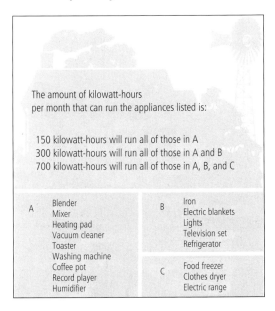

The amount of kilowatt-hours per month that can run the appliances listed is:

150 kilowatt-hours will run all of those in A
300 kilowatt-hours will run all of those in A and B
700 kilowatt-hours will run all of those in A, B, and C

A	Blender Mixer Heating pad Vacuum cleaner Toaster Washing machine Coffee pot Record player Humidifier	B	Iron Electric blankets Lights Television set Refrigerator
		C	Food freezer Clothes dryer Electric range

Average monthly power output

Output rating in watts	Blade diam- eter in feet	Kilowatt-hours at various wind speeds				
		8 mph	10 mph	12 mph	14 mph	16 mph
100	3	5	8	11	13	15
250	4	12	18	24	29	32
500	5	24	35	46	55	62
1,000	7	45	65	86	100	120
2,000	11	80	120	160	200	240
4,000	15	150	230	310	390	460
6,000	18	230	350	470	590	710
8,000	21	300	450	600	750	900
10,000	24	370	550	730	910	1100

Chart shows the output you can expect for a variety of generator sizes and wind speeds. To use the chart, locate the wind speed column most closely matching the average in your area, and read down the column. Each entry shows the kilowatt-hours (kwh) per month that will be developed by a particular generator-blade combination. For instance, if the average wind speed at a potential site is about 12 miles per hour, a 100-watt wind generator will turn out 11 kwh (scarcely worthwhile), but a 2,000-watt generator will produce 160 kwh and a 10,000-watt generator, 730 kwh.

Preferred Sites for Windmills

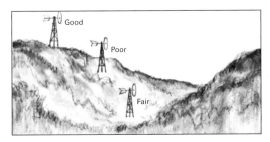

In hilly areas average wind speed can differ markedly according to location. As a guide when checking, hilltops are the best sites, hillsides are the poorest, while valley bottoms can do very well provided the direction of local prevailing winds is up and down the valley. But test each site to make sure.

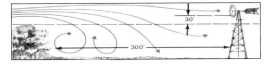

Nearby obstacles can be very detrimental to windmill power output. Even when a barrier is situated downwind from the mill it can produce enough turbulence in the area to interfere with the windmill's efficient performance. For best results, a windmill should be at least 30 ft. higher than any obstruction within a circle of a 300-ft. radius out from the windmill.

Selecting and Putting Up Towers

As towers rise in height, they also rise in cost, and eventually a point of diminishing returns is reached

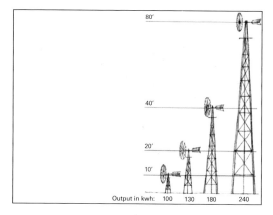

Output in kwh: 100   130   180   240

Height of windmill above the ground makes a substantial difference in power output, since wind speed in general increases with altitude. Also, windmills respond in exaggerated fashion to small changes in wind speed, their power output climbing 33 percent for each 10 percent increase in wind speed. The net effect is shown in the illustration. A wind plant that generates 100 kwh per month on a 10-ft. tower, for instance, will generate 240 kwh per month on an 80-ft. tower.

Pole-type tower must either be deeply anchored in concrete or supported by guy wires. Use a minimum of three guy-wire anchors (five are preferable). Set anchors at least one-half of tower height away from base of tower and use turnbuckles in the guy wires so that their tension can be adjusted. Some pole towers are hinged at the bottom to permit lowering for servicing and during gales.

Self-supporting tower does not need additional bracing but must have an adequate foundation—usually concrete piers in which the tower's legs are embedded or to which they are bolted. Self-supporting towers are delivered in segments by the manufacturer and must be assembled on location. They are about twice as expensive as pole-type towers of equivalent height but require no guy wires.

Homemade towers up to 30 ft. high, such as the wooden structure shown here, can be built by experienced do-it-yourselfers. They can be quite attractive (this one includes a small picnic platform in the base) but are more apt to be blown down in high winds. If you plan on building one, consult a structural engineer and site the tower in an area where danger to life and property due to the tower falling will be negligible.

speed, the type of tower used, and the cost of the windmill. For example, if a pole-type tower is to be erected, an array of at least five guy wires fanned out in different directions is preferable, an arrangement that requires more and more space as tower height increases.

It is easy to underestimate the twisting forces that a wind plant will exert in extreme winds, so it is best to use a commercial tower specifically engineered to support a windmill, especially for heights greater than 30 feet. The manufacturer will provide instructions concerning assembly and erection. You will need at least two helpers to put up the tower and install the windmill on it. The usual procedure is to prepare the foundation, assemble the tower on its side, and erect it by the gin-pole method (below). The mill is then installed part

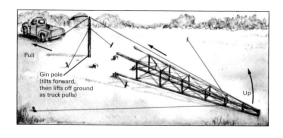

Gin-pole method for raising a tower depends for its success on carefully placed temporary guy wires that keep pole and tower from falling sideways during lifting. Wires at base of tower prevent it from sliding forward as vehicle pulls.

Note: Be sure to follow manufacturer's instructions when installing windmill; or get professional help.

Temporary crane attached to top of tower is used to raise windmill parts—first the generator, then tail vane and blades. Man on ground guides each part with guy, helping it into place at tower top, where assistant installs it.

where added tower expense is not appreciably offset by added power output. Where to draw the line will depend on your power needs and the nature of the site. Factors to consider include average available wind

by part at the top. (Do not attach the generator unit before raising the tower; the added weight increases the tower's likelihood of falling down as it is being pulled up.) Towers can also be built vertically, section by section, but this is more hazardous. In general, erecting a tower or climbing one to install equipment can be dangerous work. Never work alone and always wear strong boots, gloves, sturdy clothing, and a hard hat—tools or construction debris falling from a structure can cause serious injury.

A Wind-Electric System For Household Needs

A system such as the one shown below can supply a significant portion of the electrical needs of a one-family home. A bank of batteries installed in a

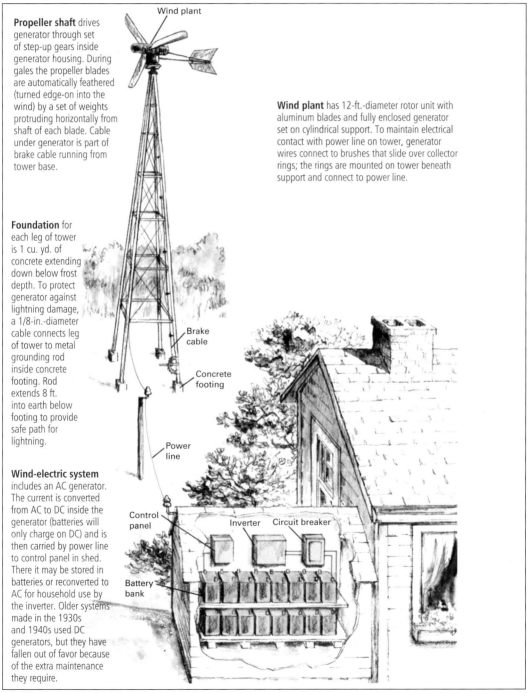

Wind plant

Propeller shaft drives generator through set of step-up gears inside generator housing. During gales the propeller blades are automatically feathered (turned edge-on into the wind) by a set of weights protruding horizontally from shaft of each blade. Cable under generator is part of brake cable running from tower base.

Wind plant has 12-ft.-diameter rotor unit with aluminum blades and fully enclosed generator set on cylindrical support. To maintain electrical contact with power line on tower, generator wires connect to brushes that slide over collector rings; the rings are mounted on tower beneath support and connect to power line.

Foundation for each leg of tower is 1 cu. yd. of concrete extending down below frost depth. To protect generator against lightning damage, a 1/8-in.-diameter cable connects leg of tower to metal grounding rod inside concrete footing. Rod extends 8 ft. into earth below footing to provide safe path for lightning.

Brake cable

Concrete footing

Power line

Wind-electric system includes an AC generator. The current is converted from AC to DC inside the generator (batteries will only charge on DC) and is then carried by power line to control panel in shed. There it may be stored in batteries or reconverted to AC for household use by the inverter. Older systems made in the 1930s and 1940s used DC generators, but they have fallen out of favor because of the extra maintenance they require.

Control panel

Inverter

Circuit breaker

Battery bank

well-ventilated shed (or basement of a house) stores excess power that the wind plant generates during low demand periods and releases during windless periods or times of peak demand. Operation is automatic. When the wind blows strongly and few appliances are on, or when the wind is down, the battery current reverses, sending just enough to the house system to make up the difference between windmill output and appliance demand.

Wind plants are generally rated according to their maximum output. The one illustrated here is rated at 2,000 watts, the rating corresponding to its power output when the wind is 25 miles per hour. Its actual output is considerably lower—in the 50- to 150-watt range for most places in the United States—since there are very few locations where wind speeds average 25 miles per hour.

The wind plant is built to stand up in winds of up to 120 miles per hour, but the propeller should be braked whenever winds above 80 miles per hour are anticipated. The brake, which is also useful for stopping the windmill for inspection and servicing, can be operated from the base of the windmill tower.

Electrical Equipment

The amount of electrical energy that can be stored by a wind-electric system depends on the capacity of its batteries. A typical home system will store enough to carry a family through two or three windless days after which some type of alternate backup supply must be switched on. If more batteries were used, more windless days could be handled, but batteries are expensive, and it is generally cheaper to use an occasional backup.

Batteries come in various storage ratings and are priced accordingly. Those shown below have a rating of 270 ampere-hours. This means, for example, if an appliance draws 10 amperes of current from such a battery, the battery will become discharged after 27 hours (10 amperes times 27 hours equals 270 ampere-hours). Appliances such as electric irons and toasters each draw about 10 amperes. This calculation can be extended to any amount of current drawn provided it is not excessive. (For instance, the batteries will not deliver 270 amperes for one hour; they are not built for it.)

Properly maintained and operated, a battery will last about 10 years. Water should be added periodically, usually every one to six months, the battery terminals should be kept clear of corrosion, and the batteries must not be permitted to become more

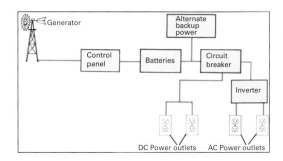

Typical wind-electric system has control panel to protect batteries from overcharging, an inverter to convert some of the DC output to AC, and a source of standby power. (Alternate systems, similar to some hydroelectric systems, can also be employed. See *Power Storage, Regulators, and Inverters*, page 76.)

than 90 percent discharged. Maintain the batteries at room temperature or above, since cold reduces battery effectiveness. However, be sure to ventilate the room in which the batteries are placed; they can emit hydrogen, a highly flammable and potentially explosive gas.

The public utility or a standby gasoline-fueled generator can be used for backup power. A standby unit requires an engine no larger than a snow thrower's, but it has a limited life span. A better backup option may be photovoltaic (PV) cells. PV cells convert sunlight to electricity and can allow greater daytime electric use.

Inverters are employed to convert DC to AC. The inverter used with the batteries illustrated below has a 2,000-watt capacity and automatically adjusts to changing loads. Such a device is quite expensive, almost as much as the wind plant shown on the previous page. If DC can be used in the house, a mixed system—one that delivers both AC and DC—is preferable; the inverter can then be smaller and less costly.

Sources and resources

Books and pamphlets
Bailey, Donna. *Energy from Wind and Water*. Chatham, N.J.: Raintree Steck-Vaughn, 1990.
Gipe, Paul. *Wind Energy Comes of Age*. New York: John Wiley & Sons, 1995.
Rickard, Graham. *Wind Energy*. Milwaukee, Ind.: Gareth Stevens, 1991.
Wind Energy Technical Information Guide. New York: Gordon Press, 1991.
Wind Power: A Source Guide. New York: Gordon Press, 1991.

Solar Energy

Earth's Private Star Holds Bright Promise For Abundant Energy

If you ever stepped barefoot on a sunbaked rock on a July afternoon, you know what solar energy is all about. Heat generated by the sun would melt a sphere of ice the size of the earth in 16.6 minutes. While only a small portion of that energy is intercepted by the earth, there is still enough to provide 646,000 horsepower for every square mile of its surface.

People have been trying to capture and use this enormous reservoir of free solar power since the dawn of history. The Greeks designed their houses around central sun-gathering courtyards 3,000 years ago. In pre-Columbian America, Indians of the Southwest carefully oriented their cliff pueblos to trap the warmth of the winter sun. During colonial times prudent homeowners built their homes with stove-warmed kitchens on the north side so that living areas would have sunny south walls. Thomas Jefferson, in designing Monticello, was keenly aware of the sun's potential for providing heat and used special windows to help trap its warmth.

Some of our most modern solar technology has its roots in the past. Functional solar systems were producing domestic hot water in 30 percent of the homes in Pasadena, California, before 1900, and by 1940 Miami had 60,000 of them. A flat-plate solar collector array built in 1907 used a sheet-iron absorber plate topped by glass. By 1914 solar collectors using copper tubes soldered to copper sheets were heating homes in California.

Today, solar systems for home heating are working almost everywhere in the country, not only in the Sun Belt but in the North too. Wherever local codes permit, you can save money and fuel with a do-it-yourself solar installation.

Solar collectors are becoming more and more common as their prices go down and oil prices go up.

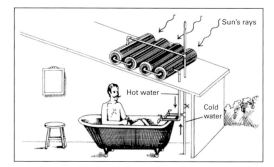

Climax solar collector, patented in 1891, consisted of a series of black tanks in a glazed box. Sun-heated water moved through tanks by convection for use in bath or kitchen below.

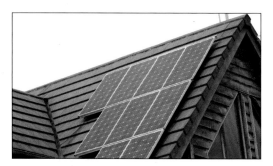

Solar panels on this south-facing roof and large windows on the east side allow the sun to warm the house during the day and provide consistent power. Costs for solar electric cells like these have dropped dramatically the last few decades and continue to become more affordable.

Where Solar Stands Today

The energy crisis of the 1970s spawned a kaleidoscope of dreams and schemes in solar home design. Some are solidly practical, some are innovative and radical, and a few resemble Rube Goldberg contraptions.

Among the most simple contrivances is a hot water system for a beach house. Tap water is run through 100 feet of black plastic hose coiled on the roof. The sun-warmed water feeds into an attic tank that is tapped as needed for showers or dishwashing. Almost as simple is a supplementary heating system that is not much more than a box sloping from the ground to the bottom of a south-facing first floor window. A black-painted divider of foam insulation suspended down the box's center permits cool air from the house to slip down the channel beneath the foam panel and up its sun-warmed topside.

At the other end of the technological scale are houses with towering glass walls and ingenious devices for trapping and storing the sun's heat. One New Hampshire home has two-story double-glazed plastic panels covering a black foot-thick concrete wall. During the day sun pouring through the panels heats the concrete. Ports at floor and ceiling allow cool interior air to circulate by convection up the wall and then reenter the building at the top after being warmed. At night and on cloudy days bushels of tiny plastic beads are blown into the

space between the double glazing to prevent escape of stored heat. Come morning, the beads are sucked out by a vacuum pump to canisters in the garage until needed again. Another unique solar home in New Mexico has south-facing walls of water-filled drums stacked in racks like wine bottles. Ends facing outward are black to soak up sun and warm the water. At night windowless walls of insulating material hinge upward to seal in the heat.

Many technological improvements are on the way, including vacuum insulated collectors and cells that can convert sunlight into electricity. Engineers in New Mexico have built a "power tower," topped by a boiler located at the focus of almost 2,000 mirrors, which has produced temperatures of 3000°F.

Will It Work in Your Home?

Solar water heaters have long been competitive with electricity, fuel oil, and natural gas in many parts of the country. Solar space heat is usually competitive wherever there is moderate to high solar radiation (see map). Even in low radiation locales, solar home heating can be a big money saver if fuel and utility costs are high.

Most successful systems take over part, not all, of the heating load. Such systems are cheaper to build and will usually pay for themselves sooner than those that rely exclusively on the sun.

For solar heating to be effective a house must have a large surface—typically a roof—facing within 10 degrees of true south. The building should also be well insulated (10 or more inches of high quality insulation in the attic and six inches in the walls for northern parts of the nation). Heating ducts or pipes should be wrapped with insulation. Storm doors and storm windows are important. All outside joints should be caulked and fireplace dampers snugly fitted and closed when not in use.

As a rule of thumb, solar heating makes good economic sense if it amortizes, or pays for itself, within 10 years. In other words, your 10-year savings in home fuel consumption should equal or exceed the cost of installing a solar system. Generally speaking, solar heating will provide the biggest savings in homes with high fuel bills: if your fuel bills run more than $3,000 a year, a $15,000 solar system can be amortized in 10 years by cutting fuel consumption in half; but if you only spend $500 to heat your home, it is doubtful that solar heating will pay. Another consideration is the relative cost-effectiveness of a switch to solar versus a simple modernization of your present heating

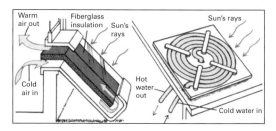

Window box collector (left) and simple hose water heater.

Solar radiation in the United States

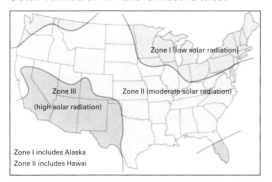

United States is divided into three main radiation areas.

Water-filled oil drums and large pulley-operated shutters of lightweight insulating material form south wall of solar pioneer Steve Baer's house in Corrales, New Mexico.

system. For example, you can often save more money by installing a fuel-efficient oil burner in place of an old one than you can by going solar.

The chart on this page can help you determine if solar energy is for you. However, a complete analysis of heating loads, site location, fuel consumption, house size, thermal efficiency, government tax incentives, and other variables is needed to make a precise appraisal. Information needed to determine the size, cost, and amortization time of a home hot water system may be available from your state energy office or public utility.

Passive Systems: The Soft Side Of Solar Heating

There are two basic types of solar heating systems: active and passive. Active systems use liquid or air to absorb and transfer the heat to its destination. They require pumps and piping or fans and ducts to do the job but are relatively easy to install in existing buildings as well as new ones. An active system is the type most often used when an older home is being remodeled and upgraded with energy-saving features.

Passive solar systems, sometimes referred to as the soft approach because they require little in the way of hardware, let nature do most of the work. They do not need pumps, blowers, or plumbing and usually have no leakage or winter freeze-up problems. They use large, heat-absorbing masses, such as concrete walls and water-filled drums, to trap solar heat as it passes through south-facing windows. Heat transfer can be by natural radiation or convection, or warmed air can be channeled to where it is needed with the help of vanes, dampers, and blowers. Because a passive system is a basic element of the house, it works best when planned as part of a new construction. However, there are many features of passive systems that can be incorporated to advantage in any house. Large glass areas on a south wall (shaded by arbors in the summer) can cut heating bills substantially in locations with moderate solar radiation. A simple

greenhouse (see image on following page) can be an effective solar supplement to the home-heating system. Another passive heat collector is the thermosiphon air panel. Heat absorbed by a black metal sheet under insulated glass vents through a duct at the top. Cool room air enters the panel through a bottom duct.

Instead of a Furnace Try a Greenhouse

Greenhouses are among the oldest and most familiar solar heating devices, but because they warm vegetables and flowers rather than men and women, most people do not think of them as replacements for a conventional home-heating device. However, what warms a plant can also warm a house, and lean-to greenhouses are being used more and more as passive solar collectors in homes with unobstructed south walls. In a typical design, such as the one shown at right, the original frame wall has been replaced by a cinder block collector wall, painted black to improve heat absorption.

The greenhouse, made with double-glazed panels of transparent plastic, is butted directly against the wall. Vents cut through the cinder blocks allow the circulation of heated air. The vents have dampers, but under most conditions the dampers are left open: the small amount of heat that escapes from the main house on cloudy days or at night helps to keep the greenhouse—and the plants growing in it—at the proper temperature. During an excessively warm day the vents would be closed and the greenhouse itself shielded from the sun.

Trapping and Storing the Sun

The simplest passive systems use double transparent glazing to admit sunlight, wall and floor masses to soak it up, and some sort of drapery or shutter arrangement to prevent the trapped heat from escaping through the glass at night or on cloudy days. Temperatures produced by such systems are relatively low, but heat builds up significantly in good storage materials, such as concrete, adobe, and ceramics, which release it slowly to the building's interior during nights and sunless days.

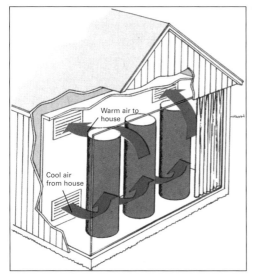

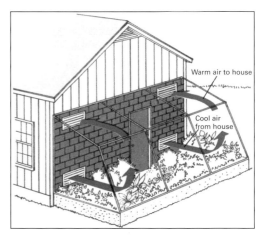

Greenhouse plus cinder block wall makes a collector and garden.

Black plastic columns filled with water collect and store heat.

In more sophisticated passive systems the sun does not penetrate the deep interior of a building but is intercepted by a heat collecting-absorbing structure located behind large double-glazed window panels and backed up inside by an interior partition. Vents at top and bottom of the partition allow natural convection of house air to pick up the stored heat from the collector and move it to the living area. In the system shown below, low-powered fans blow cooled house air through a bank of water-filled black plastic columns that serve as the solar collectors. At night sliding foam panels are moved between the columns and the windows to prevent stored heat from escaping.

Making the System Fit the Environment

A passive solar heating system must be carefully tailored to local conditions so that the best use is made of available sunlight. The key element in any passive system is the collector wall. The generally accepted rule is that the wall should face directly south, although some experts recommend angling it slightly to the east to catch more sun in the early morning when outside temperatures are lowest. The ideal collector should be aligned so that the rays of the sun strike it perpendicularly. At 40°N, which is roughly the latitude of New York, Philadelphia, Indianapolis, Chicago, Kansas City, Des Moines, Denver, and Salt Lake City, a solar wall sloping at an angle of 60 degrees to the horizontal comes close to the ideal. Farther north, the ideal angle is greater; farther south, it is smaller. Nevertheless, considerations involving snow accumulation, summer shading, high initial cost, and structural integrity generally lead solar architects to specify vertical walls despite the loss of about 10 percent in efficiency.

Collector walls are almost always sheathed in double-layered glass with an insulating airspace between the layers. This type of glass provides the best combination of transparency to sunlight plus the ability to insulate against the loss of house heat. Reflecting glass and heat-absorbing glass both provide relief

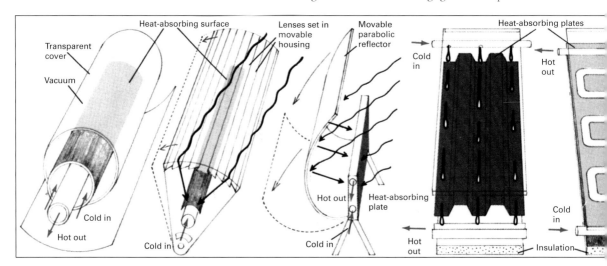

Reverse Flow: Controlling It and Putting It to Use

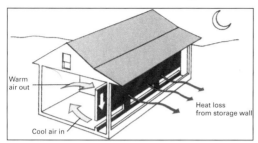

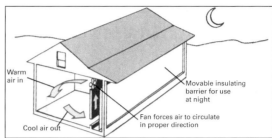

Storage walls of passive systems are often subject to an annoying reverse flow that causes cool night air to spill into the house through the floor vent while warm house air circulates out the top vent, radiating its heat to the outside.

Most common way to prevent reverse flow is to install a fan in the top vent that blows air into the house, thus maintaining positive flow. Insulating curtains or shutters behind double-paned windows further cut down on heat loss.

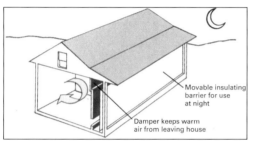

Reverse flow can also be controlled with a damper over the top vent. The damper is closed at night to prevent any circulation from behind the solar wall. This system is not as effective as a fan, since less heat is picked up from the storage wall.

Where summer nights are cool, a passive system can double as an air conditioner. The collectors are exposed at night so they can cool off. During the day a deliberate reverse flow is set up that pulls house air over the cool collectors.

from overheating in the summer but only at the cost of reduced heating ability in the winter. Intelligent landscaping and carefully designed top and side shading surfaces solve the problem even more efficiently and effectively. Proper planting can moderate summer and

winter temperatures by as much as 20°F. A curving row of evergreens bracketing the north and northeast quadrants of a building will serve as a windbreak against winter gales. Tall deciduous shade trees with high canopies placed on the south and southwest sides

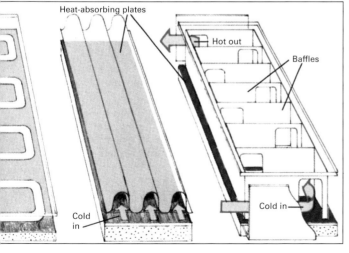

Vacuum collector is like a thermos bottle. Fluid-carrying pipes are surrounded by an evacuated insulating cylinder. Collectors can be placed on roof or against south wall.

Focusing collector is a trough, capped by lenses that bend the sun's rays so they concentrate on a water-carrying pipe along the trough's bottom. Unit swivels to track the sun.

Reflector-type solar collector has a curved mirrored surface that concentrates solar rays onto an absorber plate. The plate contains pipes that enclose liquid for heat transfer.

Trickle-type flat-plate collectors have channeled or corrugated absorber plates. Water is heated as it trickles from a pipe over the absorber to a trough at the bottom.

Another flat design uses water flowing through pipes either welded to the absorber plate or extruded as an integral part of it. As in other collectors, insulation forms the bottom.

Air is the medium of heat transfer in this flat-plate collector. Cool house air entering at the bottom warms as it passes through channels above a panel of black foam plastic.

Air transfer design of a different type warms cool house air by feeding it through a maze of baffled passages. Such baffled air systems can be driven either by a blower or by convection.

of the house will form a parasol against searing after-noon sun in summer. During winter, when the leaves have fallen, the rays of the sun can penetrate to bathe the south wall.

In addition to the collector wall, the shape and design of the house are significant factors in passive solar heating. Not surprisingly, it has been found that a house that is elongated in the east-west direction is best for collecting solar energy, since this shape

Shading the Solar Window

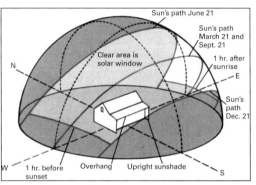

permits maximum exposure to the sun's radiation from the south. An intelligent choice of roofing and siding materials will also contribute to heating efficiency. The roof and outside walls, like the collector wall, should absorb the sun's radiation easily but reradiate little of the thermal energy from the home. Galvanized steel, black roofing material, and siding finished with flat black paint are among the most effective surfacing materials.

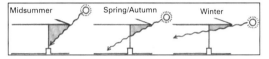

Concept of a "solar window" is important when designing shading for a collector wall. The window is shown at right on an imaginary dome around a house. Outlines of the window are the sun's path on December 21 and June 21, the winter and summer soltice respectively. As illustrated above, the roof overhang should block the midsummer sun but let the low slanting rays of the winter sun through. Upright sunshades contribute additional shading in early morning and late afternoon. During winter the solar window should be free from obstructions from one hour after sunrise to one hour before sunset.

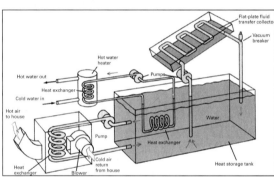

Water is the medium of heat exchange and storage in this active solar heating system. An automatic draindown device removes water from collectors when there is danger of freeze-up. Another type of system circulates antifreeze solution instead of water through collectors.

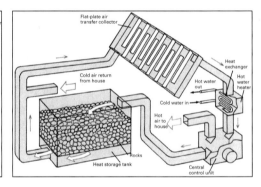

Air-type system eliminates problems of freeze-up. Key to system is the central air control unit. It contains a blower and dampers that enable it to direct air flow through collectors, storage reservoir, or hot water heater according to heating needs and sun conditions.

Active Solar Movers: Complex but Convenient

Active solar heating is an indirect process. Radiation from the sun warms an intermediate medium (either liquid or air) rather than heating the house directly. The medium is then piped into the house where its heat is extracted by heat exchangers. Excess heat is generally stored in a water- or rock-filled reservoir from which the house system draws as needed. Active solar systems are almost always paired with a conventional system that switches on automatically to tide the house through spells of cold, overcast weather. Typically, a forced hot air system is used as the backup.

The operating temperature of a typical active system is in the 120°F to 160°F range—twice as high as most passive systems. As a result, active systems can easily be put to use to produce hot water. They are also pre-ferred by many engineers for space heating because they perform better than passive systems in areas with low to moderate solar radiation. Their adaptability to existing homes and compatibility with forced air heat-ing systems are added advantages. On the debit side are their relative complexity and high initial cost, medium, the heat storage facility, a circulating pump, flow con-trols, and heat exchangers. Storage of sun-warmed water to supply heat at night and on sunless days requires a tank big enough to hold at least 1 1/2 gallons for each square foot of collector area plus an additional 2 percent allowance for expansion when the water heats up. The tank can be located in the basement, the garage, or behind a fence in the backyard. It can be aboveground or buried. It must, however, be well insulated against heat loss. If the system is to be used for domestic hot water heating only, an insulated 80-gallon tank will do the job for a family of four or five.

The Collectors Are the Key

The prime components of any active system are the collectors. These are the devices that trap the sun's heat and carry it into the building in a stream of moving air or water. There are three basic types of collectors: vacuum, focusing, and flat plate.

Vacuum collectors consist of three concentric tubes. The two inner tubes carry the transfer liquid. A vacuum between them and a transparent outer tube insulates the fluid against heat loss. The tubes are highly efficient, producing fluid temperatures over 300°F in commercial use. For domestic application, an automatic drainback system prevents overheating. The collectors work well in overcast, and are seeing increasing use in the far north where their superior fuel-saving capabilities compensate for their high initial cost.

Focusing collectors use lenses or mirrored surfaces to concentrate sunlight on fluid-carrying pipes. Such collectors can produce temperatures of several thousand degrees Fahrenheit. They are more efficient per square foot than flat-plate collectors but require a complex tracking system to keep them pointed at the sun. Not only is the tracking system expensive, but the reflectors themselves are two or three times as costly per square foot as most flat-plate types. If they drift off the sun, or if skies are overcast, they stop working completely.

Flat-plate collectors are simple, inexpensive, and can be mounted on the roof or walls of an existing home or on the ground in angled frames. Most will collect some heat in light overcast.

For maximum heat production the surface area of an array of flat-plate collectors should be equal to about one-half the floor area of the house. However, a collector array with only one-third the area of the floor will handle 40 to 60 percent of the heat load in most regions, provided the house is well insulated and has a south-facing roof on which the collectors can be mounted. Most homeowners settle for such a system, since its lower cost results in faster payback of the investment.

The pitch, or slope, at which collectors are mounted depends on how far north the house is located. Ideally, the pitch should equal the latitude plus 15 degrees. Experience has shown, however, that tilts between 20 degrees and vertical are acceptable, provided the collectors face south. Flat-plate collectors are generally fastened directly to the roof rather than mounted on frames that can rip off in a severe storm.

What Happens in Freezing Weather?

Whenever water is used as the heat transfer medium, provision must be made to prevent it from freezing and bursting the pipes on cold winter nights or dark, frigid, snowy days. In regions where there is any chance of freeze-up, active systems using a water medium incorporate what is known as a draindown, or drainback, feature. At night or when ultralow temperatures are forecast, a valve opens that drains all the water out of the collector loop. Generally, the drained water is channeled into the main heat storage tank so that neither water nor warmth is wasted. The draindown feature can be made automatic by installing a temperature-sensitive device known as a thermistor inside the piping. The thermistor triggers the draindown valve when water temperature drops too low.

With the collector loop drained, heat from the sun is no longer delivered to the house, and the storage tank comes into play. A second loop, isolated from the collectors, begins to circulate warm water from the storage tank to the heat exchanger in the return air duct. In most systems the storage tank will hold enough heat to maintain moderate indoor temperatures for two or three days. After that, the backup furnace must take over.

Underground Residences And Backyard Cookery

Underground architecture is attracting more and more attention from solar heating experts and others interested in squeezing the last drop of heating potential from the sun's output. The temperature at a depth of 10 feet or more is a nearly constant 55°F summer and winter, day and night, in the cold north and the warm south. As a result, only enough energy is needed to raise indoor temperatures by 10 or 15 degrees in order to have a comfortable year-round living climate—a requirement that is well within the reach of even the simplest solar heating systems.

Architects employ a wide variety of techniques aimed at eliminating any dampness or a cavelike atmosphere in their underground dwellings. Skylights, dropped gardens, solaria, and light wells are common features. Two particularly successful approaches are illustrated on the next page: a hillside house and an atrium-type house.

Solar homes that are built into a hillside almost always feature an exposed south side that accommodates, at the very least, double-glazed conventional windows or sliding glass doors. These south-facing expanses of glass serve as large passive solar collectors. Buried walls on the north, east, and west sides act as storage masses, soaking up solar heat during the day and releasing it to the house interior at night and on cloudy days, much as in any passive solar home. The more sophisticated and elaborate in-hill design shown at right, below, includes a broad sweep of south-facing glass along the roofline, windows backed by a concrete heat storage structure along the south-facing side of the second floor, and a solar greenhouse stretched out along the first floor's south wall. Concrete floors and walls inside the home store part of the sun's warmth; the excess is fanned through ducts to a bed of stone rubble beneath the ground floor. At night or on sunless days the same system of fans and ducts

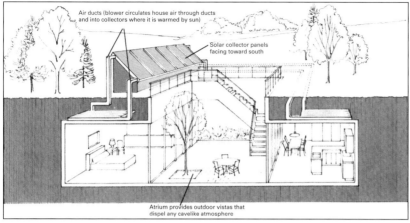

Air ducts (blower circulates house air through ducts and into collectors where it is warmed by sun)

Solar collector panels facing toward south

Atrium provides outdoor vistas that dispel any cavelike atmosphere

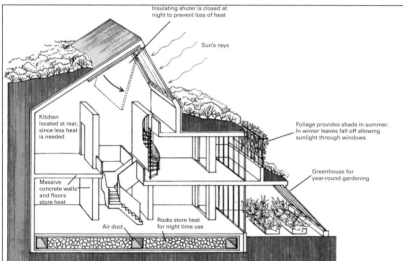

Insulating shuter is closed at night to prevent loss of heat

Sun's rays

Kitchen located at rear, since less heat is needed

Foliage provides shade in summer. In winter leaves fall off allowing sunlight through windows

Greenhouse for year-round gardening

Massive concrete walls and floors store heat

Air duct

Rocks store heat for night time use

All rooms face the garden in John Barnard, Jr.'s, subterranean house in Marstons Mills, Massachusetts (top). Aboveground solar collectors feed sun-warmed air into ducts penetrating concrete ceiling panels. Large underground complex (bottom), known as Raven Rocks, was designed by architect Malcolm Wells. Located in east-central Ohio, the house backs directly into a hill. South-facing glass walls trap heat, which is stored in rock bed under slab.

pulls stored heat from the rubble for use in warming the house. Shutters of insulating material hinge down from ceilings to prevent the loss of heat through the glass at night.

Cutaway view at top shows an atrium-type house on Cape Cod, where fuel savings of up to 85 percent are said to have been achieved. More than half the savings are attributed to the in-ground construction, the rest to 150 square feet of air-type solar collectors that circulate warmed air through tunnels in the concrete ceilings.

Constructing a Solar Cooker

The backyard solar cooker described here is simple in concept and easy to build; all it takes is a sheet of reflective material mounted so that it focuses the rays of the sun on a spit. You will need the following materials:

2 feet of 1 × 3 clear pine for uprights
2 1/2 feet of 1 × 6 clear pine for side pieces
2 feet of 1 × 10 clear pine for base
two 2 1/2-inch bolts with wing nuts
four washers to fit the bolts

Solar oven, based on the focusing reflector principle, is easily constructed with common materials and is fun to use.

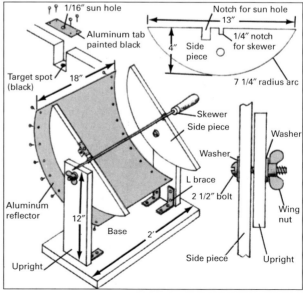

1/16" sun hole

Notch for sun hole

13"

Aluminum tab painted black

4" Side piece

1/4" notch for skewer

7 1/4" radius arc

Target spot (black)

18"

Skewer
Side piece

Washer

Washer

L brace

2 1/2" bolt

Wing nut

Aluminum reflector

12"

Base

2'

Side piece

Upright

Upright

one 16- by 18-inch piece of reflective sheet aluminum two dozen 1/2-inch aluminum brads.

The reflector is designed so that the sun's rays will focus along a line where the cooking spit is located. For proper focus it is important that the shape of the side pieces and positioning of the spit holes follow the given dimensions very precisely. Also take care to protect the mirror finish on the aluminum by taping tissue paper over it during assembly.

To construct the reflector unit, first mark and cut out the curved side pieces and plane and sand them to shape. Clamp the pieces together when shaping so that they will be identical. Next, bend the aluminum to fit the curve of the side pieces. Work carefully to avoid creasing the sheet and be sure that the shiny side is on the inner side of the curve. Clamp the side pieces 18 inches apart on a level surface with the curved edges up. Then use the brads to tack the aluminum to the side pieces.

Assemble the rest of the cooker as indicated in the diagram. An old rotisserie skewer or a 1/4-inch-square steel rod filed to a point at one end will make a serviceable spit. Note that the notches in the side pieces should be square to hold the spit in position.

While in use, the reflector must point directly at the sun. To maintain this orientation, the tilt of the reflector and the position of the cooker should be adjusted from time to time. A small sun alignment hole is built into one of the side pieces as an aid in aiming the reflector. When rays of the sun impinge directly on the target spot, the cooker is in alignment. After the entire cooker is assembled, test it on a sunny day to make sure the alignment hole is properly located. It can be adjusted by shifting the aluminum tab. Choose a clear, sunny day for cooking (a strong sun is more important than outside temperature). Wrap the food in aluminum foil, dull side out, and turn the spit occasionally. The foil keeps grease from dripping and enhances heat buildup.

Solar Water Systems: A Simple Design For Year-round Use

Solar-powered hot water systems are the most practical way for the average homeowner to take advantage of the sun's energy. They are easier to build and far less expensive than complete solar home-heating units. Moreover, since there is a year-round need for hot water, maximum use can be made of available sunlight. Complete solar water heating kits, ready to install in a new home or incorporate into an existing one, have been available for several years, and various designs have been developed to accommodate diverse conditions of weather, sunlight, and the amount of hot water needed by the user.

For families living in regions where freezing weather occurs frequently each winter, a system such as the one shown here is the best choice. It is an active system with a small electric pump to circulate the heat-transfer fluid. Instead of water, a nontoxic antifreeze solution is used for heat transfer, eliminating the need for drain-down during freezing weather. To install the system yourself, you should have a sound knowledge of basic plumbing techniques and an understanding of how the system works. If your plumbing skills and technical expertise are limited, seek professional assistance.

Theoretically, it is possible to put together a solar water heating system that will completely supply your hot water needs no matter where you live. In practice, however, the amount of solar collector area required to achieve this goal is usually so great that total reliance on solar-heated hot water would be uneconomical. The solution for most families—unless they use very little hot water or live in a particularly sunny region—is a system that produces a large percentage of their hot water needs, the rest being supplied by a conventional backup heater. During the summer such a system may provide totally solar-heated water; at other times of the year the equipment will act as an economical preheating unit for a conventional hot water system. In this latter mode the solar collectors raise the temperature of the cold water part of the way, and a standard gas, oil, or electric heater finishes the job. In many cases, the secondary system is simply the hot water heater already present in an existing home. For new homes it is likely to be a built-in feature of a water storage tank that has been specifically designed for solar heating.

As a rule of thumb, a solar hot water heater should supply about 50 to 75 percent of your yearly hot water needs in order to make it worthwhile. The collector area required to achieve this depends on the amount of sunlight in your area and the amount of hot water your household uses—80 gallons a day for a typical family of four. Assuming 24-square-foot flat-plate collectors (a standard size) and a family of four, you will need the following number of collectors: Region I, five to six collectors; Region II, three to four collectors; Region III, two collectors. (See the map on page 89 to find the region in which you live.) These are rough approximations, since even adjoining areas can differ widely due to differences in cloud cover, topography, and wind patterns. Many references carry more precise figures (see *Sources and resources*, page 99), or consult a manufacturer of solar equipment.

How the System Works

The cutaway drawing on following page shows the layout of a typical solar water heating system. All the parts can be purchased off the shelf: solar equipment manufacturers carry the collector panels, antifreeze, and the special stone-lined water storage tank with a built-in heat exchanger; the other units are standard fixtures available from plumbing suppliers. Copper piping is used throughout. Three primary subsystems constitute the overall system: the heat transfer loop, the hot water loop, and the electrical control loop.

Heat transfer loop circulates the antifreeze fluid through the solar collector panels and heat exchanger coil. Heat picked up by the fluid at the collectors is given off at the coil to warm the water in the storage

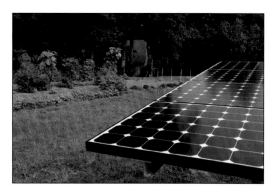

Solar water heaters will save energy all year round and are well suited for installation in existing houses. The panels can be mounted flush on the roof, provided the roof faces south and has a pitch of about 40° or more. Otherwise they must be mounted on raised metal brackets so that the sun will strike them directly. Sturdy bracing and positive anchorage is vital in case of high winds; roof mounting may even require that rafters beneath the panels be reinforced by doubling them. The panels can also be mounted on the ground. Generally, panels mounted on the ground are securely fastened to concrete piles sunk below the frost line.

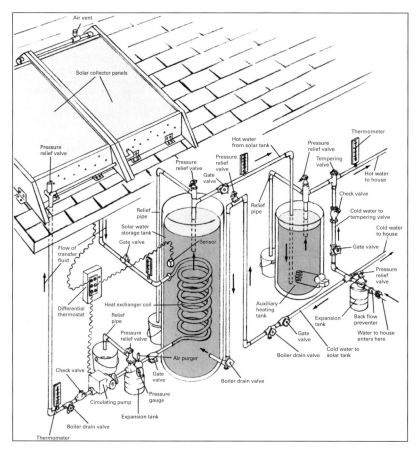

Solar heating system layout should be simple and provide easy access to components. For efficient performance minimize distances pipes must travel between collector panels and water tanks. Pipes should be insulated and routed indoors wherever possible. Consult a licensed plumber or building authority before attempting do-it-yourself installations.

tank. The loop contains an expansion tank with an air purger, plus an air vent at the highest point in the system. The expansion tank cushions pressure changes in the loop; the purger and vent bleed off any air bubbles that develop. Reverse flow of antifreeze is prevented by a check valve, and a relief valve guards against pressure buildup by providing an escape port for the fluid. A boiler drain located at the lowest point in the system is used for filling or draining the loop; gate valves at various points permit isolation of individual components for maintenance. A pressure gauge and two thermometers, one mounted on a pipe to the collectors and the other on the pipe from the storage tank, monitor the system.

Hot water loop starts at the point where the cold water enters the house from outside. A backflow preventer, expansion tank, and vacuum relief valve (positioned above the level of the water storage tank) are code requirements common to all home water systems, whether or not they are solar. Cold water feeds into the storage tank, is warmed by the heat exchanger, rises to the top of the tank, and is passed on to the auxiliary heating tank, usually a conventional water heater. For safety, a tempering valve and crossover pipe (fitted with a check valve) are installed beyond the second tank. If water should accidentally be heated above a safe temperature on a particularly sunny day, the tempering valve automatically mixes in cool water.

Electrical control loop automatically turns on the system whenever the sun is shining and shuts it off at night or on overcast days. The loop consists of a differential thermostat, plus two sensors, one that measures fluid temperature in the collector and one that measures water temperature in the storage tank. The thermostat compares the readings of the two sensors and automatically switches on the pump in the heat transfer loop whenever the water in the storage tank is more than a few degrees cooler than the collector fluid.

Assembling the Units Into a Working System

Factory-built collector panels are available as complete units. However, you can save money by making your own either by assembling them from components or by making them from scratch with ordinary building supplies and hardware. The absorber plate is the most important and the most difficult part to build. Prefabricated plates are available from firms specializing in solar heating equipment, and their efficiency and durability make them well worth the investment. If you choose to construct your own, use 7-ounce (.01-inch-thick) copper sheeting and flexible copper tubing with 3/8-inch outside diameter. Form the tubing into a grid and attach it to the sheet with a high-temperature solder (plate temperatures can reach 400°F on a sunny day). Coat the finished plate with high-carbon flat black paint.

The plate rests unanchored in the collector box on a rigid, resin-free duct insulation board (available at heating-supply outlets). A layer of soft fiberglass insulation is usually installed beneath the board. Allow a 3/4-inch airspace above the plate, then cover the collector box with one or two sheets of glass, polyester reinforced fiberglass, or plastic film. The most effective glazing is tempered iron-free glass. In most regions a single pane 3/16 inch thick is sufficient. In very cold areas use two 1/8-inch-thick panes with a 1/2-inch airspace between. A less expensive alternative is a sheet of .040-inch-thick polyester reinforced fiberglass above an inner glazing of 1-mil.-thick Teflon film, separated by an airspace of 1/2 inch. Drill 1/8-inch-diameter holes in the lower end of the collector box between the absorber plate and the glazing panel to prevent condensation. If double-glazing is used, also drill holes in the space between panes.

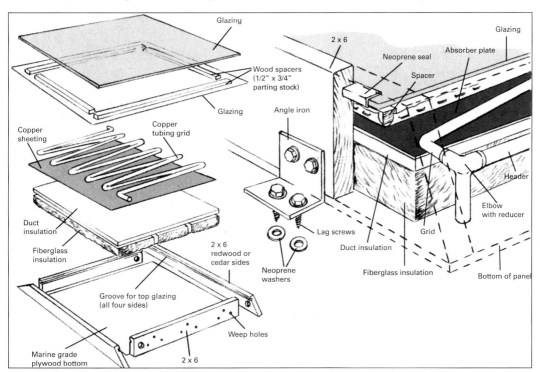

Seal edges of glazing (either glass or synthetic) with a neoprene strip to keep out moisture while allowing leeway for expansion. Caulk all other seams with silicone sealant. Header pipes linking panels are made from rigid copper tubing with 1 1/8-in. outside diameter. Sweat-solder them in place after panels are attached to roof. Use torch carefully near combustible material.

Installing the Panels

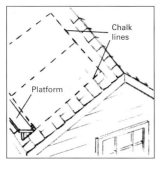

1. Lay out positions of panels using chalk line. Panel ends should be parallel to roof peak. Sides should lie along inside edges of rafters (usually spaced 16 or 24 in. apart center to center) so that they can be anchored with lag screws and angle brackets. Note platform is roof mounted to provide a safe working area.

2. Nail temporary 2 × 4 guide strip below the bottom chalk line to align the lower ends of the beveled collector box sides. Raise the panels onto the roof and position them so that they rest along the upper edge of the strip. The horizontal endpieces of the boxes should cover the top and bottom chalk lines.

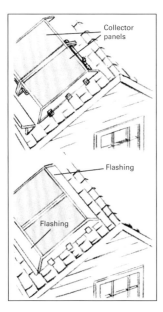

3. Attach the panels directly to the roof. Use 1/4-in. lag screws that are long enough to penetrate at least 2 in. into the rafters. Mount panels on 1/2-in.-thick neoprene washers to provide air circulation beneath collectors. Wrap screws with Teflon tape; coat heads with silicone sealant.

4. Solder headers to plate connections using high-temperature solder. Test and insulate plumbing (see p.120), then install aluminum flashing over headers to prevent debris accumulation. Flashing need not be weathertight. Screw or nail metal to sides and ends of box; fasten edges under shingles or with tar.

Pipes and Plumbing

Use copper tubing—either flexible or rigid—for the plumbing in the solar water heating system. Rigid tubing is somewhat more durable; flexible (soft-tempered)

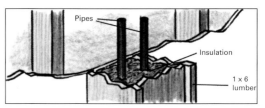

Exposed pipes can be enclosed within hollow columns built of 1 × 6 lumber filled with fiberglass insulation.

tubbing is easier to work with, less expensive, and can be connected with flare fittings or by sweat-solder fittings. Both kinds of tubing are available in type K (thick wall) and type L (medium wall), but only rigid tubing is sold in type M (thin wall). The two kinds of tubing can be used together in a single installation. Employ the rigid style for long horizontal runs and in locations where the plumbing might be subject to denting; go to the flexible tubing in places where soldering is awkward, presents a fire hazard, or where complex situations would require an excessive number of connections and fittings if a rigid pipe were used. Drain the water from existing plumbing before soldering on additional piping—pipes containing water cannot be soldered.

After the plumbing has been connected, but before the system is put into operation, the entire assembly must be pressure-tested for leaks by the procedure described below. To avoid damage to air vents, expansion tanks, valves, and other components that are sensitive to excessive pressure, omit them when first installing the plumbing. Screw in a Schrader-type valve—the kind used in automobile and bicycle tires—in the opening where the pressure gauge would normally go, and insert plugs (available from plumbing suppliers) into all the other openings. When testing is completed, remove the valve and plugs and install the final components in their place. Then cover the pipes with closed-cell foam pipe insulation, available from air conditioning, refrigeration, and solar equipment suppliers. Use 3/4-inch-thick out-

Testing the system

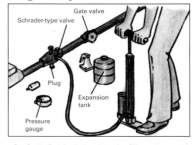

Locate leaks in finished plumbing by filling pipes with water, then raising pressure to 100 psi (pounds per square inch). With Schrader-type valve installed instead of pressure gauge, connect garden hose from main water supply to boiler drain located in heat transfer loop piping, and fill entire loop with water. Next, use high-pressure hand pump to pressurize the system; it should be able to hold the pressure for one hour. Check all connections and mark defective joints. Afterward, drain water and repair leaks. Measure water drained to determine amount of antifreeze needed.

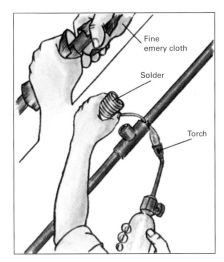

Sweat-soldering. Use 95-5 tin/antimony (high-temperature) solder throughout, especially at the collectors, to reduce lead leaching into the potable water. Scour parts to be joined with fine emery cloth until shiny, then apply thin coat of paste flux to each piece. Assemble joint, place asbestos pad behind for fire safety, and wrap nearby soldered joints with wet cloths to keep them from melting accidentally. Heat joint with propane torch until flux bubbles, then apply solder to the seam between fitting and pipe. The solder will flow into the fitting.

door-grade foam for pipes exposed to weather and 1/2-inch-thick foam indoors.

The final step is to connect the differential thermostat and temperature sensors. Follow the manufacturer's instructions and be sure to locate the thermostat in a convenient spot (it serves as the system's control box). Add the antifreeze to the heat transfer loop and the system is ready to go.

Adding the antifreeze

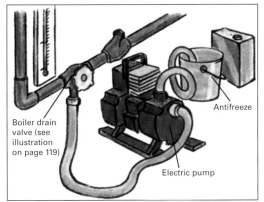

Rent a portable electric pump to force antifreeze into heat transfer loop. Pressure inside loop should be 20 to 30 psi. Check operating pressure periodically against this initial figure; any drop in pressure may indicate a leak in the loop. To avoid water contamination, only non-toxic antifreeze should be used. Solar equipment dealers carry a safe blend containing propylene glycol, distilled water, a corrosion inhibitor to protect pipes, and a colored dye that helps in the detection of an accidental leakage of antifreeze into the water supply. Manufacturer's instructions usually suggest draining loop and replacing fluid every three years.

Joining techniques

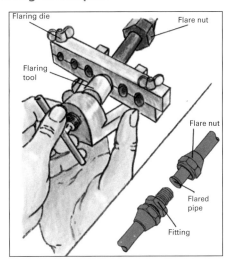

Flare fittings. These can be used only with flexible copper piping. Begin by cutting pipe ends square and removing any burrs. Slide flare nut onto pipe, and insert pipe into proper size hole in flaring die. Position pipe end even with face of die, then screw pointed flaring tool into pipe end, making certain tool is centered. Tighten tool until pipe end is flared to 45° angle. Insert fitting into flare and slide flare nut up. Tighten the nut to the fitting using two wrenches worked in opposition. Flare second pipe and attach to other end of fitting.

Sources and resources

Books and pamphlets
Anderson, Bruce, and Michael Riordan. *The New Solar Home Book.* Andover, Mass.: Brick House Publishing, 1987.
Bason, Frank C. *Energy and Solar Heating.* College Park, Md.: American Association of Physics Teachers, 1984.
Cooling Your Home Naturally. Washington, D.C.: U.S. Department of Energy, 1994.
Crowther, Richard. *Affordable Passive Solar Homes.* Boulder, Colo.: American Solar Energy Society, 1983.
DeWinter, Francis. *Solar Collectors, Energy Storage and Materials.* Cambridge, Mass.: MIT Press, 1991.
Energy Efficient Water Heating. Washington, D.C.: U.S. Department of Energy, 1995.
Freeman, Mark. *The Solar Home: How to Design and Build a House You Heat With the Sun.* Mechanicsburg, Pa.: Stackpole, 1994.
Guide to Making Energy-Smart Purchases. Washington, D.C.: U.S. Department of Energy, 1994.
Kubsch, Erwin. *Home Owner's Guide to Free Heat.* Sheridan, Wyo.: Sunstore Farms, 1991.
Reynolds, Michael. *Earthship: How to Build Your Own.* Taos, N. Mex.: Solar Survival, 1990.
Solar Electric Power Association, 1391 Connecticut Ave., suite 3.2, Washington, D.C. 2006. www.solarelectricpower.org.
Solar Water Heating. Washington, D.C.: U.S. Department of Energy, 1994.
Tomorrow's Energy Today. Washington, D.C.: U.S. Department of Energy, 1994.
Using the Earth to Heat and Cool Homes. Butte, Mont.: NCAT, 1983.

Part Three

Raising Your Own Vegetables, Fruit, and Livestock

The best fertilizer for a piece of land is the footprints of its owner.

—Lyndon B. Johnson

An 18th-century almanac cautions that "overplanted fields make a rich father but a poor son." This advice and its corollary—that good farmers are partners of the land, not exploiters—is as current now as when it was first written. Care, consideration, a little knowledge, and a lot of common sense: these are the ingredients that will ensure rich harvests year after year, whether your farm is a window ledge in the city, a backyard in the suburbs, or wide acreage in the country. "Raising Your Own Vegetables, Fruit, and Livestock" shows how to keep your land healthy while reaping bumper crops each year. It explains how to grow fruits and vegetables without resorting to expensive synthetic fertilizers or dangerous chemical pesticides. The old-time kitchen garden is treated at length, but other aspects of small-scale agriculture—some traditional, some quite modern—are also covered. Among these subjects are fish farming, keeping bees, growing grain, raising dairy animals, keeping chickens and rabbits, and using horses as draft animals.

The Kitchen Garden

Homegrown Produce: A Delicious Sense Of Self-sufficiency

It is easy to list the material benefits that a kitchen garden can bring. Your vegetables will arrive on your table garden fresh. They will probably be far tastier than the often days-old produce found on the shelves of food stores—and more nutritious too. And there will be impressive savings in your food dollar; experts say that for each $20 worth of supplies and labor invested, a return of more than $200 can be reaped.

But beyond such practical considerations are additional benefits: the pleasure of working with the soil, of watching seeds sprout and grow, and of knowing that the food on your table is a product of your own labor. It is these reasons, perhaps, more than mere economics, that account for the recent upsurge in home vegetable gardening.

The story of vegetable gardening in America goes back further than the current boom or even the victory gardens of World War II. The first gardeners, in fact, were the first Americans: the Indians who raised corn, beans, and squash in neatly tended plots. This food saw the Indians through the lean times of the year when game and fish were scarce. The colonists, like the Indians, depended on their gardens for survival. Life was hard, toil unending, and there was no room in the garden for any plant that was merely ornamental. What herbs and flowers were grown were used for flavoring, medicine, or dye.

For most people today, the home kitchen garden is no longer a necessity for survival. However, the garden still has an important role to play not only in economic terms but also in a well-earned sense of independence and accomplishment, as well as in the closer relationship with nature that working with the soil and its produce affords.

Garden goodies shown here are part of a bountiful harvest of delicious homegrown vegetables for freezing, canning, storage, and, of course, eating fresh. Even a small garden can make a big difference in your food budget, not to mention adding true garden freshness and flavor to your mealtimes. The only prerequisite is that you enjoy gardening.

Companion Planting

For centuries, observant gardeners have noticed that certain vegetables seemed to thrive in the company of one plant while doing poorly in the company of another. There is evidence that secretions given off by the roots of some plants are the cause of this effect. For example, the roots of black walnut trees exude a chemical that inhibits the growth of tomatoes. Onions apparently inhibit the growth of beans, peas, and several other vegetables. Tomatoes and basil, on the other hand, are believed to do well together, as are cucumbers and cabbage.

Another aspect of companion planting is that certain vegetables and herbs seem to repel the pests of other plants. Marigold roots, for example, exude a secretion that repels nematodes—tiny wormlike creatures that attack plant roots—and parsley is said to repel the carrot fly. Other plants lure pests away from their neighbors, as the eggplant lures Colorado potato beetles from potato plants. Although companion planting is a source of controversy among experts, it is certainly worth trying in your own garden.

The Gardener's Basic Tools

Surprisingly few tools are needed for a basic vegetable garden. To work a 15-by-20-foot plot, the only essential items are a spading fork, rake, hoe, watering can, and garden spade or round-point shovel. In addition, a string and two stakes are helpful for laying out rows, and a stout pair of gloves will protect your hands. Other useful tools are a trowel for transplanting, a mattock for dealing with rocks and roots, a hose, a soaker or sprinkler, a wheeled cultivator, and a cart for carrying sacks of fertilizer or other heavy loads. Power equipment is not necessary for the average kitchen garden except, perhaps, a rotary tiller, and this can be rented for the few days each year that it is needed.

Buy good quality tools; the extra expense will be worth it in the long run. Well-made tools last longer and are easier to use. Maintain your tools properly. Clean off soil and mud after each use and oil the tool lightly before putting it away. An occasional coat of linseed oil helps preserve wooden parts.

Old-time planting lore

Plant corn when the oak leaves are the size of a squirrel's ear or when the hickory buds are as big as a crow's bill (about 1 in. long). By then the danger of frost will be past.
Sprinkle plants with wood ashes or soot to keep bugs off.
Bury pieces of rhubarb in the row when planting cabbage to protect it against club root (a soil-borne disease).
To keep cabbage heads from splitting, give each young plant a half-twist in the ground.
When planting corn or squash in hills, be generous with the seed to allow for mishaps: "One for the woodchuck, one for the crow / One for the slug, and one to grow."
Much old-time lore involved astrological signs. Planting under Gemini—the sign of the Twins—was said to double the crop. As for the moon, farmers were enjoined to plant leafy vegetables when the moon was waxing and to plant root crops when it was waning. Such beliefs may be interesting, even charming, but their usefulness is dubious.

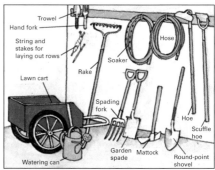

This assortment of tools will handle practically any job that needs to be done in the average home kitchen garden.

Vegetable	Does well with	Does poorly with
Asparagus	Parsley, tomatoes	_____
Beans (bush)	Beets, carrots, cucumbers, marigolds, potatoes	Fennel, garlic, onions
Beans (pole)	Marigolds, radishes	Garlic, onions
Cabbage family	Beets, celery, corn, dill, nasturtiums, onions, sage, sunflowers	Fennel, pole beans, tomatoes
Cantaloupe	Corn, sunflowers	Potatoes
Carrots	Leaf lettuce, parsley, tomatoes	Dill
Corn	Beans, cucumbers, peas, potatoes, pumpkins, squash	_____
Cucumbers	Beans, cabbage family, corn, peas, radishes	Aromatic herbs, potatoes
Eggplant	Beans	Potatoes (attacked by potato pests)
Lettuce	Carrots, cucumbers, onions, radishes	_____
Onions	Beets, cabbage family, lettuce, tomatoes	_____
Peas	Beans, carrots, corn, cucumbers, potatoes, radishes, turnips	Garlic, onions
Potatoes	Beans, cabbage, corn, marigolds, peas	Sunflowers
Pumpkins	Corn	Potatoes
Radishes	Beets, carrots, spinach	_____
Rutabagas and turnips	Peas	_____
Squash	Nasturtiums, radishes	_____
Tomatoes	Asparagus, basil, garlic, marigolds, parsley	Cabbage family, fennel, potatoes

A Successful Garden Requires Planning

To get the most out of your garden plot, it is necessary to plan ahead. Whether you have an established garden or are starting a new one, the best time to prepare is in the off season, well before planting time.

A good location is even more important than good soil. You can do a great deal to improve poor soil, but it is almost impossible to improve a bad site. The ideal kitchen garden should be sheltered from wind and have direct sunlight for at least six hours a day, preferably longer. It should be well drained; that is, the soil should not remain muddy after a heavy rain. It should be located away from trees, which can shade out light and whose roots may compete with vegetables for moisture and nutrients. Avoid locating your plot in a low spot where water and cold air tend to collect.

The garden should be near a tap, since watering will almost certainly be necessary at some time during the growing season. If you can manage to locate the garden close to the house, you will save many extra steps.

The site should be level or slightly sloping—if it slopes, a south-facing tilt is best, since it provides extra warmth in spring and fall. If the only available site is on a steep slope, terrace it to prevent soil erosion.

Another important decision is the size of the garden. This depends on the amount of arable land available and on how much of your own food you intend to grow. A garden to supply a family of two adults and two school-age children with staples the year round should cover at least 2,500 square feet (50 by 50 feet or the equivalent). However, a garden as small as 15 by 20 feet (300 square feet) can produce an amazing quantity of fresh vegetables.

Even a 6- by 8-foot minigarden can add flavor and variety to your diet while reducing the food bill.

The traditional shape for a garden is rectangular—it is the easiest to plow and cultivate with horse or machine. However, free-form shapes are becoming popular and can be adapted to the conformation of your lot as well as to obstacles such as rock outcrops and structures.

When breaking new ground for a garden, be sure either to remove the sod or plow it under so it can decay and enrich the soil. Remove stones, roots, and debris. Soil improvement is also an important part of planning. Test your soil each spring to determine what needs to be done to improve it, then set up a schedule for preparing the soil, planting your seeds, and setting out transplants.

The Right Crops Can Make All the Difference

The most obvious rule is to plant vegetables that you and your family like–it is a waste of time, labor, and garden space to raise produce that goes uneaten. You should also select vegetables that are suited to your local climate and growing season. It is a mistake, for example, to try to raise okra (a tropical plant that needs a long, warm growing season) in Maine or to plant potatoes, which prefer cool weather, in the Deep South.

Once you have decided on what vegetables to grow, you are faced with the problem of selecting the proper varieties. Seed catalogs and garden centers offer many hybrids specially bred for disease resistance, productivity, size, and flavor, as well as for rapid development. Although hybrids are higher in price than standard varieties, their special bred-in qualities often make the extra investment more than worthwhile. Avoid so-called market or cropper varieties. These are for commercial growers who want crops that ripen and can be harvested at one time. If you plant one of these varieties, you will have a glut of beans, tomatoes, or cabbages for a few days and nothing for the rest of the season.

Plan your garden so that it will yield a steady supply of vegetables once it comes into production. Succession cropping and interplanting are two methods of getting more out of your garden space. Another device is to stagger your plantings to yield a steady supply of snap beans, radishes, and other vegetables in season. Sow small batches at one- to two-week intervals. An alternative is to plant early and late varieties together.

Remember to set aside time to care for your garden—you will need about three hours a week for weeding, cultivation, harvesting, and other chores. An untended garden usually fails; only weeds grow without help. Keep the rows short for easy maintenance. If you are a first-time gardener, plant only a modest plot; the smaller the garden, the simpler it is to manage.

Vegetables should be placed where they will not shade each other. Plant tall vegetables, such as corn or staked tomatoes, on the north side of the garden or the side near a house or other light barrier. Low-growing vegetables such as beets and onions should be located on the side that gets the most light. Asparagus and other perennials should be planted out of the way of the annuals or in separate beds. So, too, should early crops such as peas; they can be plowed under and a new crop planted. The sample layout shown here can easily be expanded or altered or planted with other types of vegetables.

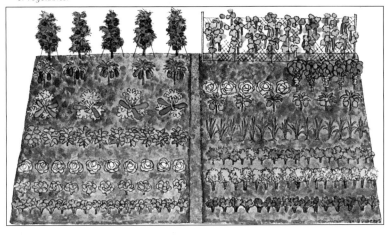

The Frost-Free Season, From Spring to Fall

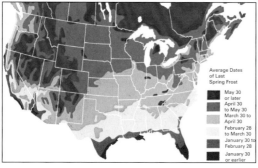

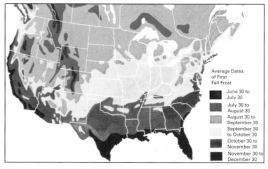

Last hard frost of spring and the first hard frost of fall mark the limits of the growing season for tomatoes, corn, melons, beans, and other tender vegetables. (A hard frost is one where the temperature falls significantly below the freezing point for several hours.) The dates shown in the maps represent averages over large regions. There is a wide variation in frost dates within each region and sometimes within the same neighborhood. Elevation, landforms, nearby bodies of water, and the proximity of big cities all affect the frost date. The presence of water and urban development both tend to increase temperature and therefore lengthen the growing season. The effect of elevation is to lower average temperatures by 3°F per 1,000 ft. of altitude. Allow a few days leeway when planting in the spring to make sure your young shoots will not be caught in an unexpected freeze. Your county agent is a good source of information on local frost-free dates. For greater precision, you can maintain your own temperature and planting records. For this purpose, special thermometers are available that record the daily highs and lows.

Shapes to Suit Your Site and Taste

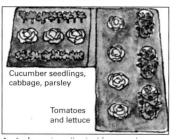

An L-shape is well suited for a garden that must follow the side of a house or is to be placed in the corner of a lot. Each arm of the L can be extended as far as you wish to create a peripheral garden space around central lawn or patio. A path at the base of the L gives improved access to both areas of the garden.

Terracing is the answer to the problem of gardening on a steep slope. Make terraces 2 to 4 ft. wide; use a carpenter's level on a 2 × 4 when laying them out. Hold the soil in place with either railroad ties, boards supported by stakes, logs, or flat stones laid on edge. Terraces can be curved to follow natural contours.

The round garden, with corn, pole beans, and squash thriving together, is based on a traditional American Indian plan. Almost any combination of tall and low-growing plants can be used. Locate the tall plants in the center where they will not choke out or shade their smaller but still desirable companion vegetables.

Two harvests in the space of one

Succession planting is a simple idea that can enormously increase your harvest. One technique is to plant successive crops of the same vegetable at one- to two-week intervals. Another is to follow an early-maturing spring crop with a fall crop planted in midsummer. The chart shows some of the best combinations, but you should experiment with others yourself. In areas with mild winters you may even get three crops by

Early crop	Late crop
Beets	Kale
Carrots	Brussels sprouts
Corn	Winter squash
Lettuce	Winter radish
Mustard greens	Bush beans
Peas	Fall cabbage
Spinach	Chinese cabbage
Turnips	Fall lettuce
Turnips	Tomato plants

following your fall crop with a hardy vegetable such as collards. A related technique is to interplant quickmaturing vegetables, such as radishes, with slow growers, such as carrots or beets.

A Life-Giving System Beneath Our Feet

Soil is a living, complex system to which our lives are linked in a very real sense. On the soil and its fertility depend the vigor and productivity of plants, the basis of our food chain.

Soil is composed of both inorganic and organic material. The inorganic components derive mainly from the slow breakdown of rocks and minerals but also include air and water held in the pores between soil particles. Organic material comprises both the remains of once-living plants and animals plus a multitude of simple life forms such as bacteria, fungi, algae, and protozoans.

Other life forms also dwell in the soil, among them insect larvae, microscopic worms called nematodes, and the familiar earthworms. Some, such as nematodes, can harm plants by attacking their roots; others, such as ants and earthworms, help plants by their constant tunneling, which aerates the soil.

Most soils are a mixture of sand, silt, and clay. Sand and silt are chemically the same as the rocks and minerals from which they are formed, while clay has undergone chemical changes that alter its properties. Clay attracts and holds water and many nutrient chemicals, while sand and silt do not. The varying proportions of sand, silt, and clay give soil its character, and soil classifications are based on which of these mineral substances predominates.

Organic matter supplies nutrients to the soil and improves soil consistency. It increases water-holding capacity and adds body to loose, sandy soils; it loosens dense, heavy clay soils, making them easier to cultivate and easier for plant roots to penetrate. Manure, compost, and mulches such as grass clippings, spoiled hay, and dead leaves are good sources of organic matter to add to your garden soil.

The ideal gardening soil is soft, loose, and crumbly. It should also be rich in organic matter and free from stones, roots, and debris. Even if your soil does not have these characteristics, you can tailor it to your requirements by removing debris and adding organic matter.

There are several simple ways to tell what kind of soil you have in your garden. One test is to place a small amount of soil—about a spoonful—in the palm of one hand. Mix it with water until it is thoroughly wet (but do not use so much water that it becomes runny). Then rub the wet soil out into a thin layer on your palm. Clay soil will feel slippery and look shiny. Sandy soil will feel gritty and look dull. Silty soil will feel slippery but will not shine. Another test is to roll the wet soil into a ball, then into a long, thin snake. Sandy soil is difficult to make into a ball; and when you roll it out into a snake, it will quickly fall part. Clay soil will hold its shape both as a ball and as a snake—the more clay, the thinner the

The Soil and Its Principal Constituents

Fill jar with one-third soil, two-thirds water. Shake well

Undecomposed organic matter floats at top

Clay
Silt
Sand

Fertile, humus-rich soil consisting largely of sand, silt, and clay is called loam. The ideal loam contains about 40 percent silt and 20 percent clay, with sand and organic matter making up the remainder. Such soils have a good balance between drainage, looseness, and retention of moisture and nutrients. To determine the makeup of your soil, mix a cupful with water and shake well in a bottle. As shown above, the soil will settle in distinct layers of sand, silt, and clay. The relative thickness of the layers indicates the proportion of each. Sand particles are big enough to see with the naked eye and are gritty to the touch. Sandy soils are loose and porous, absorbing water readily but not holding it long. Plant roots penetrate them easily, making them suitable for root crops such as carrots and beets. Because sandy soils warm up and dry out quickly in spring, they usually can be worked several weeks ahead of the denser clay soils. Clay particles are thin, flat plates, too small to see without a microscope. Clay is hard and bricklike when dry, greasy and plastic when wet. Clay soils absorb water very slowly but hold it for a long time. They also hold plant nutrients, a valuable quality in garden soils. Silt falls between sand and clay in its properties. The particles are about as fine as sifted cake flour. Silt feels powdery when dry, slippery when wet. It adds bulk and moisture-holding capacity to soil. Heavy clay soil can be lightened by digging in sand for drainage and peat moss or compost to keep the soil from compacting into a concretelike mass. However, for any type of soil the most important ingredient is organic matter.

Testing the soil

How can you tell whether your soil is acid or alkaline? In many cases the weeds and the wild plants that grow on it are natural indicators. Sorrel and knotweed, for example, thrive in acid soil; wild blueberries usually indicate a very acid soil. Sagebrush is a sign of alkaline soil. The familiar hydrangea bush blooms blue in acid soils, pink in alkaline. A carpet of moss indicates a damp soil that is poor in nutrients. For a more precise analysis, simple and easy-to-use soil testing kits are widely available from seed houses and garden-supply centers. Such kits can measure the soil's nutrient content as well as its pH. For testing a large area of soil the most practical procedure may be to send soil samples to your Cooperative Extension Service to be analyzed by experts with sophisticated equipment.

Alkaline

Neutral or sweet

Acid or sour

8.0

7.0

Slightly acid— the best pH range for most vegetables

6.0

Test kits use chemicals that change color depending on pH of soil. Color range shown is approximate

snake that can be rolled. Silty soil will feel like clay but will not hold together.

Acid or Alkaline—The Mysteries of pH

The health and vigor of plants depend to a great degree on how acid or alkaline the soil is in which they grow. This is because the degree of acidity or alkalinity controls the availability of important nutrients in the soil. If the soil is too acid or alkaline, the nutrients may be locked up in insoluble chemical compounds, and some may even become toxic to plants. Most plants do best in soil that is neutral to slightly acid, although some vegetables have different needs (see *Grower's Guide*, pp.114–122).

Acidity and alkalinity are measured by the pH scale, which runs from 0 to 14. Zero is extremely acid; 7 is neutral; 14 is extremely alkaline. Each point on the pH scale represents a factor of 10. A soil with a pH value of 5, for example, is 10 times more acid (10 times less alkaline) than soil that tests out at pH 6. A soil with a pH value of 9 is 10 times more alkaline (10 times less acid) than one with a value of 8.

For comparison, lemon juice, which is an acid substance, has a pH of about 3 and soapy water, which is alkaline, has a pH of 9. Most soils range from pH 4 to 8.5, and most vegetables thrive best between pH 6 and 6.8. Methods of correcting pH are suggested on the following pages.

Fertilizers for Productivity

Fertilizers are used to supply plants with nutrients that the soil lacks. Plants need at least 13 chemical elements for good health and growth. The big three—nitrogen, phosphorus, and potassium—are standard ingredients of almost all packaged garden fertilizers. Other necessary plant nutrients are calcium, magnesium, sulfur, and the so-called trace elements: iron, copper, manganese, zinc, boron, chlorine, and molybdenum.

The signs of a nutrient deficiency are often obvious. A lack of nitrogen, for example, shows up in the form of stunted growth and yellow leaves. Symptoms of a phosphorus shortage are stunted growth and leaves of a darker than normal green. A lack of iron appears as yellowing in new leaves. An excess of a nutrient can be bad too. An overdose of nitrogen often results in a lush growth of leaves but weak, brittle stems and little fruit. Large amounts of trace elements can be toxic to plants.

A fertilizer is considered organic if it is derived from naturally occurring materials, such as manure, dried blood, bone meal, rock phosphate, and green sand. Synthetic fertilizers are based on man-made chemicals. The numerals on a bag of fertilizer denote its percentage of nitrogen, phosphorus, and potassium, in that order. A 100-pound bag of fertilizer labeled 5-10-5, for example, contains 5 pounds of nitrogen, 10 of phosphorus pentoxide, and 5 of potassium oxide.

Organic and synthetic fertilizers both supply the nutrient chemicals that plants need. However, the trend among small-scale gardeners is toward the nat-ural and the organic, and away from the synthetic. There are practical reasons for this trend. Organic fertilizers release their nutrients slowly and over a long time; synthetic fertilizers act quickly and must be renewed more frequently. Most organic fertilizers add organic matter to the soil; synthetic fertilizers do not. Organic fertilizers often improve soil texture as well as adding nutrients; synthetics do not. Organic fertilizers naturally contain trace elements and other necessary plant foods; synthetics do not. Earthworms and other beneficial organisms are sometimes harmed by synthetic fertilizers. Synthetics are more concentrated than organic fertilizers and so are more prone to burn delicate plant roots and destroy valuable soil organisms. Perhaps most important, however, is that more and more people are making their own compost, raising animals that provide them with manure, and otherwise finding or creating their own homegrown fertilizer.

Excellent results can be achieved with either type of fertilizer, however, provided the correct amount is used—neither too much nor too little. The art of efficient fertilization consists of feeding the plants, not the soil.

Improving the Soil

Garden soil is seldom ideal when first tilled. It may be too sandy, have too much clay, or be full of roots, rocks, and debris. The pH may be too low or too high and often the soil is deficient in organic matter.

The most important soil-improvement and conditioning task is usually to add organic matter to the soil. This is best done in fall, while the soil is still warm enough to promote the activity of bacteria and fungi and when the decay process will not use up the nitrogen needed by growing crops. Manure and compost are excellent additives, as are lawn clippings, dead leaves, and so-called garden trash—the leaves and stems of plants that have died or ceased producing. But do not use plants that are diseased or insect infested. They will contaminate the soil and cause problems in future years.

If you have used organic mulch on your garden during the summer, turn it under at the end of the season. Green manure, a cover crop grown for the purpose of being added to the soil, is much used. Rye, alfalfa, and clover are favorites for this purpose, particularly alfalfa and clover, which have nitrogen-fixing bacteria growing on their roots. In addition to improving the structure of the soil, organic matter provides food for earthworms and other beneficial soil organisms.

Organic material should be thoroughly mixed into the topmost 12 inches of soil but no deeper—the roots of most common vegetables do not penetrate beyond this depth. Since organic matter is at a premium, it should be used where it does the most good.

Overly acid soil can be corrected by adding lime, which also contributes calcium—a major plant nutrient—and improves soil structure. Alkaline soils can be made more acid by adding powdered sulfur, which is slow acting but long-lived, or aluminum sulfate.

The Art and Science Of Soil Improvement

Composting is a method of converting garden trash, kitchen scraps, and other organic wastes into humus—a partly decayed form of organic matter that is an important ingredient of rich soils.

There are many variations in composting techniques, but the basic idea is to let the biological action of bacteria and fungi heat the interior of the compost pile to 150°F, killing weed seeds and disease organisms. The most efficient way to produce compost is in a bin or container to keep the material from spilling out.

A compost pile is built up like a layer cake with each layer watered as it is completed. Optimum height for a compost pile is about 4 feet. A lower pile loses too much heat; a higher one tends to pack down and interfere with the biological action. Length and width are optional, but remember that two small piles are easier to handle than one huge one. Start with a 2- to 3-inch layer of coarse materials, such as cornstalks, twigs, or straw (the purpose is to let air into the bottom of the pile). If coarse material is not available, you can use a layer of sawdust or other absorbent material or omit it entirely. In any case, only one layer of coarse or absorbent material is necessary. Next, add a 3- to 6-inch layer of organic material, such as garden trash or dead leaves. Over this place 2 to 3 inches of manure (or a light sprinkling of synthetic fertilizer) to supply the nitrogen needed for the

breakdown process. Other good sources of nitrogen are dog and cat droppings, feathers, hair clippings, and dried blood. The next layer should be a thin cover of topsoil or old compost. At this point some gardeners cover the heap with a sprinkling of lime. Repeat the process until the pile is about 4 feet high; then shape the top of the pile into a shallow saucer to let water soak in.

Moisture content is important for good composting. If the pile is too dry, the breakdown process slows to a halt; if too wet, undesirable biochemical reactions take place. The pile should be about as damp as a just-squeezed sponge. In dry weather water it every few days; in very rainy weather cover it with a tarp or plastic sheet.

The pile should be turned about once a week to aerate it. This procedure speeds decomposition, combats odor, and mixes the material so that it will decay at a uniform rate. To turn compost, take apart the old pile and put it together backward so that the material that was on the outside of the old pile is in the center of the new pile.

Compost is ready to use when the pile no longer gives off heat or odor when opened up and the material has turned brown and crumbly.

Tilling the Soil

Since the beginning of agriculture, man has tilled the soil. Tilling serves several purposes. It breaks up and buries sod and weeds that would otherwise compete with cultivated plants for space, water, and nutrients. It loosens the soil, permitting water and air to reach

A catalog of organic fertilizers

Type	Contributes	Other things you should know
Bonemeal	Phosphorus, 20–25%	Very slow acting. Will not burn roots
Compost	Organic matter, varying proportions of all nutrients	The best all round organic fertilizer; should also be used with chemical fertilizers
Cottonseed meal	Nitrogen, 6–9%; phosphorus, 2–3% potassium, 1.5–2%	Low pH, good for acid loving crops
Dried blood and tankage	Nitrogen, 5–12%; phosphorus, 3–13%	One of the best organic sources of nitrogen, aids growth of soil organisms. Quick acting
Fish meal, fish emulsion	Nitrogen, 6–8%; phosphorus, 13%; potassium, 3–4%; trace elements	Quick acting
Horn and hoof meal	Nitrogen, 7–15%	Quick acting
Manure, cow (fresh)	Nitrogen, 0.6%; phosphorus, 0.15%; potassium, 0.45%; organic matter	Relatively low in nitrogen. Can be used directly on garden without aging
Manure, goat and sheep (dried)	Nitrogen, 2.5%; phosphorus, 1.5%; potassium, 1.5%; organic matter	Relatively high nitrogen content. Should be aged or composted at least three months before using on garden
Manure, horse (fresh)	Nitrogen, 0.7%; phosphorus, 0.25%; potassium, 0.55%; organic matter	As for goat and sheep manure
Manure, poultry (dried)	Nitrogen, 4.5%; phosphorus, 3.2%;potassium, 1.3%; low in organic matter	Very high in nitrogen. Should not be used on plants directly, as it may burn them
Manure, rabbit (fresh)	Nitrogen, 2.4%; phosphorus, 1.4%; potassium, 0.6%; organic matter	As for goat and sheep manure
Rock phosphate Seaweed (dried)	Phosphorus, 24–30% Nitrogen, 1–2%; phosphorus, 0.75%; potassium, 5%; organic matter	Slow acting, nonburning A good soil conditioner because of its high content of colloids, which retain nutrients
Sewage sludge (sterilized)	Nitrogen, 4–6%; phosphorus, 3–4%; some potassium and trace elements; organic matter	May contain heavy metals that build up in the soil over the years
Wood ashes	Phosphorus, 1–2%; potassium, 3–7%	An old time standard. Has alkaline effect on soil

Refuse into compost, quickly and easily

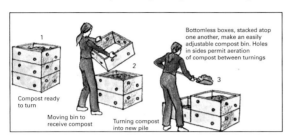

Bottomless boxes, stacked atop one another, make an easily adjustable compost bin. Holes in sides permit aeration of compost between turnings

Compost ready to turn

Moving bin to receive compost

Turning compost into new pile

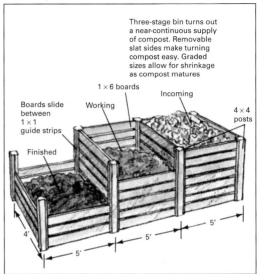

Three-stage bin turns out a near-continuous supply of compost. Removable slat sides make turning compost easy. Graded sizes allow for shrinkage as compost matures

1 × 6 boards

Boards slide between 1 × 1 guide strips

Working

Incoming

Finished

4 × 4 posts

Shredding and plenty of nitrogen are the keys to the fast 14-day method of compost making. The schedule: *1st day*. Shred the material and build pile. (Use a compost shredder or run a rotary mower over the material spread on the ground.) *2nd and 3rd days*. Check pile for heating and moisture (insert a kitchen thermometer to check temperature). If it is heating too slowly, add high nitrogen fertilizer. *4th and 7th days*. Turn pile; check temperature and moisture. *10th day*. Turn pile once more; it should be cooling off. *14th day*. Compost is ready for use.

Some easy-to-build compost bins

Screen mesh

Perforated drainpipe

Chicken wire

1 × 2 lumber

Welded wire

Sunken garbage can makes convenient compost bin when space is limited. Punch holes in bottom of can for drainage and fill with alternating layers of material. Cover with screening to keep out insects and scavengers. Perforated drainpipe in center provides aeration.

Screened compost bin is made of chicken wire and light lumber. It is easily disassembled for turning compost. Two L-shaped sections fasten with hooks and eyes. To use, simply unfasten hooks and eyes, remove sides, and set up in position to receive the turned compost. (The heap will remain standing when sides are removed.)

Wire mesh cylinder is one of the simplest of all compost bins to construct. Use mesh with heavy gauge wire; support with stakes driven into the ground. Often used for autumn leaves, it can handle any type of compost.

Rotating steel compost drum

Rotating steel drum tumbles compost each time drum is turned, mixing and aerating it. Material is loaded through a hatch. These compact, durable units are available commercially and can also be built at home using an empty oil drum and 2 × 4 lumber for frame.

the plant roots. It kills eggs and larvae of many insect pests. And it enriches the soil by turning under organic matter.

One of the oldest methods of tilling is with a spade and rake. The soil is first turned over with the spade (a broad-tined garden fork will also serve); then the rake is used to break up clods and level the surface.

Almost as old as the spade and rake is the plow, a laborsaving invention that is essentially a spade moved through the soil by man, animal, or machine. When a plow is used to till the ground, a harrow usually takes the place of a rake. There are two basic types of harrow: tooth harrows and disc harrows. A recent addition to the roster is the rotary tiller, dating from the 1950s. This motorized device combines the functions of plow and harrow and mixes the soil thoroughly.

For full-scale farming or for a very large garden (an acre or more) you will need a plow and harrow and either a tractor or draft animal to pull them. For plowing land that has been cleared of sod a small tractor of 12 to 16 horsepower may be big enough, but for breaking and plowing in sod a tractor weighing at least 1 ton and with at least 40 horsepower is necessary. It is often more practical to rent equipment or to hire someone to do the plowing and harrowing for you than to invest in expensive equipment. For an intermediate-sized garden (1/4 to 1 acre), a rotary tiller provides a good combination of high efficiency and low cost.

When tilling, go no deeper than the top 12 inches of soil. This leaves the fertile topsoil in place, where plants can utilize it. It also helps keep the soil structure, or tilth, in good condition (porous and crumbly).

The soil should be fairly dry, without any trace of muddiness or stickiness, before you work it. If the soil is worked when it is wet, soil particles will become packed together, damaging the tilth. Heavy equipment is the worst culprit in this respect, but even a man walking on the soil will cause damage if the earth is wet.

If you do not use mulch to keep the weeds down, you should till the soil lightly between rows with a rake, hoe, wheeled cultivator, or rotary tiller as the growing season

Labor savers for the garden

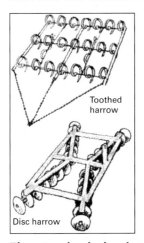

Wheeled cultivator, an old-time implement still sold by many supply houses, is valuable for cultivating between rows. Powered by hand, it gives the user more "feel" for the soil than the motorized cultivator. Rotary tiller, driven by a small gasoline engine, is meant for land that has been cleared of sod.

Device doubles as a harrow. Rotary tillers can be either bought or rented. Type with power-driven front wheels handles best.

Harrows for the farm

Toothed harrow

Disc harrow

Harrowing is done after land has been plowed. Purpose is to smooth and level the soil—the same job raking does. The toothed harrow is the simplest type. The more versatile—and usually costlier—disc harrow, which also improves soil by turning under crop residues, is widely used in commercial farming. Harrowing should be done at an angle to furrows made by the plow. Do not harrow unless soil is dry.

The standard plowing pattern

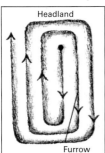

Headland

Furrow

Earth thrown off by plow should be directed to center of garden. Follow a clockwise pattern with plows that throw earth to right (as most of them do). Start at middle of one edge of field and plow from end to end. Use headlands— narrow strips of land at either end of field—for turning.

Horse vs. tractor

In recent years there has been a resurgence of interest in horses for farm work. A pair of good drafters can plow 3 acres a day. Although the rate is considerably less than a tractor's, horses provide many other benefits: they can work land too steep for a tractor, they supply manure, they are "fueled" with grasses and grains that you can raise yourself, they do not pollute the atmosphere, and they can be used for recreation and transportation. Of course, horses require daily care and skill in handling. Such massive, muscular breeds as Clydesdale, Belgian, and Percheron make the best draft horses, but any healthy horse can be used.

Contour plowing for sloping land

Plowing turns over a slice of soil with each pass of the plow, breaking up the soil as it goes. The result is the familiar pattern of ridges and furrows associated with newly plowed farmland. Hilly and sloping land should be plowed by a special technique known as contour plowing. As shown (above left), each ridge and furrow on contour plowed land stays at the same height across the slope. Such a pattern traps rainwater. letting it soak into the soil. The wrong way to plow (above right) leaves furrows running uphill and downhill. This directs the rainwater into channels made by the furrows, causing it to scour out gullies and carry off soil.

Double-digging for better soil

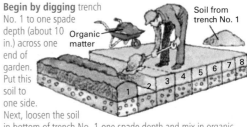

Begin by digging trench No. 1 to one spade depth (about 10 in.) across one end of garden. Put this soil to one side.

Organic matter

Soil from trench No. 1

Next, loosen the soil in bottom of trench No. 1 one spade depth and mix in organic matter. Now dig up the topsoil in trench No. 2 and use it to fill in trench No. 1; mix in organic matter and fertilizer. Continue digging and filling until you reach end of garden. Use topsoil from trench No. 1 to fill in last trench. Double-digging is hard work, so spread it over several days.

progresses. This light tilling, or cultivation, should be no deeper than 1 or 2 inches. Cultivation kills weed seedlings and reduces evaporation of water by pulverizing the soil's surface (this blocks off pores through which water vapor escapes). Cultivation also makes it easier for rainwater to soak in rather than run off.

Starting the Seeds For the Garden and for Your Table

You can gain weeks on the growing season by starting your vegetable seeds indoors, then setting out the seedlings when the danger of frost is past. Supermarkets and garden centers sell seedlings ready for planting, but serious home gardeners prefer starting their own. The cost is far lower, you can cull out all but the strongest seedlings, and you have a vastly greater choice of vegetables—typically, most outlets stock only the best-selling varieties, and some are limited to a few standbys such as tomatoes, peppers, and eggplant. Moreover, if you start your own seeds, you can be certain that no unwanted pesticides have been used. Perhaps most important, however, is the satisfaction you have of knowing that the vegetables you harvest are the products of your own labor, from seed to tabletop.

The only equipment you need to start seeds are some small containers, a suitable growing medium, and a sunny window. Vermiculite, a mineral product, is a popular growing medium because it is light, inexpensive, porous, and holds water well. Old-time gardeners often used sand, mixing it with sphagnum moss to improve its moisture-holding ability. Commercial potting compounds arc usually a mixture of vermiculite, sphagnum moss, and plant food. Compost from your compost heap is an almost ideal starting medium, but sterilize it first to kill disease organisms and insect eggs. To sterilize, bake the compost in a shallow pan in a slow oven until it reaches 180°F. You can check the temperature with a meat thermometer. Garden soil is also a satisfactory medium. It, too, must be sterilized before using it. Mix in vermiculite and sphagnum moss after sterilizing the soil in order to lighten it.

Unless the cost of seed is an important factor, do not use the tedious, old-fashioned method of starting seeds in flats (open trays) and transplanting them to pots. Instead, use small containers and sow three or four seeds in each. Although almost any small container will do, the most convenient devices in which to start seeds are peat pots, peat pellets, or fiber cubes. Since the seedlings' roots will grow right through the growing medium into the soil, there is no need to disturb the seedlings when they are set out by removing them from the container. When the true leaves appear (see opposite), cut off all but the strongest seedling in each container at soil level. Do not pull up the unwanted seedlings, as this may injure the roots of the one you want to save.

Most seeds should be started in a warm room—the kitchen is often a good choice—since the soil must be fairly warm for the seeds to germinate. You can speed germination by keeping seeds in the dark; check them daily for soil moisture and sprouting. When they have sprouted, move them into direct light.

The starting medium should be kept moist but not soggy. Excessive wetness may cause seedlings to die of damping-off, a fungus disease. A simple and efficient way to conserve moisture (and retain heat at night) is to make a mini-greenhouse by stretching plastic wrap over the seed containers. The plastic should be removed as soon as the seeds have sprouted.

When the seedlings have four to eight true leaves, they should be transplanted to the garden. If set out when older, they tend to be stunted and yield poorly. Before transplanting them, seedlings should be hardened off; that is, acclimated to outdoor conditions. About two weeks before planting time, begin putting them outdoors for short periods of time. Leave them out for about an hour the first day, gradually increasing the time until they are out all day. Protect the seedlings from the wind and do not expose them to the midday sun for the first few days. Do not feed them the last week.

Do the actual transplanting on a cloudy day or in late afternoon to avoid the drying effects of the sun. When transplanting from flats or containers with several seedlings, make sure that each seedling has as much

Homemade Starting Containers

Almost any container that is waterproof will serve for starting seeds. Yogurt cups are convenient for individual seedlings; larger containers will hold peat pellets and peat pots, or they can be used as old-fashioned flats. You can make a miniature greenhouse from a plastic milk jug, with its midsection cut out, or by rigging a plastic cover, supported on wire hoops, to fit over a plastic egg carton.

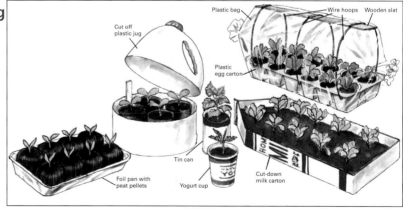

Cut off plastic jug

Plastic bag

Wire hoops   Wooden slat

Plastic egg carton

Tin can

Foil pan with peat pellets

Yogurt cup

Cut-down milk carton

From seed to seedling

Four stages in the growth of a seedling are shown below. Note the difference between seed leaves and true leaves: seedlings should be set out when four to eight true leaves appear. Seedlings do best in a window that faces south or east with at least six hours of sunlight a day; otherwise use 40-watt white fluorescent lights positioned about 6 in. above the seedlings.

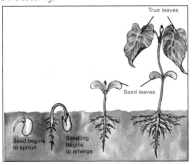

soil as possible around its roots when you remove it. (A teaspoon makes a good digger for removing seedlings.) Give each seedling a thorough watering when it is placed in the ground. Many gardeners shade their seedlings from direct sun the first few days after transplanting.

Saving Seeds for Future Use

There are two aspects to saving seeds: collecting them and storing them. Collecting seeds from your own plants is a gamble because the seeds you harvest in the fall are likely to be hybrids, or crosses, between different varieties planted nearby. These natural hybrids are unpredictable and usually inferior to the parent varieties. Many of the most popular varieties of garden vegetables produced by seed growers are specially bred hybrids (specified on the seed packet). It does not pay to save seeds from such vegetables nor from plants grown in close proximity to another variety, such as two varieties of squash that have been planted side by side.

If you decide to try your hand at harvesting seeds from your own garden, the safest course is to take seeds only from nonhybrid varieties of tomatoes, peppers, and eggplant. These vegetables are self-pollinating, and their seeds are likely to come true to type. Let the fruit become overripe on the plant. Mash it, scrape the seeds out, and let them soak in water for a day or two until they begin to ferment. Discard the pulp and the light, infertile seeds that float to the top. Dry the heavy, fertile seeds that sink to the bottom on a sheet of paper. Peas and beans are also a reasonably good risk for seed saving. Simply let the pods dry on the vine, then shell them.

Proper storage of seeds is important whether they are those you collect yourself or leftover commercial seeds from the spring planting. The key to storing seeds is to keep them dry and cool. (Moisture and warmth activate a seed's biological processes, not enough for sprouting but enough to use up the seed's food reserves.) Put seeds you have collected yourself in envelopes, label each envelope with date and vegetable type, and seal with tape. You can leave commercial seeds in their original packets; simply fold over the open end and fasten it firmly with tape, then mark each packet with the year you bought it. Place envelopes and packets in a tight container, such as a jar with an airtight top, and store them in a cool, dry location.

Sprouting Seeds for the Dinner Table

Seed sprouts, easy to grow and rich in vitamins and proteins, take only three to five days to raise. The basic techniques and equipment are simple. Seeds can be sprouted in almost any kind of household container, and the only space they require is a dark niche in a warm place, such as a kitchen cupboard.

The best-known sprouting seeds are mung bean (the sprouts are often used in Oriental dishes), soybean, and alfalfa, but many other kinds can be used including wheat, corn, barley, mustard, clover, and radish. Most health-food stores carry seeds for sprouting. Even dried peas, beans, and lentils from the grocery or supermarket make tasty, nutritious sprouts. However, you should never eat sprouts from seeds that have been sold for planting in the garden; they are generally treated with a poisonous chemical fungicide. Also avoid tomato and potato sprouts, both of which are poisonous. In addi-

Wide-mouthed jar makes a handy sprouter. Cover jar with cheesecloth held by rubber band or with wire mesh inside screw-on rim.

Rinse seeds by running water into jar and swirling it around. Method works well for small seeds, provided mesh is fine enough.

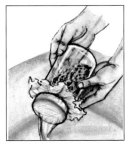

To empty rinse water, invert jar so that water drains out through mesh. Seeds should be kept constantly moist, but not wet or else they will rot.

Place sprouting jar at an angle of approximately 45° inside a large bowl to allow excess moisture to drain from sprouts between each rinsing.

The usable lifetime of common seeds

Vegetable	Yr.	Vegetable	Yr.	Vegetable	Yr.
Beans	3	Eggplant	4	Pumpkin	4
Beets	3	Kale	3	Radishes	3
Cabbage	4	Lettuce	4	Spinach	3
Carrots	1	Melons	4	Squash	4
Cauliflower	4	Onions	1	Swiss chard	4
Corn, sweet	2	Peas	1	Tomatoes	3
Cucumbers	5	Peppers	2	Turnips	5

tion, the seed sprouts of many ornamental flowers, foliage plants, and wild plants are poisonous.

The first step in sprouting is to measure out the seeds. With most seeds 1/4 cup will yield 1 to 2 cups of sprouts—enough for four average servings. Rinse the seeds thoroughly in a sieve or strainer, then soak them overnight in cool water. Allow at least four times as much water as seeds, since the seeds will absorb a great deal of moisture. The following morning, drain the seeds and place them in a clean, sterile sprouting container, such as a bowl, wide-mouthed jar, or flowerpot. Keep the seeds damp—not wet—and allow air to reach them. A shallow layer of seeds in a wide container is better than a deep layer in a narrow container.

Very small seeds, such as alfalfa and clover, are more easily sprouted on a moist paper towel than in a jar. Place the towel in a shallow bowl or dish, sprinkle the presoaked seeds onto it, and cover lightly with another paper towel. Sprinkle water over the towels from time to time to keep the seeds moist. For added flavor, give alfalfa and clover sprouts a few hours of light on the last day of sprouting.

Seeds should be rinsed in a strainer twice daily in cold water when they are sprouting. Discard any that are not sprouting properly, drain the rest, and return them to the container. The seed hulls should come off and float away during the last few rinses. Chickpeas and soybeans should be rinsed four to six times a day.

Most seeds sprout well at room temperature (60°F to 80°F); soybeans and chickpeas do best at about 50°F. For use in salads most sprouts should be 1 to 1 1/2 inches long. Peas and lentil sprouts should be the length of the seed. As a general rule, the bigger the seed, the shorter the sprout should be for maximum flavor and tenderness. Sprouts are best when eaten fresh but will keep four to six days in the refrigerator.

Damp paper towel is excellent for sprouting small seeds.

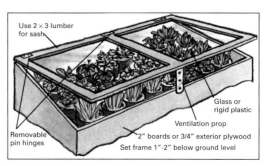

Cold frames are simple and inexpensive to build. Tailor the dimensions to fit your own needs or components at hand.

A window greenhouse

Window greenhouse at left is made out of an old storm window. (You can also make your own storm window or buy one.) Sides and floor are 3/4 in. exterior plywood fastened to the sash with 1 × 1 strips. Seal all edges with caulking compound. House heat helps keep plants warm.

Secure corners of sash with glue and dowels or with nails; reinforce with corner braces.

Trapping the Sun for Winter Farming

Cold frames, hotbeds, and greenhouses are devices for trapping the sun's energy to grow plants in cold weather. The cold frame is the simplest of the three. Basically, it consists of a bottomless box with a movable top cover of glass. Sunlight passes through the transparent top, strikes the walls and soil inside, and is converted into heat. Most of the heat waves, however, will not pass back out through the glass and are trapped inside. This is known as the greenhouse effect. Transparent plastic can be substituted for glass.

The versatile cold frame has several uses. It can be used for starting seeds in spring or for hardening seedlings that have been started indoors. In fall and winter it can provide a steady supply of such cold-tolerant crops as lettuce, spinach, and cabbage. And by adding a source of warmth, such as an electric heater cable, a cold frame is quickly converted into a hotbed for starting seedlings of tender crops even in cold weather.

When building a cold frame, make the back several inches higher than the front so that the top is tilted. This, allows rain and melting snow to drain off and helps capture more rays from the low-angled winter sun.

For starting or hardening seedlings in a cold frame, it is easiest to have the seedlings in separate containers. For raising fall or winter vegetables dig out the bed of the cold frame to a depth of 4 to 6 inches and fill it in with good garden soil enriched with compost or manure.

A cold frame should face south for maximum exposure to winter sun. If this is not possible, east is the next choice, then west. The ideal temperature inside the cold frame is 65°F to 75°F during the day and 55°F to 65°F at night. Keep an inexpensive outdoor thermometer in a shaded spot inside the frame for quick reference.

On sunny spring days raise the sash for ventilation or the temperature may rise to a point that kills delicate seedlings. Do not forget to close the sash at night. On cold nights cover the glass with hay, burlap, or an old blanket to retain warmth. In wet weather add an additional cover of waterproof material, such as a canvas tarpaulin or sheet of plastic.

A typical cold-frame measures about 3 feet by 6 feet and is 9 inches high in front and 15 inches high in back. When building a frame, the best lumber to use is a rot-resistant species such as redwood or cypress, but most woods can serve if they are treated with copper naphthenate, a wood preservative that is not toxic to plants. (The commonly used wood preservatives creosote and pentachlorophenol are both toxic to plants and should be avoided.) For the top, glass is most durable, but fiberglass is a close second. Plastic film is cheap but short lived. Old storm windows make an economical and laborsaving cover. In fact, almost any kind of window can be recycled into a serviceable cold-frame top; some economy-minded gardeners even use old window screens with plastic film tacked to them. When constructing a cold frame out of old parts, it is a simple matter to tailor the dimensions of the frame to fit what is available.

Converting a Cold Frame Into a Hotbed

The simplest way to convert a cold frame into a hotbed is to install an electric heating cable equipped with a thermostat. Cables specially designed for this purpose are sold by many garden-supply centers and mail-order houses. First dig out the soil inside the cold frame to a depth of 1 foot. Put in a 4-inch layer of coarse gravel for drainage and lay the heating cable on this. Note:

For safety and compliance with the law, make certain that your installation conforms to all local regulations governing outdoor electrical installations. Lay the heating cable in long, parallel U-shaped loops and cover it with 1/2-inch galvanized wire mesh to protect it from gardening tools. Over this goes 2 inches of builder's sand and then 6 inches of topsoil or planting medium. If you plan to plant in containers rather than soil, omit the planting medium. On sunny days the hotbed must be ventilated just like a cold frame.

You can heat a hotbed without electricity by using the warmth of fermenting organic matter. Dig a pit 3 feet deep inside the frame and fill it with a 2 1/2-foot layer of straw-rich horse manure or raw compost with a generous dose of nitrogen to speed bacterial action. Wet the organic material thoroughly and cover it with a foot of soil. It will heat up rapidly. Put in seeds or seedlings when the soil temperature drops to 75°F. The warming effect should last for several weeks.

A Do-it-yourself Greenhouse

A greenhouse is basically a giant cold frame designed to hold large numbers of plants, including ones of considerable size. In most parts of the United States greenhouses are equipped with heating devices so that even tender crops such as tomatoes and peppers can be raised in the coldest months. Greenhouses also need shading devices to protect the plants on hot, sunny days.

Ideally a greenhouse should face south to get maximum winter sunlight. If this is not possible, the next best choice is east (plants benefit from morning light). A western exposure is also satisfactory, but vegetables will not grow in a north-facing greenhouse.

Greenhouses can be bought or built in an almost infinite variety of sizes and designs, from a geodesic dome to a simple lean-to. Greenhouse manufacturers sell complete kits that the home handyman can assemble, but for economy and personal satisfaction many gardeners prefer to build their own from scratch. The simple greenhouse shown here is an economical design that uses materials available at local lumberyards.

Cross section shows construction details of rooftop vent.

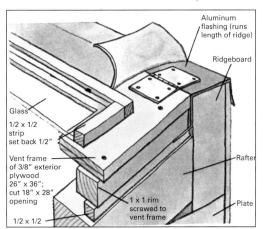

You can convert a cold frame into a hotbed using materials readily available at hardware stores and garden centers.

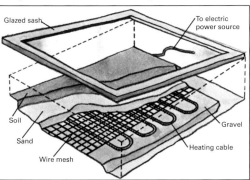

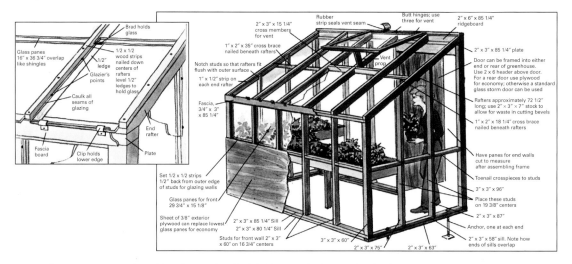

Roof panes are 16 in. wide, 36 3/4 in. long, and made of double-strength glass to reduce breakage. For the walls use ordinary window glass. The roof panes overlap like shingles and should be bedded in caulking compound to prevent water leaks and drafts. Secondhand windows or storm windows, which can be obtained from housewreckers, may be used for the walls. In this case, the studs will be farther apart, and you will need to add a 2- by 6-in. board beneath the front wall plate for reinforcement.

The plans show a freestanding unit with a rear wall of weather-resistant exterior-grade plywood. The greenhouse can also be adapted to a lean-to design by butting the rear wall against the side of the house.

Note, however, that if the greenhouse is attached to the house in a region where winter temperatures drop below freezing, a concrete foundation should be laid that extends below the frost line. Otherwise frost heaving can distort the greenhouse's frame and cause glass breakage, structural damage, and even damage to your home.

If it is freestanding, the greenhouse can rest directly on the ground or on a base of 2-inch-thick patio blocks or 8-inch-thick concrete blocks. The sills should be of rot-resistant redwood or else treated with wood preservative, especially if the greenhouse rests on patio blocks or on the ground. The floor need not be paved.

In windy areas the greenhouse should be secured to a permanent foundation or else anchored to the ground. For anchors use rods extending through the sills to 4-inch-square steel plates buried 18 inches in the soil.

From Seed to Harvest: A Grower's Guide to Garden Favorites

Home gardeners today can choose from a greater selection of vegetables than ever before. A typical seed catalog offers more than 30 varieties of tomatoes, ranging from the tiny cocktail type to 1-pound giants, from genetically engineered hybrids to old favorites like Ponderosa and Rutgers. With so many special varieties available, you can grow virtually any vegetable you want no matter what the soil type, how long the growing season, or how arid or humid the climate.

The guide that follows provides the basic information needed to select, grow, and harvest all the standard vegetables. Suggestions are given on how many to plant. They are based on Department of Agriculture recommendations and do not take account of personal tastes. When a vegetable is suitable for canning or other home preserving, an extra quantity has been allowed.

In addition to the detailed information given for each vegetable, there are a few general pointers to follow if you want a bountiful harvest. One of the most important is to leave ample space between plants. A vegetable needs enough room so it can get its share of sunlight, water, and nutrients: it is better to raise two good heads of lettuce than three runty, undernourished ones.

Another point to bear in mind is that many pests and diseases attack all members of a plant family—not just one particular species. For this reason, you should not plant members of the same family in the same spot in the garden two years in a row. The three major groups of related vegetables are: (1) tomatoes, peppers, and eggplant; (2) cabbage, broccoli, cauliflower, radishes, turnips, rutabagas, kohlrabi, and mustard; and (3) melons, cucumbers, gourds, and summer and winter squash.

Also note the following when using the guide:

Days to harvest refers to the length of time between when a plant is set out in the garden and when it is ready to harvest. It does not include the number of days a plant grows indoors after being started from seed.

Planting depth is an approximate guide. If in doubt, it is best to err on the shallow side. A handy rule is to plant the seed three times as deep as its size.

Planting in hills, in modern parlance, means planting seeds in small, compact groups. Years ago, a hill was literally that—a low mound of enriched soil.

Asparagus. A hardy perennial that yields edible spears (young shoots) in spring and early summer. A well-managed asparagus bed will be productive for 20–25 years. Since asparagus needs a

period of cold for dormancy and resting, it does poorly in areas that are warm the year round. Asparagus can be started from seed, but the usual practice is to set out year-old roots in early spring or late fall. Start about 10 to 15 plants for each member of your family. The roots are planted in trenches 4–5 ft. apart. Dig the trenches 18 in. wide and 12 in. deep. Loosen the soil at the bottom and mix well with manure, compost, or fertilizer, then cover the bottom of the trench with 4–6 in. of good soil and rake level. Set the asparagus roots on this soil 18 in. apart. Cover them with soil up to the top of the trench; if there is any extra soil it may be mounded over the top. An older technique is to barely cover the roots and fill in the trench gradually as the shoots grow. Mulch is recommended for keeping the asparagus bed free of weeds because the roots are shallow, and deep cultivation can injure the roots. Do not harvest the first spring. The next year, harvest lightly (for about two weeks). Thereafter, you may harvest freely until the spears become spindly, a sign that the roots are becoming exhausted. The harvesting season lasts six to eight weeks. Spears are ready to pick when they are tight, smooth, and about 6–8 in. tall. When they start to open up they are too old. Harvest by cutting or breaking the spears at ground level. Any surplus can be frozen or canned for an out-of-season treat.

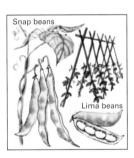

Snap beans

Lima beans

Beans. A warm-weather crop of tropical origin. Lima beans and snap (string) beans are the most popular types in American gardens. Each is available in pole varieties (requiring support) or in low-growing bush varieties. Limas are especially sensitive to cold and need a longer, warmer growing season than snap beans. Lima beans should be planted when all risk of frost is past. (Some gardeners get a jump on the season by starting limas indoors two to three weeks before the last frost date.) For bush limas, plant seeds 1 in. deep and 2 in. apart in rows 2 ft. apart. Thin later to 8 in. between plants. For pole varieties set poles 3 ft. apart in rows 4 ft. apart. Plant about six seeds per pole and thin to three or four seedlings. About 5–6 ft. of bush limas (or 2–4 ft. of pole limas) per person is ample. Supply plenty of water in hot weather. Harvest when seeds begin to plump out the pods. Pick frequently to keep plants productive. Days to harvest: 70–90. For use as dried beans let limas mature and dry on the plants. Lima beans are also excellent for freezing and canning. Snap beans are a high-yielding crop that is excellent for freezing and canning. Sow when soil is warm, after last frost date. Some gardeners gamble by planting an early batch about a week before the last expected frost. Plant bush varieties 1/2–1 in. deep, 2 in. apart, and thin to 4 in. apart. For pole varieties set poles 3 ft. apart in rows 3–4 ft. apart Plant six seeds per pole and thin later to the four strongest seedlings. You will need 5–6 ft. of bush beans or 3–6 ft. of pole beans per person. Harvest when beans are young and tender (3–4 in. long). For continuous yield plant a short row every week or 10 days, or select a variety that keeps bearing till frost. Wax beans, which are yellow instead of green, are a kind of snap bean and need the same culture. Days to harvest: 50–60 for bush varieties, 60–65 for pole varieties.

Beets. An easy-to-grow, dual purpose crop: both roots and greens (leaves) can be eaten. Beets are quite frost hardy and can be planted in spring as soon as the soil is ready to work. They do well in most types of soil except those that are highly acid. Plant 1/2 in. deep, 1 in. apart in rows 18 in. apart. Allow 3–5 ft. of row per person for the average family. Thin to 2–3 in. apart. For a fall crop, plant in late June or early July. Harvest when roots are 1–3 in. in diameter (pull up one or two to check). Beets that grow larger become tough and woody. Days to harvest: 50–70. The vitamin-rich greens may be cooked and eaten like spinach. In the warmer parts of the nation beets are often sown in early fall for a winter crop.

Broccoli. A member of the cabbage group raised for its flower buds, which are eaten before they open. (Broccoli is not edible after it goes to seed.) Broccoli prefers cool weather and can stand light frost. It will not bear in hot weather. In very mild areas it can be grown in winter. Start broccoli indoors about six weeks before the average date of the last spring frost; set out in garden two weeks before the last expected frost date. Allow three to five plants per person. Space plants 15–18 in. apart in rows 2 1/2–3 ft. apart. Harvest while flower buds are tight and heads compact. Cut off about 6 in. below the head so as not to waste the tender, edible upper stem. After the center heads (the first to develop) are cut, side shoots will develop additional heads. One plant yields six to eight cuttings over a period of 8–10 weeks. Days to harvest: 55–60, 75 for fall crops. For a fall harvest sow directly in the garden around midsummer. Broccoli retains its flavor and texture well when frozen, and it is an excellent source of vitamins A and C.

Cabbage. A cool-weather crop that can be raised for spring or fall harvest. Cabbage is a good source of vitamin C and keeps well in winter. Types include the familiar green cabbage, the mild-flavored, crinkly-leafed savoy, and the colorful red cabbage. A heavy feeder, cabbage needs a rich, nearly neutral soil that contains plenty of organic matter. For spring cabbage start seeds indoors about six to eight weeks before the last expected frost. Transplant to the garden after danger of frost is past—cabbage seedlings exposed to frost or cold grow slowly and tend to be fibrous and tough. Allow two to three plants per person for the average family. Plants should be spaced 12–18 in. apart in rows 2–3 ft. apart. For fall crops start seeds indoors in May and set out after midsummer, or sow directly in the garden June to August–the milder the winter, the later you should sow. For direct sowing plant seeds in groups of three or four, 1/2 in. deep at 1-ft. intervals in the rows; thin later to the one strongest seedling. Cabbage thrives with an insulating mulch of hay or straw to keep the soil cool. Harvest cabbage when the heads are tight and full. Days to harvest: 50–90. Fall cabbage develops larger heads and—many people think—better flavor than spring cabbage. Several soil-borne diseases attack cabbage and its close relatives, such as broccoli, cauliflower, and turnips. To avoid infection, do not plant any member of the cabbage family in soil where any of them has been grown in the last two years.

Cantaloupe. An orange-fleshed melon with a netted exterior. Cantaloupe (a kind of muskmelon) needs a long, warm growing season and full exposure to the sun. Early-maturing dwarf varieties are recommended for northern gardens. Since cold is bad for melons (cool temperatures and rain lower the quantity of sugar), they should not be planted until dependably warm weather, several weeks after the last frost. Like other melons, cantaloupes do best in sandy soil with plenty of manure and compost mixed in. To plant in rows, sow seeds 1/2 in. deep, 4–6 in. apart in rows 5 ft. apart and thin to 18–24 in. apart. Alternatively, plant three to a hill, with the hills 5 ft. apart each way. Figure on about four fruits per plant. In colder regions start the melons indoors three to four weeks ahead of planting time. Melons need ample water while the fruits are growing, but during the final ripening stage limiting the water is said to increase their sweetness. Cantaloupes are ready to pick when the fruit separates from the stem with a slight pull. Days to harvest: 60–90. If any fruits form after midsummer, pick them off the vine; they will not ripen and will take food from the others.

Carrots. One of the old standbys, high in vitamin A and with many culinary uses. Carrots are a hardy vegetable that can be planted in spring as soon as the soil can be worked. Since the seeds are slow to germinate, it is helpful to plant radish seeds along with them to mark the row. The radishes will be ready to harvest about the time the carrots start coming up. Carrots do best in rich, deep, sandy loam but will grow well in almost any soil that has been properly prepared. Dig up the soil to a depth of at least 1 ft., loosen it, and remove stones and other debris. This will allow the downward-growing carrot roots to develop properly. Heavy clay soils often cause carrots to fork. Lighten such soils by working in a goodly proportion of sand or humus. Sow carrot seeds 1/4–1/2 in. deep, 15 to 20 seeds to the inch in rows 16–24 in. apart. Allow 4–5 ft. of row per person. Thin the seedlings to 2 in. apart when they are 2–4 in. high or when the roots are about as thick as your little finger (pull up a few carrots to check root size). The tender baby carrots that have been thinned out make delicious eating. The remaining carrots may be harvested at any time, depending on how large you want them. Keep the soil moist until the seedlings have come up. For a fall crop sow in the garden in early July. Carrots keep well in the refrigerator or in winter storage.

Cauliflower. A "luxury" member of the cabbage group that is difficult for beginners to grow successfully. Cauliflower needs rich soil and constant moisture for best development. It is sensitive to heat, requiring a long, cool growing season to produce good heads. Cauliflower does best as a fall crop in most areas. For a fall crop, seeds may be sown directly in the garden in June or July, 8–10 weeks before the first expected autumn frost date for your locality. Plant seeds three or four together, 1/2 in. deep and 18–24 in. apart and thin to the strongest single seedling.

For a spring crop start indoors in February or March and set out a week before the last average frost date. Plants should be no older than six weeks when set out. Set seedlings 18 in. apart in rows 30 in. apart. Allow two to three plants per person. When heads are about 3 in. across, they should be blanched—that is, the leaves should be tied over them (this will produce white heads). Harvest while heads are compact and fairly smooth (two to four weeks after tying up, depending on the weather). Days to harvest: 50–95, depending on variety. In addition to the standard white cauliflower, seed houses offer a purple-headed variety that turns green when cooked.

Celery. One of the trickier plants for the home gardener to raise. Celery is very sensitive to both cold and heat and requires a growing season of four months. Consequently, it must be started indoors in March or April and set out in the garden between June 15 and July 15. Plants should be 6 in. apart in rows 18–24 in. apart. Celery needs a constantly moist soil very rich in organic matter; muck soils are the best. For maximum growth celery should be fertilized every two weeks. Celery stalks are naturally green but can be blanched (whitened) by various means. You can hill up dirt around the plants, place boards along the sides of the rows, or cover the plants with drain tiles, paper, or mulch. Blanching is not recommended for the home garden because of the extra space required and the danger of rot. Days to harvest: 115–135. Note: Celery may be harvested before fully mature. While celery is primarily raised for its crunchy stalks, the nutty root, or "heart," is a delicacy. The leaves are used for flavoring soups and stews.

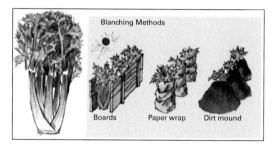

Blanching Methods

Boards   Paper wrap   Dirt mound

Collards. A loose-leafed relative of the cabbage. A traditional southern favorite, collards thrive in almost every section of the country. They are an excellent source of vitamin A. Collards tolerate cold as low as 15°F, and frost actually improves their flavor. They also tolerate hot summers better than cabbage and will grow in relatively poor soil. In areas with short, cool summers sow collards in late spring. Elsewhere, sow them in midsummer for a fall  crop. Plant seeds 1/2 in. deep and 1 in. apart in rows 24–30 in. apart. Allow 5–10 ft. of row per person. Thin so plants are 18–24 in. apart along the rows; the thinnings can be used as greens. Harvest by clipping the young leaves, including the stems. Be sure to leave six to eight leaves on the plant: they are needed to sustain growth. Do not harvest the central growing point or you will have to wait for side shoots to form to provide new leaves. Days to harvest: 75–80. In the Deep South collards are grown through the winter to furnish fresh greens. Collards can be eaten raw in salads or cooked in a variety of traditional methods, particularly as an accompaniment to ham or pork. The flavor is similar to that of cabbage but richer.

Corn. A space-consuming crop but well worth growing for its fresh-picked sweetness. Corn needs a long, warm growing season, plenty of water, and rich soil. Varieties of sweet corn (the sort grown for the dinner table) include yellow, white, and bicolored kinds, dwarf strains for the small garden, and quick-maturing hybrids for regions that have a short growing season. Plant in either rows or hills. For rows sow seeds 1 in. deep, 4 in. apart in rows 30 in. apart, and thin later to 8–12 in. For hills plant three to four seeds per hill, 2–3 ft. apart. Old-time gardeners always planted extra seeds to allow for destruction by birds, bugs, and other pests. Corn should not be planted until the soil is warm and all danger of frost is past. Harvest when the silk of the ears turns dark brown and the kernels spurt milky juice when pressed with a fingernail. Each plant will produce one or two ears of corn. Corn is best when picked just before eating; once off the plant, the sugar in the kernels turns to starch, making the corn tough and pasty. Days to harvest: 62–94, depending on variety and weather.For a continuous harvest, plant successively maturing varieties at the same time or plant successive batches of the same variety at 7-to 10-day intervals. Since corn is pollinated by the wind, it should be planted in compact blocks rather than long, thin rows. A block should have at least three rows to ensure pollination. Weed every week until the seedlings are tall enough to shade out weeds, or mulch when the corn is 3–4 in. tall. Corn plants often produce suckers–smaller extra stalks that do not bear ears. Old-time farmers removed the suckers, thinking them useless, but modern practice is to leave them, as they provide additional food for the plant and the growing ears. Popcorn and the colorful Indian corn should be planted at least 300 ft. from sweet corn to avoid cross-pollination—corn is one of the few plants in which cross-pollination affects the current year's crop. Hybrid varieties should also be planted separately from other strains of corn.

Cowpeas. A favorite in the South. Cowpeas (also known as blackeyed peas or field peas) can be grown successfully in most sections of the country. Actually a type of bean, they can be eaten green or dried. Cowpeas need a long growing season with warm days and nights; the slightest touch of frost damages them. Sow when soil is warm and all danger of frost is past. Plant seeds 1/2–1 in. deep, 2 in. apart in rows 24–36 in. apart. Thin to 4–6 in. apart. Days to harvest: 85–90. A 10-to 15-ft. row will probably be enough for four people. Cowpeas come in varieties with green, white, or brown seeds.

Cucumbers. Not the easiest vegetable to grow but a good yielder with a long harvesting season. Sow outdoors when soil is warm and danger of frost is past. Plant seeds 1/2–1 in. deep, 4–6 in. apart in rows 5 ft. apart; thin 12–15 in. to give the vines room to grow. Cucumbers can also be planted in hills 5 ft. apart each way, 5 to 10 seeds per hill; thin later to three to four plants per hill. For a headstart plant seeds indoors four to eight weeks before the last frost date. Three to six plants should produce enough for the average family. For large-scale pickle making the Department of Agriculture recommends three to five hills per person. Cucumbers

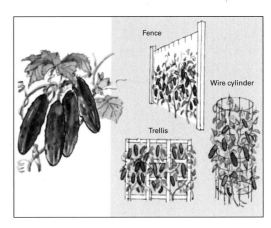

Fence

Wire cylinder

Trellis

need ample moisture and do best in a deep, rich, neutral soil. Well-rotted manure mixed into the soil is helpful. Plants should be watered throughout the growing season: insufficient water results in undersized, misshapen fruits. Mulching helps retain soil moisture and protects fruits by keeping them off the soil. Cucumber vines are eager climbers and may be trained on poles, fences, frameworks, or wire netting. These methods of saving space are preferable for the small garden. Some cucumbers are bred for pickling, others for salad use. The difference is mainly in size and shape; in other respects pickling cucumbers are perfectly good in salads, and salad varieties make fine pickles. Pick salad cucumbers when 6–9 in. long; harvest pickling types at whatever size is convenient. Note, however, that cucumbers must be picked before they turn yellow—at this stage the seeds harden and the fruit loses flavor. Keeping the vines picked stimulates them to produce until frost kills them; the presence of big, ripe cukes on the vines halts fruit production. Days to harvest: 50–70, depending on variety.
Each cucumber vine bears separate male and female flowers (except for certain all-female hybrids). No fruits are produced until the female flowers appear (identifiable by a tiny cucumber beneath the blossom). Since the vines grow from the tip only, do not break their tips off, as this will stop their growth. To avoid spreading disease, do not handle the vines or harvest the fruits when they are wet. Despite old wives' tales to the contrary, cucumbers do not cross with squash and melons.

Eggplant. A native of India related to the tomato and the sweet pep per. It is a staple of Middle Eastern cooking. The eggplant needs a long, warm growing season and will not sprout unless the soil is warmer than 75°F. Most gardening books recommend buying started seedlings.
Eggplant can be started indoors in warm soil 8–10 weeks before the last frost. Set in the garden 2–3 ft. apart in rows 3–4 ft. apart. Three to six plants yield an adequate supply for the average family. Eggplant can tolerate drought better than most vegetables. Harvest while fruit is plump and glossy; when it loses its sheen it is overripe and will taste bitter. Eggplant produces until frost. Days to harvest: 65–75.

Kale. A nonheading member of the cabbage family often grown for its ornamental, curly foliage as well as for the dinner table. It is a good source of vitamin C and thiamin. Kale can tolerate summer heat and is extremely cold hardy. It can be raised as a spring or fall crop. Sow in spring as soon as soil can be worked, 1/4 in. deep, 1

in. apart in rows 20 in. apart; thin to 12 in. between plants. About 5 ft. of row per person should furnish an adequate supply. For fall and early winter harvesting sow in midsummer. Harvest by taking entire plant or by cutting the outer leaves only, leaving the inner ones to develop. Days to harvest: 60–70, depending on variety. Kale can be covered with straw or burlap and kept fresh and green in the garden until very cold weather. South of Virginia, this protection is usually not necessary.

Kohlrabi. A cold-resistant member of the cabbage group raised for its turniplike, bulbous stem. Kohlrabi makes a good crop for both spring and fall. Sow in early spring as soon as the ground can be worked, 1/4 in. deep and 1 in. apart in rows 18–24 in. apart; thin to 3–4 in. apart. About 5 ft. of row per person should be sufficient for the average family. Kohlrabi can be eaten either raw for snacks and salads or cooked.
For a fall harvest sow in July or August. Harvest when the bulbs reach 2–3 in. in diameter. When larger, they become stringy and lose flavor. Days to harvest: 55–60.

Bibb

Iceberg

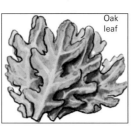
Oak leaf

Lettuce. A cool-weather crop available in either head or looseleaf types and in many varieties of each. All varieties will provide a bountiful harvest of salad greens until summer heat stimulates the plants to flower, which makes them tough and bitter. Lettuce can also be sown in late summer for a fall crop. Lettuce is one of the easiest vegetables to raise from seed. Sow thinly in early spring, 1/4 in. deep in rows 16 in. apart. Thin gradually to 12 in. between plants for loose-leaf types, 16–18 in. for head types. (Head lettuce is often started indoors in flats and set out when the soil is ready to work.) Allow 4–5 ft. of row per person. Thin ruthlessly—lettuce needs a lot of room to grow in. Thinnings may be transplanted or used thriftily in a garden-fresh salad. To be tender and free from bitterness, lettuce should grow quickly. It needs plenty of water and nitrogen. To keep leaf lettuce producing for a maximum length of time, harvest only the outer leaves so that the plant continuously produces new leaves for use. With head lettuce the entire head must be harvested. Head lettuce is more sensitive to heat than is loose-leaf lettuce. The growing season for both types can often be prolonged by planting them in a partly shaded area of the garden.

Days to harvest: 40–83. For a fall crop sow in August. Lettuce seeds will not sprout when the soil temperature is more than 80°F, but they can be forced to germinate by chilling them in the refrigerator in damp peat moss and sand for five days.

Mustard. Another southern favorite that can be raised anywhere that radishes will grow. Esteemed for its pungent green leaves, mustard is a fast-growing, frost-hardy, cool-season crop. Sow in spring as soon as the soil can be worked, 1/2 in. deep and 1–2 in. apart in rows 16 in. apart. A 20- to 25-ft. row provides ample supplies of mustard greens for the average family. Thin the plants to 4–6 in. apart. Harvest when leaves are 3–4 in. long (sooner if you like). Snap or cut off the leaves, leaving the growing point to produce more. For a fall crop sow in August or September. In areas with mild winters mustard can be grown for a winter supply of fresh greens. Days to harvest: 25–50. Pulverize the seeds, and mix with water to make fresh old-time mustard.

Seeds

Okra. A tall warm-weather plant related to hibiscus and cotton that is raised for its edible pods. Although considered a southern vegetable, okra may, with luck, be grown as far north as southern Canada. It thrives in almost any fertile, well-drained soil. Sow when soil is thoroughly warm, 1/2–1 in. deep and 18 in. apart in rows 3 ft. apart. To speed germination, soak the seeds in water overnight. Plant three or four seeds at each spot; when seedlings are 1 in. tall, remove all but one. Allow three or four plants per person. Okra may also be started indoors about a month before the last expected frost date. Harvest pods when they are 3 or 4 in. long or three to four days after the blossom petals fall off. For best flavor pick just before cooking. For continued production keep the pods picked. Days to harvest: 55–60. Okra is used in stews and in soups, especially the famous gumbo of New Orleans.

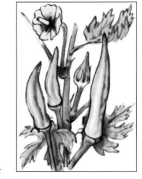

Onions. Hardy members of the lily family raised for their pungent bulbs. Onions do best in loose, fertile soil. They are heavy feeders, so the soil should be enriched by digging in manure or compost before planting time. Onions may be raised from seed, from immature bulbs called sets, or from young plants. Because onions have a long growing season, home gardeners generally prefer sets or plants over seeds. Whatever the choice, onions can be planted as soon as the soil can be worked. Place sets or plants 1 in. deep

Young transplants
Ready to harvest
Young onions

and 4 in. apart in rows 12 in. apart. If grown from seed, thin seedlings to 3–4 in. apart when they are 3 in. tall. The thinnings can be used as young green onions or transplanted. Allow 4–5 ft. of row per person for average use. Days to harvest: 80-110 from seed, 50–60 if sets or young plants are used. To harvest onions for storage, bend the tops down to the ground when they start to go yellow. After the tops turn brown, pull up the onions and spread them out to dry for a week (longer if the weather is damp). Then braid the tops together and hang the onions indoors to store; or cut tops off an inch above the bulbs and store the onions in mesh bags or shallow open boxes in a cool, airy place. They should keep from two to four months.

Parsnips. A slow-growing relative of the carrot; resembles a large white carrot. Parsnips do best in fertile, loamy soils. Heavy clay soils and stony soils distort and toughen the roots. Sow seeds in spring as soon as the soil can be worked. Since they may take several weeks to germinate, mark the row with radishes, which will be ready to pull when the parsnip seedlings emerge. Loosen the soil to a depth of 12 in. to let the roots grow properly. Plant seeds thickly 1/4 in. deep in rows 18 in. apart. Thin to 3–4 in. apart. Allow 4–5 ft. of row per person.

Parsnips can either be dug (not pulled) in fall and stored in damp sand, or they can be left in the ground for use as needed throughout the winter. Freezing temperatures improve their naturally sweet flavor. Days to harvest: about 100.

Peas. A cool-weather crop with both bush and tall (requiring support) varieties. Green peas (known in the South as English peas) are raised for their immature seeds. Snow peas, or sugar-pod peas, are eaten pod and all when very young. Peas do well in most kinds of soil as long as it contains plenty of organic matter. Plant peas in spring as soon as the soil can be worked. Dig in compost, manure, or other organic matter. Plant seeds 1–2 in. deep, 1 in. apart in rows 3 ft. apart. If you plant double rows (8–12 in. wide), allow 40 in. between rows. Many authorities recommend planting peas in a shallow trench, which is filled in with soil as the pea vines grow, but this is not necessary. Give peas plenty of water. Mulch to retain water and keep soil cool. Allow about 10 ft. of row per person. Tall-growing varieties should be supported on branches or brush stuck in the ground when the vines begin to get bushy. They can also be trained on wire, twine, or netting strung between stakes. Dwarf, or bush, varieties can be grown without support but are easier to care for and harvest if supported. Pick green peas when the pods are well filled but the peas inside are not hard. Pick snow peas when the pods are just beginning to plump out. All peas are at their best if cooked within a few hours after picking. If left too long on the vine, peas become tough and unappetizing, so check the vines every couple of days. However, if you wish to dry peas for storage, let them mature on the vine until they are completely hard, then remove from vine, shell, and dry them in an oven at low heat. They make a hearty pea soup. Peas are also excellent for freezing fresh. Days to harvest: 55–78, depending on variety. In areas with above-freezing winters peas can be sown from midsummer on for a fall or winter crop.

Peppers. A frost-tender crop that needs a long, warm growing season. In their tropical home pepper plants are perennials and reach the size of small trees. In the mainland United States they are raised as annuals and grow about 2 ft. tall. There are sweet and hot types of peppers. All varieties have much the same cultural requirements as tomatoes, to which they are related. They do best on a slightly acid soil with full sun and plenty of moisture. For most areas of the United States peppers should be started indoors about eight weeks before the last expected frost date and set out in the garden when the soil is warm. The plants should be 18–24 in. apart in rows 24–36 in. apart. Three to five plants per person are sufficient. The fruits of both sweet and hot peppers may be harvested at any stage of growth. Sweet peppers, also known as green or bell peppers, turn red or yellow at maturity. At this stage they are sweeter. Some hot peppers turn red or yellow soon after the fruits are formed. Be careful when picking peppers: the plants are brittle, and you may end up with a whole branch in your hand instead of a fruit. You can avoid the problem by cutting the fruits off, not picking them.

Peppers are temperamental plants. They set fruit only when nighttime temperatures are between 60° and 70°F. If they do not get enough moisture, they drop blossoms and fruits. However, under favorable conditions they bear plentifully. Sweet peppers are rich in vitamin C and freeze well; hot peppers can be stored by stringing them up and letting them dry. In fall sweet peppers can be kept for two to three weeks by pulling up the entire plant and hanging it, roots uppermost, in a cool (but not freezing) indoor location. Pepper plants can be grown indoors in pots in wintertime or where garden space is limited.

Hybrid bell pepper

Pimiento

Cubanelle

Sweet banana

California Wonder

Cherry

Cayenne

Hot red

Sweet red

Common long red

Potatoes. One of the world's major food crops. Native to the bleak Andean highlands of South America, the potato is related to the eggplant, pepper, and tomato. Though killed by frost, potatoes do best in cool weather. They thrive in light, sandy, acid soil. If you can spare the space in your garden (potato plants are sprawling and take up a good deal of room), potatoes are well worth planting for the rewards of tender, young new potatoes or full-sized tubers from your own soil. Potatoes can be raised from sets (small tubers) or seed potatoes (medium-sized tubers specially bred for propagation). A set is used whole; seed potatoes are cut into pieces about the size of a small hen's egg, each containing one or more eyes. Potatoes sold in food markets are not recommended as

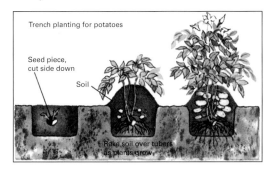

Trench planting for potatoes

Seed piece, cut side down

Soil

Rake soil over tubers as plants grow

seed pieces—they are often contaminated with disease, and many are treated with chemicals that inhibit them from sprouting. If you are using seed potatoes, spread the seed pieces on a clean surface and allow the cut surfaces to dry out for 1 to 10 days. This permits the cut surfaces to heal over and reduces the chance of infection from decay organisms. The seed pieces can be dusted with a fungicide for further protection. Potatoes should be planted in spring as soon as the soil can be worked–if late frosts are common in your area, plant them about three weeks before the last expected frost. Plant sets or seed pieces 3 in. deep and 12–18 in. apart in rows 24–36 in. apart. The tubers form close to the surface of the soil, so cultivate no more than an inch deep to avoid injuring them. As the vines grow, mound up soil, mulch, or compost around them to shield the tubers from light: sunlight not only turns potatoes green but generates a poisonous alkaloid called solanine in the green portions. If a potato should have a green portion, cut it away before cooking. For new potatoes harvest when vines blossom. For mature potatoes, intended for storage, dig up when vines have died. Dry tubers for several hours and store them in a cool, dark place, preferably between 40° and 45°F.

Another method of planting is to set the seed pieces directly on the bare, prepared soil, press them in lightly to ensure good contact, and cover them with a 12-in. layer of straw, salt hay, or other light organic mulch. When the mulch settles, add 6 in. more. Potatoes raised this way are cleaner and easier to harvest, since no digging is necessary. You need only pull the mulch away. Days to harvest: 100–120. Potatoes will not form tubers when the soil temperature reaches 80°F. For this reason they do poorly in warm regions.

Pumpkin. A kind of squash first cultivated by American Indians. Whether they are the vine or bush type, pumpkins require a great deal of space; however, in a small garden they can be grown on a trellis with the fruits supported by slings. Pumpkins grow 7–24 in. in diameter, depending on type. In general, the smaller varieties are better for eating. Large pumpkins were used for stock feed on the old-time family farm. There are also special varieties that are raised for their tasty seeds. Frost tender, as are all members of the gourd family, pumpkins should not be planted until all danger of frost is past and the soil is warm. They may be started indoors three to four weeks before the last expected frost date. For outdoor planting plant seeds in hills 8–10 ft. apart for vine types, 4–6 ft. for bush types. Plant six seeds to the hill; when seedlings are about 6 in. tall, thin out all but the two or three strongest ones. A shovelful of manure or compost mixed in with the soil will get the plants off to a good start. For pumpkins started indoors use two or three to a hill. Pumpkins may also be planted in rows, with 3–4 ft. of space between plants and at least 6 ft. between rows to allow room for the sprawling vines. Mulching is recommended to keep down weeds, conserve soil moisture, and keep the fruits off the dirt. On the old-time farm pumpkins were often planted with corn, a practice settlers had learned from the Indians. To grow huge exhibition-type pumpkins, plant seeds of a large variety such as Big Max or Mammoth. Allow only one fruit to develop on each vine and water the plants heavily. Pumpkins are normally left on the vine until the vine is killed by frost or deteriorates from age. (The fruits, with their thick skins, are not harmed by a light frost.) The best practice is to cut the stem a few inches above the fruit. Store pumpkins in a cool, dry place. Days to harvest: 100–120 for most varieties.

Radishes. A fast-growing, hardy, virtually foolproof cool-weather crop related to cabbages and turnips. Radishes are often sown together with seeds of other, slower germinating vegetables such as carrots and parsnips. This practice makes double use of the garden space, marks the location of the second vegetable, and loosens and aerates the soil when the radishes are pulled up for harvesting. Plant as soon as the soil can be worked, two or three to the inch, 1/2 in. deep. Rows can be as close as 6 in. apart. Thin seedlings to 2 in.

apart soon after they emerge. Radishes become tough, pithy, and increasingly hot to the taste as they get old. Plant small batches at intervals of a week to 10 days to get a continuous supply of young, mild, tender radishes. Hot weather and lack of water also make radishes hot. Do not plant radishes in the hottest part of summer (when daytime temperatures average over 80°F). They will not bulb up. Sow them for a fall crop when the weather cools off. Radishes are ready to harvest when the bulbs are about 1 in. in diameter, although some people prefer them smaller. If the top of the bulb shows above the ground, the radish is usually ready to pick. Alternatively, probe the soil at the base of the leaves with your finger to estimate the size of the bulb. Days to harvest: 22–30, depending on variety. Winter radishes, much larger and slower growing than ordinary radishes, should be sown in early summer for a fall crop and around midsummer for late fall and winter use. Thin to 6–8 in. between plants. Dig in late fall and store in damp sand in a location safe from freezing. They will remain fresh and crisp for several weeks. Winter radishes may also be cooked using any recipe suitable for turnips. Days to harvest: 55–60.

Rhubarb. A hardy perennial raised for its tart, edible stalks. Rhubarb thrives in any deep, well-drained fertile soil as long as it has a good supply of moisture.

Rhubarb is almost always raised from roots, which are planted in early spring 3–4 ft. apart each way. (It does not come true from seed.) Do not harvest the first year. Thereafter, harvest when stalks reach 1 in. in diameter. **Caution: Do not use the leaves; they contain oxalic acid, a dangerous poison.** Pull stalks, do not cut them. Most varieties of rhubarb send up a seed stalk noticeably taller than the leaf stalks. It should be cut off at ground level to keep the plant producing.

Mammoth Gold

Cushaw type

Cinderella

American

Every five to seven years, when the stalks become markedly thinner, dig up the plants, split up the root clumps, and replant them. Where possible, select the plants that in past years have yielded the best stalks for replanting.

Spinach. A hardy cool-weather vegetable that yields both spring and fall crops. Spinach is rich in vitamin A and a good source of iron. Most spinach contains small amounts of oxalic acid, an agent that causes loss of calcium from the blood. New strains are available, however, that have almost none of this substance. Spinach thrives on well-drained, fertile soils with plenty of organic matter. The soil should be slightly acid; on very acid or very alkaline soils spinach does poorly. Plant seeds four to six weeks before the last expected frost date, 1/2 in. deep and about 1 in. apart in rows 14 in. apart. Thin to 4 in. between plants. Plan on 5–10 ft. of row per person. Harvest spinach by picking the outer leaves as soon as they reach edible size. Should buds form at the center, it is a sign that the plant will soon bolt (send up its flower stalk) and its leaves will become tough and unpalatable. At the bud stage the plants are still good and can be salvaged by pulling them up or cutting them off at ground level. Long days and hot weather in combination stimulate spinach to bolt. For a fall crop, plant in late August or early September. Because of its short growing life, spinach should be planted in small batches at two-week intervals. Spinach can be grown as a winter vegetable in areas where temperatures do not dip much below the freezing point. Days to harvest: 40–50. Spinach can be eaten raw as well as cooked and is excellent for freezing.

Squash. A large group of vegetables belonging to the gourd family. Summer squash have soft skins and moist, succulent flesh; they are eaten while young and tender. Popular summer squash include zucchini, yellow straightneck, and scallop. Winter squash, which are picked in fall and eaten fully ripe, have hard, thick skins and a rather dry, fibrous flesh, a combination that helps them keep for months. Acorn, buttercup, butternut, hubbard, and turban are standard types of winter squash. Most summer squash are bush varieties; most winter squash grow on sprawling vines. All require a good deal of space, although bush kinds are more compact. Cultural requirements are the same for all types of squash. Squash are frost tender and should not be planted until danger of frost is past and the soil is warm. Where the growing season is short, squash plants should be started indoors. Squash should have a rich, loamy, slightly alkaline soil and plenty of moisture; otherwise the fruits may be undersized. Squash can be planted in hills or in rows. Plant seeds 1–2 in. deep. For hills plant five or six to the hill, thinning later to the two or three strongest seedlings. Hills should be 4–6 ft. apart in each direction for bush squash, 8–10 ft. for vine squash. When row-planting bush varieties, place seeds 24–30 in. apart in rows 36 in. apart; for vine varieties 2–3 ft. apart in rows 9–12 ft. apart. Plant three or four seeds together as insurance against cutworms, slugs, and other garden pests; thin later to the strongest seedling. Squash do well with mulch. Summer squash are best picked when they are about 1–2 in. in diameter and while the skin can still be pierced with a fingernail. (Zucchini, however, can be allowed to grow much larger and still be used for baking.) Scallop squash can be picked when 3 or 4 in. across. Cut fruits off with a knife to avoid injuring plants. Days to harvest: 48–55. Keep plants picked for continuous production. Winter squash should be picked in fall when their skin is so hard that it cannot be scratched by a fingernail. Harvest by cutting stems about 3 in. from the fruit. For maximum storage life cure in a warm room for about 10 days, then move to a cool, dry area (avoid freezing). Days to harvest: 80–115.

Sweet potatoes. Not a true potato but a member of the morning glory family. Sweet potatoes are a good source of many vitamins, particularly vitamin A. They need a very long growing season—four to five months without frost—and require warm temperatures. For this reason they are grown mainly in the South, where they are often known erroneously as yams. Sweet potatoes do best in sandy soil that is low in organic matter. (Too rich a soil makes them run to vines instead of roots.) Once the vines are established, they are quite drought tolerant. In fact, too much moisture in the soil rots the tubers. Sweet potatoes are raised from transplants (slips cut from sprouting tubers). The slips should be 8–10 in. long and have several leaves. Plant them 15 in. apart in rows 3–4 ft. apart. Set the slips about 6 in. deep, leaving at least two leaves aboveground, and water well. They will root quickly. Rooted plants are also available. In heavy, moist soils, the soil should be raised into flat-topped ridges 8–15 in. high—the wetter the soil, the higher the ridge. Harvest after the first frost blackens the vines. In frost-free areas harvest about four months after planting. Cure the tubers in a warm, dry place for about two weeks after picking them. Store in a cool, humid place with good air circulation (not below 50°F or they may spoil). Days to harvest: 120–150.

Swiss chard. A type of beet bred for its large, crisp leaves and fleshy leaf stalks rather than for its root. Chard is rich in vitamin A and a good source of vitamin C. It tolerates both frost and hot weather—a single planting can give a continuous yield from spring to late fall. The leaves of chard may be prepared like spinach, the stalks like asparagus. Plant Swiss chard in early spring as soon as the soil can be worked and there is little danger of a severe frost. Set the seeds 1/2 in. deep and 1–2 in. apart in rows 18 in. apart. Thin later to 12 in. between plants. Chard should be harvested while the leaves are still tender and succulent. Cut the outer leaves off with a sharp knife about an inch above the ground. Be careful not to injure the inner leaves and central bud, which produces new leaves. Harvest regularly throughout the summer and fall in order to keep new leaves coming. Days to first harvest: 50–60.

Tomatoes. Once shunned as poisonous but now the most popular garden vegetable in the United States. A member of

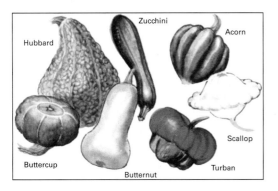

Zucchini

Acorn

Hubbard

Scallop

Buttercup

Turban

Butternut

White   Red

Yellow — Burpee's Big Boy — Cherry — Plum — Pear — Ponderosa — Snowball

the nightshade family, the tomato is closely related to eggplant, pepper, potato, and tobacco. Tomatoes are among the best yielders of all vegetables but need a long growing season with moderate temperatures—they will not set fruit when nighttime temperatures are below 60°F or above 75°F, to many a gardener's puzzlement and dismay. Years of experimentation, research, and controlled breeding have resulted in a profusion of special varieties. Tomatoes are available that range in size from giant 1-lb. Big Boy hybrids down to tiny plum and cherry tomatoes. There are egg-shaped and pear-shaped tomatoes. In addition to the familiar red, there are orange, yellow, and pink tomatoes (orange and yellow types tend to be sweeter, with less bite). There are bushy dwarf strains that can be grown in a pot or window box. Early, midseason, and late-ripening varieties have also been developed. Most early types are so-called determinate tomatoes—the vines grow to a certain length, bear their fruit over a short period, and then die. Midseason and late-season varieties are usually indeterminate—the vines continue to grow and bear fruit until the onset of cold weather stops them. Since tomatoes are killed by frost and grow poorly at cooler temperatures, they are usually started indoors in all but the warmest parts of the country. Start the seeds six to eight weeks before the last expected frost date, and set out when the weather is safely warm. To save time and trouble, you can buy ready-to-plant seedlings at most garden-supply centers and supermarkets and at many neighborhood stores as well. However, only the top-selling varieties tend to be available. The number of plants you will want to grow depends on the type grown, the amount of canning you plan to do, and your family's appetite for tomatoes. Three to five plants each of early varieties and midseason varieties are enough for the average family. Tomatoes do best in slightly acid soil and need plenty of water. Before setting out the seedlings, dig compost, well-rotted manure, or damp peat moss into the soil to improve its moisture-holding capacity. Place the plants 2–3 ft. apart in rows 3 ft. apart. The vines may either be allowed to sprawl on the ground, which gives a higher yield, or trained on stakes, fences, or other supports. A popular method is to train the vines on a circular "tower" of heavy wire. The advantage of training is that the vines yield cleaner fruit and are easier to inspect and pick. Mulching is helpful,

Trellis — Stake — Sucker — Sucker

especially if the vines have been left to grow on the ground. Tomatoes that are trained above the ground should be pruned to one or two main stems. This is done by pinching or cutting off the suckers next to the main stems. (Suckers are shoots that grow in the joints where the leaf stems meet the main stem; if allowed to grow, they divert energy from fruit production.) Suckers should be pinched off throughout the growing season. However, do not remove foliage to let sunlight reach the fruits. Instead of aiding them to ripen, it causes sun scald, a discoloration and toughening of the skin. Tomatoes are ripe when they separate easily from the stem. If cool or rainy weather delays ripening, they may be picked as soon as they start to change color and ripened on a sunny windowsill. To pick unripe tomatoes, twist them off the vine. Tomatoes can be stored for several weeks in fall by pulling up the entire plant and hanging it upside down in a cool, shady place. The tomatoes will ripen slowly on the vine. Unripe tomatoes may also be picked and stored in a single layer. Rich in vitamins A and C, tomatoes are excellent for canning and freezing. Days to harvest: 52–90, depending on variety.

Turnips and Rutabagas. Two related root crops of the cabbage family. Most turnips have white flesh, while most rutabagas have yellow flesh. Rutabagas are larger than turnips and are often called yellow turnips or Swedish turnips.

Turnips are raised for their tops, or greens, as well as their roots. A quick-growing, hardy cool-weather crop, they can be planted for spring or fall harvest. Sow in spring as soon as the soil can be worked, 1/2 in. deep and two or three seeds to the inch in rows 18 in. apart. Thin seedlings to 2 or 3 in. apart. Turnips should be harvested when they are about 2 in. in diameter. In most cases they get tough, pithy, and bitter if allowed to grow longer. For a fall crop sow in midsummer. Days to harvest: 35–60.

Rutabagas are slow growing and are planted for fall harvest. For table use, plant as for turnips about three months before the first expected fall frost date. Thin to 6 in. between plants. Harvest when roots are 3–6 in. in diameter (quality declines when they grow larger). Harvest rutabagas and turnips by pulling them up by their tops. Days to harvest: 90–100.

Watermelon. One of the gourd family raised for its sweet, juicy fruit. Watermelons need a warm growing season, plentiful moisture, and full sun for proper growth and flavor (even a light frost can kill them). Standard melons reach sizes of 20 lb. and up and are best grown in the warmer sections of the country. For cooler regions midget varieties are available. They weigh 4–15 lb. and mature in a shorter time. In all but the warmest areas watermelons should be started indoors about four weeks before the last expected frost date and set out when the nights are reliably warm (above 55°F). Watermelons are usually planted in hills, at least 6 ft. apart in each direction, two seedlings to a hill. If planted in rows, the plants should be 2–3 ft. apart in rows 6–7 ft. apart.

Super Sweet seedless hybrid — Sugar Baby — Charleston Gray

Mulch is very helpful in preventing the fruit from rotting. There is no sure way of telling when a watermelon is ready to harvest. One traditional method is to thump the melon; a hollow sound indicates it is ripe. Another is to examine the underside of the melon. When it turns yellow, the melon is probably ripe. Days to harvest: 70–95, depending on variety.

Mulch and Water: Helping Nature The Natural Way

Mulching is a traditional practice that has found new favor. Properly applied, a blanket of organic mulch smothers weeds, conserves soil moisture, and adds organic matter to the soil as it decomposes. Mulch insulates the soil, keeping the temperature even and aiding the growth of plant roots. It provides food and habitat for earthworms and burrowing insects, whose tunnels loosen and aerate the soil. It controls gullying and erosion. It prevents the rotting of fruit-type vegetables such as squash, melons, and cucumbers by keeping them away from ground moisture.

Mulch should be applied to the garden in the spring, after the soil has warmed up. Otherwise, by keeping the soil cold, it may retard plant growth. The thickness of mulch to be applied depends on the nature of the material. Loose, porous mulch such as straw should be 6 to 8 inches thick to keep sunlight from reaching weeds; denser materials such as sawdust need only be 1 1/2 to 2 inches thick. If possible, weeds should be removed before applying mulch, even though a thick layer of mulch will smother them. When placing mulch on the soil, be careful not to cover the vegetable seedlings.

It is best to turn the mulch under at the end of the growing season. If you wait until spring for this chore, be sure to add extra nitrogen fertilizer, since decay organisms, activated by warm weather, will rob the soil of much of its nitrogen as they break down the mulch.

A wide variety of materials can be used for mulch, ranging from hay and straw to chipped bark, ground corncobs, and cocoa bean hulls. Some of the best mulches cost nothing. Lawn clippings and leaves, for example, are both excellent; they function not only as mulches but add nutrients and humus to the soil when plowed under. In addition to organic materials, strips of black plastic film are often used as mulch.

Mulch is not entirely problem free. It may contain weed seeds and can also serve as a shelter for slugs, destructive insects, and field mice. (For dealing with these and other pests, see pp.148–153.) Mulch must also be replenished from time to time, since it breaks down gradually. Nevertheless, a properly applied mulch is one of the simplest and most effective ways for saving labor, improving the soil, and getting better crops.

Watering: How, When, How Much

Vegetables cannot live—much less grow and yield an abundant harvest—without water. If natural rainfall does not supply enough water, then the gardener must supply it. In the arid Southwest artificial watering or irrigation is a necessity. Even in the more humid North-east dry spells of several weeks are not uncommon.

For large commercial farms, open irrigation ditches are one answer to the problem of delivering water to where it is needed. For the home gardener there are less costly, more efficient methods of supplying water. The familiar oscillating and spinning types of lawn sprinklers duplicate natural rainfall, as does a permanently installed overhead sprinkler system or even the simple hand-held garden hose. Perforated hoses are much more economical of water. Laid on the ground, they deliver a long, soaking trickle of water directly onto the soil with minimal loss from evaporation or runoff. A wide variety of such hoses are sold by garden-supply centers.

For the ultimate in water-saving efficiency there are buried plastic pipes, also perforated, that deliver moisture directly to the root zones, where it is most needed. (Water must reach the roots to be effective—a light watering that wets only the surface of the ground leaves plants thirsty.) Experts recommend a heavy watering once a week rather than a light one every day. The watering should be heavy enough to saturate the soil 10 to 12 inches deep. (Check the depth of water penetration by opening a slit with your spade.) Clay soil requires more time and more water to saturate it than sandy soil but also holds water longer and so needs less frequent waterings. Experiment with varying amounts of water to determine how much your garden actually needs. No matter what method you use to water your garden, the watering pattern should be spread evenly over the entire area. This is because water tends to move downward through the soil rather than sideways. Water has a limited sideways spread, ranging from about 1 foot in clay soils to 2 feet in sandy soils.

How do you tell when your garden needs watering? The simplest way is to watch your plants. If they wilt in the sun and do not recover when it cools off, they need watering. (Remember, though, that any vegetable may wilt temporarily on a hot summer afternoon, no matter how wet its roots are.) The best time to water is in late afternoon, when little water will be wasted by evaporation and the air is still warm enough to dry the foliage.

Wood chip mulch discourages weeds and keeps the dirt moist around this Gerber daisy. Mulch absorbs the energy of falling rain and permits the water to soak gently into the underlying soil instead of running off.

A survey of mulching materials

Sawdust (1) can be obtained from lumberyards and sawmills. If you heat with wood, save the sawdust from your own wood-cutting operations. Let the dust rot until it is dark before use. Apply 1 1/2–2 in. thick.

Leaves (2) are abundant and easy to come by in most regions of the country. You can usually obtain additional supplies from neighbors or from your local park and highway departments. Apply 4–6 in. thick.

Pine needles (3) are cheap and plentiful in many areas. Their resin content makes them long lasting, and they have a neat appearance. Apply 4–6 in. thick.

Hay and straw (4) can be obtained from local farmers, garden-supply centers, or your own fields. Spoiled hay, which is unfit for animals, and salt hay, from tidal flats, make excellent mulches. Apply 6–8 in. thick.

Black plastic film (5) is sold by most garden-supply and hardware stores in 25-, 50-, and 100-ft. rolls of a standard 3-ft. width. Weed and till soil before spreading plastic on it. Bury edges of plastic film in shallow trenches to hold it in place, or weight edges down with stones or dirt. Leave a path for walking between plastic strips (never walk on the plastic itself, as it tears easily). Cut holes as needed to plant seeds. Also cut X-shaped slits at intervals to admit water. Black plastic warms the soil, aiding the growth of many crops.

Cocoa bean hulls (6) are attractive but expensive. They are alkaline and so help to sweeten soil; do not use on acid-loving vegetables. Apply 3–6 in. thick.

Old newspapers (7) can be recycled as mulch, but avoid colored newsprint—it may contain lead. Apply papers in layers at least six sheets thick, and weight them down to keep them from blowing. Paper is biodegradable.

Wood chips (8) can often be obtained from power or telephone companies, whose road crews chip up the brush and limbs they clear. Wood chips are durable and slow to decay. Apply 3–6 in. thick.

Lawn clippings (9), considered a problem by many homeowners, can be used productively as mulch. Clippings should be allowed to dry out before use as mulch, since they tend to mat together when fresh. Apply 3–6 in. thick.

Compost (10) is one of the best garden mulches. It supplies nutrients in addition to performing the other functions of a mulch. However, for maximum effectiveness compost for mulching should be only partly broken down; otherwise it may encourage, rather than deter, the growth of weeds. Apply 3–6 in. thick.

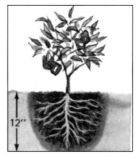

The roots of most vegetables grow in the top 8–12 in. of soil, although some, like tomatoes, may reach 4–5 ft. down in deep, loose soils. When watering, it is important to saturate the root zone about 1 ft. deep, not just wet the surface. Shallow watering encourages roots to grow close to the surface, where they are likely to dry out during hot spells with resultant damage to the plants.

Other ways to wet the soil

Connected saucers or basins for watering are a refinement of the traditional irrigation ditch. They confine water to root zones and also collect rainfall. The series of saucers should be graded to let water flow slowly down the whole length of the chain.

Surprising seaweed mulch

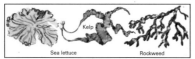

Sea lettuce   Kelp   Rockweed

Those who live near the shore can harvest their own supply of one of the finest natural mulches—seaweed. Rich in potassium and trace elements, seaweed is also a good fertilizer and a desirable addition to the compost pile. It should be dried in the sun before using in the garden.

Perforated cans or milk cartons, placed in the soil at planting time, conserve water by letting it ooze slowly into the root zone. Fill them by hand or with a hose. A variant on this idea is a short piece of pipe inserted in the soil at a convenient angle for a hose.

(Wet foliage is susceptible to fungus infections.) Early to midmorning is also a good time for watering. Avoid watering the garden in midday or after sundown.

Do not overdo it when watering. Overwatering wastes water, leaches nutrients out of the soil, damages roots, and encourages the growth of lush, disease-prone foliage. In arid areas it can also cause a buildup of salts in the soil: mineral-laden water, moving upward by capillary action, evaporates leaving a saline residue.

Sources and resources

Books

Arms, Karen. *Environmental Gardening*. Savannah, Ga.: Halfmoon Publishing, 1992.

Bartholomew, Mel. *Square Foot Gardening*. Emmaus, Pa.: Rodale Press, 1981.

Berry, Susan, and Bradley, Steve. *Plant Life: A Gardener's Guide*. North Pomfret, Vt.: Trafalgar Square, 1995.

Burke, Ken, and Walter Doty. *All About Vegetables*. San Francisco: Ortho Books, 1990.

Clevely, A.M. *The Total Garden: A Complete Guide to Integrating Flowers, Herbs, Fruits and Vegetables*, Avenal, N.J.: Random House Value, 1988.

Crockett, James. *Crockett's Victory Garden*. Boston: Little, Brown, 1977.

Engelken, Ralph, and Engelken, Rita, eds. *The Art of Natural Farming and Gardening*. Greeley, Iowa: Barrington Hall Press, 1981.

Loewer, Peter. *The New Small Garden: Plans and Plants That Make Every Inch Count*. Mechanicsburg, Pa.: Stackpole, 1994.

Raver, Ann. *Deep in the Green: An Exploration of Country Pleasures*. New York: Knopf, 1995.

Thomson, Bob. *The New Victory Garden*. Boston: Little, Brown, 1987.

Overhead sprinklers cover a wide area and can be fed by hose or buried pipelines. They are much used by commercial vegetable growers and their spray radius is easily adjusted. However, they waste much water through evaporation.

Water-saving drip irrigation

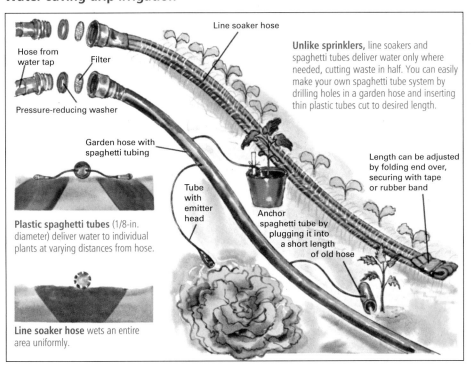

Hose from water tap

Filter

Pressure-reducing washer

Line soaker hose

Unlike sprinklers, line soakers and spaghetti tubes deliver water only where needed, cutting waste in half. You can easily make your own spaghetti tube system by drilling holes in a garden hose and inserting thin plastic tubes cut to desired length.

Garden hose with spaghetti tubing

Tube with emitter head

Anchor spaghetti tube by plugging it into a short length of old hose

Length can be adjusted by folding end over, securing with tape or rubber band

Plastic spaghetti tubes (1/8-in. diameter) deliver water to individual plants at varying distances from hose.

Line soaker hose wets an entire area uniformly.

Gardening in Limited Space

For Big Results Think Small

High-rise living, cluster-zoned developments, and an increasing scarcity of land are giving rise to a new class of farmer: the urban gardener. Using simple space-saving stratagems, city dwellers and suburbanites are growing an impressive variety of vegetables. With the help of intensive culture (very close planting) the yield per square foot can be multiplied. Intercropping and succession planting can also bring impressive increases in crop size. Where soil is poor or space extremely limited, you can get excellent results by raising vegetables in containers.

Lack of sunlight, as well as a shortage of space, often limits the kinds of plants an urban gardener can grow. Crops that are raised for their fruits, such as tomatoes and cucumbers, need at least six hours of sunlight a day. Root crops, such as beets and turnips, can get along with less. Lettuce and other leaf crops can be grown with as little as four hours a day of direct light. Best choices for the minigarden are plants that give a high yield and take little space: leaf and salad crops, plus those that can be trained vertically.

The French Intensive Method

Developed nearly a century ago by French truck farmers, the French intensive method combines special soil preparation with heavy feedings of organic fertilizers to support a dense planting of vegetables.

To prepare the soil, first rototill or double-dig it (see *The Kitchen Garden*, p.101). Then work compost or well-rotted manure into the soil until the top 12 inches are one-third to one-half organic matter. In clay soils build up the proportion of sand to one-third.

Adding these materials will increase the volume of your soil so that it forms a low mound, which aids drainage. Rake the mound smooth; then top it with a 2-inch layer of manure plus a light sprinkling of bone-meal and wood ashes. Work these into the top 3 or 4 inches of soil and rake smooth. (For succession crops repeat this feeding each time a crop is replaced.)

Soak the soil deeply a day or two before you sow seeds or set out transplants and mark off the areas where you plan to plant each vegetable. Spread seeds thinly in their designated areas. As the seedlings grow, thin them to about half the spacing recommended for an ordinary garden. A laborsaving trick is to drag a steel rake lightly across them when they are 1 inch tall; thin by hand later. Large seeds, such as peas and beans, can be sown so that no thinning will be necessary later. Transplants of tomatoes and other large vegetables should be set a little more than half as far apart as in an ordinary garden.

Leafy vegetables, such as lettuce and Swiss chard, should be left close enough for their leaves to form a continuous canopy over the soil, thus shading out weeds, conserving moisture, and creating a favorable microclimate for plant growth.

Careful soil preparation and dense planting are the keys to success with the French intensive method: (1) Gardener works organic matter into well-loosened soil. (2) The soil is raked into a smooth mound. (3) Seeds are broadcast thinly (not sown in rows) to cover the soil. (4) The resulting crop forms a soil-protecting canopy with its densely growing leaves.

Raised Beds and Planters

Raised beds, originally developed to cope with infertile or poorly drained soils, are increasingly popular. They are convenient for planting, weeding, and other garden tasks; they give excellent drainage; and they warm up, several weeks ahead of regular garden plots in the spring.

For best results, raised beds should be at least 12 inches high. Fill them with enriched garden soil or a special mix, such as the one described on the next page. If the soil level is kept 2 or 3 inches below the top of the beds, they can be covered with glass and made to serve as cold frames.

When a bed runs along a wall or is otherwise accessible from only one side, it should be no more than 3 feet wide so that you can tend it without having to step on the soil. When both sides are accessible, the width may be up to 6 feet. Raised beds may be any length desired, but they are easier to manage when they are short. Popular sizes are 4 by 4 feet and 3 by 9 feet.

Farming in Containers

Container gardening is one of the most efficient methods for growing vegetables in limited space. Almost any vegetable can be grown in a container—even corn or pumpkins—although plants that take up a great deal of space are not practical. Miniature varieties of vegetables are especially suited to container growing: they require less space than full-sized varieties and mature earlier.

Many vegetables can be container-raised indoors as well as outdoors. Leaf crops can be grown indoors even in winter with the aid of fluorescent lights. Fruit crops, such as tomatoes, can be grown indoors but need warm temperatures and at least six hours of summer sunlight. Most root crops, however, are best grown outdoors.

Raised beds can be made of treated 2-in.-thick boards held in place by stakes or fastened at the corners with angle irons. If 2 × 12 boards are not available, combine narrower boards to gain the needed height. The higher the bed, the less stooping is required to tend the plants.

Stepped boxes, a variant of the raised bed, give plants better exposure to sunlight and can be tucked in a corner or against a wall. The separate levels are easy to tend. Boxes and stand can be made separately for easy disassembly and moving.

Narrow strip beside the house is thriftily utilized with a raised bed made of railroad ties. Pole beans or other climbers are trained up a trellis for maximum sunlight. The bed can also be made of brick, stone, concrete, or cement blocks. Whatever material is used, be sure drainage is adequate.

Bag of planting mix becomes instant planter.

Salad tree is made of long shelf board and semicircle of wire with tub to hold planting mix.

Box planter is easily built of new or scrap lumber and can rest on stringers or feet.

Many variations of the container idea are possible. The movable bookcase-type planter shown above holds several levels of plants growing in slits in its wire or plastic lining. Water and fertilizer are supplied through perforated pipes. Casters make the planter easy to move, an idea that is adaptable to other heavy, bulky containers.

Almost any sturdy, water-resistant receptacle can be used for container gardening: plastic or galvanized iron garbage cans, redwood planters, 2-gallon or 5-gallon buckets, even a plastic garbage bag. Of course, any type of container must be provided with holes for drainage. Recommended practice is to drill drainage holes just above the bottom rather than in it.

For best results, use an artificial planting medium rather than garden soil. Artificial mixtures do not compact, even after repeated waterings, and they are much lighter in weight than soil. As a result, it is much easier to move the containers, an important feature since one of the advantages of raising vegetables in containers is that they can be shifted indoors on a cold night or around the yard to follow the sun. A good homemade mix can be made from peat moss, vermiculite (or perlite), and fertilizer. To make 1 gallon of mix, use 1/2 gallon peat moss, 1/2 gallon vermiculite, 1 teaspoon lime, 1 1/2 teaspoons of 5-10-10 fertilizer, and 1/2 teaspoon superphosphate. About 9 gallons of mix will fill a bushel container.

Because of the intensive care they get, container-grown plants can be spaced much closer together than if they were planted in an ordinary garden. The chart at right gives recommended space and soil allowances for a number of popular vegetables.

Plants grown in containers need watering more frequently than they would in a garden—as often as once a day in hot, dry weather. To check for moisture, probe the top 2 inches of soil with your finger. If the soil is dry, soak it thoroughly until water runs out at the bottom of the container. You should also add fertilizer every three weeks. Use light doses, however; overfertilizing can damage or kill plants that are grown in containers.

Windowsill Farming Indoors and Out

Apartment dwellers can use windowsills, balconies, and rooftops to raise surprisingly large crops of homegrown vegetables. According to one expert, as many as 100 carrots, 50 beets, and 50 cherry tomatoes can be harvested from a dozen 8-inch pots.

The most practical vegetables for the windowsill farmer are those that need little space and give high yields. The nature of your space also determines what you can grow. If you have balcony or rooftop space, climbers—such as standard tomatoes, pole beans, and cucumbers—are practical. For a windowsill concentrate on such low-growing vegetables as lettuce, spinach, carrots, and dwarf tomatoes.

Daylight exposure is also important, since indoor plants have the same needs for light and warmth as those grown

Selected vegetables for containers

Vegetable	Minimum container size	Number of plants per container
Beans (bush)	2 gal.	6 plants; in larger containers space 2"-3" apart
Beans (pole)	4 gal.	6 plants
Beets	1 pt.	2-3 plants; in larger containers space 2" apart
Broccoli	5 gal.	1 plant
Brussels sprouts	5 gal.	1 plant
Cabbage	5 gal.	1 plant; in larger containers space 12" apart
Chinese cabbage	1 gal.	1 plant
Carrots	1 pt.	3-4 plants; in larger containers space 1"-2" apart
Corn	10 gal.	4 plants; space 4" apart. Plant at least 12 for pollination
Cucumbers	5 gal.	2 plants. Train vertically
Eggplant	5 gal.	1 plant
Kale	5 gal.	3-4 plants; in larger containers space 16" apart
Lettuce	1/2 gal.	1 plant; in larger containers space 10" apart
Mustard greens	1 pt.	1 plant; in larger containers space 4" apart
New Zealand spinach	2 gal.	1 plant (good for hanging basket)
Onions	1/2 gal.	16 green onions. For full-sized onions use larger containers; space 2"-3" apart
Peppers	2 gal.	1 plant
Radishes	1 pt.	4-5 plants per pot; in larger containers space 1" apart
Spinach	1 pt.	1 plant per pot; in larger containers space 5" apart
Summer squash and zucchini	5 gal.	1 plant
Swiss chard	3 1/2 gal.	4-5 plants; in larger containers space 8" apart
Tomatoes (dwarf)	5 gal.	1 plant
Tomatoes (standard)	1 1/2 qt.	1 plant
Turnips	5 gal.	Space 2" apart

outdoors. For an east-facing window the choice is limited to leafy vegetables and radishes. Southern and western windows are suitable for most vegetables. Warmth lovers, such as tomatoes and beans, do best in a southern exposure. A northern window is unsuitable for vegetables unless artificial lighting is provided as a supplement.

Gardening Under Lights

Vegetables need ample light to flourish, especially rays from the blue and red ends of the spectrum. Normally these rays are supplied by the sun, but fluorescent tubes can take the place of natural sunlight. An equal number of cool-white (rich in blue) and warm-white or natural tubes (rich in red) seem to give the best result. Tubes especially designed for indoor gardening, high in both blue and red wavelengths, are also available.

Some growers use incandescent lamps to augment the red end of the spectrum, but these consume much more electricity for the light produced. In addition, they must be used with caution because of the heat they generate.

Fluorescent tubes should be positioned 6 to 12 inches above the plants: light intensity diminishes rapidly as distance increases. A fixture with four 4-foot tubes provides enough light for a 3- by 4-foot area.

Vegetables require 13 to 18 hours of artificial light per day. They also need a resting period of darkness. Leafy and root vegetables are easiest to grow under lights; tomatoes require extra care.

What to grow where

For the windowsill:	
Carrots	Radishes
Cress	Spinach
Lettuce	Tomatoes
Mustard	Zucchini
For balcony, rooftop, or windowbox:	
Any windowsill vegetables plus:	
Beans	Peppers
Broccoli	Potatoes
Brussels	Squash
sprouts	Tomatoes
Cabbage	Turnips,
Corn	other root
Cucumbers	vegetables
Indoors under lights:	
Beets	Cucumbers
Carrots	Endive
Celery	Onions
Chinese	Radishes
cabbage	Watercress

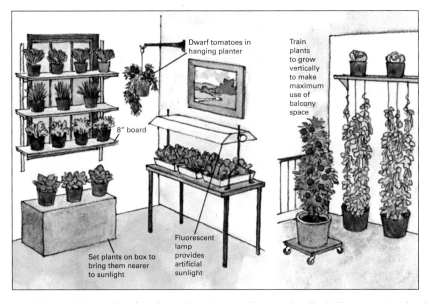

Dwarf tomatoes in hanging planter

Train plants to grow vertically to make maximum use of balcony space

8" board

Set plants on box to bring them nearer to sunlight

Fluorescent lamp provides artificial sunlight

Growing space can be increased by a number of simple expedients. You can widen a windowsill to hold more containers by adding an 8-in. board supported by brackets. Most windows can accommodate two or three boards placed across them, again supported by brackets. Hanging containers are fine for dwarf tomatoes, but be sure not to make them too heavy for their supports. Bulky plants can be placed on a table in front of the window or on an up-ended box on the floor to raise them to window level. Unused bureau tops, tables, bookshelves, and even closets become planting areas with the aid of easily installed fluorescent light fixtures. On a balcony or other outdoor area you can make use of vertical space by training vegetables on stakes, strings, or against a wall as well as by using hanging containers and wall brackets.

Fruits and Nuts

Tree, Bush, or Vine: A Lifetime Harvest of Fruits and Nuts

By raising your own fruits, you gain freshness and a range of flavor that cannot be matched by store-bought fruit, which is often limited to a few varieties more pleasing to the eye than to the taste. You can grow such historic favorites as the Spitzenburg apple, relished by Thomas Jefferson, and the famous Concord grape, plus fine modern varieties including the Reliance peach, so hardy that it defies the severe winters of New Hampshire. You can enjoy such unusual treats as yellow and purple raspberries or fresh currants and gooseberries, not to mention pies, jam, cider, or wine made with your own fruit. And fruits yield beauty as well as food: clouds of fragrant blossoms in spring, colorful clusters of fruit in fall.

Almond trees in full bloom. Fruit and nut trees can be beautiful as well as practical.

Nut trees, while needing more space than fruit trees, thrive with minimal care and live for generations, often reaching giant size. They provide welcome shade in summer and valuable timber, as well as bountiful crops of nuts—a source of pleasure long after your own lifetime. As an added benefit, both nut and fruit trees provide food and habitat for many species of wildlife.

It is easy to grow your own fruit and nuts if you have enough space for a couple of trees or a few berry bushes. They need less care than flowers and vegetables; and although fruit-bearing plants take one to five years before they come into production, with care most of them will keep on producing for many years—even for generations.

Starting Your Orchard

The most important step you can take for your newly purchased stock is to plant it properly. An old adage advises that you should plant a $5 tree in a $10 hole, meaning that the hole should be large enough to give the roots ample room to spread. Cramped roots grow poorly and may even choke one another.

If you buy a tree or bush from a local nursery, it is probably either growing in a container of soil or balled-and-burlapped. (Balled-and-burlapped, or B & B, means that the roots are embedded in a ball of soil and wrapped in burlap.) Stock from a mail-order nursery, which offers a far wider range of choices, will arrive with its roots bare, packed in damp moss or excelsior. For B & B or container-grown stock, planting is simple: make the hole as deep as the root ball and a foot wider, place the plant in position, loosen the top of the burlap, and replace the soil. Bare-root stock needs more care (see below).

Ideally, stock should be planted as soon as it arrives. If this is not possible, it can be stored. B & B stock can be held for several weeks by placing it in a shady location and keeping the root ball moist. Bare-root stock can be kept up to 14 days by opening the base of the package and keeping the roots moist. If kept over 14 days, it should be "heeled in" until you are ready to

Hardiness Zones

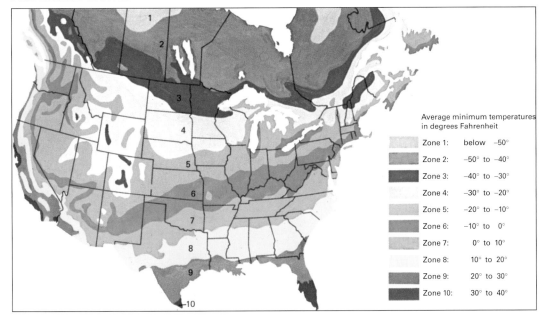

Zone 1:	below	−50°
Zone 2:	−50° to	−40°
Zone 3:	−40° to	−30°
Zone 4:	−30° to	−20°
Zone 5:	−20° to	−10°
Zone 6:	−10° to	0°
Zone 7:	0° to	10°
Zone 8:	10° to	20°
Zone 9:	20° to	30°
Zone 10:	30° to	40°

Average minimum temperatures in degrees Fahrenheit

Climate is a critical survival factor for fruit trees, nut trees, bushes, and vines. Fruit- and nut-bearing plants vary widely in hardiness (resistance to subfreezing temperatures). Many require an extended period of chilling below 45°F to bear fruit. The map shows average minimum temperatures for winter over broad zones. Local features, such as hills and valleys, wind patterns, and urban areas, can cause sharp variations within each zone. Frost dates and length of growing season can also affect the kind of fruit or nuts that can be raised in your area. Contact your county agent for varieties that do well locally.

plant: remove the plants from their package, place them roots down in a shallow trench, and cover the roots with soil. Keep the plants out of the sun, and keep the soil moist.

When planting, do not expose bare roots to sunlight or air any longer than necessary. If they dry out, the plant may die. To avoid this, keep roots immersed in a pail of water or wrapped in a wet cloth until the hole is ready. Fruit or nut stock can be planted in either spring or fall provided the plants are dormant and the soil is not frozen. In Zones 3 and 4 and the northern part of Zone 5 spring planting is safer. Choose a site that has at least eight hours a day of full sunlight during spring and summer. The best locations are on high ground or on slopes to permit cold air to drain off. Avoid areas that are wet for most of the year.

If the soil is poor, mix peat moss or compost with it before planting the stock, but do not use fertilizer when planting: it may burn the roots and cause severe damage to the plant. Give newly planted stock plenty of water during the first growing season. If rainfall is insufficient, provide each young plant with a laundry pail of water once a week. Young trees have thin bark that is easily scalded (injured) by winter sun. To avoid sunscald, loosely wrap the trunks of newly planted trees from the ground to their lowest branches for the first few years. Use burlap, kraft paper, or semirigid plastic spirals (obtainable from nurseries). It may be removed in summer or left on year round as protection against deer, rodents, and farm animals.

Any vegetation close to the young tree, including grass, competes with it for water and nutrients. Therefore, the soil around the tree should be clean cultivated or heavily mulched from the trunk out to the drip line (the ends of the branches). If mulch is used, place a collar of hardware cloth around the base of the trunk to protect against field mice and other small nibblers.

After the first year, fruit and nut plants can be lightly fertilized. Overfeeding makes them produce a profusion of leaves and branches with fruit of poor quality. Manure, compost, wood ashes, and fertilizers high in nitrogen, phosphorus, and potassium are recommended.

Organic-minded fruit growers are usually willing to accept some blemishes and even the loss of some fruit as the price for avoiding sprays. However, in many areas spraying is necessary to get a crop at all. Organic insecticides include pyrethrum, rotenone, nicotine sulfate, and ryania. Also available are man-made insecticides that do not have a long-lasting toxic effect.

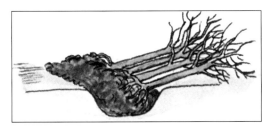

Heeling-in is a method of storing plants for up to a month.

How to Plant a Tree

1. Dig hole at least 2 ft. deep and 2 ft. wide for nut trees, 1 1/2 ft. deep and 1 1/2 ft. wide for fruit trees, to give roots room. When digging hole, keep sod, topsoil, and subsoil separate. Loosen soil at bottom of hole and place sod upside down on it. Then make a low cone of topsoil in the center of the hole.

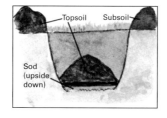

2. Prune broken or damaged roots with a sharp knife or pruning shears. Also remove roots that interlace or crisscross. Shorten any roots that are too long to fit the hole. Do not allow the roots to dry out during this operation, and avoid crowding them into the hole when positioning the tree.

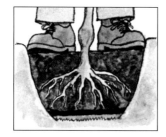

5. Add soil until roots are covered, then work it around the roots with your fingers, leaving no air pockets. Fill hole almost to top and pack the soil by treading it. Gently pour a pail of water onto soil to settle it further. Fill in remainder of hole, leaving a shallow saucer for watering. Do not pack this soil.

6. Prune off all but the three or four strongest branches, and head these back a few inches to a strong bud. Lowest branch should be about 18 in. above soil. These "scaffold" branches will be the tree's future framework. Tie tree to stake with soft material, such as a rag, to avoid injury to the bark.

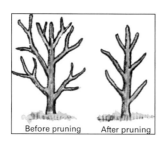

Before pruning   After pruning

3. If tree is grafted, the graft union will appear as a small bulge near bottom of trunk. Standard trees should be planted so graft is about 2 in. below soil level. For dwarf trees the graft should be 2 in. above soil level to prevent the upper part of the tree from forming its own roots and growing to full size.

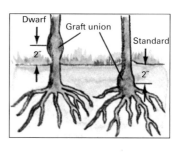

Dwarf   Graft union   Standard   2″   2″

4. Newly planted trees need support. Set a temporary stake in hole before planting tree to avoid damage to roots. Place tree on cone of topsoil with roots spread out evenly. If necessary, adjust height of cone to bring graft union to proper level; a board laid across the hole makes a handy depth gauge.

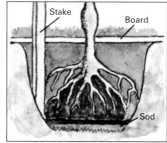

Stake   Board   Sod

Less Means More: Pruning, Grafting, and Espaliering

Pruning, grafting, and espaliering are skills that will keep your plants productive, help you propagate special varieties, and enable you to shape your trees so they can be grown on a wall or along a fence.

Pruning is the art of selectively trimming or removing parts of a living plant. Properly done, pruning will promote the formation of flowers and fruit, eliminate dead and diseased wood, and control and direct the growth of the tree, bush, or vine. Pruning can also compensate for root damage at transplanting time. One of the most important rules is not to injure the bark when making a cut. The inner bark, or cambium, is the lifeline of woody plants, whether trees, bushes, or vines. This thin green layer of living tissue, only one cell thick, is not only the actively growing part of the tree, it is also the pathway that transports nutrients from the leaves to the roots. Whenever the cambium is injured or destroyed, the tissue around the injury will also die back.

When a limb is removed, the cambium forms a scarlike tissue called a callus and gradually begins to grow back over the exposed wood surface. A small wound often heals over in a single growing season, thereby excluding decay organisms. Wounds larger than a 50-cent piece should be painted to keep out rot, which weakens the tree and shortens its life, besides ruining the wood.

The traditional time for pruning is in late winter or early spring, while the tree is dormant and the weather is not excessively cold. (Pruning should not be attempted when the temperature is below 20°F, since dieback may result.) In general, summer pruning is not recommended, since it encourages plants to put out new growth to replace what has been removed. The new growth seldom has time to harden before frost comes; as a result, it is usually killed. The exceptions to the rule against summer pruning are dead, diseased, or damaged branches, and so-called water sprouts or suckers, which should be cut off as soon as they appear. Water sprouts are vigorous, vertical shoots that spring from a tree's trunk and limbs; suckers are similar but spring from the roots.

An important function of pruning is to keep branches from crowding one another; thus weak and interlacing branches should be removed regularly. A light pruning every year is better—and easier—than a heavy one every two or three years.

Pruning Tools for Every Job

One-hand pruning shears sever branches up to 1/2 in. in diameter and are handy for light work.

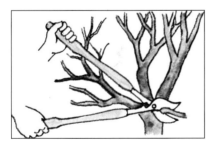

Two-hand lopping shears are used on branches up to 1 1/2 in. in diameter and for extending reach.

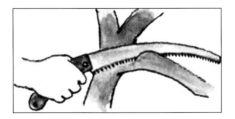

Small-toothed pruning saw can handle branches up to 5 in. thick if necessary.

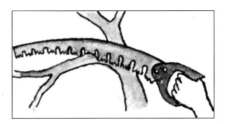

Speed saw, with large teeth, cuts fast but coarsely; do not use it for branches under 3 in.

Pole saw is for work too high to reach without a ladder. Many models include cord-operated shears for twigs.

Fundamentals of Good Pruning

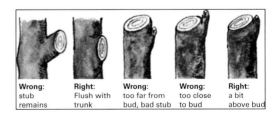

| **Wrong:** stub remains | **Right:** Flush with trunk | **Wrong:** too far from bud, bad stub | **Wrong:** too close to bud | **Right:** a bit above bud |

"Leave no stubs" is the pruner's first commandment. Stubs soon die, creating an entryway for decay organisms and harmful insects. Make your cut flush with the main stem or as close to it as possible without injuring the bark. Such a cut will soon begin to heal over. When heading back a branch, leave at least one strong bud to ensure that the branch survives. Use a slanting cut just beyond the bud to promote healing. Select a bud that points in the direction in which you wish to direct the growth of the branch after pruning.

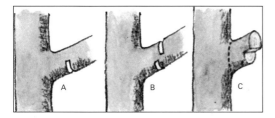

Pruning off large branches can injure trees if not done properly, since the weight of the branch may cause it to break loose when partly cut through, tearing away large areas of bark or even splitting the tree. To prevent this, first cut upward from the lower side of the branch, about 6 in. from the trunk or main stem (A). This undercut should go a third of the way through the branch. Then cut down through the branch an inch or two farther out (B). The undercut prevents tearing when the branch falls. The stub can now be removed with a cut flush to the trunk (C).

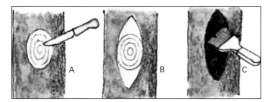

To speed healing, trim the bark around the edge of the wound with a sharp knife and smooth off rough spots and projections on the bare wood (A). If the wound is large, use a wood rasp for smoothing, and trim the bark lengthwise in a diamond shape (B). This eliminates bark that would die because sap cannot reach it. Wounds more than 1 to 1 1/2 in. in diameter (about the size of a 50-cent piece) should be painted with shellac or water-soluble asphalt-based tree wound paint to seal them against decay organisms and insects (C).

Espaliers for Fence or Wall

The ancient art of espaliering is finding new popularity with space-conscious modern gardeners. The technique, which dates back to ancient Rome, was revived in

Bud grafting

First year. At planting cut tree back to three buds just below bottom wire. One bud will form new vertical leader; the others will become lateral branches. Keep all other shoots that sprout later pruned back to 6 in. to encourage fruit buds to form.

Second year. Cut leaders back below second wire. Gently bend the two laterals and tie them to wire with a soft material such as twine. Remove all other first-year shoots. Leave three strong buds at top of leader to develop into new leader and new laterals.

Third year. Tie down second tier of laterals to wire. Cut back leader slightly below wire. Remove shoots from trunk and leader as before. Trim all side shoots on laterals to three buds. Do not cut back ends of laterals until they reach desired length.

medieval times by monks who needed to utilize every inch of their cramped monastery gardens. It has also been part of the New World tradition since colonial days.

Despite its high-sounding French name, espaliering is simply a method of training fruit trees or ornamentals to grow flat against a wall or on supports. Espaliered trees occupy a minimum of space and can be planted in spots that would otherwise be unproductive. When grown against a wall, they benefit from reflected light and heat so that their fruit often ripens early.

Espaliering is most easily done with dwarf trees. They may be trained on trellises, on wires strung between spikes in a wall, or on fence rails. In the North espaliers should have a southern exposure; in the South and Southwest an eastern exposure is favored. Since a healthy tree needs balanced growth, espaliers are often trained in symmetrical geometric patterns that combine economy of space with beauty.

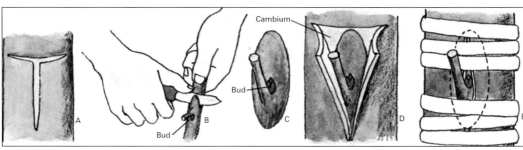

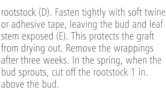

Bud grafting, or budding, is done in late summer. With a sharp knife or razor blade make a small T-shaped cut in the bark of the rootstock (A). Cut a twig from the tree you wish to propagate and snip off the twig's leaves, leaving about 1/2 in. of each leaf stem. At the base of each leaf stem is a bud that will produce the next year's growth. Cut toward the tip from just behind the bud (B). You should get a broad, shallow slice of bark and cambium and a little inner wood (C). Spread the flaps of the T-cut and insert the bud so that its cambium contacts that of the rootstock (D). Fasten tightly with soft twine or adhesive tape, leaving the bud and leaf stem exposed (E). This protects the graft from drying out. Remove the wrappings after three weeks. In the spring, when the bud sprouts, cut off the rootstock 1 in. above the bud.

Shown below are the basic steps for training a one-year-old tree into an espalier. The pattern is the double horizontal cordon. A new tier of laterals can be added each year until the desired height is achieved; after that, keep the leader trimmed back.

Grafting for Propagation

Because of their complex genetic makeup, cultivated fruit and nut plants do not come true from seed, and the vast majority of seedlings are of poor quality. The only way to ensure that a young plant has all the desirable qualities of its parent is to propagate it nonsexually by grafting, layering, or division. Grafting is used principally with fruit and nut trees; layering (see page 134) is used to propagate grapes and some bush fruits; division (see page 146) is used with bush fruits.

Cleft grafting

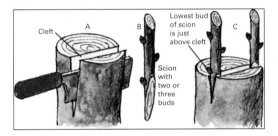

Cleft grafting, the simplest way to graft, is done in early spring before growth starts. Cut off the rootstock a few inches above the ground. With a cleaver, heavy knife, or wide chisel, split the rootstock stem near one edge 2 to 3 in. deep (A) and wedge the split open. Take a scion (a short section of a shoot with several buds) and cut one end to a wedge shape (B). Insert the scion at one side of the cleft so that cambium touches cambium (C). Cover all cut surfaces with grafting wax to prevent drying out. As insurance, use two scions: if both take, cut off the weaker one.

Whip grafting

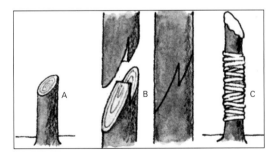

Whip grafting is used when the scion and rootstock are of equal size and less than 3/4 in. in diameter. It is done in early spring. With a sharp knife, cut off the rootstock diagonally about 6 in. above the ground (A). Make a matching cut on the scion. The cuts should be smooth and clean. Now cut a slanting tongue in the rootstock and another in the scion and fit the two pieces together so that cambium meets on both sides (B). Fasten firmly with twine, waxed thread, or adhesive tape and cover the top of the scion with grafting wax (C) to prevent it from drying out.

Grafting is the most complex of these techniques but is still simple enough for amateurs to master. It has been practiced at least since the days of the ancient Romans. Grafting involves joining the top of one variety to the roots or trunk of another. Old-time farmers propagated their best fruit trees by grafting and gave buds and scions (young shoots) to their friends. The famous McIntosh apple was propagated in this way from a single wild seedling discovered on a pioneer farm in the Canadian bush in 1811. All McIntosh apples in existence today are descendants of that one seedling.

In addition to propagating desirable varieties, grafting is used to impart special characteristics such as hardiness, extra-small tree size, or disease resistance. Three common grafting techniques are shown below.

Apples and Pears Are Old Favorites

Apple and pear trees are closely related and have similar cultural requirements. Both grow best in a deep, rich, well-drained, slightly acid soil but can be grown in almost any type of soil that is not excessively acid or alkaline. The orchard should be sited on a north-facing slope if possible to delay blossoming and reduce the danger of frost damage.

Both apple and pear trees need a period of cold and dormancy to set flowers and fruit. Apples thrive best in Zones 5 to 7 (see map on p.131), although there are hardy varieties that succeed in Zone 4 and a few heat-tolerant ones that grow in Zones 8 and 9. Pears, more delicate than apples, do best in areas with mild winters and cool summers, such as the Pacific Northwest, but can be grown in Zones 5 to 7.

Most varieties of apples and pears are not self-fertile; that is, they need at least one other variety planted close by to set fruit. Even those listed in catalogs as self-fertile produce better when they are cross-fertilized by another variety. Standard apple trees should be planted 20 to 30 feet apart, with the same distance between rows; for standard pear trees the figures are 20 feet apart and 20 feet between rows. Dwarf trees can be planted as close as 10 by 10 feet or even 6 by 10 feet. Semidwarfs should be at least 12 feet apart.

Like other fruit trees, apples and pears are prey to a variety of diseases and insect pests. For a good crop of unblemished fruit, commercial growers must spray as often as 13 times a year. Home growers can get by with six sprayings—fewer if they do not mind a few blemishes.

Both types of trees bear fruit on spurs–short, gnarled twigs that grow from the branches and produce blossoms for several years in a row. Spurs can be identified in winter by their buds—fruit buds are plump and rounded, while leaf buds have a slenderer, more pointed shape. With a little practice it is not hard to tell the difference. For best results the fruit should be thinned three to six weeks from the time it first forms, after the early summer "June drop." First eliminate any wormy, diseased, and undersized fruits. Then space out the remaining fruits to

Chenango Strawberry apple ripens early.

Rome Beauty is a large apple used for cooking.

Rhode Island Greening, a cooking apple, dates from colonial days.

Spitzenburg was the favorite apple of Thomas Jefferson.

Winesap is an old favorite cider apple.

York Imperial, an excellent keeper, comes from eastern Pennsylvania.

Grimes Golden is a richly flavored winter apple.

Roxbury Russet ripens late and gains sweetness in storage.

Jonathan apple, discovered in 1826, is good for eating and cooking.

Dwarf trees for efficiency

Where space is limited, dwarf trees can be the answer. Dwarf trees, produced by grafting standard varieties onto special rootstocks or by inserting a special stem section, bear full-sized fruit but seldom grow more than 8 to 10 ft. tall. Because of their small size, they are easy to prune and care for, and the fruit can be picked without climbing a ladder. Dwarf trees usually bear much sooner than standard (full-sized) trees, and as many as 10 dwarfs can be planted in the space required by one standard tree. This not only increases the yield but allows you to plant more varieties. On the debit side dwarf trees require more care than standards and must usually (except for interstem dwarfs) be staked permanently to prevent them from toppling under the weight of a heavy crop.

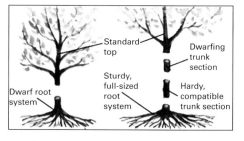

Dwarf trees are created by two methods: using dwarf rootstock or interstem grafting.

to 40 years, but with care a tree will survive, blossom, and bear fruit for as long as 100 years.

Both apples and pears have early, midseason, and late-ripening varieties. The early and midseason varieties do not keep well and should be eaten soon after picking or else be dried or canned. Late varieties are picked before they are fully ripe and attain peak flavor and aroma in storage.

Training for Better Trees

Left to themselves, fruit trees grow into a nearly impenetrable jungle of branches that yield small, inferior fruit and leave the trees vulnerable to destruction in storms or under the weight of snow. The fruit grower's aim is to direct the growth of the tree into a shape that is structurally sound, easily cared for, and requires little pruning. This training should begin when the tree is two to four years old and the branches are still pliable. The best configuration for apple and pear trees, known as the central leader shape, features a tall main trunk surrounded by lateral, or scaffold, branches. The lowest scaffold branch should be 18 inches from the ground. Each succeeding scaffold branch should be at least 8 inches above the one below it. No two scaffold branches should be directly opposite each other.

Scaffold branches should grow at an angle between 45 and 90 degrees to the main leader; a narrow crotch is structurally weak, and vertically growing branches produce fewer fruit buds. If possible, select scaffold branches that grow naturally at this angle. If the tree has none—and many varieties are upright growers—you can force them to grow horizontally with the aid of spreaders (see

6 or 7 inches apart. Thinning produces larger and more flavorful fruit and also reduces the danger of branches breaking from too heavy a load. Be careful not to break off fruit spurs when removing the fruits.

The fruits are ready to harvest when their stems separate easily from the tree. Pears should be picked before they are ripe, when their color changes from deep green to light green or yellow. Apples should be tree ripened and have reached their mature coloration. Pears should be ripened in a cool, dark place for immediate use or held in storage in the refrigerator.

When picking fruit of any kind, try to keep the stem on the fruit—removing it creates an entry for rot. Place fruits gently in a basket or other container rather than dropping them in; bruises cause rapid spoilage.

Apples and pears should begin to bear at 5 to 10 years of age for standard trees and 2 to 3 years for dwarfs. Owners of commercial orchards replace their trees at 25

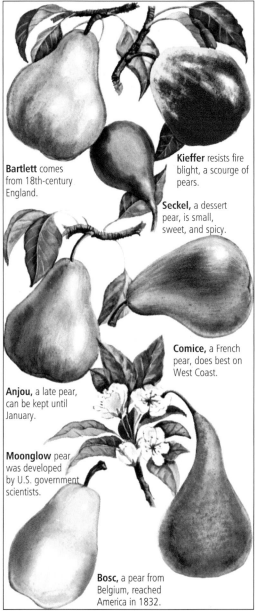

Bartlett comes from 18th-century England.

Kieffer resists fire blight, a scourge of pears.

Seckel, a dessert pear, is small, sweet, and spicy.

Comice, a French pear, does best on West Coast.

Anjou, a late pear, can be kept until January.

Moonglow pear was developed by U.S. government scientists.

Bosc, a pear from Belgium, reached America in 1832.

Central-leader system produces a strong tree that resists breakage. The shape allows sunlight to reach the lower branches.

Modified central leader tree has a main leader that is headed fairly low and scaffold branches nearly as long as the leader.

Open-center system is best for peaches and other stone fruits but experts no longer recommend it for apple or pear trees.

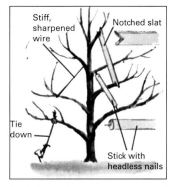

Train branches to the best growing position by tying them down to stakes or by using spreaders like the homemade types above.

Stiff, sharpened wire

Notched slat

Tie down

Stick with headless nails

illustration on right). Prune the trees to maintain a Christmas-tree profile so light can reach the lower branches. The central leader should be headed back each year to encourage the scaffold branches to grow—the leader will produce new shoots to continue its own growth. Head back the laterals, too, to keep them within bounds and promote formation of fruit spurs.

Trees that naturally tend to produce more than one leader can be trained on the modified central leader plan. The traditional open-center plan should not be used for apple and pear trees. It tends to produce lots of water sprouts and makes the tree vulnerable to splitting.

Rejuvenating Old Trees

An old, overgrown apple or pear tree, picturesque but unproductive, can often be restored to fruitfulness by pruning and feeding. The first task is to head the tree back to a manageable height, such as 15 to 20 feet (some varieties may reach 35 to 40 feet), and to cut off all dead, diseased, and damaged branches. Next, eliminate branches that are weak, crisscross, grow downward, or have narrow crotches, and cut off water sprouts and suckers. Paint wounds with tree-wound compound.

If the tree has a major limb that can serve as a central leader, save it and try to select branches that form a natural scaffold. If there is no leader, prune the top into an open vaselike shape to let in light and air. In addition to pruning, a neglected tree almost certainly needs cultivation and feeding. Rototill or spade up the soil, starting near the trunk and moving out to the drip line of the branches. This frees the tree's feeder roots from the competition of sod and weeds. It is helpful to till in compost or rotted manure. Another way to feed the tree is by using a crowbar to make a circle of 12-inch-deep holes around the drip line 18 inches apart and filling them with 10-10-10 fertilizer. Apply a thick layer of mulch around the tree to keep down weeds, but leave an 18-inch circle clear around the trunk to discourage rodents.

The Stone Fruits: Cherries, Peaches, Apricots, and Plums

The stone fruits—cherries, peaches, nectarines, apricots, and plums—get their name from the hard, stony pits that encase their seeds. In general, the stone-fruit trees are smaller and come into bearing sooner than apple and pear trees. They are also shorter lived, although with reasonable care they can remain productive for 20 to 40 years, depending on type.

All the stone fruits need well-drained soil, and good drainage is particularly important for peaches and cherries. Like apples and pears, the stone fruits need a period of winter chilling to blossom and produce fruit. Plant standard-sized trees 20 feet apart and dwarfs 10 feet apart. Some dwarf varieties can be grown even closer together; the nursery from which you buy them should supply details on planting and care.

The stone fruits are highly perishable and keep only a few days in storage. However, they are excellent for canning, drying, and, in some cases, freezing. All of them make fine preserves.

Cherries. There are two basic types of cherries: sweet and sour. Sweet cherries can be eaten fresh or cooked; sour cherries, also known as pie cherries, are used mainly for pies and preserves, although some are sweet enough to eat from the tree. The black cherry, a wild native American tree, yields small, sour cherries that can be used in pies; they are also a favorite food of songbirds.

Sweet cherries are grown in Zones 5 to 7 (see map, p.131); pie cherries in Zones 4 to 7. Bush cherries, a different species, grow throughout Zones 3 to 7 and bear small, sour fruits. Sweet cherry trees are upright in form and reach 25 to 30 feet if not pruned back. Most sour cherry trees are spreading and reach 15 to 25 feet, although the black cherry, an upright tree, occasionally grows as high as 100 feet. Sweet cherries should be trained as central-leader trees (see p.137). Sour cherries do better on the modified-leader plan.

Sour cherries are self-fertile, but sweet cherries must be cross-pollinated by another variety of sweet cherry if they are to bear fruit. Check with your county agent for compatible varieties, since certain types are not mutually fertile. Bush cherries also require cross-pollination, but they are not as finicky as sweet cherries. Sweet cherries rarely cross-pollinate with sour varieties.

Commercial varieties of both sweet and sour cherries live 30 to 40 years; bush cherries about 15 to 20 years. Wild black cherry trees live much longer; individual trees that are 150 to 200 years old have been found. Sweet cherries begin bearing about five years after they are planted, sour cherries usually bear three years after planting, and bush cherries often bear after the first year. All of them produce their fruit on spurs. Thinning is seldom needed for cherries. Robbing by birds can be countered by covering the trees with netting.

Peaches and nectarines. Often thought of as warmth-loving southern fruits, the peach and its smooth-skinned variant, the nectarine, flourish in Zones 5 through 8. Several hardy varieties, such as the Reliance peach, produce fruit in Zone 4. Peaches and nectarines must have a substantial winter chilling period to blossom—the number of hours of chill required differs with the variety. A few recently developed varieties produce fruit in the cooler parts of Zone 9.

Peaches and nectarines grow best on slightly acid soil (pH 6 to 7), but their prime requirement is good drainage. Late spring frosts often kill blossoms; to avoid this danger, plant the trees on high ground.

Peach and nectarine trees should be trained to the open-center or modified-leader plan with three or four scaffold branches. They bear on shoots that were formed the previous year, not on spurs like apples, pears, and cherries. Most peaches and all nectarines are self-fertile. Thin the fruits to 6 to 8 inches apart. Thinning is especially important with peaches and nectarines to get fruits of good size and flavor and to avoid weakening the tree by overproduction.

Peaches and nectarines should ripen on the tree. They should be picked when they feel soft under gentle pressure and when they separate readily from their stems. They keep only a few days in cool storage but are excellent fruits for freezing and canning. The quality is better if they are frozen in syrup or sugar.

Apricots. Although little grown for home use, apricots are not difficult to raise. The prime requisite for success is protecting these early-blossoming trees from spring frosts. Planting them on a north slope or on the north side of a building helps by delaying blossoming. If the tree is small, it can be covered on a frosty night. Apricot trees themselves are quite hardy and can be grown in Zones 4 through 8.

Standard apricots, if left unpruned, will reach a height of 20 feet and a spread of 25 to 30 feet; dwarfs reach a maximum height of 8 feet and a spread of 10 feet. Both produce better when kept pruned back.

Apricots should be trained on the open-center plan (see p.137), with three or four main scaffold branches beginning between 18 and 30 inches from the ground. Each scaffold branch should have one or two secondary scaffold branches arising 4 to 5 feet above ground level.

Apricots bear fruit on short-lived spurs. Almost all apricots are self-pollinating and set heavy crops without the aid of another variety. The fruit should be thinned conscientiously to 6 inches apart. Apricots normally begin to bear two or three years after planting and can produce for as long as 70 years.

For eating fresh and for drying, apricots should be harvested when they are fully ripe and separate easily from the stem. For canning, harvest the fruit while it is still firm.

Napoleon is a golden red sweet cherry.

Black Tartarian, an early sweet cherry, is a long-time favorite.

Emperor Francis, a yellow cherry with firm flesh, is seldom harmed by birds.

Bing, a sweet cherry, ripens in midsummer.

North Star, a very hardy sour cherry, grows on a dwarf tree.

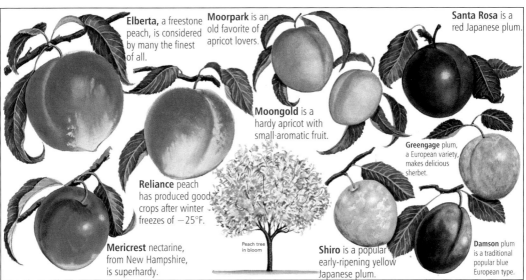

Elberta, a freestone peach, is considered by many the finest of all.

Moorpark is an old favorite of apricot lovers.

Santa Rosa is a red Japanese plum.

Moongold is a hardy apricot with small aromatic fruit.

Greengage plum, a European variety, makes delicious sherbet.

Reliance peach has produced good crops after winter freezes of −25°F.

Mericrest nectarine, from New Hampshire, is superhardy.

Peach tree in bloom

Shiro is a popular early-ripening yellow Japanese plum.

Damson plum is a traditional popular blue European type.

Some nurseries have developed strains of apricots with edible kernels. (The kernels of most varieties of apricots, like those of most stone fruits, contain enough cyanide to render them bitter and even poisonous if eaten in quantity.)

Plums. Plums fall into two major groups: European and Japanese. Japanese plums are mostly round and red; European plums are mostly oval and blue. There are also green and yellow varieties, such as the Greengage and Yellow Egg, both old European-type favorites. Most European plums are self-fertile; all Japanese plums require another variety of Japanese plum as a pollinator. Certain European varieties with a very high sugar content are called prunes, and dried prunes are made from their fruits. They are also delicious fresh.

Plums thrive on soils with a pH of 6.0 to 8.0. European plums do best in Zones 5 to 7; Japanese plums in Zones 5 to 9. A few hardy varieties, produced by crossing European or Japanese plums with native American species, will bear fruit in Zone 4.

Standard plum trees reach a height and spread of 15 to 20 feet; dwarfs reach 8 to 10 feet. European plums do best when trained on the modified-leader plan; Japanese plums on the open-center plan. Plums usually bear three to four years after planting. The fruit, borne on long-lived spurs, should be thinned to 3 or 4 inches apart.

For eating fresh or for drying, pick plums when they are soft and come away from the tree easily. For canning, pick them when they have acquired a waxy white coating and are springy to the touch but still firm.

The Warmth-Loving Citrus Fruits

Citrus fruits are semitropical plants requiring a warm frost-free climate the year round. They do best in Zone 10 and the warmer parts of Zone 9 (see map, p.131). The members of the genus vary in their resistance to cold. Limes are the most cold tender; tangerines are the hardiest. Kumquats, which belong to a related genus, are even hardier. Cold hardiness is influenced by the weather just before a freeze: cool weather makes the trees hardier. However, citrus trees rarely survive prolonged exposure to temperatures in the lower teens.

Citrus trees grow best in a slightly acid soil (pH 6.0 to 6.5). They can be planted at any time of the year, but the winter months are preferred because less watering is necessary then. No pruning is needed except to remove dead wood and to shape the tree to fit the available space. Citrus trees reach a height of 20 to 40 feet, with an equal spread; kumquats usually reach half this size.

Both grafted and ungrafted citrus trees are available. Most are sold in containers. Look for plants with large healthy leaves; reject any that are potbound, that is, whose roots have grown until they fill the containers.

Grafted citrus trees begin to bear when they are two to four years old. Ungrafted plants bear much later; in addition, they are quite thorny and tend to become very large. Citrus trees are long-lived—some that are more than 100 years old are still producing.

Temple orange, a Florida specialty.

Tangelo is a cross between a tangerine and a grapefruit.

Valencia, an orange good for juice and marmalade.

Lemon is a prolific bearer and yields tasty honey.

Lime gained fame as a scurvy preventive in Britain's navy.

Kumquats are hardy and easy to raise.

Grapefruit can have white, pink, or red flesh.

Most citrus trees produce fruit without pollination, although some of the tangerine hybrids do need cross-pollination. Citruses can be prolific bearers: a mature navel orange tree will yield more than 500 pounds of fruit per year, and large lemon trees can bear even more. The fruits should be allowed to ripen on the tree for the best flavor. Color is usually, but not always, a guide to ripeness. (Cool weather enhances color while delaying ripening.) The fruit also becomes softer as it gets ripe, usually about 8 to 12 months after bloom. In the cool coastal areas of California it can take 24 or more months for the fruit to mature, and three crops of fruit can be found on the trees at the same time. Tangerines should be harvested by clipping their stems to avoid tearing the loose rind; other citrus fruits can be pulled off by giving the fruit a slight twist. Citrus fruits keep well in cool storage. Most citrus varieties can be left on the tree for long periods without the fruit developing any symptoms of deterioration.

Protecting trees from frost

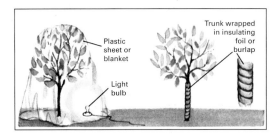

When temperatures drop below 26°F, citrus trees need protection, either by covering them or providing artificial heat. Smudge pots—containers of burning oil—are seldom used anymore.

Grapefruit can have white, pink, or red flesh and is available in seeded and seedless varieties. Grapefruit trees tend to be larger than orange trees and need more warmth. When ripe, the fruit grows to 6 inches in diameter, usually with a thick, pale yellow rind. Best quality is reached after Christmas.

Kumquats are valued as ornamentals as well as fruit producers. The bright orange fruit is eaten whole, rind and all. Kumquats have a tart, spicy flavor and are commonly made into preserves. Limequats, a pale yellow lime-kumquat hybrid, are useful lime substitutes in climates where limes will not survive.

Lemons grow very vigorously and are thorny; thus they are suitable only for very large gardens. Their sensitivity to cold limits them to Hawaii, southern Arizona, coastal California, and the Gulf Coast. The Meyer lemon, a semihardy hybrid, is a good choice for home gardens. Lemons bloom and bear fruit the year round, but the main crop is usually set in summer.

Limes, like lemons, tend to fruit the year round. They are very cold tender and are common only in southern Florida. The Key lime is small, sour, and seedy and thrives only in the warmer areas of Florida.

Oranges are divided into early, midseason, and late varieties; these in turn can be subdivided into seeded and seedless types. The best-known early orange is the navel orange. The most common late variety is the Valencia.

Tangelos and tangors are common garden trees in the citrus belt. Tangelos are crosses between tangerines and grapefruits, tangors between tangerines and oranges. The temple orange is a well-known tangor.

Tangerines, also called mandarins, are hardier than most other citrus fruits. They have a loose skin that is easily peeled and are best when eaten fresh. As with oranges, there are early, midseason, and late varieties, most of which are well suited to home gardens.

Long-lived Nut Trees For Food and Shade

Nut trees adapt to a wide range of climates and soils, although they prefer a deep, rich, crumbly soil that is neutral or slightly alkaline. (An exception is the Chinese chestnut, which does well in acid soil.) Nut trees even thrive in rough or otherwise uncultivatable land, provided the drainage is good. Full sunlight is needed for best results. Most nut trees do not succeed where minimum temperatures fall below –20°F, and they need a frost-free growing season of at least 150 days to produce a crop. Nut trees also need ample summer heat for their nuts to develop properly.

Nut trees are planted like fruit trees. However, walnuts and hickories have a single deep taproot rather than a branching root system. Since the taproot should not be cut back or bent, dig the hole deep enough to accommodate it. At planting time the top of the tree should be cut back by a third to a half to force it to grow a strong new sprout that will mature into the main trunk. Nut trees need little pruning except to maintain a strong central leader during the first years of growth and to remove dead and crisscrossing branches.

Nut trees can be propagated from seed, but in many cases the extraction of the kernels will be so difficult that it is hardly worth the effort. As a result, with the exception of Chinese chestnuts and Carpathian walnuts, only grafted trees of named varieties should be planted. However, seedlings can be grafted with buds or scions of named varieties after they have become established.

Well-cared-for grafted nut trees usually begin to bear at three to five years of age. For proper pollination it is advisable to plant two or more of each kind of tree. With cultivated strains plant at least two varieties. When mature, nuts will fall from the tree by themselves or with the aid of gentle shaking. For best quality they should be gathered as soon as they fall; when allowed to lie on the ground, they deteriorate rapidly if not eaten by squirrels and other wildlife.

The nuts should be husked and dried in a shaded spot until the kernels are brittle—usually about three weeks. The dried nuts, stored in a cool place, will remain in good condition for a year. Freshness can be restored by soaking them in water overnight. Shelled nuts will keep indefinitely if stored in a plastic bag in the freezer. (Chestnuts should be boiled for three to five minutes before freezing them.)

Almonds are grown mainly on the West Coast because of their climatic needs: a long, warm growing season with low humidity. For other sections nurseries sell hardy strains that can be raised where peaches succeed, but the kernels are toxic to some people.

Butternuts are a species of walnut and the hardiest of all native nut trees. They grow in Zones 4 to 8 (see p.131). The oil-rich nuts can be pickled when immature as well as eaten ripe. A gray-brown dye can be made from the bark. The nuts can be dried with their husks on.

Chinese chestnuts are resistant to the blight that wiped out the native American chestnuts. About as hardy as peach trees, they succeed in Zones 5 to 8. Chinese chestnuts yield large crops of high-quality nuts, borne in sharp-spined burrs that split open at maturity. Each burr contains from one to three nuts. When fresh, chestnuts are high in starch and low in sugar, which gives them a taste like potatoes. However, as the nuts dry out the starch changes to sugar.

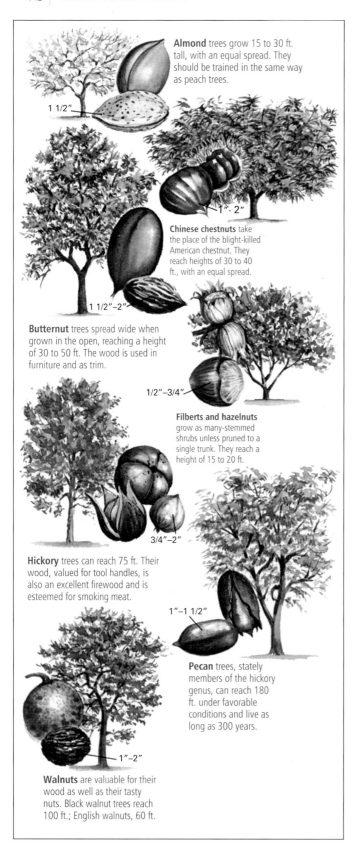

Almond trees grow 15 to 30 ft. tall, with an equal spread. They should be trained in the same way as peach trees.

1 1/2"

Chinese chestnuts take the place of the blight-killed American chestnut. They reach heights of 30 to 40 ft., with an equal spread.

1"- 2"

1 1/2"–2"

Butternut trees spread wide when grown in the open, reaching a height of 30 to 50 ft. The wood is used in furniture and as trim.

1/2"–3/4"

Filberts and hazelnuts grow as many-stemmed shrubs unless pruned to a single trunk. They reach a height of 15 to 20 ft.

3/4"–2"

Hickory trees can reach 75 ft. Their wood, valued for tool handles, is also an excellent firewood and is esteemed for smoking meat.

1"–1 1/2"

Pecan trees, stately members of the hickory genus, can reach 180 ft. under favorable conditions and live as long as 300 years.

1"–2"

Walnuts are valuable for their wood as well as their tasty nuts. Black walnut trees reach 100 ft.; English walnuts, 60 ft.

Filberts and hazelnuts are closely related. (The name filbert is generally used for the European species, hazelnut for the native American species.) There are also numerous hybrid varieties. American hazelnuts grow in Zones 4 to 8; European filberts are hardy in Zones 5 to 8.

Hickory trees are native to North America and grow over most of the eastern half of the United States in Zones 5 to 7. Two species, the shagbark and the shellbark, produce edible nuts that are hard to crack. However, cultivated varieties with meatier kernels and thinner shells have been developed and are sold by nurseries.

Pecans belong to the hickory clan. Essentially a southern tree, the pecan's native range is the Southeast and lower Mississippi Valley. Papershell pecans grow in Zones 7 to 9. There are hardy northern varieties that grow in Zones 6 to 9, and even one that survives in Zone 5. However, pecans in the North often fail to produce nuts when summer is cool or frost comes early.

Walnuts include the native American black walnut; the English, or Persian, walnut native to Central Asia; and the heartnut, a Japanese walnut variety. The roots of black walnuts give off a substance that is toxic to apples, tomatoes, potatoes, and a number of other plants. Do not plant these susceptible plants within 30 feet of a black walnut. The black walnut can be raised in Zones 5 to 9. English walnuts reach a height and spread of about 60 feet. Easier to shell than black walnuts, they are hardy in Zones 5 to 9. Heartnuts are low, spreading trees that reach 30 to 40 feet in height. They are hardy in Zones 4 to 8. The nuts, which grow in clusters of 8 to 10, resemble butternuts in flavor.

Tasty Strawberries Give Vitamin C Too

Strawberries, though short-lived, are one of the most adaptable of fruits. They can be grown from Florida to Alaska, and since the plants are small, they can be raised in containers, in

Sparkle, a late-blooming variety for northern gardens, escapes late spring frosts.

Ozark Beauty, an everbearer, keeps on producing until killing frosts.

Wild strawberries, small but prolific, are one of the ancestors of today's large succulent garden strawberries.

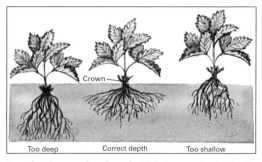

Strawberries must be planted with their crowns level with soil.

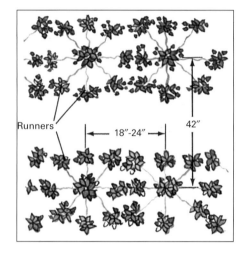

Matted-row system requires very little main-tenance. However, the yields are lower and the berries are smaller than they are under other systems of culture. In the matted-row system almost all the runners are allowed to root. The plants are spaced 18 to 24 in. apart in single rows with about 42 in. between rows.

Three Culture Systems

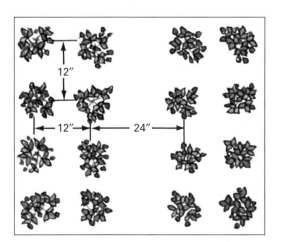

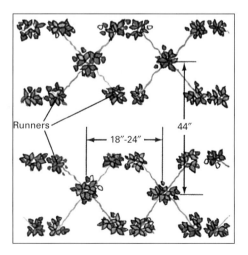

Hill system requires that all runners be kept pruned off the plants. Plants are spaced 12 in. apart. Growers usually plant double or triple rows with 12 in. between rows and a 24-in. alley between each set of rows. The hill system gives high yields and large berries, but it requires a great deal of labor and attention.

Spaced matted-row system is popular with home gardeners. It is a compromise between the hill and matted-row systems. The plants are spaced 18 to 24 in. apart in a single row; only four to six runners per plant are allowed to develop. The spaced matted-row system gives good yields and high quality.

ornamental borders, or among vegetables, provided they have full sunlight.

Once established, strawberries spread by sending out numerous slender stems, or runners, along the ground. When a runner is about 8 inches long, it bends sharply upward. At this bend the runner sends roots down into the soil and begins to form leaves. Once the new plant is formed, it sends out runners of its own.

The best planting time for strawberries is in the early spring, although in the South they can be planted in the fall. Plant them in well-tilled soil mixed with compost or rotted manure. Spread the roots out fanwise in the hole and pack the soil firmly around them. Some growers find that trimming the roots to 4 inches simplifies planting. Proper planting depth is critical for strawberries (see diagram on previous page). Spacing depends on which system of culture you choose: hill, matted-row, or spaced matted-row.

Most strawberries bear fruit in May or June, depending on the local climate. There are also so-called ever-bearing varieties that produce a crop of berries in early summer and another in late summer or early fall.

Strawberries will produce blossoms the year they are planted, but these blossoms should be pinched off to strengthen the plants and ensure a good crop the next year. The yield is greatest on two- and three-year-old plants. Production tends to drop sharply after three years, and the recommended practice is to replace the plants, preferably putting them in a new bed to avoid soil-borne disease. You can use runners that rooted the previous year in the old bed, but it is safer to order new certified virus-free plants from a nursery.

Strawberries thrive when mulched between the rows and under the plants. The plants should be covered with 6 inches of straw, leaves, or pine needles after the ground has frozen. Remove the mulch cover in late spring when new leaves are about 2 inches long.

Grapes: A Variety For Every Palate

Three types of grapes are raised in the United States. Labrusca grapes are descended from the native eastern wild grape. They are grown in the northern two-thirds of the country east of the Rockies in Zones 5 to 8 (see p.131). Muscadine grapes are grown in the Southeast, where they are natives, in Zones 7 to 10. Vinifera (European) grapes, the kind usually found at fruit stores, do best in Zones 6 to 9 and are raised mainly in California and Arizona (in other areas they are subject to disease and pests). In addition to the basic types there are many hybrids that combine the tastiness and the winemaking qualities of European grapes with the hardiness and resistance of American grapes. Most Labrusca and European grapes are self-fertile; most muscadines are not.

Grapes can be propagated easily by rooting cuttings of dormant stems in damp sphagnum moss or by layering—bending a shoot down and burying part of it in the soil, while leaving a few leaves or buds at the tip uncovered. This should be done in spring; roots will form along the buried portion during the growing season. Early the next spring, before growth starts, cut the newly rooted portion away from the parent vine and transplant it.

Grapes are produced on each year's new growth, and the best fruit is produced from the new shoots formed on canes from the previous year. The year-old canes are easy to recognize at pruning time: they are about as thick as a pencil and have light, smooth bark whereas older canes are stouter and have dark, fibrous bark. Remove blossoms and fruits from the vines the first two summers for a good crop the third year. Grapevines are long-lived and may produce for a hundred years. Although they will yield fruit in poor soil, they do better in fertile soil. However, overfertilization will produce masses of shoots and leaves with inferior fruit. The vines should be heavily mulched or clean-cultivated, since grass and weeds rob grapes of nutrients. Cultivate no deeper than 4 inches to avoid injuring the shallow roots.

Planting and Training Grapes

Grapes grow in a wide variety of soils as long as the organic content is high. They should be planted

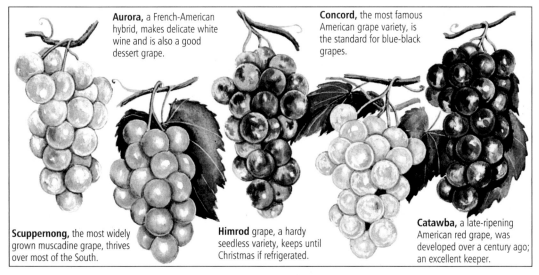

Aurora, a French-American hybrid, makes delicate white wine and is also a good dessert grape.

Concord, the most famous American grape variety, is the standard for blue-black grapes.

Scuppernong, the most widely grown muscadine grape, thrives over most of the South.

Himrod grape, a hardy seedless variety, keeps until Christmas if refrigerated.

Catawba, a late-ripening American red grape, was developed over a century ago; an excellent keeper.

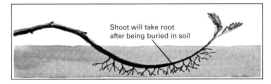

Layering a grapevine, a simple means of propagation.

in spring. Try to plant your vines on a slope so that cold air and water will drain off. Set new vines 8 to 10 feet apart in holes 12 inches wide and 12 inches deep. Trim the roots to fit the hole and prune off all canes (branches) but one. Prune that cane back to two buds.

Grapes must be trained on supports to keep the fruit off the ground and provide air circulation. A sturdy wire trellis is the most common form of support. Training should begin at planting time: the vine should be trained on a stake to form a straight main stem, or trunk. Training on the wire trellis begins the second year. While grapes can be trained in a myriad of forms, the most used system is the four-arm Kniffin (below). The first year, at pruning time, leave about three buds above the lower wire and two buds below it. Remove all other buds and side shoots. Head the trunk back a few inches above the lower wire. As the new shoots grow from the buds, select the straightest one above the wire to be the main leader and tie it to the upper wire when it is long enough. Train the shoots from the two lowest buds along the lower wire to become the next year's fruiting arms. Train two shoots along the upper wire as they develop.

The third spring prune back the fruiting arms to 6 to 10 buds each. Remove other lateral canes, but leave two stubs, or spurs, near the fruiting arms to produce next year's fruit. Follow the same procedure each year for steady crops of fruit. Muscadine grapes, however, are treated slightly differently. They should have fruiting spurs of three or four buds left along the fruiting arms, which need to be renewed only every four or five years.

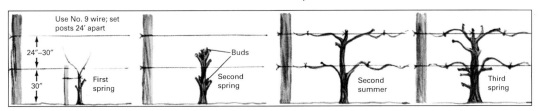

Newly planted vine (left) should be tied to stake. After two additional springtimes vine will be well established on wire trellis.

Fast, Prolific Bearers: The Bush Fruits

The cultivated bush fruits include raspberries, blackberries (and their relatives), blueberries, currants, and gooseberries. (There are numerous other fruit-bearing bushes, but they are not cultivated on any significant scale.) All are hardy and productive. Most are shallow rooted. All need to be pruned every year to keep them from becoming overgrown. All prefer well-drained humus-rich soil, and all need at least eight hours of sunlight. Although not as long-lived as fruit trees, most of the bush fruits can be kept going for several decades with a modest amount of care.

Raspberries are divided into two basic types: red and black. Yellow raspberries are considered a variant of red, and purple raspberries of black. Varieties of differing hardiness grow from Zones 3 to 8 (see p.131). Raspberries bear fruit the year after planting, and a raspberry bed will generally last for 7 to 10 years before production declines, usually due to one of the many viruses to which raspberries are susceptible. The plants should then be replaced with new ones, preferably in a different bed, and the old bed should not be used for raspberries or blackberries for at least five years.

Spring planting is best for raspberries, except in the South. The soil should be well cultivated and free of sod and weeds. Dig a small hole 4 inches deep for each plant, or plow a 4-inch-deep furrow. Set the plants with the crowns just below soil level. Cover the roots with loose soil and pack it down gently. Fill the remainder of the hole or furrow with loose soil. Space plants 3 feet apart in rows 5 to 8 feet apart.

Raspberries produce their fruit on two-year-old canes, that is, stems that sprouted the previous summer. In most varieties the canes die after one crop. The exceptions are the everbearing varieties, which yield a small crop in the fall on the tips of one-year-old canes and a second small crop lower down on the same canes the following summer. Once a cane has borne its full crop of fruit, it should be cut off at ground level and removed as a sanitary measure. Many growers prefer to treat ever-bearers as fall bearers only. They cut the canes down to soil level after the end of the growing season; the next year's new canes will then produce a heavy fall crop. Some growers use a rotary lawn mower at the lowest setting to cut down their old everbearing canes. Red and yellow raspberries produce numerous suckers from their roots. Most of these must be pulled out to keep the bed under control, but a few of the strongest from each plant should be saved to become next year's bearing canes. Excess suckers can be dug up with a bit of root and replanted to become new bushes. As the plants fill in, they may be grown in clumps or in hills 3 feet apart, with 6 to 10 canes per hill. They can also be grown in hedgerows 1 to 2 feet wide with no more than five canes per square foot of row. Leave at least a handbreadth of space between canes to permit air circulation. Raspberries are most easily managed when wire trained.

Latham is a very popular red raspberry.

Bristol, a black raspberry, is a heavy bearer.

Darrow, an improved blackberry strain, bears inch-long fruit.

Black and purple raspberries produce few if any suckers; they increase instead by tip layering. In late summer the bearing canes arch down to the ground and push their tips into the soil. The buried tips produce roots and new shoots that can be clipped free the next spring and replanted if necessary.

Although raspberry roots strike as deep as 4 feet, most of the roots are in the upper 12 inches of soil. Since so much of the root system is shallow, mulching is preferable to cultivation.

Prune red raspberry canes back to 4 or 5 feet in spring. The canes of black raspberries should be cut back to 18 to 24 inches their first summer. This stimulates them to form the lateral branches on which they will bear their fruit. Shorten the laterals to 8 to 10 inches the next spring. Black raspberries treated this way will not need a trellis for support.

Since raspberries bloom over a period of several weeks, the harvest season is correspondingly long. By planting successively maturing varieties you can extend the harvest season from midsummer to heavy frost. Raspberries are ready to pick when they separate easily from the stem, leaving the core of the berry behind.

Blackberries that are sold for cultivation are larger, juicier, sweeter cousins of the widespread wild blackberry. Not as hardy as raspberries, blackberries do best in the South, but there are varieties that are hardy as far north as Zone 3. Boysenberries, loganberries, and youngberries are hybrids of blackberries and either dewberries (another species of bramble fruit) or red raspberries. They are relatively cold tender and prosper best in Zones 7 to 9. Thornless blackberries are not reliably hardy north of Zone 5. Within their climate range they are a desirable choice because they lack thorns.

There are bush and vine types of blackberries. The bush types, which are hardier, are planted and propagated like red raspberries. Vine types are treated like black raspberries. Like raspberries, blackberries bear fruit on two-year-old canes. Bush-type canes should be pruned back to 5 feet at midsummer during their first year to aid in the formation of laterals. The next spring head back the laterals to 12 to 18 inches. Vine-type canes can be pruned like black raspberries. Blackberries should not be picked until they are dead ripe, separating from the stem at the slightest touch.

Blueberries thrive wherever their relatives, azaleas or rhododendrons, grow. They demand a very acid soil, ideally close to pH 4.8. Blueberries will not survive in alkaline soil. If your soil has a pH over 6.5, grow your blueberries in containers or raised beds filled with an acid soil mix. Do not plant blueberries in soil that has been limed in the last two years. Two species of blueberries are cultivated in the United States: the highbush blueberry in the Northeast, Midwest, upper South, and Pacific Northwest, and the rabbiteye blueberry in the Deep South. The highbush grows to 10 feet or taller if unpruned; the rabbiteye can reach 20 feet.

Highbush blueberries should be planted 4 to 5 feet apart in rows 8 to 10 feet apart; rabbiteye blueberries should be spaced 5 to 6 feet apart with 10 to 12 feet between rows. Dig a hole about 6 inches deep and 10 inches in diameter and set the plants with the crowns at soil level. If the soil is poor in humus, mix in compost. Be sure to keep the soil moist the first year—blueberries are very sensitive to drought. A 6-inch mulch of leaves or rotted sawdust will maintain soil moisture, add to the soil's organic content, and keep down weeds. Cultivation is apt to injure the shallow root systems of blueberries.

Rabbiteye blueberries very seldom need pruning except to remove weak or dead branches. Highbush blueberries should be pruned annually beginning the third year after planting. Remove old canes (stems) by cutting them off at soil level when they become twiggy. New canes arising from the root system will take their place. The desired result is a bush with clean, sparsely branched canes with a few fat buds on each branch. If necessary, head back lateral branches to three buds each.

Commercial growers propagate blueberries by rooting cuttings in sand or sphagnum moss. Better systems for the home gardener are mounding (a form of layering) and division, a technique familiar to flower gardeners. In mounding, pile soil, compost, or a mixture of peat moss and rotted sawdust around the base of the blueberry bush about a foot deep. Keep the mound damp. New roots will form on the covered portions of the canes, which can be severed below the roots and replanted. In division, use a sharp spade to split the bush into two or more parts, each with its own roots and stems. Head back each portion about one-third and replant.

Highbush blueberries are moderately self-fertile but produce better crops if two or more varieties are planted together. In addition, by combining early, midseason, and late varieties, you can stretch out your harvest so that it lasts more than two months. Rabbiteye blueberries

Bluecrop is a hardy, dependable blueberry.

Wild blueberry is found in many areas.

Red Lake is the leading currant in the United States.

Pixwell gooseberry turns pink when ripe.

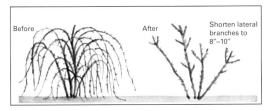

Pruning red raspberries keeps the bushes within manageable size, removes dead canes, and permits air circulation.

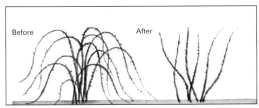

Shorten lateral branches to 8″–10″

Black raspberries produce lateral branches where the fruits are borne. These branches should be headed back in spring.

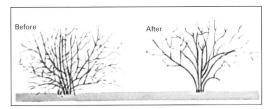

When pruning highbush blueberries remove old canes and twigs that interlace. Crowded bushes produce poorly.

require cross-pollination. Blueberries are ready to harvest when they separate from the stem at a light touch and are sweet to the taste.

Currants and gooseberries, close relatives of each other, are the most cold loving of the bush fruits, thriving as far north as Zone 2 but doing poorly from Zone 7 south. Unfortunately, both species are hosts to white pine blister rust, and raising them is governed by strict regulations (check your own state's regulations with your county agent). Some states ban them entirely.

Well-drained soils are best for both currants and gooseberries, although they tolerate damp ground better than other bush fruits. They should be planted in fall in holes 12 inches across and 12 inches deep, with 2 to 4 feet between plants and 8 to 9 feet between rows. Bushes may be propagated by layering branches or by taking 8- to 10-inch cuttings of the current season's shoots in fall and sticking them in the ground, leaving two buds exposed. Currants form roots in one year; gooseberries can take as long as two years.

Currants and gooseberries bear fruit the year after planting, and production is heaviest on two- and three-year-old canes. Canes more than three years old can be removed after harvest. The canes darken as they grow older, a clue to their age. Let a few new canes develop each year as replacements. Little pruning is needed except to keep the bushes open and to remove the nonproductive overage canes.

Many people find currants too tart to eat fresh, but they make excellent jelly, jam, and fruit syrup. Gooseberries can be eaten fresh, in pies, or as preserves.

Sources and resources

Books and pamphlets
Clarke, J. Harold. *Growing Berries and Grapes at Home.* New York: Dover, 1976.
Ferguson, Barbara J. *All About Growing Fruits and Berries.* San Francisco: Ortho Books, 1982.
Hedrick, U. P. *Fruits for the Home Garden.* New York: Dover, 1973.
Hessayon, D.G. *The Fruit Expert.* New York: Sterling Publishing, 1995.
Hill, Lewis. *Fruits and Berries for the Home Garden.* Pownal, Vt.: Storey Communications, 1992.
Kains, Maurice G. *Five Acres and Independence.* New York: Dover, 1973.
Seymour, John. *The Self-Sufficient Gardener: A Complete Guide to Growing and Preserving All Your Own Food.* Garden City, N.Y.: Doubleday, 1979.
Smith, Miranda. *Backyard Fruits and Berries.* Emmaus, Pa.: Rodale Press, 1994.
Van Atta, Marian, and Wagner, Shirley. *Growing Family Fruit and Nut Trees.* Sarasota, Fla.: Pineapple Press, 1993.

Pest Control

Protecting Your Crops Without Poisoning Them

Gardens and orchards are threatened by three enemies: disease, insects, and animals. During the last few decades the standard defense against most of these pests has been massive doses of man-made poisons. For large-scale farmers there may be no practical alternative, but the home gardener has an arsenal of nonchemical and organic methods from which to choose.

Some are as simple as picking pests off plants by hand or employing basic preventive hygiene to keep them from breeding; others are as sophisticated as electronic traps that lure insects, then electrocute them. Some strategies enlist the aid of nature herself to fight pests by encouraging natural predators or cultivating pest-repellent plants near valued crops. Fences bar the larger animals, while traps and barriers defend against a variety of insects and small animals. As a last resort there are organic sprays and dusts—naturally occurring insecticides usually derived from plants.

The underlying theme of natural pest control is the recognition that a garden or orchard is part of an ecological whole and that the entire system must be in balance for the garden or orchard to be healthy. Those who practice ecological gardening do not try to eliminate pests completely, since in so doing they will eliminate the food supply of many beneficial organisms. Instead, the aim of organic pest control is to keep the number of pests low enough so that they do not do serious damage, while at the same time maintaining the predator population that feeds on the pests.

Nonchemical controls entail more time and labor than chemical methods, and the nonchemical gardener must be prepared to lose some crops to "bugs." But an increasing number of people find this a price worth paying.

Using Natural Controls

Japanese beetles feed on leaves of fruit and shade trees and also destroy much fruit directly. The larvae, which feed on the roots of grass, are major lawn pests.

One of the easiest ways to combat pests is to protect and encourage such natural allies as birds, toads, spiders, nonpoisonous snakes, and insects that feed on other insects. In many cases this simply involves no more than tolerating the predator (such as a snake or spider) instead of killing it or destroying its habitat. With a little more effort you can provide suitable habitats for insect destroyers; for example, an inverted flower pot for toads or a special birdhouse for purple martins. Another solution is to stock your garden or orchard with beneficial insects. Ladybug and praying mantis eggs are sold by

A Rogue's Gallery of Common Insect Pests

Aphids are probably the most common garden pests. They suck sap from leaves and stems, weakening plants. They also spread virus and fungal diseases.

Codling moth larvae are serious pests to apples. They tunnel their way into the hearts of young fruits, emerging on the far side and leaving worm holes behind.

Colorado potato beetles attack potatoes, eggplant, tomatoes, and peppers. The adults and larvae both devour foliage and may kill entire plants if unchecked.

Spotted or Striped cucumber beetles feed on every part of cucumber plants, including the roots, and spread bacterial wilt They also attack squash, melons, beans, peas, and corn.

June beetles (also called May beetles in some locations) can cause extensive damage to the roots of lawns and shrubs.

Plant louses feed on plant juices and can damage both indoor and outdoor plants.

many garden supply houses; both insects prey on a variety of common pests. Another natural predator is the trichogramma wasp, which lays its eggs inside the eggs of many species of caterpillar. The wasp larvae feed on caterpillar eggs, destroying them.

The introduction of specific insect diseases is a proven biological method of pest control. Milky spore disease, available as a white powder, can be dusted on the soil to infect and kill the larvae of the Japanese beetle. Bacillus thuringiensis—BT for short—is a bacterium that infects many destructive caterpillars, including the cabbage worm and gypsy moth. It is applied as a spray and has an effective life of seven days. Both milky spore and BT are harmless to humans, domestic animals, and such beneficial insects as honeybees.

More sophisticated biological controls have been developed, although as yet they are practical for large-scale usc only and are therefore beyond the scope of the home gardener. One such method is the rearing and release of huge numbers of sterile male insects. By competing with normal males in mating, these sterile insects reduce the number of offspring. Another technique is to spray caterpillars with juvenile hormones; the caterpillars never mature to have young, cutting down tremendously on the size of the next generation.

Natural predators are one of the gardener's most powerful weapons for fighting pests; moreover, they require no care and need only be left alone to do their work. Some of the more commonly found predators that feed on insect pests are shown above. All are harmless to humans and should be encouraged in your garden, berry patch, or orchard.

So-called trap crops take advantage of the food preferences of various insect pests by luring them away from more valuable crops. For example, nasturtiums lure aphids away from nearby vegetables, while Japanese beetles are attracted to white geraniums, white or pastel zinnias, and odorless marigolds. Radishes lure root maggots away from cabbage crops, eggplants draw flea beetles away from potato plantings, dill attracts tomato hornworms, and mustard greens are a good trap crop for harlequin bugs. Pests concentrated on the trap crop can be picked off by hand and destroyed, but this must be done regularly or the trap crop will not be effective. Kill the pests by dropping them into kerosene or into water that has a thin layer of kerosene on it.

Do-it-yourself Defenses for Foiling the Enemy

Repellents are often effective in deterring pests, thereby protecting crops without having to resort to poisons. Many gardeners report success with homemade sprays based on hot peppers, onions, and garlic. As with poison sprays, add a few drops of liquid detergent or 1/3 cup of soap flakes per gallon of spray to increase the spray's sticking power and effectiveness. Another type of repellent spray is made by liquifying the pests in a blender. It is said to be effective on slugs, snails, and insects, but each liquified pest repels its own species only.

Some plants are natural repellents. Mints and other aromatic herbs interplanted with vegetables discourage a number of insects, especially those that attack the cabbage family. Radishes have been successful in repelling pests of melons and other vine crops. Garlic is one of the most potent repellent plants and will protect nearby fruit plantings from Japanese beetles and aphids. If planted around fruit trees, it is said to keep borers away. (For more information on companion planting, see *The Kitchen Garden*, p.101.)

Tar paper repels cutworms by its odor. Use 3-inch squares of tar paper laid on the ground, with holes in the centers for the stems to pass through, to protect seedlings from these pests. Aluminum foil laid on the ground has been found to be effective against aphids and squash-vine borers. Plants also appear to benefit from the extra reflected light. A simple way to remove aphids from foliage is to knock them off with a jet of water from the garden hose; few return to the plants.

There are a number of botanical poisons—natural chemicals produced by plants for their own protection—that are deadly to many insects but virtually harmless to humans and other warm-blooded animals. These substances break down into harmless by-products soon after use. The best known are ryania, rotenone, and pyrethrum. Nicotine, another powerful natural insecticide, is very dangerous to humans, animals, and bees.

Preventive measures stop trouble before it starts

Gardens, like human beings, can be kept healthy and productive more cheaply and more easily with an ounce of prevention than with a pound of cure.

Prevention begins with the soil. Till your garden in the autumn as well as spring to expose subsoil insects and larvae to predators and the weather. Since well-nourished plants have greater resistance than poorly nourished ones, keep the soil's organic content high. Compost, organic mulches, and well-rotted manure are excellent additives. Sanitation is a simple but effective preventive technique, useful against both disease microorganisms and insect pests. Locate your garden in a spot with good drainage and air flow; quick drying discourages fungi. Disease organisms can be kept from spreading from sick plants to healthy ones by removing all sick plants from the garden, the orchard, and the surrounding area. The diseased material should be burned or buried—do not use it for compost. Branches and canes pruned from fruit trees, bushes, and vines should be disposed of in the same way. If they are left on the ground near plants, they can act as breeding grounds for boring insects and fungus disease. Fallen fruit should be picked up twice a week and buried or fed to livestock. Vegetable plants should be removed from the garden at the end of the growing season. They can safely be composted in a fast-acting compost pile (see *The Kitchen Garden*, p.101).

Crop rotation is an effective measure, especially against soil-borne disease. By shifting a crop to a new area yearly, pathogens and pests that may have developed the previous year are deprived of their host. In a small garden it may be difficult to rotate crops, but the same effect can be gained by changing the type of vegetables planted. For example, if squash is grown one summer, plant a member of a different family the next. If you are fond of a certain vegetable, plant different varieties each year and concentrate on pest-resistant strains.

Diatomaceous earth is a different sort of pesticide, working mechanically rather than chemically. It is sold as a fine dust made up of the skeletons of tiny one-celled sea organisms. The dust particles have sharp spikes that pierce the skins of such soft-bodied insects as aphids, causing them to die of dehydration.

Harmless pest killers can be made from a number of common household substances. A safe old-time remedy for cabbage worms is to sprinkle flour on the developing cabbage heads. The worms ingest the flour, which swells up inside them and bursts their intestines. Finely powdered sugar sprinkled on the plants can kill cabbage worms by dehydration. Salt sprinkled on slugs causes them to exude masses of orange slime and die. Insect eggs on the bark of trees can be smothered by painting the bark with a mixture of old cooking oil and soapy water during the dormant season—a homemade variation on the standard dormant spray. A good dormant spray can also be made by adding one part superior oil (sold in garden stores) to 15 parts water. No detergent is needed to emulsify superior oil. (Vegetable oil can be used instead, but it needs an emulsifier.)

Countering the common insect pests

Pest	Control
Aphid	Spray with dilute solution of clay or quassia extract; soapy water is also effective, but be sure to rinse off plants immediately after application (kills)
Cabbage worm, imported	Apply sour milk in the center of the cabbage head (repels). Or dust with a mixture of 1/2 cup salt to 1 cup flour (kills)
Codling moth	Spray with ryania, fish oil, or soapy water (kills)
Colorado potato beetle	Dust plants with wheat bran while they are wet (kills). Or pick off by hand
Corn earworm	Apply mineral oil to the silk just inside the tip of each ear—use a medicine dropper or small oil can (repels)
Flea beetle	Dust with soot mixed with slaked lime or wood ashes (repels). Or spray with rotenone (kills)
Harlequin bug	Spray with pyrethrum (kills)
Mexican bean beetle	Spray with garlic or cedar extract (repels)
Tarnished plant bug	Dust with sabadilla, an organic insecticide (kills)
Thrips	Spray with rotenone, oil-water mixture, or tobacco extract (kills)

Formulas You Can Make at Home

Homemade pesticides and repellents tend to be safer than synthetic substances in terms of undesirable side effects. Nevertheless, they should be treated with respect. Wash fruits and vegetables before eating them, and use the sprays as sparingly as possible to avoid unnecessary ecological damage.

Biodynamic spray. Mix powdered clay and an organic insecticide such as rotenone with enough water to make a thin fluid. Spray on fruit trees in early spring before leaves appear to suffocate eggs of insect pests.

Buttermilk and flour spray. Mix 1/2 cup buttermilk and 4 cups wheat flour with 5 gallons of water; kills spider mites and other mites by suffocation.

Cedar extract. Boil 1/4 pound cedar chips or dust in 1 gallon of water for two hours; strain and dilute the liquid with three parts water; spray on plants to repel Mexican bean beetles and other troublesome beetles.

Garlic and hot pepper spray. Steep 1/2 teaspoon each of crushed garlic and crushed hot peppers in 1 gallon of water for 10 to 24 hours. Use full strength on woody plants; dilute 25 percent for annuals and vegetables. Spray repels many sucking and chewing insects.

Glue mixture. Dissolve 1/4 pound of fish or animal glue in 1 gallon of warm water. Spray trees and bushes to trap and kill aphids, spider mites, and scale insects. (It removes pests from trees when it flakes off on drying.)

Green soap spray. Mix 1 cup of green soap tincture with 3 gallons of water; kills nonfurry caterpillars on contact. Green soap is available in drugstores. Laundry soap can be used instead in the ratio of 1/2 cake of soap to 1 gallon of hot water. If used on nonwoody plants, rinse off with clear water immediately after applying.

Quassia spray. Boil 1/4 pound of quassia chips in 1 gallon of water for two hours, strain the liquid, and mix with three to five parts water. The spray poisons aphids and caterpillars but is harmless to ladybugs and bees. Homemade organic sprays can also be made from infusions of larkspur seeds, rhubarb leaves, or tobacco. Such sprays are nonpersistent and are effective against a variety of insect pests—larkspur against aphids, thrips, and several species of chewing insects; rhubarb against aphids; tobacco against a wide assortment of soft-bodied insects. However, these preparations are highly poisonous to humans and animals. If you do use them, be sure to wash the produce thoroughly before eating it.

Traps and Barriers

Proper fencing and netting will protect fruits and vegetables against most of the larger animals, including deer, rabbits, raccoons, woodchucks, dogs, and birds. Raccoons can be a bother because of their ability to climb, but extra-high chicken wire or an electric fence line across the top will discourage them. Some simple yet effective barriers are shown at right.

Many of the smaller common garden pests can be caught in simple traps. A shallow pan filled with beer is deadly to slugs and snails: the odor of the beer lures the mollusks into the pan where they drown. Using flour to thicken the beer will increase its effectiveness.

Aphids are attracted by the color yellow. Fill a yellow plastic dishpan with a solution of soap and water and place it near infested plants. Other containers, such as a 5-gallon oil can, can be used; paint the inside bright yellow (the outside can be any color other than red, which repels aphids). Japanese beetles are also attracted by yellow. An effective Japanese beetle trap is a yellow container with a scent lure, such as geraniol or oil of anise. Another Japanese beetle trap consists of a glass jug containing an inch or two of a fermenting "soup" of water, sugar, and mashed fruit scraps. Japanese beetle traps should be placed well away from your plants, since they attract beetles from a wide area.

Codling moths, apple maggot flies, and many other flying orchard pests can be trapped in empty tin cans or glass jars filled with a mixture of one part molasses and 1 1/2 parts water, plus a little yeast. Hang the traps in the fruit trees when the moths or flies appear. To catch earwigs, use rolled-up newspapers or hollow bamboo tubes. The insects will seek shelter in the tubes toward evening. Shake them out into kerosene each morning.

Fencing, barriers, and traps prevent pests from reaching valuable crops. Fencing can be costly but is long-lasting and relatively trouble free if set up properly. Many traps can be made at home from scrap materials. All avoid the use of harmful chemicals.

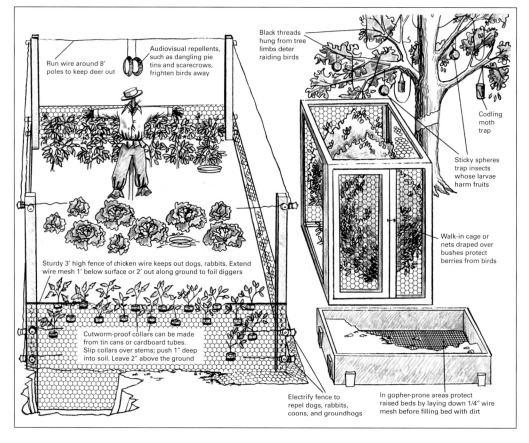

Run wire around 8' poles to keep deer out

Audiovisual repellents, such as dangling pie tins and scarecrows, frighten birds away

Black threads hung from tree limbs deter raiding birds

Codling moth trap

Sticky spheres trap insects whose larvae harm fruits

Walk-in cage or nets draped over bushes protect berries from birds

Sturdy 3' high fence of chicken wire keeps out dogs, rabbits. Extend wire mesh 1' below surface or 2' out along ground to foil diggers

Cutworm-proof collars can be made from tin cans or cardboard tubes. Slip collars over stems; push 1" deep into soil. Leave 2" above the ground

Electrify fence to repel dogs, rabbits, coons, and groundhogs

In gopher-prone areas protect raised beds by laying down 1/4" wire mesh before filling bed with dirt

Caterpillars can be trapped by smearing bands of Tanglefoot, a sticky commercial preparation, around the trunks of fruit and other trees. Experimenters have also found that destructive flying insects can be trapped on colored spheres 3 to 6 inches in diameter, hung from the trees and coated with Tanglefoot or homemade flypaper stickum. Construct the spheres of any lightweight material, such as small gourds or styrofoam, and paint them orange, dark red, or black.

The tomato hornworm and other destructive caterpillars, such as the armyworm, cutworm, peach borer, and corn earworm, are actually larvae. The moths are easily caught at night in traps that use an ultraviolet bulb to lure the moths into a container. Another version of this type of trap has an electric grid around the bulb that kills the insects on contact. Check such traps regularly; if too many beneficial insects are being caught, discontinue their use.

Sources and resources

Books and pamphlets
DeBach, Paul. *Biological Control of Natural Enemies.* New York: Cambridge University Press, 1974.
Pleasant, Barbara. *The Gardener's Bug Book: Earth Safe Insect Control.* Pownal, Vt.: Storey Communications, 1994.
Yepsen, Roger B., Jr. *The Encyclopedia of Natural Insect and Disease Control.* Emmaus, Pa.: Rodale Press, 1984.

Grains and Grasses

Raising Food and Forage For the Small Place

Grains and grasses were staples of the old-time self-sufficient farm. Grasses, in the form of hay or fresh pasturage, supplied the bulk of the diet for the farm animals. Grains provided flour for homemade bread, supplementary feed for the livestock, and raw materials for everyday needs. An acre of corn can fill a year's grain requirements for a pig, a milk cow, a beef steer, and 30 laying hens. Still another use for pasture plants and grains is green manure—crops that are raised for the purpose of being turned under the soil to improve it.

Raising grain or grass does not require large acreage or costly machinery. Indeed, if you can grow a lawn, you can raise grains and grasses as crops. A plot of land only 20 by 55 feet can supply all the wheat an average family of four will need in a year. The crop can be harvested, threshed, and winnowed with hand tools and ground into flour in a tabletop mill.

Like any other crop, grains and grasses require soil preparation, fertilization, and attention. However, they require much less care than a good-sized vegetable garden.

Planting rates

Type of grain	Amount of seed per acre	Land area needed to grow 1 bushel
Wheat	75–90 lb.	10′ × 109′
Oats	80 lb.	10′ × 62′
Field corn	6–8 lb.	10′ × 50′
Barley	100 lb.	10′ × 87′
Rye	84 lb.	10′ × 145′
Buckwheat	50 lb.	10′ × 130′
Grain sorghum	2–8 lb.	10′ × 60′
Note: These figures are estimates; actual yields may be affected by weather, soil, and variety of seed		

Sowing the Cereal Grains

The most important food plants in the world are the cereal grains. Whether eaten directly, processed into

Barley
Rye
Buckwheat
Corn
Oats
Sorghum
Wheat

Grains are the seeds of certain members of the grass family, such as wheat, corn, and rye, that are used for food and animal feed. Buckwheat is also considered a grain, although the plant is not a grass but a member of the knotweed family.

Corn and wheat are the two most widely grown grains in the United States, accounting for hundreds of thousands of acres and millions of bushels. The major use of wheat is for flour; the major use of corn is for animal feed. Both also have many industrial applications. The other grains have more specialized uses, but all are nutritious, high yielding, and good for small-scale farming.

bread, or used as animal feed, they provide the basic nutritional needs of almost every man, woman, and child on the face of the earth. North America is particularly suitable for growing grain. Almost every one of the major grains flourishes over vast regions. The sole exception is rice, a crop whose cultivation is restricted to the Deep South and southern California.

Wheat, barley, and other hardy grains can be grown as either spring or winter crops. Winter crops are sown in early fall, grow a little, and then go dormant during the cold months. When spring returns, they shoot up and are ready to harvest in midsummer.

Spring crops are usually grown where winters are too severe for fall-sown grains. They are sown about the time of the last killing spring frost and are ready for harvest in early fall. In general, the winter crops yield more heavily. There are separate varieties for spring and fall sowing. Spring wheat will not survive the winter if planted in fall; winter wheat may not have time to mature before autumn frost kills it if it is planted in spring, especially if the growing season is short.

Most grains do best on well-tilled soil of average fertility—too much nitrogen makes them grow overly lush and topple over. Corn, however, needs highly fertile soil. Before planting, the soil should be plowed and disked or rototilled and lime and fertilizer added as needed. The seeds can be broadcast (flung out) by hand or with a hand-cranked seeder, as in planting a lawn. To ensure even coverage, go up and down the plot lengthwise as you sow; then go over it again at right angles to your first direction. After sowing, till or rake the soil to work the seeds in. If the plot is large, sow the grain with a drill, a mechanical device that spaces out the seeds in straight rows at precise depths. Except for field corn and sorghum, grains need virtually no care until harvest time. Corn and sorghum should be planted in widely spaced rows so that they can be cultivated while small.

To prevent soil depletion and the buildup of pests and pathogens, grain crops should be raised as part of a rotation system with other crops. Your county agent can advise you on the best rotation plan for your area. A typical plan might be corn the first year, followed by alfalfa, winter wheat, vegetables or soybeans, and pasture in succeeding years.

The Major Grains

Wheat, the world's leading bread grain, requires a cool, moist growing season and about two months of hot, dry weather for ripening. Wheat grows 3 to 4 feet tall and turns golden brown when ripe. It is ready to harvest when the grain is hard and crunchy between the teeth.

Wheat can be sown in fall or spring. Winter wheat should not be sown before mid-September: it may grow too much before cold weather arrives and be killed by freezing as a result. Early planting also exposes winter wheat to attack by the destructive Hessian fly.

Five kinds of wheat are commonly grown in the United States and Canada. They are hard red winter wheat, used for bread; soft red winter wheat, used in cakes and pastries; hard red spring wheat, the best for bread; white wheat, used mainly for pastry flour; and durum wheat, used for spaghetti. Wheat supplies the best-balanced nutrition of all the grains.

Oats are the highest in protein of all grains. They are a hardy crop that thrives in a cool, moist climate and cannot tolerate drought. Oats are sown as a spring crop except where winters are mild. A mature oat plant stands 2 to 5 feet tall. Oats can be harvested while they still have a few green tinges. They should be gathered into shocks and left to dry in the field.

Rye, once a major bread crop, is now grown mainly for stock feed and whiskey. It is also much used for green manure and as a cover crop. Rye grows 3 to 5 feet tall and is almost always sown in fall. Although its per-acre yield is less than that of wheat, it can produce crops on poorer soil than wheat and tolerates cold, drought, and dampness better. Most rye bread contains at least 50 percent wheat flour. Old-timers often mixed rye and corn flour to make a bread called Rye-and-Injun.

Buckwheat is raised for its nutlike, triangular seeds. Its dark, strong-flavored flour is excellent for pancakes. Buckwheat grows about 3 feet high; it prefers moist, acid soil and hot weather. Because it matures rapidly (60 to 90 days), buckwheat is often used as a second crop after winter wheat or early vegetables.

Barley does best with a long, cool ripening season and moderate moisture but adapts well to heat and aridity. It also tolerates salty and alkaline soils better than most grains. In warm regions barley is usually planted as a fall crop; in colder areas it is planted in early spring. Barley is used for animal feed, beer, and malt. It is also used in soup and as a whole-grain dish.

Sorghum resembles corn but with narrower leaves and no ears. There are four types of sorghum: grain, sweet, grass, and broomcorn. Grain sorghum grows to about 4 feet tall, and its seeds are used mainly for animal feed. They also make nutritious porridge and pancakes. Sweet sorghum is raised for syrup and silage, grass sorghum finds use as pasturage and hay, and broomcorn is valued for the long, springy bristles of its seed heads, used in making brooms. Sorghum tolerates heat and drought well. Plant it about 10 days after corn.

Corn, first domesticated by American Indians thousands of years ago, leads all other grains in the United States in acreage and harvest.

Corn raised for grain is not sweet; it is called field corn to distinguish it from the sweet corn we raise as a vegetable. Field corn is used for animal feed, cornstarch, hominy, grits, and a variety of breakfast cereals and snack foods. A limited amount is used for corn bread. Field corn is taller and yields more heavily than sweet corn but is planted and cultivated in the same way. It can be harvested easily after the plants are dead and dry by snapping the ears off the stalks. The ears of corn should be taken under shelter as soon as possible to protect them from rain and mold. The corn should be husked before storing.

Corn can be fed to animals while still on the ear, but for most purposes it should be shelled—that is, the kernels should be removed from the cob. Shelling can be done by rubbing an ear of corn briskly between your hands, or you can buy a hand-powered sheller.

Corn: America's unique contribution is an Indian discovery

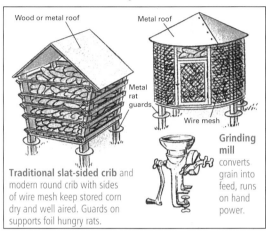

Wood or metal roof

Metal roof

Metal rat guards

Wire mesh

Grinding mill converts grain into feed, runs on hand power.

Traditional slat-sided crib and modern round crib with sides of wire mesh keep stored corn dry and well aired. Guards on supports foil hungry rats.

From Field to Flour

Harvesting is the same for all grains other than corn. After the grain has been cut, gather the stalks into sheaves and stack them to dry in the field until no trace of green is left. To thresh the grain, lay the sheaves on an old sheet on a hard surface and hit the seed heads with a flail, broomstick, or baseball bat to knock the seeds loose. To separate the grain from the chaff, or loose husks, toss it in a sheet outdoors on a breezy day, or pour grain and chaff back and forth from one container to another. On a calm day a fan can supply the air current.

Store grain in covered metal trash can or a wooden bin that has been rat proofed with wire mesh. Stored grain must be kept thoroughly dry to prevent mold. Grain can be ground in a small mill designed for home use (some are equipped with revolving stones that duplicate the old-time stone-ground flour). Small batches can be run through a heavy-duty food blender.

Grassland Management For Hay and Pasture

If you have a horse, a cow, or other livestock and an acre or two of unused land, an excellent way to put that

1. Make a sheaf by tying an armful of grain stalks into a bundle. Use twine or twist grain stems into a cord.

2. Stack sheaves together to make a shock. Leave them outdoors to dry in the sun. Do not store damp grain.

Flail

Chaff

Grain seeds

3. Thresh the grain to separate the kernels. A simple flail can be made of two sticks joined loosely.

4. Final step is winnowing threshed grain by using the wind to blow away chaff and other small particles.

land to work is by planting it to grass. In addition to providing essential pasturage and hay for the animals, grass protects the soil from erosion and furnishes a habitat for a myriad of small creatures.

Managing a grassland is like managing a small ecosystem. The trick is to keep various plant species—not just grasses but also such legumes as clover and alfalfa—in balance so as to provide a nutritious diet for livestock while at the same time maintaining or increasing the fertility of the soil. By regulating the intensity of grazing, by mowing, and by minor adjustments of the soil's mineral content, the landowner can favor the growth of one plant species or another and keep many troublesome weeds under control without resorting to chemicals.

Grasslands fit well into crop rotations, and for maximum production you may wish to establish a grassland on a cultivated field. Such rotation also prevents the buildup of pests and pathogens by depriving them of hosts. You may also decide to put steep, uneven, or rocky land into permanent grassland. The only prerequisites are sunlight for at least half the daylight hours and sufficient moisture. In areas of low rainfall moisture can be supplied by irrigation or sprinklers.

To establish a pasture on cultivated land, plow and harrow the soil and lime it, if needed, to bring the pH to between 6 and 7 (slightly acid). Till in manure, compost, or an all-purpose chemical fertilizer. The seed can be broadcast or planted in very close rows using a seed drill. For hay you may wish to plant only one crop, such as alfalfa or timothy. For pasture a mixture is preferable, since livestock suffer from bloat on a pure diet of fresh legumes. Consult your county agent for the best combination of forage plants. A mixed pasture is ecologically sound. A variety of plants lessens their vulnerability to pests and disease, and the legumes supply nitrogen, which the grasses need for good growth.

Do not let livestock graze in a pasture until the plants are well established and about a foot tall. This gives them time to build up food reserves in their root systems. Repeated grazing closer than 3 or 4 inches depletes the food reserves of the forage plants, so they grow back poorly. Eventually they die off, leaving the land open to invasion by weeds and brush. However, properly controlled grazing and mowing help keep weeds and brush under control.

Legumes: green nitrogen factories

Legumes add nitrogen to the soil in which they grow by means of symbiotic bacteria that form nodules on their roots. These bacteria convert nitrogen from the air into forms that plants can use. However, each type of legume needs a different strain of bacteria, and the proper type may not be in the soil when the legume is planted. Legumes will grow without their bacteria, but they then take nitrogen from the soil instead of adding it. To ensure success, inoculate the soil with the proper bacteria, obtainable at most garden supply stores.

When scything, cut with a rhythmic, sweeping motion of the upper body. Stand with your feet well apart for balance. Keep the scythe blade sharp, and wear heavy work boots for greater safety.

Let hay dry partially on the ground after cutting; then rake it into long piles, or windrows, to complete drying in the open air. Windrows should be 6 to 12 in. high and loosely heaped so that air can circulate freely. Turn the windrows over periodically.

To renovate an old or run-down pasture, plow it up thoroughly, apply lime and fertilizer, and reseed the land with desirable varieties. Grasses will often come back vigorously from their roots in the soil, so little reseeding may be required. Legumes, however, must usually be reseeded, sometimes every year. If the old pastureland is overgrown, as it often is, grub out brush and young trees or keep them mowed close to the ground. Eventually they will be starved out.

Hay and Haymaking

Although the terms "hay" and "straw" are often confused, the two are actually quite different. Hay is made from grass, legumes, or other forage plants that have been cut while young and tender and cured by drying. Straw consists of the stalks of grain after threshing or the dried stalks and stems of other farm crops. Hay is palatable, nutritious livestock feed; straw is useful as bedding but contains little food value. Legume hay is an excellent source of protein for livestock; clover and alfalfa are leading legume hay crops.

Whether made from grasses or legumes, the best hay comes from plants that are cut in the early blooming stage: at this point they have their highest nutritive value. If allowed to set seed before cutting, the plants become tough, dry, and woody, like straw. Hay can also be made from immature oats and other grains, which should be cut while the kernels are soft and milky.

It is important to cut your hay on a clear day so that the hay can dry on the ground in the sun's heat. After drying for a day or two, rake the cut hay into long parallel rows. These rows, known as windrows, should be turned over periodically with a pitchfork or by machine to expose all the hay to sun and air. The hay is ready to store when its moisture content is down to 15 percent. A simple way to judge its readiness is to pick up a handful of stems and then bend them in a U shape. If they break fairly easily, they are ready for storing. If they are pliable and take a lot of twisting to break, the hay is still too damp. If the stems are so brittle that they snap off easily, the hay is too dry—safe to store but with much nutritional value lost. Hay that is too dry is also subject to leaf shattering—the leaves, which are the most nutritious portions of the plants, break off and are lost.

Grasses

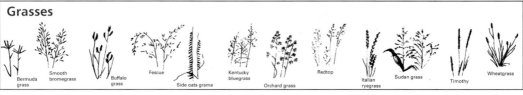

Bermuda grass · Smooth bromegrass · Buffalo grass · Fescue · Side oats grama · Kentucky bluegrass · Orchard grass · Redtop · Italian ryegrass · Sudan grass · Timothy · Wheatgrass

Legumes

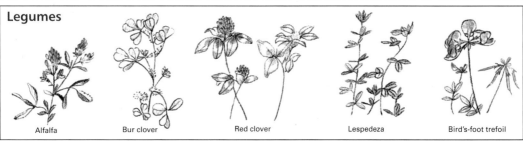

Alfalfa · Bur clover · Red clover · Lespedeza · Bird's-foot trefoil

Selected forage crops

Variety	What you need to know
Alfalfa	Perennial legume; the leading hay crop in all sections but the Southeast. Grows 2'–3' tall; deep roots (8'–30') tap moisture in subsoil and make plant drought resistant. Tolerates alkali; fails on acid soils. Very rich in protein; raised chiefly for hay but also used in pasture together with grass
Bermuda grass	Perennial grass; grows best in Southeast. Forms sod. Primarily a pasture grass, though some strains grow tall enough to cut for hay; a good companion for legumes. Tolerates heat well
Bromegrass, smooth	Vigorous perennial grass; 3'–4' tall. Forms dense sod. Thrives in Corn Belt and Pacific Northwest; under irrigation on Great Plains. Used for pasture, hay, erosion control. Withstands drought, extreme temperatures
Buffalo grass	Low-growing perennial native to Great Plains; forms dense, matted turf 2"–4" tall. Noted for tolerance of drought, heat, cold, alkaline soil. Withstands heavy grazing
Bur clover	Annual legume related to alfalfa. Used for winter pasture; needs mild, moist winters
Clover	Important genus of legumes; five species predominate in United States: red, white, alsike, ladino (giant white), crimson. Height ranges from a few inches to 3'. May behave as annuals, biennials, or perennials depending on climatic variations and soil. Used for hay, pasture, silage, green manure
Fescue, tall	Perennial grass can be grown in most parts of United States; important in Southeast and Pacific Northwest. Used for pasture and hay; grows 3'–4' tall; very tolerant of wet soils
Grama grass	Perennial grass; native to Great Plains. Several species; height ranges from 2"–3". Primarily used for pasture
Kentucky bluegrass	Perennial grass; grows in most of United States except Southwest and at extreme elevations. From 12"–30". tall; best suited to permanent pasture. Leading pasture grass of Canada and United States
Lespedeza	A cloverlike legume. Two annual species important in United States. Height from 4"–2". Most important in southern Corn Belt and South. Used chiefly for pasture; in South grows tall enough for hay also
Orchard grass	Perennial grass; vigorous, long-lived. Tolerates shade and wide range of soil types; likes moisture. Forms bunches 2'–4' tall; used for hay and permanent pasture
Redtop	Perennial grass; tolerates heat, cold, acid, and run-down soils. Grows up to 3' tall. Used for hay and pasture; often sown with timothy
Ryegrass, Italian	Fast-growing annual, 2'–3' tall. Used for winter pasture in South; hay and pasture in Pacific Northwest. Excellent poultry pasture
Sudan grass	A grasslike sorghum; annual; reaches 3'–8' in height. Tolerates heat, drought. Used primarily for pasture and fresh chopped feed; also makes excellent hay. Most important in South but grows as far north as Michigan
Timothy	One of the oldest cultivated grasses; perennial. Thrives in cool, moist climate. Grows in bunches 20"–40" tall. Primarily used for hay, especially for horses
Trefoil, bird's-foot	Hardy perennial legume. Tolerates damp, acid, and infertile soils. Raised from Vermont to eastern Kansas, also Pacific Northwest. Grows 20"–40" tall; used for pasture and hay
Wheatgrass	Perennial grass; five important species, some native to West. Grows 2'–4' tall. Some types form sod; others are bunch grasses. Important in dry lands of West; used for hay and pasture

Good hay often has a tinge of green even though thoroughly dry. (Alfalfa hay should be bright green.) Hay can be stored loose or in bales. In either case it should be protected from the weather. Wet hay may rot into good compost, but it makes bad feed. It can go moldy and may then poison the animals to which it is fed; in extreme cases it will ferment, and the heat produced will start a fire. If you have no barn or shed, a tarpaulin over the hay will provide a fair degree of protection from the effects of rain and snow.

Sources and resources

Books and pamphlets
Elkins, Donald M. and Darrel S. Metcalf. *Crop Production: Principles and Practices.* New York: Macmillan, 1980.
Nation, Allan. *Grass Farmers.* Jackson, Miss.: Green Park, 1993.
Willis, Harold L. *How to Grow Great Alfalfa . . . & Other Forages.* Wisconsin Dells, Wis.: H. L. Willis, 1993.

Beekeeping

One Small Hive Can Keep You in Honey All Year Round

Few projects yield so much satisfaction in return for such a small investment in money and labor as beekeeping. Once the bees are established, a single hive can easily produce 30 pounds or more of delicious honey each year—enough to supply the needs of the average family of four or five plus plenty to give away or even sell. In return, bees need only minimal attention and a little feeding to carry them through the winter.

Bees gather food from an astonishing variety of plants. Wild flowers, fruit blossoms, shrubs, trees—even weeds—are sources of the nectar that the bees convert to fragrant honey and of the pollen that supplies their vital protein needs. Bees also perform the valuable service of pollinating many plants. So efficient are they that commercial fruit growers often import bees to pollinate their orchards.

Beekeeping in America dates back to the early colonial period when British settlers first brought honeybees to the Colonies (they are not native to the New World). Some swarms escaped and established themselves in the wild; these free-living bees spread slowly westward to the edge of the Great Plains, where the lack of hollow trees for nesting stopped them. It was not until the 19th century that bees reached the Far West, carried there in the wagons of homesteaders.

In colonial times, and long afterward, bees were kept in hives of straw, called skeps, or in hollow logs. Lacking scientific knowledge, beekeepers often found their hives wiped out by disease. Honey yields were often low. However, thanks to a series of advances since the 1850s, beekeeping today is a scientifically based, thoroughly up-to-date enterprise.

Choosing a Site for Your Hive

The right location will get your colony off to a good start and help ensure a productive future. One of the first

Early types of hives

things to look for is good drainage—dampness leads to disease and encourages the growth of mold. Ideally, the hive should be set on a gentle slope so that rain and melting snow can drain off rapidly. Avoid hollows or low spots where water can collect. Raising the hive above the ground on bricks, cinder blocks, or other supports helps to combat dampness.

The site should be sheltered from wind. Bees are susceptible to cold, and even a mild breeze can chill them enough to reduce their efficiency as honey collectors. Severe cold can kill bees, and in winter a good windbreak may mean the difference between survival and death for an entire colony of honeybees.

Another important factor is adequate sunlight to warm the hive. (To maintain the hive's normal inside temperature of 93°F, bees must "burn" honey, thereby reducing the yield.) Experienced beekeepers orient the hive entrance toward the east or south to take advantage of the warming effect of the morning sun. Afternoon shade is also important—especially in the hotter sections of the country—since excessive heat can be as deadly to bees as excessive cold.

Be sure there is a good supply of forage plants (sources of nectar and pollen) before setting up a hive. Since bees can easily forage as far as two miles from the hive, this is seldom a problem except in densely built-up areas.

If neighbors live close by, screen the hive with a tall hedge or board fence. This protects the hive from molestation and forces bees to fly high above passersby.

Setting Up Shop As a Beekeeper

Start your colony in early spring so the bees can build up their numbers before the honey flow begins. Start on a small scale with one or two hives. Two hives have an advantage, since if one queen dies, the colonies can be combined. Of the various strains available, Italian bees are the best for beginners. They are gentle, good foragers, and disease resistant. Caucasian, Carniolan, and Midnite bees, also popular, tend to swarm and stray.

Major mail-order houses and bee-supply specialists offer complete beginners' kits, including bees, hive, tools, protective gloves and veil, and instructions. As the season progresses, you can purchase extra supers and frames. Bees need plenty of fresh water. A nearby stream

Straw skep is the traditional symbol of beekeeping. It is cheap and snug but unsanitary. The only way to remove honey from a skep is to kill the bees and cut the combs out.

Early settlers frequently used bee gums—hollow sections of the gum tree or tupelo—to hive their bees. Bears often raided these backwoods apiaries to feast on bee larvae and honey.

The Standard Hive

1. **Outer cover,** metal-sheathed for durability, protects hive from rain snow, and hailstones.
2. **Inner cover** has hole for ventilation.

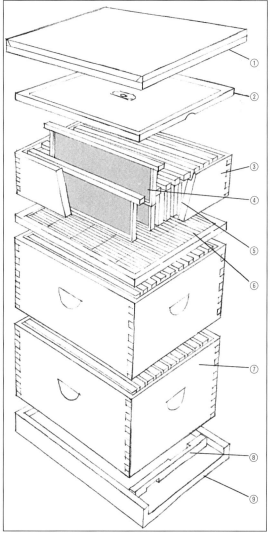

3. **Shallow super,** usually employed for honey to be harvested, is lighter and easier to handle than a deep super (40 lb. versus 75 lb. when filled with honey).
4. **Frames** contain wax foundation sheets stamped with a honeycomb pattern to guide bees in building regular combs with uniform cells
5. **Bee space,** about 5/6 in., surrounds frames on all sides.
6. **Queen excluder** is a flat grille that prevents the queen from leaving her brood chamber to lay eggs in honey supers. Workers, being smaller, can pass freely through to all parts of the hive.
7. **Brood and food chambers** are deep supers in which the queen lays eggs to maintain and increase the hive's population. Food supplies for winter are also stored in these supers.
8. **Entrance cleat,** a movable wooden block with different-sized openings, allows entrance to be widened or narrowed.
9. **Bottom board.**

Identifying the bee castes

Queen: About 1 in. long (larger than drones or workers) with a long, shiny abdomen. Queens leave the hive only during mating or swarming. They lay as many as 2,000 eggs a day and live as long as four years. Queens develop from larvae that are fed royal jelly by nurse bees.

Worker: A bit over 1/2 in. long with furry abdomen and long tongue for collecting nectar. Carries brightly colored pollen in "baskets" on hind legs. Workers make honey, build the comb, and tend larvae. They live one month during honey flow, three in winter.

Drone: About same length as a worker but with larger eyes and thicker body. Drones buzz lo dly but harmlessly: they have no stingers. The drone's only function is to mate with the queen; it dies in the act. Drones still alive in late autumn are turned out of the hive by the workers. Unable to feed themselves, they die.

Birth of a bee

New larva

Egg, larva, pupa: A bee begins life as an egg about as big as the dot on an *i*. In three days the egg hatches into a wormlike larva. At eight days the larva spins a cocoon and nurse bees seal the cell. Workers emerge after 21 days, queens after 16, drones after 24.

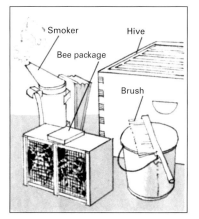

Smoker
Hive
Bee package
Brush

1. The best time for hiving is late afternoon or early evening, when the bees are quietest and least likely to fly off. Place the package of bees near the hive, which you have assembled beforehand. Light the smoker and have a pail of syrup handy. Wear protective clothing for safety.

Tools and equipment

Hat and wire veil protect head, face, and neck, the body's most vulnerable parts.

White coveralls or light-colored clothing is recommended. (Dark colors irritate bees, making them likelier to sting.)

Loose-fitting gloves and stout boots protect hands and feet, which bees are apt to go for.

Smoker for quieting bees burns wood scraps (such as cedar pet litter) or rags.

Hive tool is used to pry hive open, loosen frames.

Uncapping knife is electrically heated, makes cutting easier by softening wax of comb.

Centrifugal extractor, hand or motor powered, removes honey without damaging combs.

Some favorite bee blossoms

Alfalfa
Light-colored honey with mild, delicate flavor. One of the major sources for commercial production.

Aster
White, minty honey; granulates readily. It is a major source of fall honey and pollen.

Basswood
Light, aromatic honey. Prolific nectar producer. Often mixed with other honeys for sale.

Clover
Light, delicate honey. Because of its abundance, clover is one of the leading sources of honey.

Dandelion
Important early spring source of nectar and pollen. Honey is yellow to amber, with strong flavor.

Goldenrod
Excellent fall source of pollen and nectar. Thick, golden honey mostly used as winter food for bees.

Orange and other citrus
One of the most popular honeys. Fragrant and mild. Often used for blending with other honeys.

Sage
Important in West. Light colored, mild in flavor. Most sage honey does not granulate.

Tupelo
Mild greenish-amber honey. Known for not granulating. A favorite in health-food stores.

Bees are shipped in packages with wire-screen sides, usually containing a mated queen, 2 1/2 pounds of bees (about 6,000 bees), and a can of syrup to feed them en route. The queen is in a small cage inside the package with several workers to tend her. The exit hole of the queen cage is usually closed with a plug of soft candy that the other bees will gnaw through to release her. Check your bees on arrival to make sure that they are healthy and that the queen is alive. You should contact your county agent before ordering bees. He can advise you on diseases, parasites, pesticides, and regulations.

Once the bees have been installed, open the hive as little as possible; every one or two weeks is enough to check on your bees' welfare.

Bees sting only when they feel threatened. Nevertheless, it is important to wear protective gear. A hat and veil are basic; coveralls, gloves, and stout boots are recommended. However, many experienced beekeepers work without gloves for greater dexterity and because bee stingers left in gloves release a scent that stimulates other bees to sting. Move slowly and gently—violent or abrupt motions alarm bees. If you want to open the hive, quiet the bees first with your smoker.

When a worker bee stings, its barbed stinger becomes trapped in the skin and is torn loose when the bee escapes. (The bee later dies.) The venom sac remains attached to the stinger and continues to pump poison into the wound. Scrape off the stinger as quickly as possible with a fingernail or knife blade. Do not try to pull it out. You will only squeeze more venom into the

or pond, a pan of water with a wooden float for the bees, or a slowly dripping hose will supply them.

2. Lay the package on its side and brush or spatter some syrup on the wire mesh. The food will help to calm the bees and make them easier to handle. Repeat feeding until they stop eating. When they are full, rap the package on the ground to jar bees to bottom of package.

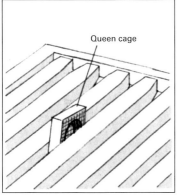

Queen cage

3. Pry cover off package with your hive tool; again jar bees to bottom. Remove queen cage and replace cover. Remove cover from candy plug and make a small hole in plug so that bees can gnaw through and release queen. Wedge queen cage between two frames in hive.

Several frames have been removed to make room for bees

4. Knock bees down again and remove cover and syrup can from package. Pour half of bees over queen cage, the rest into empty space in hive. Place package on ground facing hive to let remaining bees make their way in. Replace all frames but one; replace it in a few days.

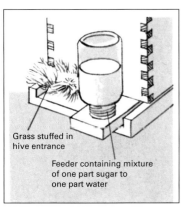

Grass stuffed in hive entrance

Feeder containing mixture of one part sugar to one part water

5. Place inner and outer covers on hive. Be careful not to crush any bees. A puff of smoke will send bees down between frames to safety. Fill feeder and place in position. Stuff entrance lightly with green grass to keep bees inside until they feel at home. Remove queen cage after a few days.

wound. Ammonia or baking soda paste helps neutralize the venom. Most persons develop immunity after a few stings. However, those who have severe reactions should consult their physicians.

Swarming and How to Avoid It

Swarming occurs when the queen bee and a large number of workers abandon the hive to establish a new colony, leaving behind other workers, eggs and larvae, and a crop of contenders for the new queenship. In the wild, swarming spreads the bee population and prevents overcrowding the colony. For the beekeeper, however, it results in the loss of both bees and honey production.

By far the major cause of swarming is overcrowding although excessive heat, poor ventilation, or an overanxious owner who opens the hive too frequently can also cause the bees to swarm.

One warning that bees are preparing to swarm is the near-cessation of flight in and out of the hive during honey season. The bees, instead of going out to gather nectar, remain in the crowded hive and gorge on stored honey in preparation for flight. Another sign is the presence of peanutlike cells on the brood combs, in which new queens are being reared.

A simple preventive measure is to give the bees more room. Add a shallow super early in spring and add extra supers as needed. Switching the two lowest supers every five to six weeks also helps. Bees tend to work upward; so by the time the upper chamber is filled with eggs and larvae, the lower chamber will be empty.

If you suspect the hive is overheating, rig a shade of boards or burlap. To improve ventilation, tilt the top cover up at one edge and remove the entrance cleat.

Harvesting Honey

An established hive will yield 30 to 60 pounds of honey a year. You will usually have to wait a year for your

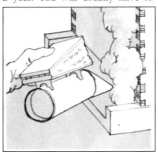

1. Choose a sunny, windless day for harvesting honey, since bees are calmest then. The first step is to drive the bees away from the honeycombs. Begin by blowing smoke through the hive entrance to quiet the bees. A few puffs are all that are needed; too much smoke may injure the bees.

2. Wait a few minutes for the smoke to take effect. Then pry the outer cover loose with your hive tool and lift it off. Blow more smoke in through the hole in the inner cover. Remove the inner cover and blow smoke across the tops of the frames to drive bees downward and out of the way.

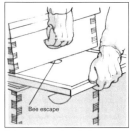

Bee escape

3. Instead of smoke, the bees can be cleared out with an escape board, which lets bees move down but not up. Using the hive tool, pry up the super you want to remove and slide the escape board beneath it. Install the board about 24 hours in advance to give the bees time to leave the super.

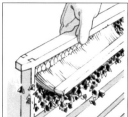

4. Remove the super and pry the frames loose with the hive tool. Be careful not to crush any bees (a crushed bee releases a scent that stimulates other bees to attack). Gently brush off bees that cling to the frames. A comb is ready to be harvested if it is 80 percent sealed over.

5. Uncap the combs in a bee-proof location, such as a tightly screened room. (If the bees can get at the honey, they may steal it.) Slice off the comb tops with a sharp knife warmed in hot water—a heavy kitchen knife is fine. It is best to use two knives, cutting with one while the other is heating.

6. If an extractor is available, place the frames of uncapped comb in it and turn it on. (If it is a manual model, turn the handle at moderate speed to avoid damaging the combs.) Return emptied combs to the hive for the bees to clean and use again. Combs can be recycled for 20 years or more.

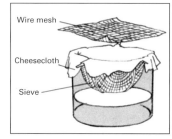

Wire mesh

Cheesecloth

Sieve

Double layer of damp cheesecloth in a wire sieve makes a good honey strainer. Use another sieve or a piece of window screen above strainer to catch larger bits of foreign matter, such as wax and dead bees.

first harvest, however, since newly hived bees must build up the strength of the colony and rarely produce much honey beyond their own needs in their initial season.

Plants yield nectar in two main flows. The spring flow starts with the blossoming of dandelions and fruit trees and lasts into July in most parts of the country. The fall flow begins around September and ends when hard frost kills the last flowers. Honey can be extracted after each flow, but many amateur apiarists prefer to wait until the end of the fall flow.

One way to extract honey is to let it drip from an uncapped comb into a clean pan. Another is to crush the combs and squeeze the honey out through cheesecloth. However, bees must then build new combs, which takes time and honey (they consume 8 pounds of honey to make 1 pound of wax). Centrifugal extractors are widely available but expensive. One option is to build your own extractor (see below, right).

Storing Honey

Newly extracted honey should be strained through cheesecloth to remove wax and other impurities. Let the strained honey stand several days so that air bubbles can rise to the top; then skim them off. To prevent fermentation and retard crystallization, heat the honey to 150°F before bottling it. To do this, place the honey container in a water bath on a stove. Check the temperature carefully with a candy thermometer, since overheating will spoil the flavor. Next, pour the honey into clean, dry containers with tight seals; mason jars or their equivalent are excellent. Store the honey in a warm, dry room (the ideal temperature is 80°F). If the honey crystallizes—a natural process—it can be liquified by heating in hot water and stirring occasionally.

Getting your hive ready for winter

The goal of winter management is to bring as many bees through the winter alive as possible. A good food supply is vital. Leave one deep super filled with honey and pollen for the bees. (Bees need pollen as a protein source, and larvae will not develop without it.) Supplement with syrup; check feeder regularly. Bore a 1-in. hole in top super for ventilation—dampness can be fatal to bees. This will let out warm, moist air and provide an extra hive entrance.

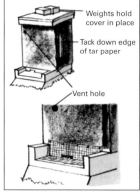

Weights hold cover in place

Tack down edge of tar paper

Vent hole

Wrap hive in a layer of tar paper to protect bees from sudden temperature changes. Fasten paper with tacks or staples. Leave vent hole and entrance open. Remove tar paper in spring.
Mice move into beehives in fall and nest in combs, destroying them. To keep mice out, bend 1/2-in. wire mesh into an L-shape, and tack or staple over hive entrance. Mesh lets bees pass but excludes mice.

Sources and resources

Books and pamphlets
Dadant, C.P. *First Lessons in Beekeeping*. New York: Scribner's, 1982.
Gojmerac, Walter L. Bees, *Beekeeping, Honey and Pollination*. Westport, Conn.: AVI Publishing, 1980.
Graham, Joe M., ed. *The Hive and the Honey Bee*. Hamilton, Ill.: Dadant & Sons, 1992.
Hubbell, Sue. *The Book of Bees and How to Keep Them*. New York: Random House, 1988.
Melzer, Werner. *Beekeeping: An Owner's Manual*. Hauppauge, N.Y.: Barron, 1989.
Morse, Roger, and Flottum, Kim, eds. *The ABC and XYZ of Bee Culture: An Encyclopedia of Beekeeping*. Medina, Ohio: A.I. Root, 1990.

Fish Farming

A King-sized Aquarium that Feeds a Family

You do not have to be an expert to raise fish successfully; basically, it is like managing an oversized aquarium. Fish are raised commercially in large artificial ponds or complex structures, but for individual homeowners and homesteaders a simple backyard tank can produce a significant proportion of a family's protein needs. An aboveground wading pool, 12 feet across and 2 feet deep, can yield 50 to 100 pounds of tasty trout, catfish, or other species in a single growing season of five to six months.

Good Water Is the Key to Productivity

The types of fish you can raise as well as the poundage you harvest depend on three factors: oxygen content of the water, water quality, and water temperature.

Oxygen content. Fish must have oxygen to survive. When oxygen dissolved in the water falls too low, the fish suffocate and die. Oxygen enters water by diffusion from the air and by the action of algae and other water plants. Oxygen content drops on a sunless day, when plants photosynthesize slowly, and in hot weather, because warm water holds less oxygen than cold water. The fish farmer can get around natural deficiencies by using an aerator to supply needed oxygen. In fact, constant aeration can double the fish harvest, since fish are healthier and grow faster when they have plentiful oxygen.

Many models of aerators are sold by aquaculture supply houses. Some bubble air up from the bottom via perforated pipes or hoses; others spray a fountain of water up into the air. The latter type of aerator has the advantage of providing circulation as it splashes down on the surface of the tank. For a small-scale home operation a sump pump with a short hose attached to jet the water back into the tank can serve as an aerator.

Water quality. The pH (degree of acidity or alkalinity) and the presence of such impurities as heavy metals and organic waste play a part in determining water quality. Fish will not thrive in water with a pH much lower than 6 (acid) or much higher than 8 (alkaline). The ideal pH is 6.5 to 7. Check the pH of your water regularly: add lime to reduce acidity; add gypsum to reduce alkalinity. Before setting up your tank, have the water tested for such heavy metals as iron, lead, and copper. Even in concentrations as low as three parts per million these substances are toxic to fish. If your water supply chlorinated, filter it through charcoal before using it.

Fish give off nitrogenous wastes in large quantities. These must not be allowed to accumulate. Algae are effective purifiers in ponds and lakes; but if you are raising fish in a tank, particularly if you are raising trout you will need a recirculating filter. An efficient filter can be made at home from a clean 55-gallon drum filled with crushed rock, gravel, sand, seashells, or special plastic ringlets. Naturally occurring bacteria that grow on the filter medium convert the fish wastes to harmless substances. A small electric pump circulates water to the filter; gravity feeds it back to the tank.

Water temperature. Trout do best in water be-tween 54°F and 56°F, but they can survive lower temperatures as long as the water does not freeze. If the temperature rises to 85°F they will die. A steady supply of water from a cold spring is close to ideal. Catfish, in contrast, thrive at 80°F to 90°F and become torpid below 40°F. If your climate permits, raise trout in the colder months and catfish in the warm season. For best results, match your fish to the climate and let nature work for you.

Setting Up a Backyard Fish Tank

Breeding your own fish entails an extra investment in equipment and labor. Most fish farmers, from large-scale trout ranchers to backyard hobbyists, find it easier to obtain their stock from commercial hatcheries. Fish are purchased as 2- to 6-inch fingerlings and harvested after one growing season (it is seldom economical to carry them longer). The bigger the fingerlings, the bigger the fish you will harvest.

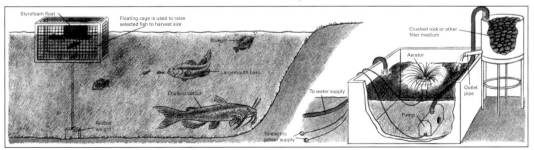

Self-sustaining fish pond contains a balanced mixture of life: algae and other plankton, tiny animals that feed on the plankton, small fish that feed on the plankton eaters, and so on up the chain to the big fish. The pond shown above contains a combination of fish species recommended by government experts: bluegill sunfish, largemouth bass, and channel catfish. Each fish utilizes a different source of food.

Backyard fish tank is easy to manage and produces plenty of fish for family use. The system requires few components. Tank can be built of cement block painted with waterproof epoxy compound. It can also be made from fiberglass or from wood lined with plastic sheeting. Even a standard child's wading pool will serve.

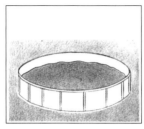

1. Set up your tank in a level area as close to a water outlet as possible. Fill the tank, then check that the filter and aerator are functioning properly.

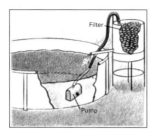

2. Run the system for two weeks before the fish arrive to condition the water and permit waste-neutralizing bacteria to become established in the filter.

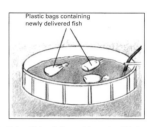

3. Fish will be delivered in water-filled plastic bags. To avoid thermal shock, place bags in tank until temperatures are equalized, then release fish.

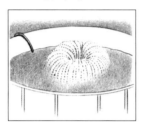

4. Keep the water thoroughly aerated; a good oxygen supply is vital to the health of the fish. A small submersible fountaintype aerator is shown operating here.

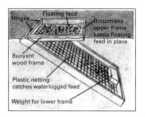

5. Feed can be broadcast on the water, but a floating feed rack, easy to make at home, will provide better sanitation and will waste less feed.

6. Harvest fish with a dip net or by draining the tank. If the fish are in a pond, a drag net can be used to harvest large numbers of them at one time.

During the growing season water must be added to the tank regularly to replace water lost by evaporation. When the time comes to harvest the fish, drain out most of the water and scoop the fish up in nets. The fish can be frozen, eaten fresh, or preserved in a variety of other ways (see *Preserving Meat and Fish*, pp.212–223).

If you lack experience in fish farming, plan on stocking about 1 pound of fingerlings for each cubic foot of water—more could overload the system. (Fish farmers think in terms of total fish weight, not numbers.) It is possible to stock more than one species together; in fact, studies show that polycultures outyield monocultures provided the species are selected so as not to compete with each other for food or living space. For a sustained yield in farm ponds experts recommend a mixture of 100 largemouth bass and 500 bluegill sunfish per surface acre. The bluegills feed on small water organisms, and the bass feed on the bluegills. Some pond owners, however, stock bass only, since bluegills tend to overbreed.

The leading types of fish raised in the United States are trout and channel catfish. Both are best raised in monocultures, since they do not compete effectively with other species for food and oxygen. Under proper conditions both gain weight rapidly, and both are excellent for eating.

A tropical fish, the tilapia, holds promise for tank culture in temperate areas, but providing warm water (75°F) for the five-month growing season they need to reach a half-pound size can be a problem. Tilapia are tasty, cheap to feed (they can live largely on algae and garden waste), and tolerant of less-than-perfect water quality. Because they are prolific and might pose an ecological threat if they escaped, tilapia are banned in some states. However, since they die when the water temperature falls to 50°F, they are no problem in northern states.

Carp are also an excellent fish for tank culture. They were among the first species to be raised by man (ancient Chinese records describe their culture as long ago as 500 B.C.), and they are mainly vegetarian. Israeli carp and several species of Asian carp do well in polycultures. Since carp are banned in many states, check with your conservation officer before stocking them.

Feeding Your Fish

For intensive fish culture supplementary feeding is required. If the fish are to reach harvesting size (1/2 to 1 pound) in one growing season, trout and catfish need high-protein rations. Commercial feeds supply protein, vitamins, and minerals in the correct proportions; fish scraps are an acceptable substitute. Experimenters have devised mixtures of chopped earthworms, soy flour, grain meal, and midge larvae. Tilapia and carp have been raised successfully on a diet of algae and grass clippings fortified by small doses of animal manure. Feed your fish at the same time every day, gradually increasing the rations as they grow so that they receive about 3 percent of their body weight daily. (Estimate a gain of about 1 pound for every 2 to 3 pounds of feed.) When feed is left over, use less the next day. Overfeeding can cause sanitation problems.

Sources and resources

Books
Bardach, John E., John H. Ryther, and William O. McLarney. *Aquaculture: The Farming and Husbandry of Freshwater and Marine Organisms.* New York: John Wiley, 1974.
Bennett, George W. *Management of Lakes and Ponds*, 2nd ed. Melbourne, Fla.: Krieger, 1983.
Huet, Marcel. *Textbook of Fish Culture: Breeding and Cultivation of Fish.* Cambridge, Mass.: Blackwell Scientific Publications, 1994.
Spotte, Stephen H. *Fish and Invertebrate Culture: Water Management in Closed Systems.* New York: John Wiley, 1979.
Yoo, Kyung H., and Boyd, Claude E. *Hydrology and Water Supply for Pond Aquaculture.* New York: Chapman & Hall, 1993.

Raising Livestock

Animals Pay Their Way With Meat, Milk, Eggs, and Heavy Work Too

Vast grazing lands, fertile soil for feed grains, and the demand for protein have helped make meat, milk, and eggs mainstays of the American diet. Our hunger for beef financed the railroads that opened the West to intensive settlement. Our love of pork and lard made the fast-growing hog the traditional "mortgage lifter" for on-the-move farmers.

To keep pace with America's demand for meat and dairy products, farmers have worked to find new ways to make animals grow bigger, gain weight faster, and produce more abundantly. But their advances have not been without some drawbacks. Animals that are scientifically fed for fast growth simply do not have the flavor of ones on a varied diet. Growth-stimulating hormones and medicated feed may have long-term side effects that are as yet unknown. And in spite of record-high productivity, meat, milk, and eggs are becoming increasingly expensive.

But you need not remain bound by the limits—and costs—of mass production. If you like animals, have a little extra space (a few square feet is all it takes to raise rabbits), and can put in a little time daily, you can have cream-rich milk, fresh eggs every day, and full-flavored, chemical-free meat that you have produced yourself. You can also learn to keep costs to a minimum—by feeding discarded greens, stalks, and bumper crops that would otherwise go to waste or by turning unused land into pasture.

Do not let anyone tell you that raising animals is easy. It may take only a few minutes a day, but you can never skip a day. Nonetheless, there is an abundance of rewards, not the least of which is the satisfaction of watching animals prosper.

Self-sufficient lifestyle of 19th-century farm families was based on the use of animals for heavy work as well as for food.

An Ounce of Cleanliness Is Worth a Pound of Cure

Cleanliness is the single biggest contributor to livestock health. Feeding and shelter requirements vary from one farm animal to another, but all require good sanitation to stay in top condition. Begin with good planning. Be sure the feeding and watering equipment is protected from contamination and that the shelter is easy to clean. If you have a pasture, it should be free of boggy areas, poisonous weeds, and dangerous debris. Use fencing and traps to protect your animals from rodents, and guard against flies by installing screens. Daily care is important too. Wash equipment after each use, keep bedding dry, and check animals daily for early signs of trouble.

Once or twice each year thoroughly scrub and disinfect your animals' shelter. Haul all the old bedding to the compost heap and replace it with some that is clean, new, and dry. Take all movable equipment outside, wash it thoroughly, and let it dry in the sun—sunlight is an excellent disinfectant. Scrub the inside of the house with a stiff bristled brush to remove caked dirt, then go over everything again with a disinfectant formulated for use with livestock. Follow the directions that come with the disinfectant and allow adequate drying time before letting the animals back into the house. The same sanitary procedures should be followed in the event of an outbreak of disease or before bringing a new animal into the shelter—for instance, if you are putting a new feeder pig into the pen used by last year's feeder.

Try to keep strange animals away from your livestock. If you buy a new animal, keep it quarantined until you are sure it is healthy. If you take an animal to a livestock show, isolate it for awhile when you return before reintroducing it into the herd. Some farmers go so far as to pen new animals with a member of the established herd to be sure the new ones are not symptom-free disease carriers. If they are, only a single animal need be lost, not the entire herd. Many chicken raisers slaughter their entire flocks and start with a new batch of chicks instead of trying to introduce a few new birds at a time. Remember: a clean environment is the best way to guarantee healthy, profitable, attractive livestock.

Keeping Records of Productivity

Good records are essential if you want to know whether your animals are paying their way and how the cost of raising them stacks up against going to the supermarket. Keep track of all expenses, including veterinary bills, and write down exactly how much feed you provide each day. If possible, record the amount fed to individual animals. Keep track of productivity too. Note how many offspring each animal produces, whether the offspring survive to maturity, and how fast they gain weight. If you have dairy animals, weigh their milk at each milking. Count the number of eggs laid by each of your chickens, ducks, or geese and the percentage of the eggs hatched. Maintaining records is not a time-consuming chore. The most convenient system is to keep a looseleaf notebook or box of file cards near your animals' shelter. Carefully kept records will tell you which animals are producing efficiently and which should be culled. They will also increase the worth of any animals you choose to sell and help you decide which offspring will make the most valuable additions to your stock.

Learn Before You Leap

Before buying animals, learn as much as you can about keeping them. Books, breeders' magazines, and government pamphlets are helpful, but do not expect to become an expert just by reading. Talk to your county agent and other knowledgeable people. Attend shows and exhibits to learn what distinguishes good specimens. Check costs of feed, equipment, fencing, and building materials. And be certain there is a veterinarian available who will be able to treat your animals. If you are interested in selling produce, find out what markets are available, what laws restrict its sale (the sale of milk is particularly strictly regulated), and what price it is likely to bring. You might also want to make sure that there is someone in the area to slaughter your livestock—or to help you learn to do the job yourself.

Before you commit yourself to purchasing any animals, check at town hall to determine whether they are permitted in your area. Be sure that you have ample space as well as clean, sanitary shelter. If you plan to range-feed, make sure your pasture is of sufficiently high quality. It can take years to develop top-quality grazing land, and if yours is not, you will have to buy hay. Before the animals arrive you should have on hand all necessary equipment, such as feed pans, milk pails, watering troughs, halters, and grain storage bins. You should also be prepared to store what your animals produce. Milk and eggs must be refrigerated, and meat must be salted, smoked, or kept frozen until you are ready to eat it.

Chickens: Best Bets For the Small Farmer

Most chickens are bred to produce either eggs or meat but not both. The best egg producers remain thin no matter how much they eat, while meat types become plump quickly but lay fewer eggs. There are a number of dual-purpose breeds and hybrids, however, that provide plenty of eggs as well as meaty carcasses.

You can buy chickens at almost any stage of their development, from day-old chicks to old hens who are no longer very productive. (You can even buy fertilized eggs, but they are unlikely to hatch successfully for a beginner.) If possible, obtain your birds from a local hatchery or breeder. However, buying chicks through the mail is very common and may be the only way you can get them. Purchasing started pullets—females about four months old that have just begun to lay—is an easy way for a novice to start a flock. Pullet eggs are small, but the birds will soon be laying full-sized eggs.

Day-old chicks are cheaper but require extra attention and special equipment until they are grown. They are

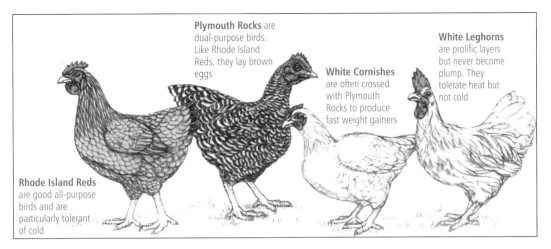

Plymouth Rocks are dual-purpose birds. Like Rhode Island Reds, they lay brown eggs

White Cornishes are often crossed with Plymouth Rocks to produce fast weight gainers

White Leghorns are prolific layers but never become plump. They tolerate heat but not cold

Rhode Island Reds are good all-purpose birds and are particularly tolerant of cold

available either sexed (that is, differentiated as to sex) or unsexed. If you are interested in egg production only, buy all females, since a rooster is not necessary unless you want fertilized eggs.

The number of birds you need depends upon the number of eggs you want. A good layer will produce an egg almost every day but none during the annual molt (shedding of feathers). If you want a dozen eggs a day, you will need about 15 birds. This allows for decreased productivity and for any deaths. If you buy unsexed chicks, buy twice that number plus a few more to allow for higher mortality among the younger birds. Butcher the males for meat when they become full grown at about 5 to 6 pounds live weight.

Try to obtain birds that have been vaccinated against pullorum, typhoid, and any other disease that might be prevalent in your area. If the birds have not been vaccinated, have a veterinarian do the job. It is also advisable to buy chickens that have been debeaked to prevent pecking later in life. Most hatcheries routinely vaccinate and debeak all birds.

Whatever type of bird you decide to raise, be sure to make arrangements well in advance. Start by checking with your county agent; he will be able to advise you on what breeds are popular in your area and what diseases are prevalent. Send in your order early.

Troubleshooting

Symptoms	Treatment
Cannibalism (pecking)	Increase feed and space. Keep bedding dry and let birds scratch in it
Egg eating	Increase feed and calcium. Darken nest boxes. Gather eggs often
Lice	Dust birds and coop with louse powder
Change of habit, listlessness	Isolate sick bird. Call veterinarian. If bird dies, bury deeply or burn

Feeding Your Poultry

The quality, quantity, taste, and appearance of a chicken's meat and eggs depend on proper feeding and watering.

Fresh water must be available at all times and must be kept from freezing in winter. Each bird will drink as much as two cups a day, particularly while laying, since an egg is almost entirely water.

Mash purchased from a feed supply store is the most commonly used chicken feed. It is a blend of many components: finely ground grains, such as wheat, corn, and oats; extra protein from such sources as soybean meal, fish meal, and dried milk; calcium from ground oyster shells and bone meal; and vitamin and mineral supplements. There are a variety of special mixes, such as high-protein mash for chicks and high-calcium mash for laying hens. There are also all-purpose mashes containing plenty of everything, but these are generally more expensive. On the average, each bird will eat 4 to 5 ounces of mash per day but will require more food during peak production periods or in cold weather.

You can save money by feeding your chickens with homegrown scratch (unground grain) and food scraps in addition to commercial mash. Most chicken raisers consider it wasteful to scatter scratch on the ground, where it gets dirty and is not eaten. Instead, load the feeder at one end with scratch and the other end with mash, or sprinkle the scratch on top of the mash. When scratch is used for feed, it is necessary to provide the birds with grit—bits of pebble and sand—that collects in their gizzards and helps them digest the grain.

Extra protein and calcium must also be provided when feeding scratch. (Protein should make up 20 percent of a chicken's total diet, but most scratch grains are only 10 percent protein.) Birds that can range freely get protein from bugs in the ground. Table scraps and dried milk are other good sources or you can use mash with an extra-high protein content. To supplement calcium in the diet, feed the chickens ground egg or oyster shells, but be sure to grind the eggshells thoroughly. Otherwise the birds may develop a taste for them and eat their own eggs. (Egg eating can also mean the birds lack calcium.)

Birds also like and benefit from very fresh greens, such as grass clippings and vegetable tops. Feed only as much of these greens as the birds will eat quickly—in about 15 minutes. Remember, scraps can affect the taste of eggs and meat. Do not feed anything with a strong flavor.

Most chicken raisers keep food available to the birds at all times but fill the feeders no more than halfway so that the feed is not scattered and wasted. Mash and grains may be stored in airtight, rodent-proof containers, such as plastic garbage pails. Do not store more than a month's supply of mash, since it quickly becomes stale.

A Shelter Planned for Comfort and Minimum Care

Whether you are converting an unused shack or starting with a new building, you will want a chicken house that is warm, dry, draft free, and easy to clean. It should have at least 2 square feet of floor space per bird. A dirt floor—the cheapest and simplest type—is adequate for a small flock. Concrete is easier to clean and gives more protection against rodents but is expensive. If the floor is wooden, it should be raised at least 1 foot off the ground (build it on cinder blocks) as a protection against rats as well as to reduce dampness.

Cover the floor with a litter of wood shavings, shredded sugarcane stalks, or other cheap, absorbent material. Start with about 6 inches. Whenever the litter becomes dirty, shovel away any particularly wet spots and add a new layer of absorbent material. The litter absorbs moisture and provides heat and natural antibiotics as it decomposes. It should be completely replaced at least once or twice a year. Add the dirty litter to the compost heap—it makes excellent fertilizer—then clean and disinfect the coop before spreading new litter.

Insulation in the ceiling and walls will moderate the temperature and help to keep it near 55°F, the level at which chickens are most comfortable and productive. Adequate ventilation is needed to cool the coop, dry the litter, and disperse odors. It can be provided by slots high in the walls, double-hung windows open at the top, or windows that tilt inward at the top. The windows should face away from the wind but in a direction where they can let in the winter sun.

You may want to let your birds out of their house during the day to range free on your land (be sure they are all safely inside at night), but they will be better protected against dangerous dogs, foxes, weasels, and rats in a wire-enclosed run. The run should have a wire-mesh covering or a fence high enough to keep the birds inside. (The smaller the breed, the higher the birds can flutter.) Birds allowed out-of-doors are less likely to develop boredom-induced problems, such as egg eating and pecking. They will also be supplied with plenty of free vitamin D from the sun.

Eggs and Meat

Most small flocks are kept primarily for their eggs, with meat as a valuable by-product. Eggs are less likely to crack or get dirty if they are gathered frequently—at least once a day or even twice a day if possible. Avoid washing the shells, since water removes the protective layer that slows evaporation and protects against disease. If you must wash an egg, use warm water (cold water will be drawn through the shell and into the egg), and eat the egg promptly. A fresh high-quality egg has a thick white and a yolk that remains at the center when hard-boiled. As the egg ages, water evaporates, the air pocket enlarges, and the albumen (white) breaks down.

When a hen is two or three years old, its laying rate falls off and it should be butchered. Be sure it has not had antibiotics for a week or two (check the instructions on the medicine) and that it has not eaten for 24 hours before it is killed. To kill the bird, hold legs and wings firmly with one hand while you chop off the head with the other. Then hang the carcass upside down by the

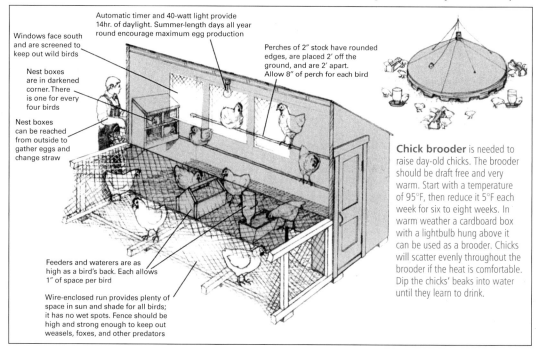

Automatic timer and 40-watt light provide 14hr. of daylight. Summer-length days all year round encourage maximum egg production

Windows face south and are screened to keep out wild birds

Nest boxes are in darkened corner. There is one for every four birds

Nest boxes can be reached from outside to gather eggs and change straw

Perches of 2″ stock have rounded edges, are placed 2′ off the ground, and are 2′ apart. Allow 8″ of perch for each bird

Feeders and waterers are as high as a bird's back. Each allows 1″ of space per bird

Wire-enclosed run provides plenty of space in sun and shade for all birds; it has no wet spots. Fence should be high and strong enough to keep out weasels, foxes, and other predators

Chick brooder is needed to raise day-old chicks. The brooder should be draft free and very warm. Start with a temperature of 95°F, then reduce it 5°F each week for six to eight weeks. In warm weather a cardboard box with a lightbulb hung above it can be used as a brooder. Chicks will scatter evenly throughout the brooder if the heat is comfortable. Dip the chicks' beaks into water until they learn to drink.

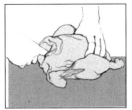

1. Insert finger to pry lungs and organs loose.

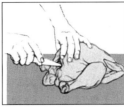

2. Cut around vent, being careful not to cut into it.

3. Carefully pull out vent and attached intestines.

4. Pull out entrails. Do not rupture gall bladder.

feet for 10 minutes to let the blood drain. To loosen the feathers for plucking, scald the carcass briefly in 150°F to 190°F water. Start the butchering by slitting the neck skin open, cutting off the neck, and pulling out the windpipe and gullet. Eviscerate as shown below, and finish by thoroughly washing the carcass.

For Food Without Fuss Try Geese and Ducks

Geese and ducks are extremely hardy and will forage for most of the food they need. They are also amusing pets and, in the case of geese, make excellent lookouts that squawk loudly whenever a stranger approaches. To start a small flock, raise day-old birds to maturity or buy young birds—ducks about seven months old or geese about two years old—that are ready to start breeding.

One male and six females is a good number of ducks to start with. Geese tend to be monogamous, so it is best to buy a pair. Buy the birds a month before breeding season (early spring) to give them time to adjust. By midsummer there should be plenty of fertile eggs.

Incubation. A goose can hatch only 12 of the 20 or so eggs it lays, while domesticated ducks (except the Muscovy breed) rarely sit on their eggs at all. Since machine incubation is difficult, use broody hens (ones that want to sit on eggs) as foster mothers. Dust the hen and nest with louse powder and put five eggs under the bird. Keep water and food nearby so that it will not need to leave its nest for more than a few minutes. The hen will turn the eggs daily if they are not too heavy; if this does not happen, turn them yourself to keep the yolks from settling. Mark one side of each egg with a grease pencil so that you can tell which need to be turned. Sprinkle the eggs with water every few days to maintain the high humidity that a duck or goose provides naturally with its wet feathers. About five days after incubation begins, hold each egg up to a bright light in a dark room and look for the dark spot inside, which means the egg is fertilized. Hatching takes 28 days for ducks, 30 days for geese.

Brooding. Newborn birds must be kept warm and dry until they grow protective feathers at about four weeks of age. For birds raised by their natural mothers, this is no problem, but if the young are raised by a hen, take special precautions. First, as each bird emerges, remove it to a warm brooder until all are born. Otherwise, the hen may think the job is finished and leave the rest of the eggs before they hatch. Then confine the hen and babies in a small area for the first few days.

If you are using a brooder like the one shown on page 168, provide 1 square foot of floor space per bird and keep it at 85°F. As the birds grow, gradually increase the floor space and reduce the temperature by 5°F a week for four weeks. Give starter feed and plenty of water to the newborns. If it is warm and dry outside, two-week-old goslings can be let out to eat some grass. After four weeks begin to shift the little ducklings and goslings entirely to range feeding.

Indian Runners are egg-laying ducks that gain little weight

Emden geese are excellent for meat and the 40 eggs per year each produces makes them among the best layers of any breed of geese

Khaki Campbell ducks can lay more then 300 eggs a year, rivaling chickens in productivity, but they grow to only 4 1/2 lb.

Pekin ducks are the most popular breed for meat thanks to fast weight gain and white feathers that leave skin clear and attractive once plucked

Choose the right breed: a small laying type of duck for eggs, a heavy breed of duck or a goose for rich, flavorful meat.

Feed. At least 1 acre of range is needed for 20 mature birds. To prevent overgrazing, divide the area into three sections and shift the birds from one to the other as the supply of grass dwindles. Carefully fence any young trees on the range area, since geese love to eat their tender bark. You can supplement foraging with pellet feed placed in covered self-feeders right on the range. Supply laying birds with ground oyster shells to provide calcium, and provide plenty of fresh drinking water at all times or the birds will choke on their food. Water troughs must be deep enough that a duck can submerge its bill (to clear its nostrils) and a goose its entire head.

Eggs, Meat, and Down

Duck eggs are larger than chicken eggs and have a stronger taste but can be treated and used just the same way. Butchering too is the same, but be prepared to spend much more time plucking, especially with geese, since the feathers of waterfowl are harder to remove. If you are not planning to save the down, paraffin can be used to help remove the pin feathers. Melt the wax, pour it over the partially plucked bird, and then plunge the carcass into cold water to harden the wax. Many of the pin feathers will come out as you peel off the hardened wax. Ducks are ready to be butchered at 8 pounds live weight and geese at 12 pounds live weight.

Feathers and down tend to blow about, so do not pluck a bird in a drafty area or in a spot where you might mind finding feathers later. To save the down, stuff it loosely into pillowcases and hang them to dry. Down is the warmest insulator for its weight that is known. Once dry, it can be used as stuffing for soft pillows, comforters, and sleeping bags. You can even make your own feather bed.

Troubleshooting

Symptoms	Treatment
Droopiness, change in habit, diarrhea	Call veterinarian for diagnosis. Isolate bird. Improve sanitation
Slow weight gain	Check for worms and use dewormer if necessary. Improve sanitation
Lice, ticks, mites	Use appropriate insecticide. Follow directions carefully

Rabbits: Good Protein In a Limited Space

Rabbits are excellent animals to raise for meat. Not only are they delicious, prolific, and hardy, but they are also inexpensive to feed. In fact, they yield more high-protein meat per dollar of feed than any other animal.

Food. Specially prepared rabbit pellets provide the best diet. These can be supplemented with tender hay, fresh grass clippings, and vegetable tops—but greens should be fed sparingly to a rabbit that is less than six months old. Root vegetables, apples, pears, and fruit tree

A simple shed with 5 to 6 sq. ft. of floor space per bird is all that ducks or geese need for shelter. Good ventilation and sanitation are necessities, and litter should be spread and tended as for chickens. The birds enjoy a place to swim, but a pond or other open body of water is not needed to raise them successfully.

leaves are also favorites. Water is essential (change it at least once a day). Many raisers also provide a salt lick.

Mating. Medium-weight types, such as the New Zealand, are ready to breed at about six months old. Signs to look for in the female are restlessness, attempts to join other rabbits, and a tendency to rub its head against the cage. Once a doe has reached maturity, it is fertile almost continuously, with infertile periods lasting only a few days. Simply place the female in the male's cage; mating should take place immediately. If it does not, bring the doe back to its own cage, wait a few days, and then try again. Never bring the male to the female; fearing an intruder, the female may attack.

Birth. Ten days after mating, check for pregnancy by feeling the area just above the pelvis. Try to locate the small marble-shaped embryos. If you feel nothing, check again a week later and rebreed if necessary.

Birth—called kindling—occurs 31 days after conception. Five days before the young are due, put the nesting box—with a good supply of straw in the bottom—in the doe's hutch. The young will probably be born at night. Leave them alone for a day or two until the doe is calm.

New Zealand White, the most popular rabbit for meat, is a medium-weight breed of about 5 lb. Buy the best animals you can afford, since the quality of future litters will depend upon them. Be sure they are alert, bright-eyed, and clean, with dry ears and nose and no sores on the feet. Start with rabbits six months old. To pick up a rabbit, grip it as shown. Never hold it by the ears.

Then distract the mother with some food and look inside the nest to see if there are any dead or deformed babies that must be removed. Start feeding the doe a special high-protein nursing diet as soon as the young are born, and make sure that the family is not disturbed. Otherwise the doe may kill the young. The rabbits will suckle for about eight weeks.

A Basic Wire-Mesh Hutch

Butchering a Fryer

When the rabbits are 8 to 12 weeks old, they are ready to be butchered as fryers. They should be about 4 pounds live weight and will weigh only about half as much after they are fully skinned and dressed.

For one day before butchering, do not feed the rabbit. To kill it, administer a sharp blow directly behind its ears. Use a heavy pipe or piece of wood, and hold the animal upside down by its feet or place it on a table

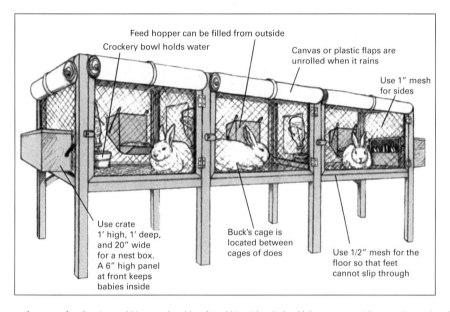

Feed hopper can be filled from outside
Crockery bowl holds water
Canvas or plastic flaps are unrolled when it rains
Use 1" mesh for the sides
Use crate 1' high, 1' deep, and 20" wide for a nest box. A 6" high panel at front keeps babies inside
Buck's cage is located between cages of does
Use 1/2" mesh for the floor so that feet cannot slip through

Housing can be very basic, since cold is no real problem for rabbits. A hutch should, however, provide protection against drafts, rain, and intense heat, and each rabbit should have its own cage. Individual cages can be hung in a garage or empty shed. Or build an outdoor hutch of lumber and 1 in. wire mesh or hardware cloth. Individual cages should be about 3 ft. wide by 3 ft. deep by 2 ft. high with mesh sides and floors. Set them up at a convenient height for feeding and cleaning. If the cages are not in the shade, they need to have a double roof to help keep them cool. For easy cleaning, place trays beneath the cages to catch droppings. Clean the trays regularly, and scrub and disinfect the cages between litters.

1. Slit skin along back legs and center of belly.

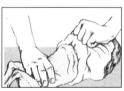

2. Pull skin down toward the animal's front legs.

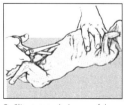

3. Slit carcass, being careful not to cut into anus.

4. Carefully remove insides. Do not cut into gall bladder.

to deliver the blow. Next, immediately hang the animal by its feet, cut off the head just behind the ears, and let the blood drain out. Cut off the feet, then follow the steps below to skin and dress the carcass. After dressing, immediately chill the meat, including the liver, heart, and kidneys, all of which are edible. Discard the other entrails or feed them to other animals.

Troubleshooting

Symptoms	Treatment
Refusal to eat	Check water. Call veterinarian if refusal persists
Runny nose, sneezing, diarrhea	Destroy sick animal or isolate it and call veterinarian
Sore hind feet	Keep floor of cage scrupulously clean and dry

Pork for the Year From a Single Hog

Pigs are the most intelligent of barnyard animals. They can be taught to perform as many tricks as a dog and even seem to be able to puzzle out answers independently—for example, the way to open a complicated gate latch. For anyone with a good source of leftover produce, pigs can be profitable as well as amusing animals to raise. They will eat almost any type of food, including table scraps, restaurant garbage, an unexpected bumper crop of vegetables, a summertime oversupply of goat's milk, or alfalfa and grain from the pasture.

Owning a sow and raising the two or three litters of 10 or so piglets produced each year is likely to provide too much pork for even a large family. Instead, buy a just-weaned pig, called a shoat, in the early spring and fatten it during the summer. When, in the fall, it reaches 220 pounds, it will be ready for butchering into 150 pounds of edible cuts. Your larder will be full and you will be free from the daily chores of animal tending.

In choosing a shoat, health and vigor are more important than breed. Buy from a reliable breeder who maintains a clean, healthy herd. Make arrangements with him well in advance, for his litters may be in great demand. When the time comes, pick the biggest and best of the litter. Look for an animal that is long, lean, and bright-eyed. Never accept a runt, even if it is offered at a greatly reduced price. It will take too much extra feed to fatten, since a runt needs extra food throughout its life.

The shoat should be six to eight weeks old at the time of purchase. A good rule to follow is to select one that weighs between 30 and 40 pounds; if it weighs less, it is either too young or a runt. If your shoat was not free to range for its food, it should have received an iron shot, since pigs born in confinement are anemic. It also should have been inoculated against hog cholera and any disease prevalent in your area (check with your county agent). If it is a male, be sure it has been castrated.

Troubleshooting

Symptoms	Treatment
Lice, mites	Apply disinfectant according to directions. Improve sanitation
Slow weight gain	Check for worms. Deworm regularly. Improve sanitation
Joint pain, skin blotches	Consult veterinarian. Move pig to new pen or pasture

Summertime Fattening

A pig must eat 3 pounds of feed to gain a pound of weight, or a total of 600 to 700 pounds to reach slaughtering weight. Commercial feeds provide the right balance of vitamins, minerals, proteins, and carbohydrates, but so do many less expensive substitutes.

One partial substitute is pasture. Up to six pigs can forage on 1 acre of such high-quality pasture as clover, grass, and alfalfa. Alfalfa, a legume, is especially valuable because it provides the precise amount of protein—16 percent—required in a pig's diet. In addition to eating plants, pigs on a range will get valuable minerals and trace elements when they root through and ingest the dirt in the field. Divide the pasture into three or more areas and rotate the animals from one to another to minimize the buildup of parasites harmful to pigs.

Range feeding must be supplemented with a small amount of coarsely ground grains, usually 2 to 4 pounds per animal depending upon the quality of the pasture. Traditionally, corn has been the most commonly used grain supplement, but oats, barley, and rye are also good. Despite their reputation, pigs will eat only as much food as they need, not enough to make themselves sick. This simplifies feeding, since the grain can be put into self-feeding hoppers set inside the grazing area.

If acreage is too scarce for foraging, raise the pig in a pen. Supplement grain or commercial feed with table scraps, garbage, and garden or orchard wastes, such as vegetable tops, stalks, and rinds. Discarded food from

Chester Whites are always white. They are of medium size, weighing 600 to 700 lb. at maturity

Yorkshires are also white. Mature boars can weigh as much as 1,000 lb.

Durocs are noted for their red color. They are fast weight gainers, reaching a 200-lb. slaughtering weight in as little as five months

Hampshires

Crossbred hogs

restaurants and school cafeterias can make an excellent feed supplement if it is properly prepared.

To process discarded garbage, sort through and remove inedible items. Also pick out all chicken bones (they will splinter and choke the pig) and pork scraps (a seemingly healthy pig can carry germs to which your animal is susceptible). Cook the remaining garbage at 212°F for 30 minutes to kill dangerous bacteria. If you must feed pork scraps, thorough boiling is especially important. Otherwise you risk the spread of trichinosis, a parasitic disease that is dangerous to humans. (The parasites live in the pig's intestines and muscles but are killed when heated to 137°F. Use a meat thermometer, and cook the pork slowly until the thermometer reads 170°F for small roasts, 185°F for thick roasts.)

If you have a goat or cow, its milk will provide an excellent source of supplemental protein. Up to 1 1/2 gallons of milk per day may be fed. To provide trace minerals, let the pig root through clumps of dirt or sod that you have carried to the pen. Be sure that the dirt does not come from a field fertilized with hog manure (it can contain harmful bacteria) or sprayed with chemicals. Provide plenty of fresh, clean water for your pig.

Housing Should Be Cool and Sturdy

In summer almost any unused shed will make a good home for a pig, or you can build a simple A-frame, either permanently sited or movable like the one shown above. As protection from the sun's heat, the structure should be set under a tree or have a double roof with several inches of space between the two levels. Good ventilation will also help to keep the house cool.

To keep a 220-pound hog confined, strong fencing is essential. A wire fence usually proves the most practical for a range. Set the posts at least 3 feet deep to make the fence strong enough so that the animal cannot knock it over. A strand of barbed or electrified wire placed 3 inches above the ground may be needed to keep the hog from burrowing under the mesh.

If you are raising your pig in a pen, provide as much outdoor space as possible; the absolute minimum for a single pig is 100 square feet. Fence the pen with closely spaced boards so that the shoat cannot catch its head between them. The boards must also be strong enough to keep a grown hog inside. Nail all boards to the inside

A-frame on skids is a popular hog shelter. Windows or doors are put at front and rear to provide maximum cooling and ventilation, since overheated pigs gain weight slowly. Skids permit the house to be moved to different parts of the pasture or pen.

of the posts so that the pig cannot push them loose, and bury the bottom board several inches deep in the ground to keep the pig from burrowing underneath.

A hog has very few sweat glands to keep it cool and will appreciate a wallow in its pen or range area. Use a garden hose to make a big, muddy area or fit the hose with a spray nozzle to provide a light shower.

Careful Butchering Is Key to Quality Meat

The hog must be kept quiet and in a pen by itself for at least three days before slaughtering. Bruises, overheating, and excitement will damage the meat's flavor and texture and cause unnecessary spoilage during the butchering. For the last day before butchering, withhold food, but provide as much water as the pig will consume.

Sticking is the best method of killing. The animal can be shot or stunned first to make the job easier, but experts warn that this hampers efficient bleeding. Hang the freshly killed animal head downward, and collect the blood for use in sausage, as a protein supplement for other animals, or as fertilizer.

Once all the blood is drained, remove the hog's body hair as quickly as possible. To loosen the hair, immerse the entire hog in 145°F water for several minutes. An old bathtub set on concrete blocks and with a fire underneath is an easy way to heat the 30 to 40 gallons of water necessary for this task. After scalding, hoist the carcass onto a table where two or more people with special

Breeding for leanness

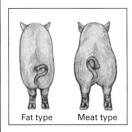

Fat type   Meat type

Modern hogs are bred to be lean and meaty, not fat like the ones popular 50 years ago when lard brought high prices. You can recognize a meat-type hog from its wide, straight stance; its long, lean, muscular physique; and its thick shoulders and hams (upper back legs).

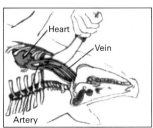

Heart

Vein

Artery

To stick a hog, hang it head down or flip it on its back. Insert knife under breastbone between ribs. Move knife up and down to sever main artery that comes out of heart. Do not damage heart, which must keep pumping to ensure proper bleeding.

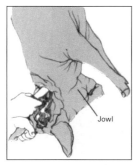

1. Remove head (except for jowl) by cutting from back of neck toward jawbone.

2. Slit carcass open by cutting upward from throat, downward from hams.

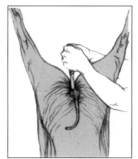

3. Cut circle around anus to begin removal of bung (lower end of intestine).

4. Pull bung away from body cavity. Bung must not be cut, torn, or punctured.

5. Use hand or knife to sever fibers joining entrails to body. Do not cut gall bladder.

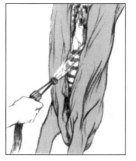

6. Pull entrails out and place in cold water. Hose out body cavity with cold water.

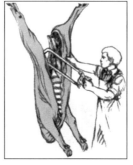

7. Slit backbone, pull out lard, and hang carcass for 24 hours at 34°F to 40°F.

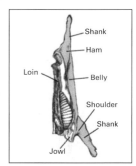

8. Cut carcass into parts. Use innards and blood for sausage and scrapple.

bell-shaped hog scrapers can scrape off the hair. Finally, rehang the carcass and butcher as shown below.

Sheep: Gentle Providers of Meat and Fleece

For homespun yarn, homegrown meat, lustrous shearling skins, and the companionship of a few amiable yet profitable animals, consider raising sheep. Their moderate size and gentle disposition make them easy to handle, their shelter needs are minimal, and they can graze for most of their food.

To start a small flock, buy grade (nonpurebred) ewes, but find out as much as you can about their background. If you can find a ewe that is a twin and born of a mother that is also one of twins, that animal is likely to bear many twins to build your flock. When purchasing a ram, pick the best purebred you can afford. The good qualities will gradually improve the overall excellence of the entire flock.

When shopping for sheep, go to a reliable breeder and select alert animals that are close to two years old (the age they begin to breed). Make sure they are free of any indication of disease, particularly sore feet, teats, or udders, and that they have no sign of worms. Color is another consideration. Sheep raisers have tradition-

ally sought animals with pure white fleece that can be dyed a variety of colors. But many modern handspinners enjoy working with the fibers from their black and brown ewes.

Pasturage, Hay, and Grain

Sheep, like cows and goats, are ruminants whose stomachs have special bacteria that break down grass into digestible food. Unlike nonruminant animals that derive little food value from grass, sheep can get all the nutrients they need from good-quality pasturage.

A sheep pasture must be well fenced, as much to keep out predators as to keep the sheep inside. Build a 4-foot-high fence of medium-weight wire field fencing attached to heavy wooden posts. Set the posts at least 3 feet deep in the ground and no more than 15 feet apart. Install a strand of barbed wire at the bottom and another one or two strands at the top to protect sheep from dogs and other enemies. Barbed wire, however, will not prevent sheep from wandering through a broken fence. Their thick wool coats protect them against the barbs—and against electric shock as well if the fence is electrified. As a result, you must check the fencing regularly and repair any weak spots or holes through which the sheep can pass.

One acre of good-quality pastureland containing about half tender grass and half legumes will feed four sheep for most of the summer. To be sure that the animals do not overgraze and ruin the pasture, rotate the grazing

Corriedales are fast growing, easy to handle, and produce good spinning wool

Columbias yield good meat, and fleece that is easy to spin

Romneys are a favorite among spinners who like the long, silky fleece

Merinos are raised for their beautiful wool but are not desirable for meat production

When choosing a sheep, look for such traits as hardiness, fast growth, ability to forage, quiet disposition, and spinnable fleece.

area. Use at least three separate sections, and move the sheep from one to another when they have cropped the tops off the plants. The older, tougher parts—which the sheep dislike—will send up new shoots, so the pasture will regenerate. Another precaution that helps to keep the pastureland in good condition is to exclude the sheep in the very early spring before the new growth has had a chance to become well established.

When good pasture is not available or when extra demands are placed on a sheep's body during pregnancy and nursing, its diet must be supplemented with grain. In the spring, when the ewes are being prepared for breeding, begin giving them whole grains, such as oats, corn, and wheat. Feed them each 1 pound of grain per day. A mother nursing twins requires 1 1/2 to 2 pounds of grain per day. During winter provide each sheep with 1 pound of grain per day along with all the top-quality hay it will eat. The hay should be tender and green with plenty of legumes, and it should never be moldy. Put it in a hayrack, where it will stay fresh and not be scattered on the ground and wasted.

For good health and fast growth, feeding must be managed carefully. If a grain supplement is being used, measure it out carefully and give half the daily amount in the morning and half in the afternoon. Keep the feeding times constant, and make any change in diet extremely gradual, especially when changing from winter hay to summer pasture. Sheep unaccustomed to grass can develop bloat (excess gas in the stomach), which is painful and can cause death.

Whether they are grazing or being fed hay and grain, the sheep need salt (in the form of a salt lick). Medication for internal worms, a major danger to sheep, as well as extra minerals can also be supplied in the lick. Plenty of fresh water is also vital.

Troubleshooting

Symptoms	Treatment
Weight loss	Check for worms, deworm regularly
Limping, inflamed feet	Check hooves and trim semiannually, avoid wet pasture, use footbath
External worms, ticks, mites	Dip, dust, or spray, especially after shearing
Change in habits, weakness	Consult veterinarian for diagnosis and proper medication

Housing a Small Flock

Sheep thrive in cold weather and, as a result, their housing requirements are minimal. A three-sided shed is adequate in most climates unless there is to be a midwinter lambing. In that case, you will need a warm place for the lambs. The shelter should be roomy enough to provide at least 12 square feet of space per animal and preferably 15 square feet or more. A wide door is another essential so that pregnant ewes will not be crowded as they enter and leave the building. Good ventilation will keep the shed cool and minimize dampness.

The floor can be dirt or concrete but not wood, and it should be covered with about 1 foot of litter. Sheep manure is normally dry and can be allowed to accumulate in the litter, where it will warm the floor. Remove the dirty litter once a year, and clean and disinfect the floor and building. If damp spots develop before the year is up, they must be removed and fresh litter added. Similarly, if the litter becomes wet and smelly, it should be changed.

Teeth indicate age of sheep. When an animal is about one year old, it gets its first two adult teeth. It will add two more permanent teeth each year until there are eight in all. In old age, tops of adult teeth wear down to leave short, narrow bases with spaces between them.

Lambs need a creep, an area only they can enter. To set up one install a fence diagonally across one corner of the shelter. The fence palings should be 9 in. apart—enough space for lambs, but not sheep, to get through. Use heat lamp to warm creep.

Shed must have ample space because sheep dislike crowding.

At lambing time a few additions to the sheep shed are necessary. A fenced-off stall should be provided for each ewe—most sheep raisers keep a supply of gatelike panels that can be set in place at lambing time to create temporary stalls. A lamb creep—a small area with a barrier that permits the lambs but not the sheep to enter—is also needed to protect the lambs' special feed.

Shearing

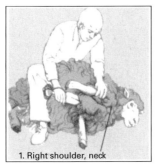

1. Right shoulder, neck

Shear sheep every spring. A good shearer will cut close to the skin and remove the entire fleece in one piece. Second cuts—made by going back over previously clipped areas—are not desirable. Use your knees to hold sheep in position and to keep the animal calm. Proceed to shear, following order shown in illustrations starting at left. Either electric or hand shears can be used.

The Breeding Season

Since most breeds of sheep mate just once each year, managing the breeding season is not difficult. The season begins in the fall. A few weeks before, check the ewes for worms, sore feet, and other problems. At the same time put them on a high-protein diet to bolster their health and improve their chances of bearing twins.

Lambing time is 148 days after mating. In the normal birth, feet come out first, followed by the head resting

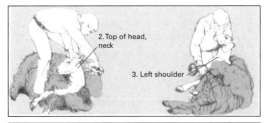

2. Top of head, neck

3. Left shoulder

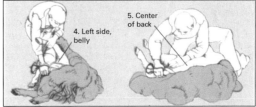

4. Left side, belly

5. Center of back

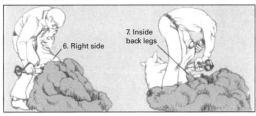

6. Right side

7. Inside back legs

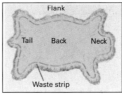

Flank

Tail   Back   Neck

Waste strip

Cleanest fibers are at the fleece's center—which was on sheep's back before shearing. Outermost 3 in. around edge of fleece comes from sheep's tail, legs, and belly. This strip is usually too dirty and matted to spin and must be cut off and thrown away.

between the legs. A number of complications can arise, including breech birth (tail first delivery) and other positions that cause the lamb to get stuck in the birth canal. Until you accumulate enough experience to recognize signs of trouble, it is wise to seek the help of someone who is knowledgeable—either a veterinarian or a neighbor who has raised sheep for some time.

Be prepared to take good care of the lambs as soon as they are born. Wipe the lamb dry—particularly around the nose so that it can breathe—and put it in a small, warm box until its mother can tend it. Make sure that each lamb gets some of the ewe's first milk, called colostrum, which contains vital antibodies and vitamins. Occasionally a ewe will not feed its lamb. If this should happen, you will have to bottle-feed it every two to four hours for the first few days. After that, bottle-feed the lamb twice a day until it is two months old; at that time it can be weaned. Use special sheep's milk replacer (from a feed supply store) rather than cow's milk, which has too little fat. You can also get another ewe to adopt the lamb. Disguise the lamb's smell by washing it in warm water and rubbing it with the afterbirth from the adoptive mother's own lamb. Or rub it with something tasty, such as molasses.

Keep each ewe and its lambs together in a separate stall for the first few days after birth or until they learn to recognize each other. Before the young are two weeks old, vaccinate them for tetanus and castrate any males that are to be used for meat. You may also want to remove, or dock, their tails to prevent dirt from collecting. A suckling lamb whose diet is supplemented with grain will gain about 5 pounds per week and is ready for sale at 40 pounds. Or a lamb can be gradually switched to grazing and fattened until it reaches about 100 pounds. Lambs are usually shipped live to market, but one or two might be butchered like pigs for home use.

Dairying on a Scale That Fits a Family

The easy-to-handle size, quick wit, excellent foraging ability, and moderate production level (3 to 4 quarts per day) of goats make them ideal dairy animals for a family or small farm. Their milk is fully comparable in flavor and nutritive value to cow's milk and, in fact, in some ways is superior. It is naturally homogenized—the fat particles are so small that they do not separate from the rest of the milk—and as a result is easier to digest. In addition, it is less likely than cow's milk to provoke an allergic reaction.

The most important consideration in buying a dairy goat is milk production. Several breeds of goat are available, all of them satisfactory producers, but it is not necessary to purchase a purebred to get good productivity. The surest course is to buy a milking doe (a female already producing milk) with a good production record. If you are buying a goatling (young female), the productivity of its mother and sisters will provide an indication of how much milk you can expect. Young kids, though inexpensive, are usually not a good choice for beginners, who do not have the expertise to raise them and who will probably have to purchase most of their feed—with no return of milk until the young goats give birth to kids.

A goat's appearance is indicative of good productivity. Look for an animal with a large well-rounded udder with smooth elastic skin and no lumps; a straight back and broad rib cage, which show that the doe can consume large quantities of feed for conversion into milk; and a long trim body, which indicates that the doe will convert most of its feed into milk, not body fat. But avoid does with any signs of disease or lameness. Bright eyes and a sleek coat are good signs of health. You should be sure the animal you buy has been tested for brucellosis and tuberculosis. Although both diseases are rare among goats in the United States, they are dangerous, since they can be transmitted to humans through milk. Annual testing of milkers is essential.

Before you buy a milking doe, make sure you know how to milk it correctly. If you fail to empty the udder completely at each milking, milk production will slacken and can even stop completely. Once this happens, the doe will give no more milk until it bears another kid. Many first-time goat owners buy a bred doe that has not yet borne a kid so that they can become accustomed to caring for the animal before having to milk it.

Bucks (male goats) are not usually kept by people interested in producing only a small quantity of milk. Bucks have a strong smell that can easily taint the flavor of the doe's milk and must therefore have separate quarters. Since it is easy enough to take a doe to a neighbor's buck for breeding, most small farmers avoid the added bother and expense of keeping a buck.

Feed According to Productivity

Good-quality forage will satisfy almost all the nutritional needs of dry (nonmilking) does. Unlike pasture for cows and sheep (which, like goats, are ruminants), a goat's pasture should include a variety of leaves, branches, weeds, and tough grasses to supply essential vitamins, minerals, and trace elements. Legumes are also needed, since they provide necessary protein. When pasturage is unavailable, feed well-cured hay. Goats will not eat hay off the ground; so place it in a rack or manger, or hang it in bundles from the walls.

Unlike a dry doe, a milking doe needs the additional protein of a mixed-grain supplement in its diet. Between

Saanens are vigorous, gentle, and excellent, producers

Toggenburgs are hardy, affectionate, and excellent browsers. They are moderate milkers but also eat somewhat less than other breeds

Nubians are famed for the butterfat content of their milk

Grade (mixed breed) goats can produce as much milk as purebreds and are much cheaper. But purebreds can be a good buy if there is a demand for purebred kids.

2 and 4 pounds of grain per day—in two evenly spaced feedings—is an average amount of grain to feed, although top producers need more than poor ones. A combination of corn, oats, and wheat bran with some soybean oil meal or cottonseed oil meal (for even more protein) is the most common supplement. Molasses is often added to this combination for extra moisture, sweetness, and vitamins. If a good-quality, fresh premixed feed is not available, buy a calf starter or horse grain mixture.

Overfeeding of grain is dangerous, since it can lead to less efficient digestion of roughage and in extreme cases cause bloat—a serious buildup of gases that can cause death. To prevent overeating, feed the grain only after the goats have eaten plenty of grass or hay. Place the goats in separate stalls or lock them in separate feeding slots in front of a common manger to be sure that each gets only its own ration. A goat's stomach can also be disturbed by changes in its diet, so feed your animals at the same time each day and make any dietary changes very gradually. This is especially important when changing from wintertime hay to spring pasturage.

Plenty of fresh, clean water is important to any milk-producing animal. The more a goat drinks, the more feed will be converted into milk instead of body fat. If you do not have an automatic waterer, change the water twice each day when you feed grain.

Troubleshooting

Symptoms	Treatment
Listlessness, weight loss	Test for worms, and deworm if necessary. Rotate pasture grazing
Pain, distended stomach, heavy breathing	Call veterinarian immediately to treat bloat. Massage stomach. Keep goat moving if possible
Flakes or clots in milk, hot udder	Have veterinarian treat for mastitis, an udder disease. Isolate goat, milk it last, and disinfect hands

The Goat Barn

Quarters for one or two milking does can be fairly simple, but their sleeping area should be draft free and well bedded. Goats do not mind cold weather, but they cannot withstand drafts on their skin. Overheating can be almost as bad; a goat that has been kept unnaturally warm for an extended period of time is likely to get sick if it is accidentally exposed to the cold.

Provide access from the barn to a fenced-in outdoor area for browsing and exercise. The fence must be at least 4 feet high—though even this may not be high enough for an unusually agile goat. If you cannot provide a fenced area, you can tether your goats, but tethering should be a last resort. It not only limits access to food and confines the goat close to its own droppings, but by inhibiting exercise it reduces milk production and increases the danger of disease.

Whether tethered or fenced, goats should be pastured on well-drained ground to avoid foot rot. They should also have access to shade and to temporary shelter in case of wind and rain. If possible, include a large boulder or other object for the goat to climb on within the exercise area. Rocks are especially valuable because they help keep the goat's feet trimmed.

Breeding and Milking

When does reach 18 months, they should be bred once each year to ensure a continuing supply of milk. They can mate as young as six months old, but waiting until they are fully developed guards against permanent stunting that the double burden of pregnancy and continuing maturation can cause. The breeding season for goats begins in the fall and lasts through early spring. During these months a doe will come into a two-day-long heat every 21 days until pregnant. Arrange well in advance for the services of a neighbor's buck. Then when you notice signs of heat—restlessness, tail twitching, bleating—take your doe to be serviced. At the end of five months watch for signs such as bleating, reduced feeding, engorged udder, and white vaginal discharge that mean the young are about to be born.

Newborn kids (goats often bear twins) must receive colostrum, the doe's antibody-rich first milk. After that they should be separated from their mother and fed from a pan or bottle. Give them 1/2 to 1/3 pint of milk three times daily for the first two weeks. Then gradually reduce the amount of milk and substitute grain and fresh green hay.

A doe freshens (begins producing milk) after giving birth. Rebreed the goat six months after freshening. You can continue to milk for three months longer, but then allow the doe to dry off by stopping the daily milkings. Otherwise its strength may be overtaxed. Establish a familiar milking routine by spacing milkings as evenly as possible. A 12-hour interval is ideal but not vital. At milking time keep the atmosphere calm and allow the doe to settle down, then lift or walk it onto the milking stand. Put the doe's head in the stanchion, where a bucket of grain should be waiting. Next, wipe the udder with a warm, moist cloth. This cleans the area and stimulates secretion of a hormone that relaxes the muscles holding the milk in place. Milk each teat alternately, using the technique shown below. When the flow subsides, stop and gently massage the udder from top to bottom to stimulate the flow; then begin milking again.

For good-tasting milk, cleanliness is essential. Even a minute quantity of dry goat manure or dust will damage the milk's flavor if it should fall into the milk bucket. To prevent this, milk in an area that is easy to clean, has few ridges or niches to collect dust, and is separated from the feeding and bedding areas. Keep the hairs around the goat's udder clipped short to minimize the spread of dust that the doe may be carrying, and keep the doe's coat free of dirt by frequent brushing. The person who is doing the milking and the equipment that is used must be scrupulously clean. Clothes should be clean and hands well washed. (For more information on dairy hygiene, see *Making Your Own Dairy Products*, pp.224–232).

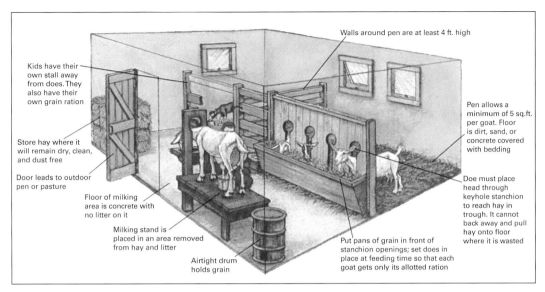

Kids have their own stall away from does. They also have their own grain ration

Store hay where it will remain dry, clean, and dust free

Door leads to outdoor pen or pasture

Floor of milking area is concrete with no litter on it

Milking stand is placed in an area removed from hay and litter

Airtight drum holds grain

Walls around pen are at least 4 ft. high

Pen allows a minimum of 5 sq.ft. per goat. Floor is dirt, sand, or concrete covered with bedding

Doe must place head through keyhole stanchion to reach hay in trough. It cannot back away and pull hay onto floor where it is wasted

Put pans of grain in front of stanchion openings; set does in place at feeding time so that each goat gets only its allotted ration

Ideal goat shelter provides a well-ventilated but draft-free stall and an easy-to-clean, dust-free space for milking.

The technique of milking, step by step

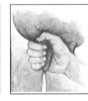

Milk by pressing gently upward against udder, then closing successive fingers; when flow decreases, massage udder.

Protein by the Gallon, Courtesy of Old Bossy

The dairy cow was a nutritional mainstay of the 19th-century homestead, helping to fatten pigs and hens and feed the family. It can perform the same functions for modern homesteaders, exurbanites, and first-time farmers provided it is given the care and attention it needs.

A cow is a major responsibility. It is a big animal—often over 1,200 pounds—and requires relatively large quantities of food. Before obtaining one, be sure that you have at least 2 acres of high-quality, well-drained pasture, a well-ventilated, roomy shed, and a place to store several tons of hay and straw. Also, find out if artificial insemination is locally available; your cow will not continue to produce milk unless bred once a year.

The cow you choose should be gentle, accustomed to hand milking, and have several good years of milking ahead of it. A bred heifer—a cow carrying its first calf—is often an economical choice for a beginner. Since it cannot be milked until after the calf is born, the novice has a chance to adjust to other cow-tending chores. Another good choice is a four- or five-year-old cow in its second or third year of milking. If you have a source of feed and some experience nurturing young animals,

you might try buying a three-day-old calf and raising it to maturity, but this is a demanding job.

The cow you buy should have a trim body, clear eyes, and a smooth, elastic udder. The udder should not be lumpy, but protruding veins are typical of a good producer. Try to see the cow milked several times and watch out for any signs of trouble, such as stringy milk or clots and blood in the milk. Some breeders will show you milk production records for their cows, while others will give only a general estimate. In either case buy from a reliable breeder with a reputation for standing behind his promises. He should have proof that his cow is free from tuberculosis and brucellosis, diseases that are rare today but are dangerous because they can infect humans. The breeder should also guarantee in writing that the animal he sells you is able to bear calves.

Feeding the Dairy Cow

Cows, like sheep and goats, are ruminants and can absorb nutrients from pasture grasses and leaves. Their pasture should also contain legumes, such as clover, alfalfa, or lespedeza, since grasses and leaves alone do not provide adequate protein and high-energy sugars for prolonged milk production. To get maximum food value from any plant, the cow must eat it when it is tender and green. Most dairy farmers turn their cows onto a pasture when the grass is 5 1/2 to 6 inches tall. After the

Guernsey is also a relatively small breed. Guernsey milk has a slight yellowish tint

Jersey is the smallest breed, averaging 1,000 lb. Its milk is extremely rich in butterfat

plants are eaten, but before the land is overgrazed, the cows are moved to a new pasture so that the first area can rejuvenate itself. By rotating pastures, the cows are assured a steady supply of nutritious roughage.

During winter months cows must be fed hay. Like fresh pasturage, hay should be tender and green. It is best when cut just as it blooms. From 2 to 3 pounds of top-quality hay per 100 pounds of body weight will meet a cow's daily nutritional needs. When fed excellent hay or pasturage alone, most cows will produce 10 quarts per day during peak production months. This amount, which represents 60 to 70 percent of maximum capacity, should be more than enough for the average family. To boost productivity or to supplement average-quality hay or pasturage, feed a mixture of grain and highprotein meal. Ground corn, oats, barley, and wheat bran are the most popular grains. High-protein meal is the pulp left over after the oil has been extracted from cottonseed, linseed, soybeans, or peanuts. Feed stores sell these supplements already mixed in proper proportion for lactating cows. They also sell high-protein mixtures specially designed to be diluted with your own grain. Feed the high-protein mixture twice daily—it is usually fed during milking—in measured amounts, and make any changes in diet very gradually. Otherwise the cow may develop bloat, a dangerous stomach disorder.

Up to a point the more grain and meal you feed a cow, the more milk it will produce. Beyond that point the extra grain is wasted. To achieve maximum production, gradually increase the grain ration until the increase no longer results in higher productivity. Then cut the ration back slightly. Conversely, when grain rations are cut—or when pasture quality deteriorates—milk production will fall. A rule of thumb is to feed 1 pound of grain for every 3 pounds of milk the cow produces. When fed about half this grain ration, together with good-quality pasture, most cows produce 90 percent of their top capacity.

Besides good feed, the other essentials to top milk production are free access to salt and plenty of water. For best results provide a salt lick and water in the pasture as well as in the cow's stall. Change the water at least twice a day or else install a self-watering device.

Breeding and Milking

A cow must freshen, or bear a calf, in order to produce milk. Heifers (young females) can be bred when they are as young as 10 months old, but it is best to wait until they are 1 1/2 years old or weigh at least 600 pounds.

Today most breeding is done by artificial insemination. Your county agent will help you find a professional inseminator. Arrange well in advance for his services, since the cow will be fertile for only 12 hours after the onset of heat. Signs to watch for are restlessness, bellowing, a swollen vulva, and reduced milk flow. When 21 days have passed after the cow is serviced, watch again for signs of heat. If they reappear, the cow is not settled (pregnant) and must be serviced again.

Carrying a calf while producing 10 or more quarts of milk a day is a tremendous drain on a cow's system. Watch your pasturage carefully to be sure that it is tender, green, and rich in legumes. If the crop shows signs of browning off (as is likely to happen during a hot summer) or if the cow is losing weight, provide some high-energy food supplement. Avoid overfeeding, however, especially during the last months of pregnancy, since this too can cause illness. To keep from overtaxing the cow and to protect future milk production, stop milking two months before the calf is due; the cow will go dry for the remainder of its pregnancy.

The calf will be born 280 days after settling. Bellowing and restlessness are signs that freshening is imminent. Once actual labor begins, check its progress periodically but avoid disturbing the cow. If labor lasts for more than a few hours, call a veterinarian for help.

When the calf is born, be sure it begins to suckle and gets colostrum, the cow's first milk that is rich in vitamins and disease-fighting antibodies. The cow will produce colostrum—which humans should not drink—for five days after freshening. After the first two or three days

Troubleshooting

Symptoms	Treatment
Distended stomach, pain	Call veterinarian immediately to treat bloat. Keep cow moving
Clot or blood in milk, swollen udder	Discard milk. Consult veterinarian to treat mastitis. Improve sanitation. Disinfect hands after milking
Swollen feet, pain in legs (foot rot)	Clean foot thoroughly. Apply copper sulfate as powder or salve. Keep bedding and pens dry and clean

separate the calf and mother. The calf's new quarters must be clean, dry, and draft free. Cold temperatures are not harmful, but dampness, drafts, and sudden exposure to cold can cause pneumonia. Teach the calf to drink from a bucket by pulling its mouth down to the pail when it is hungry. The calf should receive a daily ration of 1 quart of milk for every 20 pounds of body weight. Provide the milk in three or four equally spaced feedings. When a milk-fed calf is about eight weeks of age, it is ready to be sold as veal.

Begin milking as soon as the calf is removed from its mother. Cleanliness is essential. Keep the milking area free from dirt and sanitize all milking utensils. Pay atten-

tion to the cow too. Clip long hairs near its udder and brush the cow daily to remove dirt. (See *Making Your Own Dairy Products,* pp.224–232, for additional information on dairy hygiene.) It is important to maintain a relaxed atmosphere during milking: milk at the same times each day and avoid disturbances.

At milking time lead the cow to its stanchion, where a pail of grain should be waiting. Wipe the udder with a warm, wet cloth, then start to milk as you would a goat. The cow's teats are much larger and will require more strength to milk, but the basic action is the same. The first milk from each of the cow's four teats should be collected in a strip cup, a special cup with a filter on the top. If strings, clots, or blood spots appear on the filter, discard the milk and call a veterinarian.

After testing the milk proceed to milk two of the teats, holding one in each hand and squeezing them alternately. Eventually, their milk flow will slacken. When this happens, change teats and milk the other pair. (It makes no difference which two teats you milk together.) As you empty the second pair, more milk is secreted from the udder into the first pair. Work back and forth, milking one pair and then the other until they do not refill. Then rub the udder with one hand as you strip the teats with the other. To strip, close the thumb and forefinger tightly around the top of the teat, then continue to squeeze as you pull your hand down its length.

Milking Shed and Pens for Cow and Calf

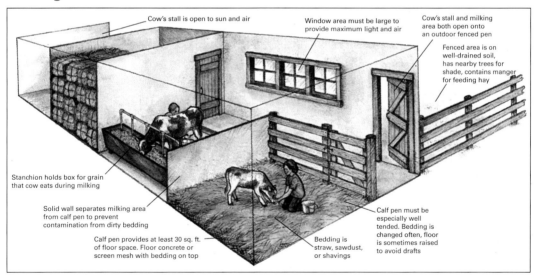

Simple three-sided shed provides the healthiest environment for a cow. With the open front facing away from prevailing winds—usually toward the east or south—the shed ensures plenty of ventilation and allows warm, drying sunlight to reach all the way inside. Rotting, manure-laden bedding on a dirt floor supplies enough heat to keep a cow comfortable in climates as cold as North Dakota's.
The milking area needs careful planning. While a cow can be milked almost anywhere, a well-planned, easy-to-clean area close to the cow's sleeping shed will make the job easier and more sanitary. Floors should be concrete, sloping toward a drain or gutter. Running water is helpful for hosing down walls and floors. There should be ample room to store grain for feeding at milking time.
The same building might contain a calf pen or a spot where a temporary one can be constructed from movable panels when necessary. A lean-to on the cow's shed provides a place to store straw or other bedding material as well as hay, which must be kept dry to protect its nutritive value.

Percherons are not quite as large as Belgians but move somewhat faster and with a livelier, more spirited gait

Clydesdales have a distinctive high-stepping gait that has made them popular for pulling showy wagons

Belgians, the largest of the draft horses, are quiet, docile, and slow moving but immensely powerful

Horses have filled so many different roles throughout history that there is amazing diversity among breeds. Drafters such as these, weighing 2,200 lb. and standing 17 hands to the top of the shoulder (a hand equals 4 in.), have provided pulling power for centuries.

Strong and Spirited, The Working Horse Will Pull Its Weight

For a small amount of acreage a horse can be an efficient substitute for a tractor. While the horse is slower, it is also much cheaper to buy, fuel, and repair. It does less damage to the soil, and it can work in areas too wet and hilly for a wheeled vehicle. Purebred draft horses are the ideal types for farm work. Used at one time to carry medieval knights in full armor, these horses have the size and strength necessary for long hours of strenuous labor. Buying a purebred Belgian, Percheron, or Clydesdale is an expensive proposition, however; a more economical alternative would be to purchase a crossbreed. One such cross would be a draft horse sire with a utility-type mare; such crossbreeds have the size—about 1,200 pounds—and steadiness for farm work, though they are not as powerful as drafters. The mule, a cross between a horse and an ass, is another good draft animal. Riding horses are too light for extensive plowing, but if properly taught, some can do light pulling.

Whatever horse you purchase, it should be trained for the work you expect it to do. As a beginner, you will almost certainly be unable to train the animal properly, and you can easily damage its personality by trying. A 7 to 10-year-old gelding or mare would be ideal, but an older horse is better than one that is too young and playful for hard work. Never buy stallions because they are too unpredictable for a novice to handle.

Buying from a reliable breeder is essential, but it is no substitute for close inspection. Examine the horse's stall for any signs of kicking or biting the walls. Watch as the horse is harnessed to be sure it is not head-shy or dangerous to approach. Before it has had a chance to warm up, look for indications of stiffness, such as shifting of weight from one front leg to the other or failure to rest its weight equally on both front feet. Next, see the animal doing the work you will be asking of it and make sure it neither balks nor is too frisky to handle the job. Its gait while working can provide clues to soundness. Shortened stride, nodding of hip or head, unusually high or low carriage of head, and unevenness of gait may mean the horse is lame. After watching the animal work, listen to its breathing to be sure it is not winded. Finally, examine the horse as it cools down; look for any signs of stiffness and for unusual lumps or knobs on the legs.

Feed According to Work Performed

A top-quality, well-fertilized pasture can provide the nutrients an idle horse needs. Provide per horse 2 to 3 acres of grasses combined with high-protein alfalfa, clover, or birds'-foot trefoil. Since horses are destructive of turf, protect the pasture by practicing rotation and by closing off the land whenever it is wet or soggy. When pasturage is unavailable, feed 8 to 12 pounds per day of fresh, green, leafy legume hay.

A working horse—whether used for riding or pulling—needs more energy than can be provided by pasturage and hay alone. Oats are the best grain supplement to feed. They are high in protein, contain plenty of

Troubleshooting

Symptoms	Treatment
Upset stomach (colic)	Call veterinarian immediately. Keep horse standing. Improve feed
Sore feet (founder)	Consult veterinarian. Be careful not to overfeed or feed while hot
Hoof odor	Consult veterinarian. Treat with salve
Teeth worn to sharp edge	Have veterinarian file teeth so feeding is not disrupted

Shetland ponies stand about 10 hands. They descend from miniature drafters of Scotland's Shetland Islands

Morgans, a spirited breed averaging 14 to 15 hands, can do many kinds of farm work

Quarter horses, noted for dexterity and speed, are favorites for working cattle

Speed, agility, steadiness, and spirit are among the qualities that have been cultivated in horses of various breeds. Nonpurebreds, too, exhibit marked differences in personality and aptitude. Know which traits are important to you before you buy a horse.

Stabling Your Horses

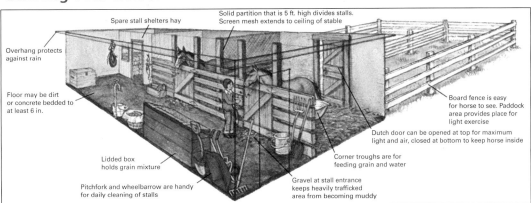

Overhang protects against rain

Spare stall shelters hay

Solid partition that is 5 ft. high divides stalls. Screen mesh extends to ceiling of stable

Floor may be dirt or concrete bedded to at least 6 in.

Board fence is easy for horse to see. Paddock area provides place for light exercise

Dutch door can be opened at top for maximum light and air, closed at bottom to keep horse inside

Lidded box holds grain mixture

Corner troughs are for feeding grain and water

Pitchfork and wheelbarrow are handy for daily cleaning of stalls

Gravel at stall entrance keeps heavily trafficked area from becoming muddy

Stall measuring 12 ft. by 12 ft. is ideal for a horse. A dirt floor is best; although it is more difficult to maintain than concrete, it is easier on a horse's feet. Make the floor several inches higher than the surrounding ground and rake it periodically to keep it level. From time to time dig out the dirt and replace it with a clean new layer. If you own more than one horse, each will need its own stall, with floor to ceiling partitions between stalls.

The horse should have access to a paddock or pasture. The more time it spends there, the better its muscle condition will be. The best pasture fences are of boards or the traditional post and rail (see *Fences*, pp.52–56); both styles are safe, secure, and highly visible. An electrified wire can be run along the top to discourage an especially spirited animal. If you use wire fencing instead, choose a small mesh size so that the horse's hooves cannot get caught, and tie rags to the top so the horse can see the fence. Avoid barbed wire, since it can damage your animal. Set windows high in wall and screen them against flies and other insects.

Checking teeth and conformation

Placement of legs beneath body, slope of shoulders, and slant of ankles are all aspects of a horse's conformation that affect leverage and, therefore, pulling power. Teeth give a general idea of a horse's age. In a young horse they are nearly vertical; in a 20-year-old horse they slant forward.

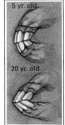

5 yr. old

20 yr. old

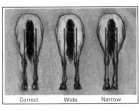

| Correct | Wide | Narrow |

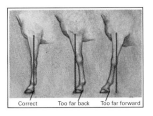

| Correct | Too far back | Too far forward |

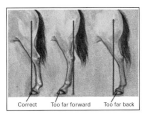

| Correct | Too far forward | Too far back |

bulky roughage, and are unlikely to cake in the horse's stomach. Wheat bran is another high-protein, bulky feed. Corn is relatively high in carbohydrates but is not high enough in protein. If the grain is dusty, mix it with molasses to reduce dustiness, improve flavor, and provide extra energy. The exact amount of grain to feed depends upon the size of the horse, strenuousness and duration of work, and the quality of pasturage. An underfed horse will lose weight, but overfeeding on rich pasturage or grain can cause founder (laminitis), a painful inflammation of the lining of the hoof wall. For light work a daily supplement of 1/3 pound of grain per 100 pounds of horse is sufficient. This can be raised as high as 1 1/4 pounds of grain per 100 pounds of live weight during heavy work.

Horses have delicate stomachs and must be fed carefully. Eating and drinking while overheated from exercise—like overeating—can cause laminitis and colic. For best health, feed a horse at the same times each day—morning and evening for light work; morning, noon, and night for strenuous work. Make changes gradually, and avoid turning a horse suddenly into a lush pasture.

Fresh water should be available at all times—in the pasture as well as in the horse's stall. Change the water twice a day if you do not have an automatic waterer. A salt lick is also essential. Many owners provide one containing trace minerals especially balanced for horses.

Hardworking Drafters Need Considerate Care

Whether you intend to hitch your horse to a plow or show it in a ring, daily grooming is essential to good health as well as appearance. A good brushing before every workout prevents painful hard-to-cure skin injuries caused by dirt matted beneath the harness, saddle, or other tack. Another brushing is necessary after a hard day's work to remove the sweat and dust that will have accumulated in the horse's coat.

For proper grooming you will need a currycomb, a stiff-bristled brush, and a brush or comb for the mane and tail. The currycomb is used first. Rub it in a circular motion over the horse's neck and sides to remove dirt caked on the surface. Avoid using it near bony, sensitive areas, such as the legs, where a bump from its metal or rubber ridges would be extremely painful. After currying, brush the coat to remove embedded dirt and distribute the natural oils. Press the brush firmly enough against the horse's body so that the bristles penetrate the coat but not so hard that you hurt the tender skin beneath. Always brush in the direction of the coat hairs. Pay special attention to the lower legs and ankles—they get extremely dirty and yet are very sensitive. As a result, they need slow, gentle treatment.

Wipe the horse's face and then the area beneath its tail with a clean cloth wrung out in warm water. A bit of mild soap can be added to the water for washing the tail area if it is particularly dirty, but be sure to rinse the soap off thoroughly. Sponges are sometimes used instead of a cloth, but they are more likely to spread disease because they are difficult to sterilize. Gently comb or brush the mane and tail. When doing the tail, stand beside the horse, not behind where you can get kicked.

If the horse is confined in a paddock or stall, its hooves should be cleaned daily to remove any manure, debris, or stones embedded between the shoe and the frog (the sensitive pad at the back of the foot). At the same time check to be sure the shoes have not worked loose and that the hoof walls are not overgrown. Hooves should be trimmed and reshod every six to eight weeks. Like fingernails, they grow slowly—1/4 inch to 1/2 inch per month—but the toe grows faster than the heel. If the toe becomes too long, the horse's weight will be forced back toward the heel and

An acre per horse per day is an old rule of thumb that tells how much land a team of horses can be expected to plow. Few farm chores are harder. By way of comparison, a single horse can harrow, cultivate, plant, or mow as much as 7 to 10 acres in a day.

Special implements will help you to groom your horse's coat and to comb out its mane and tail.

Currycomb

Brush

Comb

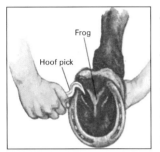

Frog

Hoof pick

Clean hooves regularly. To lift horse's foot, face toward rear of horse, run hand down its leg to ankle, and lift. (A horse will usually lift its foot.) Starting near hoof wall, run the hoof pick from heel toward toe to remove accumulated dirt. Check hoof wall for dryness and apply salve if it is needed.

A mule is the sterile offspring of a jack (a male ass) and a mare. Mules have more endurance than horses and are noted for being tough, strong, and surefooted. A female ass, or jennet, bred to a stallion produces a hinny. Jacks weighing 1,100 lb. and standing 15 to 16 hands tall can be bred to average-sized mares to produce mules strong enough for drafting. If they are to breed with mares, the jacks must be separated early from other asses and raised exclusively with young horses until thoroughly trained.

its stance changed in a way that can damage its legs and feet. On an unshod horse an overgrown hoof can break off unevenly, causing a cracked hoof. A farrier will cut and file the hoof walls to just the right length and shape them before fitting a new set of horseshoes. Never try to do this job yourself. Proper shoeing can only be learned by years of training with an expert. Poor shoeing can permanently injure the horse.

Hitching a Team

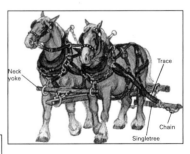

Neck yoke

Traces

Driving lines

Singletree

Doubletree

3. Arrange driving lines on a team as shown. For safety keep lines in top condition.

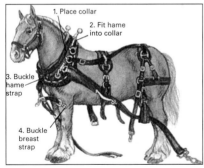

1. Place collar

2. Fit hame into collar

3. Buckle hame strap

4. Buckle breast strap

1. Start by putting collar on horse. Fit hame into collar, spread out harness, and buckle straps.

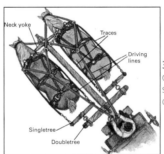

Neck yoke

Trace

Chain

Singletree

4. To hitch wagon, clip breast straps to neck yoke and attach chains to the singletrees.

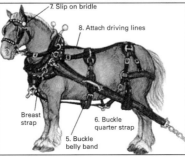

7. Slip on bridle

8. Attach driving lines

2. Buckle harness straps under horse's belly, then put on bridle and driving lines.

Breast strap

6. Buckle quarter strap

5. Buckle belly band

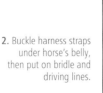

Pulling and Plowing

The only sure way to learn to use a team for plowing is to be taught by someone with experience. Horses must be handled firmly and consistently; even a well-trained team can be ruined by a poor driver. Use the command words that your horses were trained to obey. In America standard commands are "whoa" (stop), "get up" (go), "gee" (turn right), and "haw" (turn left). Learn to maintain steady control of the reins; keep them taut, but never pull so hard that you damage a horse's mouth.

Be careful and considerate of your animals. Talk kindly and quietly to them so that they learn to recognize and trust your voice. During breaks in work loosen their collars so they can relax too. Never leave a hitched horse unattended. If you must tie it up temporarily, use the bridle, not the harness straps, and be sure it is tied securely to something immovable. A team that has been idle during the winter needs to get back into condition gradually. Start with small amounts of light work and build up gradually to such heavier jobs as plowing. Keep your equipment in top condition and do not let anyone inexperienced drive your team. With care you will avoid injuring either yourself or your valuable horses.

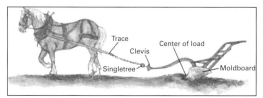

Hitch singletree to clevis. Note alignment of trace, clevis, and center of load on moldboard.

Sources and resources

Books and pamphlets
Poultry
Bartlett, Tom. *Ducks and Geese: A Guide to Management*. North Pomfret, Vt.: Trafalgar Square, 1991.

Mercia, Leonard S. *Raising Poultry the Modern Way*. Charlotte, Vt.: Garden Way Publishing, 1990.
Raising Geese. Washington, D.C.: U.S. Department of Agriculture, 1983.
Rabbits
Attfield, Harlan D. *Raising Rabbits*. Arlington, Va.: Volunteers in Technical Assistance, 1977.
Bennett, Bob. *Raising Rabbits Successfully*. Charlotte, Vt.: Williamson Publishing, 1984.
Hogs
Baker, James K., and Elwood M. Juergenson. *Approved Practices in Swine Production*. Danville, Ill.: Interstate Printers and Publishers, 1979.
Beynon, Neville. *Pigs: A Guide to Management*. North Pomfret, Vt.: Trafalgar Square, 1994.
Sheep
Simmons, Paula. *Raising Sheep the Modern Way*. Charlotte, Vt.: Garden Way Publishing, 1989.
Goats
Belanger, Jerome. *Raising Milk Goats the Modern Way*. Charlotte, Vt.: Garden Way Publishing, 1990.
Dunn, Peter. *Goatkeeper's Veterinary Book*. Alexandria Bay, N.Y.: Diamond Farm Books, 1994.
Jaudas, Ulrich. *The New Goat Handbook*. Waltonville, Ill.: Barton, 1989.
Luttmann, Gail. *Raising Milk Goats Successfully*. Charlotte, Vt.: Williamson Publishing Co., 1986.
Mackenzie, David. *Goat Husbandry*. Winchester, Mass.: Faber & Faber, 1993.
Cows
Etgen, William M., et al. *Dairy Cattle: Feeding and Management*. New York: John Wiley & Sons, 1987.
Juergenson, Elwood M., and W.P. Mortenson. *Approved Practices in Dairying*. Danville, Ill: Interstate Printers and Publishers, 1977.
Van Loon, Dirk. *The Family Cow*. Charlotte, Vt.: Garden Way Publishing, 1975.
Horses
Evans, J. Warren, and others. *The Horse*. San Francisco: W.H. Freeman and Company, 1995.
Lorch, Janet. *From Foal to Full Grown*. North Pomfret, Vt.: Trafalgar Square, 1993.
Telleen, Maurice. *The Draft Horse Primer*. Waverly, Iowa: Draft Horse Journal, 1993.

Draft horses can also be trained to pull a sleigh in the wintertime.

Part Four

Enjoying
Your Harvest
The Year Round

Once the harvest is in, the next job is to make sure it does not go to waste. Countryfolk call this process putting by: storing up today's surplus against tomorrow's shortage. Putting by is a happy skill because most of the old-time methods of preservation add delicious flavors to the food. Nowadays, such products as cheese, yogurt, smoked meat, sauerkraut, pickles, and jams and jellies are prepared more for their taste than because they keep well on the shelf. In "Enjoying Your Harvest the Year Round" all the ways to put food by are explained along with plenty of delicious recipes that will add special tang to the preserved foods. There are instructions on maple sugaring too and detailed descriptions and recipes for making cheese, pickles, sausage, and more. Finally, directions for making homemade bread are described and illustrated along with a simple recipe for white bread that can be used as a base for all kinds of bread making adventures.

Preserving Produce

One Harvest Can Provide A Year-round Feast for Your Whole Family

In the not too distant past, drying, salting, and live storage were the only ways known for preserving produce. The Indians of North and South America depended on sun-dried foods. American settlers survived bitter winters by eating salt-cured produce or vegetables stored live in root cellars. Caesar's army carried pickled food with it, and the builders of the Great Wall of China dined on salt-cured vegetables.

Nowadays we can choose among a much larger variety of processes, including canning, freezing, and jellying. Besides being more convenient, these newer methods have helped to transform the job of preserving food from a mere necessity into a full-fledged culinary art.

A Survey of Ways to Preserve Fruits and Vegetables

Food spoils for two reasons: the action of external biological agents, such as bacteria and molds, and the digestive actions of naturally occurring enzymes. The art of "putting food by," as canning and other preserving methods were known in the old days, consists of slowing down or halting both types of spoilage while at the same time preserving nutritive values and creating food that tastes good. No system of preservation fully achieves all these goals, but no system fails to contribute something of its own—in taste, in food value, in convenience, in simplicity, in economy.

Live storage—either aboveground or belowground—preserves produce with minimum alteration in taste, color, and vitamin content. However, such storage requires certain temperature ranges: winters must be cold enough

Red peppers, like mushrooms, peas, corn, and many other vegetables, can be dried in the sun. A few long, hot days with low humidity should do the trick.

to slow down food deterioration, but food must not be allowed to freeze. In addition, only certain fruits and vegetables can be stored by this method, notably apples, pears, and root crops.

Canning involves heating to high temperatures, resulting in vitamin loss and changes in taste. Water soluble vitamins can be retained by conserving the cooking liquid, but some others are destroyed. If food is canned in jars, store it in a dark place to avoid loss of riboflavin by exposure to light. A cool area—below 65°F—also helps retain nutrients: at 80°F vitamin C will be reduced by 25 percent after one year, vitamin A by 10 percent, and thiamine by 20 percent.

Freezing, the most modern method of food preservation, has a minimum effect on flavor and food values if the food is properly prepared and carefully packaged. Only vitamin E and pyridoxine (B^6) are destroyed by the freezing process. For best results, frozen foods should be stored at 0°F or below. Vitamin C is easily oxidized and as much as half can be lost if food is kept at 15°F for six months. Length of storage time also affects nutrients. Even at 0°F, most of the vitamin C can be lost if produce is stored for a year.

Salt curing alters the taste of the food (although in the case of pickling and fermenting, the results are delicious). If salt curing is done in a strong salt solution, nutritional value is greatly reduced because the food must be thoroughly washed before it can be eaten, a process that will rinse away vitamins and minerals. A weaker salt solution will preserve more nutrients, but there will be a greater risk of spoilage. Nor is salt curing reliable for truly long-term storage: pickles, sauerkraut, and relishes must be canned if they are to be stored for more than a few weeks after the three- to five-week salt-curing process is finished.

Jellying changes the taste of the food because of the large amounts of sugar, honey, or other sweetener that are needed in order to form a gel. In addition, some vitamins are lost during the heat processing required to sterilize fruit and make an airtight seal.

Drying retains a high percentage of most vitamins. But if dried foods are stored for long periods, considerable destruction of vitamins A, C, and E can result because of oxidation, especially if food has not been properly blanched. In addition, vitamins A and E and some B-complex vitamins are broken down by light; as a result, considerable food value can be lost by drying outdoors in direct sunlight.

Choosing the right storage method

Almost every fruit and vegetable can be stored by one of the common preserving methods: live storage (root cellars and in-ground storage), canning, freezing, salt curing, jellying, and drying. The table gives the methods that are considered most successful in preserving flavor, texture, appearance, and nutrients in various produce.

Produce	Recommended storage methods
Apples	Live storage, canning, jams and jellies, drying
Apricots	Canning, jams and jellies, drying
Asparagus	Canning, freezing
Beans (green)	Canning, freezing, salt curing
Beans (lima)	Canning, freezing, drying
Beets	Live storage, canning, salt curing
Broccoli	Freezing
Cabbage	Live storage, salt curing
Carrots	Live storage, canning, freezing
Cauliflower	Freezing, salt curing
Celery	Live storage
Cherries	Canning, jams and jellies
Corn	Canning, freezing, salt curing
Cucumbers	Salt curing
Onions	Live storage
Parsnips	Live storage
Peaches	Canning, jams and jellies, drying
Pears	Live storage, canning, salt curing, jams and jellies, drying
Peas	Canning, freezing, drying
Peppers	Freezing, salt curing
Plums	Canning, jams and jellies, drying (prunes)
Potatoes	Live storage, canning
Pumpkin	Live storage, canning
Radishes	Live storage
Raspberries	Jams and jellies
Rutabagas	Live storage, salt curing
Spinach	Canning, freezing
Squash (summer)	Canning, freezing
Squash (winter)	Live storage, canning
Sweet potatoes	Live storage
Tomatoes	Canning, salt curing
Turnips	Live storage, salt curing

Maintaining a Winter Garden

The simplest method of preserving garden produce is to leave it right where it is—in the garden. The technique is particularly suitable for root crops, such as radishes, beets, carrots, and parsnips, but even tomatoes can be kept beyond their normal season. With little more than a covering of earth and straw to help maintain a temperature of 30°F to 40°F, many vegetables can be safely left in the ground from the end of one growing season to the start of the next. The main requirement for successful in-garden preservation is wintertime temperatures that are near or just below freezing.

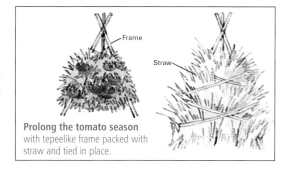

Prolong the tomato season with tepeelike frame packed with straw and tied in place.

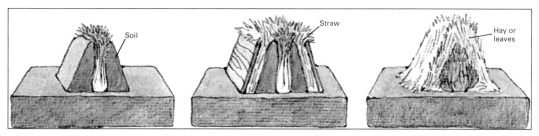

Bank soil around late celery (left). As temperature drops, cover plants completely. In near-freezing weather add straw held down by boards (center). Cover kale, collards, parsnips, and salsify with 2 in. of hay or leaf mulch (right).

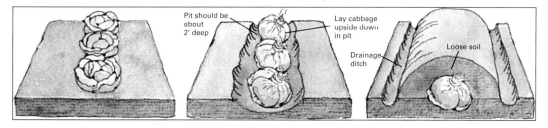

Cabbages can be stored in a long pit dug in the garden as well as in a root cellar (p.191) or conical mound. Dig storage pit about 2 ft. deep, pull cabbages out by the roots, set them upside down, and cover them completely with soil.

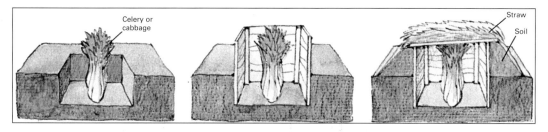

Trenching preserves both cabbages and celery. Dig shallow trench for cabbage, a deep one (2 ft.) for celery. Place plants, roots down, in trenches; then replace soil. Build frame high enough to cover plants, bank soil against it, and top with straw.

Keep Produce Fresh In Cold, Moist Air

If you live in an area where fall and winter temperatures remain near freezing and fluctuate very little, you can store root vegetables, apples, and pears in a wide variety of insulated structures and containers. These range from a simple mound in the garden to a full-fledged root cellar. In each case, the storage unit must maintain temperatures in the 30°F to 40°F range with humidity between 80 and 90 percent. The high moisture content of the air prevents shriveling due to loss of water by evaporation. An old-fashioned, unheated basement is an ideal spot for a root cellar, but a modern basement can be used if a northerly corner is available. Construction

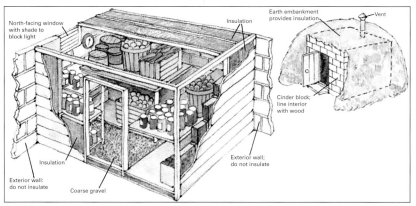

North-facing window with shade to block light

Insulation

Earth embankment provides insulation

Vent

Cinder block; line interior with wood

Insulation

Exterior wall; do not insulate

Exterior wall: do not insulate

Coarse gravel

Root cellars can be part of the house, as shown at left, or completely separate. A small well-insulated shed or a concrete block structure (above) with soil banked along three walls are both time-tested designs. A wood-lined excavation dug in well-drained soil with a hatch to get in is simpler yet and still quite serviceable. Air vent should be provided for circulation; humidity control is the same as for indoor root cellar.

Basement root cellar is particularly convenient, since produce is near at hand.

details are given below. Root cellars can also be built outside the house, either above the ground or embedded in earth.

Different vegetables can be stored together in a single container, but fruits should never be stored with vegetables nor should different fruits be stored together. Be sure to check stored produce every week or two, and cull out any that is spoiling. The old saying "One rotten apple spoils the barrel" still holds true.

In addition to the basement, many warmer areas within the house can be utilized for preserving crops. Onions, pumpkins, and squash, for example, do best at temperatures between 50°F and 55°F with a humidity of 60 to 70 percent. An unheated attic or an upstairs room that is closed off for the winter months are excellent storage sites for these vegetables.

Onions and herbs can be strung and hung upside down above the hearth or in the kitchen for preservation. Tomatoes that have been picked green can be stored for several weeks by letting them ripen slowly. Set the tomatoes on a rack or shelf, spacing them 6 inches apart to allow for air circulation.

Setting Up a Simple Root Cellar

An 8-foot by 10-foot root cellar will accommodate 60 bushels of produce, more than enough for most families. Indoor root cellars are the most convenient to use and easiest to build. Try to use a northeast or northwest corner of your basement that has at least one outside wall and is as far as possible from your oil burner or other heat source. One north-facing window is desirable for ventilation. The interior walls of the root cellar should be constructed of wood, and if the basement is heated, they should be insulated. The precise amount of insulation needed depends on the average basement temperature, but standard 4-inch-thick fiberglass batting with a foil or plastic vapor barrier should be more than adequate. Install the insulation with the barrier against the wood. Add an insulated door and fit the window with shades to block out light. To keep humidity high, spread 3 inches of gravel on the floor and sprinkle it

Window Wells and Stairways

Basement window well can be used as a mini root cellar. Cover the well with screening and wood to keep in heat and keep out animals. When temperatures drop below freezing, open window so that heat from the house can warm the storage area. If outside temperatures rise into the 70s, open window to allow cool basement air to circulate in storage area.

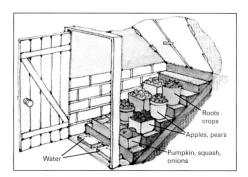

Roots crops

Apples, pears

Pumpkin, squash, onions

Water

Outdoor basement entrance can make an excellent root cellar. Install a door at the bottom of the steps to block off house heat. The top steps near the outside door are coolest, the bottom steps are warmest. Store root crops, such as potatoes, on top steps; warmth-loving pumpkins, squash, and onions at bottom; apples and pears in between. Place pans of water at the bottom of the stairwell to provide necessary humidity.

Heap up root crops and store them right in the garden

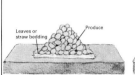 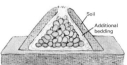 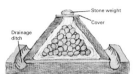 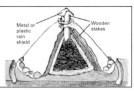

1. Spread several inches of leaves or straw as bedding. Stack produce in cone shape.

2. Cover produce with bedding and 4 in. of soil. Let bedding extend through soil for air.

3. Small drainage ditches and wood or metal covering protect cone from rainfall and runoff.

4. Cover large stacks with tarp; provide additional ventilation with wide central opening.

Create a storage chamber out of bales of hay

 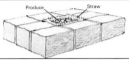  

1. Form hay bales into rectangle. Central opening will be used as storage area.

2. Line opening with straw and stack produce. Spread hay over each item, then over stack.

3. Use additional bales as a lid over the opening. Raise bales on 2 × 4 for ventilation.

4. During periods of severe weather remove the 2 × 4 in order to seal opening.

Store apples in an upright barrel

  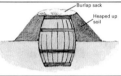 

1. For apple storage, start by burying wooden barrel or metal drum halfway in ground.

2. If metal drum is used, line it with sawdust at bottom and between produce and sides.

3. Fill barrel or drum with apples. Cover with leaf-filled sack, then pile soil around sides.

4. Dig a 6-in. ditch around barrel for drainage; put rocks on sack to keep it in place.

Turn the barrel on its side and store other types of produce

1. Dig space for barrel in well-drained area. Put bedding under barrel and fill with produce.

2. Slant open end down so any moisture will run out, then place board over the opening.

3. Cover sides and upper end of barrel with 18 in. of soil. Cover lower end with 3 in. of soil.

4. Cover everything with straw. Place boards on top to keep straw from blowing away.

occasionally with water. You can also maintain humidity by storing the produce in a closed container, such as a metal can lined with paper.

High-Heat Processing Eliminates Spoilage

Canning has been one of the most popular methods of preserving food since 1809, when the technique was first developed by the Frenchman Nicolas Appert. Today over 40 percent of the families living in the United States do some home canning, and the percentage is increasing. The principle behind canning is simple: decay and spoilage are caused either by enzymes in the food itself or by bacteria and other microorganisms. During the canning process, food is heated to a high temperature to stop the action of the enzymes and to kill all decay organisms. The food is then stored in sterile, airtight containers to prevent contamination.

Different foods require different processing temperatures. Low acid vegetables—and this includes every type other than tomatoes—can harbor heat-resistant bacteria and must be heated to at least 240°F, a temperature that can only be achieved by pressure canning. High acid foods, including tomatoes and most fruits, can be processed at the temperature of boiling water—212°F— since the only spoilage microorganisms present in them will be destroyed at this lower temperature. Pickled vegetables can also be processed in a boiling water bath.

Cans and jars

Home canners generally do their canning in glass jars rather than tin cans. Jars are easier to use, cost less, and allow you to see the contents. In addition, they can be reused many times and are chemically inert with respect to all types of food. The tin can's immunity to breakage is its only significant advantage. Two commonly used jar designs are shown at right, along with an old-fashioned clamp-type jar. Jars—and tins as well—come in a variety of sizes ranging from 1/2 pint (1 cup) to 1 gallon and larger.

If you plan to can in tins, you will need to purchase a sealing device. To check that the sealer is properly adjusted, seal an empty can, then immerse the can in warm water for several minutes. No bubbles should rise from the can. When canning in tins, the food should be packed while it is hot (more than 170°F) or else heated

Specialized Canning Utensils

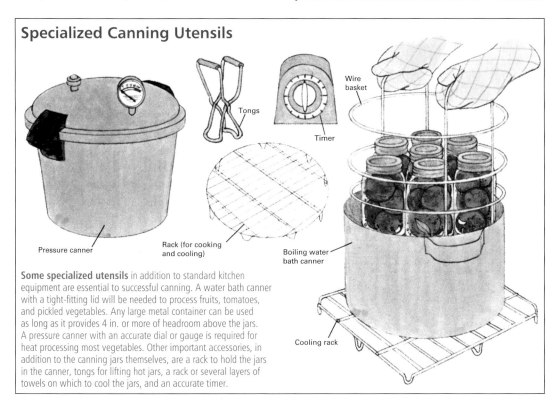

Some specialized utensils in addition to standard kitchen equipment are essential to successful canning. A water bath canner with a tight-fitting lid will be needed to process fruits, tomatoes, and pickled vegetables. Any large metal container can be used as long as it provides 4 in. or more of headroom above the jars. A pressure canner with an accurate dial or gauge is required for heat processing most vegetables. Other important accessories, in addition to the canning jars themselves, are a rack to hold the jars in the canner, tongs for lifting hot jars, a rack or several layers of towels on which to cool the jars, and an accurate timer.

Porcelain-lined cap consists of screw top and rubber ring. To seal, fit wet ring against shoulder of jar, screw on cap firmly, then back off a quarter turn. When jar is removed from canner, immediately screw cap tight.

Self-sealing cap consists of lid with sealant around its rim and a screw-on band that holds lid against lip of jar. Tighten band firmly before processing and do not loosen again. Band can be reused but not the lid.

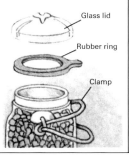

Bailed jar with glass lid and wire clamps is rarely sold now. Lid is held in place with long clamp during processing, then short clamp is snapped down for a tight seal. Decorative replicas should not be used for canning.

Tin cans are sealed by machine. Plain tin cans are safe for all foods, but to avoid discoloration of produce enamel-lined tins are used for corn, beets, berries, cherries, pumpkin, rhubarb, squash, and plums.

to that temperature in the can. Seal the can immediately after heating, then process it by the appropriate method shown on the next page. Processing is similar to jar canning except that steam pressure can be reduced immediately after the heating period is completed.

The ABCs of Canning

Vegetables and fruits must be pretreated before they are packed into jars for heat processing. Wash all produce, and cut vegetables into pieces. Berries and other kinds of small fruits can be left whole, but larger fruits, such as peaches, pears, and pineapples, should be pitted, if necessary, and sliced. Fruits are often dipped in ascorbic acid (vitamin C) and packed in sugar syrup to preserve their shape, color, texture, and flavor.

There are two ways to pack the produce into jars: raw (raw packed) or cooked (hot packed). To hot pack most fruits or vegetables, steam them, or heat them to boiling in juice, water, or syrup; then immediately pack them into the containers. (Tomatoes and some fruits can be cooked in their own juices.) For raw packing, load clean produce tightly into containers and pour on boiling juice, water, or syrup, leaving the proper amount of space at the top of the jar above the packed fruit or vegetables. Wipe the rim and sealing ring to remove any

Boiling water bath canning

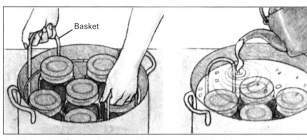

1. Fill canner halfway with hot water, load jars in basket, and put inside.

2. Add boiling water to 2 in. above jars. Do not pour directly on jars.

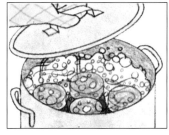

3. Cover canner. Bring water to rolling boil and start timing.

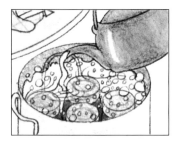

4. Reduce heat, but maintain rapid boil. Add boiling water if needed.

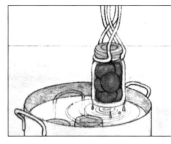

5. When processing time is up, remove jars immediately with tongs.

6. Tighten lids if needed. Set jars on rack, leaving space between them.

Pressure-cooker canning

1. Pour 2 to 3 in. of boiling water into bottom of pressure canner.

2. Place jars on rack set at bottom of canner. Jars must not touch.

3. Fasten lid. Turn heat to maximum. Let steam exhaust 10 minutes.

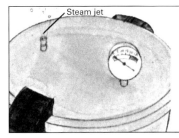

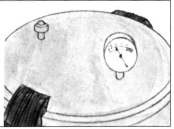

4. When the first inch of the steam jet is nearly invisible, close the vent.

5. At 8-lb. pressure lower heat slightly. Let pressure rise to 10 lb.

6. At 10-lb. pressure start timing. Hold pressure for full canning period.

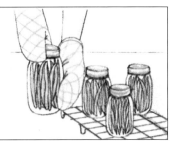

7. Remove canner from heat and let cool. Do not pour cold water on it.

8. When pressure is zero, open vent, then lid. Tilt lid as shown for safety.

9. Set jars on rack leaving spaces between jars. Tighten lids if necessary.

particles of food, then close the jar and proceed with the canning process: boiling water bath for fruits and high acid vegetables, pressure canning for low acid vegetables. After canning, store food in a dark place, since light can cause discoloration and loss of nutrients. Be sure to date and label all jars.

It Pays to Be Careful When Canning Food

Canning must be carried out with scrupulous care if bacterial contamination and spoilage are to be avoided. Most types of spoilage cause only minor illness at worst, but one type—botulism—is extremely dangerous and often fatal. This form of food poisoning is caused by toxins produced by germs that multiply rapidly in the low-oxygen, low-acid environment of canned vegetables. To prevent botulism as well as other food poisoning, it is essential that care be taken at every step of the way.

The first rule is to can only perfect produce. Overripe or damaged fruits and vegetables are prone to spoilage. Inspect jars, lids, and sealing rings to be sure they are in perfect condition, then wash and scald them before use. Wash all produce thoroughly, and pretreat it according to a reliable recipe and the principles described in this chapter. Be sure to use the correct time, temperature, and method of processing. (Because the spores that cause botulism are killed only at temperatures well above boiling, all vegetables except tomatoes must be pressure canned.) When canning with the boiling water bath method, use a lidded container and keep the jars totally immersed in rapidly boiling water. Before start-

ing to pressure can, test the canner according to the manufacturer's instructions. After processing, check the seal on every jar: when you push down on a self-sealing lid, it should stay down. Test porcelain lids by turning jars upside down; if you see a steady stream of tiny air bubbles, the seal is not airtight.

There are further safety precautions to take after the processed food is on the shelf. Discard any jar whose contents appear foamy or discolored, whose lid bulges or is misshapen, or whose rim is leaking. Be sure that

Store canned goods in a cool, dark place—a root cellar is ideal. Jars let you see all the produce easily, but they must still be dated either on the lid or on a label. Also list such additives as salt, sugar, and spices.

the canned produce is normal before you eat it; discoloration, odor, mold, and spurting liquid are all reasons to discard it. When disposing of suspect food, place it where animals or humans cannot accidentally eat it. Home-canned vegetables, except tomatoes, should be cooked before they are served. Bring the vegetables to a rolling boil, then boil an additional 20 minutes for corn or spinach, 10 minutes for other vegetables.

Choose the Proper Canning Method and Follow Procedures Exactly

The specifics of canning vary from one fruit or vegetable to the next. For high-acid produce, use the boiling water bath method; start to time only when the bath reaches a rolling boil. For low-acid produce, use a pressure canner. Let steam vent for 10 minutes to expel all air from the canner, then close the vent to let pressure build. Start timing after pressure in the canner reaches 10 pounds. If pressure falls below 10 pounds at any time during processing, start timing over again. Processing times for both methods depend upon the size of the jar used.

Vegetable	Time to maintain pressure for pints	Time to maintain pressure for quarts
Asparagus	25 min.	30 min.
Beets	30 min.	35 min.
Carrots	25 min.	30 min.
Corn	55 min.	–
Cowpeas	35 min.	40 min.
Lima beans	40 min.	50 min.
Potatoes	35 min.	40 min.
Pumpkin	55 min.	90 min.
Snap beans	20 min.	25 min.
Winter squash	55 min.	90 min.

Fruit or vegetable	Time in boiling water bath for pints		Time in boiling water bath for quarts	
	Hot pack	Raw pack	Hot pack	Raw pack
Apples	15 min.	–	20 min.	–
Apricots	20 min.	25 min.	25 min.	30 min.
Berries	10 min.	10 min.	15 min.	15 min.
Cherries	10 min.	20 min.	15 min.	25 min.
Peaches	20 min.	25 min.	25 min.	30 min.
Pears	20 min.	25 min.	25 min.	30 min.
Plums	20 min.	20 min.	25 min.	25 min.
Rhubarb	10 min.	–	10 min.	–
Sauerkraut	15 min.	15 min.	20 min.	20 min.
Tomatoes	35 min.	40 min.	45 min.	50 min.
Tomato juice	35 min.	–	35 min.	–

Adjustments for high altitudes

If you live in an area that is more than 1,000 feet above sea level, the reduced atmospheric pressure causes water to boil at temperatures lower than 212°F. To compensate, you must increase processing times for boiling water baths. You must also increase pressure settings for pressure canning to attain the required 240°F temperature. Add time or pressure according to the table.

Altitude above sea level	For boiling water bath:		For pressure canning, add
	of 20 min. or less, add	of more than 20 min., add	
1,000'	1 min.	2 min.	1/2 lb.
2,000'	2 min.	4 min.	1 lb.
3,000'	3 min.	6 min.	1 1/2 lb.
4,000'	4 min.	8 min.	2 lb.
5,000'	5 min.	10 min.	2 1/2 lb.
6,000'	6 min.	12 min.	3 lb.
7,000'	7 min.	14 min.	3 1/2 lb.
8,000'	8 min.	16 min.	4 lb.
9,000'	9 min.	18 min.	4 1/2 lb.
10,000'	10 min.	20 min.	5 lb.

Simple Recipes With a Delicious Flavor Difference

Try a variety of flavorings and combinations when canning fruits and vegetables. Sugar or salt can be added or deleted from any recipe without changing the processing requirements; so too can vinegar, lemon juice, or spices. Tomatoes can be flavored in a number of ways to make condiments and sauces. But be careful when adding any other vegetable, such as onions, peppers, and celery, to tomatoes: the mixture will be less acid than tomatoes alone and *must* be pressure canned. In addition, changes in density can affect processing time, so do not try to mix a variety of vegetables unless you have a reliable recipe that includes canning instructions.

Fruit Puree

3 lb. Fruit   Sugar to taste

Wash and cut up fruit, remove any pits. Simmer fruit pulp until soft (about 15 min.), adding water as necessary and stirring frequently to prevent sticking. Put pulp through food mill or strainer. Add sugar to pureed pulp. Simmer pulp for five minutes more. Pack hot puree into jars, allowing 1/2-in. headroom. Adjust lids. Process in boiling water bath for 10 minutes for either pint or quart jars. *Makes 1 quart*.

Pear Honey

8 cups ripe pears, peeled   1 lemon, juice of and rind
  and chopped   cut into pieces
5 cups sugar

Put all ingredients into large heavy pot. Bring slowly to a boil and simmer until thick (about 45 minutes). Stir frequently to avoid burning. Pour boiling mixture into jars, leaving 1/2-in. headroom. Process in boiling water bath for 20 minutes for either quarts or pints. *Makes 1 quart*.

Applesauce

3 lb. apples, quartered   1/4 tsp. cinnamon
   and cored   sugar to taste

Place apples in a saucepan with 1/2 cup water. Bring slowly to a boil, then reduce heat and simmer until soft (about 10 minutes). Add cinnamon and sugar and stir. Pack hot applesauce into jars, allowing 1/2-in. headroom. Insert knife to pierce any air bubbles. Adjust lids. Process in boiling water bath for 10 minutes for either pint or quart jars. *Makes 1 quart.*

Tomato Preserve

2 cups red tomatoes,   1 small lemon, juice of
   peeled and chopped   and grated rind
2 cups sugar   1 stick cinnamon
                                   1/4 tsp. powdered ginger

Cover tomatoes with sugar. Let them stand for 12 hours. Drain juice and boil pulp until thick, stirring often to prevent scorching. Add lemon juice, grated rind, cinnamon, and ginger. Cook until thick. Pour into pint jar. Process in boiling water bath 15 minutes. *Makes 1 pint.*

Freezing Produce

Freezing is not only simple and reliable but also retains flavor and nutrients better than any other preservation method except live storage. It prevents deterioration by slowing enzyme action and halting bacterial growth. For best results, store foods in moisture-proof containers and cool the food quickly to 0°F or below. Rigid containers of glass, metal, and heavy plastic are impermeable to all moisture and vapor. Other products made especially for freezing are resistant enough to prevent deterioration. These include paper cartons lined with a heavy coat of wax, freezer paper, heavy plastic wraps, and heavy plastic bags. Waxed paper, cartons lined with only a thin layer of wax, and thin plastic containers, bags, or wraps should not be used.

For rapid freezing, pack produce that is already cool; work with small quantities, filling only a few packages at a time, and freeze the packages immediately. Place them against or as close as possible to the freezer coils, and allow ample air space around each package. Once the food is frozen, rearrange it to make the best use of freezer space. Put no more food into the freezer than will freeze within 24 hours.

Frozen produce will keep for as long as a year. Label and date all packages and make a list showing the kind of produce and the date frozen. Put the list near the freezer and cross off entries as food is used. Once frozen fruits and vegetables are thawed, they deteriorate rapidly; so use the thawed food immediately and do not try to refreeze it.

How to freeze fruits

1. To prevent discoloration, dip light-colored fruits in a solution of ascorbic acid (vitamin C) and water. Use 1 teaspoon per cup of water for peaches and apricots, 2 1/4 teaspoons per cup of water for apples.
2. For a dry pack, sprinkle fruit with 1/2 cup of sugar per pound of fruit. For a wet pack, make a light syrup by mixing 1 cup of sugar with 2 1/2 cups of water.

3. Pack fruit into rigid containers or plastic bags. In a wet pack, cover fruit with liquid; leave 1-inch headroom in glass jars, 1/2 inch in plastic containers.
4. Label and date containers, and freeze at 0°F.

How to freeze vegetables

1. Blanch vegetables in boiling water or steam to destroy enzymes that break down vitamin C and convert starch into sugar. (See page 208 for blanching instructions.)
2. Cool vegetables quickly by immersing them in cold water. Drain on absorbent toweling.
3. Pack and freeze as you would dry-pack fruit, but do not use any sugar.

Salt Enhances Flavor and Shelf Life Too

Salt was a treasured commodity in the ancient world not only for its flavor but also for its preservative properties. When produce is impregnated with salt, moisture is drawn out and the growth of spoilage-causing bacteria inhibited. There are four basic methods of salt curing: dry salting, brining, low-salt fermentation, and pickling.

Dry salting and brining require heavy concentrations of salt during processing. In general, the more salt used, the better the food is preserved, but the greater the loss in food value, particularly since heavily salted food must be soaked and rinsed to make it palatable—a process that further depletes vitamins.

Modern cooks are more likely to choose a salt-curing method for its distinctive flavor than for its preservative properties. As a consequence, low-salt fermentation (the process used to make sauerkraut) and pickling remain popular today in spite of drawbacks as means of preservation. In both methods bacteria convert natural sugars in the produce into lactic acid, a substance that enhances flavor, improves preservation, and is said to promote health. The chief difference between low-salt fermentation and pickling is the use of vinegar, herbs, and spices in the pickling process. In either method salinity is low enough for the produce to be eaten without first being freshened (rinsed in water).

Almost any vegetable or fruit can be preserved by one or more of the salt-curing methods. Once cured, the produce will remain fit for consumption for periods of up to three weeks, provided it is kept at a temperature of about 38°F. If you want to keep the produce for longer periods or if the 38°F storage temperature is impossible to maintain, can the food by the boiling water bath method as soon as possible after it is thoroughly cured. For salt curing, choose vegetables and fruits that are firm, tender, and garden fresh without any trace of bruises or mold. Store-bought produce can be employed, but avoid vegetables that have been waxed (cucumbers and rutabagas are frequently coated with paraffin), because the curing solution will not penetrate. Wash the produce thoroughly under running water, and scrub each fruit or vegetable individually.

Curing containers should be enamelware, stoneware, or glass (avoid metal, since it may react with the brining solution). Do not cure with table salt—it contains additives that will discolor the food. Instead, use pickling or canning salt.

For Unbeatable Taste Add Vinegar and Spice

Pickling serves two purposes: it preserves and it adds delicious flavor. Choose firm, fresh vegetables and fruit

Dry Salting

Severest method of salt curing is dry salting. Corn, beans, green vegetables, cabbage, and root crops are the foods most frequently dry salted. Use additive-free, finely granulated salt (coarse salt takes too long to dissolve) in the proportion of one part salt to four parts vegetables by weight. Produce must be "freshened" (thoroughly rinsed of salt) before it is eaten. To freshen, soak food for 10 to 12 hours in fresh water, changing the water every few hours.

Pickling is an excellent way to preserve a small bumper crop and make it last for the first few months of the fall. If you want sharp, spicy pickles all winter, can them. Pickled foods are relatively easy to can because their acidity eliminates any chance of botulism growth. As a result, they can be processed by the boiling water bath method rather than the more complicated steam canning method required for unpickled vegetables.

for pickling—green tomatoes and underripe fruit can be used for greater firmness—but avoid vegetables that have been waxed. (Wax prevents the pickling solution from penetrating.) Use only pickling-type cucumbers.

There are two methods of pickling—fresh-pack pickling and fermentation pickling. Both rely on brine and vinegar as the primary preservatives; sugar, herbs, and spices are often added for additional flavor. The vinegar should have an acid content of 4 to 6 percent. Either cider vinegar or distilled white vinegar is acceptable; the latter has a sharper, more acid taste. Do not use homemade vinegar unless you are sure of its strength. For sweeteners, honey or granulated white or brown sugar is generally specified. Salt should be the pure granulated variety (often sold as "pickling salt") with no additives. Herbs and spices should be fresh and the water soft if

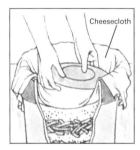

5. After 24 hours juice should cover produce. If it does not, add a solution of 3 tbsp. salt mixed into 1 cup of water.
6. Store container in cool area (38°F). Change cloth when

soiled. Use glass or china cup to dip out food.
7. Before eating salted produce, soak and drain it in several changes of fresh water until saltiness is gone.

1. Blanch vegetables in steam over rapidly boiling water (see *Blanching*, p.207). Cool by plunging into cold water.
2. Weigh produce and divide into batches that will make

1-in. layers. Weigh out 1 lb. salt per 4 lb. produce.
3. Fill crock with alternate layers of salt and 1-in.-thick layers of produce. First and last layers should be salt.

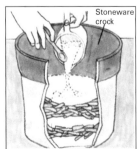

4. Leave 4-in. headroom above final salt layer. Cover with cheesecloth weighted down with a plate or board.

Brining

Salt solution is used to cure food by the brining method. Prepare the brine in advance by mixing 1 lb. salt per gallon of water. You will need 1 gal. of brine for each 2 gal. of produce. While the food is being brined, a process that will take four to eight weeks, keep it at room temperature (65°F to 70°F). Rinse food in several changes of cold water before eating it.

1. Weigh and blanch food, then place in crock and add brine to 4 in. of top.

2. Cover produce with cheesecloth; weight with plate to keep submerged.

3. The next day, add salt on top of cloth—1/2 lb. for each 5 lb. of produce.

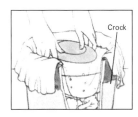

4. After one week add 1/8 lb. salt for every 5 lb. of produce. Repeat each week.

5. Check container every few days and remove any scum that appears on the surface.

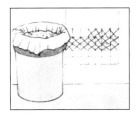

6. Maintain at room temperature until no bubbles rise (four to eight weeks).

7. Store brined food in cool area (38°F) in container covered with tight lid.

Low-Salt Fermentation

Do not blanch food when using the low-salt method, since fermentation organisms would be destroyed. Let the produce ferment at about 70°F, then store at 38°F in a tightly lidded container. For long-term storage, can by boiling water bath method (see p.194). Low-salt fermentation is particularly suitable for such vegetables as turnips and cabbage.

1. Wash and dry cabbage, then shred into small pieces so salt can penetrate.

2. Weight out 1 oz. salt per 2 1/2 lb. of cabbage. Thoroughly mix salt into cabbage.

3. Pack salted cabbage into container. Press down firmly to help extract juices.

4. Cover with cheesecloth weighted down with plate. Check after 24 hours.

5. If brine does not cover cabbage, and solution of 1 tsp. salt per cup of water.

6. Check fermentation regularly. Remove scum and change cloth if dirty.

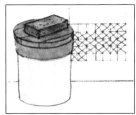

7. Keep at room temperature until no bubbles rise to surface (one to four weeks).

Making Dills by Fermentation Pickling

Cucumbers and green tomatoes are the vegetables most frequently treated by fermentation pickling. The method is similar to low-salt fermentation (p.199), but a stronger salt solution is employed, and vinegar and spices are generally added. After pickling is completed (a matter of one to three weeks), the pickles can be stored for up to three weeks in a refrigerator or cool (38°F) location. For long-term storage, can the pickles with the boiling water bath method (p.194). If the pickling brine is cloudy, make a fresh one to use in canning. You will need the following ingredients:

1/2 gal. water	1/3 cup salt
1/2 cup vinegar	4 lb. pickling cucumbers
	(4 to 5 in. each)
15 sprigs dill	30 peppercorns
15 cloves garlic (optional)	

1. Line bottom of 1-gal. crock with half of dill and other spices, then add cucumbers.

Prepare the brine by mixing water, salt, and vinegar. Clean and scrub cucumbers (especially the flower end) thoroughly, and be sure the crock and all other utensils are clean.

2. Top cucumbers with the remaining dill and spices. Add brine to cover all ingredients.

3. Keep produce submerged with a heavy plate so that it is under at least 2 in. of brine.

4. Remove scum daily. When bubbles and scum stop forming, fermentation is completed.

possible. If the tap water in your area is hard, you can use rainwater or bottled soft water.

Pickled products should be heat treated (canned) unless they are to be consumed soon after pickling. The boiling water bath canning procedure described on page 194 can be used for all pickled products; processing times vary from recipe to recipe. The usual precautions should be followed during canning and afterward: the jars of pickles should be labeled, dated, and stored in a cool, dry location. If there is any sign of spoilage—a bulging lid, bad smell, poor pickle consistency, sliminess, discoloration—do not eat any of the food in the jar.

Pickling Recipes

There are pickling recipes to suit every taste. All kinds of fruits and vegetables can be combined, and vinegar, salt, sugar, and spices can be adjusted in an almost endless variety of ways. The results are piquant relishes, chutneys, and sauces—as well as pickles with sweet, sour, or sweet-and-sour taste combinations. Although pickling is of limited use as a means of preserving fruits and vegetables—it prolongs shelf life only a few weeks—it does simplify long-term storage, since pickled produce has a high enough acid content to be processed by the boiling water bath method (see pp.194–195). The recipes given below include processing times.

Tomato-Apple Chutney

6 lb. tomatoes, peeled and chopped	2 cups seedless white raisins
1 qt. white vinegar	5 lb. apples, peeled,
4 tsp. salt	cored, and chopped

2 lb. brown sugar	2 medium green peppers,
tsp. ground ginger	seeded and chopped
1/4 cup mixed whole pickling spices	4-5 medium onions, peeled and chopped

Combine all ingredients except the mixed whole pickling spices. Put the spices in a spice bag and add to the mixture. Bring to boil and cook slowly, stirring frequently until mixture thickens (about one hour). Remove spice bag. Pack boiling mixture into sterile pint jars, leaving 1/2-in. headroom. Process in boiling water bath for 10 minutes. *Makes 7 pints.*

Sour Pickles

3 tbsp. mixed whole pickling spices	3 gal. hot water
3 tbsp. pickling dill	9 horseradish roots and leaves, or to taste
40 well-scrubbed cucumbers	9 garlic cloves, or to taste
9 peppercorns, or to taste	21/4 cups salt
	3 cups white cider vinegar

Put half the mixed whole pickling spices in the bottom of a large stone crock and cover with half the dill. Add cucumbers. Put remaining pickling spices and dill on top of the cucumbers. Make a pickling brine by dissolving 1 1/2 cups salt in mixture of 2 cups vinegar and 2 gal. hot water. Cool brine and pour it over the cucumbers. Cover with a plate weighted down to hold it beneath the brine. Keep crock at room temperature (68°F to 72°F) for two to four weeks. Remove scum daily.

When pickles are an even olive color without any white spots, they are ready for packing. Make a new brine of 1 gal. hot water, 3/4 cup salt, 1 cup white cider vinegar, horseradish roots, and peeled garlic; bring to boil. Pierce each pickle on the ends and once in the middle with a sterilized ice pick or knitting needle. Divide pickles among quart jars and add at least one peppercorn and one horseradish leaf to each jar. Pour hot brine over pickles, cover, and process by the boiling water bath method (p.194) for 15 minutes. *Makes 8 to 9 quarts.*

Making Dills by Fresh-Pack Pickling

1. Soak cucumbers overnight in brine solution; then drain and pack into 1-qt. jars.

2. Divide spices among jars. Mix together vinegar, salt, sugar, and water, and bring to a boil.

3. Pour boiling mixture over cucumbers to 1/2 in. from top of jars. Put lids on jars.

Not only cucumbers but beets, cauliflower, green beans, pears, peaches, tomatoes, and watermelon rind are suitable for fresh-pack pickling. Each type of fruit or vegetable can be processed individually, or several can be combined to make a relish or chutney. Details of processing vary from recipe to recipe depending on the ingredients used. Vegetables are frequently marinated overnight in brine before being heat processed; fruits and relishes are often simmered in a syrup of sugar, vinegar, and spices before processing. The procedure shown here for making fresh-pack dills is typical. As for any pickle recipe, use only ripe, perfect produce, and wash it thoroughly. You will need the following ingredients:

4 lb. pickling cucumbers	1/2 gal. brine (1/3 cup salt in 1/2 gal. water)
4 cloves garlic (2 per qt.)	8 heads dill (4 per qt.)
4 tsp. mustard seed (2 per qt.)	11/2 cups vinegar
3 tbsp. salt	1 tbsp. sugar
3 cups water	

4. Process jars in boiling water for 20 minutes. Set jars several inches apart on rack to cool.

Watermelon Pickles

6 lb. watermelon rind with green rind and pink meat removed	9 cups sugar
	3 cups white vinegar
	1 tbsp. whole cloves
3/4 cup salt	6 1-in. cinnamon sticks
3 3/4 qt. water	1 lemon, sliced thin
2 trays ice cubes	

Cut rind into 1-in. squares (it makes about 3 qt.). Dissolve salt in 3 qt. water, add ice cubes, and pour over watermelon rind. Allow to stand five to six hours. Drain rind and rinse in cold water. Cover with cold water and cook until fork tender (about 10 minutes). Drain. Combine sugar, vinegar, and remaining 3 cups water; then add a spice bag filled with cloves and cinnamon sticks. Boil five minutes and pour over rind. Add lemon slices and marinate overnight. Boil rind in syrup until rind is translucent (about 10 minutes). Pack boiling pickles into hot, sterilized pint jars. Remove cinnamon sticks from bag and divide among jars. Cover with boiling syrup, leaving 1/2-in. headroom. Process in boiling water bath for 10 minutes. *Makes 6 pints.*

Sauerkraut

5 lb. tender young cabbage, washed and thinly shredded	3 tbsp. salt

Mix cabbage and salt in a large pan and let stand 15 minutes. Pack mixture into clean nonmetal container, pressing it down firmly with wooden spoon. Juices must cover cabbage. Allow 4 to 6 in. of headroom above cabbage. Cover cabbage with clean white cheesecloth tucked down inside container. Weight down the cloth with a flat, tight-fitting lid that is heavy enough for the juice to rise up to but not over it. The cabbage should not be exposed to any air. Ferment at room temperature (68°F to 72°F) for five to six weeks. Skim off any scum that forms, and replace cloth and lid if they are scummy. When fermentation stops (bubbles will no longer rise to the surface), cover container with clean cloth and sterile lid, and move sauerkraut to a cold area (38°F), or process it in boiling water bath. To process, bring sauerkraut to a simmer (do not boil), and pack it into hot, sterile jars, leaving 1/2-in. headroom. Process in boiling water bath 15 minutes for pints, 20 minutes for quarts. *Makes 1 to 2 quarts.*

Homemade Horseradish Sauce

2-4 horseradish roots, washed peeled, and grated	1/2 cup white vinegar
	1/2 tsp. salt

Mix ingredients, pack into a clean jar, and seal tightly. The horseradish sauce can be used immediately, or it can be stored in refrigerator for up to four weeks. (Heat processing destroys the sharp bite of homemade horseradish.) *Makes 1 cup.*

Combine water, 2 cups sugar, and vinegar. Put spices into a spice bag, add to liquid, and bring to boil. Cook peaches a few at a time until barely tender (about 5 minutes). When the last batch has been removed, add 2 more cups sugar to syrup, and return to boil. Pour syrup over peaches and let stand 12 hours. Reheat peaches and syrup, then pack peaches into quart jars. Add final cup of sugar to syrup, bring to boil, and pour over peaches. Process in boiling water bath for 20 minutes. *Makes 6 quarts.*

Spiced Pears

8 cups sugar	2 tbsp. whole cloves
4 cups white vinegar	2 tbsp. whole allspice
2 cups water	8 lb. pears, peeled
8 2-in. cinnamon sticks	

Mix sugar, vinegar, water, cinnamon sticks, spice bag filled with cloves and allspice. Simmer 30 minutes. Add pears. Simmer 20 minutes more. Divide pears and cinnamon sticks among pint jars, and cover with boiling liquid, leaving 1/2-in. headroom. Process in boiling water bath for 20 minutes. *Makes 8 pints.*

Sweet and Savory Ways to Store Your Fruits

Just as salt and vinegar preserve vegetables and fruits through pickling, so sugar acts as the preserving agent in jellies, jams, conserves, marmalades, preserves, and fruit butters. Since most fruits are high in sugar to begin with, they are natural candidates for preservation in one of these forms.

In order to achieve proper gelling of a sugar-preserved product, three key ingredients must be present in correct proportion: sugar, pectin (the gelling agent), and acid. The best way to ensure good results is to follow a recipe and measure all ingredients carefully. All fruits need added refined white sugar or other mild-tasting sweetener, such as light corn syrup or honey. Very few recipes use brown sugar, molasses, or maple syrup because the flavors of these sweeteners are too strong and will overpower the taste of the fruit.

Many fruits contain sufficient natural pectin and acid for gelling, but others require extra amounts of one or the other. Some fruits have enough pectin or acid if they are sour or just barely ripe but not when they are fully ripe or overripe. To test for pectin, mix 1 teaspoon of cooked fruit with 1 tablespoon of rubbing alcohol. If the mixture coagulates into a single clump, there is sufficient pectin. (Do not taste the mixture, since rubbing alcohol is poisonous.) To check a fruit for acid, compare its taste to that of a mixture consisting of 3 tablespoons of water, 1 teaspoon of lemon juice, and 1/2 teaspoon of sugar. If the fruit is less tart than the lemon juice mixture, it needs more acid.

Pectin can be purchased in either liquid or powdered form, or you can make your own from apples (below right). A pectin substitute, low-methoxyl pectin, forms a gel when combined with calcium salts or bonemeal and lemon juice. It can be used to make jelly without any added sweeteners. If fruits lack sufficient acid, add lemon juice or citric acid when you add sugar.

Making Jelly Without Added Pectin

While any sugar-preserved product needs a good recipe, accurate measuring, and precise timing, nowhere is care more important than in the preparation of jelly without added pectin. The first requirement is that the fruit has enough natural pectin for gelling; either select a high-pectin fruit from the list on page 203 or test for pectin content as described on the same page.

To collect juice for jellymaking, cook the fruit, then hang it in a jelly bag made of muslin or several layers of cheesecloth. Squeezing the bag or pressing it with a spoon hastens the flow of juice but can cause cloudy jelly—it is better to let the juice drip naturally. If you do squeeze the jelly bag to collect extra juice, strain the juice a second time through a clean cloth.

Prolonged cooking turns the sweetened fruit juice into jelly by boiling away water until the sugar reaches just the right concentration. Timing is critical: overcooking leads to jelly that is stiff or full of sugary crystals; undercooking will produce thin, runny jelly. Because of the precision required in the process, work with the exact amounts specified in recipes: do not double a batch for extra jelly, make two separate batches instead.

An accurate thermometer provides the simplest and safest way to tell when the sugar has reached the proper concentration. Start by measuring the exact temperature at which the mixture first boils (it will vary depending on weather as well as altitude, so take a new reading each time you make a batch of jelly). As cooking progresses and water boils away, the sugar concentration will rise and the temperature go up. When the thermometer registers 8°F to 10°F above the initial boiling point, the jelly is done. As an additional test, dip a cold metal spoon into the mixture and hold the spoon away from the heat. If the jelly runs off in a sheet rather than individual drops, it is ready. A third test is to put a spoonful of jelly on a plate and put it in a freezer. If the sample becomes firm after one or two minutes, the jelly is ready. The freezer test can also be used for jams and preserves, the sheet test cannot.

The traditional way to seal jelly is with paraffin. Melt clean paraffin in a double boiler or small pan set in a larger wide-bottomed pan filled with water. (Do not melt paraffin directly over a flame or it may catch fire.) Prepare the paraffin in advance so that you can use it as soon as the jelly is done. Once the sealed jars are cool, put on lids to protect the paraffin from being accidently broken. For surer long-term storage, use canning jars and lids, and process the jars of jelly for 5 to 10 minutes in a boiling water bath (see p.194). For best retention of color and consistency, store the sealed jelly in a cool, dark place and use it within three months.

Equipment for making jams and jellies

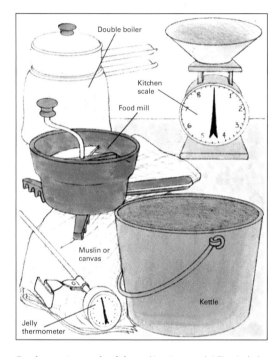

Double boiler

Kitchen scale

Food mill

Muslin or canvas

Kettle

Jelly thermometer

Equipment required for making jams and jellies includes all the standard canning supplies plus a few others. Buy a jelly thermometer, double boiler, and strainer. You will also need 1/2 yd. of a strong fabric, such as unbleached muslin or canvas, to make into a bag for straining jelly. A heavy kettle (less likely to let fruit scorch than a thin one), a food mill for pureeing, and a kitchen scale for precise measurement are also helpful.

Gelling properties of common fruits

Fruits with sufficient acid and pectin to gel	
Apples (sour)	Gooseberries
Blackberries (sour)	Grapes
Lemons	
Crabapples	Loganberries
Cranberries	Plums
Currants	Quinces

Fruits that may need added acid or pectin	
Apples (ripe)	Grapefruit
Blackberries (ripe)	Grapes (California)
Cherries (sour)	Loquats
Chokecherries	Oranges
Elderberries	

Fruits that always need additional acid or pectin	
Apricots	Pears
Figs	Prunes
Grapes (Western Concord)	Raspberries
	Strawberries
Guavas	
Peaches	

A Variety of Confections To Please Every Taste

Unlike jelly, which is made from fruit juice, other sugar-preserved foods contain parts of the whole fruit. Fruit butter is mashed pulp simmered with sugar until the pulp is thick; in the other fruit products pieces of fruit float in a light gel. Jam consists of gelled, mashed pulp; preserves are made of fruit pieces in a thin gel; and marmalade contains bits of fruit and citrus rind in a stiff, clear gel. Conserves contain a high proportion of mixed, chopped fruits in a small amount of gelled juice; nuts are often stirred into the gel just before it starts to set.

In all these products, with the exception of the fruit butters, the concentration of pectin, acid, and sugar are critical to proper setting, particularly if extra pectin is not being added. As in making jelly, best results are achieved by following a recipe carefully—do not

---

Making and using pectin

To manufacture your own pectin, wash 10 lb. of tart apples, remove stems quarter the fruits (but do not core), and place in a kettle. Cover apples with cold water and bring to a boil over moderate flame. Then cover kettle and simmer until the fruit is soft (about 30 minutes). Drain fruit in jelly bag overnight (see p.215) and collect juice (there should be about 3 qt.). Boil down juice to make 1 1/2 to 2 cups pectin.

Adding liquid pectin to fruit. Cook fruit until it is soft, add sugar, bring to a full boil, then boil fruit and sugar together for one full minute. Add the pectin. No additional cooking is required.

Adding powdered pectin to fruit. Stir pectin into softened, cooked fruit, bring fruit and pectin mixture to a boil, and add sugar. Return mixture to a boil, then boil one minute. Jelly will then be ready.

Blackberry Jelly Step-by-step

1. You will need 5 qt. of berries (about one-fourth should be underripe) to make 2 qt. of juice. Remove stems, wash fruit, and place in heavy kettle.
2. Crush berries with potato masher, add 1 1/2 cups water, cover, and bring

to boil. Reduce heat and simmer, stirring occasionally, until tender (five minutes).
3. Pour mixture into dampened jelly bag, suspend bag over bowl or pan, and let juice strain overnight. Cover bag and bowl with cloth to protect from dust.

4. If you are going to seal with paraffin, cut fresh paraffin into chunks, and add a few at a time to double boiler until all are melted. Hold until jelly is done.

5. Pour 2 qt. of juice into heavy kettle and add 6 cups of sugar. Place kettle over a high flame and heat the liquid to a full rolling boil that cannot be stirred down.

6. Stir juice, insert thermometer so that bulb is covered but does not touch pan, and note temperature at which juice reaches full rolling boil.

7. Continue heating until temperature reaches 8°F to 10°F above initial boiling point. At this temperature sugar is concentrated enough for product to gel.
8. Pour jelly into hot, sterile jars, leaving 1/2-in. headroom. Process by boiling water

bath method (p.194), or cover with 1/8 in. of paraffin, using pin to break bubbles.
9. Let jars stand undisturbed on rack overnight. Then put on lids over paraffin seal; label with name, date, and batch number; and store in a cool, dark place.

double or triple ingredient measures to make a bigger batch. Instead, make several small batches. Be sure pectin and acid content are high enough by using plenty of underripe high-pectin fruit or by testing for pectin and acid as described on page 202. You can tell if the sugar concentration is correct by measuring the temperature of the sugar-fruit mixture as it cooks. First, find the temperature at which water boils. Then cook the fruit and sugar until it reaches 8°F to 10°F above the

boiling point of water. If you do not have a thermometer, use the freezer test described on page 202. When making jams or other fruit products with added pectin, you need not cook down the fruit mixture to make it gel, but precise measurements and accurate timing are still important.

Jams, marmalades, preserves, conserves, and butters must undergo further processing to eliminate spoilage-causing organisms if the product is to be stored for

Jams, Marmalades, Preserves, and Conserves Without Added Pectin

1. Wash fruit, remove pits, and peel if called for in recipe. Cut up large fruits, such as peaches. Measure exact boiling point of water.

2. Put fruit into kettle, first crushing bottom layer. (Add water if fruit has arecipe instructions.

3. Add sugar (and lemon juice if acid content is low). Insert thermometer. Return mixture to boiling, stirring constantly to prevent scorching.

4. Boil rapidly, stirring constantly, until temperature reaches 8°F to 10°F above boiling point of water. Remove from heat immediately.

5. To prevent fruit from floating in finished product, let mixture cool for about five minutes and stir several times during cooling.

more than two or three weeks. Certain recipes specify freezing; all others require canning by the boiling water bath technique described on page 194. Use hot, sterile canning jars, and leave a 1/2-inch space above the fruit.

Apple Jelly

2 1/4 lb. just-ripe tart apples	3/4 lb. underripe tart apples
2 tbsp. lemon juice (if apples are not sufficiently tart)	3 cups sugar

Wash apples and cut into small pieces without paring or coring. Put apples and water into heavy kettle, cover, bring quickly to a boil. Reduce heat and simmer until apples are soft (about 20 minutes). Pour cooked apples into jelly bag and collect juice as it drips. Return 4 cups juice to heavy kettle, add sugar and lemon juice. Place over high heat, and boil rapidly until temperature rises to 8°F to 10°F above boiling point of water. Remove from heat immediately, skim, and pour into hot, sterile jelly jars. Seal. *Makes four to five 1/2-pt. jars.*

Grape Jelly

3 1/2 lb. underripe Concord grapes	1/2 cup water
1 tart apple, cut into eighths but not peeled or cored	3 cups sugar

Wash grapes and remove stems. Put grapes into heavy kettle and crush. Add apple sections and water, cover, and bring quickly to a boil. Reduce heat and simmer until grapes are soft (about 10 minutes). Pour grapes into a jelly bag and collect juice as it drips. Let collected juice stand in a refrigerator or other cool place for 8 to 10 hours, then strain juice through two layers of cheesecloth to remove any crystals.

Return 4 cups juice to heavy kettle, and add sugar. Place over high heat, bring to a full boil, and continue rapid boiling until temperature rises to 8°F to 10°F above boiling point of water. Remove from heat immediately, skim, and pour into hot, sterile jelly jars. Seal. *Makes three to four 1/2-pt. jars.*

Mint Jelly

1 cup tightly packed mint leaves	3 1/2 cups sugar
5 drops green food coloring	1 cup water
3 oz. liquid pectin	1/2 cup cider vinegar

Wash mint, remove stems, and coarsely chop leaves. Put mint leaves, water, vinegar, and sugar into heavy kettle, and bring quickly to a full boil, stirring constantly. Remove kettle from heat, add food coloring and pectin, return liquid to a full boil, then boil 30 seconds. Remove immediately from heat, skim, strain through two layers of damp cheesecloth, and pour into hot, sterile jelly jars. Seal. *Makes three to four 1/2-pt. jars.*

Apple Butter

8 cups applesauce	2 cups brown sugar
1/2 tsp. cloves	1/2 tsp. cinnamon
1/2 tsp. allspice	Grated rind of one lemon

Mix all ingredients and spread in shallow baking pan. Bake at 275°F, stirring occasionally, until thick (about four hours). Pack into hot, sterile canning jars. For long-term storage, process in boiling water bath for 10 minutes. *Makes two 1/2-pt. jars.*

Peach Jam With Powdered Pectin

3 lb. peaches	1 3/4 oz. powdered pectin
1/4 cup lemon juice	5 cups sugar

Making Fruit Butters

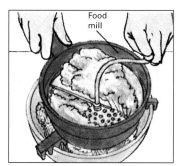

1. Wash and cut up fruit, remove pits, and crush fruit into a pulp with potato masher. Measure pulp and put into a heavy kettle.

2. Add half as much water by volume as there is fruit pulp. Cook over low heat, stirring almost constantly to prevent scorching, until pulp is soft.

3. Press fruit pulp through a colander or strainer to get rid of all pits and skin. Then put it through a food mill or blender to make a smooth puree.

4. With kettle removed from heat, pour pureed pulp back in, and stir in 1/2 cup of sugar per cup of fruit pulp. Return kettle to low heat.

5. Cook mixture over low heat, stirring constantly and watching carefully to prevent scorching. Simmer until fruit is thick and glossy.

Wash, peel, pit, and crush peaches; there should be 3 3/4 cups. In a heavy kettle mix fruit, lemon juice, and pectin. Bring quickly to a full boil, stirring constantly. Add sugar. Return mixture to boil, then boil rapidly, stirring constantly, for one minute. Remove immediately from heat, skim, and pour into hot, sterile canning jars. For long-term storage, process 10 minutes in boiling water bath. *Makes six 1/2-pt. jars.*

Blueberry Peach Jam

4 lb. fully ripe peaches	1/2 tbsp. whole cloves
1 qt. firm blueberries	1/4 tsp. whole allspice
2 tbsp. lemon juice	5 1/2 cups sugar
1/2 cup water	1/2 tsp. salt
1 stick cinnamon	

Wash, peel, pit, and chop peaches; there should be 1 qt. Wash and sort blueberries. In a heavy kettle mix fruit, lemon juice, and water; then simmer, covered, until fruit is soft (about 10 minutes). Tie cinnamon, cloves, and allspice in a cheesecloth bag, and add bag, along with sugar and salt, to fruit. Bring mixture quickly to a full boil, and boil rapidly, stirring constantly, until mixture reaches 8°F to 10°F above the boiling point of water. Remove immediately from heat, skim, and remove spices. Pour jam into hot, sterile canning jars. For long-term storage, process in boiling water bath for 10 minutes. *Makes six 1/2-pt. jars.*

Uncooked Berry Jam

1 qt. fully ripe berries	1 3/4 oz. powdered pectin
4 cups sugar	1 cup water

Wash berries and remove stems. Place fruit in bowl and crush; there should be 2 cups. Add sugar, and let stand for 20 minutes, stirring occasionally. Meanwhile, mix pectin and water, bring to a full boil, then boil one minute. Pour pectin solution into berries, and stir for two minutes. Pour into sterile jars or freezer containers. Store in refrigerator for up to three weeks or in freezer for up to one year. *Makes five 1/2-pt. jars.*

Strawberry Preserves

2 qt. firm, tart strawberries	4 1/2 cups sugar

Wash berries and remove stems and leaves. Arrange alternate layers of whole berries and sugar in a large bowl, and let stand in refrigerator or other cool place for 8 to 10 hours to bring out juice. When juice has accumulated, place fruit-sugar mixture in heavy kettle over medium-high heat. Bring quickly to a boil, stirring gently so as not to break berries. Boil mixture rapidly; stir frequently to prevent scorching until temperature reaches 8°F to 10°F above the boiling point of water. Remove fruit mixture immediately from heat, skim, and pour into hot, sterile canning jars. For long-term storage, process 10 minutes in boiling water bath. *Makes four 1/2-pt. jars.*

Orange Marmalade

1 1/2 cups orange peel, cut into thin strips	6 oranges
1/3 cup lemon peel, cut into thin strips	1/3 cup lemon juice
3 cups sugar	

Cover orange and lemon peel with 1 qt. cold water and simmer, covered, until tender (30 minutes). Drain. Section oranges, remove filaments and seeds, and cut into small pieces. In a heavy kettle mix oranges, lemon juice, drained peel, sugar, and 2 cups boiling water. Bring quickly to a full boil, then boil rapidly, stirring often, until temperature reaches 8°F to 10°F above the boiling point of water. Remove immediately from heat, skim, and pour into hot, sterile jars. For long-term storage, process in boiling water bath for 10 minutes. *Makes three 1/2-pt. jars.*

Let Sun and Air Preserve for You

When 80 to 90 percent of the moisture in food is removed, the growth of spoilage bacteria is halted and the food can be stored for long periods of time. By exposing your produce to a flow of hot, dry air, you will not only remove moisture quickly but also concentrate natural sugars for a delicious, sweet flavor while reducing volume for easy storage. In addition, proper drying can preserve many of the natural nutrients in foods.

Careful preliminary treatment is an important contributor to high vitamin retention, good flavor, and attractive appearance. To fix the natural color in sliced fruits, dip the pieces of fruit in pure lemon juice or a solution of ascorbic acid (vitamin C) as soon as they are cut. You will need about a cup of lemon juice to process 5 quarts of cut fruit; or mix 3 teaspoons of pure ascorbic acid with 1 cup of water. Vitamin C tablets in the proportion of 9,000 milligrams per cup of water can also be used to prepare the dipping solution, but the tablets are expensive and difficult to dissolve.

Sulfuring and blanching are the most common ways of preserving vitamin content and preventing loss of flavor in produce that is to be dried. Of the two techniques blanching is preferable, since sulfuring destroys thiamine (vitamin B^1). In addition, sulfuring may impart a sour taste to food. In general, the sulfur method is best for fruits, where the tartness may be an asset to flavor.

High vitamin retention also depends upon striking the right balance between the relatively fast drying made possible by exposure to heat and slower drying at lower temperatures. Generally, the faster the food is dried, the higher will be its vitamin content and the less its chance of contamination by mold and bacteria. Excessively high temperatures, however, break down many vitamins. Most experts recommend drying temperatures in the range between 95°F and 145°F; 140°F is the optimum suggested by the U.S. Department of Agriculture. Exposure to bright sun also speeds up drying, but sunlight is known to destroy some vitamins.

Blanching

Blanching—brief heat treatment in either steam or boiling water—helps preserve both color and vitamin content by deactivating plant enzymes. It also speeds the drying process by removing any wax or other surface coating on the produce and makes peeling easier by loosening the skins. Blanching in boiling water is recommended for fruits whose skins are to be peeled. Steam blanching is recommended for most other fruits and vegetables.

Onions, garlic, leeks, and mushrooms should be dried without blanching.

Boiling water blanching. Immerse produce in boiling water for the time listed on the chart. Use your largest pot and add fruit a little at a time so that the water will return to a boil quickly. After blanching, immediately dip the produce in cold water to cool it, then either peel the skin or crack it by nicking with a knife in order to aid in evaporation during drying.

Steam blanching. Place a 2 1/2-inch layer of cut vegetables in a strainer or colander. Bring 2 inches of water to a boil in a large kettle. Set the strainer on a rack above the water, cover the kettle tightly, and process for the time specified on the chart.

Sulfuring Protects Vitamins and Bright Colors

Sulfuring should be done outdoors—the fumes are not only unpleasant but also dangerous. You will need a heavy cardboard box large enough to allow 6 to 12 in. of space on all sides of a stack of drying trays. Cut a flap at the bottom of one side of the box to aid in air circulation.

To prepare fruit for sulfuring, cut it up, weigh it, and spread it in single layers—with cut sides up and no pieces touching—in nonmetal trays (sulfur fumes will corrode most metals). Stack the trays 11/2 in. apart (set pieces of wood at the corners to keep trays separated), and support the stack on cinder blocks or bricks.

You will need about 2 tsp. of sulfur per pound of fresh fruit. Sulfur is sold at most pharmacies; a standard 2-oz. box contains about 16 tsp. Heap the sulfur about 2 in. deep in a clean, disposable container, such as a tuna fish can, and set it next to the stack of trays. Place the cardboard box over the trays and sulfur, then pile dirt around the box's edges to seal them. Light the sulfur through the flap and check frequently to make sure that it keeps burning. (If the sulfur will not stay lit, poke a venthole in the box at the top of the side opposite the flap.) When the sulfur is entirely consumed, seal both the flap and the vent and let the fruit sit in the fumes until it is bright and shiny. Dry the fruit immediately after sulfuring is completed.

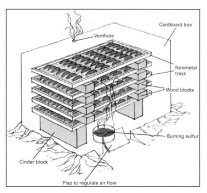

Sulfuring times

Fruit	Time
Apples	45 min.
Apricots	2 hr.
Nectarines	8 min.
Peaches	8 min.
Pears	5 hr.
Prunes	1 hr.

Outdoor Drying

If you live in an area with clean air, a dry climate, and consistently sunny weather, the simplest way to dry produce is to do it right in the garden. Peas and beans can be left to dry on the vine if the growing season is long enough. Store vine-dried peas in mesh bags in an airy spot. When you are ready to eat them, whack the bag with a stick to remove the shells. Vine-dried green

Blanching: preparation and timing

Produce	Preparation	Steam	Boil
Apples	Peel, core, slice 1/8' thick	5 min.	2 min.
Apricots	Leave whole to boil; otherwise halve and pit	3-4 min.	4-5 min.
Beans	Cut into 1' pieces	2 1/2 min.	2 min.
Broccoli	Cut into flowerettes	3-3 1/2 min.	2 min.
Brussels sprouts	Halve lengthwise	6-7 min.	4 1/2-5 1/2 min.
Cabbage	Core, slice 1/8' thick	2 1/2-3 min.	1 1/2-2 min.
Carrots	Peel, slice 1/8' thick	3-3 1/2 min.	3 1/2 min.
Cauliflower	Cut into flowerettes	4 min.	3-4 min.
Celery	Remove leaves, slice stalks	2 min.	2 min.
Corn	Remove husks	2-2 1/2 min.	1 1/2 min.
Grapes (seedless)	Remove stems	No blanching necessary	
Nectarines, peaches	Leave whole; halve and pit after blanching	8 min.	8 min.
Pears	Peel, halve, core	6 min.	–
Spinach	Trim, wash leaves	2-2 1/2 min.	1 1/2 min.
Summer squash	Trim, slice 1/4' thick	2 1/2-3 min.	1 1/2 min.
Tomatoes	Peel, section or slice	3 min.	1 min.

and wax beans must be blanched and then oven cured by baking them for 10 to 15 minutes at 175°F before storing. Oven curing will kill any insect eggs and ensure thorough drying. For long-term storage, string the beans together and hang them in a dry place, such as the attic. Onions can also be allowed to dry in the garden. Pull them up and let them lie on the ground in the sun for four to six days. When the tops turn stiff and strawlike, braid them together with a length of strong twine.

While outdoor drying is convenient, there are some drawbacks. The longer the fruits and vegetables are exposed to air and sunlight, the more vitamins they lose. Moreover, even mild air pollution can contaminate food—in rural areas the fumes from trucks and automobiles can be a serious problem.

Drying on trays

Produce that is not suited to garden drying can still be dried outdoors on trays made from parallel wooden slats or from nonmetallic screening. (Metal screening should not be used, since some metals are poisonous while others destroy vitamins.) The mesh should be tacked or stapled to wooden frames. Old metal window screens covered with brown paper are sometimes used for drying, but they are not recommended because the metal may still contaminate despite the paper.

When your food is ready for drying, spread it on trays in single layers so that the pieces do not touch one another. Choose a warm drying spot, such as a heat-reflecting driveway or a rooftop, and set the trays out, raising them on blocks to 6 inches above the ground for better air circulation. For even more heat tilt the trays so that they face the sun. To protect against insects, shield the food with cheesecloth placed above the tray. Drape the cloth over wooden blocks to keep it from touching the food, and weight its edges down with stones. Put out the trays as soon as the morning dew has evaporated. At dusk either bring the trays indoors or cover them with canvas or plastic.

Drying Indoors Is Most Efficient

In many parts of the country indoor drying is the most convenient and practical way to remove moisture from food. Not only is indoor drying independent of the weather, but it is faster than open-air drying because it continues day and night. As a result, vitamins are conserved and there is less chance of spoilage.

The simplest way to dry food indoors is in an oven. Start by preparing the food as described on page 207, including blanching or sulfuring. Next, preheat the oven to 145°F. (Buy an accurate thermometer to check the oven temperature.) Spread the pieces of fruit and vegetable in single layers on cookie sheets, making sure that the pieces do not touch one another. Place the sheets on racks inside the oven, leaving at least 4 inches above and below the trays for air circulation. With the oven door slightly ajar for ventilation, turn the temperature down to 120°F, then gradually increase it to 140°F. Be sure that the food is exposed to 140°F temperatures for at least half the full drying time. From time to time rearrange the trays and shift the food to ensure even drying. A number of commercial devices are available for drying food in the home, or you can make one of the simple driers shown on these pages. Such driers generally do the job more

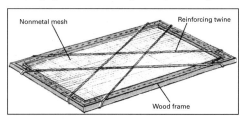

Make a drying tray from wooden slats or by stretching nonmetal mesh on a wooden frame. Reinforce bottom with twine.

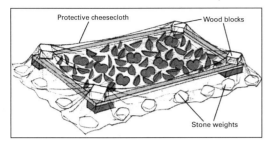

Cover trays with cheesecloth to allow maximum air and heat circulation while protecting against insects and birds.

slowly than an oven but have the advantage of using less energy. In addition, they free the oven for more routine tasks, such as cooking dinner or baking bread.

Drying on top of the stove

Stove-top driers designed for wood-burning stoves can be used on gas and electric stoves as well. In this type of drier the drying tray is separated from the direct heat of the burner by a 3-in-deep reservoir of water. All burners are lit, but they are turned very low. As in other drying techniques, food must be spread in a single layer with space between pieces.

Keep a watchful eye and add water to the reservoir as needed to prevent burning of food.

Tests for dryness

Drying times vary considerably depending on weather as well as size and moisture content of produce. Fruit is dry if it appears leathery and tough and no moisture can be squeezed from it. Vegetables should be so brittle and crisp that they rattle on the tray. Check weight too. If food has lost half its weight, it is two-thirds dry. The table gives approximate drying times.

Produce	Time in drier
Apples	6-12 hr.
Apricots	24-36 hr.
Beans	8-18 hr.
Broccoli	12-15 hr.
Brussel sprouts	12-18 hr.
Cabbage	10-12 hr.

Easy-to-make indoor driers

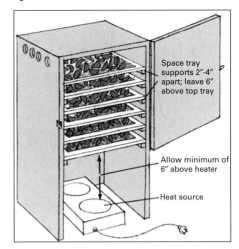

Home dehydrator (above) holds trays 2 to 4 in. apart and leaves 6 in. above top tray for circulation of heated air.

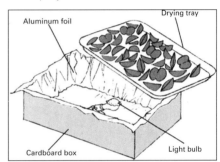

For simple drier (above) line box with foil and place light bulb inside box, but not touching the box. Blacken bottom of tray and set on top of box. Spread food on tray.

Carrots	10-12 hr.
Cauliflower	12-15 hr.
Celery	10-16 hr.
Corn	12-15 hr.
Grapes (seedless)	12-20 hr.
Nectarines	36-38 hr.
Peaches	36-48 hr.
Pears	25-36 hr.
Spinach	8-10 hr.
Summer squash	10-12 hr.
Tomatoes	10-18 hr.

Storage and Rehydration

After food has been dried it should be pasteurized in an oven to be sure no insect eggs or spoilage microorganisms are present. Final pasteurization also helps ensure thorough drying. To pasteurize, preheat the oven to 175°F. Spread food 1 inch deep on trays, and put the trays in the oven for 10 to 15 minutes.

Even though a batch of fruit or vegetables may have been meticulously dried and pasteurized, small pockets

Solar driers

Solar driers collect heat from the sun and use it to speed up air circulation and reduce the moisture content of the air. They are especially useful in areas, such as the Southeast, where there is plenty of sunlight but the humidity is relatively high. The simplest design has glass or plastic panels that trap sunlight to warm a box. A more elaborate drier, made from an oil drum, circulates sun-heated air around stacks of drying trays. The key to successful solar drying is to check the apparatus

frequently. If sunlight is blocked even partially, the air inside the drier will cool, fail to circulate, and become damp. The result is increased risk of deterioration of food.

Ingenious drier designed by New Hampshire sun enthusiast Leandre Poisson uses curved layers of plastic as solar collectors. Heated air travels by natural convection into the oil drum, where food is spread on trays. Electric light bulb and small fan increase reliability by maintaining the temperature and a balanced flow of air if sun dims.

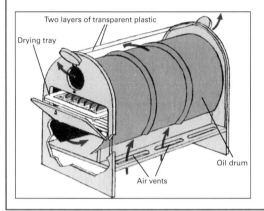

Two layers of transparent plastic
Drying tray
Oil drum
Air vents

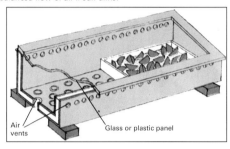

Air vents
Glass or plastic panel

Simplest solar drier is like a cold frame with glass panels tilted toward sun. Specially placed vents maximize air circulation.

of residual moisture always remain trapped. Additional conditioning helps spread this moisture evenly throughout the produce. The conditioning is accomplished by placing the cooled, dried produce in open enamel, glass, or ceramic containers, such as mason jars. The food is then stirred thoroughly twice a day to distribute any remaining moisture. If the food seems moist at the end of five days, return it to the drier.

After the fruits and vegetables have been conditioned, they are ready for long-term storage. Dried food is best kept in sterilized glass jars or plastic bags. Metal containers can be used, provided they are lined with brown paper—dried food should never be allowed to come in direct contact with metal. A perfect seal of the sort required in canning is not necessary, but the containers should have secure, tight-fitting lids to keep out dirt, dust, and insects. For best results, store dried food in a dark place where the temperature is below 60°F. Produce will sweat if stored in a warmer area, so refrigerate it during warm periods. Check periodically for condensation (it encourages mold), and return the food to the drier if any moisture is present.

Dried fruits may be eaten without reconstitution for snacks or in cereals, desserts, and salads. Vegetables, however, should be rehydrated by infusing them with enough water to replace the moisture removed during the drying process. Most fruits and vegetables can be rehydrated by pouring boiling water over them in the ratio of 1 1/2 cups of water to 1 cup of dried food and letting the food soak until all the water has been absorbed. Vegetables generally rehydrate in about two hours, but dried beans and fruits require overnight soaking. If all the water is absorbed but the food still appears shriveled, add more water a little at a time. Avoid adding

excess liquid, however, since it will dissolve nutrients and waste them.

Rehydrated fruits need not be cooked, but vegetables must be. Cover the vegetables with any water left over from soaking and add fresh water if necessary to prevent scorching. Bring the water to a boil, reduce the heat, and simmer until the vegetables are tender. Reconstituted fruits and vegetables can be eaten plain or combined with other foods and flavorings.

Recipes

Substitute reconstituted dried food for fresh in almost any recipe (generally the volume of soaked food will be four times that of dried), or take advantage of the concentrated flavor of tomato paste and vegetable powder to enrich soups and stews.

Apple Leather

4 qt. apples, peeled, cored, and cut in pieces	Cinnamon, cloves, and nutmeg to taste
1-1 1/2 cups apple cider	Honey to taste
Cornstarch or arrowroot powder	

Crush apples in a blender or food mill. Catch the juice and return it to mixture. Put ground apple mixture in a heavy kettle and add enough apple cider to prevent scorching. Bring mixture to a boil over low flame. Add honey and spices to taste. When mixture is as thick as apple butter, spread it in a 1/4-in.-thick layer on oiled cookie sheets or cookie sheets covered with freezer paper. Cover sheets with cheesecloth and place in a warm, dry area until dry (one to two weeks) or in a 120°F oven or a food drier. When fruit leather is dry enough to be lifted from sheets, lay it on cake rack so both sides can be dried at once. When leather is no longer sticky, dust with cornstarch or arrowroot. Wrap each sheet in freezer paper, wax paper, or aluminum foil, stack sheets, and cover with more paper. Store in a cool, dark place.

Sun-Cooked Preserves

4 cups mixed fruit, such as peaches, pears, and berries

1 cup honey

Wash fruit and cut large types into 1/2-in. chunks. Place fruit in saucepan, add honey, and bring to a boil, stirring constantly. Spread boiled mixture 1/2 in. deep in cookie sheets, making sure fruit is spread in a single layer. Cover trays with cheesecloth stretched taut, and put them in direct sun or drier for two to seven days to dry. When preserves are thick, pack into sterilized jars and refrigerate or freeze.

Vegetable Powder

Use any thoroughly dried vegetable for this recipe. Grind vegetables in blender and store. Add dried powder to boiling water to make instant vegetable soup, or add to stews and casseroles to enhance flavor.

Tomato Paste

Italian plum type tomatoes, which have less juice, are best for this recipe, but any type of tomato may be used. Put tomatoes into heavy kettle and crush to bring out juice. Cook until very soft (about one hour), then put through blender or food mill to puree. Return puree to kettle and simmer, stirring often, over very low heat until reduced by half (two to four hours). Spread puree 1/2 in. thick on cookie sheets and place in sun or drier until no longer sticky (about two days). Roll dried paste into 1-in. balls and let dry at room temperature for another one to two days. Store in airtight jars. Add balls of tomato paste to soups, stews, sauces, and gravies to enhance flavor, or add to cooked tomatoes to make tomato sauce. For variety add such herbs as basil and parsley when making tomato paste.

Sources and resources

Books and pamphlets

Bailey, Janet. *Keeping Food Fresh*. New York: Harper Collins, 1993.

Brennan, Georganne, and Kleinman, Katherine. *The Glass Pantry: Preserving Seasonal Flavors*. San Francisco: Chronicle Books, 1994.

Chesman, Andrea. *Summer in a Jar: Making Pickles, Jams and More*. Charlotte, Vt.: Williamson Publishing, 1985.

Chioffi, Nanci, and Gretchen Mead. *Keeping the Harvest*. Pownal, Vt.: Storey Communications, 1991.

Holm, Don, and Holm, Myrtle. *Don Holm's Book of Food Drying, Pickling and Smoke Curing*. Caldwell, Ind.: Caxton, 1978.

Home Canning of Fruits and Vegetables. Home and Garden Bulletin No. 8. Washington, D.C.: U.S. Department of Agriculture, 1983.

Home Freezing of Fruits and Vegetables. Home and Garden Bulletin No. 10. Washington, D.C.: U.S. Department of Agriculture, 1971.

Humphrey, Richard. *Saving the Plenty: Pickling and Preserving*. Kingston, Mass.: Teaparty Books, 1986.

Hupping, Carol. *Stocking Up*. New York: Simon and Schuster Trade, 1990.

Innes, Jacosta. *The Country Preserves Companion*. San Francisco: Collins Publishers, 1995.

Kinard, Malvina. *Well Preserved*. New Canaan, Conn.: Keats Publishing, 1994.

Lesem, Jeanne. *Preserving Today*. New York: Knopf, 1992.

Nichols, Naomi. *Food Drying at Home*. New York: Van Nostrand Reinhold, 1978.

Pyron, Cherry, and Clarissa M. Silitch, eds. *The Forgotten Arts: Making Old-Fashioned Pickles, Relishes, Chutneys, Sauces and Catsups, Mincemeats, Beverages and Syrups*. Dublin, N.H.: Yankee Books, 1986.

Stoner, Carol Hupping, ed. *Stocking Up III*. New York: Fine Communications, 1995.

U.S. Department of Agriculture. *Complete Guide to Home Canning, Preserving and Freezing*. New York: Dover, 1994.

Preserving Meat and Fish

The Old Methods Survive Not Just for Practicality But for Unsurpassed Flavor

The problem of storing meat and fish for use the year round is as old as mankind. Most of the traditional methods involve processing with salt, smoke, and spices that not only preserve but add flavor as well. Although modern refrigeration has made food storage simpler, many of the old ways are still popular, primarily because they make meat and fish taste so good.

Curing and smoking were once the standard ways of preserving, and many popular products—Smithfield hams, corned beef, lox, pastrami—are still made by one or both of these techniques. Sausages, too, were and are popular. The recipes by which sausages are made vary according to climate. In warm areas traditional recipes call for cured meat laced with plenty of herbs and spices; the result is sausages that tend to be hard and dry. In colder climates, where storage is less of a problem, sausages are generally milder and are made from fresh, uncured meat.

Some old-time methods of preservation are now all but forgotten. Poultry, cooked and deboned, was stored for months beneath a covering of lard or butter. Roasts were kept fresh for up to a week by immersing them in cold running water—when the meat began to float, it was time for it to go into the oven. Charcoal, a strong antibacterial agent, was often ground and rubbed into the surface of meat; fish would be kept fresh by replacing the innards with a lump of charcoal. American Plains Indians perfected the art of drying, or jerking, meat and then grinding the jerky to make pemmican; modern outdoorsmen have rediscovered this ancient food, and today a small jerky-making industry flourishes, catering to the needs of hikers, campers, and skiers.

Short-term Storage, Hanging, and Sanitation

Fresh meat (including poultry) deteriorates rapidly in temperatures above 40°F, so it is important to refrigerate it as soon as possible and to keep it under refrigeration until it is cooked or processed. In addition, a period of chilling, or hanging, can improve the flavor and texture of most meats by giving natural enzymes time to break down tough muscle fibers. The temperature range for hanging is 33°F to 40°F. Freshly killed poultry should be hung for 12 to 48 hours, depending on the size of the bird. Pork and veal should hang for one or two days; beef, mutton, and lamb for as long as a week. Game should be gutted first, and any scent glands should be removed. If you cannot maintain a temperature at or below 40°F, do not attempt to hang meat. Instead, cure it, freeze it, or otherwise process it

Smoking meat, fish, and poultry is much easier than it might seem. This unique smoker is crafted to look like a bull, but really no specialized equipment is required beyond a firepit, where the hardwood smolders, and a ventilated smoke chamber (a wooden crate or even a cardboard box could serve). The smoke helps to preserve meat, partly by coating it with smoke-borne preservative chemicals. Thoroughly cured and smoked meats, such as the South's famous Smithfield hams, can be kept for years. (Smithfields have reputedly been stored for as long as 25 years—from a girl's christening until her wedding.) Nowadays, many people use smokers to add a delicious woodsy flavor to a piece of fresh meat or fish.

for preservation immediately. Fish rots very quickly, so it should never be hung; process it immediately or else freeze it.

When handling meat and fish, make sure your hands are clean, as well as all your tools and utensils. Scrub or scrape wooden cutting boards, wash them with hot, soapy water, and scald them with boiling water before and after each use. You will probably need several different knives for preparing different cuts of meat. The knives should be not only clean but sharp. High carbon blades are the best; use a butcher's steel to give them a final edge after sharpening.

Special precautions are required when processing or preparing pork, since fresh pork may contain trichinae worms, which cause the disease trichinosis. These worms can be killed by heat or by cold. Always cook pork to a minimum of 137°F *throughout*. (To be safe, cook it to 145°F to 150°F.) For cuts of pork less than 6 inches thick the worms can also be destroyed by freezing at –10°F for 10 to 12 days or at 0°F for three to four weeks.

Freezing In Fresh Flavor

Since World War II freezing has become the most popular way to store meat and fish; it is quick and easy, and preserves both the nutritional value and flavor of the fresh food. The only drawback is that freezing is dependent on a consistent supply of electrical power. The best way to freeze meat and fish is to flash-freeze at –15°F, then store at 0°F. Most chest-style freezers have the capability of reaching –15°F, but some uprights may not. Set your freezer's control to its coldest setting several hours before using it as a flash-freezer. Shift the food that is already in the freezer to one side; try to leave about 1 cubic foot of freezer space for every 2 pounds of meat or fish to be flash-frozen.

Chill meat or fish before you freeze it to make it easier to cut and package and to decrease the chance of spoiling other food in the freezer. Wrap all pieces securely in individual moisture-proof packages to prevent freezer burn (caused by dehydration) and to avoid contaminating one meat with the odors of another. There are many brands of freezer wrap available that give durable protection for frozen goods. Label each package with the type and cut of meat or fish it contains and the date it was frozen. Then load the packages into the freezer. To protect the frozen food, be sure to keep the unfrozen packages from touching any of the already frozen food. When all the food is hard frozen, return the control to normal (0°F). In the event of freezer breakdown or power failure, do not open the freezer—it will maintain its temperature for several hours. During longer breakdowns keep the empty space in the freezer packed with dry ice. Once meat is thawed, it should not be refrozen.

All meats begin to deteriorate if they are left in the freezer too long. Cured meats, such as ham and bacon, and very fatty meats, such as sausage, do not keep well under refrigeration and should not be kept frozen for more than a month. Ground meat, stewing meat, pork chops, liver, and kidneys can generally be left frozen for up to three months. Steak, chops, fish, and roasts will last as long as six months. The best way to thaw frozen

Wrapping meat for the freezer

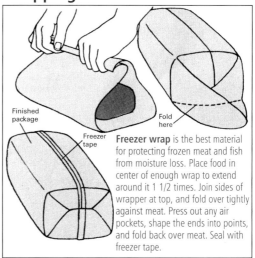

Finished package

Fold here

Freezer tape

Freezer wrap is the best material for protecting frozen meat and fish from moisture loss. Place food in center of enough wrap to extend around it 1 1/2 times. Join sides of wrapper at top, and fold over tightly against meat. Press out any air pockets, shape the ends into points, and fold back over meat. Seal with freezer tape.

food when you are ready to use it is to place it in the refrigerator, still in its sealed package, and let it warm gradually. For quick thawing run cold water over the package. You can cook frozen meat without thawing by allowing extra cooking time.

Canning for Convenience

Canning is convenient and economical. Canned foods are not endangered by power failures, they are easy to transport, and they keep a long time. Both meat and fish can be safely preserved either in glass jars or in tin cans, but jars are generally recommended because they cost less, are more convenient, and do not require a mechanical sealing device.

The greatest danger in canning is botulism, a severe and often fatal form of food poisoning caused by bacteria that thrive in dark, airless conditions. To be sure of killing the bacteria, you must treat the food and containers for an extended time at 240°F. To reach this temperature requires a pressure canner with its control set for at least 10 pounds. (For instructions on pressure canning, canning terminology, and canning equipment, see "Preserving Produce", pp.188–196.)

Meat, fish, and poultry can be canned by either the raw-pack or hot-pack method. Raw-packed food is put into containers before it is cooked; hot-packed food is cooked first. In both cases the presence of fat on the rim of the jar may spoil the canning seal, so it is safest to trim off as much fat as possible before packing. For raw packing cut the food into pieces, pack it loosely in sterilized jars, and add 1/2 teaspoon of salt per pint but no liquid. Place the uncovered jars in an open saucepan of water, and heat gently until a thermometer inserted in the middle of the meat reads 170°F—the temperature at which air is driven out and all yeast and mold spores are killed. This process, known as exhausting, may take an hour or longer. Cap the jars immediately according to the manufacturer's directions; then process them in a pressure canner.

To hot pack, cook the food thoroughly in salted water, and pack it loosely into jars, leaving 1-inch headspace. Next, fill the jars to within 1 inch of the top with boiling water or cooking broth. Make sure the rims of the jars are clean and free of fat before putting the caps on, then carry out the standard pressure canning procedure.

After the jars have been pressure processed and allowed to cool, check for a perfect seal. Metal lids should be slightly concave and should give a clear metallic ring when you tap them. If one fails to do so, either discard it or open it and reprocess the contents from the beginning. After they are checked, label all jars with the contents and date. Store them in a cool, dry, dark location (direct light can discolor the contents).

If a lid bulges during storage, or if the contents spurt or show any sign of being under pressure when the jar is opened, do not use the food. Botulism is extremely virulent, yet affected food may not show the usual signs of spoilage. When disposing of the food, be sure it will not be eaten by an animal or other person.

A guide for canning

Meat	Preparation	Time at 240°F (sea level)
Chicken, duck, goose, rabbit, squab, turkey, and other poultry and small game	Bone in: remove meat from breast; break legs and wings into short pieces	1-pt. jars . . . . .65 min. 1-qt. jars . . . . .75 min. No. 2 cans . . . . . 55 min. No. 2 1/2 cans . . . 75 min.
	Boneless: cut meat into chunks with skin attached	1-pt. jars . . . . .75 min. 1-qt. jars . . . . .90 min. No. 2 cans . . . . . .65 min. No. 2 1/2 cans . . .90 min.
Beef, lamb, pork, and veal	Cut raw meat into strips or chunks, or grind and cook as patties	1-pt. jars . . . . .75 min. 1-qt. jars . . . . No. 2 cans . . . . . 100 min. No. 2 1/2 cans . . .135 min.
Mackerel, salmon, trout, and other fish	Fillet large fish, for saltwater fish add 1 tbsp. vegetable oil per pt.	1/2-pt. jars . . . . . .90 min. 1-pt. jars . . . . . . .110 min. 1/2-lb. flat tins . . . 90 min. No. 2 cans . . . . . 100 min.
Smoked salmon	Use C-enamel cans	1/2-pt. jars . . . . . .95 min. 1/2-lb. flat tins . . .90 min. No. 2 cans . . . . . 100 min.

Curing and Smoking For Lasting Flavor

Curing, the first step in the smoking process, is essential for good flavor. In the old days a strong brine cure was the rule—pioneer women judged that there was enough salt and other ingredients in the brine when a raw potato floated. Such a powerful mixture resulted in meat that had excellent keeping qualities but was extremely salty. Before the meat was eaten it was generally desalted by soaking in cold water. Modern refrigeration has opened the way for mild, sweet cures in which flavor is more important than long-term preservation.

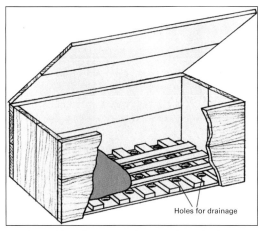

Hardwood box for dry-curing has a wooden rack at bottom for drainage space. Holes drilled in the bottom allow the escape of juices drawn from the meat or fish by the salt.

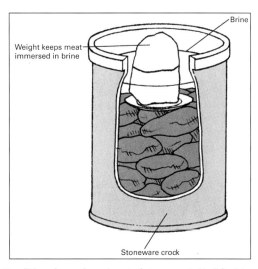

Traditional crock made out of stoneware is ideal for brine-curing, but any large container of pottery, plastic, or glass—even a sterile plastic garbage can—will serve the purpose. Do not use a metal container: salt water is highly corrosive, and the meat or fish can be contaminated. A seasoned hardwood barrel is also good for the job; avoid barrels made of softwood, such as pine, because the resins in the wood will leach into the brine and impart a bitter flavor to the meat or fish.

Not only curing methods but smoking methods as well have changed over the years. In former times meat was kept for days or even weeks in chambers filled with cool, dense smoke (the temperature rarely topped 110°F). The result was strongly flavored meat that would keep for a very long period. Modern methods of hot smoking require temperatures of at least 170°F in the smoke chamber. In this heat the meat cooks as it smokes, and to prevent dehydration it must be removed from the smoke chamber after a relatively short time. The only purpose of hot smoking is to add flavor—hot-smoked meat does not keep significantly better than other cooked meat.

Hot smoking can be done all year round, but lengthy curing and cold smoking are best accomplished when the weather is cool enough to prevent the meat from spoiling but not so cold that the meat freezes. For these reasons the best time to start a cold-smoking project is in the autumn, when nighttime temperatures approach freezing and the days are consistently cool.

How to Cure: Two Methods

Salt is the only essential ingredient for curing. It retards spoilage by drawing water out of meat or fish while simultaneously killing decay-causing microorganisms. Meat cured with salt alone will store well but will be tough and dry. Sugar or honey is often added for flavor as well as to keep the meat moist and tender. Herbs and spices can be included in the curing mixture according to personal taste, but do so cautiously; some combinations give unsatisfactory results. Garlic and pepper, for example, can overpower the flavor of a cure.

There are two curing methods: brine-curing and dry-curing. Dry-curing is faster, but many people prefer brine-curing because the results are more consistent and the flavor milder. In either case do not use ordinary table salt; the iodine it contains can discolor meat and fish. Pickling salt is the best type for curing. It has no additives, it is inexpensive, and since it is finely ground, it dissolves readily in brine cures and is quickly absorbed by the meat in dry cures. Other acceptable salts include rock salt, kosher salt, dairy salt, and canning salt.

Brine-curing. For a brine cure the curing mixture is dissolved in pure water. Boil questionable water first to kill bacteria and diminish chlorine, then let it cool. Lay larger pieces of meat or fish, skin side down, on the bottom of a watertight, nonmetal container, such as a stoneware crock, then pack smaller pieces on top. Fill the container with brine until the pieces start to shift. To keep the meat or fish submerged, cover it with a plate on which several weights have been placed; make sure no air pockets are trapped under the plate. Maintain the brine at 36°F to 40°F. After three to five days remove the meat from the brine, spoon off any scum, stir the brine up, and repack the crock. This procedure need be done only once for most cuts of meat; but if the pieces are large (a whole ham, for example), it should be repeated once a week until the cure is complete.

To check progress, cut off a small piece of meat, wash it, cook it thoroughly, and taste it. When the meat is cured to your taste, remove each piece from the crock and rinse it first in warm water, then in cold. Use a scrubbing brush to remove any encrustations of salt, and hang the pieces in a warm place to dry. When dry, red meats will generally have a glossy film of dissolved protein that helps to preserve them.

Dry-curing. In this process the meat or fish is packed directly in a mixture of salt and seasoning. Start by coating each piece; rub it in well and press extra mix into the crannies on the cut ends, especially around projecting bones. Cover the bottom of the curing box with a thick layer of curing mix and place the pieces of meat (or fish) on it. Pack more mix on and between the pieces, making sure each piece is well covered, especially where chunks touch, then put down another layer of meat. Continue until the final layer of meat is packed and covered. After three days remove the pieces of meat and recoat any surfaces that are not well coated. This process of checking and replenishing should be repeated every five days thereafter.

Making and Using a Smokehouse

The difference between a smokehouse designed for hot smoking and one designed for cold smoking is largely a matter of the distance between the smoke chamber and the fire: the greater the distance, the cooler the smoke. Proper ventilation is important with either smoking method, since smoke that is trapped in the chamber too long becomes stale and gives food a bitter taste. Too much ventilation, however, dissipates the smoke. Your best guide is the temperature inside the chamber; install a thermometer that can be read from outside, then open or close the vents as needed.

Meats are cold smoked for flavor or for long-term preservation. When the aim is preservation, the temperature should be between 70°F and 90°F; the maximum is 110°F, although large hams are sometimes smoked at higher temperatures. Locate the fire pit about 10 feet from the smoke chamber on the side from which the prevailing winds blow. The top of the pit should be about a foot lower than the bottom of the chamber with a stovepipe or tile-lined tunnel between.

Hot smoking requires temperatures of 170°F to 210°F, so the smoke chamber should be insulated. Smoke is produced inside or directly beneath the chamber. If you use an electric burner to produce smoke and heat, the job of maintaining a proper temperature is made easier.

The flavor that smoke adds depends on the wood being burned. Softwoods should not be used—their resins are ruinous to smoked food—but almost any hardwood is usable. The best smoke is produced from hickory, apple, or cherry. To use an electric burner, fill a 1-pound coffee can with damp shavings or chips, and place it on the top of a burner set to *low*; you will need to replenish the fuel about once an hour. Otherwise, start a fire with dry hardwood and let it burn to a bed of glowing coals before adding damp chips or shavings. Do not use a chemical fire starter—the odor will linger in the smoke.

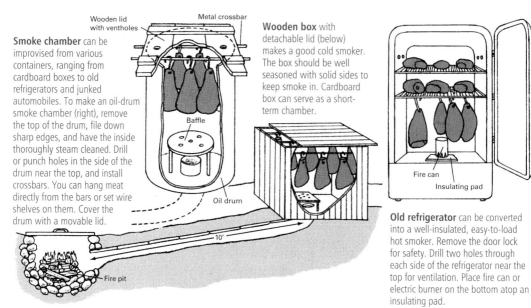

Smoke chamber can be improvised from various containers, ranging from cardboard boxes to old refrigerators and junked automobiles. To make an oil-drum smoke chamber (right), remove the top of the drum, file down sharp edges, and have the inside thoroughly steam cleaned. Drill or punch holes in the side of the drum near the top, and install crossbars. You can hang meat directly from the bars or set wire shelves on them. Cover the drum with a movable lid.

Wooden lid with ventholes

Metal crossbar

Baffle

Oil drum

10'

Fire pit

Wooden box with detachable lid (below) makes a good cold smoker. The box should be well seasoned with solid sides to keep smoke in. Cardboard box can serve as a short-term chamber.

Fire can

Insulating pad

Old refrigerator can be converted into a well-insulated, easy-to-load hot smoker. Remove the door lock for safety. Drill two holes through each side of the refrigerator near the top for ventilation. Place fire can or electric burner on the bottom atop an insulating pad.

When the chamber is filled with smoke and the temperature is right, load in the meat or fish. The best method is to hang the food from crossbars near the top. It can also be placed on mesh shelves of stainless steel or aluminum—not brass, copper, or galvanized steel. During smoking, continue to add damp fuel to maintain dense white smoke; should the smoke turn blue, it means the fuel supply is running low. If your smoke chamber is lined with metal, it is important to avoid the buildup of smoky deposits that will make new batches of smoked food bitter; clean and scrub the walls of the smoke chamber after every third or fourth use. Wooden walls are more difficult to clean, but they absorb much of the deposits and need not be scrubbed as often.

How to build a smokehouse

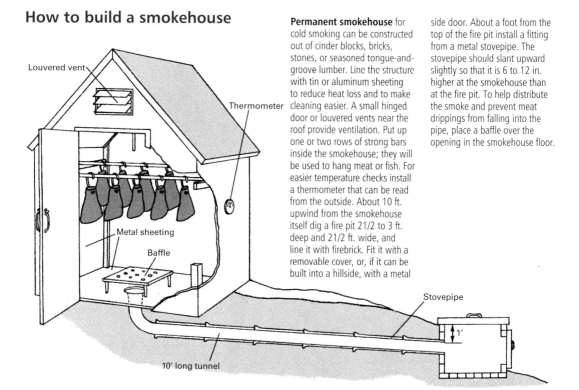

Louvered vent

Thermometer

Metal sheeting

Baffle

10' long tunnel

Stovepipe

Permanent smokehouse for cold smoking can be constructed out of cinder blocks, bricks, stones, or seasoned tongue-and-groove lumber. Line the structure with tin or aluminum sheeting to reduce heat loss and to make cleaning easier. A small hinged door or louvered vents near the roof provide ventilation. Put up one or two rows of strong bars inside the smokehouse; they will be used to hang meat or fish. For easier temperature checks install a thermometer that can be read from the outside. About 10 ft. upwind from the smokehouse itself dig a fire pit 21/2 to 3 ft. deep and 21/2 ft. wide, and line it with firebrick. Fit it with a removable cover, or, if it can be built into a hillside, with a metal side door. About a foot from the top of the fire pit install a fitting from a metal stovepipe. The stovepipe should slant upward slightly so that it is 6 to 12 in. higher at the smokehouse than at the fire pit. To help distribute the smoke and prevent meat drippings from falling into the pipe, place a baffle over the opening in the smokehouse floor.

Recipes and Techniques For Curing Poultry, Pork, Beef, and Game

Curing and smoking are inexact arts, and any attempt at precise instruction concerning the strength and duration of the cure, or the time spent in the smokehouse, will be frustrated by variables. The type of meat and its weight, size, and quality are considerations. So are temperature and the density of the smoke, both of which vary with humidity and air pressure. The way the salt is ground makes a difference, as does the kind of wood burned for smoke. The greatest variables of all are the tastes and intentions of the person doing the smoking.

If your purpose in curing and smoking a piece of meat is to preserve it, use a strong, salty brine cure, and cold smoke for the full recommended time. If you are not interested in long-term storage but merely wish to add tenderness and flavor, soak the meat in a marinade, or dry-cure it briefly in seasoned salt before hot smoking. The length of time a piece of meat should be hot smoked

Country-Style Ham and Other Pork Cures

The majority of traditional curing recipes are designed for pork. One reason is that the meat's rich taste is ideally complemented by curing and smoking. Another is that pork was the staple meat among early settlers, and smoking was the most practical way to store hams, pork shoulders, sides of bacon, and other large cuts.

Pumping a ham. To prevent rot at the heart of a large piece of pork, inject brine cure close to the bone. A brine pump to do the job can be bought at most agricultural supply stores. Sterilize the pump and fill it with 1 oz. of brine for each pound of meat. Thrust the needle deep into the meat; then press the plunger gently and steadily as you withdraw it. Pinch the opening closed to prevent brine from oozing out. Make four or five separate injections to distribute the cure evenly.

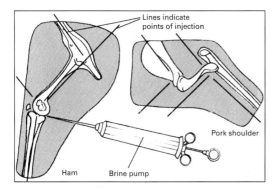

Lines indicate points of injection

Pork shoulder

Ham   Brine pump

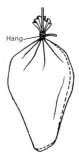
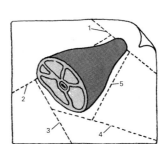

Protection from insects

Hang

Insect infestation is a major enemy of stored meat. To protect a ham after it has been cured and smoked, first wrap it in heavy brown paper according to the numbered sequence shown above. Place the wrapped ham in a fitted bag of strong sackcloth, tie the top with string or wire, and suspend the sack in a cool place. Inspect regularly for signs of insects, such as greasy spots or holes in the sackcloth. If the meat has been attacked, trim away all affected parts and use the remainder as soon as possible. Remove all meat from the storage area and spray room surfaces with a methoxychlor solution (1/2 lb. powder per gallon of water). When you replace the meat, do not allow it to contact sprayed surfaces.

Long-term preservation of large pieces of pork calls for thorough curing and cold smoking. The process, known as hard-curing, can take from 10 to 90 days, depending on the size and cut of meat. The result is the familiar, rich flavor of country-style ham, pork shoulder, and bacon. Of the many old-time methods of preservation with all their regional variations, this is still the most popular. The chart at right gives curing and smoking times.

You can also cure and smoke pork for flavor alone rather than for preservation. Cut the meat into pieces of no more than 4 pounds. Dry-cure up to a week or brine-cure up to nine days, then rinse and scrub the pieces, and hang them to dry. Smoke for one to four hours at 110°F to 120°F.

The cure recipes given at right can be used for either type of smoking. Always cook pork well before eating it. varies with temperature. The best guide is a reliable meat thermometer stuck deep into the meat.

Meat that has been cured and cold smoked for long-term preservation keeps best at 55°F to 60°F. It should be suspended to allow good air circulation, and pieces should not touch each other. Before storing smoked meat, clean the storage area thoroughly, and seal all cracks where dirt can collect or insects might breed.

The following basic curing recipes can be used with a variety of meats:

Sweet Pickle Brine

4 oz. pickling spices   3 cloves crushed garlic
21/2 gal. water   1 lb. sugar
21/2 lb. salt

Simmer spices in a cup of boiling water for 10 minutes, then mix with remaining water and other ingredients. Chill brine to 35°F, and add meat. Maintain temperature throughout curing.

Spicy Seasoned Salt

1 cup salt	1 tbsp. celery salt
4 tbsp. sugar	2 tsp. onion powder
4 tbsp. black pepper	2 tsp. garlic powder
4 tbsp. white pepper	1 tsp. sage

Mix all ingredients and store for several days in an airtight jar to allow the flavors to blend before applying to meat.

Curing Beef

Any cut of beef can be cured and smoked for preservation, but only the cheaper cuts, such as rump, chuck, and brisket, are really improved by the process. To give a smoky flavor to steaks and other good cuts without losing too much moisture, cook them first, then cold smoke them for a short time to taste. In curing beef for preservation, avoid dry cures; use a brine cure that is rich in sugar or molasses.

Corned Beef

2 1/2 lb. salt	1 lb. brown sugar
10 lb. brisket of beef	4 cloves garlic
1 gal. Water	4 tbsp. pickling spices

Rub 2 lb. of the salt into the meat, then place meat in a clean container for 24 hours. Boil water, and mix in sugar and remaining salt. Let cool, then pour brine over meat. Add garlic and spices, weight meat down, and cure for 30 days in refrigerator at 38°F to 40°F, turning meat every five days. Remove meat as needed; rinse in fresh water for a few hours before cooking. Keep remaining meat submerged in brine at 38°F to 40°F.

Pastrami

1 1/2 gal. water	6 crushed garlic cloves
3 lb. salt	2 tsp. black pepper
3 cups brown sugar	1 tsp. onion powder
4 tbsp. pickling spices	1/2 tsp. cayenne
8 crushed cloves	Whole brisket of beef

Mix all ingredients except brisket. Submerge brisket in brine and cure three to four days for each pound. Rinse and dry. Cold smoke for four hours, then finish by cooking in slow oven until center of meat reaches 140°F. Store in refrigerator.

The Ancient Art of Jerking

The word "jerky" is an Anglicized version of the Spanish *charqui*, which itself comes from the Peruvian *ch'arki*, meaning "dried meat." Jerky is a product that is so hard as to be nearly indestructible. It was a staple of American Indians as well as the Incas, and frontiersmen were quick

Cut of meat	Type of cure	Quantity of cure	Length of cure	Smoking
Ham or shoulder	Dry	1 lb. for every 12 lb.	2 days per lb.	1–4 days at 100°F –120°F
	Brine	To cover meat	4 days per lb.; 28 days max.	
Bacon or loin	Dry	1/2 lb. for every 12 lb.	11/2 days per lb.; 25 days min. for cuts over 2" thick	
	Brine	To cover meat	15–20 days	

Brine Cure for Pork

2 gal. water
3 lb. salt
1 lb. brown sugar
2 tbsp. black pepper
5 crushed cloves
1 tbsp. white pepper

Dry Cure for Pork

3 lb. salt
1 1/2 lb. brown sugar
5 crushed cloves
2 tbsp. black pepper
3 crushed bay leaves
1 tbsp. cinnamon

to learn jerking for their own survival. Today, jerky and its derivative, pemmican, are popular among campers and backpackers. The meat is nutritious, lightweight, and compact, and will remain edible for months or even years if stored in containers that have a bit of ventilation. Any meat can be jerked, but lean beef and venison produce the best results.

Brine-cured jerky. Cut lean meat into long, wide slabs about 1 inch thick, and cure for three to six days in the sweet pickle brine described on the opposite page. Then rinse and dry in a cool place. Use a very sharp knife to slice the meat lengthwise into 1/4-inch-wide slices (it will help to chill the meat to near freezing first). Hang the slices on racks and cold smoke at 75°F to 85°F for 12 to 36 hours. If the jerky snaps when it is bent rather than merely folding, it is ready.

Quick-cured jerky. Cut lean raw meat into very thin slices. Dip into a dry-curing mix (pure pickling salt will do) and suspend from racks. Smoke at 100°F to 120°F for two to four hours. Rinse off any encrustation of salt, and dry the meat between paper towels; then lay flat in baking trays and place in a cool oven (175° to 200°F) until meat is stiff and dry. Leave the oven door open to allow moisture to escape.

Pemmican. Pound some jerky into a powder or run it through a meat grinder. Add nuts, seeds, or dried fruit that have been finely chopped or ground. Bind the whole mixture together with melted beef fat and roll it into balls. Store in a lidded container in a cool, dry place.

Curing Poultry

Large birds with a high fat content, such as ducks, geese, and capons, respond well to smoking. Turkeys and large chickens can also be smoked but tend to become dry and tough unless they are basted frequently either with cooking oil or with their own juices. Because dry cures tend to make the problem worse, they are seldom used with any poultry—and never with chicken or turkey. For flavor the bird can be rubbed with a basic seasoning mixture, such as the spicy seasoned salt on this page. The more usual method is to brine-cure before smoking. Prepare the bird by cutting off its lower legs, head, and neck. Then remove the entrails and internal organs and wash the central cavity to remove all blood clots.

After brine-curing the bird, hot smoke it at 200°F to 225°F to taste, basting often to prevent drying. Alternatively, cold smoke until the skin turns a golden brown or deep reddish brown, then cook in oven. While cooking, keep the bird moist by wrapping it in tightly sealed aluminum foil along with a few tablespoons of water. Once the bird is smoked, use it immediately, since neither procedure contributes to preservation.

Brine Cure for Poultry

6 cloves	1 tbsp. onion powder
3 gal. water	1 tbsp. sage
3 lb. salt	Ginger, nutmeg, paprika
3 1/2 cups brown sugar	to taste (optional)
2 tbsp. dill salt	

Crush the cloves, and mix the ingredients in a crock. Submerge the bird in the mixture, and let it cure at 38°F to 40°F for 24 to 36 hours per pound. Rinse and dry the bird.

Dressing and Curing Game

All wild game should be field dressed as soon as it is killed. Start by removing any musk glands from the legs. Next, open the body cavity from the base of the tail to breastbone, cutting around the anus to free it. Remove the entrails, cut around the diaphragm and through the windpipe and gullet, and remove the heart and lungs. Roll the animal facedown to let the blood drain, then clean the body cavity by rubbing it with grass, paper, or cloth—do not wash it, since moisture speeds spoilage. Keep the carcass chilled if possible.

Bear. Use the same recipes and smoking techniques for bear as for pork. Bear meat, like pork, must be thoroughly cooked as a precaution against trichinosis.

Deer, elk, moose. Venison is even less fatty than beef. Use the sweet brine cure given below before smoking large pieces, or cut the meat into strips for jerky.

Sweet Brine Cure

3 gal. water	6 crushed bay leaves
5 1/2 lb. salt	3 tbsp. black pepper
3 1/2 cups brown sugar	

Small Game Marinade

1 cup wine	3 bay leaves
1 cup vinegar	1 tbsp. oregano
1/2 cup olive oil or	1 tsp. nutmeg
vegetable oil	2 cups water
1 medium onion, chopped	3 tbsp. sugar (optional)

Small game animals, such as rabbits and squirrels, are too lean to smoke well, but their flavor is enhanced by soaking in this marinade before cooking.

Smoking and Drying Food From the Sea

Almost every type of fish responds well to curing and smoking. The flavor of oilier fish, such as salmon and eel, is particularly enhanced by the process. Less juicy fish, such as pike, should be basted often while they are smoking to prevent them from becoming dried out.

Because fish rot quickly, they should be cleaned and dressed as soon as they are caught, then kept on ice

Jerking meat the American Indian way

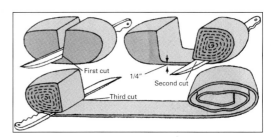

Indian women could produce a sheet of meat 1/4 in. thick by several yards long from a single chunk of lean meat. The technique was to cut down through the center to within 1/4 in. of the bottom, then outward in one direction, unwrapping the meat as the cutting proceeded until half the chunk was sliced. The chunk was then reversed and the other half cut the same way.

until they are processed. The processes of curing and smoking are quicker and easier with fish than with most meats. Only a brief period in the cure followed by a few hours in the smokehouse is sufficient to add a delicious flavor; with slightly extended treatment you can achieve long-term preservation.

A fish that is to be cold smoked should first be cured to extract surplus moisture. Removing water firms the flesh and helps preserve the fish during smoking. First soak the dressed fish in a solution of 1 cup of salt per gallon of water for half an hour, then either dry-cure for up to 12 hours or else brine-cure for two to four hours (see p.221). After curing, rinse the fish in fresh water, removing any lumps of salt with a stiff brush, then hang it to dry in a warm, shaded, well-ventilated place.

When the surface of the fish is absolutely dry, put it in the smokehouse. How long you smoke the fish depends on your personal taste and on how long you intend to store it. If you plan to eat the fish within a week, 24 hours of cold smoking should be sufficient. If you intend to keep it for several weeks, smoke the fish for up to five days, depending on its size and thickness: fillets will be ready the soonest, but steaks may require a few extra days. In either case expose the fish to light smoke by keeping the vent open for the first third of the total smoking period, then increase the density of the smoke, but keep the temperature in the chamber below 90°F.

Fish that is to be hot smoked need not be cured first; in fact, the combination of curing and smoke cooking will probably make it dry and tough. If you wish to add flavor, soak the fish briefly in a marinade or rub it with seasoned salt before moving it into the smoke chamber. Smoke it at a temperature of about 100°F for the first two to four hours, then gradually increase the temperature in the chamber to 140°F until the flesh is flaky. Eat the fish immediately, or let it cool, wrap it in wax paper, and refrigerate it.

Dressing Fish for Curing and Smoking

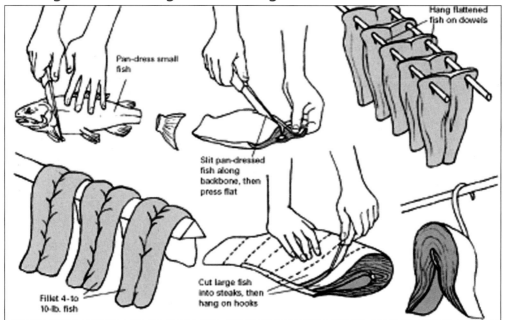

Prepare small fish (up to 4 lb.) for smoking by splitting and pressing. Start by pan-dressing the fish; then carefully cut down the length of the backbone, and press the fish flat. Pierce the flattened body through the upper corners with dowels, and hang it for smoking.

Fillets and steaks. Fillet a 4- to 10-lb. fish and hang the fillets over wooden bars in the smoke chamber. Cut larger fish into 1- to 2 in. thick steaks. First, pan-dress; then use a sharp knife to slice the body crosswise. Hang on hooks or place on mesh grills as with red meat.

Two Cures and a Marinade

The three recipes given below are good, basic formulas for curing almost any type of fish. For more tang you can add dried mustard, bay leaf, or other spices. The marinade only adds flavor but does not aid in preserving. After either cure, the fish should be left to dry until a glossy layer, called the pellicle, appears on its skin.

Dry Cure for Fish

1 lb. salt	2 tbsp. white pepper
1 lb. dark brown sugar	1 tbsp. onion powder
1 tbsp. garlic powder	

Combine ingredients 24 hours before cure is needed, and store in airtight container to allow flavors to blend.

Fish Marinade

1 cup pineapple juice	1/2 tsp. black pepper
8 tbsp. lemon juice	1 crushed garlic clove
4 tsp. soy sauce	

Brine Cure for Fish

5 qt. water	2 tbsp. onion powder
3 lb. salt	2 tbsp. oregano
2 cups brown sugar	

Smoked Salmon

A salmon's large size and oily flesh make it a prime candidate for smoking, and there are nearly as many recipes for smoked salmon as there are for smoked ham. Lox, a traditional favorite, is thoroughly cured and cold smoked and eaten raw. Other recipes use hot smoking.

Dress the salmon by removing the strip of fat near the dorsal fin but not the rest of the skin. Clean the central cavity, then fillet the fish, or—if the salmon is large—cut it into thick steaks. The salmon can be dry-cured in the spicy mixture described below or brine-cured by submerging the fillets or steaks in a very salty brine for one to two hours, then letting them drain.

Spicy Dry Cure for Salmon

1 lb. salt	2 oz. mace
2 lb. sugar	2 oz. white pepper
2 oz. allspice	2 oz. crushed bay leaves
2 oz. crushed cloves	

Mix ingredients thoroughly. Pack salmon fillets or steaks in mixture and cure for 8 to 12 hours. Rinse and dry fish. Smoke at 90°F for eight hours in light smoke, then increase density of smoke for 18 to 48 hours, depending on the flavor you like. (Or you can hot smoke the fish at 170°F until the flesh becomes flaky.) Store the salmon in a refrigerator.

Drying Fish in the Open Air

In an area where warm sun and low humidity can be relied on for at least a week at a time, the flesh of lean fish can be preserved without smoking by air drying it. Properly dried, a fish will keep without refrigeration for a year or longer, provided it is protected from moisture.

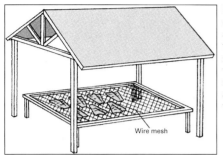

Fish should be dried in open air but shaded from direct sun. Ensure ventilation by spacing fish well apart on racks of wire mesh.

Wire mesh

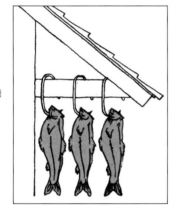

Small fish can be hung to dry under the eaves of a house or barn. Suspend each fish on its own metal hook. Bring fish inside at night and stack in a location that is dry and well ventilated.

Drying is not practical for salmon, catfish, and other species whose oil content exceeds 5 percent.

The only cure that is needed before drying is packing in salt. Finely ground pickling salt is best for the job. Clean and dress the fish as soon as it is caught; split and press fish that weigh less than 2 pounds and fillet larger fish; if the fish is large enough to require steaking, it is probably too fatty to be dried. Rinse the meat in a brine made from 1 cup of salt per gallon of water, towel it dry, then coat in salt, allowing about 1 pound of salt for every 4 pounds of dressed fish. Spread a layer of salt on the bottom of a dry-curing box (see p.214), and place a layer of fish, skin side down, on it. Cover with more salt, then add more layers of fish in the same manner. The last layer of fish should be placed skin side up. A small batch of fish may cure in 48 hours in warm weather; allow up to seven days for a large batch in cool temperatures.

When the weather is right—warm and dry but not too hot—take the fish from the curing box, rinse them, and clean off all salt, scrubbing with a stiff brush to remove any visible salt encrustations. Hang the fish or lay them on racks in a shady, well-ventilated place (direct sun will cause spoilage). Bring the fish inside every evening and stack them one atop another, head to tail, with the skin side down, except for the top fish, which should be placed skin side up. Then cover them, and press them with a weight about equal to the weight of the stacked fish.

Six warm days are usually required for thorough drying. To test for dryness, push on the flesh with your finger; if the impression remains, the fish is not yet dry. Should the weather turn before drying is complete, take the fish inside and wait for another good day. They can

be kept for up to two weeks in a cool, dry place, provided that every second day you restack them, putting the bottom fish on top and putting a little salt on each layer.

Preserving Fish in Brine

Oily fish that are not suitable for drying can be preserved without smoking by using their own juices to produce a strong brine. About 25 pounds of fish can be preserved in this manner in a 2-gallon stone crock.

Dress the fish according to size and score the flesh so the salt will penetrate faster. Soak them for an hour or two in a mild brine (1/2 cup salt to 1 gallon water). After draining, coat the fish with dry salt (allow about 1 pound for every 3 pounds of fish). Next, sprinkle a layer of salt in the bottom of the crock and place a layer of fish on top of it. Cover with another layer of salt, then another layer of fish. Continue in this way until the container is full. Weight the fish down. Within 2 to 10 days, depending on the size of the cuts, the salt and fish juices will have combined to make a thick brine. At this point remove the fish, rinse and brush them. Scrub the crock and replace the fish; then cover with strong brine (2 2/3 pounds of salt to 1 gallon of water). Store in a cool, dark place. Change the brine at least once every three months. If the weather is hot, change the brine more often.

Sausages and Scrapple: Delicious Techniques For Avoiding Waste

Autumn was the traditional time for slaughtering and putting up meat: the animals had been fattened during the summer, and cooler fall temperatures helped keep just-slaughtered meat fresh. Almost no part of a carcass was allowed to go to waste. Large joints of meat were carefully cured and smoked; organ meats were consumed immediately, and fat was rendered into lard for soap, candles, and shortening. Hides were fleshed and tanned, large bones used for broth, heads were boiled down to make headcheese, and the feet, or trotters, of pigs were stewed, jellied, or pickled. With all this accomplished, there were still many scraps of meat, fat, and innards that remained, waiting to be put to good use. Nowadays, such bits and pieces are discarded or ground up for pet food. In the old days, however, they were converted into sausage or scrapple with the intestine of a freshly slaughtered animal serving as casing.

Although sausages, scrapple, and headcheese are still produced commercially, traditional recipes and ingredients are seldom used. If you want to enjoy their special flavors, you will probably have to make them yourself—and when you make your own, you can include just the right blend of meats and spices to suit your own taste. The only special tool you will need is a meat grinder.

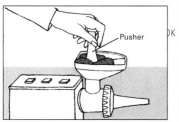

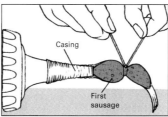

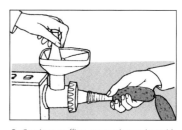

1. Meat grinder ensures that the meat is cut into fine ribbons rather than pulped. Use pusher, not your fingers, to press meat into the grinder.

2. Rinse casing thoroughly. Place it over nozzle, stuff a small section, and tie off tightly in the middle in order to give an airtight seal to the first sausage.

3. Continue stuffing, supporting casing with free hand to prevent kinks and bends. Tie off or twist each link. Tie off end, leaving a little meat outside.

Electric grinders do the job quickly and effortlessly but are expensive and, in general, designed for the processing of larger quantities of meat than you are likely to need. Food processors can be used to grind meat but have only limited value, since they will only produce a fine grind. Old-fashioned hand-cranked meat grinders call for a bit of elbow grease but are still best for home use; they will not overheat the meat while it is being ground, and they come with several cutter plates for finer or coarser grinds plus an attachment for stuffing sausages.

Plastic casings and other types of artificial casings are available in various sizes but are difficult to use. For the home sausagemaker the best casings are probably those made from the small intestine of a hog or sheep. They can usually be bought from a butcher who makes his own sausages. If you want to try making your own casings, you will need the intestine from a freshly slaughtered animal. Clean it thoroughly, scraping both sides to remove all traces of fat and mucus (this is a time-consuming job). Rinse the intestine in several changes of water, and store it in brine until it is needed. Hog casings can be used for sausages up to 1 1/2 inches in diameter; larger casings are commonly made of light weight muslin.

Any kind of meat, poultry, or game can be used for sausage, from the cheapest to the most expensive. The lower the quality of the meat, however, the poorer the sausage is likely to be. Although pork and beef are commonly used, lamb, veal, and poultry will also serve the purpose—and venison sausage is a rare treat. No matter what type of meat is employed, it is important to strike a balance between fat and lean meat: about two parts lean meat to one part fat is satisfactory in most cases. Too little fat results in hard, dry sausages; too much fat results in greasy sausages that shrink when they are cooked. When stuffing the sausage casings, it is important to avoid air bubbles, since they can become pockets of spoilage; if any exist in the finished sausage, prick them with a needle. To give a soft texture and consistency to the meat so that it will fill the casings easily, it is a good idea to add a little water or wine.

Many types of sausage and scrapple must be eaten soon after they are prepared or else stored in a freezer. Other types, such as hard sausages, benefit from aging and will keep unrefrigerated for considerable periods of time. If you plan to preserve your sausages by freezing there are certain seasonings to avoid: garlic loses its flavor, sage produces an off flavor if it is kept frozen too long, and salt may cause a rancid taste after about a month of freezing.

Old-fashioned Pork Sausage

4 lb. lean pork	3 tsp. pepper
2 lb. pork fat	1 1/2 tsp. sugar
3 1/2 tsp. salt	3/4 tsp. ground clove 6
tsp. sage	2/3 cup cold water

Thoroughly chill meat and fat and put them separately through grinder with 1/2-in. cutting plate. Chill meat again. Combine all seasonings and mix into meat, then put through grinder with 1/8-in. cutting plate. Mix meat and fat in a bowl and add just enough water to make a soft dough. Stuff into casings of muslin or hog intestine, taking care to avoid air bubbles. Hang sausages in a cool, dry place (or in the refrigerator) for one to two days. These sausages gain from being cold smoked at about 80°F for 10 to 14 hours until they turn a deep, dark brown. Store under refrigeration. Cook before serving.

Traditional Recipes for Sausage, Scrapple, and Headcheese

The different regions of America developed sausage recipes tailored to local food resources and ethnic traditions. Another influence was weather: sausages that are stuffed with cured meat and then smoked afterward have superior keeping qualities in warm climates. Many sausages are made with uncooked pork; they must be thoroughly cooked before they are eaten.

Indiana Farm Sausage

This herb-flavored sausage is delicious fried for breakfast, especially with eggs or pancakes and syrup.

4 lb. lean pork	2 tsp. thyme
1 lb pork fat	2 tsp. basil
2 cloves garlic, minced	4 tsp. salt
2 tsp. black pepper	2 tbsp. sage
2 tsp. chili powder	2 tbsp. parsley

Manual and electric grinders usually come with a stuffing attachment. A variety of other sausage-stuffing devices are available, including a stuffing tube with matching wooden plunger and a funnel through which the meat is pressed by hand.

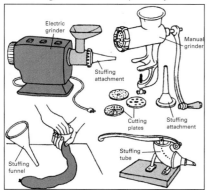

| 2 tsp. cayenne | 2 onions |
| 2 tsp. marjoram | 6 tbsp. iced water |

Cut meat and fat into chunks, add seasonings, and grind with medium cutting plate. Grind onions. Knead ground meat and onion in bowl and add iced water to give a soft dough consistency. Stuff into hog casings. Store in refrigerator.

Southwestern Sausage

Although well-flavored and spicy, this Spanish-Indian sausage is not quite as hot as the Mexican *chorizo*.

2 1/4 lb lean pork	1 tsp. black pepper
3/4 lb. kidney suet or fat	1 tsp. ground coriander
5 cloves garlic, minced	1 1/2 tsp. cumin
4-6 chili peppers, chopped	Salt to taste
1/2 cup onion, finely chopped	1/2 tsp. Tabasco
1/4 cup brandy	1/2 cup vinegar
1/3 cup chili powder	

Grind lean pork and fat together with coarse cutting plate. Combine garlic, peppers, onion, brandy, and seasonings. Mix into meat along with Tabasco and vinegar. Stuff into casings, lying off each link at 4 in. Hang in a warm, breezy, insect-free place to dry for 24 hours. Store in refrigerator.

Summer Sausage

Although the traditional recipe contains some pork, beef and beef fat can be used throughout.

6 lb. lean beef	2 lb. lean pork
Sweet Pickle Brine	2 lb. pork fat
(see p.226)	8 whole black peppercorns
4 tbsp.salt	2 tbsp. coriander seed
4 tsp. garlic powder	Pinch mustard seed
3 tbsp. white pepper	2 1/2 cups dry red wine

Cut the beef into 2-in. chunks and place in a crock. Cover with brine; use weight to keep meat submerged. Remove the meat and stir the brine every four days. After 8 to 12 days remove beef, rinse it, and place it in the refrigerator to drain for 24 hours; then cut it into smaller chunks, and mix with the salt, garlic powder, and white pepper. Grind the beef, pork, and pork fat twice through 3/16-in. plate, and mix. Mix in other seasonings and wine; let stand for 48 hours in refrigerator. Stuff into muslin casings. Cold smoke at 80°F for 12 to 14 hours until the skin turns dark brown (the sausage will dry and shrink by as much as one-third). Hang the sausage in a refrigerator or other cool place for at least two weeks. Use in salads and for snacks. Store in refrigerator.

For a faster recipe grind pork and beef through coarse cutting plate and mix in 14 oz. of Dry Cure for Pork (see p.218). Regrind through same plate, knead meat in a glass or plastic bowl, and place in the refrigerator for 48 hours. Then mix in salt and other ingredients and continue as with brine-cure recipe.

Old-Style Frankfurters

Turn of the century cartoonist Tad Dorgan deserves credit for the name "hot dog"; his drawing of a frankfurter as a dachshund encased in a bun inspired the term. Store frankfurters under refrigeration.

1 1/2 lb. pork loin or shoulder	1/2 tsp. coriander
1 lb. pork fat	1/2 tsp. nutmeg
2 tbsp. salt	1/2 tsp. cinnamon
1 tsp. white pepper	

Cure the meat for three days in the Brine Cure for Pork (p.218); then grind it two times, along with the fat, through a coarse cutting plate. Mix in salt and seasonings, and grind again through a medium-fine cutting plate. Slowly add 1 cup of iced water and mix thoroughly. Stuff into hog casings about 18 in. long. Secure at both ends and twist in the middle to make two long, thin sausages from each length of casing. Hang to dry for 24 hours; then cold smoke for eight hours or until sausages turn deep brown. To cook, simmer in boiling water for 10 minutes.

Scrapple

This Pennsylvania Dutch delicacy, once popular in many parts of America, has slowly lost favor; a shame because it is tasty, economical, and easy to make.

5 lb. pork scraps, including	3 cups cornmeal
bony meat, liver, kidneys,	Freshly ground
and heart	pepper, sage, thyme, 1
gal. Water	and salt to taste

Boil liver, kidney, and heart in salted water until tender. Remove from pot and cut into small pieces. Mix with other meat and return to water. Boil until meat shreds when tested with two forks (there should now be about 3 qt. of broth). Remove any bones, then slowly add cornmeal to pot, stirring constantly until the mixture starts to thicken. Continue to cook until the scrapple has a thick, mushy consistency. Season with plenty of pepper plus sage, thyme, and salt. Pour into greased molds and allow to cool. To cook, cut into 1/4 to 1/2-in. slabs, coat in flour, and fry in butter. Serve with eggs for breakfast or as a tasty trimming with roast game birds. Philadelphia scrapple is made the same way but only shoulder and neck meat is used. Store in refrigerator.

Sources and resources

Books and pamphlets

Ashbrook, Frank G. *Butchering, Processing and Preservation of Meat*. New York: Chapman & Hall, 1973.

Dubbs, Chris, and Dave Heberle. *The Easy Art of Smoking Food*. New York: Winchester Press, 1978.

Eastman, Wilbur F., Jr. *The Canning, Freezing, Curing & Smoking of Meat, Fish & Game*. Charlotte, Vt.: Garden Way Publishing, 1975.

Sleight, Jack, and Raymond Hull. *Home Book of Smoke Cooking Meat, Fish and Game*. Harrisburg, Pa.: Stackpole Books, 1982.

Stoner, Carol Hupping, ed. *Stocking Up III*. New York: Fine Communications, 1995.

U.S. Department of Agriculture Staff. *Complete Guide to Home Canning, Preserving and Freezing*. New York: Dover, 1994.

Making a muslin sausage casing

Sew here

To case extra-large sausages (more than 4 in. in diameter), fold and sew a piece of muslin into a tubular shape, turn it inside out, and dampen with water just before stuffing.

Making Your Own Dairy Products

Savory Dairy Treats Preserve Fresh Milk's Nutritional Values

Dairying–the collection and processing of milk into such foods as cheese, butter, and yogurt—has been practiced since man first domesticated wild animals. Cheese, in fact, is one of the first man-made foods: well-preserved cheeses were found in the tombs of the pharaohs, and in 1948 a 2,000-year-old cheese was discovered in Siberia—reportedly still edible.

The reason for most milk processing is preservation. Milk is an almost perfect food, containing most of the essentials for human nutrition: protein for growth and muscle development, fat for digestion and warmth, carbohydrates for energy, vitamins and minerals for general health and well-being. But milk spoils rapidly in its natural state. By converting it into dairy by-products, its nutritive value can be retained for long periods of time.

Different regions of the world have developed their own recipes and methods for handling milk. In Eastern Europe and the Middle East yogurt is particularly popular. Calabash, an African specialty, is a form of fermented milk named for the dried and hollowed gourds in which it is made and stored. In Europe and America more than a thousand varieties of cheese have been developed over the centuries.

If you have your own milk animals or a supply of raw milk or unhomogenized pasteurized milk, you can separate cream to use fresh or make into butter, buttermilk, and ice cream. The remaining skimmed milk can be converted into yogurt or cottage cheese. With a plentiful supply of raw milk you can also learn the intricacies of cooking, pressing, and aging your own cheeses.

Good Milk Makes Good Dairy Foods

Almost all milk sold in supermarkets and grocery stores has been pasteurized to destroy bacteria and homogenized to break up butterfat particles. This commercial milk can be used for making yogurt and kefir but will only make soft low-quality cheeses and cannot be used at all for making butter, since

Over the centuries a variety of butter churns were developed, all designed to ease the tedium and effort involved in the weekly butter-churning chore. The Victorian advertisement at left features the latest in 19th-century centrifugal churns, a sophisticated model that is geared for rapid churning and can be operated with only one hand. The drum of the churn is made of wood, a material that does not react with the lactic acid in milk. Many old dairying items are now sought-after antiques. Cheese presses, decorative butter stamps, molds, scales, and ice cream makers all command premium prices. In addition, a lively business has sprung up in working replicas of these old implements. As a result, almost any dairying tool you need is available in its old-fashioned form as well as its modern equivalent.

the cream will not separate out. Reconstituted instant dried milk will produce a good soft cheese and some simple hard cheeses. However, to make a full range of dairy products, you will need a source of raw milk. If you do not have your own milk animals, you may be able to buy raw milk from health food stores or other outlets. In some states you can purchase raw milk direct from the farm, but be sure that the animals have been tested for disease and have been milked under hygienic conditions.

The diet of milking cows and goats will affect the quality and flavor of their milk. Goats should be allowed to browse over weeds and scrub, since such plants provide the extra minerals and proteins that the animals need. Cows will produce their best milk on rich pasturage. Any strong-smelling foodstuff, including turnips, wild onions, or garlic, can flavor the milk.

After an animal gives birth do not use its milk for four days (in the case of goats) or for two weeks (in the case of cows). During these periods the milk is of a special type called colostrum, high in protein, minerals, vitamins, and antibodies but low in sugar and fats. It is unsuited for most dairy uses. Moreover, colostrum is essential to the health of the newborn animals. You should also avoid using milk from cows or goats that appear to be sick. If an animal is treated with antibiotics or other drugs, wait at least three days after the treatment before using its milk. When processing or storing milk or cream, use wooden, glass, ceramic, enamel, or stainless steel equipment; milk contains lactic acid, a substance that reacts with many metals.

About 6 percent of Americans have difficulty in digesting cow's milk. In infants the problem is usually manifested by symptoms of stomach upset. As the baby grows older and its digestive system develops, the problem often disappears, but in some cases a more-or-less permanent allergy develops. If undetected, the allergic reaction can be severe, even fatal, particularly in infants less than six months old. Goat's milk is often helpful for children and adults who have problems digesting cow's milk. It is easier to digest and does not contain some of the complex proteins found in cow's milk, which are the usual causes of allergy.

Hygiene Is Vital When Processing Milk

All fresh milk contains bacteria, most of them harmless, some beneficial to the human digestive system, and others vital in the production of cheese and butter. Certain strains, however, are pathogenic and can transmit diseases, such as brucellosis (undulant fever) and tuberculosis. If you intend to use raw milk for dairying purposes, it is of the utmost importance that it be taken from cows or goats that have been tested and found free of disease. This is just as important whether the milk is from your own animals or has been purchased elsewhere.

Even though your milk may be good to start with, it can quickly go bad. Your dairy hygiene should aim to prevent contamination by pathogenic bacteria and inhibit the excessive multiplication of all bacteria. If you milk your own animals, maintain strict standards of cleanliness while milking, and take the milk from the milking shed to your dairy room as soon as it is collected. Once in the shed, cool the milk quickly to about 40°F and maintain it at that temperature until it is used. To eliminate any possibility of harmful bacteria, pasteurize your milk by heating it gently to 145°F for 30 minutes or to 158°F for 15 seconds. Cool it immediately after it has been pasteurized. Pasteurization, however, can interfere with some dairying processes.

The dairying room should be cool, dust free, well ventilated, and well lit. All dairying equipment must be kept scrupulously clean and should be free from cracks, sharp corners, nicks, or other spots where dirt can collect. Clean the equipment immediately after it is used. First rinse it in cold water, then wash it in warm water with a dairy detergent. (Standard detergents may leave a residual flavor that will spoil the taste of the milk.) Next, scald the equipment by pouring boiling water over it. The equipment can then be left to air dry. Every few weeks, completely sterilize all your dairy implements by washing them in a chlorine solution or placing them in an electric oven at 250°F for 15 minutes. From time to time clean off any milkstone—a hard, transparent milk residue—that may have formed on your equipment. Use commercial milkstone solvent, a product that is available from dairy suppliers.

Keep milk away from any strong barnyard, household, or food smells, since milk, particularly goat's milk, absorbs odors very easily, and never use milk that seems abnormal. An unusual flavor in fresh milk can mean contamination and a high bacteria count. If fresh milk tastes off or sour, check your dairy hygiene and the health of your livestock as well as their diet.

Separating Cream From Milk

To extract cream from cow's milk, put fresh, chilled milk in shallow dishes in a cool place. After 12 to 24 hours the cream will have risen to the surface. Gently skim it off with a spoon or ladle until you come to the bluish "skim milk" underneath. Store the cream in the refrigerator in a clean, covered jar.

The cream obtained from goat's milk, unlike cow's cream, is pure white. It is also lighter, easier to digest, and whips to a greater bulk. Unfortunately, goat's cream is very finely emulsified within the milk and several days are needed for even a small amount to rise to the surface. During this period the cream, which picks up odors very easily, often takes on an unpleasant flavor. Although separation can be speeded by adding cow's milk, the best way to obtain significant quantities of goat's cream is to use a separator, a centrifugelike device that automatically splits whole milk into skim milk and cream. Separators are expensive, however, unless you are lucky enough to find a used one—even a low-priced separator will cost several hundred dollars if it is bought new. As a result, a cream separator is worthwhile only if you are milking several animals. If you are thinking of getting a separator, be sure it can be adjusted finely enough to work with goat's milk.

One solution to the problem of getting cream quickly and easily is to make Devonshire cream. Set whole cow's or goat's milk in heat-proof pans for 12 to 24 hours, then warm the pans gently to 187°F. When the surface of the milk begins to wrinkle and crack, remove the pans from the heat. When the milk is cool, skim off the surface. This will produce a rich, delicious, thick-textured cream.

A time-honored way to get cream is to leave fresh cow's milk overnight in large, shallow pottery bowls. The next day the cream can be scooped off with a wooden or brass skimmer.

Churning Fresh Butter Out of Your Cream

Butter can be made from cream that has been ripened (slightly soured) or from fresh cream. Ripened cream churns more rapidly and produces butter with more flavor; sweet cream butter is comparatively bland. To ripen cream, let it stand at room temperature for 12 to 24 hours until the surface appears glossy and the cream has a slightly acid taste. If it is allowed to stand longer, the butter may have a sour flavor.

Any form of agitation—the dairyman's term is concussion—that brings together the globules of butterfat that are suspended in cream will yield butter. The equipment need not be expensive. Even a hand whisk or an electric beater will work for small quantities of cream. Some people churn butter simply by shaking cream in a covered jar. In the Middle East butter was once made by filling leather bags with cream, then strapping the bags onto the backs of horses. If you intend to make butter for your family on a regular basis, however, it would pay to invest in a home churn. Most are powered by an electric motor and can process from 1 to 5 gallons of cream at a time, but several types of manual churns are available.

Bring the temperature of the cream to about 60°F before churning. This is an important step; if you churn cream at a higher temperature, the butter will be soft and keep poorly, while if you churn at a lower temperature, the butter will take much longer to form, or come.

After 15 minutes of churning, the cream should begin to feel heavy. If it does not, check the temperature. When using goat's cream, it helps to add a tablespoon or two of cold skimmed cow's milk at this stage. After another 10 to 20 minutes the cream should separate into buttermilk and grain-sized pellets of butter.

Once the granules have formed, stop churning, drain the buttermilk from the churn, and thoroughly rinse the butter with cold water. The buttermilk should be saved for later use—it can be used in baking or consumed directly by drinking it plain or in milkshakes. The butter can be rinsed in the churn, but a better way is to place it on a cheesecloth in a colander and let cold water run over it. Next, work the butter granules together with a butter paddle or wooden spoon. You will probably want

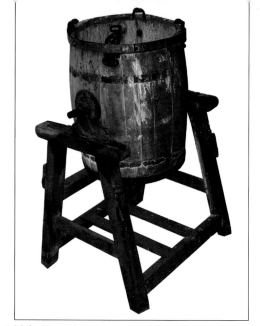

Old-fashioned wooden barrel churn allows more cream to be processed at once. Buttermaking equipment is available from mail order firms, online sources, and country stores.

to add salt at this time—1/4 to 1/2 teaspoon per pound of butter—since unsalted butter spoils quickly. Wrap the finished butter in wax paper and place it inside a refrigerator to protect it from light and air.

If you use ripened cream, you can avoid any risk of an unpleasant taste by pasteurizing it first. Heat the cream in a double boiler to a temperature of 180°F to 200°F for 40 minutes. Then let the cream cool for 12 hours, and add a small amount of starter, such as cultured buttermilk, sour cream, or yogurt, before churning. Follow the same procedure if the cream comes from an animal that is near the end of lactation; cream taken at that time will be difficult to churn into butter.

For Flavor and Health Try Fermented Milks

Any milk or cream that is allowed to stand at room temperature will soon ferment and curdle because of bacterial action. With careful timing, thorough sterilization of the milk or cream, and the use of pure cultures of desirable bacteria, this natural spoiling process can yield such healthful and delicious cultured milk products as yogurt, sour cream, buttermilk, and kefir.

Cultured milks not only taste good, but they are also easy on the stomach. Part of the reason is that lactose, a complex, hard-to-digest milk sugar, breaks down during fermentation. In addition, the bacteria used in making cultured milks help relieve certain stomach upsets and can restore the natural bacterial balance of the stomach after antibiotic treatments.

Raw milk, pasteurized milk, powdered milk, and homogenized milk can all be used to make cultured milk products. Raw milk must be pasteurized before it is used, but pasteurized milk need not be repasteurized if the containers are kept sealed until use.

In addition to the milk or cream that will form the base of your yogurt or other fermented product, you will

Making Butter With a Hand Churn

1. Bring cream to temperature of 60°F before churning (a degree or two warmer if the dairying room is cold). Temperature can be adjusted by placing cream jar in warm or cool water.
2. Fill churn partway with cream (one-third for maximum

concussion), and begin churning immediately. Butter should "come" within 30 minutes. If it does not, check temperature.
3. Pour off buttermilk, and rinse butter granules several times in cold water until the water runs completely clear.

Any buttermilk left behind will make the butter taste sour.
4. Work the butter with a butter paddle to remove remaining moisture and to mix any salt that has been added. Put butter in molds or shape pats with paddles and stamps.

need a starter—a culture of the proper strain of bacteria. The safest and surest way is to buy a fresh, unadulterated starter from a dairy supplier. You can also achieve good results, with less work, by using a portion of a store-bought fermented milk product as your starter, provided it does not contain flavoring or sweetener. Check to make sure that the product has not been repasteurized after culturing, since repasteurization destroys most of the desirable bacteria. Preservatives will also affect the bacteria adversely.

Once you begin producing a cultured milk, you can keep making it again and again by reculturing—using a portion of the old batch to begin a new batch. It is important to reculture within 10 days after the first batch has been made, since the bacteria will be destroyed by long refrigeration. Cover all containers tightly during culturing and refrigeration (except for kefir), and maintain strict hygienic standards to avoid contamination. Eventually, however, a starter will lose its vigor. If the flavor of a freshly cultured milk product appears to be inferior or the product takes longer to thicken, it is time to buy a new starter. The flavor and texture of cultured milk products will improve if they are refrigerated for at least a few hours after being cultured.

Buttermilk is a term applied to two different products. One is simply the milk fraction left over after butter is made; the other, cultured buttermilk, is produced like yogurt—by the fermentation of skim milk. Buttermilk from churned butter varies in taste depending on whether the cream was ripened or not and on which bacteria happen to develop. To make cultured buttermilk—a much more consistent product—allow 1 quart of low-fat milk to reach room temperature, then add 1/4 to 1/2 cup of previously cultured buttermilk and leave overnight in a warm place (80°F to 85°F). Refrigerate as soon as the milk reaches the desired level of acidity. Buttermilk adds flavor and lightness to baked goods and is useful as a starter for cheeses.

Yogurt, a centuries-old favorite of Middle Eastern peoples, has become the best known and most popular cultured milk product sold in America. By making your own yogurt, you can experiment with different milks,

starters, incubation temperatures, and culturing times to produce the flavor you like best.

Begin by sterilizing a quart of low-fat milk by heating it briefly to 180°F. Allow the milk to cool to about 105°F (just above body temperature). Add 2 tablespoons of starter from a dairy supplier or 4 tablespoons of store-bought yogurt. Stir in thoroughly, then set the cultured milk to incubate undisturbed at 105°F to 112°F for two to three hours. Yogurt can be cultured at any temperature between 70°F and 120°F, but it takes longer to thicken at the lower temperatures and may have a sour flavor. As soon as the yogurt retains the impression of a spoon pressed into its surface, stop incubation and refrigerate. This will prevent the yogurt from becoming very acid and help it keep longer. If the yogurt is lumpy, it means too much starter was used.

For a richer, sweeter yogurt, use whole milk or a mixture of milk and cream. For a thicker curd, add up to 3 tablespoons of powdered milk per quart of milk. After the yogurt has thickened, you can add fresh fruit, fruit preserves, nuts, honey, maple syrup, or even a strong brew of sweetened coffee as flavoring.

Sour cream is thicker and stronger tasting than yogurt and is generally eaten in conjunction with other

Cultured milks must be kept warm while they develop. The top of a refrigerator or warming oven of a wood stove are good locations. A pan set on top of a radiator or stove-top pilot light also works well. Another method is to place the warmed containers in a picnic carrier filled with crumpled newspaper.

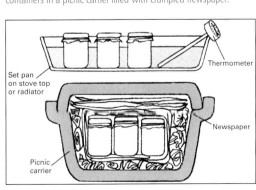

Set pan on stove top or radiator

Thermometer

Newspaper

Picnic carrier

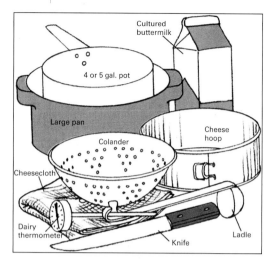

Cheesemaking implements should be made of stainless steel, enamel, glass, or wood and should be kept scrupulously clean. You will need a 4- or 5-gal. pot and a somewhat larger pan that can hold the pot. When heating the milk, fill the pan partway with water and set the pot in it so that the combination functions as a double boiler; leave enough space between to test the temperature of the water. Other useful supplies include a good dairy thermometer, a long knife for slicing the curdled milk, a large ladle, and several yards of cheesecloth. A cylindrical mold, or cheese hoop, and a cheese press—both required for making hard cheese—can be improvised or purchased.

foods. It makes an excellent base for dips and goes well with salads, potatoes, and some soups. Use fresh, heavy cream that has been pasteurized at 150°F to 160°F for 30 minutes. Mix 1 cup of cream with 11/2 cups of pasteurized whole milk, then add 1/2 cup of cultured buttermilk. Raise the temperature of the mixture to that of a warm room (68°F to 70°F), and let it stand for 12 to 24 hours or until it is sufficiently sour and thick enough to cling firmly to a spoon. Keep it in the refrigerator until you want to use it. For a richer, heavier sour cream combine 2 cups of pasteurized heavy cream with 5 teaspoons of cultured buttermilk and incubate as before. For better texture refrigerate for 24 hours before serving.

Kefir, sometimes called the champagne of milk, is similar to yogurt but thinner, milder, and easier to culture. Kefir starter consists of individual grains made up of a combination of yeast and several strains of bacteria. The yeast gives kefir a slight fizz and a small alcoholic content. Kefir grains are difficult to obtain. Some firms sell them in a milk base or in freeze-dried form. The more widely available powdered cultures do not seem to produce as good results as the grains.

To make kefir, add 1/2 to 1 cup of grains to a quart of skim milk. Cover, but do not seal the mixture, and allow it to stand at room temperature for 12 to 48 hours until it has a mild acid taste and has achieved the desired degree of carbonation. Strain the grains from the milk and rinse them thoroughly in cold water, then add them to a new batch of milk. Refrigerate the cultured milk. To slow down the process, culture the kefir at a lower temperature of 55°F to 60°F.

The grains multiply rapidly, so some must be removed periodically to prevent the kefir from becoming too

thick. To preserve grains that have been removed, wash them thoroughly, then let them dry between two pieces of cheesecloth in an airy location. To revive dried grains, place them in a cup of milk for 24 hours; drain, rinse, and add another cup of milk. After two days the amount of milk can be gradually increased to a quart.

Cheese: The Most Varied Of the Milk By-products

According to legend, cheese was discovered by a Middle Eastern traveler named Kanana, who was carrying milk in a bag made from a lamb's stomach. When Kanana paused to drink, he noticed that his milk had coagulated into a custardlike mass. More daring than most, he sampled this odd substance and found it surprisingly pleasant. What had happened was that rennin—an enzyme found in the stomachs of newborn lambs, kids, and calves—had transformed the milk into curds and whey. The process is known as curdling, and it is the fundamental step in the production of all cheeses.

There are two types of cheese: soft and hard. Soft cheeses are made from unpressed curds and must be eaten within a week or two. Hard cheeses take longer to prepare but keep better in storage. Cow's milk is the most popular base for both types of cheese. Goat's milk cheese can be quite mild when fresh but tends to develop a strong ammonia taste if kept for long. Sheep's milk is employed for genuine Roquefort, while traditional mozzarella is made from the milk of the water buffalo. The richest, creamiest cheeses are made from whole raw milk. However, skim milk and reconstituted dried instant milk can be used for most cheese recipes and are particularly suitable for cottage cheese. If you use pasteurized milk, ripen it by adding cultured buttermilk or a cheese starter. Do not use homogenized milk; it will produce weak curds and a watery cheese.

Rennet, the substance that contains the chemical agent rennin needed to curdle the milk, is available at dairy suppliers and some pharmacies, often being stocked as junket tablets. If you use junket tablets, be sure they are unflavored. Originally, rennet was simply dried pieces of stomach from newborn calves.

Making Basic Hard Cheese

Large cheeses tend to ripen better, so start with at least a gallon of milk–enough to make 11/2 to 2 pounds of cheese. Either raw milk or unhomogenized pasteurized milk is satisfactory. The ideal milk for making cheese is a blend of equal parts of raw morning milk (fresh milk that has just been collected) and evening milk (milk that was collected the night before and allowed to stand at room temperature overnight). If pasteurized milk is to be used, it must first be ripened. Heat the milk in a double boiler to 86°F and stir in 1 cup of unpasteurized, preservative-free cultured buttermilk per gallon of milk. Let the milk stand for 30 minutes if you want a mild cheese or up to three hours for a sharp, strong-tasting cheese.

Once the milk is ready, the next step is to add rennet to coagulate, or curdle, it. Rennet tablets are sold for use in junketmaking and, in more concentrated form, for cheesemaking. For basic hard cheese, use one-eighth of a cheese rennet tablet or 1 1/4 junket tablets per gallon of milk. Dissolve the rennet in 30 to 40 times its volume of cool water before putting it in the milk. Once the rennet is added, stir the milk thoroughly and place it in a warm location where it will not be disturbed.

After about 45 minutes a thin layer of watery whey will appear on top, while the firm, custardlike curds will form beneath. Cut the curds immediately, since they soon begin to deteriorate. Slice them into even-sized cubes so they will all cook at the same speed. Cubes measuring about 1/2 inch will produce a moist cheese; smaller 1/4-inch cubes will give a dry cheese. Next, mix the cut curds for 10 minutes, then start to heat the curds and whey very slowly. If the curds are heated too quickly, they will become tough

Cream cheese: an easy-to-make treat

Combine 2 cups heavy cream with 2 tbsp. buttermilk, then suspend the mixture in a clean piece of cloth over a bowl for 24 hours or until the cream thickens. (The longer you leave it suspended, the drier the cheese will be.) Season with salt and herbs to taste. For a tangy cream cheese with less fat, use yogurt in place of the cream and buttermilk.

Two presses you can build yourself

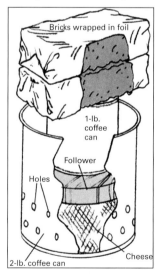

Simple cheese press is made from an empty coffee can. Use an awl to pierce the bottom and sides of the can. These are the holes through which the whey will escape. Pierce from the inside out so that metal will not project inward. Next, use a coping saw to cut a circular "cheese follower" out of 3/4-in.-thick wood. The circle need not be precise but the follower must be able to slide inside the can easily. Several bricks serve as weights to press the follower downward and squeeze the whey out of the curds. Sterilize the bricks first, then wrap them in foil. Place a smaller coffee can on the follower, then stack the bricks on it.

on the outside but remain watery inside. When stirring the curds, do so gently to avoid crushing them.

After the curds are cooked (they will be slightly firm and will not stick together), strain off the whey and mix in approximately 3 teaspoons of salt per gallon of milk. Salt improves flavor while slowing the ripening process. Put the curds in the cheese press, applying gentle pressure for the first hour or two to avoid bruising them. Later, for a harder cheese with improved keeping qualities, add more weight. After the cheese has been pressed, allow it to dry in a cool, airy place for four to five days, turning it over twice a day. Next, coat the cheese with paraffin, butter, vegetable oil, or salt, and allow it to ripen in a cool, well-ventilated area. Most cheese will improve in flavor for several months. After a month, sample the cheese and reseal it if it is not ready. If mold develops, scrape off the moldy parts, rub with salt, and reseal. Date your cheeses, making a note of any special method used so that you can develop your own recipes.

Old-time Favorites For the Adventurous

Early settlers in America, more concerned with survival than with gourmet dining, made only simple cheeses. As the population grew and living conditions became less harsh, a number of entirely new cheeses were created, often inspired by recipes brought over by immigrants. Together with the nation's immense dairy production, these new local varieties have helped make the United States one of the world's major cheese producers.

One of the best known of the homegrown American cheeses is Monterey Jack, a descendant of a cheese developed by early Spanish settlers in California. Its name comes from a California Scotsman named David Jacks, who began manufacturing the cheese in 1916, exporting it from Monterey. In taste and consistency Monterey Jack is a member of the Cheddar family. Another cheese developed in America is Colby. The first Colby cheeses were manufactured in Wisconsin in 1882 by Ambrose and J. H. Steinwand. Colby is related to Plymouth cheese, a granular variety still produced in small quantities in Vermont. Liederkranz and Wisconsin brick are two entirely new cheeses created in America.

Cheesemaking is not an easy art, and homemade cheeses can vary from batch to batch depending upon temperature, humidity, and which bacteria are most active. However, with careful hygiene they should almost all be good tasting and long lasting. And if a cheese is not quite good enough to eat plain, it can be used for cooking, salad dressing, or in a cheese spread. If you are interested in trying your hand at cheesemaking, start with a simple hard cheese or cottage cheese. Once you feel confident with a basic cheese, try making Cheddar, Colby, or Wisconsin brick cheese.

Cottage and Farmer Cheese

The key to success for both small-curd and large-curd cottage cheese is to warm the curds gently and gradually.

Step by Step From Raw Milk to Finished Cheese

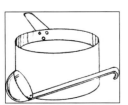

Curd

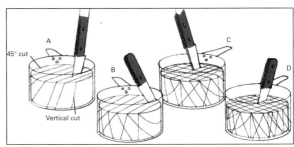

45° cut

A

B

C

D

Vertical cut

1. Allow milk to stand for a few hours at room temperature. Mix in rennet and leave milk to stand undisturbed in a warm place (86°F).

2. When the white curd can be separated cleanly from the side of the pot with a knife, the milk has coagulated and is ready for cutting.

3. The cuts should be 1/2 in. apart across the curd. Make the first cut at a 45° angle, but change gradually so that final cut is vertical (A). Using the same surface marks, make similar cuts sloping the other way (B). Turn the pot and make similar cuts at right angles to the first two sets (C and D).

After mixing, replace curds in pot; or mix them directly in pot

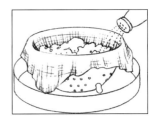

4. Mix the curds gently with your fingers to break up any large pieces. Continue for 10 to 15 minutes to give the curds time to release the whey.

5. Heat curds for about an hour to 102° F. Increase heat by no more than 2°F every five minutes and stir frequently. Remove from heat.

6. Leave curds in hot whey until they separate after being held together in your hand. Strain through cheesecloth and add salt a little at a time.

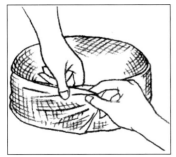

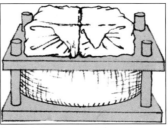

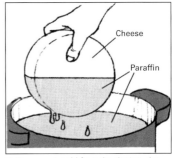

Cheese

Paraffin

7. Leave curds in cloth, and either put into mold or bandage with a strip of strong material folded double. Push curds into shape to avoid airspaces.

8. Fold cloth over top, put cheese in press, and weight lightly for about two hours. Turn cheese, and increase weight for another 12 hours.

9. To prevent mold from developing, dry cheese for four days, then coat in hot paraffin. Dip one half, allow to dry, then dip other half.

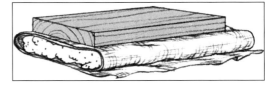

When rinsing cottage cheese, first remove cooked curds from heat. Drain through cheesecloth, allow to stand for a minute or two, then lift up the corners of the cheesecloth to make a bag. Dip the bag several times into warm water, rinse for two minutes in ice water to chill the curds, and let the water drain off.

Farmer cheese can be made by using either of the cottage cheese recipes, but use whole milk rather than low-fat milk. After coagulation cut curd into 1/4-in. cubes. Heat slowly to 104°F and continue to cook until curds retain shape after being pressed. Drain, rinse, and pour into oblong shape on a clean, folded cheesecloth. Wrap cloth over and press lightly with board.

Small-curd sharp cottage cheese is made by allowing the milk to coagulate, or clabber, without rennet. Heat a gallon of skim milk to about 72°F and add 1/2 cup of buttermilk. Stir thoroughly. Cover the milk and let it stand undistubed in a warm place for 16 to 24 hours until it coagulates. You can use raw milk, but because of the risk of unfavorable bacteria developing, you will probably have better results with pasteurized milk. Do not let the temperature drop below 70°F during clabbering, as this will slow the process, increasing the likelihood of bacterial growth.

When the milk has clabbered, cut the curds into 1/4-inch cubes, mix, and allow to rest for 10 minutes. Then slowly raise the temperature to 104°F, increasing it by 5°F every five minutes. Continue to cook at 104°F for 20 to 40 minutes or until the curds feel firm. The curds should not stick together when squeezed, and the inside of the curds should appear dry and granular. If necessary, raise the temperature as high as 120°F. When the curds are cooked, drain and rinse them. Add a teaspoon of salt for every pound of curd. For a creamed cottage cheese add 4 to 6 tablespoons of sweet or sour cream.

Large-curd sweet cottage cheese is made with rennet. Heat 1 gallon of skim milk to 90°F (no higher), and add 1/4 cup of buttermilk. Dissolve 1 1/4 junket tablets or an eighth of a cheese rennet tablet in a glass of cool water, add it to the milk, and let stand at 90°F. Test the milk for coagulation after a few hours. When the milk has coagulated, cut the curd into 1/2-inch cubes, allow them to rest for 10 minutes, then heat to 110°F by raising the temperature 5°F every five minutes. Test as for small-curd cottage cheese, and raise the temperature as high as 120°F if the curds are not ready. Drain, rinse, and cream as for small-curd cottage cheese.

Cheddar Cheese

The basic Cheddar recipe was developed in Somerset, England, four centuries ago as a way of reducing contamination in the local cheeses. The word "Cheddar" comes from Cheddar Gorge, where the cheeses were ripened, and the term "cheddaring" has come to mean the reheating process used in making the cheese.

To make a 1 1/2-pound cheese, combine 2 gallons of whole milk with 3/4 cup of buttermilk, and allow the mixture to ripen at room temperature overnight. The next day warm the milk gently in a double boiler to 86°F, mix in one cheese rennet tablet dissolved in a glass of cool water, and let the mixture coagulate undisturbed. When the milk curdles (about 45 minutes later), cut the curds into 3/8-inch cubes. Mix the curds and allow them to stand 15 minutes, then heat very slowly to 100°F. Cook for about an hour until a piece of cooled curd retains its shape when squeezed. If it crumbles, it needs more cooking. Drain the curds for a few minutes and rinse out the double boiler, then cheddar the curds as shown for two hours (longer for a strong flavor). After cheddaring, cut the resultant cheese strips into cubes and gradually mix in 1 tablespoon of salt, being careful not to bruise the curds. Let the curds stand for 10 minutes, put them into a cheesecloth, and press them with 15 pounds for 10 minutes, then with 30 pounds for an hour. Remove the cheese from the press, unwrap it, dip it in warm water, and fill in and smooth off any cracks or unevenness. Rewrap in a

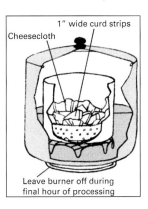

Cheddaring imparts a characteristic nutty flavor and dense texture to cheese. After the curds have been drained, return them to the double boiler and spread over a rack lined with cheesecloth. Cover and reheat at about 98°F for 30 to 40 minutes until the curds form one solid mass. Remove the curds, cut them into strips 1 in. wide, and return them to the pan. Turn the strips every 15 to 20 minutes for an hour.

clean cheesecloth and weight with 40 pounds for 24 hours; then remove from the press and let the cheese dry for four to five days in a cool, airy location. Turn the cheese twice a day during this period, and wipe it dry each time with a clean cloth. When a hard, dry skin has formed, rub it with oil or seal it with paraffin. Cheddar can be eaten after six weeks but is best if aged six months or more. American cheese is actually a mild variety of Cheddar.

Colby Cheese

Making Colby cheese involves the unusual step of adding cool water to the curds after they are cooked. The result is a mild, moist, porous cheese. Because of its high moisture content, Colby does not keep well.

To reduce the risk of the Colby having an off flavor, use pasteurized whole or skim milk. Heat 2 gallons of milk to 88°F and add 1/2 cup of buttermilk. Stir thoroughly and allow to stand for 30 minutes. Dissolve 1/4 cheese rennet tablet or 2 1/2 junket tablets in a glass of water and add to the milk, stirring vigorously to mix it well. Allow the milk to coagulate (about 30 minutes), then cut the curds into 3/8-inch cubes. After mixing the curds for 10 minutes, heat them very gently to 98°F, increasing the temperature about one degree every three minutes. Continue to cook at this temperature for 40 minutes, then slowly add cool water until the temperature drops to 80°F and remains stabilized at that point. Turn off the heat and gently mix the curds for 15 minutes.

Drain the curds and gradually mix in 6 teaspoons of salt. Put the curds into a cheese hoop or mold and press them lightly for half an hour, then add more weight for an hour and a half. Coat with paraffin when the surface has dried, or rub with vegetable oil or salt. Ripen in a cool place (40°F to 45°F) for two to three months.

Wisconsin Brick Cheese

To make Wisconsin brick, first warm 2 gallons of whole, pasteurized milk to 90°F. Next, add 2 tablespoons of buttermilk. Stir thoroughly, and add half a cheese rennet tablet dissolved in water. When the milk coagulates, cut the curd into 1/4-inch cubes, and mix gently for 15 minutes. Then increase the temperature 1°F every five minutes to 96°F. Maintain this temperature for 20 minutes while stirring gently, then remove from heat, spoon out as much whey as possible, and transfer the curds into a mold with plenty of drainage holes. (A perforated bread

1. Rennet is added to a kettle of milk that has been warmed by an open fire.

2. Curdled milk is cut with a traditional five-pronged curd cutter.

3. Large, shallow ladle is used to remove as much whey as possible from curds.

4. Curds are transferred to old-style ashsplint basket lined with cheesecloth.

5. Curds are gathered up in the cheese cloth to put inside a cheese hoop.

6. Curds are gently pushed into the shape of the hoop to remove airspaces.

7. Extra cheesecloth is neatly folded over the curds before adding the follower.

8. Cheese is slid into an old-fashioned press. Note follower and wooden block.

9. Final step is to rub cheese with salt to prevent mold and help form hard skin.

pan will give the characteristic brick shape.) Add the follower and weight with a brick.

After 12 hours remove the cheese from the mold and weight it so it stays submerged in a salt solution (1 teaspoon of salt per cup of water). After 24 hours remove the cheese and rub its entire surface with rind from a piece of Wisconsin brick or Limburger. Each day for the next two weeks, rub the surface with a mild brine solution (1/2 teaspoon of salt per cup of water). During this period, keep the cheese at about 60°F in a very moist atmosphere. (Place it in a sealed container along with two or three bowls of water, sprinkling it with water occasionally.) The last step is to apply paraffin and age the cheese in a cool place (about 40°F) for eight weeks.

Making Cheese in Colonial Days

Before the development of thermometers, cheesemaking was a very inexact skill. Housewives heated their milk in large copper pots in front of an open fire until it was warm to the touch. For rennin they added either brine solution in which a calf's stomach had been kept or a fingernail-sized piece of dried calf's stomach. Another method was to use a little of the dried contents of a newborn calf's stomach. The cheese being made below follows a recipe that was used in the Hudson Valley in the late 18th century. The curds are pressed directly after being cut and drained. After several days in the press the cheese is removed and rubbed several times with salt before being stored on long benches in a cool dairy room. Cheese made this way did not have any distinctive flavor. Its main virtue was that it preserved the summer surplus of milk for use during the winter.

Sources and resources

Books and pamphlets

Carroll, Robert, and Ricki Carroll. *Cheesemaking Made Easy:* 60 *Delicious Varieties.* Charlotte, Vt.: Garden Way Publishing, 1982.

Duback, Josef. *Traditional Cheesemaking: An Introduction.* New York: Intermed Technology Development Group of North America, 1988.

Hobson, Phyllis. *Making Cheese and Butter.* Charlotte, Vt.: Garden Way Publishing, 1984.

Hunter, Beatrice Trum. *Fact Book on Yogurt, Kefir and Other Milk Cultures* New Canaan, Conn.: Keats Publishing, 1973.

Stoner, Carol Hupping, ed. *Stocking Up III.* New York: Fine Communications, 1995.

U.S. Department of Agriculture. *Cheeses of the World.* New York: Dover, 1972.

Maple Sugaring

Two Quarts of Syrup From One Maple

The art of making maple syrup and maple sugar is uniquely American. In the days before the coming of the white man, Indians of the Northeast would cut slashes in the bark of the sugar maple, collect the sap that ran off, and boil it down in a hollowed-out cooking log by continually adding heated rocks. Early settlers in the New World soon learned the skill and improved on the Indian system by using iron drill bits to tap the trees and copper buckets to evaporate the sap into syrup and sugar. Small-scale family sugaring has long been an American tradition, and recently the rising cost of syrup has provided additional incentive for the backyard sugarer. A good maple will yield 15 to 20 gallons of sap during a single sugaring season—enough to make about 2 quarts of pure, preservative-free maple syrup.

The Tools and Techniques of Tapping

The larger the diameter of the trunk and the greater the spread of limbs at the crown, the more sap a healthy tree will yield. Trees with trunks smaller than 10 inches should not be tapped; the yield will be low and the tree may be injured. There are several sap flows, but by far the best time to tap is in late winter or early spring before the buds open: sugar content is high, flavor is at its peak, and the cool nights inhibit bacterial action.

Tap holes can be drilled on any side of the tree, although production from the south side is generally greater early in the season. Drill 2 to 3 inches into the sapwood—no deeper. Greater penetration will not produce much more sap and may injure the tree. Use a brace and bit and drill at a slight upward angle (10° to

Spile is gently driven into hold at slight upward angle. Gray, somewhat scaly bark is typical of black maple.

20°). The hole diameter should be less than that of the spout, or spile, to be inserted: 7/16 inch for a standard 1/2-inch spout. Tap holes can be located anywhere from 2 to 6 feet above the ground. A big tree (over 2 feet in diameter) can be tapped in four or more spots. One or two taps is safer for a small tree. A new hole in a tree that has been tapped previously should be about 6 inches from tap scars.

As soon as a hole is drilled, the spile should be inserted. Do this by tapping the spile rather than hammering it; if excessive force is used, the bark may split, damaging the tree and creating a leaky tap. Metal spiles, tapered to fit snugly and with built-in bucket hooks, are widely available in rural areas, or you can make your own spiles by hollowing out 4-inch lengths of sumac with a heated awl or other reaming instrument. (Be sure to select only red-berried sumacs; white or light green berries indicate a poison sumac.) If you use a wooden spout, hammer a nail in the tree above it to support the sap bucket.

Collect the sap in covered containers. Galvanized 2- to 3-gallon buckets are traditional, but plastic 1-gallon milk containers serve well, and their narrow necks do away with the need for a cover. Clean the container thoroughly and suspend it beneath the spile by a wire or strong string. You can store sap outdoors in large containers, such as clean plastic trash cans, for up to three days as long as the weather remains cold. A warming trend is a signal to process the sap more rapidly and to remove the spiles. The tree will heal by midsummer.

Sap Into Syrup

As soon as you have collected enough sap to make an appreciable amount of syrup, you should begin boiling it down. Almost any outdoor heating device will do, from a simple bonfire to a commercial evaporator working on bottled gas. Kerosene stoves, gasoline-fired camp stoves, and old coal-burning ranges have all been used successfully. Wood is the fuel of choice, however, since it is safe, inexpensive, and there is less risk of spoiling the taste of the syrup. If you have an outdoor barbecue pit, you can do your evaporating there. If not, you can construct a temporary evaporator out of cinder blocks. Do not boil sap down inside your house, however. The result will be a sticky deposit of sugar on walls, furniture, and floors. Whatever the fuel used, shield the evaporating device from the wind to conserve fuel.

Boiling down sap takes a lot of fuel, so be sure to have plenty on hand. If you are using wood, you will need about a quarter cord for every 4 gallons of syrup produced. The evaporator pan should be clean, have a large heating surface, and hold at least a gallon of sap, preferably more. A big roasting pan will do for small-scale sugaring. You will also need a stirring spoon, a candy thermometer, a 1- or 2-gallon "finishing" pot, and a kitchen strainer. In addition, have some heavy felt cloth or paper toweling on hand to filter the finished syrup.

Fill the evaporator pan about half full of sap and bring the sap to a boil over the fire. Unprocessed sap is mostly water, and its boiling point is the same as that of water (212°F at sea level, 1°F lower for each 550 feet of eleva-

Stalking the sugar tree

For sugaring, the sugar maple and black maple are best, with the Norway maple a close third. Other maples can be used, but syrup production is lower. The sugar maple's ash-gray bark is often broken into hard flakes. The bark of the black maple is smooth and gray when young; scaly, furrowed, and darker when old. The range of both trees extends from New England west to Minnesota, north into Canada, and south to Tennessee. Identify trees in summer and mark them for spring tapping.

Very tight angle

Sugar maple

Tight angle

Black maple

Wide angle

Norway maple

Highest grade syrup (left) is pale and delicately flavored; it is made from clear sap that has been boiled down quickly. Home sugarers, however, often prefer the richer-tasting, darker syrup.

tion). As the water vapor is driven off, the boiling point slowly rises. When the temperature reaches 7°F above the boiling point of water, the syrup is done.

During the course of the evaporation process, skim off surface froth with the kitchen strainer. Whenever the sap gets low in the pan, add more to prevent burning or scorching. As the syrup nears the ready stage, it tends to boil over, so most sugarers finish the syrup on a stove whose heat can be easily controlled. When the syrup is 6°F above the boiling point of water, it is ready for finishing. Remove the evaporator pan from the fire and pour the syrup into the finishing pot, at the same time filtering it through felt cloth or paper towels placed in the strainer. (Be extremely careful when handling the pan; hot sap will stick to the skin, producing severe burns.) The purpose of filtering is to remove any impurities, particularly the granular calcium compound known as sugar sand, which is found in all maple sap. Once the syrup is finished, it should be bottled immediately while still hot. Some sugarers filter the syrup a second time, as it is being poured into the storage jars, to remove any traces of sugar sand that may remain.

Storing and Processing Maple Syrup and Sugar

Pure maple syrup can be stored for extended periods of time without the addition of artificial preservatives. The most practical method for long-term storage is by canning in airtight glass, plastic, or metal containers. Of the three, glass containers, such as mason jars, are best because they do not rust, do not affect the flavor as some plastics do, and allow the syrup to be inspected without opening the container. Pour the hot syrup (it must be at least 180°F) directly from the finishing pot into the containers, seal the containers, and let the syrup cool slowly to avoid risk of contamination. Store the bottles of syrup in a cool, dark place such as a basement or pantry.

Syrup will also keep in nonairtight containers for several months provided they are refrigerated. It can even be frozen, but this may result in loss of flavor and will also cause the syrup to crystallize and separate.

Soft maple sugar and hard maple sugar will both stay fresh for long periods of time if stored in moisture-proof containers and protected from contaminants. To make soft maple sugar, cook maple syrup in a pot to about 30°F hotter than boiling water, let it cool to 155°F, and stir until it becomes thick and viscous. Then pour into molds. Hard sugar is made by bringing syrup to 33°F above boiling water, cooling to 150°F, and stirring until crystals form. While you are sugaring, you can also enjoy an old-fashioned treat simply by pouring some of the hot syrup (about 230°F) on snow or crushed ice. The result is a taffylike confection known as Jack wax.

Sugar shack in Nova Scotia, Canada is well-ventilated to allow steam from evaporator to escape. As the sap cooks, it is checked periodically with a candy thermometer. When temperature reaches 7°F above the boiling point of water, syrup is ready. About 1/4 cord of dry hardwood will boil down 200 gal. of sap.

Baking Bread

First Master the Basics And the Rest Is Easy

Nothing smells quite so good as the aroma of bread baking in the oven. And the incomparable taste and texture of a loaf of wholesome, homemade, preservative-free bread is well worth the effort, especially since breadmaking is not nearly as time-consuming as many people believe. Measuring, mixing, kneading, and shaping can be accomplished in 30 minutes or less. Rising takes longer; but this is a process that occurs by itself, leaving you free to handle other chores or simply to sit back, relax, and contemplate the warm, fresh bread you will soon be enjoying.

Ingredients and Supplies: What Goes Into a Loaf of Bread and Why

Bread is a simple food. Few ingredients and little equipment are required to make it. The basic components of bread are yeast and flour: yeast to make the dough rise, flour to provide substance and structure.

Yeast. When yeast, a plant with millions of living cells, is placed in warm water and is fed sugar and flour, it grows and multiplies, giving off the carbon dioxide gas that makes dough rise. Yeast adds vitamins, gives bread its airy texture, and contributes to aroma and flavor.

You can buy yeast in two forms: active dry and compressed. Active dry yeast is granulated and will remain fresh for months without refrigeration. Before it is used, it is generally dissolved in warm (110°F) water or milk. However, it is sometimes added directly to the other dry ingredients and then mixed with the water or milk at a somewhat higher temperature—120°F to 130°F.

Compressed yeast in cake form is more perishable: it should be refrigerated or frozen immediately. Refrigerated, it will keep about 10 to 14 days. Frozen, it can be stored for much longer periods. When you are ready to make bread, thaw the yeast at room temperature and use it immediately by dissolving it in water or milk that has been warmed to no more than 95°F

You can also make your own yeast as old-time homesteaders did. Mix together 1 cup of cooked mashed potatoes, 1/4 cup sugar, 2 teaspoons salt, and 1 cup of warm water (105°F to 115°F). Pour the mixture into a 1-quart glass jar, cover with a cloth, and leave in a warm place (80°F to 85°F) for two days or until it ferments and bubbles up. One cup of this mixture is equivalent to one package of active dry yeast or one cake of compressed yeast. Every time you use a cupful, replenish the starter by stirring in 3/4 cup of flour and 3/4 cup of potato water, water, or milk. Allow to ferment for a day or so and return, covered, to the refrigerator. It is best to use the starter once a week. If you do not, stir it down after three or four weeks, discard half of it, and replenish the balance with flour and one of the liquids.

Tools and ingredients for making bread are simple. Start with a basic bread recipe and then experiment by using different grains, nut, seeds, fruit, etc.

Flour. The gas emitted by the growing yeast must have a framework that will hold it. This structure is provided by the flour, more strictly by gluten, a sticky combination of proteins that is developed by stirring and kneading moistened flour. The gluten traps the minute pockets of gas given off by the yeast, causing the bread to rise. Hard-wheat flour, also known as bread flour, is the richest in gluten and produces loaves of greater volume than other flours. Neighborhood bakeries sometimes sell hard-wheat flour, or you may be able to purchase it from a health food store. So-called all-purpose flour is widely available and is satisfactory for both yeast and quick breads. Buy it unbleached—it gives the bread a better texture. Rye, whole wheat, and buckwheat flour are low in gluten and must be combined with all-purpose flour. Used alone, they produce heavy, compact breads.

Other ingredients. In addition to yeast and flour, salt, sweetener, shortening, and eggs are often used in bread recipes. Salt adds flavor and controls the yeast action. Sweeteners add flavor, help in browning, and provide food for the yeast. White cane sugar is the type most often used, but brown sugar, honey, and molasses can be substituted in many recipes. Shortening, generally butter or lard, provides additional flavor, makes bread more tender, improves keeping quality, and helps form a brown crust. Eggs give yeast breads color, texture, and flavor. However, dough that has been enriched with shortening or eggs takes longer to rise.

Special equipment. Several bread pans and, perhaps, a heavy-duty mixer are the only special implements you will need. The size of the pan is important, so be sure to use the one specified in the recipe. If the pan is too large, the dough will rise properly but will not expand over the top of the pan to make a dramatic-looking loaf. If the pan is too small, the dough will rise too high and slide over the sides of the pan. As a rule of thumb, the dough should fill two-thirds of the pan.

Some experienced bakers prefer dark-colored bread pans to help absorb heat and give a browner crust. Special black steel pans are best, but aluminum pans are satisfactory. Darken aluminum pans before using them by heating them in a 350°F oven for five hours. Pans of heat-resistant glass are also popular.

Basic White: Template for Breadmaking

The instructions for making basic white bread can be used as a guide for almost all other yeast breads. Master it and you will be on the way to mastering the entire art of breadmaking from the simplest recipes to the most complex. You will need two 9- by 5- by 3-inch bread pans plus the following ingredients:

2 cups milk	1/2 cup warm water
1 tbsp. salt	(105°F-115°F)
2 tbsp. butter	2 tbsp. sugar
1 package active dry yeast	6-7 cups unsifted hard-wheat or all-purpose flour

Making the dough. *Heat the milk, salt, and butter in a saucepan until bubbles appear around the edges of the pan. Remove from the heat and let cool to about 110°F.*

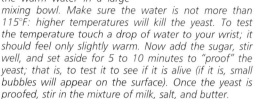

Sprinkle the yeast over the warm water in a large mixing bowl. Make sure the water is not more than 115°F: higher temperatures will kill the yeast. To test the temperature touch a drop of water to your wrist; it should feel only slightly warm. Now add the sugar, stir well, and set aside for 5 to 10 minutes to "proof" the yeast; that is, to test it to see if it is alive (if it is, small bubbles will appear on the surface). Once the yeast is proofed, stir in the mixture of milk, salt, and butter.

Add 3 cups of flour. Stir to mix, then beat with a wooden spoon until smooth—about two minutes. Gradually add more flour, mixing it in with your hands until the dough tends to leave the sides of the bowl. The secret of making bread is to use as little flour as possible and still be able to handle the dough; any flour beyond this amount will tend to make the bread heavy and tough. Remember that the amount of flour given in a bread recipe can only be an approximation, since flours vary greatly in their ability to absorb moisture, differing from one locale to another and from batch to batch. Experience will help you judge the correct amount.

Kneading the dough. *The purpose of kneading is to distribute the yeast cells throughout the dough and to develop the gluten in the flour, which traps the gas produced by the yeast, causing the bread to rise. Turn out the dough onto a lightly floured board, marble slab, or countertop. Sprinkle the dough lightly with flour. As shown in the illustration at bottom left, knead by folding the dough toward you, then push down with the heels of your hands. Fold the dough over again, give it a quarter turn, and repeat the kneading; try to develop a rhythmic motion. Continue kneading and turning for 10 minutes or until the dough is smooth and elastic. To test the dough to see if it has been kneaded sufficiently, press two fingers into it about 1/2 in. deep; the dough should spring back. Form the dough into a ball.*

First rising. *Grease a large mixing bowl with about 1 tbsp. of softened butter. Place the ball of dough into the bowl and roll the dough around to cover it with butter. This will keep the surface from drying out and cracking as the dough rises. Cover with a kitchen towel or plastic wrap, and let rise in a warm, draft-free place (80°F to 85°F) for 1 to 1 1/2 hours or until doubled in bulk. If the room is cold, put the dough in a bowl, cover, and place the bowl in a pilot-lighted oven, or on a rack over a pan of hot water, or near (not on) a radiator. If you have a wood stove, the warming oven over the range is ideal for rising.*

To test if the dough has risen sufficiently, make an indentation by pressing two fingers into the dough about 1/2 in. deep. If dough does not spring back, it is ready. If the dough has risen a little too much, it will not be seriously affected; however, excessive rising can change the texture and flavor of the finished product.

Punch the dough down with your fist to deflate it. Turn it out on a lightly floured board, then knead well about two minutes. Cut the dough in half with a sharp knife and shape each half into a smooth ball. Cover with a towel and let rest about five minutes.

Shaping the dough. *Use a rolling pin to shape each ball of dough into a 9- by 12-in. rectangle, then roll the dough up tightly from the short sides (above left). Next, press the ends together to seal them, and fold the ends so that they are underneath the rolls (above right). Lift the loaves carefully and place them in the greased pans with their seam sides down.*

Second rising. *Brush the top of each loaf with 1/2 tbsp. melted butter. Cover pans with a towel. Let rise as before in a warm, draft-free place until the dough has doubled in volume or when a finger pressed lightly near the edge leaves a dent. The purpose of the second rising is to give the dough a finer grain. This rising will take less time than the first rising; 3/4 to 1 1/4 hours is typical.*

In case of an interruption. If at any time during the first or second rising you cannot complete the breadmaking, punch the dough down as you did after the first rising, and place it in a buttered bowl. Set a clean plate on top of the dough, weight it down with a brick or other heavy object, and place the bowl in a refrigerator. The cold plus the weight will bring the action of the yeast almost to a halt.

Baking the bread. *For glazed loaves, gently beat one egg yolk with 1 tbsp. of milk. Lightly brush the top of each loaf with this mixture just before putting the bread in the oven.*

Bake the loaves 40 to 50 minutes on the lower rack of an oven that has been preheated to 400°F. Place the bread pans so that their tops are as close to the center of the oven as possible. In order to permit adequate circulation of hot air, however, the pans should not touch each other or the sides of the oven. To check if the bread is ready, tap the top of a loaf with your middle finger (left). If it is done, the bread will sound hollow. To test further, take a potholder in each hand, turn the loaf out of the pan, and tap the bottom of the bread with your finger (right); it should sound hollow. If it is soft on the bottom, return the loaf to the pan, bake an additional 5 to 10 minutes, and test again.

Remove the pans from the oven, turn the loaves on their sides on a rack, and place in a draft-free location. For easy slicing, the bread should cool completely—about two to three hours. To store the bread, put it in plastic bags and tie securely or keep it in a bread box or freezer. Bread will keep at least a month in the freezer. If you use only a small amount of bread at a time, slice the loaf before freezing and remove slices from the freezer as needed. For quick thawing of a whole loaf, wrap it in aluminum foil and heat in a 300°F oven about 25 to 40 minutes.

Part Five

Skills and Crafts For House and Homestead

Handicrafts were once part of everyday life. People thought no more of making their own candles, spinning their own yarn, or mixing their own paints and glues than modern folks think of vacuuming a rug or screwing in a new light bulb. In those days crafts were not just for artists and hobbyists— they were the survival skills of average men and women. Today, Americans are beginning to rediscover these old-time home skills: for fun, for economy, but most of all for the feeling of independence that comes when one makes do for oneself. Many of the topics covered in "Skills and Crafts for House and Homestead," such as spinning, tanning, and soapmaking, can be practical money savers as well as enjoyable creative activities. And a few, among them weaving and basketry, yield satisfaction on many levels: pride of accomplishment, pleasure in artistic creativity, and the gratification of doing something with your own hands.

Natural Dyes

A Rainbow of Color
From Common Plants

Indigo blue and madder red were the favorite colors of early migrants to the New World. Both had to be imported, but the permanent, deep shades they produced made them worth the expense. Experimentation did occur, however, and settlers learned to create rich yellows and beiges from natural dyestuffs native to America. The bark of the American black oak tree became a particularly valuable source of bright yellow and was eventually used by commercial dyers throughout Europe. When home dyers needed mordant (one of several chemicals that make dye colorfast), they turned to an apothecary or tanner. In areas lacking these suppliers, settlers relied on the metal leached from the copper or iron pot in which the dye was cooking or else employed a concoction of stale urine and ashes. Then, as now, color results varied from batch to batch—but, with luck and skillful use of dyes and mordants, the tones were rich, mellow, and durable.

Naturally dyed yarn at a market. Marigolds and dahlias are among the several kinds of flowers that give bright, long-lasting dyes. Most flower heads will produce a shade of yellow no matter what color their petals.

Start by Scouring

Because all fibers contain oils that keep mordants and dyes from penetrating, it is necessary to clean or scour them before beginning the dye process. To scour 1 pound of fiber takes about 3 gallons of water. As with all dyeing procedures, soft mineral-free water is best. If the tap water in your area is hard, use rainwater instead or add commercial water softener to the tap water. To scour grasses, do not use any detergent or soap; simply soak them in water until they are soft. For other fibers, once the water is softened, add enough mild detergent to make it sudsy, then immerse the yarn and gradually raise the temperature. Silk should be allowed to simmer for 30 minutes and wool for 45 minutes. For cotton or linen, also add 1/2 cup of washing soda to the detergent solution to make the scouring bath, and boil the fibers rather than simmering them for one to two hours. When scouring is completed, allow the bath to cool, then rinse the fibers in soft water until no suds remain.

How to Prepare and Use a Dyebath

A dyebath is prepared by soaking and cooking the raw dyestuff in water. Use either an enamel or stainless steel pot (unlike aluminum, copper, and cast iron, these materials will not give off chemicals that affect the dye). Your dye pot should be large—4 gallons or more—and you will also need a wooden spoon or dowel for stirring and some cheesecloth in which to wrap the dye substance.

Prepare the dyestuff so that as much color as possible can be extracted. Leaves and blossoms should be shredded. Twigs, bark, and roots should be cut up into small pieces, and nut hulls should be crushed. Pick out foreign particles and remove extraneous parts of plants.

Wrap the dye substance in cheesecloth, put it into the pot, and cover with water. (Some dye materials must first be soaked in cold water.) Cook until the dyebath becomes richly colored, adding more water as needed to keep the dye substance covered. After cooking, remove the cheesecloth bag and its contents or strain the liquid through a sieve. To the concentrated dye, add enough cold water to make a bath in which the yarn can float freely—4 gallons is adequate for 1 pound of wool. Wet the fibers, add them to the bath, and bring slowly to a simmer for animal fibers or to a boil for plant fibers. Cook until the desired shade is reached, turning the fibers occasionally with the wooden spoon or dowel so the bath penetrates evenly. Then allow the fibers to cool, either in or out of the bath, and rinse until the water runs clear. You may also cool the yarn by rinsing it in successively cooler baths. After gently squeezing out excess moisture, hang the skeins to dry.

If there is any color left in the dyebath, you may reuse it to produce lighter shades. A dyebath can be stored for several days by refrigerating it. Freezing will keep it for several months, and by adding 1 teaspoon per gallon of the preservative sodium benzoate, you can preserve the dye for a month without refrigeration.

Collecting and Storing Dyestuffs

The first step in making your own dyes is to gather the dyestuffs. The chart on pages 242–243 is a guide to common, naturally occurring sources of dyes and to the colors they will produce. In general, the plants are easy to identify; if you need more information, consult a good botanical guide that illustrates leaves, flowers, bark, buds, and other distinctive characteristics.

You not only need to collect the right plants, you also need to collect them at the right times. Flowers should be picked just after they reach full bloom. Roots, bark, and branches should be from mature plants—do not pick new branches. Nuts should be fully ripe and even a little aged (but should not have lain on the ground through the winter). Acorns, for example, are best just after they have fallen from the tree, while black walnuts benefit from lying on the ground until they become spotted. Berries make the best dyes when picked fully ripe.

Although fresh dyestuffs produce the strongest dyes, most plants can be stored for later use. Twigs, leaves,

nuts, blossoms, bark, and roots can be dried. Spread them in a single layer in a shady, well-ventilated spot, turning them occasionally for faster drying. A window screen set on bricks makes a good drying rack because it lets air circulate underneath as well as on top. Plants with stems may be hung in bundles to dry. Once drying is complete, store the dyestuffs in brown paper bags or other containers through which air can circulate. Berries should not be dried but can be kept for several months if frozen. Freeze them unwashed, either whole or pulverized into juice.

Mordants: The Stuff That Makes Dyestuffs Colorfast

Mordants are chemicals that help to keep dyes from fading, changing color, washing out, or rubbing off. They may also affect the final color so that a single dye can produce a variety of shades depending on what mordant is used with it. Textiles may be mordanted either before or after dyeing, or the mordant may be added directly to the dyebath. It is simplest to do the mordanting first. Once the fibers are mordanted, you can soak them in the dyebath for as long as necessary to achieve the desired shade without worrying that long exposure to the mordant will damage the yarn.

For mordanting, use an enamel or stainless steel pot for cooking and a wooden rod or spoon for stirring. Dissolve the chemical in about 4 gallons of lukewarm soft water (use commercial water softener if necessary), then thoroughly prewet the textile and immerse it in the mixture. Bring the bath slowly to a simmer or boil. Once mordanted, the yarn may be dyed immediately or dried and saved for future use.

The most commonly used mordants are alum, blue vitriol, chrome, copperas, tannic acid, and tin.

Alum (aluminum potassium sulfate) causes least change in color. Use 1 ounce per gallon of water and simmer one hour to mordant wool, silk, or other animal fibers. For cotton or linen use 1 1/3 ounces of the mordant per gallon of water and boil the fibers for one hour.

Blue vitriol (copper sulfate) sometimes colors fibers green. Use 1/4 ounce per gallon of water and simmer one hour to mordant animal fibers. For cotton and linen use 1 ounce per gallon and boil for one to two hours.

Chrome (potassium dichromate) often strengthens colors. Use 1/8 ounce per gallon for animal fibers and simmer for one hour. With linen or cotton use 1/2 ounce per gallon and boil for one to two hours. Because chrome mordanted fibers are turned brown by exposure to light, keep mordant pot covered and dye the yarns immediately or store them in complete darkness. Keep the pot covered when dyeing the chrome-mordanted fiber.

Copperas (iron sulfate) grays colors. For wool use 1/8 ounce per gallon of water and simmer for 30 minutes. For linen or cotton use 1 ounce per gallon and boil for one hour. For greater color fastness add 3/4 ounce of oxalic acid, dissolved in water, to the mordant bath. Some dyers sadden colors (dull them) by adding 1/8 teaspoon of copperas to 4 gallons of dyebath for the last few minutes

Dyeing with indigo

Because indigo is not water soluble, special techniques are employed to dissolve it and to use it as a dye. Start by mixing 1 oz. of washing soda in 4 oz. of water, then add 1 tsp. of indigo paste. Shake 1 oz. of hydrosulfite (available from a pharmacy) over the solution and stir gently. Next add 2 qt. of warm water, heat to 350°F, and let stand for 20 minutes. To complete the dyebath, shake another ounce of hydrosulfite over the top and stir gently again. Immerse wet yarn in the yellow-green solution for 20 minutes. When the yarn is removed from the bath and exposed to air, it will turn blue.

of dyeing premordanted fibers. Dissolve the mordant in a little water and remove the fibers from the bath before adding the solution.

Tannic acid tends to turn fibers brown. For animal fibers use 1 1/4 tablespoons per gallon of water and simmer one hour. Use 2 1/2 tablespoons per gallon for plant fibers and boil them for one to two hours.

Tin (stannous chloride) brightens colors, particularly reds and yellows, but it can easily damage fibers. To prevent damage, mordant fibers for as short a time as possible and wash them thoroughly after mordanting. For both animal and plant fibers use 1 ounce per gallon of water and simmer for one hour. Some dyers use tin in combination with another mordant by adding 1/8 teaspoon of tin to 4 gallons of dyebath for the last few minutes of dyeing. As with copperas, remove fibers, add the tin in solution, then replace the fibers.

Mordants are sold by most pharmacies and chemical supply houses. They are available in a range of purities. The so-called chemical grade, which is less expensive than purer grades, is sufficient for dyeing purposes. **Mordants are strong chemicals and must be handled carefully. Use them in a well-ventilated place and keep the mordanting pot covered to prevent chemicals from escaping into the air. Never use mordant pots to cook food. Chrome requires particular care since it is highly poisonous.**

General Tips on Textiles, Fibers, and Dyes

Fibers derived from animals, particularly wool from sheep, tend to take dye more easily than either plant fibers or synthetics. In addition, the colors you get with wool and other so-called protein fibers will be darker and brighter than any you could obtain with plant fibers.

Animal fibers must be treated carefully during the dyeing process. Cooking time is shorter than for vegetable fibers. Yarns should be simmered in the dye solution, not boiled, and should be handled as little as possible when wet. Turn them over gently in the water to keep them from settling to the bottom of the pot and avoid wringing or twisting them. Wool will shrink if subjected to abrupt temperature changes. Always immerse it in room-temperature water, then raise the temperature slowly, allowing at least half an hour to reach a simmer. Be sure that dye and mordant baths are the same temperature if you move yarn from one to another.

Plant fibers such as cotton and linen do not absorb color easily and must be scoured and mordanted at higher temperatures and for longer periods than those from animals. They must then be boiled for as long as one to two hours in the dyebath. Grasses can also be dyed but must be treated gently. To minimize handling, mordant and dye them in the same bath.

Yarn is the easiest textile to dye since slight unevenness of color is unnoticeable. To keep yarns from tangling during dyeing, loop them into skeins, then tie the skeins with string at various points. Make the ties very loose so that dyes and mordants can reach the yarn. To store yarn between steps, you may either wrap it wet in a towel and keep it for a day or two (or for as much as a week if refrigerated) or dry it and keep it indefinitely. To dry, gently squeeze out excess moisture, then hang the skeins. Turn the yarn several times during the drying so that it will dry evenly. Before immersing dry fibers in a mordant or dye, rewet them in clear water to promote deep, even penetration.

No two dyebaths made from natural dyes are quite the same. Colors made from identical plants will vary according to when and where they were collected, the chemistry of the water in which they were cooked, and even the weather conditions during their growing season. The chart on pages 242–243 gives formulas and cooking times for a variety of colors from several popular, widely available dye materials. While these recipes provide good guidelines, the colors you create will be your own and, as you gain experience, you will enjoy experimenting with other recipes.

Sources and resources

Books and pamphlets
Adrosko, Rita J. *Natural Dyes and Home Dyeing*. New York: Dover, 1971.
Bemiss, Elijah. *The Dyer's Companion*. New York: Dover, 1973.
Dye Plants and Dyeing. Portland, Oreg.: Timber Press, 1994.

Dyestuff	Gathering the dye material	Preparing the dyebath	Dyeing instructions
(Mordants are indicated in parentheses)	Most of the dye materials listed here are commonly available in the wild or can be grown in your garden; others can be purchased. Quantities given will make 4 gal. of dyebath, enough for dyeing 1 lb. of wool	Unless otherwise noted, begin by wrapping dyestuff in cheesecloth and placing it in enough water to cover. Simmer for time indicated, remove the dyestuff, and add sufficient water to make 4 gal. of dyebath	Unless otherwise noted, start with 1 lb. of premordanted wool (see p. 242 for ways to mordant). Wet the wool with water, add it to the dyebath, heat the bath slowly, and simmer the wool for time indicated. Let the bath cool, rinse the wool until rinse water runs clear, and dry the wool.
Coreopsis (alum)	Pick 2 bushels flower heads when in full bloom	Simmering time: 1/2–1 hr.	Simmering time: 1/2 hr.
Sophora (tin and cream of tartar)	Pick 1 bushel flower heads when in full bloom	Boil (instead of simmering) for 1/2 hr.	Simmering time: 1/2 hr.
Goldenrod (alum)	Pick 2 lb. fully bloomed flower heads and stems	Simmering time: 1/2 hr.	Simmering time: 1/2 hr.
Lily of the valley (alum)	Gather 2 lb. fresh, green leaves	Simmering time: 1 hr.	Simmering time: 20 min. Note: When using chrome mordant, put 1/8 oz. of it directly into dyebath, then add 1 lb. wet unmordanted wool
Lily of the valley (chrome)			
Privet (alum)	Gather 1 lb. fresh, green leaves	Simmering time: 1/2–1 hr.	Simmering time: 20 min.
Queen Anne's lace (alum)	Pick 1 bushel fully bloomed flower heads and stems	Simmering time: 1/2 hr.	Simmering time: 1/2 hr.
Rhododendron (alum)	Gather 3 lb. fresh, green leaves	Soak leaves in water overnight, then boil (not simmer) 1 hr.	Simmering time: 1/2 hr. Note: When using iron sulfate mordant, put 1 tsp. of it directly into dyebath, then add 1 lb. wet unmordanted wool
Rhododendron (iron sulfate)			
Logwood (copperas)	Purchase 4 oz. of chips from a dye supplier	Soak chips in water overnight, then boil 45 min.	Simmering time: 1/2 hr.
Logwood (alum)			
Onion skin (alum)	Collect 2 lb. dry outer skins	Simmering time: 20 min. Do not overcook	Simmering time: 20 min.
Smartweed (tin)	Gather 2 bushels fully bloomed whole plants except roots	Boil (instead of simmering) for 20 min.	Simmering time: 1/2 hr.
Marigold (alum)	Pick 2 bushels flower heads when in full bloom	Simmering time: 1 hr.	Simmering time: 1/2 hr.

Dyestuff	Gathering the dye material	Preparing the dyebath	Dyeing instructions
Pokeberry (alum)	Gather 16 qt. fully ripe berries	Boil 1/2 hr. in water to which 1 cup of vinegar has been added	Simmering time: 1/2 hr.
Madder (alum)	Purchase 1 oz. dried root from a dye supplier	Soak dried root in water overnight, then simmer 1/2 hr.	Simmering time: 1/2 hr.
Butterfly weed (alum)	Pick 1 bushel blossoms when in full bloom	Soak blossoms in water for 1 hr., then boil 1/2 hr.	Simmering time: 1/2 hr.
Tea (no mordant)	Purchase 1/4 lb. dried leaves	Cover leaves with boiling water, then steep for 15 min.	Simmering time: 20 min. Use unmordanted wool
Cochineal (alum)	Purchase 1 1/2 oz. dried powder from a dye supplier	Soak powder in water to dissolve (about 30 min.), then boil 15 min.	Simmering time: 1/2 hr.
Coffee (no mordant)	Purchase 1/2 lb. grounds	Boil (instead of simmering) for 15 min.	Simmering time: 1/2 hr. Use unmordanted wool
Tobacco (alum)	Purchase 1 lb. cured leaves	Boil 1/2 hr. in water to which 1 oz. cream of tartar has been added	Simmering time: 1/2 hr.
Acorn (alum)	Gather 7 lb. nuts that have already fallen to ground	Soak nuts in water overnight, then boil 2 1/2 hr.	Simmering time: 1 hr.
Acorn (copperas)			
Indigo (alum)	Purchase 1 oz. of prepared paste from a dye supplier	Prepare dyebath by special technique given on page 242	Gradually heat wool, then immerse and simmer in dyebath for 20 min.

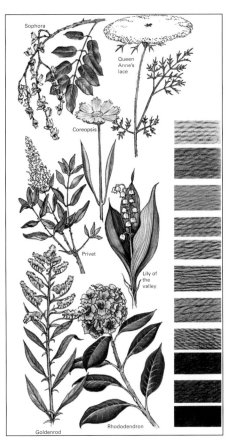

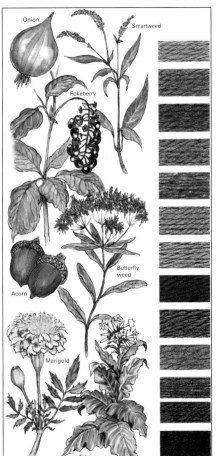

Spinning

The Relaxing Art Of Twisting Fleece Into Yarn

The basics of spinning are easy to learn, especially if you begin with a drop spindle; a flick sets the spindle whirling, then your fingers draw out the fleece into yarn. A bit more persistence will be needed to learn the hand and foot motions of the treadle wheel, but once they are mastered, you can concentrate on making fine thread and specially textured yarns; or you can simply relax, daydream, chat with neighbors, and delight in the feel of the fleece as it slips through your fingers.

In preindustrial America a homestead wife was more likely to spin her own thread than to perform any other traditional craft. Not only was spinning a virtual necessity of life, but the equipment required was small, light, and easily accommodated in a corner where it could be turned to in free moments. The craft even became fashionable among rich upper-class ladies, many of whom not only owned elegant parlor wheels but also had special visiting wheels to take with them when paying social calls on their neighbors. In the East, where sheep were scarce, linen was the most commonly spun thread. In the Southwest, wool yarn was the staple. A little cotton was sometimes spun, and occasionally someone experimented with silk.

Wool is by far the easiest fiber to spin. You may be able to buy fleece from a local herder; ask your county agent where one can be found. Otherwise, contact spinning supply companies and stores (check advertisers in spinning magazines) for fleece as well as for more exotic fibers. Other spinnable fibers that may be locally available are angora rabbit fur, goat hair, wild cotton, and dog hair. It is surprising how many spinners treasure a sweater made of hair combed from a favorite pet.

Low wheel twists fleece into yarn and winds it onto spindle in a continuous sequence. Many spinners enjoy the relaxed rhythm of treadling almost as much as the yarn that results.

1. Start carding by pulling fleece across a card so that fibers catch on teeth. Spread fleece evenly across card.

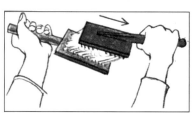

2. Pull upper card gently across fleece. Stroke several times until half the wool is distributed on each card.

3. Transfer fleece from top card to bottom one by first reversing top card, then pulling it across bottom one.

4. Stroke the fleece several more times, repeating Steps 2 and 3 until fibers are evenly distributed and fluffy.

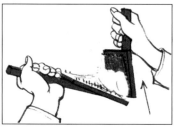

5. Remove fleece from cards by first transferring all to bottom card, then pulling top card across as shown.

6. Shake wool from card, then roll between palms to form a "rolag" (long roll of evenly distributed fiber).

Using the Drop Spindle

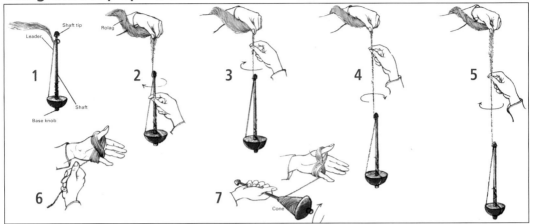

1. Tie leader (a scrap of previously spun yarn) to base of spindle shaft. Wrap leader around base knob, then up to and around shaft tip as shown. Fan out end of leader.

2. Fan out rolag end and lay end of leader to overlap it by 2 in. Hold ends between thumb and forefinger of one hand as you start spindle turning with the other hand.

3. As rolag end twists around leader, shift lower hand up to hold juncture of ends. With top hand start drawing out fleece until only a few fibers remain between hands.

4. When ends are joined, move lower hand up again to pinch fleece at point just below top hand. Twist can now run farther up rolag but not above pinch. Maintain pinch until filaments below lower hand are twisted as tight as you wish.

5. As you pinch, use top hand to pull out more fibers. The aim is to thin out the fibers so that yarn will be as thin and even as desired. Repeat Steps 4 and 5, pinching with one hand and pulling out fibers with other. As whirling slows, reach down and twist spindle shaft with your fingers. Do not spin rolag all the way to its end. Instead, add new rolag as in Step 2.

6. When spindle reaches floor, wrap spun yarn in a figure eight around thumb and fifth finger of one hand. Do not release grip at end of spun yarn or it will untwist.

7. Unwrap yarn from tip of spindle and wind onto shaft. Wind more yarn at shaft base and less above so yarn will form cone. Rewrap yarn as in Step 1 and continue to spin.

Preparing the Fleece

Many spinners prefer to spin "in the grease"—that is, with unwashed fleece—because the natural lanolin coating lets the fiber slide more easily through the fingers, making spinning faster and more comfortable. In addition, garments knitted from yarn that still contains lanolin from the sheep are naturally waterproof.

However, if a fleece is very dirty it must be washed. You will need a large basin for the job (two would be better) or a large sink. For 1 pound of fleece, fill the basin with 4 gallons of lukewarm soft water and add mild soap. Lay the fleece on the surface of the water (do not pour water over it); submerge and squeeze the fleece gently. When the first bath is dirty, make a second, similar bath and shift the fleece to it. Most of the dirt tends to collect at the tip of each lock of sheep's wool. Gently scrape with your thumbnail to remove the dirt lodged there. Rinse the wool and dry it on a rustproof window screen.

Washed fleece should be sprayed lightly with thinned lanolin oil to recondition it. A good recipe is one part of any lanolin-containing hand lotion to five parts water. Spray one or two squirts of the mixture over each 1/2 pound of fleece and let it stand overnight.

Carding the Fleece

Wool, as it comes from the sheep, is kinky, matted, and may contain dirt and burrs if it has not been washed.

To prepare the wool for spinning, the fibers must be separated from one another and the foreign matter removed. The method by which this is accomplished is called carding, after the pair of paddle-shaped wire brushes, or cards, that are used in the process. (Long fibers can also be separated and cleaned by combing with a metaltoothed dog comb or even an ordinary hair comb, but working with these tools is too tedious for anything except a small quantity of fleece.)

Cards are rated by fineness. The finer the card, the thinner the wires in the mesh and the tighter the mesh itself. As a rule, No. 8 cards are adequate for wools of medium weight. For lighter wools use a finer (higher numbered) card; for heavier wools use a lower numbered card. When you buy your cards, it is a good idea to mark one card for the right hand and one for the left. Then as you use them, the pitch, or angle, of their teeth will adjust to your particular stroke. Prepare the fleece for carding by teasing it apart with your fingers. Then follow the steps for carding.

Wheels to Speed The Spinning

You can spin yarn six times as fast on a low wheel as on a drop spindle, primarily because the spun yarn is wound onto the bobbin automatically. The other great advantage of this wheel is its foot-powered treadle, which turns the flyer, the whirling mechanism that twists fibers into yarn and winds it onto the bobbin.

Handling the fleece is almost the same as with a drop spindle, but coordinating the hand and foot movements takes practice. You should familiarize yourself with treadling before you try to spin yarn. First, adjust the tension of the drive band by turning the tension screw. The band must be almost—but not quite—tight. If it is too loose, it will slip; if it is too tight, it will turn the flyer very fast and the yarn will be kinky. When the band is adjusted, start the wheel turning clockwise by pushing it gently with your right index finger, then treadle as slowly and smoothly as you can without letting the wheel stop or go backward. Many spinners remove their shoes to increase control over the treadle. Others chant a simple song or recite a nursery rhyme as they work to help maintain the slow, steady rhythm that is required.

When you are ready to begin spinning, arrange several rolags side by side over one knee. Tie a leader to the bobbin—a beginner will find it easiest to use a 2-foot-long leader—and start spinning as shown below. When you have spun almost to the end of the first rolag, attach a new one just as you attached the first one to the leader.

As the spindle fills with yarn, you will need to tighten the drive band occasionally to keep the flyer turning as fast as it did when empty. This is accomplished by turning the tension screw. As you work, strive for yarn of even thickness and uniform twist. This will be difficult to accomplish at first, but in the meantime take satisfaction in the rich character of your homespun.

Spinning on a High Wheel

When using the high wheel, the spinner keeps the wheel constantly turning with one hand while drawing out the fleece with the other. As on the low wheel, the

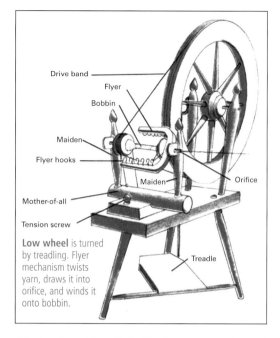

Low wheel is turned by treadling. Flyer mechanism twists yarn, draws it into orifice, and winds it onto bobbin.

drive band must be adjusted to the proper tension and a leader ttached before starting. Then when the rolag fibers are wrapped around the tip of the spindle and pulled away from it at just the right angle, the whirling spindle can twist the fibers into yarn. As it does, the spinner pinches the rolag until fibers between fingers and spindle are spun to the desired tightness. Then additional fleece is allowed to slip through the spinner's fingers so that it can be spun. As the fleece slips through, the spinner must step back from the spindle in order to draw out even more fleece. Eventually, when the wheel can barely be reached, the spinner walks forward to wind the yarn onto the spindle. Because the spinner must continually walk back and forth alongside the wheel—as much as 20 miles in a day during colonial times—the high wheel is sometimes called a walking wheel. It is also known as a wool wheel, since it is so often used to spin wool.

Using the Low Wheel

1. Tie leader to back of bobbin, then pass it over flyer hooks. Draw leader through orifice with crochet hook or with hook made of bent wire. **2.** Fan out ends of rolag and leader and hold them

together with one hand. Use other hand to start wheel by pushing a spoke clockwise. **3.** Treadle slowly and evenly. Allow rolag end to twist around leader so that they are joined. Meanwhile,

leader is drawn toward orifice. **4.** Pinch juncture of leader and rolag with right hand. Use other hand to draw out fleece to thickness

appropriate to the size of your yarn.

  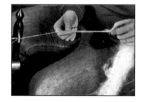

5. When rolag and leader are joined, move right hand to pinch drawn-out fibers at a spot farther back on rolag. Twist can now run farther up fleece.

6. As yarn spins to tightness that you desire, continue to draw out fibers between left and right hands. Spun yarn is drawn into orifice.

7. When enough fibers are drawn out, open fingers to let twist travel farther up rolag. Continue to draw out fibers; add new rolag as needed.

8. Flyer hooks determine where yarn winds onto bobbin. First

wind yarn at ends of bobbin, then move it from hook to hook to build even layers.

High wheel is turned by hand. Spindle tip twists yarn, then spinner unwinds yarn from tip and winds it up on back of spindle.

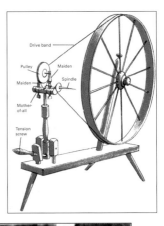

1. Tie leader yarn at back of spindle. Then hold yarn parallel to wheel, turn wheel clockwise, and wind leader onto spindle in even layer.

2. Wrap leader around spindle tip, pull leader away from spindle at angle shown (approximately 120°), and hold ends of leader and rolag together.

3. Turn wheel clockwise with free hand in order to start spindle turning. End of rolag twists around end of leader so that the two will be joined.

4. Keep turning wheel and slide hand farther back on fleece. Pull out fibers, then pinch so that fleece in front of hand is spun. Then slide hand back again.

5. When a length is spun, turn wheel counterclockwise to free yarn. Hold yarn parallel to wheel and turn clockwise to wind into cone on spindle.

6. Return yarn to spinning position and draw out fibers again. When necessary, add new rolag by holding ends together and joining as in Step 3.

After the yarn is spun

The spindle or bobbin must be emptied periodically whether you use a drop spindle, low wheel, or high wheel. To unwind yarn from either type of wheel, you must first take off the wheel's drive bands. Next, the yarn is wound onto a wooden frame called a niddy noddy. Do not unwind all the yarn. Instead, leave the last few feet on the spindle to use as a leader. The distance around a niddy noddy is about 2 yd., though the size varies from one to another. You should wrap 40 lengths before unloading it. This is about 80 yd., or 1 knot, of yarn. (A skein contains 560 yd., or 7 knots.) When you have wrapped a knot of yarn, tie cotton string around it at several points before taking it off the niddy noddy. Now wet or steam the entire knot, tie a 1/2-lb. rock or similar weight at one end, and hang the knot up by its other end to dry. This will set the twist of the yarn. To store a knot or skein of yarn, twist it as shown at far right.

To wind yarn on niddy noddy, tie end of yarn to a crosspiece, grip shaft, and wrap in path shown above.

Store wound yarn by twisting it several times, then pulling loop at one end through loop a other end.

Sources and resources

Books and pamphlets

Hecht, Ann. *The Art of the Loom: Weaving, Spinning and Dyeing Across the World.* New York: Rizzoli, 1990.

Hobdeen, Eileen. *Spinning and Weaving: A Practical Guide.* Portland, Oreg.: International Specialized Book Services, 1987.

Hochberg, Bette. *Handspinner's Handbook.* 33 Wilkes Circle, Santa Cruz, Calif.: Bette Hochberg, 1980.

Leadbeater, Eliza. *Handspinning.* Newton Centre, Mass.: Charles T. Branford Co., 1976.

Ross, Mabel. *The Essentials of Handspinning.* McMinnville, Oreg.: Robin & Russ Handweavers, 1988.

Simmons, Paula. *Spinning and Weaving with Wool.* Petaluma, Calif.: Unicorn Books for Craftsmen, 1991.

Tanning and Leatherwork

A Sensible Craft Whether for Necessity Or Just as a Hobby

Tanning and leatherwork call for a comparatively small investment in tools but can yield a great amount of satisfaction. There is a real sense of achievement in converting a rabbit skin, which a hunter might otherwise throw away, into a soft, lustrous fur and then into warm mittens or a fine hat. With experience, tanning and leatherwork can also become profitable sidelines. Hunters are frequently glad to pay to have the pelt of an animal made into pliable leather, a fur rug, or a trophy to hang on the wall.

The craft of tanning is older than civilization itself. Chemical tanning, as it is practiced today, existed at least 5,000 years ago—there are Egyptian wall paintings showing tanners at work with their tubs and mixing vats. Long before that, our prehistoric ancestors used the hides of animals to clothe themselves. At first, they must have worn the skins just as they came from the animal. Untreated hides, however, are stiff, crack easily, decompose rapidly, and, in addition, may emit an obnoxious odor. Eventually it was discovered that a hide could be treated to make it durable as well as comfortable. The earliest leather-conditioning methods probably involved nothing more than scraping off all the flesh and hair from the hide. The result must have been close to rawhide, a material the American Indians used to make drumheads, lashings, saddles, knife handles, sandals, and snowshoe thongs. The next development probably involved the application of animal fat or other substance—the Indians used animal brains—to soften the leather and make it more water resistant. Other skin-dressing procedures included smoking, soaking in urine, and rubbing with plant or animal oil.

Different Leathers and Where to Get Them

Hunting, trapping, or raising your own livestock are the most direct ways of obtaining the hides you need to make fur or leather. Remember, however, that there are strict regulations governing where, when, and how you may hunt and trap game. There are also endangered species that must not be taken at any time of the year.

Another potential source of hides, especially for rabbit skins, is your local butcher. He may also be able to obtain cow, goat, sheep, and pig hides from a local slaughterhouse, or you can try the slaughterhouse yourself. Some hunters and trappers will sell animal pelts at relatively low prices; a hunter may even let you have them for free, since many hunters are more interested in an animal for sport or food than for its hide. A farm that slaughters its own animals can be another economical source of untanned leather. If you do not care to do the tanning yourself, you can obtain leather from stores listed in the classified telephone directory. Many of these stores cater to the hobbyist and carry a wide variety of hides. Generally, they will also stock a complete line of leatherworking equipment, such as needles, heavy thread, awls, and punches, as well as buckles, lacing, snaps, dyes, leather lubricants, and varnishes.

The First Step Is to Remove the Hide

The object of skinning is to remove the animal's pelt cleanly, neatly, and with minimum damage to either hide or fur. To skin an animal perfectly requires experience. The first time, you are almost certain to damage the hide by slicing too close or else by cutting too cautiously and leaving large chunks of flesh that will mean extra work during the fleshing operation.

Practice skinning a few times with an inexpensive hide before trying your hand on more costly leather. A chipmunk, or even a mouse, is suitable for your first attempts, especially since they are more difficult to skin than larger specimens and so help attune you to the fine points of the skinner's craft. Another good choice for a first attempt would be a freshly killed rabbit from the butcher; if you slash through the hide, you can at least console yourself with a rabbit dinner.

The best tool to use is a skinning knife, an implement with a thin, curved blade specially designed for the job. However, good results can be obtained with almost any blade, provided it is razor sharp. For this reason, keep a sharpening stone handy, particularly since even the best edge will dull during the skinning operation. Note that while a single-edge razor blade can be used for making the first incisions, it should not be employed for the actual skinning: there is too much risk that the blade will slip, cutting either you or the hide.

Once the incisions are made, pull the skin gently away until you run into resistance. When this happens, it means the skin is being held by a membrane or other tissue. Use the knife to cut restricting tissue loose, then resume pulling. Throughout the skinning operation the animal must be held tightly to keep it from shifting.

All animals are skinned in much the same fashion. Generally, the skin on the animal's head and paws is not removed. Instead, incisions are made around the neck and feet, and the rest of the pelt is pulled off. Large animals, such as a bear whose skin is to be made into a rug, may have the head and paws left on the hide.

Once the skin is off the animal, the next step is to flesh it; that is, to remove bits of fat and meat that still adhere to the underside. To make fleshing easier, first soak the unfleshed skin in a solution of either salt or borax to loosen the clinging bits of flesh. Instructions for pre-soaking as well as for fleshing are given at the

Animal	Use	Comments
Bear	Rugs	Hard, durable
Beaver	Coats	Wears well
Calf	Slippers, purses, wallets	Soft, durable
Cow	Jackets, gloves, belts, luggage, shoes	Rough, wears well
Deer	Gloves, moccasins	Soft, pliable, wears very well
Fox	Fur coats, jackets	Fairly durable, warm
Goat	Purses, wallets, gloves	Very fine leather
Muskrat	Fur coats	Wears well
Pig	Wallets, gloves	Wears well
Rabbit	Gloves	Delicate fur
Raccoon	Hats, coats	Fairly delicate
Sheep	Gloves, slippers, rugs	Soft, warm
Squirrel	Fur coats	Wears well
Wolf	Coat trimming	Warm, sheds snow
Woodchuck	Gloves	Delicate

right. To make a salt solution, dissolve 1 pound of ordinary table salt per 2 gallons of soft water. For a borax solution dissolve 1 ounce of borax per gallon of water. Use hot water when dissolving the borax, but let it cool off before immersing the skin. An agitator-type washing machine will speed the soaking process and also help reduce hair loss from the pelt by avoiding oversoaking.

Converting a Hide Into Leather

There are almost as many formulas for tanning solutions as there are tanners, each one swearing by his own mixture. The recipe given here has two advantages: it will not overtan and it has no dangerous acids or toxic vapors. Nevertheless, when working with this tanning solution, as with all others, always use rubber gloves; tanning chemicals are not good for the skin. Use a large plastic or wooden container or nonmetallic washbasin for both mixing and tanning. To make the tanning solution, add 5 lb. of ordinary salt to 10 gal. of warm water. The water should be soft—rainwater will do. Next, mix 2 lb. of alum in enough hot water to dissolve it, then combine both solutions, stirring with a wooden paddle until the ingredients are thoroughly mixed. The solution can be used cold or warm but not hot.

Immerse the hide into the tanning solution and stir gently about twice a day with a wooden paddle. For a perfectly tanned piece of fur or leather make certain the tanning solution reaches every cranny and wrinkle in the hide. The larger the hide, the longer it takes to tan it. A rabbit skin will take about two days, a raccoon about three days. A deer may take from six to eight days, while a sheepskin may take a little less.

The ABCs of Tanning

Tanning converts an animal hide, which would otherwise decompose rapidly, into fur or leather that will stay soft and odor free for years. Originally, tanning was accomplished using tannic acid obtained from trees and vegetables, but most tanners today employ alum. To do a professional job, you must take time to tan the hide thoroughly and to work it until it is pliable.

After the hide has been soaked in the tanning solution for several days, cut off a tiny piece near one edge. If the color is uniform all the way through, then the hide is tanned. But if there is a difference in color between the center and edges, return the skin to the solution for an extra day or two. The most common mistake is to take a pelt out before tanning is complete.

Tanning procedures are the same whether you are processing leather or a fur. However, if the hair is to be removed, it must be removed from the hide before tanning takes place. The easiest way to get the hair off is to start by soaking the hide in a dehairing solution. Use 1 pound of hydrated lime per 8 gallons of soft water and soak for about five days (longer in cool weather) in a wooden container. Move the hide around occasionally with a wooden paddle. (Lime is caustic, so avoid contact with it.) When the hair is loose, rinse the hide, then place it fur side up on a smooth log, and scrape off the hair and loose surface skin with the dull edge of your fleshing knife. Use the same log or type of log that was employed for fleshing (see "Fleshing the hide", p.251).

Rawhide: A Material for All Seasons

Rawhide is untanned leather—usually dehaired—that has been cured by being stretched and dried. To the Plains Indians, buffalo rawhide was a vital all-purpose material, serving as lumber, nails, cord, and cloth. Nowadays rawhide is commonly made from deer or cow skin and can be used for moccasin soles, knife handle grips, boxes, construction lashing, lacing for snowshoes, and drumheads for tom-toms. A special quality of rawhide is that it shrinks as it dries, tightening and forming itself around any object to which it is attached.

Use a fresh pelt when making rawhide. Skin and flesh the animal in the usual fashion, but do not salt the pelt. The next step is dehairing. You can use a dehairing solution of lime and water (see "The ABCs of Tanning", p. 260) or one of wood ash and water, which combine to form lye. For the latter method make a paste of hardwood ashes and water, spread it on the hair side, then roll the skin up over the paste and place the roll, weighted down with a rock, in an ash and water solution. Wear rubber gloves as you work, since the water and ash mixture is caustic. Leave the hide in the dehairing bath until the hair can be pulled out easily—usually several days—then scrape off the hair with a blunt knife. Finally, rinse the hide thoroughly, wring it out, stretch it on a frame, and set it out to dry in a shady spot. It will dry into a hard, flat, platelike sheet.

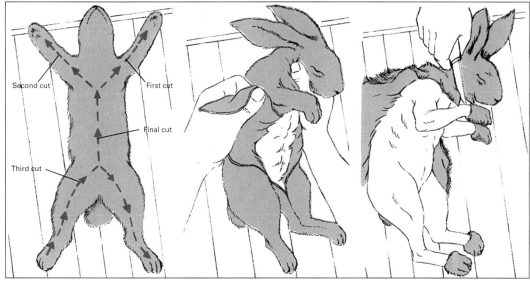

Make the first incision at the breastbone. Starting at this point, cut to the heel of one front leg and then to the heel of the other front leg. Next, cut from the heel of one back leg to the other. Now make one long incision joining both leg cuts as indicated in the drawing. Be sure to use a knife that is razor sharp.

Skin can be pulled off a rabbit with little additional cutting. However, with most other animals the skin must be pulled off a bit at a time, as though it were a very tight glove, until the hide resists further pulling; then use the knife to free the hide. Cut close to the skin, but be careful not to cut into the hide.

Last step in skinning is to free the pelt by incising a circle around the neck and around each leg near the paw. After the skin is off, use a dull knife or the back of the skinning knife to scrape off any flesh or fat that can be removed easily. Leave on pieces that adhere tightly; they will be removed in the fleshing operation.

1. After the hide is tanned, remove it from the solution; then rinse it with a garden hose or in a sink with many changes of water.

2. Hang the hide fur side up over a railing. It should be out of direct sunlight, and air should be able to circulate around the hide.

3. After several days, while the hair and hide are still slightly damp, fold the hide flesh side to flesh side, roll it up, and leave it overnight.

4. If the hide has dried before you are able to roll it up, use a wet sponge to dampen the flesh side. Then fold it as described in Step 3.

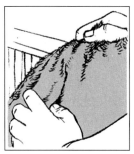

5. Work the hide by stretching it, pulling it over a smooth edge, and twisting it with your hands. Continue working until it is pliable.

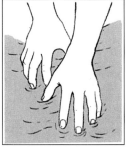

6. Use the tips of your fingers to rub in neat's-foot, cottonseed, corn, or leather lubricating oil. Warm the oil to speed up the work.

7. To clean the matted fur, fill plastic bag with dry oatmeal or hardwood sawdust. Then place hide in bag and shake until fur is clean.

8. Brush and comb fur until it is entirely fluffed up. Go over rough spots on underside of leather with coarse sandpaper wrapped around a block.

Fleshing the hide

Before you flesh the hide, soak it in a brine or borax solution to make the flesh easier to remove. Let the hide soak about 12 hours—overnight will do. The next morning, rinse the hide in fresh water and let it drain. Then, while it is still moist, rub in salt until the flesh side is completely covered (avoid getting salt into the fur side). When the first application of salt has been absorbed, apply a second. Fold the hide in half lengthwise, flesh side to flesh side, roll it up, and place it on a slanting surface so that it can drain. Begin fleshing the next day. Place the hide on a smooth log, fur side down, and scrape away fat and gristle with a fleshing knife, butcher's knife, or drawknife. The log should be about 4 ft. long and 8 in. in diameter. Split it so one side is flat and work on the other side, which should be very smooth. Scrape carefully and evenly. The membrane on the hide's inner surface must be removed for tanning to be successful. Scrape with the blunt edge of the knife blade occasionally to help soften the leather. After fleshing is complete, wash the hide in a soapy solution, then rinse quickly and thoroughly.

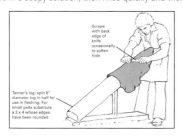

Scrape with back edge of knife occasionally to soften hide

Tanner's log: split 8" diameter log in half for use in fleshing. For small pelts substitute a 2 x 4 whose edges have been rounded

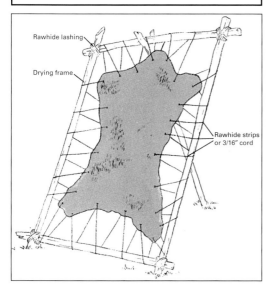

Rawhide lashing

Drying frame

Rawhide strips or 3/16" cord

Rawhide lacing—or any type of leather lacing—is made by cutting a spiral in the hide. Place the leather on a board and drive a nail through, near the center, pinning the leather to the board. With a very sharp knife held vertically, cut a circular spiral. Start from the outside and work in toward the nail. When the nail is reached, remove the leather strip and stretch it out.

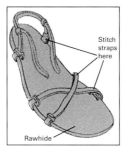

Stitch straps here

Rawhide

Moccasins with soles made of rawhide rather than tanned leather were used by some High Plains tribes. An equivalent contemporary use would be sandals—some believe rawhide to be the best sandal material. The width of the sandal should be 1/2 in. wider than the foot all the way around. Straps can be sewn, stapled, riveted, or simply laced through slots. Make them of soft leather.

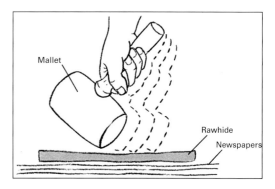

Mallet

Rawhide

Newspapers

Drying frame for rawhide should be built of stout branches lashed solidly together. Make the frame considerably larger than the hide. Use an awl or leather punch to make holes around the edge of the skin, then lash the skin to the frame by lacing rawhide strips or 3/16-in. cord through one hole, around the frame, and back through the next hole until the hide is stretched taut. After it is dry, rawhide can be lightened in color and made pliable by pounding it over its entire surface with a heavy, smooth implement, such as an ax, small sledgehammer, or mallet. Lay the hide on a thick mat of newspapers over a hard, smooth surface and strike it with short, glancing blows.

Sources and resources

Books and pamphlets
Farnham, Albert B. *Home Tanning and Leathermaking Guide.* Columbus, Ohio: A. R. Harding, 1950.

Hobson, Phyllis. *Tan Your Hide.* Charlotte, Vt.: Garden Way Publishing, 1977.
Hunt, W.B. *The Complete How-to Book of Indian Craft.* New York: Collier Books, 1973.
Ickis, Marguerite, and Reba S. Esh. *The Book of Arts and Crafts.* New York: Dover, 1965.
Seymour, John. *The Forgotten Crafts.* New York: Knopf, 1984.

Soapmaking

A Simple Miracle To Perform Yourself In Your Kitchen

According to Roman legend, soap was discovered after a heavy rain fell on the slopes of Mount Sapo (the name means "Mount Soap" in Latin). The hill was the site of an important sacrificial altar, and the rainwater mixed with the mingled ashes and animal fat around the altar's base. As a result of this fortuitous coincidence, the three key components of soap were brought together: water, fat, and lye (potash leached from the ashes). As the mixture trickled down to the banks of the Tiber River, washerwomen at work there noticed that the mysterious substance made their job easier and the wash cleaner.

Over the centuries the basics of soapmaking have remained essentially unchanged from the Roman prescription. To this day in parts of rural America soap is being made much as it was in ancient Rome: out of potash, rainwater, and animal tallow. Even commercial soap is manufactured by much the same process. Other than obvious differences in the scale of the operation and the use of automated equipment, the chief innovations in the commercial product are the substitution of sodium hydroxide for potash and the use of a variety of vegetable oils as supplements to the animal fats.

Homemade soaps can duplicate or improve on the commercial product, usually at considerably less cost. Scents, coloring agents, and decorative effects are all within the scope of home soapmakers who also have the advantage of knowing exactly what ingredients are in the soaps that they produce. The result is that more and more people are trying their hand at making soap, often experimenting with ingredients to devise their own favorite blends.

Making soap can be very simple or more involved depending on the desired product. For very evenly shaped and sized bars, a basic mold with slits like this one can be constructed.

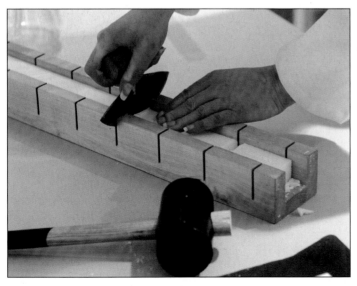

One Substance, Many Varieties

Although, by definition, every soap is made by the saponification (chemical combination) of lye, water, and fat, one soap will differ from the next depending on the kind of fat, the kind of lye, and how much of each is used. Lye made from wood ash, for example, produces soft soap, so-called because of its jellylike consistency. In contrast, soap made from commercial lye (sodium hydroxide) will be hard. Soaps containing coconut oil tend to lather well in cold water but may have a drying action on the skin. Superfatted soaps, such as castile, that contain excess amounts of unsaponified fat are particularly gentle and make excellent toilet soap.

For the sake of convenience or for some special use, soap can be altered in consistency and appearance. Jellied soap for doing the dishes is obtained by slicing off shavings of hard soap and boiling them in water until they dissolve; about 1 pound of shavings per gallon of water should be used. To produce soap flakes for laundry use, simply grate any ordinary hard soap, then add a few tablespoons of borax to improve water softening ability and quicken sudsing action. The preparation of liquid soap is somewhat more complicated. It is generally based on vegetable oils rather than animal fats and requires the addition of glycerine and alcohol during the soap-making process, followed by filtering. If you want soap that floats, gently whip the warm soap solution with an egg beater just before pouring it into molds; when the soap hardens, the trapped air bubbles will make it float.

The Basics Are the Same No Matter What the Soap

The three ingredients needed to make soap—fat, water, and lye—are all readily available. Lye in the form of sodium hydroxide is sold as dry crystals in many supermarkets and hardware stores, while lye in the form of potash can be made at home from wood ash (see p.288). Because all types of lye are highly caustic substances that react with plastic, aluminum, and tin, soapmaking utensils should be made of wood, glass, enamel, stainless steel, or ceramic. Fat for soapmaking can be almost any pure animal or vegetable oil from reclaimed kitchen grease to castor oil. (See "Rendering and Clarifying", p.287, for more information.) The water should be soft. If you are in a hard water area, treat the water with a commercial softener or add a few tablespoons of borax to it. You can also collect rainwater and use it to make soap. The following equipment is needed for soapmaking:

1. A container to hold the lye solution. A 2-quart juice bottle will do. Punch two holes in the cover, one on the opposite side from the other, so you will be able to pour the lye over the fat later on.

2. A 10- to 12-quart pot to hold the fat and lye.

3. A wooden spoon to stir the lye solution and fat.

4. A candy or dairy thermometer that is accurate to within 1°F in the 80°F to 120°F range. For convenience you may want to have two such thermometers.

5. Rubber gloves. Wear these as a precautionary measure, since lye will burn if it touches the skin.

6. Molds for the soap. Prepare the molds by lining them with plastic or greasing them with Vaseline.

7. Insulation to keep the soap warm after it is poured into the molds. Cardboard, styrofoam, or an ordinary blanket can be used.

8. Enough newspapers to cover work surfaces and floor areas where you will be working.

Prepare the lye solution before beginning the soap-making process so that it will have a chance to cool. To make the lye solution, pour cold water into an enamel-ware pot, then add the lye slowly while stirring the solution steadily with a wooden spoon. The reaction between the lye crystals and water will generate temperatures over 200°F. The container can be placed in a basin of cold water to hasten cooling. Once the solution has cooled, pour it carefully into the 2-quart glass container. If you are going to use animal fat for your soap, you should also prepare it in advance to allow it to cool down (the rendering process takes place at well above the temperatures needed to make soap). Fats can be refrigerated and then brought to soapmaking temperature by warming in a basin of hot water. The type of fat you should use and the relative amounts of fat, lye, and water that should be combined depend on the particular type of soap being made. The standard recipe calls for 6 pounds of beef fat, 2 1/2 pints of water, and 13 ounces of lye crystals. (See p.288 for other recipes).

Saponification is the chemical process by which soap is formed from lye, water, and fat. In order for saponification to take place, the temperature of the lye solution and fat has to be carefully controlled. The simplest method is to bring both the lye and the fat to a temperature of 95°F to 98°F before mixing them together. Some experts recommend that the fat be at a higher temperature than the lye: about 125°F for the fat and 93°F for the lye when beef tallow is used, 83°F and 73°F when lard is used, 105°F and 83°F for half lard, half tallow.

Occasionally, saponification does not take place and the soap mixture separates into a top layer of fat and a bottom layer of lye solution. Generally, the mixture can be reclaimed by heating it to about 140°F while gently stirring with the wooden spoon. Then remove from the heat and keep stirring until the mixture thickens into soap. To test your soap solution, spoon up a bit and let a few drops fall on the surface of the soap; if the surface

Some plants are natural cleaners

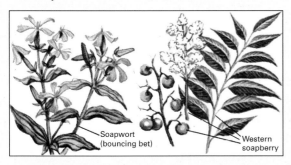

Soapwort (bouncing bet)

Western soapberry

American Indians and early settlers were familiar with a number of plants whose roots, leaves, or berries contain saponin, a natural ingredient that foams and cleans like soap. The best known and most frequently used of these plants is soapwort, or bouncing bet, a pink-blossomed perennial that grows wild throughout most of the United States; the juice from the root produces a lather when mixed with water. Another soap plant is the yucca found in Mexico and the Southwest. Its roots, broken into pieces and mixed with water, form a gentle soaplike compound for the skin and hair. California soap root, a member of the lily family, contains a liquid in the middle of its bulb that makes an excellent antidandruff shampoo; simply crush the bulb center and mix it with water. The fleshy berries of both the southern soapberry tree, found in southern Florida as well as South America, and the western soapberry tree of the American Southwest contain seeds that produce lather in water and closely duplicate the cleansing action of soap.

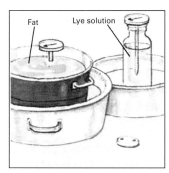

1. Bring both fat and lye solution to between 95°F and 98°F by placing their containers in basins of hot or cold water, depending on whether they need to be warmed or cooled.

2. To ensure thorough mixing, stir the fat before the lye is added. Pour in the lye solution in a steady stream while continuing to stir with an even, circular motion.

3. The mixture will turn opaque and brownish, then lighten. Soap is ready when its surface can support a drop of mixture for a moment; consistency should be like sour cream.

4. Add colorants, scents, and other special ingredients (adding them earlier would probably have interfered with saponification). Pour liquid into molds and place in warm location.

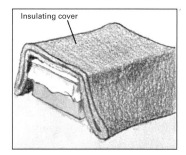

5. Cover molds with cardboard, styrofoam, or blankets. Soap should be removed from the molds after 24 hours, then left uncovered in freely circulating air for two to four weeks.

supports the drops for a moment or two, the soap is ready for the molds.

Caution: Lye is highly caustic and should be washed off immediately with cold water if it comes in contact with the skin. Avert your face to avoid inhaling the fumes while mixing lye. Always mix lye with cold water, and pour the lye into the water rather than the water into the lye.

From Humble Origins Of Fat and Potash Come Fancy Soaps

Rendering and Clarifying

Any animal fat and most vegetable oils can be used in soapmaking. A combination of rendered beef fat (tallow) plus pig fat (lard) makes a most satisfactory basic soap and is the mixture most commonly recommended in books, pamphlets, and by manufacturers of lye. Poultry fat alone is too soft but may be used in combination with other fats, and so can most vegetable oils. Coconut oil produces high-quality kitchen and toilet soaps, while palm oil soap is gentle and pleasant smelling. Soy bean, cottonseed, corn, and peanut oils all yield low-foaming, medium-quality soap. The whitest, best-smelling soaps are made from pure rendered fats and oils. However, reclaimed kitchen grease and drippings from the frying pan if properly treated make good soaps.

Rendering is the process of melting and purifying solid fats. Start with twice the weight of fat called for in the soap recipe. Cut the fat into small pieces, and heat over a low flame. Do not let the fat burn or smoke. Although most of the fat will liquify, solid particles called cracklings will remain. After rendering, strain the liquid into a clean container and refrigerate until it is needed.

Grease and drippings can be reclaimed for soapmaking by clarifying them. Place the fat, an equal amount of water, and 2 tablespoons of salt in a pan and bring to a boil. Remove from the fire, cool slightly, and add cold water—about 1 quart per gallon of hot liquid. The mixture will separate into three layers: pure fat at the top, fat with granular impurities next, and water at the bottom. Spoon off the pure fat and save it for soapmaking. Even if the unclarified drippings were rancid, they can be rescued by using a mixture of one part vinegar to five parts water in the clarifying process instead of plain water. To deodorize fat, cook sliced-up potatoes in the clarified fat. Use one potato for each 3 pounds of fat. To bleach fat, mix it with a solution of potassium permanganate, a powerful oxidizing and bleaching agent; then warm and stir. Use 1 pint of solution for each pound of fat. To make a pint of solution, dissolve a few crystals of potassium permanganate (available at some hobby supply stores) in a pint of soft water.

Soap as Art

For centuries soap has been a medium of artistic expression. It has been carved, painted, sculpted, packaged, and inlaid with pictures and patterns. Soap decoration begins with the mold. Almost any conveniently sized container can be used; for example, custard cups, cake pans, boxes of all sorts, jello molds, and ashtrays. Once the soap has set, designs can be pressed or cut into the surface of the

Dried fruit or flowers can be pressed into soap while it's hardening for a decorative and aromatic touch.

individual bars, or the soap can be carved into almost any conceivable shape. The only equipment you need for carving is a small, sharp knife. If the soap is relatively soft, it can be worked like dough. Roll it into balls, or flatten it with a rolling pin, and cut shapes out of it with cookie cutters. An unusual decorative technique is to embed a picture or decal in the top of a bar of soap, then cover the picture with a thin layer of melted paraffin. The paraffin protects the design from water, keeping it intact as the soap wears away around it.

Making Your Own Lye the Old-time Way

From pioneer times to the present the traditional way to make lye has been to leach it from wood ashes. Lye produced in this manner is known as potash and consists mostly of potassium carbonate, a less caustic substance than commercial lye. Any large wooden container can be used for the lye-making process—the bigger the better, since the more ashes the water seeps through, the more concentrated will be the lye solution. A barrel or large tub with a hole drilled as near to the bottom as possible is excellent for leaching.

Place the barrel on cinder blocks or other supports so that a crock or enamel pot can be placed beneath it to collect the solution as it seeps out. Set up the barrel at an angle, with the opening at the lowest point, so that the lye will run out of it and into the crock. Line the bottom of the barrel with straw to prevent ashes from sifting into the lye solution and pack the barrel with ashes—almost any hardwood will do, but oak, hickory, sugar maple, fruit woods, beech, and ash produce the strongest lye. Finally, scoop out a depression at the top large enough to hold 2 to 3 quarts of water.

To make the lye, fill the depression with rainwater heated to boiling, and let the water seep down through the ashes. When the water has all seeped away, add more. It will be a while before the lye begins to trickle out the bottom—perhaps as long as several days if the ashes have been packed tightly—but do not try to hurry the process by adding extra water prematurely.

The single bar method

If you want to experiment with a variety of scents, colors, and ingredients, the simplest and most economical way is to prepare a single bar of soap rather than a large batch. You will need the following ingredients:

1/2 cup cold soft water   1 cup melted beef tallow
2 heaping tbsp. commercial lye

Slowly add the lye to the water, then bring both lye solution and tallow to about body temperature. Combine the two in a glass bowl and mix slowly and steadily with an egg beater until the consistency is that of sour cream. Pour mixture into mold and age according to standard procedure.

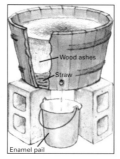

After lye is made test it by cracking in a raw egg. If the egg barely floats, the lye is good for soapmaking.

Although soap can be made directly from the lye solution, it is often convenient to have the lye in crystalline form, since crystals permit more precision in the soapmaking process. To extract crystalline potash from lye water, boil down the solution in a stainless steel or enamelware pot. At first a dark residue called black salts will form. By maintaining heat, additional impurities can be driven off, leaving the grayish-white potash.

A Survey of Soap Recipes

The standard batch recipe makes an excellent hard soap for laundry and bathing. The recipe calls for one can (13 ounces) of commercial lye, 2 1/2 pints of water, and 6 pounds of fat. About 9 pounds of soap result, enough to make 36 bars of toilet soap. These can be molded separately, or the soap can be poured into a large container, such as a shoebox, and later cut into bars. A combination of half tallow and half lard is usually suggested. Most other soaps—and there are as many formulas as there are soapmakers—are variations on the standard recipe. A number of attractive recipes are given here, but much of the fun in making soap comes from experimenting with your own combinations of fats, oils, and additives. Except where noted, the soaps are prepared by the procedure described on pp.253–254.

Beauty soaps

Beauty soaps are made by adding scents, oils, and special purpose substances or by replacing some of the water and fat in the standard recipe with new ingredients. The most popular variation is in the amount and type of fat or oil used. Extra fat or oil makes the soap superfatted—that is, the soap becomes enriched with excess fat left unaffected by the saponification process. The result is an especially gentle soap suitable for delicate complexions.

Avocado soap. For sensitive skin. Use the recipe for castile soap but substitute 6 oz. of avocado oil for an equal amount of olive oil.

Castile soap. Simple but expensive with a hard consistency that is good for carving; named for the kingdom of Castile in north-central Spain where it was first produced.

1 lb. 9 oz. olive oil	10 1/2 oz. lye
3 lb. 10 oz. tallow	2 pt. water

Coconut and olive soap. Cream colored with rich, gentle lather, even in cold water.

1 lb. 7 oz. olive oil	11 1/2 oz. lye
1 lb. 7 oz. coconut oil	2 pt. water
1 lb. 7 oz. tallow	

Cold cream soap. Thoroughly mix 2 oz. of commercial cold cream into standard soap just before pouring it into molds.

Lanolin soap. Recommended for dry skin. Add 2 oz. pure liquid anhydrous lanolin to the standard recipe before pouring into molds.

Milk and honey soap. Nourishing for the skin. Thoroughly mix 1 oz. each of powdered milk and honey into any soap while it is still in liquid form, then pour it into molds.

Palm soap. For dry skin. Substitute 3 lb. lard, 1 lb. bleached palm oil, and 2 lb. olive oil for the tallow-lard mixture in the standard recipe.

Rose water soap. Slightly astringent for oily skin. Substitute 4 oz. of rose water for plain water when mixing the lye.

Scented soaps

Essential oils—powerful aromatic substances extracted from flowers, herbs, and animals—can be obtained from specialty druggists and added in small amounts to your soap before it is poured. Popular fragrances are bayberry, rosemary, jasmine, carnation, and musk. You can also make your own infusions, or strong teas, from various herbs and flowers. Steep the plant in boiling water, strain off the solids, and substitute the infusion for some of the water in the recipe. If the infusion is strong enough, you can get the same result by adding it to the soap mixture just before pouring it into molds. However, do not add over-the-counter perfumes or toilet waters: the alcohol they contain will interfere with saponification. Generally, 6 tsp. of scent mixture will be sufficient for the standard batch. *Savon au bouquet* and cinnamon are among many old-time scent mixtures. You can experiment with other combinations yourself.

Cinnamon. Traditionally, cinnamon soap was colored with yellow ocher. A few drops of oil of lavender can also be added.

6 tsp. oil of cinnamon	1/2 tsp. oil of bergamot
1/2 tsp. oil of sassafras	

Savon au bouquet. In French the name simply means "perfumed soap." A 19th-century recipe for *savon au bouquet* advises: "The perfume, and with it the title of the soap, can be varied according to the caprice of fashion."

4 1/2 tsp. oil of	1/2 tsp. oil of thyme
bergamot	1/2 tsp. oil of sassafras
1/4 tsp. oil of clove	1/2 tsp. oil of neroli

Colored soaps

Roots, bark, leaves, flowers, fruits, and vegetables can be used for colorants. Spices such as turmeric and natural dyes such as chlorophyll can be added directly to the soap mixture before pouring into molds. Candle dyes and liquid blueing also work well. Food coloring, however, does not mix well with soap. To obtain your own dyes, make an infusion by pouring boiling water over dyestuff until a deep color is achieved. Strain out the solid pieces and use 4 to 10 oz. of the liquid in the standard recipe as a substitute for an equal amount of water when mixing up the lye solution. Or add the dye just before pouring the soap into the molds. (See *Natural Dyes*, pp.239–243, for more information.) A marbleized effect can be obtained by gently swirling the colorant into the mixture.

Shampoo soap for blonds. Add 3 oz. each of infusions made from camomile, mullein flowers, and marigolds before pouring into molds.

Shampoo soap for brunettes. Add 3 oz. each of infusions made from rosemary, raspberry leaves, and red sage before pouring into molds.

Special purpose soaps

Old-time soap recipes included special formulas for almost every conceivable purpose—insect repellent soaps, antiseptic soaps, medicinal soaps, abrasive soaps, dandruff remover soaps, louse-killing soaps, fungicide soaps. Some were useful, many were not, and several were downright dangerous, such as soaps containing mercury chloride for "the itch." Kerosene was a favorite additive but did little except make the soap harsh. Below are two safe and useful recipes.

Grease remover. For use on hands with ground-in dirt and grease. Add 1 oz. of almond meal, oatmeal, or cornmeal to the castile recipe before pouring into molds.

Vegetable soap. For strict vegetarians; reddish in color, soft enough to mold into balls. Vegetable soap is extremely mild and gentle. It can also be used as a base for a dry hair shampoo soap. Simply add a mixture of 11/2 oz. glycerine and 11/2 oz. castor oil to the liquid soap just before pouring it into molds.

2 lb. 10 oz. olive oil	2 pt. water
1 lb. 7 oz. of solid-type	1 lb. coconut oil
vegetable	10 1/4 oz. lye
shortening	

Sources and resources

Books

Bacon, Richard M. *The Forgotten Arts.* Book 1. Dublin, N.H.: Yankee, Inc., 1975.

Bramson, Ann. *Soap: Making It, Enjoying It.* New York: Workman Publishing, 1975.

Cavitch, Susan M. *The Natural Soap Book: Making Herbal and Vegetable-Based Soaps.* Pownal, Vt.: Storey Communications, 1995.

Seymour, John. *The Forgotten Crafts.* New York: Knopf, 1984.

White, Elaine C. *Soap Recipes: Seventy Tried and True Ways to Make Modern Soap with Herbs, Beeswax and Vegetable Oils.* Starkville, Miss.: Valley Hills Press, 1995.

Candlemaking

Time-tested Methods Of Working With Wax

Autumn was candlemaking time in early America. Housewives spent long hours boiling down the fat of newly slaughtered beef and sheep into tallow. Not only was the job hot and sweaty, but the odor of the rendering fat was also unpleasant and the product was far from perfect: the candles burned too rapidly, buckled in warm weather, and gave off fumes and smoke.

Other sources of wax were available—notably bayberry and beeswax—but both were expensive, and candles made from them were reserved for special occasions. It was not until the discovery of paraffin in the 1850s that the average family could enjoy the luxury of bright, steady, smokeless illumination.

Waxes

Paraffin has come to be the chief ingredient in almost all candles. Beeswax is expensive, and tallow, a staple in years gone by, is seldom used today because of its many drawbacks: there are few more effective ways to dampen enthusiasm for the "good old days" than to spend a chilly winter's evening in the smoky, sputtering glow of an old-fashioned tallow candle.

Paraffin, a petroleum by-product, comes in five grades, the hardest of which is sold by craft shops for use in candlemaking. One 10-pound slab, the usual size, makes about 4 quarts of liquid wax. For firmer, brighter burning candles add 3 tablespoons of powdered stearin per pound of paraffin.

Beeswax, always a scarce commodity, is in shorter supply than ever, primarily because modern hives allow honey to be harvested without harvesting the comb in the process (see "Beekeeping", pp.158–162). However, you

Hand-dipped candles are beautiful but time consuming to make. Dipping several wicks at once helps to hasten the process; another way is to add alum to the mixture, since alum will cause the wax to form thicker layers.

Candles from beeswax sheets

Sheets of beeswax that are used to start new hives can be rolled into candles without being melted. Buy sheets from suppliers of beekeeping equipment or from craft shops. Sheet widths vary, but the standard length is about 16 in. On a warm day your hands will provide enough heat to make the sheets pliable. In cold weather set the sheets in a warm (80°F to 85°F) spot to soften before shaping. Cut a sheet so that the top edge slants downward about 1 in. from corner to corner. Then roll up the sheet around the wick.

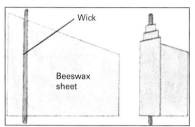

Wick

Beeswax
sheet

Roll beeswax sheet around wick to make a sweet-burning candle.

Wick types and their uses

Kind of wick	Wick size	Candle diameter
Flat-braided wick	15 ply	1"–21/2"
Square-braided wick	24 ply	3"–4"
Square-braided wick	30 ply	More than 4"
Metal-core wick	Small	Less than 2"
Metal-core wick	Large	2"–4"
Metal-core wick	Extra large	More than 4"

along the New England coast. Old-timers gathered the berries in autumn, then sorted them to remove leaves and twigs. Next, the berries were boiled in hot water for two hours, and the muddy green fat that floated to the top was skimmed off, reboiled, and strained. Today, most bayberry bushes are protected by law and the berries cannot be picked, but artificial colors and scents can be used instead to make paraffin candles that look like and smell like the old-fashioned bayberry ones.

Wicks

Wax is the fuel of a candle, and the wick is its burner. The wick must blot up the molten wax, provide a surface for the wax to burn on, and yet not burn up too quickly itself. To make wicks the colonial way, soak heavy cotton yarn for 12 hours in a solution of 1 tablespoon salt plus 2 tablespoons boric acid in a cup of water. (A mixture of turpentine, lime water, and vinegar will also serve.) After the yarn is dry, braid three strands together to form the wick. Wicks can also be purchased. Be sure that any wicks you buy fit the candles you plan to make as indicated in the chart: too large a wick will cause a smoky candle; too small a wick and the flame will be doused in melted wax.

The Basics of Paraffin Candles

Candlemaking is a simple job requiring little in the way of special equipment. You will need an accurate candy thermometer to measure the temperature of the molten wax and plenty of newspaper (spilled wax is difficult to clean up). Whether you are making dipped candles or molded ones, the first step is to melt the wax. Wax is flammable, so never try to melt it in a container set

can still buy beeswax at craft stores or you can make your own if you have a hive and are willing to sacrifice some honey (bees use up 10 pounds of honey to make 1 pound of comb). First extract the honey from the comb. Rinse the empty comb in cold running water, and place it in a pan along with 2 cups of water to prevent the wax from catching fire. Gently heat the comb until it is melted, and continue cooking for an hour. Pour the still-molten wax onto cheesecloth above a tub of cold water, and press the wax through the cloth to remove any impurities. If you are economy minded, use the beeswax as an additive only. Candles with as little as 10 percent beeswax have a better aroma and are harder than ones made entirely of paraffin or tallow.

Tallow for candlemaking is obtained by rendering animal fat (see "Soapmaking", p.285). Beef fat is best, but sheep fat can also be used. To harden the candles and make them burn cleaner, add 1/2 pound of alum and 1/2 pound of saltpeter to each pound of melted tallow.

Bayberry candles, a Christmas favorite, are made from the tiny gray-green, wax-coated fruit of the bayberry, a spicy, woody shrub that grows in sandy soil

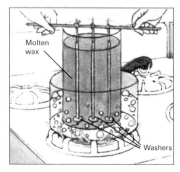

Molten wax

Washers

1. Dip wicks in hot wax held in tall can set in hot water. Remove wicks; let drip.

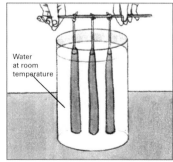

Water at room temperature

2. Dip in water, blot with paper towel, and lay on waxed paper 30 seconds.

Waxed paper

3. Dip repeatedly; roll candles on level surface occasionally to straighten them.

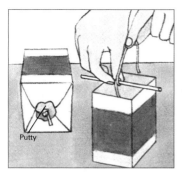

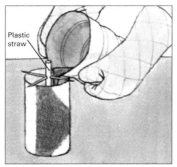

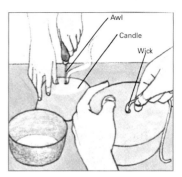

Wick-in-mold method. Cut hole in center of mold, tie washer to wick bottom, and thread wick through hole. Hold wick end in place; plug hole with putty. Pull wick taut and tie around pencil resting on top.

Plastic straw method. Stand straw in mold, then fill mold with wax. After wax hardens, pull out straw, tie foil to one end of wick, and thread other end through. When candle is lit, wax will fill hole.

Hot-awl method. Bore hole in hardened candle with heated awl or metal knitting needle. Knot one end of wick and thread other end through hole. When the candle is used, melted wax will fill in hole.

directly over a flame. Instead, fill a wide-bottomed pan (one that is large enough to cover the burner completely) half-full of water, and place it over a low flame. Then put several chunks of wax in a can, and set the can in the center of the water-filled pan. As the chunks of wax melt, add additional pieces. If, despite your precautions, the wax should catch fire, douse the flames by covering the can with a lid or by pouring baking soda over them. Do not use water, since wax floats on it.

Once the wax is melted, add stearin (3 tablespoons per pound) and coloring. Use a liquid, solid, or powdered dye made especially for candles. Add it a little at a time, and test the color by dripping a bit on a white plate.

Making dipped candles

Two cans are needed for candle dipping—one to hold molten wax, the other to hold cool water. The cans must be taller than the candles you wish to make; 48-ounce juice cans are a convenient size. Keep the melted wax at 150°F to 180°F during the dipping procedure. The water in the cooling can should be about room temperature.

Cut wicks 4 inches longer than the finished candles, and tie a washer to the lower end of each wick for weight. Dip the wicks individually or tie several to a dowel and dip them together. After cooling the first dip pull the wicks straight. It will take 30 to 40 dips to make a candle 1 inch in diameter. To harden the candle's outer layer and make the candle dripless, add an extra tablespoon of stearin per pound of wax for the final dip. After dipping is complete, cut the candle base straight with a sharp, heated knife, and trim the wick to 1/2 inch.

Making molded candles

Milk cartons, jars, cans, plastic cups, cardboard rolls, and many other common containers make interesting candle molds. Start by coating the interior of each mold with cooking oil or silicone spray to prevent sticking. (Waxed containers need not be coated.) If the mold is cardboard, wrap string around it so that it will hold its shape when filled. Next, prepare the container for the wick by one of the methods shown at right.

Use a coffee can for melting wax. Bend its rim to form a spout. Heat the wax to 130°F for cardboard, plastic, or glass molds; 190°F for metal molds. Turn off the flame, lift the can with potholders, and pour the wax into the molds. Let the molds cool overnight, then refrigerate them for 12 hours. Cardboard or plastic molds can be peeled off. Turn glass or metal molds upside down and tap until the candles slide out. If the candle sticks, dip the mold briefly in hot water. Smooth rough spots on the candles by rubbing with a nylon stocking. Candles should age for at least a week before use.

Sources and resources

Books

Constable, David. *Candlemaking*. Woodstock, N.Y.: A. Schwartz & Co., 1993.

Guy, Gary. *Easy-to-Make Candles*. New York: Dover, 1980.

Ickis, Marguerite, and Reba S. Esh. *The Book of Arts and Crafts*. New York: Dover, 1965.

Innes, Miranda. *The Book of Candles*. New York: Dorling Kindersley, 1991.

Meldrum, Sandie. *Traditional Candlewicking*. Cincinnati, Ohio: Seven Hills Books, 1994.

Seymour, John. *The Forgotten Crafts*. New York: Knopf, 1984.

Basketry

Beautiful and Versatile: There Is a Basket Style For Almost Every Job

Basketmaking has proven itself an invaluable skill to Americans from pioneer times to the present. Few tools besides a sharp knife are needed to make a basket, the basic techniques can be easily adapted to whatever materials are locally available, and an endless variety of basket shapes and sizes can be created to fill almost any need that may arise. A soft, lightweight willow basket can serve for gathering eggs or one of sturdy splintwork for apples. A big, flat-sided basket can be strapped onto a horse to carry major loads, while a large, lidded basket—designed to let in air but keep out sunlight—will store dried fruits and vegetables all winter long. An open weave makes a good strainer; a tightly wrapped coil can be virtually watertight.

Old-time basketmakers often specialized in just one technique and handed down its secrets from one generation to the next. Modern practitioners see basketry as an art form. They explore a variety of approaches and strive for imaginative combinations of colors, textures, and forms. They also take advantage of the wide availability of basketry materials, combining everything from wire, string, and feathers with the traditional splints and grasses. Craft stores supply an abundance of imported and machine-milled splints and reeds, whose uniform size and flexibility make them easy to manipulate. There is also a nearly limitless supply of free basketmaking materials growing in the countryside. Tall grasses and weeds alongside a highway, honeysuckle that has overgrown its boundaries, and thin shoots pruned from a tree or bush all make beautiful, serviceable baskets.

Brand-new or centuries old, all baskets are handmade because no way has yet been found to weave them by machine. While many modern baskets are primarily decorative, the old ones were absolute necessities. Settlers in isolated areas, working with homegrown or locally gathered materials, used baskets in place of scarce metalware and pottery.

How to Use Easy-to-Find Materials

Some of the most useful and widely available natural basketry materials are listed in the chart on the opposite page, but these represent only a few of the many possibilities for making beautiful baskets. Experiment with whatever vines, grasses, and leaves are available to you and try all the different methods of preparing them.

Gathering and Preparing Natural Basketry Materials

Material	What to gather	When to gather	Preliminary preparations	Soaking instructions
Blackberry, raspberry (green)	Shoots, 1–2 yr. old	Late fall	Strip off thorns by pulling through heavily gloved hand. Use at once	20 min. in lukewarm water
Blackberry, raspberry (brown)	Any older canes	Anytime	Dethorn as for green shoots, but boil 3–4 hr. as for honeysuckle	20 min. in lukewarm water
Cattail leaves	Fully grown leaves	Early fall	Clean off slime at base and spread or hang leaves to dry	5–10 min. in lukewarm water
Cattail stalks	Fully grown stalks	Early fall	Remove top, clean base, split in half to dry, then in quarters	5–10 min. in lukewarm water
Corn husks	Pale green inner leaves	When corn is ripe	Spread or hang to dry slowly. Drying should take 1 wk.	1–5 min. in lukewarm water
Grasses (green)	Ripe green grasses	Spring or summer	Hang or spread to dry in cool, dark place or spread in sun	1/2 hr. in cold water
Grasses (brown)	Dry brown grasses	Late summer or fall	Use immediately or store in cool, dry place	1/2 hr. in cold water
Honeysuckle	Vines, 1–2 yr. old	Late fall to early spring	Boil for 3–4 hr. Rub briskly with towel to remove bark	20 min. in lukewarm water
Iris, crocus, daffodil (green)	Full grown green leaves	Late spring through summer	Spread to dry in sun to bleach or in darkness to retain color	Dip in water or spray lightly
Iris, crocus, daffodil (brown)	Brown, wilted leaves	After 1st frost	May be used immediately or spread to dry in shade	Dip in water or spray lightly
Maple, dogwood, other hardwoods	Thin 1st-yr. growth	Spring or fall	Use immediately, either peeled or unpeeled. May be split	Most shoots need not be soaked
Pine needles (green)	Long, green needles	Anytime	Hang branch full of needles upside down or spread on ground to dry	Until pliable in lukewarm water
Pine needles (brown)	Long, brown needles	Any dry day	No preliminary preparation except cleaning is necessary	Until pliable in lukewarm water
Straw	Nearly ripe stalks	Late summer or early fall	Spread on ground or hang upside down to dry slowly	10–20 min. in lukewarm water
Willow (green)	Green 1st-yr. growth	Spring	May be used immediately or dried for future use	1/2–hr. in warm water
Willow (brown)	Older growth	Late fall or winter	Boil 4–6 hr. or soak for 3–4 days. Peel off bark	1/2–hr. in warm water
Wisteria, ivy, grape	Any long, pliable vines	Fall or early spring	Hang to dry in cool, dark place. Peel off bark if it is loose	Overnight in lukewarm water

The easiest materials to work with are ones that are long and pliable: grasses and leaves that are mature but have not yet started to brown off, first-year branches and saplings, and spring or fall vines in which the sap is running. However, the rich colors of hard-to-handle dried grasses, leaves, and vines make them well worth learning to use too. The chart gives special instructions for preparing plants gathered after they are dry.

Most of the materials you collect will need some preliminary preparation to strengthen and preshrink them, since any shrinkage after a basket is finished tends to loosen the construction. Once the preparatory steps are completed, materials can either be used immediately or dried and stored. Dry the plants slowly in a cool, dark place unless you want to achieve the bleached effect of drying in full sun. To prevent mildew and general deterioration, store dried material in a location that is cool, airy, and free of moisture. Brown paper bags are good for storing small leaves and grasses. Vines can be coiled. Long grasses should be tied into loose bundles and hung.

When you are ready to make a basket, soak the dried material in water until it is pliable. Soaking time varies greatly. In general, the thicker and harder the plant is, the more soaking it will require. To avoid oversoaking, wrap the soaked material in a damp towel rather than letting it sit in water as you work.

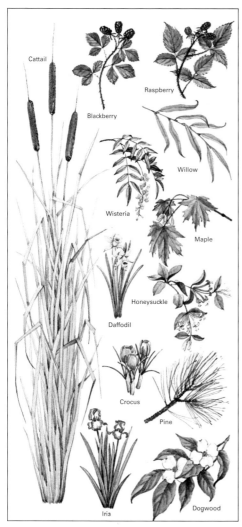

Cattail

Raspberry

Blackberry

Willow

Wisteria

Maple

Honeysuckle

Daffodil

Crocus

Pine

Iris

Dogwood

Constructing a Basket From Coils of Straw

Even a weak and brittle material, such as straw or grass, can be made into a strong basket when it is coiled. Gather 1 to 2 pounds of straw and 75 to 100 willow branches to use as wrapper for the straw. Choose long, straight first-year willow shoots with no side branches. Weeping willow is good if gathered in winter, or gather shoots from a basket willow anytime.

When you are ready to make a basket, soak the willow in water overnight and split it as shown below. Prepare the straw by removing short, broken pieces. The easiest way to do this is to take a small handful at a time (a bunch about 1 1/2 inches in diameter is easy to handle), slap it against your knee, and comb your fingers through so that the broken pieces fall out. Soak the straw for 10 minutes to make it pliable enough to coil. Keep it wrapped in a damp towel as you work so it does not dry out. As you coil the basket, strive for evenly spaced willow stitches and straw bundles of uniform thickness.

Bread basket is made of bundles of broom straw that were wrapped with strips of willow as they were coiled into a spiral. Grass or pine needles could be used instead of straw. The coils are 1/2 in. thick and the willow turns are 1/2 in. apart.

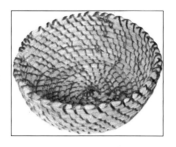

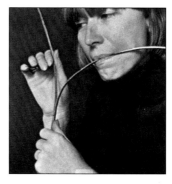

To split willow, cut with a sharp knife 2 in. into end of branch and pull halves apart with exactly equal force. Pull one side with teeth; use free hand to help control force. It takes practice to keep split centered so that one of the halves does not tear off in a short piece. After splitting, shave any lumps off split side of each half, and cut small end to a point.

Basic Coiling Techniques

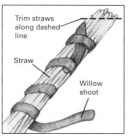

Trim straws along dashed line

Straw

Willow shoot

1. Wrap a willow strip around its own end to anchor it to top of straw bundle. Trim off ends of the straws close to willow.

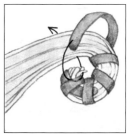

2. After four wraps, curl straw bundle into spiral, draw willow through center, and pull tight. Repeat five times.

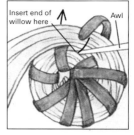

Insert end of willow here

Awl

3. Open a hole with the help of an awl, then stitch willow through straw under a wrap made in Step 1. Pull tight.

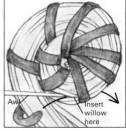

Awl

Insert willow here

4. Continue wrapping willow strip around straw and stitching through straw bundle to make a continuous coil.

Making the Basket

1. As basket grows, add more straw by interweaving new ends among old.

2. To add more willow, draw new strand through, then hide ends between coils.

3. When base measures 6 in., gradually curve spiral upward to form bowl.

4. When sides of bowl reach a heightof 5 in., cut off ends of straw at an angle.

5. Wrap tapered ends of straw with closely spaced willow stitches.

6. Reinforce rim by overstitching in direction opposite to first round of stitches.

Use Corn-Husk Braids To Make a Place Mat

To make a corn-husk mat, you will need husks, raffia or other stitching material, a blunt needle, and a place to anchor the braid. For a good anchor, hammer a nail at one end of a plank, hook your braid over the nail, sit on the plank's other end, and pull the braid tight.

Dry the corn husks according to directions in the chart on page 261. A screen makes an excellent drying rack, or spread the leaves on a tabletop or board. Drying will take two to four days, depending on the weather. Prepare the husks by clipping off the ends to make them straight and even. Then soak them for five minutes. Finish the mat with a row of fringed braid.

Weaving Strong Baskets Out of Wood Splints

Black, or basket, ash is the ideal tree for making splints because it has tough annual growth rings separated from one another by relatively soft, spongy layers. The tough rings are torn apart into long, thin strips to make splints. Red maple, white maple, hickory, elm, poplar, and sassafras are other sources of splints, but they are more difficult to process than ash.

Whatever tree you choose, it should be 4 to 6 inches in diameter with at least 6 feet of straight, branch-free trunk. (Branches produce knots, which interfere with splintmaking.) One processing method is to soak the

Corn husks, braided into a long rope and sewn into a spiral, make a sturdy, heat-resistant place mat. Use the husk's soft inner leaves or buy packaged husks at a Mexican grocery. Sew with raffia (available at craft shops), cotton thread, or narrow strips of leather.

whole log in water for a month or longer and then pound it with a club to break up the spongy layers so that the tough rings will separate from one another naturally. In another method the log is first split into eighths using hardwood wedges and a froe, an old-fashioned home-steading and carpentry tool that was used to make shakes, shingles, and clapboards. The eighths are then cleaved into splints. Froes can still be purchased from specialty-tool mail-order houses. A sharp ax or cleaver makes a good substitute for starting the split in the log. Splints made by either method are fairly rough. They can be used as is or smoothed with sandpaper or by scraping with a sharp knife.

Drawknife is used to peel bark from whole log or from sections of a log that have been split into eighths.

Drawknife

Making the Mat

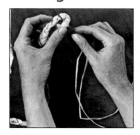

1. To start spiral, curve braid around and stitch through knot in end with raffia.

2. Secure center by stitching downward through section of braid opposite knot.

3. Continue sewing braid into a spiral. Stop as necessary to make more braid.

4. Add new raffia by joining ends of new and old strands with square knot.

5. When mat measures 12 in., braid the fringe using technique shown below.

6. Sew fringe to mat, cut end, bind with raffia, and sew bound end in place.

Braiding the husks

To start the braid, tie together narrow ends of three husks. Hook knot over nail and pull husks taut as you braid. Add new husk by laying its narrow end inside wide end of braided husk.

How to make the fringe on the final row

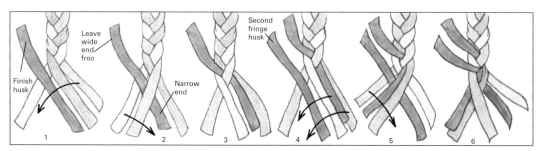

Finish mat with a decorative fringe. Add husks one at a time to the braid. Incorporate the narrow end of each husk you add into the braid; let the wide end stay free to form the fringe. Husks are shown in color to aid in identification.

Splints From a Whole Log

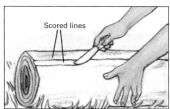

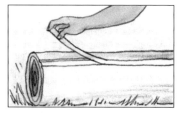

1. Score parallel lines along trunk of log that has first been soaked for one month and then stripped of bark.

2. Pound log end vigorously with wooden club until strip ends separate, then pound between score lines all along log.

3. Pull up strips. When necessary, repeat pounding at any spots where strips fail to separate easily from trunk.

Splints From a Split Log

1. Stand 6-ft. log on end, and place froe or other blade so that it cuts directly across centermost growth ring. Pound froe into log.

2. Pull handle of froe toward you to pivot blade and split trunk, then work froe down; repeat until froe is worked several inches into log.

3. Remove froe and lay log on ground. Insert tip of wedge into split opened up by froe. Pound wedge all the way into the tree trunk.

4. Pound in second wedge. Work wedge over wedge down log, then repeat process to split halves into quarters and then eighths.

5. Remove dark heartwood. First cut partway down line where dark wood meets light, then pull sides apart with hands. Peel off bark.

6. Remaining light outer wood must be split exactly in half, repeatedly, to make splints. Start split by cutting into center of end.

7. Complete the split by pulling halves apart with equal force. If split drifts off center, recenter by pulling down harder on thinner half.

8. Resplit halves again and again to make successively thinner splints. For very thin splints control force with thumb and fingers.

Weaving Splints to Form the Basket Body

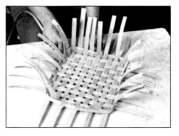

1. With smooth sides up weave a 20-in splint through three 22-in.-long splints.

2. Weaving on right and left sides alternately, add ten 20-in. splints.

3. Weaving on near and far sides alternately, add six 22-in. splints.

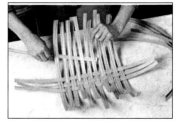

4. With a sharp knife score splints lightly along edge of woven portions.

5. Turn basket over, bend up splints, and weave circumference with 6-ft. splint.

6. Weave half-width splints for next five rounds, then finish with a wide splint.

7. Cut off ends of all splints that are on the inside of the top round.

8. Cut half the width from each splint that comes up on outside of top round.

9. Cut half-width splints to a point, fold over, and tuck point into weaving.

Steps for making a hickory handle

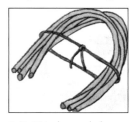

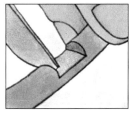

1. Tie 10-in.-long soaked shoots into U-shape. Let dry.

2. Mark width of splint on each side of hickory handle.

3. Cut notches between lines marked on handle.

4. Sharpen handle ends and insert into side of basket.

Finishing the edge

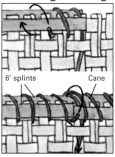

Reinforce rim with two 6-ft.-long splints lashed in place with cane. On inside of basket insert cane end through weaving. Then lay a 6-ft.-long splint against each side of upper edge (top left), and lash with cane all the way around rim. (Long splints can be held in place temporarily with clothespins.) When you reach handles, lash around them and continue. Where splint ends meet, double-wrap with cane (bottom left).

Ash splints make a lightweight basket that is excellent for storing balls of yarn. You can make your own splints or buy machine-made ones from a craft shop.

A Square Basket Made From Ash Splints

To make a 10-inch by 12-inch yarn basket, you will need 1-inch-wide ash splints cut to the following lengths: 9 splints that are 22 inches long, 11 that are 20 inches long, and 7 that are 6 feet long. You will also need cane to reinforce the rim and two 1/4- to 1/2-inch-diameter hickory shoots for handles. Prepare the handles in advance by soaking the shoots overnight, then bend them into U-shapes. Finish the basket body, then fit the handles.

Before starting to weave, cut three 6-foot-long splints in half lengthwise. The halves will be used to create varied texture in the basket sides. Next, find the rough sides of the splints by bending them first one way, then the other. Splinters will be raised on the rough side when you bend a splint with its rough side facing out. The rough side will form the basket interior. Finally, soak the splints for 20 minutes in room-temperature water.

Sources and resources

Books

Allen, Laura G. *Basket Weavers: Artisans of the Southwest.* Flagstaff, Ariz.: Museum of Northern Arizona, 1993.

Hart, Carol, and Dan Hart. *Natural Basketry.* New York: Watson-Guptill, 1978.

Harvey, Virginia I. *The Techniques of Basketry.* Seattle, Wash.: University of Washington Press, 1986.

Hoppe, Flo. *Wicker Basketry.* Loveland, Colo.: Interweave Press, 1989.

Mason, Tufton O. *American Indian Basketry.* New York: Dover, 1988.

Pollock, Polly. *Start a Craft: Basket Making.* Edison, N.J.: Book Sales Inc., 1994.

Tod, Osma G. *Earth Basketry.* West Chester, Pa.: Schiffer Publishing, 1986.

Tod, Osma G., and Oscar H. Benson. *Weaving With Reeds and Fibers.* New York: Dover, 1975.

INDEX